THE
LETTERS
OF
H. P. BLAVATSKY

H. P. BLAVATSKY
COLLECTED WRITINGS

THE LETTERS OF
H. P. BLAVATSKY

VOLUME 1

Edited by John Algeo
Assisted by Adele S. Algeo and the
Editorial Committee for the Letters of H. P. Blavatsky:
Daniel H. Caldwell, Dara Eklund, Robert Ellwood,
Joy Mills, and Nicholas Weeks

QUEST BOOKS
THE THEOSOPHICAL PUBLISHING HOUSE
Wheaton, Illinois, and Chennai (Madras), India

The Theosophical Society acknowledges with gratitude the generous support of the Kern Foundation and the John A. Sellon Charitable Trust for the publication of this book.

First Quest Edition 2003
First Printing 2003

The Theosophical Publishing House
P. O. Box 270
Wheaton, Illinois 60189-0270

Book design and typesetting by Kirsten Hansen

Library of Congress Cataloging-in-Publication Data

Blavatsky, H. P. (Helena Petrovna), 1831–1891.
[Correspondence]
The letters of H. P. Blavatsky / edited by John Algeo . . . [et al.].
—1st Quest ed.
   p.   cm.
"H. P. Blavatsky, Collected writings."
Includes bibliographical references and index.
ISBN 0-8356-0836-0
1. Blavatsky, H. P. (Helena Petrovna), 1831-1891—Correspondence.
I. Algeo, John.   II. Blavatsky, H. P. (Helena Petrovna), 1831–1891. Works.
1950.   III. Title.
BP585.B6.A4 2003
299′.934′092--dc21
[B]   2003046614

Printed in the United States of America

Contents

CONTENTS

CONTENTS

CONTENTS

Preface

This collection of the letters of H. P. Blavatsky aims at including all known correspondence written by her. A few letters intended for publication that were not included in her *Collected Writings* are also included here. But letters that were sent to periodicals for publication and are in the *Collected Writings* are omitted from this series. This first volume contains letters written before Blavatsky's arrival in India in February 1879. Subsequent volumes will continue the correspondance.

Editorial Principles

For each of the letters, an effort has been made to establish the most authentic text, that is, the one closest to what she wrote. Whenever possible, autograph letters have been sought out and transcribed verbatim, without changes of grammar, wording, spelling, or punctuation. When autograph letters are not available, the earliest or best-known copy has been used.

No effort has been made to improve Blavatsky's texts in any way, including the correction of obvious or presumed errors. The aim is to let HPB (as she will usually be referred to in editorial matter) speak with minimal editorial intervention between her and the reader. Some of what present-day editorial style would correct was, in her time, variant usage. It does not serve HPB well to impose upon her our sense of stylistic propriety, which she would doubtless have labeled, with one of her favorite dismissive terms, "flapdoodle." Nor have *sic*'s generally been inserted to call attention to departures from current use, as their number would be oppressive. When corrections have been judged important to a reader's understanding of the text, they have been suggested in endnotes or more rarely inserted in square brackets within the text itself.

The punctuation and capitalization in HPB's handwriting are often very difficult to interpret. She uses dashes of various lengths (all represented by a standard one-em dash in the transcriptions). Her periods and commas are often difficult to distinguish, and she sometimes uses a dot with spaces on either side (transcribed here as a comma following the preceding word). Some capital letters have distinct forms from their lower-case versions, but others are only the small letter written larger, with the size difference continuous rather than discrete.

Word spacing is frequently variable and thus uncertain. Items that today would be written solid (such as *today*) are often spaced in HPB's handwriting (*to day*) and are so transcribed here. Occasionally, in her more carelessly written letters, HPB runs adjacent words together with no space between them. In such cases, if her usual practice is to write the words separately, a space has been silently added.

When original letters in HPB's own handwriting have not been available (as is very often the case), the earliest copy or published version has been used. Such texts are obviously less reliable as representations of HPB's intention, but have been used for lack of any better. The same editorial policy as that used for the autograph letters has been applied to the other texts. Although the usage thus recorded may often be that of a copyist or editor, rather than HPB's, it is impossible to distinguish one from the other with certainty, so the available texts are presented with such commentary as seems helpful.

Commentary and glosses to the letters are provide in the following ways:

- Introductory comments and related materials are given in headnotes before the letters.
- Subsequent comments and related materials are in endnotes after the letters.
- Words and terms are glossed if they are not in a general desk dictionary, for which *Merriam-Webster's Collegiate Dictionary*, Tenth Edition (1993), has been taken as representative. If a word or term is in that dictionary, it is not glossed unless it has some unusual feature, as of spelling or sense, in a letter. A term found mainly in a single letter is glossed by a numbered explanatory note following that letter. Terms found in several letters or of more general interest are glossed in the Glossarial Index at the end of the volume rather than repeated for every letter in which they occur.
- Foreign words and expressions (not listed in *Merriam-Webster's Collegiate Dictionary*) are glossed in square brackets at the point where they occur in the text of a letter.

- When a letter is not explicitly dated, a date—exact or approximate—is put in square brackets and the reason for that dating given in a date note following any numbered explanatory notes to the letter.
- The source used for the text of a letter in this edition, along with any related information, is identified in a source note following any other notes for the letter. A statement in such notes that a letter has also been published elsewhere does not imply that the other published version is identical with the text in this volume. Other published versions of the letters have often been edited or altered in at least minor ways. And often there are extensive differences, suggesting that published versions have been based on different copies of the same letter. In such cases, when the original autograph letter is not available, significant differences are mentioned in notes or strikingly different versions are both (or all) presented.

REFERENCES

References, including those for quoted matter, are indicated in the text in three ways: in full, or by the name of the author and when necessary a short form of the title, or by an abbreviation for often cited works (e.g., *CW* for Blavatsky's *Collected Writings*). Full bibliographical information for the references and explanations of the abbreviations are in the bibliography at the end of the volume.

TRANSLITERATION

The Russian alphabet can be variously transliterated into English. In editorial matter, Russian personal names are given in the spelling used in the *Collected Writings* for ease of reference to that standard edition of HPB's works, even when such spellings are not the ones commonly used elsewhere. For example, the given name of HPB's cousin, Serguey Yulyevich de Witte (as it is spelled in the *Collected Writings*) is give as "Sergey" in *Merriam-Webster's Collegiate Dictionary*, 10th ed., and the *Encyclopædia Britannica*, and as "Sergei" in Theodore von Laue's biography *Sergei Witte and the Industrialization of Russia* (1963). When there is variation of spelling in the *Collected Writings* (as there is, for example, between "Aksakoff" and "Aksakov"), the form in volume 15, the *Cumulative Index*, is used.

Translations

In this volume, letters written originally in Russian and French are given only in English translation. It is the editor's intention later to publish separately the original language versions of such letters. Efforts have been made to provide translations that are accurate to both the sense and the tone of the originals. Boris de Zirkoff's translations of the Russian letters in Solovyov's *Sovremennaya* are based primarily on the English translation by Walter Leaf in *Modern Priestess*, with the further translation of the French expressions in them and some revisions based on Solovyov's Russian versions.

Order

The letters are for the most part ordered chronologically, to the extent that their chronological order can be determined or guessed at. Many letters are undated, so internal evidence of their date of composition must be relied upon. In a few cases, other ordering principles may be preferred, particularly when two or more letters are closely related in subject matter but would be widely separated according to chronology.

History of the Project

The project to publish the collected letters of H. P. Blavatsky was conceived and begun by her relative (second cousin, once removed), Boris de Zirkoff, as part of his great plan to publish all the writings of his distinguished kinswoman in a uniform edition. In preparation for that project, de Zirkoff gathered all letters of whose existence he knew and tentatively dated them. It is a great regret of all students of Blavatsky and her writings that de Zirkoff was not able to complete his work on the letters before his death, as no one else had the detailed knowledge of her life and works that he did.

Conscious of the need to secure the future of the project after his death, Boris de Zirkoff left his library, his manuscripts and notes, and all materials related to the Collected Writing series to the Theosophical Society in America. It was hoped at first that Joy Mills, who knew Boris, would be able to take on the task of producing the volumes of HPB's correspondence, but as other duties called her, she was instrumental in arranging that the task should be passed to John Cooper, a widely admired Theosophical historian.

Consequently, the Theosophical Publishing House asked Cooper to become the editor of the letters and passed on to him copies of all the letters that de Zirkoff had collected and the Theosophical Society in America had registered with the Library of Congress for copyright purposes. John, who had extensive knowledge of Theosophical history and was a very skillful collector of materials, located a number of additional letters unknown to Boris de Zirkoff because of their obscurity or because they had come to light only after Boris's death. His expansion of the known corpus of Blavatsky letters was his most significant contribution to the project.

Because Cooper lived in the Australian outback with limited technological resources (he generated his own electricity), the Theosophical Society in America gave him extensive technical support, entering all the letters into electronic form and printing out the texts that he wanted to use as the thesis for his doctoral degree. Unfortunately, John died before completing the project or even his doctorate, which was awarded posthumously.

After John Cooper's death, it became clear that, for several reasons, his work on the letters could not be used directly. One of those reasons was the discovery that the texts of many of the letters—both those de Zirkoff had collected but not fully edited and those Cooper had added to the known corpus—were not accurate. Consequently, when the Theosophical Society in America resumed the task of preparing the letters for publication and appointed John Algeo as its new editor, assisted by the Editorial Committee for the Letters of H. P. Blavatsky, all of the texts had to be regathered to assure their accuracy and fidelity to the best original sources. That task was performed personally by John and Adele Algeo for most of the letters.

It is too much to hope that the present volume is either complete or error-free. There is an old tale that Jewish scribes, when copying manuscripts, always deliberately left something out or introduced an error—to show that only God is perfect. In that respect, all of us who work with texts are Jewish scribes, perhaps not in our intention, but certainly in our results. The editor and the publisher will be most grateful to any reader who points out lacunae or errata, so that they can be corrected in future printings of the volume.

Acknowledgments

More thanks than I can express are due to my wife, Adele S. Algeo, who has worked with me on every aspect of this project, particularly in copying original letters and proofreading the work at various stages of its production, as well as more generally in making it possible for me to devote time to the project by her care and attention to matters that should have been my dharma.

Notable thanks are due to the members of the Editorial Committee for the Letters of H. P. Blavatsky, who have helped in many ways, but especially by reading and commenting on the draft versions of this work, as well as in individually particular ways:

- Daniel H. Caldwell (for his early help with bibliographical sources and references and his deep knowledge of HPB and her history),
- Dara Eklund (for the knowledge she has from long association with Boris de Zirkoff and the *Collected Writings* project, as well as her keen editorial eye),
- Robert Ellwood (for his extensive knowledge of religious history and his scholarly expertise),
- Joy Mills (for her long association with the Letters project and her Theosophical sensitivity), and
- Nicholas Weeks (for his indefatigable skill in tracing down allusions and enlisting the support of others).

Primary thanks are due to Boris de Zirkoff, who began the Letters project as part of the *Collected Writings* of H. P. Blavatsky and gathered the primary collection of letters on which this volume is based, as well as for his comprehensive knowledge of HPB and her writings and his meticulous annotation of materials.

Thanks are due to many other persons, not all of whom can be listed here, and with apologies to any of those who have been inadvertently omitted from the following list:

Miss Mary Anderson, International Secretary of the Theosophical Society, for help in translating several French letters.

Ms Laura E. Beardsley, Research Services Coordinator, and Ms Sandra Rayser Ragonese, Reference Specialist, the Historical Society of Pennsylvania, Philadelphia, for their assistance in providing a copy of HPB's letter to M. D. Evans.

Mr. and Mrs. James and Ina Belderis, Librarians, Theosophical Society with international headquarters in Pasadena, for making the library's facilities available to us during the day and after hours.

Mrs. Betty Bland, National President of the Theosophical Society in America, for her encouragement and support in many ways and for many years of friendship and collaboration.

Mr. John Buescher for identifying several references to persons and events in early Spiritualism.

Dr. Radha Burnier, President of the Theosophical Society, for generously allowing us access to the Archives of the Theosophical Society at Adyar.

Mr. Charles C. Carr for information about the LeMoyne Crematorium.

Mr. Leonard DeGraal, Archivist, Edison National Historical Site, West Orange, NJ, for his kindness in searching for relevant material and providing xerographic copies of the correspondence between Thomas A. Edison and several Theosophists.

Mme. Diana Dunningham-Chapotin for help in translating French and kindly putting us in touch with Jean-Louis Siémons.

Ms Diane Eisenberg for her devoted and skillful entering of all the letters into electronic format.

Mr. R. A. Gilbert for helping us to obtain access to the archives of the Grand Lodge of England in Freemason's Hall, London.

Dr. Joan Houston Hall, Chief Editor of the *Dictionary of American Regional English*, for her help with language history.

Mr. Obadiah Harris, President and Chairman of the Board, Philosophical Research Society, Los Angeles, for making available a photocopy of a letter in that Society's archives.

Mr. Anatol Kagan for help with the translation of several Russian letters.

Mr. John Kern for his longtime support and advice on matters relating to the work of the Theosophical Society, and the Kern Foundation for its generous financial support of this project and of the Theosophical Publishing House, Wheaton.

Dr. Grace Knoche, Leader, Theosophical Society with international headquarters in Pasadena, for access to letters in the Society's archives and for hospitality while we consulted them, as well as to all her staff for their cordiality and helpfulness.

Dr. Richard A. LaFleur, Professor of Classics, University of Georgia, for help with the translation of Latin.

Ms Jennie Lee, archivist of the College of Psychical Studies, London, for her help in locating and copying material from that archive.

Mr. John McChesney-Young, Berkeley, California, for help with the translation of Latin.

Ms Susan Szasz Palmer, Head of Public Services, Division of Rare and Manuscript Collections, Kroch Library, Cornell University, Ithaca, NY, for providing copies of correspondence between Louisa Andrews and Hiram Corson.

Mr. Leslie Price for helping us obtain access to archives of the Society for Psychical Research and the College of Psychical Studies.

Mrs. Willamay Pym for help in proofing the texts of many of the letters.

Mr. Hari Har Raghavan for help with Sanskrit.

Mrs. Ananya Rajan for research assistance and proofreading.

Mr. Amarnath Rao, Superintendant of the Headquarters Attendants at Adyar, for many kindnesses including also opening the Archives beyond normal hours.

Mr. and Mrs. David and Nancy Reigle for help with Sanskrit, Buddhist technical terminology, and HPB's sources.

Ms Idarmis Rodríguez, Secretary to the President of the Theosophical Society, for copying documents and helping us with electronic communication.

The John A. Sellon Charitable Trust for encouragement and generous financial support for the editorial work and publication of this project.

M. Jean-Louis Siémons for providing translations, editing French texts, and explaining allusions to help clarify the texts.

The Society for Psychical Research for permitting us access to their archives in the University of Cambridge Library.

Ms Joan Sutcliffe for supplying photocopies of the letters from H. P. Blavatsky to Hiram P. Corson in the HPB Library, Toronto.

Mr. R. M. Tolani, Acting Officer in charge of the Archives of the Theosophical Society at Adyar, for his kind assistance in helping us to find material and keeping the Archives open for us beyond the normal hours, as well as in interpreting some Sanskrit and Hindi.

Mrs. Elisabeth Trumpler, Librarian of the Henry S. Olcott Memorial Library, Wheaton, Illinois, for assistance in locating materials and in translating Russian.

Mr. David Wietersen, Archivist, Theosophical Society with international headquarters in Pasadena, for assembling the originals of several letters and related documents.

Dr. Leonard Zwilling, General Editor and Bibliographer for the *Dictionary of American Regional English*, for his help with etymology.

I have depended heavily on standard reference works for the facts reported in the notes and commentaries, but especially noteworthy is John Grimes's highly useful *Concise Dictionary of Indian Philosophy*.

—J. A.

Background Essay A

HPB's Early Life

[The following account is based primarily on the biographical sketch of HPB's early life by Boris de Zirkoff, "Helena Petrovna Blavatsky: General Outline of Her Life Prior to Her Public Work," in *Collected Writings* 1:xxv–lii, supplemented by other sources, such as A. P. Sinnett's *Incidents*.]

Much of H. P. Blavatsky's early life is poorly documented, and reports of it are sometimes contradictory (with different reports even by Blavatsky herself). The following sketch presents some of the surest or at least likely facts about her life before the first known letter, and subsequent essays give background for other letters. These essays are not a biography of HPB (as Blavatsky preferred to be called by those who knew her), but supplementary material to help explain her correspondence.

Birth and Ancestry

Ekaterinoslav (since 1926 called Dnepropetrovsk) is a town on the bank of the Dnieper River toward the southeast of the Ukraine, which was formerly part of the Russian Empire. Shortly after its founding in 1783, Ekaterinoslav became a provincial center, where trade was carried on by people from the surrounding region. There, probably in the early morning hours of August 12 (which was July 31 by the Julian calendar then used in Russia) in the year 1831, a baby girl was born to Helena Andreyevna and Artillery Captain Peter Alexeyevich von Hahn.

A cholera epidemic was sweeping the land, and the baby girl was premature, so she was baptized immediately and given her mother's Christian name, Helena. (A Russian has as a second name a patronymic, that is, a name based on the father's first name, so the baby was Helena Petrovna, "daughter of Peter.") The ceremony of her baptism was a small disaster. Throughout the lengthy Russian Orthodox ritual, participants stood with candles in their hands. One of them in the very front of all the assembled relatives, the infant's aunt but herself only a little child, grew weary and slumped down on the floor. The godparents were in the process, on behalf of the infant Helena, of renouncing the devil and all his works. At that point the little girl on the floor, toying with the lighted candle she was holding, accidentally set fire to the long flowing robes of the officiating priest. The result was a great blaze that severely burned him and several others who tried to put out the fire. People said it was a sign that the infant Helena's life would be full of trials and troubles.

Helena's father, Peter Alexeyevich von Hahn (1798–1873) was the son of Lieutenant General Alexis Gustavovich von Hahn and Countess Elizabeth Maksimovna von Pröbsen. The family was from Mecklenburg, a branch of the Counts Hahn von Rottenstern-Hahn, who a century or so earlier had emigrated to Russia, where their last name was Russianized as "Gan." Vera de Zhelihovsky, HPB's sister, says that Helena inherited her curly hair and her vivaciousness from her paternal grandmother. Helena was her parents' first child, and at the time of her birth, her father was in Poland, fighting in the Russo-Polish War of 1830–1.

Helena's mother was Helena Andreyevna (1814–42), the oldest daughter of Andrey Mihailovich de Fadeyev and Helena Pavlovna.

Helena's maternal grandfather was a civil officer of some distinction, at various times a Privy Councillor, Civil Governor of the Province of Saratov, Director of the Department of State Lands in the Caucasus, and a member of the Council of the Viceroy of the Caucasus. Helena's maternal grandmother was the daughter of Prince Paul Vassilyevich Dolgorukov and Henrietta Adolfovna de Bandré-du-Plessis, of French descent. Because the maternal grandmother, Helena Pavlovna, had been born as Princess Dolgorukova, her parents objected to her marriage with a commoner. She was an accomplished woman, with proficiency in botany, history, archeology, and numismatics. She corresponded with scientists from various countries of Europe, including Alexander von Humboldt. Lady Hester Lucy Stanhope called Helena Pavlovna "an outstanding woman-scientist, who would have been famous in Europe, but who is completely underestimated due to her misfortune of being born on the shores of the Volga river, where there was none to recognize her scientific value."

The de Fadeyevs had several other daughters who survived infancy, in addition to HPB's mother. They included Nadyezhda Andreyevna (1828-1919), HPB's aunt who was only three years older than she, who never married, and who was to be for some years a member of the Council of the Theosophical Society; and Katherine Andreyevna, who married Yuliy F. de Witte and one of whose sons was Count Serguey Yulyevich de Witte, Russian Minister of Finance (1892–1903) and first constitutional Prime Minister of the Russian Empire (1905–6), who sought to Westernize Russia.

HPB's mother, Helena Andreyevna, was also an accomplished woman. She became a published novelist at the age of twenty-three. When just sixteen, she married Peter Alexeyevich, who was nearly twice her age. Her marriage exemplified the truth of the opening line of Tolstoy's *Anna Karenina*: "All happy families are alike; every unhappy family is unhappy in its own way." Helena Andreyevna's cultured background did not fit the tenor of military camps. Her novels depicted the plight of women in nineteenth-century Russia and were early examples of feminist protest. She died of tuberculosis at the age of twenty-eight, when her first child, Helena Petrovna (HPB) was eleven. She had borne three other children as well: a son, Alexander, who died in infancy; a daughter, Vera, four years younger than HPB and a frequent correspondent of hers; and another son, Leonid, born two years before his mother's death.

FROM CHILDHOOD TO WIFEHOOD

During her first ten years, Helena Petrovna moved repeatedly, partly because, like all military men, her father had frequent changes of post and partly because her mother's health led her to travel to various places in search of cures or relief from the rigors of military life. In 1834, her grandfather, Andrey Mihailovich de Fadeyev, was appointed to a post in Odessa, on the shore of the Black Sea. His daughter, recovering from the birth and infant death of a son, Alexander, brought young Helena to live with her grandparents. The next year, Helena's sister, Vera, was born in Odessa.

The following years saw Helena traveling with her mother in the Ukraine, to St. Petersburg, and to Astrakhan, a city and province at the delta of the Volga River into the Caspian Sea. In 1836, Helena's grandfather was appointed Trustee for the nomadic Kalmuck tribes in Astrakhan. Her mother took Helena and Vera to live there for about a year. Then Helena's mother, with the two girls, resumed her travels—to a spa in the Caucasus; to Poltava, where Antonya Christianovna Kühlwein joined them as the girls' governess; and to Odessa, for more mineral water treatments. In 1839, a Yorkshire English governess, Augusta Sophia Jeffers, joined the family. Late that year, they moved to Saratov on the Volga River, where Helena's grandfather had been appointed as governor of the province. Helena's brother Leonid was born there in 1840.

In 1841, Helena went with her mother, sister, and brother to join their father in the Ukraine, moving again the following year back to Odessa. In July 1842, Helena's mother died, and her children returned to Saratov to live with their grandparents for about three years. But Helena continued her travels, visiting the Ural Mountains, which divide European Russia from Siberia, and beyond.

In 1846, Helena, Vera, and Leonid moved with their aunt Katherine de Witte and her family to a house in the country, but at the end of the year they returned to Saratov. The following year they journeyed to Tiflis (now called Tbilisi) in Russian Georgia, on the eastern shore of the Black Sea, where their grandparents had settled. The journey, an arduous one by boat and horse carriage, took nearly two months. The years 1847–8 saw further travels around Tiflis.

During the winter of 1848–9 Helena was engaged to Nikifor Vassilyevich Blavatsky. There are several explanations of how and why the engagement came about, but the most widely cited and perhaps most probable is that given by her aunt, Nadyezhda Fadeyev (*Incidents* 54):

> She cared not whether she should get married or not. She had been simply defied one day by her governess to find any man who would be her husband, in view of her temper and disposition. The governess, to emphasize the taunt, said that even the old man she had found so ugly, and had laughed at so much, calling him "a plumeless raven"—that even he would decline her for a wife! That was enough: three days after she made him propose, and then, frightened at

4

what she had done, sought to escape from her joking acceptance of his offer. But it was too late.

Nikifor Blavatsky had held various civil posts in the Russian
provincial governments in the Ukraine and Georgia (in the Caucasus)
and was to be appointed vice governor of a newly organized Province of Yerivan (Yerevan) in Armenia, near the eastern border of
Turkey. He was an undistinguished but competent civil servant.

In the following spring 1849, Helena seems to have run away
from home, perhaps in an effort to avoid her approaching marriage.
In July 1849, however, Helena married Nikifor and went with him
to a resort near Yerevan in Armenia. She again tried unsuccessfully
to run away during this trip. The Blavatskys stayed at the resort,
however, until late August, when they were briefly visited by her
family, after which they all went to Yerevan.

In October 1849, HPB left her husband to return to Tiflis,
where her grandparents were. They sent her to St. Petersburg to
join her father, who had remarried and was to meet his daughter at
the Black Sea port of Odessa. With two servants, she traveled over-
land from Tiflis to Poti, a port in Caucasian Georgia on the eastern
shore of the Black Sea, where she was to take passage to Odessa.
However, either accidentally or purposefully, HPB missed the ship
she was supposed to take to Odessa and instead got passage on an
English vessel, the SS *Commodore*. On it she sailed northwestward
on the Black Sea to the city of Kerch at the eastern tip of the
Crimea. Helena sent her servants ashore to arrange for her arrival
in Kerch the next morning, but instead of debarking herself, she
remained on board when the ship sailed that night for the city of
Taganrog, on the north shore of the Sea of Azov, and then back
across the Black Sea to Constantinople. Thus at the age of eighteen, Helena Petrovna Blavatsky began her long wanderings around
the world.

EARLY TRAVELS

From Constantinople, HPB may have traveled during 1849–50
in Greece, eastern Europe, Asia Minor, and Egypt, meeting Paulos
Metamon, a Coptic occultist in Cairo. During 1850–51, she was in
western Europe, particularly Paris and London, where she met a

family friend, Princess Bagration-Muhransky. During her London stay, she lived variously in a flat on Cecil Street, in a hotel called Mivart's (now Claridge's), and in another hotel between the City and the Strand.

According to Countess Constance Wachtmeister, HPB said that she first met Master Morya face to face in Hyde Park, London. She identified the time to A. P. Sinnett as "the year of the first Nepal Embassy," which was 1850. Both the date and place, however, are problematical. HPB wrote in her Sketchbook that she met her teacher at Ramsgate on her twentieth birthday (August 12, 1851), but also told Constance Wachtmeister that "Ramsgate" was a blind. HPB also told the Countess that her father was in London at the time and she consulted him about the Master's offer for her to cooperate "in a work which he was about to undertake."

It is, according to Boris de Zirkoff (*CW* 1:xxxix, citing Sinnett, *Incidents* 62–6), "fairly certain or at least probable" that HPB traveled to Canada in fall 1851 and stayed at Quebec, going from there to New Orleans to study the practice of voodoo. But being warned in a vision of the dangers of voodooism, she continued through Texas to Mexico. During 1852, she seems to have traveled through Central and South America to visit the ancient ruins there. She also went to the West Indies, where she arranged with "a certain Englishman" she had met in Germany two years before and a Hindu chela she had met in Honduras to sail by way of the Cape of Good Hope to Ceylon and Bombay.

HPB made an unsuccessful attempt by herself to enter Tibet through Nepal. She traveled around north India, as far east as Dinajpur (in what is now Bangladesh). In a letter of December 5, 1881, to Prince Dondukov-Korsakov, she says she "stayed there nearly two years, traveling about and receiving money each month—from whom I have no idea." Thereafter, HPB seems to have traveled back to England by way of Java and Singapore. In *From the Caves and Jungles of Hindostan* (272), HPB says of her Master, "Long ago, very long ago, more than twenty-seven years, I met him in the house of a stranger in England, where he had come in the company of a dethroned native prince." The latter was presumably young Prince Dhuleep Singh of Lahore, who sailed from India on April 19, 1854, and arrived at Southampton on June 18, 1854.

Later in 1854, HPB again traveled to America, landing in New York and passing through Chicago on her way across the Rockies to San Francisco with a caravan of emigrants, probably in a covered wagon (Sinnett, *Incidents* 66-7). Her precise whereabouts thereafter are unknown, but she probably stayed in the Western Hemisphere until fall 1855. At that time, she left for Calcutta, India, by way of Japan.

In India, HPB traveled widely, at Lahore meeting a German ex-Lutheran minister named Kühlwein, an acquaintance of her father's and perhaps a relative of her old governess, who was accompanied by his two brothers. The four laid plans to enter Tibet. They traveled through Ladakh in eastern Kashmir to Leh, one of the highest permanently inhabited towns in the world, in the company of a Tartar Shaman on his way home to Siberia. HPB may at this time have crossed the border into Tibet with the aid of the Shaman, who also helped her out of a difficult situation by mentally summoning the help of native horsemen. Her adventures on this occasion are described, with some artistic license, in *Isis Unveiled* (2:598-602, 626-8). She may also have traveled in Burma, Thailand, and Assam at this time, leaving India by summer 1857.

RETURN HOME

By early 1858, HPB was apparently back in Europe, traveling through France and Germany and then returning to Russia in fall 1858, for her first visit home in nine years. The approximate time of her return to Russia is fixed by a letter from her husband, Nikifor Blavatsky to HPB's aunt and confidant, Nadyezhda de Fadeyev (the Russian original of which is in the Archives of the Theosophical Society, Adyar, and has been translated in the *Theosophist* 80 [Aug. 1959]: 295-6). The letter, which is dated from Erevan, November 13, 1858, reads in part:

> Until now I knew nothing of H. P.'s [Helena Petrovna's] return to Russia. To tell you the truth, this ceased to interest me long ago. Time smooths out everything, even every memory. You may assure H. P. on my word of honor that I will never pursue her. I wish ardently that our marriage be annulled, and that she may marry again. It is possible that

I too may marry again, from calculation or inclination, feeling myself not yet unsuited to family life. So make every effort, by uniting your forces, and let her also do her best to annul the marriage. I did my best, but Exarch Isidor [the bishop who headed the Orthodox Church in Caucasian Georgia] refused to do it. Therefore I do not intend to start a new lawsuit any more, or even to obtain the divorce by applying to the Emperor [five illegible words] because I consider it entirely useless after having received your letter. I beg you instantly to endeavor to end the matter, to the satisfaction of both of you. Whether she finishes or reopens the subject, in any case, I repeat, I shall not attempt to pursue her or make inquiries in order to find out where she is living. You know that a man loses less, in public opinion, than a woman, in whatever circumstances he may happen to be. In whatever manner I might behave morally, I would be justified sooner than a woman.

In this way I have been living since the time of my misfortune [his marriage to HPB]. And in consequence of it I have been working on my character in order that I may become unaffected by anything. Very often I even laugh at the stupidities which I committed, and I comfort myself by realizing that not only I but other people too make the same mistakes in this strange world.

One can become accustomed to anything. So I have got used to a joyless life in Erivan. Whatsoever may happen I shall remain unaffected. My plan is to retire entirely from active service. I would then go to my estate, in that hidden corner which nobody knows of, and live there surrounded by the delights of a lonely life.

Your always devoted, N. Blavatsky

At Christmas 1858, HPB visited her sister Vera, whose husband, Nikolay de Yahontov, had recently died and who was therefore living temporarily with her father-in-law in Pskov, in northwest Russia near southeast Estonia. During her short stay there, HPB became an object of considerable local interest because of reports of her parapsychological abilities. In spring 1859 HPB visited St. Petersburg with her father and her half sister Liza, a child of his second marriage, before they traveled on to the house Vera had inherited from her late husband in the province of Pskov. There HPB had an attack of a recurring illness, involving the reopening of a wound near her heart. These attacks involved a deathlike trance and spontaneous recoveries.

HPB and Vera traveled to Tiflis to visit their grandparents in spring or summer 1860, and HPB remained there for about a year. While she was there, in August 1860, her grandmother, Helena Pavlovna de Fadeyev, died. About this time HPB was reconciled with Nikifor Blavatsky and they lived in the same house for about a year, but then HPB once again left.

At some point during this period, or shortly before, HPB—and apparently Nikifor—acquired a ward, a young boy named Yury, at a time and under circumstances that are unknown, except that she says she took the child to protect the honor of another person. It has been proposed (Fuller, *Blavatsky and Her Teachers* 18, 54-6) that the other person was a Nathalia Blavatsky, perhaps a relative of Nikifor's, but the facts are probably beyond recovery. The existence of the child is attested by a passport issued to HPB on August 23 (Julian calendar), 1862, in Tiflis and signed by the Civil Governor, Orlovsky. The passport was issued "in pursuance of a petition presented by her husband, to the effect that she, Mme. Blavatsky, accompanied by their infant ward Yury, proceeds to the provinces of Tauris, Cherson, and Pskoff for the term of one year." Pskoff (Pskov) is the city and province in northwest Russia where the estate Vera inherited from her late husband was located, but nothing is known about the reason for this trip or even whether it was actually taken.

～⌒

Introduction to Letter 1

In 1863, before returning once more to Tiflis for about a year, HPB traveled widely in Caucasian Georgia, especially to mountainous and wild country, and apparently studied with native magicians called *kudyani*, becoming known for the healing and parapsychological powers she was developing. During this time, she began to experience a "double life," which she described in a letter to her relatives. There are two recorded versions of the surviving extract from this letter. The notes give variants from the later version, which were apparently made by HPB herself when A. P. Sinnett was editing the letter for use in his book, *Incidents in the Life of Madame Blavatsky* (1886).

Letter 1

To her relatives   *[between 1861 and 1864]*

Whenever I was called by name, I opened the eyes upon hearing it and was myself, in every particular. As soon as I was left alone, I relapsed into my usual, half dreamy condition and became *somebody else*.[1] . . . In cases when I was interrupted during a conversation in the latter capacity—say, at half a sentence either spoken by me or some of my *visitors*—invisible of course to any other, for I was alone to whom they were realities—no sooner I closed my eyes than the sentence which had been interrupted[2]—continued from the word[3] it had stopped at. When awake and *myself* I remembered well who I was in my second capacity[4] and what I was doing. When somebody else[5]—I had no idea of who was H. P. Blavatsky. I was in another far off country, quite another individuality, and had no connection at all with my actual life.

NOTES:

1. From the leader dots down to "no sooner," *Incidents* has instead: "I had simply a mild fever that consumed me slowly but surely, day after day, with entire loss of appetite, and finally of hunger, as I would feel none for days, and often went a week without touching any food whatever, except a little water, so that in four months I was reduced to a living skeleton. In cases when I was interrupted, when in my other *self*, by the sound of my present name being pronounced, and while I was conversing in my dream-life,—say at half a sentence either spoken by me or those who were with my second *me* at the time,—and opened my eyes to answer the call, I used to

answer very rationally, and understood all, for I was never delirious. But no sooner . . ."

2. *Incidents* adds: "was completed by my other self,"

3. *Incidents* adds: "or even half the word,"

4. *Incidents* adds: "and what I had been"

5. *Incidents* adds: ", i.e., the personage I had become, I know"

DATE: Unknown, but the events correspond to HPB's experiences at this time and the letter is cited in "Mystical History" and *Incidents* in connection with her stay in the Caucasus.

SOURCE: Russian original unavailable. Copied from a translation in "Mystical History" 527n. Significant variations and additions in *Incidents* 147–8 (2nd ed. 116) are given in the notes.

ᔌᔍ

Introduction to Letter 2

The year 1865 was a watershed in HPB's life. As a result of her experiences in the Caucasus during the preceding few years, her parapsychological powers, which had been active to varying degrees since her childhood, came increasingly under her conscious control, and her life took a new direction. In a letter of March 1, 1882, to Prince Dondukov-Korsakov, HPB says, "Between the Blavatsky of 1845–65 and the Blavatsky of the years 1865–82 there is an *unbridgeable gulf.*" When HPB finally left the Caucasus to go to Italy in 1865, she was never to return there again. Her sense of freedom and release is expressed in a letter to her relatives, probably written about the time she left the Caucasus.

Letter 2

To her relatives   *[1865]*

Now I will never be subjected any longer to external influences. The last vestiges of my psycho-physiological weakness is gone to return no more. . . . I am cleansed and purified of that dreadful attraction to myself of stray spooks and ethereal affinities (?). I am free, free, thanks to Them whom I now bless at every hour of my life.

DATE: As in "Mystical History"; in *Incidents,* the letter is dated 1866.

SOURCE: Russian original unavailable. Letter fragment copied from a translation in "Mystical History" 553. Also published in *Incidents* 152 (2nd ed. 120) with minor variations.

⟵⟶

BACKGROUND ESSAY B

The Lost Years

HPB's whereabouts during the five or so years after she left the Caucasus are poorly documented; they are consequently sometimes referred to as the "veiled years." Vera de Zhelihovsky, her sister, wrote ("Mystical History" 553): "From her letters we learned only that she was always travelling, rarely settling for any length of time in one place." HPB seems to have traveled in the Balkans, Greece, Italy, Egypt, Syria, Lebanon, and perhaps Persia. She had contact with the Druzes and other esoteric and mystic groups in the Near East.

Boris de Zirkoff (*CW* 1:xlvii) comments on the only certain information we have about HPB during this period:

> To this period belong her travel-notes written in French and contained in a small Notebook now in the Adyar Archives. Although these notes are undated, H.P.B. mentions one or two historical facts which provide a key to the dating of the trip she describes. It appears that she was at Belgrade when the Turkish garrison yielded the Fort and the commander, Al Rezi Pasha, withdrew from the territory. This was April 13, 1867. H.P.B. travelled by boat on the Danube, and by coach between various towns of Hungary and Transylvania; she visited, among others, Brassó, Szeben, Féhervár, Kolozsvár, Nagyvárad, Temesvár, Belgrade, Neusatz,

Esék, etc. These travel-notes are the only definite information concerning her whereabouts during a period which presents a great deal of uncertainty.

In 1867, HPB was in Bologna, with young Yury, who had apparently been with her all this time. The child was sickly, and HPB's efforts to keep him alive did not succeed. She returned to Russia briefly to bury her ward, but did not contact her relatives on that trip, instead returning immediately to Italy. She was at Mentana in November 1867, when the popular hero and nationalist Guieseppe Garibaldi led his volunteer forces against the French. She is said to have participated in the battle, which ended in defeat for the Italian patriots and during which she was wounded five times.

In early 1868, HPB traveled from Florence, through Constantinople, to India. On this trip she entered Tibet, meeting for the first time the Master KH and staying for a while in his sister's house in Shigatse, a city in south central Tibet near the Tashilhunpo Monastery, the seat of the Panchen Lama. During this period HPB was out of contact with her relatives, but on November 11, 1870, her aunt Nadyezhda de Fadeyev, received a letter from the Master KH saying that HPB was well and would return to the family before "18 moons."

HPB returned from India through the newly opened Suez Canal in late 1870, traveling to Cyprus and Greece, where she met the Master Hilarion. Subsequently she boarded the SS *Eunomia* at Piraeus (the port of Athens) to travel to Egypt. It carried a supply of gunpowder as protection against pirates, but as the ship sailed southward, its powder magazine exploded with great loss of life and property. HPB was not injured and eventually reached Alexandria, but with only meager resources. By the end of 1871 she was in Cairo, where she met Emma Cutting (later Mme. Alexis Coulomb) who provided her temporary financial assistance.

⌒

Introduction to Letter 3

In Egypt, HPB became interested in the phenomenon of Spiritualism. Although HPB rejected the notion that the spirits of the departed communicate through mediums, she did not doubt that what she called "spooks," the postmortem remains of a personality, could manifest in various ways, as shown in the following account from a letter to her sister, Vera de Zhelihovsky, who introduces the account:

During the latter years many were the changes that had taken place in our family: our grandfather and aunt's husband (who had both occupied very high official positions in Tiflis) had died and the whole family had left Caucasus to settle permanently in Odessa. H. P. Blavatsky had not visited the country for nearly seven years, and there remained in Tiflis but her younger sister with her family, and a number of old servants, ancient serfs of the late General Fadeyeff's, who, once liberated, could not be kept without wages in the house they had been born in and had been gradually all sent away. These people, some of whom were unable owing to old age to work for their living, came constantly for help to Mme Jelihovsky. Unable to pension so many she did what she could for them. Among other things she had obtained a permanent home at the City Refuge Home for two old men, late servants of her family: a cook called Maxim and his brother Piotre—once upon a time a very decent footman, but at the time of the event—an incorrigible drunkard who had lost his arm in consequence.

On that summer Madame Yahontoff (who had during the interval married her second husband V. Jelihovsky) had gone to reside during the hot months of the year at Manglis, the headquarters of the Regiment of Erivan—some thirty miles from town. She had just received the news that her sister had returned from India and was going to remain for some time in Egypt. The two sisters corresponded very rarely, at long intervals, and their letters were generally short. But after a prolonged silence Mme Jelihovsky (Yahontoff) received from HPB a very long and interesting letter. A portion of it consisted of flying sheets torn out from a note-book and these were all covered with pencil writing. The strange events they recorded had been all put down on the spot, some under the shadow of the great Pyramid of Cheops, and some of them inside Pharaoh's Chamber. It appears that Mme B. had gone there several times, once with a large company, some of whom were Spiritualists. Some most wonderful phenomena were described by some of her companions as having taken place in broad daylight in the desert when they were sitting under a tent; while other notes in Mme Blavatsky's writing recorded the strange sights she saw in the cimmerian darkness of the King's Chamber when she had been left alone in the Pyramid comfortably seated inside the sarcophagus. But as her narrative in the notes is very broken, consisting as it does of rough notes, we leave a description of what she saw to herself when she is ready to give it out. We rather narrate the strangest case of clairvoyance that ever came under our personal notice. It is a striking case of what Spiritualists generally call "spirit identity". We give a fragment of Mme Blavatsky's letter.

Letter 3

To V. de Zhelihovsky   *[early 1872]*

Let me know, Vera, whether it is true that the old Piotre is dead? He must have died last night or at some time yesterday?[1] Just fancy what happened! A friend of mine, a young English lady and medium,[2] stood writing mechanically on bits of paper, leaning upon an old Egyptian tomb. The pencil had begun tracing perfect gibberish—in characters that had never existed nowhere as a philologist told us—when suddenly, and as I was looking from behind her back, they changed into what I thought was Russian letters. My attention having been called elsewhere, I had just left her when I heard people saying that what she had written was now evidently in some existing characters, but neither she nor any one else could read them. I came back just in time to prevent her from destroying that slip of paper as she had done with the rest, and was rewarded. Possessing myself of the rejected slip, fancy my astonishment on finding it contained in Russian an evident apostrophe to myself!

"*Barishnya*" (little or "young miss"), "dear *baryshnya!*" said the writing. "Help, oh help me, miserable sinner! . . . I suffer: *drink, drink, give me a drink!* . . . I suffer, suffer!" From this term *baryshnya*—a title our old servants will, I see, use with us two even after our hair will have grown white with age—I understood immediately that the appeal came from one of our old servants and took therefore the matter in hand by arming myself with a pencil to *record what I would myself see.* I found the name Piotre Koutcherof echoed in my mind quite distinctly, and before me an undistinguishable mass, a formless pillar of grey smoke, and thought I heard it repeat the same words. Furthermore I saw that he had died in Dr Gorolevitch's hospital attached to the City Refuge—the Tiflis Work House I suppose. Moreover, as I made out, it is you who had placed him in company with his old brother, our old Maxim, who had died a few days before him. You had never written me about poor Maxim's death. Do tell me whether it is so or not.

NOTES:

1. Vera adds a parenthesis at this point: "the date on the stamp of the envelope showed that it had left Egypt ten days previous to the one it was received."

2. More information about the young lady, including her possession by an astral "spook" desirous of wine and her subsequent sickness for several weeks, is given in Sinnett's *Incidents* 167n and *CW* 14:488-9.

Vera concludes her comment on the episode with these remarks:

Further on followed her description of the whole vision as she had it, later on in the evening, when alone, and the authentic words pronounced by "Piotre's spook" as she called it. The "spirit" (?) was bitterly complaining of thirst and was becoming quite desperate. It was a punishment it said—and the spook seemed to know it well—for his drunkenness during the lifetime of that personality! . . . "An agony of thirst, that nothing could quench . . . an ever living fire!" as she explained it.

Mme Blavatsky's letter ended with a postscript in which she notified her sister that her doubts had all been settled. She saw the astral "spooks" of both the brothers—one harmless and passive, the other active and dangerous.

Upon the receipt of this letter, her sister was struck with surprise. Ignorant herself of the death of the parties mentioned, she telegraphed immediately to town and the answer received from doctor Gorolevitch corroborated the news announced by Mme Blavatsky in every particular. Piotre had died on the very same day and date as given in HPB's letter, and his brother two days earlier.

DATE: According to Boris de Zirkoff, HPB was in Cairo between October or November 1871 and April 1872. This letter must have been written during that time; it shows none of the disillusionment with Spiritualist manifestations and mediums that ended HPB's efforts to form a society for their investigation toward the end of her time in Cairo. Consequently a date sometime in early 1872 seems probable.

SOURCE: Russian original unavailable. Copied from a translation in "Mystical History" 558–9. Russian text published in *Blue Hills* ix–x and in *Rebus* 2 (Nov. 27, 1883): 419. English translation in *Incidents* 165–6 (2nd ed. 129–30) with minor variations.

❧

Introduction to Letter 4

In Cairo, HPB attempted unsuccessfully to organize a "Société Spirite" for the investigation of the phenomena of Spiritualism, her first effort at organizing a group. Because she felt the need of practical demonstrations, HPB decided to seek mediums who might come to Cairo and therefore wrote to a London Spiritualist journal, *The Medium and Daybreak: A Weekly Journal Devoted to the History, Phenomena, Philosophy, and Teachings of Spiritualism*, requesting it to announce her search. *Medium and Daybreak* did not publish her letter, but years later, after HPB had become something of a celebrity, the journal (March 15, 1889, 20:165) recalled having received it: "As far as we can remember, her letter was accompanied by a printed circular, stating the objects of the society she was then attempting to promote. Her communication would be received by us early in

1872." The journal did publish a short description of the society in its issue of February 9, 1872 (3:55), which was probably derived from the "printed circular":

THE CAIRO SOCIETY OF SPIRITUALISTS.

A society of Spiritualists has been formed in Cairo, Egypt, under the direction of Madame Blavatsky, a Russian lady, assisted by several mediums. Seances are held twice a week, namely on Tuesday and Friday evenings, to which members alone are admissible. It is intended to establish, in connection with the society, a lecture room, and a library of spiritualistic and other works, as well as a journal under the title, *La Revue Spirite du Caire* [*Fr.* The Spiritualist Review of Cairo], to appear on the 1st and 15th of each month. The following is a synopsis of the general rules of the society:—

1. Each annual member will have the right to a seance on his private affairs. 2. Both sexes are admissible to membership. 3. No member is allowed to introduce a stranger on pain of paying the price of an annual ticket, or of being excluded from the society. 4. All members provoking, by misconduct, the manifestation of evil spirits, or otherwise disturbing the tranquillity of the seance, will be subject to exclusion for the rest of the evening. 5. All frivolous or personal questions, not interesting to the society, must be submitted to the president. Lastly, All questions concerning the Government are strictly forbidden.

Later in the year, however, *Medium and Daybreak* (April 26, 1872, 3:150) did publish an announcement of the sort HPB wanted:

D. K. C. writing from Egypt, sends his kind regards to Mrs. Berry and others whom he used to meet at Mr. Herne's seances at the Spiritualist Institution, 15, Southampton Row. Mediums visiting the East would do well to pay a visit to Cairo. Madame Blavatsky has lately formed a society of Spiritualists, now numbering thirty-seven members. She offers board and lodging to any good mediums as long as they please to stop. Her address is Madame Blavatsky, Société Spirite, Rue d'Abdin, near the Viceroy's Palace, Cairo, Egypt.

That same month (April 1872), a sister London publication, *Human Nature: A Monthly Journal of Zoistic Science and Intelligence, Embodying Physiology, Phrenology, Psychology, Spiritualism, Psychology, the Laws of Health, and Sociology* (6:190), printed a paragraph "compiled from her letter and circular" (as later attested by *Medium and Daybreak*, March 15, 1889, 20:165):

> CAIRO, EGYPT.—A Society of Spiritualists has recently been founded in this city by a Russian lady, from whom we have received a very kind and encouraging letter. In a country of ignorance and superstition, she is meeting with much difficulty and opposition, and it is not an easy matter to maintain an association in such a state of society. She expresses herself as greatly in want of mediums to demonstrate the existence of spiritual beings, and says that any physical medium, such as Messrs. Herne and Williams, would meet with a cordial reception. She would give such a medium board and lodging in her own house, free from all expense, as long as he might choose. This lady's address is:—Madame Blawatsky, Societé Spirite, Rue d'Abdin, Cairo, Egypt. A postscript contains the following:—

Letter 4

To The Medium and Daybreak   *[ca. January 1872]*

I should like to subscribe for your valuable publication, *The Medium*. Please to let me know what the price of subscription will be. If you should chance to see Mr. D. Home, medium, please tell him that a friend of his late wife "Sacha"[1]—a St. Petersburg friend of past years—sends him her best compliments, and wishes him prosperity.

NOTE:

1. "Sacha," the nickname of Alexandrina de Kroll.

DATE: Estimated from the date (February 9, 1872) of the first announcement of the Cairo Société Spirite and the editor's recollection that the letter was received "early in 1872."

SOURCE: Original unavailable. Copied from *Human Nature* 6 (April 1872): 190.

Introduction to Letter 5

HPB's view of mediumship was not that of Spiritualists generally. Her private thoughts about Spiritualism are contained in fragments from a letter (or letters) to her relatives. In introducing these fragments, her sister, Vera de Zhelihovsky wrote:

> Mediums she held in as little esteem as ever, for she considered them one and all as weak, passive creatures, sickly sensitives with no will of their own. But she was bound she said, to prove to the world of the Spiritualists that by no means all of the agents 'behind the veil'—the producers of those meaningless, brutal physical phenomena that so rejoice the hearts of our unphilosophical wonder-hunters—are 'spirits' of departed mortals; that mediums, the high-priests of the new religion of the day and their parishioners, the Spiritualists, were both in the wrong box:

Letter 5

To her relatives   *[ca. March or early April 1872]*

[a] Their spirits are no spirits but spooks—rags, the cast off second skins of their personalities that the dead shed in the astral light as serpents shed theirs on earth, leaving no connection between the new reptile and his previous garments.

[b] They know no better and it does me no harm—for I will very soon show them the difference between a passive medium and an active *doer*. [1]

NOTE:

1. In fragment [b] from the same letter or from another written about the same time, HPB explained her reason for seeking to establish the Société Spirite. Vera comments:

   > In the meantime she determined to establish a *Société Spirite* for the investigation of mediums and phenomena according

to Allan Kardec's theories and philosophy, since there was no other; to give people a chance to see for themselves how mistaken they were. She would first give room to an already established and accepted teaching and then, when the public would see that nothing was coming out of it, she would then offer her own explanations. To accomplish this object, she said, she was ready to go to any amount of trouble—even to allowing herself to be regarded for a time as a helpless medium.

DATE: The subjects of these two fragments suggest the period when HPB was attempting to form her Société Spirite.

SOURCE: Russian original unavailable. Copied from a translation in "Mystical History" 554. The two fragments may be from the same or different letters.

⟜

Introduction to Letter 6

The attempt to found the Société Spirite and to find appropriate mediums for investigation was unsuccessful. HPB reported the collapse of her efforts in a letter that Vera introduces with the following remarks:

A few weeks later we received a new letter. In this one she showed herself full of disgust for the enterprise which proved a perfect failure. She had written, it seems, to England and France for a medium and had no response. *En desespoir de cause* [Fr. as a desperate shift, as a last resort] she had surrounded herself with *amateur* mediums—French female spiritists, mostly beggarly tramps when not adventuresses in the rear end baggage of M. de Lesseps' army of engineers and workmen on the canal of Suez.

Letter 6

To her relatives   [ca. late April 1872]

They steal the Society's money, they drink like sponges and I had caught them cheating most shamefully our members, who come to investigate the phenomena, by bogus

21

manifestations. I had very disagreeable scenes with several persons who held me alone responsible for all this. So I gave orders that their fees of membership (20 francs) should be returned to them and I will bear myself the costs and money laid out for hire of premises and furniture. My famous *Société Spirite* has not lasted one fortnight—it is a heap of ruins, less majestic but as suggestive as those of Pharaoh's tombs. . . . To wind up the comedy with a drama I got nearly shot by a madman—a Greek clerk who had been present at the only two public seances we held and got possessed, I suppose, by some vile spook. He premised by running about the bazaars and streets of Cairo with a cocked revolver, screaming that I had sent to him during three nights running a host of she-demons, of *Spirits* who were attempting to choke him!! He rushed into my house with his revolver, and finding me in the breakfast room, declared that he had come to shoot me and would wait till I had done with my meal. It was very kind of him, for in the meanwhile I *forced* him to drop his pistol and to rush out once more out of the house. He is now shut up in the lunatic asylum and I swear to put an end forever to such public seances—they are too dangerous *and I am not practised and strong enough* to control the wicked spooks that may approach my friends during such sittings. . . . I had told you before: how that this kind of promiscuous seances with mediums in the circle are a regular whirlpool—a maelstrom of bad magnetism during which time the so-called spirits (vile *Kikimora*!) feed upon us, suck in, sponge-like our vital powers and draw us down to their own plane of being. But you will never understand this without "going over a portion, at least, if not the whole range of writings that exist upon this subject."

DATE: As the letter refers to the collapse of the Société Spirite, it must have been written shortly before HPB left Cairo, which Boris de Zirkoff dates as about April 1872.

SOURCE: Russian original unavailable. Copied from a translation in "Mystical History" 554–5. Abridged version in *Incidents* 159 (2nd ed. 125) with minor variations; cf. *CW* 14:487–8.

⌣⟩

Introduction to Letter 7

When she left Cairo after the collapse of the *Société Spirite*, HPB traveled through Palestine, Lebanon, Syria (where she visited Palmyra), and Constantinople. In Lebanon, she met Countess Lydia Alexandrovna de Pashkov and traveled with her for a while. She returned to her family in Odessa in July 1872 (close to the predicted "18 moons" mentioned in background essay B), but left again in April 1873.

While in Odessa, contemplating renewed foreign travels, she may have written the following letter, addressed to the Director of the Third Section or Department, which had been formed by Tsar Nicholas I in 1826 as a secret police force responsible for political security but was closed in 1880 largely because of a proliferation of false reports. The genuineness of this letter has been questioned by a number of researchers. Several attempts to obtain a photocopy of the original, in order to compare the handwriting, have not been successful.

This letter was referred by the Third Department to the Police Department of the City of Odessa, which replied on January 27, 1873, that "Mme. Blavatsky's request has been left without consequences," meaning that no action was to be taken. The file on this application is labeled "Case of the Third Department of His Imperial Majesty's own office of the Third Dispatch Office Regarding the wife of the Councilor of State, Helena Blavatsky. Commenced January 9, 1873. Completed January 27, 1873 on 14 folios." The 14 folios are presumably the number of pages of the letter.

Letter 7

To the Director of the Third Department   December 26, 1872
                                                Odessa

Your Excellency!

I am the wife of Councilor of State Blavatsky. I was married at the age of 16 but, by mutual agreement, we separated several weeks after the wedding. Since then I have been living abroad almost continuously. During those 20 years I became well acquainted with the whole of western Europe. I zealously watched current politics, not with any specific aim, but because of an inborn passion arising from the habit of entering into the minutest details of a case in order to understand events better and to be able to foretell them. For this purpose I endeavored to make the acquaintance of all outstanding personalities among the politicians of the different powers, both on the Government side, as well as on the extreme Left. A whole sequence of events, intrigues, and revolutions took place before my eyes. . . . Many times I had the opportunity to be useful to Russia with my findings, but in the past, I kept quiet out of fear, due to my youthful stupidity. Later on, family misfortunes distracted me somewhat from such a task.

I am a direct niece of General Fadeyev,[1] a writer on military subjects, who is known to Your Excellency. Being involved in Spiritualism, I acquired the reputation, in many places, of being a powerful medium. Hundreds of people believe absolutely and will continue to believe in spirits. But I, who am writing this letter to offer my services to Your Excellency and to the Motherland, am obliged to tell you the whole truth, without any concealment. Therefore I confess that, on three-quarters of the occasions, the spirits spoke and answered in my own words and out of consideration for the success of my own plans. Rarely, very rarely, was I unsuccessful, by using this trap, in eliciting from the most secretive and serious people, their hopes, plans, and secrets. Being carried away little by little, they tried to find out from the spirits the future and the secrets of others, but in so doing they unwittingly betrayed to me their own. However, I acted cautiously, and rarely used my knowledge for my own benefit.

The whole of the last winter I spent in Egypt, in Cairo, and through the late Lavison,[2] our Vice Consul, I knew all that was happening at the Khedive's, of his plans, the cause of intrigues and so on. Lavison was so carried away with spirits, that in spite of all his cunning, he continuously divulged information. Thus I found out about the secret acquisition of a huge quantity of arms left behind by the Turkish Government; I found out about all the intrigues of Nubar-Pasha,[3] and of his talks with the German Consul General. I found out about all the ramifications of the exploitation by our agents and consuls of the estate of Raphael Abet, worth millions, and about much else. I founded the Spiritualist Society, and the whole country came into commotion. Some 400-500 people, the whole of society, Pashas and others, daily hurled themselves at me. Lavison was continuously at my place. Secretly he daily sent for me, and at his place I saw the Khedive, imagining that I would not recognize him in a different guise, obtaining information of the secret plans of Russia. He did not find any secret plans, but disclosed much to me. Several times I wanted to get into contact with Mr. de Lecs,[4] our Consul General. I wanted to offer him a plan, according to which so much could become known in Petersburg. All the consuls visited me, but whether it was because I was friendly with Mr. Pashkovsky and his wife,[5] while Mme. de Lecs was hostile to them for one reason or another, all my attempts remained in vain. Lecs forbade the whole Consulate to belong to the Spiritualist Society, and even insisted that all this was nonsense and charlatanism, which was unpolitic of him.

To put it briefly, the Society, deprived of government assistance, collapsed within three months.

It was then that Father Grégoire, of the Papal Mission in Cairo, who visited me every day, began insisting that I should get in touch with the Papal Government. In the name of Cardinal Barnabo,[6] he offered me 20 to 30 thousand francs yearly, for me to act through spirits, using my own discretion in view of Catholic propaganda, and so on. I listened and kept silent, since I have an inborn hatred of the whole Catholic clergy. Father Grégoire brought me a letter from the Cardinal, offering me all the blessings in future, saying: Il est temps que l'ange des ténèbres devienne l'ange de la lumière [*Fr.* It is time that the angel of darkness should become the angel of light], and offering me a place without equal in Catholic Rome, urging me to turn my back on heretical Russia. The result was that after I had taken 5 thousand francs from the Papal envoy for the time spent with him, I made many promises for the future, and then turned my back, not on heretical Russia, but on them, and departed. At the same time I informed the Consulate about this, but they only laughed at me, saying how stupid I had acted by not agreeing to accept such a favorable offer, and that patriotism and religion were a matter of taste, of stupidity, and so on.

I have now decided to turn to Your Excellency, fully certain that I will be more than useful to my Motherland, which I love more than anything in the world, and to our Emperor, whom we all deify. I can speak French, English, Italian, as well as Russian, I easily understand German and Hungarian and a little bit of Turkish. By birth, if not by my position, I am descended from the best aristocratic families of Russia, and can therefore move as easily in the highest circles as in the lowest strata of society. My whole life was spent in such leaps up and down. I have played all the parts and can turn myself into any sort of person; this is not a flattering portrait, but I am obliged to reveal the whole truth to Your Excellency, and to present myself as I have been molded by people, circumstances, and the eternal struggle of my whole life, which has exacerbated my cunning to equal that of a Red Indian. Seldom have I failed to achieve the desired result in any objective that I have pursued. I have experienced all temptations, and I repeat, that I have played parts in all strata of society. I can find out everything through spirits and by other means, and can extract the truth from the most secretive person. Until now all this achieved nothing and was wasted. If my abilities had been applied to the practical advantage of the State, the greatest results in governmental and political relations could have brought a not insignificant profit. Instead the results were microscopically limited for my own use.

My aim is not profit, but rather protection and help that is more *moral than material*. Although I have limited means of livelihood, and subsist by translations and commercial correspondence, I have, until now, consistently rejected all offers that could place me indirectly against the interests of Russia. In 1867 an agent of Beyst offered me various blessings, because I am a Russian and the niece of General Fadeyev, who is hated by them. This occurred in Pest;[7] I rejected the offer, and was subjected to most severe annoyances. The same year, in Bucharest, General Tiur, a Hungarian in the service of Italy, also pleaded with me—before the very conclusion of peace between Austria and Hungary[8]—to serve them. I refused. Last year in Constantinople, Mustafa Pasha,[9] the brother of the Egyptian Khedive, offered me a large sum of money through his secretary, Wilkinson, and once even by himself—after making my acquaintance through his French governess—asking that I should return to Egypt and supply him all information on the activities and intentions of his brother, the

Vice-King. Not knowing well how Russia would be looking at this business, and being afraid to tell General Ignatieff[10] about it, I declined this assignment, although I could have carried it out admirably.

In 1853, after losing a game of roulette in Baden Baden, I accepted an offer from a gentleman unknown to me—a Russian who had been watching me for some time. He offered me two thousand Francs if I could, by some means, get hold of two letters written in German (the contents of which remained unknown to me), and which had been very cunningly concealed by Count Kvilecky, a Pole in the service of the King of Prussia. The Russian was a military man, and every Russian had my sympathy. I had no money, I could not at that time return to Russia and was very upset by this. I agreed to the offer, and within three days, and with the greatest difficulties and subject to greatest danger, I obtained those letters. Then this gentleman told me that I have enough *talent* to be of use to the Motherland, and that it would be better for me to return to Russia. And if I should decide to change my way of life and to engage in serious work, then I need only apply to the Third Department and leave there my address and name. Unfortunately, at the time, I did not avail myself of this suggestion.

All this gives me the right to believe that I can be of use to Russia. I am alone in the world, although I have many relatives. Nobody knows that I am writing this letter.

I am completely independent, and feel that it is not simply a boast or an illusion if I say that I am not afraid of the most difficult and dangerous assignments. Life does not offer me anything either pleasant or good. Love of struggle and perhaps for intrigues is in my character. I am stubborn, and will go through fire or water to achieve an objective. I did not bring much benefit to myself; let me bring benefit at least to the Government of my Motherland. I am a woman without prejudice, and if I see the benefit of some cause, I look only on its bright side. Perhaps after finding out about this letter my relatives will curse me, blinded by their pride. But they will not find out, and it doesn't matter to me if they do. They never did anything for me. I had to serve them as a domestic *medium*, them, as well as their society.

Forgive me, Your Excellency, if I have dragged unnecessary domestic squabbles into a business letter. But this letter is my confession. I am not afraid of a secret investigation of my life. Whatever evil I have done, in whatever circumstances of life I have found myself, I have always been true to Russia, true to her interests. In sixteen years I committed only one illegal act, I left Poti[11] for abroad without a passport and dressed in male attire. But I was escaping not from Russia, but from an old hated husband, who had been imposed on me by Countess Vorontsova.[12] But in 1860 I was forgiven, and Baron Bruno,[13] the London Ambassador, gave me a passport. I had many incidents abroad defending the honor of the Motherland. I had arguments more than once during the Crimean War.[14] I don't know how I have not been assassinated, or how I have not been put into jail.

I repeat, I love Russia and am prepared to devote all my remaining life to her interests. Having revealed to Your Excellency the whole truth, I ask you respectfully to take notice of all this, and if necessary, to try me out. At present I live in Odessa with my aunt, the wife of General Witte,[15] on Polizeyskaya Street, house of Haas, No. 36. My name is Helena Petrovna Blavatskaya. If I do not hear from you within a month, I shall leave for France, since I am seeking a position as a correspondent in some business office. Your Excellency, please accept assurances of boundless respect and complete devotion, and of the readiness to be of service to you of Elena Blavatskaya.

NOTES:

Those introduced by [Mildon:] are translated from the Russian of
V. I. Mildon, editor of the letter in *Literaturnoe Obozrenie*.

1. Rostislav Andreyevich de Fadeyev, HPB's maternal uncle.

2. [Mildon:] Eduard Lavison (? –1872), Russian Vice-Consul in Cairo,
   1856–72.

3. [Mildon:] Nubar Pasha, the prime minister in the government of
   the Khedive Ismail.

4. [Mildon:] Ivan Mikhailovich Leks (1834–83), Russian Consul
   General in Cairo, 1868–83.

5. Perhaps Lydia Alexandrovna de Pashkov (Carlson, *Theosophical
   History* 5 [1995]: 228n).

6. [Mildon:] Alexander Barnabo (1801–?), Cardinal from 1856; he
   brought about a link between the Papal throne and foreign missions.

7. Pest, the Hungarian city on the left bank of the Danube River that
   was united with Buda, on the right bank, in 1872 to form Budapest.

8. The peace between Austria and Hungary of 1867 formed the
   Hapsburg Kingdom of Austria-Hungary, which lasted until 1918.

9. [Mildon:] Mustafa Pasha, military governor of Egypt under the
   Khedive Ismail.

10. [Mildon:] Nikolay Pavlovich Ignatieff, Count (1832–1908), Russian
    ambassador in Turkey, 1867–77.

11. Poti, the port on the Black Sea where HPB eluded the servants
    escorting her to meet her father after she had left her husband and
    instead sailed on an English ship bound for Constantinople to
    begin her world travels and independent life.

12. Perhaps the wife of Prince Mikhail Semyonovich Vorontsov
    (1782–1856), Viceroy of the Caucasus, 1844–56 (Carlson, *Theosophical History* 5 [1995]: 230-1n; *CW* 1:371). No connection between
    Countess Vorontsova and HPB's marriage is otherwise known.

13. [Mildon:] Baron Bruno, in Russian transliteration Philipp Ivanovich Brunnov (Brunov) (1796–1875), Russian ambassador in Great
    Britain, 1860–74.

14. Crimean War, fought by Russia against Britain, France, and Turkey from October 1853 to February 1856, during part of which time HPB was in England and India.

15. HPB's maternal aunt Katherine. [Mildon:] Wife of General Witte—presumably Ekaterina Andreyevna Fadeyeva, mother of S. Y. Witte.

SOURCE: Russian original in TsGAOR, the Central State Archive of the October Revolution, MS no. 109.3.22. Published in *Literaturnoe Obozrenie* 6 (1988): 111-2, from which translated here by Anatol Kagan. Also translated by Maria Carlson in *Theosophical History* 5 (July 1995): 227-31 and partially quoted in her *No Religion* 214.

◡◠◠

BACKGROUND ESSAY C

Early Days in New York

When HPB left Odessa in April 1873, she went by way of Bucharest to Paris, where she stayed with her cousin, Nikolay Gustavovich von Hahn, the son of her paternal uncle Gustav Alexeyevich. While in Paris, she became friendly with Monsieur and Mme. Leymarie, who were active in French Spiritualism. HPB had not been in Paris long when she was instructed by the "Brothers" to go to New York. Years later, she wrote a letter (undated and otherwise unknown) to her relatives about her sudden departure for America, a fragment of which is preserved in "Mystical History" 28; cf. *CW* 14:488:

> In June of the same year [1873] she was in Paris where she had intended to reside for sometime, when suddenly she received a letter—"an advice I have neither the desire, or possibility of resisting" as she explained it to us in her correspondence—from one of her Teachers in the far East. Hardly after two month's rest she had to pack up her trunks once more and cross over to the U.S. of America. She did this, as we all know it, unhesitatingly and at two days' notice. She arrived at New York on July 7th 1873 . . . .

31

As usual, HPB was short of cash. In New York, consequently, she resided in a cooperative-living arrangement with about forty working women, some of whom got her employment producing illustrated advertising cards, ornamental leather work, artificial flowers, and neckties. Later she resided in a widow's house, with whom she began to hold Sunday gatherings.

HPB's father Peter von Hahn died on July 27, 1873, but because the family did not know where she was at the time, she did not hear the news until several months later, after which she also received some money as her share of the estate. With that, she moved into quarters of her own, residing in several locations in New York City: a furnished top-floor room in a house on the northeast corner of Fourteenth Street and Fourth Avenue, and also on Union Square and on East Sixteenth Street. She visited Saugus, Massachusetts, and Buffalo, New York.

On June 22, 1874, HPB contracted a business arrangement with a French woman named Clementine Gerebko. As partners, they bought a tract of farmland on Long Island, to which HPB moved in July. The partnership ended with a quarrel and a lawsuit, eventually tried by jury on April 26, 1875, with judgment in HPB's favor filed on June 15, 1875 (background essay H).

Shortly after HPB's ill-starred business venture, events were set into motion that were to result in her meeting Henry Steel Olcott and the formation of the Theosophical Society. Olcott had earlier been interested in Spiritualism, but had turned his attention to other matters. However, one day in July 1874, while working in his New York law office, Olcott felt the urge to see what new developments there might be in Spiritualism. So he bought a copy of the Boston Spiritualist journal, the *Banner of Light*, and found in it a description of some remarkable phenomena at a Chittenden, Vermont, farmhouse belonging to a pair of brothers, Horatio and William Eddy. His curiosity aroused, Olcott went to investigate. Following a visit of several days, he came back to New York and wrote a description of his observations that was published in the *New York Sun*. As a result of that article, another New York newspaper, the *Daily Graphic,* asked him to go to Chittenden again so that he might investigate more thoroughly and write a series of articles on the subject. On September 17, 1874, Olcott returned to the Eddy farmhouse with an artist to do sketches, intending to stay about twelve weeks.

On September 22, HPB applied to be naturalized as an American citizen. Then, having read some of Olcott's newspaper articles, on October 14 HPB went to Chittenden to view the phenomena herself and to meet Olcott. HPB's presence at the Eddy séances considerably affected the manifestations. A number of apparitions—she called them "portrait-pictures"—of persons connected with her began to appear (*People* 310–38, 355–60; *ODL* 1:8–9). The first of these was Mihalko, a servant of her aunt, Katherine A. de Witte. On her first day at the farm, HPB met Olcott at the midday meal (*ODL* 1:1–5; *People* 293–306). After about ten days at Chittenden, during which HPB experienced a recurrence of her chronic illness—the reopening of the wound below her heart—she returned to New York City, where she was living at 124 East Sixteenth Street.

<hr>

Introduction to Letter 8

Having returned to New York, HPB wrote an account of her experiences at the Eddy farm in refutation of a skeptical article by Dr. George M. Beard; this was her first published article, "Marvellous Spirit Manifestations," appearing in the *Daily Graphic* on October 30 (*CW* 1: 30–4). Between its composition and publication, she wrote the following letter to the Russian author and Spiritualist researcher Alexander Aksakoff.

Letter 8

To A. N. Aksakoff   *October 28, 1874*
                                                                           New York

Pardon the liberty I take in so unceremoniously addressing one to whom I am entirely unknown.... This is what I have in mind: I have been living in America for about a year and a half, and have no intention of leaving. All my life is centered here, that is, of course, my inner life, as I am too old to take much interest in the outer life. . . . An attempt should be made to explain at home what is now going on in America, England, and France. Spiritism here is no laughing matter. The eleven million spiritists in the United States, according to the latest report, have grown to eighteen million, almost fifty percent, since the moment when pamphlets appeared in defense of spiritism, by men such as Alfred Wallace, Crookes, Varley, etc. . . . The entire press has begun to talk all at once. Attempts at ridicule, condemnation, and censure are rarer and rarer. Last year it was barely possible to find in any so-called respectable newspaper any article on the facts of spiritism; but now hardly a day passes without the papers being full of hundreds of facts, proofs, and so on. The papers send reporters and artists to mediums in every direction. Only last week I returned from the Eddy brothers, well-known mediums in Rutland, Vermont, where I spent two weeks. The house and the neighboring lodgings were full of correspondents. At the Eddy's the spirits of the departed walk about almost in full daylight. Several times they have appeared without the help of the medium, and in the evening during the *séance* from fifteen to twenty spirits appear as though in the flesh before the eyes of the spectators. I talked for five minutes on the platform in Russian with my *father*, my *uncle*, and other relations, as though they were alive. Seven persons of my acquaintance, long dead, of different nations, appeared and talked to me, each in his own language, and walked away. Would it not be possible for me to send you, or, rather, to keep sending from here translations of articles on the facts of spiritism, not by unknown people, but by persons such as Robert Dale Owen, Colonel Olcott, and the best writers here? I know many of them and they gladly give me the right of translating their productions. Olcott is a correspondent sent expressly to the Eddy brothers in Vermont by one of the best illustrated journals of New York, the *Graphic*. He has already spent more than two months there, and his illustrated articles are creating a *furore*. I am myself working for the *Graphic*, and can send my articles regularly, translated and fair-copied, with copies of the illustrations drawn in pen and India ink. You have probably also heard about the posthumous work of Dickens—the second part of his novel *Edwin Drood*, which was left unfinished at his death. I have translated this second part, and it is lying ready before me. . . . Whether the spirit of Dickens wrote it, or the medium James himself, this second part is accepted by the whole American and European press (with few exceptions) as a perfect *facsimile* of Dickens's style and his inimitable humor. . . . I again apologize for the unceremonious character of my letter. I hope you may perhaps find a spare moment to send me a few words in reply. I should very much like to see the completion of Dickens's novel, mentioned above, published in Russia. I have worked hard at it, translating it from James's manuscript, which he wrote under the dictation of Dickens's spirit.

SOURCE: Russian original unavailable. Translated by Boris de Zirkoff from Solovyov's *Sovremennaya* 255-6. Another English translation by Walter Leaf in *Modern Priestess* 225-7.

⌣⟶

Introduction to Letter 9

After their meeting at Chittenden, HPB wrote to Olcott several times. The letters do not survive, but were referred to and quoted from in *Old Diary Leaves*, from which the following account is taken:

Letter 9

To H. S. Olcott   *[ca. October 31 and November 6, 1874]*

[Olcott summarizes and quotes:] In her very first letter to me, written from New York within a week after she left me at Chittenden (October, 1874) addressing me as "Dear Friend" and signing herself "Jack," and in her second one, dated six days later and signed "Jack Blavatsky," she entreats me not to praise the mediumistic musical performance of one Jesse Sheppard, whose pretence to having sung before the Czar, and other boasts she had discovered to be absolutely false; as such a course on my part would "injure Spiritualism more than anything else in the world."[1] "I speak to you," she tells me, "as a true friend to yourself and (as a) Spiritualist anxious to save Spiritualism from a danger." In the same letter, referring to a promise given her by "Mayflower" and "George Dix," two of the alleged spirit-controls of Horatio Eddy, that they would help her by influencing the judge before whom was pending her lawsuit to recover the money put into the Long Island market-garden co-partnership—she says: "Mayflower was right, Judge——came in with another decision in my favour."[2]

NOTES:

1. H. S. Olcott adds a footnote: "Led by his unlucky star, Sheppard—she writes—had brought her a lot of his St. Petersburgh credentials, in Russian, to translate. Among them she found a Police license to sing at the Salle Koch, a low lager-bier saloon and dance hall, resorted to by dissipated characters of both sexes, and a music-master's bills for 32 roubles, for teaching him certain Russian songs—which we heard him sing at Eddy's, *in a dark séance when he was ostensibly under the control of Grisi and Lablache!* I give the facts on her authority without prejudice."

2. See background essay H, "HPB's Lawsuit in America."

DATE: HPB left Chittenden about October 25, according to Boris de Zirkoff's Chronology (*CW* 1:liii), so the first letter written "within a week" would be before November 1, and the second was "six days later."

SOURCE: Original unavailable. Copied from *Old Diary Leaves* 1: 68-9.

HPB also entered into correspondence with the younger of the two Eddy brothers, Horatio, who was at the time about 32 and semiliterate. Her letters to him have apparently not survived, but one of his replying to her is in the Archives of the Theosophical Society, Adyar:

Chittenden Vt   Nov 4th 1874

Dear Friend Madam I just reseived your letter and will Hasten to answer it it found us all well and glad to hear from you. I did not see your Don't in the Graffic But trust you will give that contemptle puppy, all he wants—Before you git threw with him hoping you will Be sustaind and know you will by the Spirit world, don't mind the Babbone monkey nor the Rabits [?] as it will be to much trouble for you the Spirits all Send Love to you and all the rest hoping ear long we Shall See you and your Law Suit—will all Be Seteld up

From your trew friend Horatio
[Horatio B. Eddy]

Introduction to Letter 10

Early in November 1874, HPB moved to 16 Irving Place, where Olcott visited her when he came back from Chittenden (*ODL* 1:10), and then to 23 Irving Place. HPB's first article, "Marvellous Spirit Manifestations" (*Daily Graphic*, October 30, 1874, in *CW* 1:30-4) was quickly followed by a second, "About Spiritualism" (*Daily Graphic*, November 13, 1874, in *CW* 1:36-44). Both were directed against Dr. George M. Beard, a critic of Spiritualism.

On November 12, HPB went to the office of the *Daily Graphic* newspaper to deliver her second article on the Eddy phenomena (*CW* 1:36-44). There she was interviewed by a reporter, and the interview was published as "About Spiritualism: Mme. Blavatsky's Visit to *The Daily Graphic* Office" in the paper's November 13 issue.

Olcott (*ODL* 1:31) quotes a letter from HPB relating to this event, with the following introduction:

> In November, 1874, signing her letter 'Jack the Pappoose,' she wrote to ask me to get her an engagement to write weird stories for a certain journal, as she would soon be 'hard up,' and gave me a rollicking account of her family pedigree and connexions on both sides; talking like a democrat, yet showing but too plainly that she felt that she, if anyone, had reason to be proud of her lineage. She writes me how the *Daily Graphic* people had interviewed her about her travels and asked for her portrait. Considering how many thousand copies of her likeness have since been circulated, the world over, it will amuse if I quote a sentence or two about this first experience of the sort:

Letter 10

To H. S. Olcott   *November [ca. 12,] 1874*

Don't you know, the fellows of the *Graphic* bored my life out of me to give them my portrait? Mr. F. was sent to get me into conversation after I came out [HSO comments: "for the Eddys, she means"], and wanted them to insert my article against . . . Beard. I suppose they wanted to create a sensation and so got hold of my beautiful nostrils and splendid mouth. . . . I told them that nature has endowed and gifted me with a potato nose, but I did not mean to allow them to make fun of it, vegetable though it is. They very seriously denied the fact, and so made me laugh, and you know *"celui qui rit est désarmé"* [Fr. The one who laughs is disarmed].

SOURCE: Original unavailable. Copied from *ODL* 1:31–2.

HPB's views on Spiritualism published in the *Daily Graphic* elicited a response from Elbridge Gerry Brown, the editor of the *Spiritual Scientist* of Boston, written on November 14, 1874 (*CW* 1:45–6):

> I have read your article in the *Daily Graphic*, and am so much pleased with the statements therein, and the powerful

refutations of Dr. Beard's so-called "arguments," that I hasten to acknowledge to you, as editor of the *Scientist*, my gratitude for the service you have done Spiritualism in re-opening the eyes of the skeptical world.

Should you ever be in Boston, I beg that you will grant me permission, to call on you that I may learn more of the Eddy Family from one who has had so wonderful an experience and presents it in so interesting and attractive style.

I have taken the liberty, to send you a copy of the *Scientist*.

Hoping you will pardon my enthusiasm, which thus seeks expression, I have the honor to subscribe myself, with respect, truly yours, Gerry Brown.

The Spiritual Scientist: A Weekly Journal Devoted to the Science, History, Philosophy, and Teachings of Spiritualism, published in Boston, was patronized by HPB and Olcott, who hoped to use it as a journal devoted to the philosophical aspects of Spiritualism, rather than merely to the phenomena. For that purpose, HPB set about raising support for the journal, in both subscriptions and contributions by writers of repute, and she and Olcott both contributed to the journal themselves.

As a Christmas present in 1875 and doubtless in acknowledgment of HPB's past support, the editor, E. Gerry Brown, presented her a bound volume of the first issues of the journal, from September 10, 1874, through the supplement of July and August, 1875 (the first two numbered volumes). On the recto of the flyleaf, he inscribed the gift:

> Mdme Helen P Blavatsky
> Compliments of
> December 25 75   E Gerry Brown

HPB later made a gift of the volume, inscribing the flyleaf, just below Gerry Brown's inscription to her, as follows:

> presented to the National Association of Spiritualists
> with the good wishes of
> H. P Blavatsky.
> October 1877
> New York.

The volume eventually came into the possession of the London book dealer John Watkins, who in turn made a gift of the book, with the following inscription at the bottom of the inside front cover, opposite the earlier inscriptions:

> Presented to the L.S.A. [London Spiritualist Alliance]
> Library
> by John M Watkins
> June 30th 1920.

The volume is still in the archives of that body, in 1970 renamed the College of Psychic Studies. Of interest in this particular volume, in addition to its peregrinations from the editor of the *Spiritual Scientist* through HPB to its present resting place, is the fact that HPB annotated one of its articles, whose subject was herself, with marginalia. The article (*Spiritual Scientist*, November 19, 1874, 121-2) reported HPB's visit to the office of the New York *Daily Graphic* newspaper, which resulted in a biographical sketch of the Russian woman who was attracting attention among Spiritualists and the general public. The article took liberties with some of the facts it reported, thus eliciting HPB's self-deprecating scorn upon some of its inaccuracies, although there are other specific ones that she might also have pilloried, but did not. The article, as reprinted in the *Spiritual Scientist* from the *Daily Graphic* of November 13, and HPB's marginal comments on it (here reproduced in notes) are as follows:

MORE ABOUT MATERIALIZATION.

AN INTELLIGENT AND LOGICAL SPIRITUALIST.—
A MEDAL BROUGHT FROM A GRAVE IN RUSSIA BY A SPIRIT.—
HOW THE EMPEROR OF RUSSIA WAS CONVERTED.

ME. [*i.e.,* Mme.] BLAVATSKY visited the Daily Graphic office Thursday, and excited a great deal of interest. She exhibited the silver jewel of the Order of St. Ann, which was buried with her father at Stavropol, and which the spirit of George Dix conveyed to her during her recent seance at the Eddy homestead in Vermont. Her object in visiting them was to hand to the chief editor a letter *apropos* of the Olcott-Beard discussion. The lady expressed herself with great vivacity in favor of the Eddy brothers, and seemed very much exercised about the Beard letter. Mme. Blavatsky has traveled in almost every quarter of the world, has met with many romantic adventures, and is a remarkably good natured and sprightly woman.[1] She is handsome, with full voluptuous figure, large eyes, well-formed nose, and rich, sensuous mouth and chin. She dresses with remarkable elegance, is *bien gantee* [*Fr.* well-gloved], and her clothing is redolent of some subtle and delicious perfume, which she has gathered in her wanderings in the far East.

"I was born in 1834, at Ekaterinoslav," she said, "of which my father, Col. Hahn-hahn was Governor. It is about two hundred versts from Odessa. Yes, he was a cousin of the Countess Ida Hahn-hahn, the authoress. My mother was a daughter of Gen. Fadeef, and I am a granddaughter of the Princess Dolgorouki. My mother was an authoress, and used to write under the *nom de plume* of Zenaida R * * * va.[2]

"When my father died,"[3] she proceeded, "I went to Tiflis, in Georgia, where my grandfather was one of the three Councillors of the Viceroy Woronzoff. When I was sixteen years of age, they married me to M. Blavatsky, he was the Governor of Erivan. Fancy! he was seventy-three and I sixteen. But mind, I don't blame anybody,—not my friends, not in the least. However, at the end of the year we separated. His habits were not agreeable to me. As I had a fortune of my own I determined to travel. I went first of all to Egypt. I spent three nights in the Pyramid of Cheops. Oh, I had most marvelous experiences. Then I went to England. And in 1853, I came to this country. I was recalled to Russia by the death of my grandmother, Mme. Brajation. She left me a fortune, but if I had been with her before her death I should have had much more. She left eight millions of roubles to the convents and monasteries in Moldavia,—she was a Moldavian herself. I went back to Egypt, and penetrated into the Soudan. I made a great deal of money on that journey."

"How?"

"Why, by buying ostrich feathers. I did not go there for that purpose, but as I found I could do it I did it. Oh! ostrich feathers that would sell for five or six guineas you could buy there for a cent. Then I went to Athens, Palestine, Syria, Arabia, and back again to Paris. Then I went to Homburg and Baden Baden, and lost a good deal of money at gambling, I am sorry to say. [From here to the end of the paragraph, HPB underlined the text.] In 1858, I returned to Paris, and made the acquaintance of Daniel Home, the Spiritualist. He had married the Countess Kroble, a sister of the Countess Koucheleff Bezborrodke, a lady with whom I had been very intimate in my girlhood. Home converted me to Spiritualism."[4]

"Did you ever see any of his 'levitations,' as they are called?"

"Yes, I have seen Home carried out of a four-story window, let down very gently to the ground, and put into his carriage. After this I went to Russia. I converted my father to Spiritualism. He was a Voltairean before that. I made a great number of other converts."

"Are there many Spiritualists in your country?"

"Yes. You would be suprised to know how large a number of Spiritualists there are in Russia. Why, the Emperor Alexander is a Spiritualist. Would you actually believe it?—the emancipation of the serfs was caused by the appearance of the Emperor Nicholas to the Emperor Alexander."

"This is a very remarkable statement."

"It's true. The Cæsarewitch was one day telling Prince Bariatinsky of it. He said, 'Oh, your Imperial Highness, I cannot believe it.' The Emperor came forward and asked what they were talking about. Prince Bariatinsky told him what the Cæsarewitch had said about the appearance of the spirit of the Emperor Nicholas. The Emperor Alexander turned as pale as a ghost himself, and said, 'It is true.'"

"That is very remarkable. Where did you travel subsequently?"

"I went to Italy and then to Greece. As I was returning from the Piræus to Napoli, when we were off Spezzia, the boat in which I was making the voyage, the Evmonia, blowed up, and of four hundred persons on board only seventeen were saved. I was one of the fortunate ones. As I laid on my back I saw limbs, heads and trunks all falling around me. This was the 21st of June, 1871. I lost all my money and everything I had. I telegraphed to my friends for money. As soon as I got it I went to Egypt again, and to the Soudan. I never saw a white face for four months. I translated Darwin into Russian while I was in Africa. I have also translated Buckle into Russian. I have contributed to the Revue des deux Mondes and several Parisian journals, and have acted as correspondent of the Independance Belge. I am a member of the order of Eastern Masonry, the most ancient in the world. I was initiated in Malta." Here Mme Blavatsky showed the writer the jewel of one of the most celebrated orders in existence, the name of which, however, he is not at liberty to give. "There are not more than six or seven women in the world who have been admitted to this order. I shall probably stay in American a long time. I like the country very much."[5]

NOTES:

1. [HPB added a footnote to the bottom of the page:] A *lie* Number 1°. H.P.B.

2. [HPB's footnote:] Lie Number 2. Stolen from C. Olcott's "People from it. [*i.e.,* the Other World"]

3. [HPB underlined the words "my father died" and added this footnote:] Lie Number 3. My father died three years ago.

4. [HPB's footnote:] The biggest lie of all. *I never saw in my whole life* either D. D. Home or his wife; I never was in the same city with him for half an hour in my life. From 1851 to 1859 I was in California, Egypt and India. In 1856–58 I was in Kashmere and elsewhere.

5. [In the right margin of the first page of the article, HPB wrote the following annotation, which seems to apply to the whole article:] These lies were circulated by American reporters with which this land of "canards" and unwarrantable exaggeration so freely abounds. H. P Blavatsky.

~~~~~

Introduction to Letter 11

HPB continued her correspondence with Aksakoff and her relatives in Russia.

Letter 11

To A. N. Aksakoff   *November 14, 1874*
                                    23 Irving Place, New York

It is barely a week since I wrote to you,[1] and I already bitterly repent it! This morning, as usual, when I was in town, I was sitting with my only friend, Andrew Jackson Davis, who is highly respected by all here; he has received your letter in French, and, as he does not understand the language well, he asked me to read it and to translate it. In this letter you write: "I have heard of Madame Blavatsky from one of her parents, who spoke of her as a rather strong medium. Unfortunately her communications reflect *her morals, which have not been very strict.*" Whoever it was who told you about me, they told you, the *truth*, in essence, if not in detail. God only knows how I have suffered for my past. It is clearly my fate to gain no forgiveness upon Earth. This *past*, like the seal of the curse on Cain, has pursued me all my life, and pursues me even here, in America, where I came to be far from it and from the people who knew me in my youth. You are the innocent cause of my being obliged now to escape somewhere even farther away—where, I do not know. I do not accuse you; God is my witness that while I am writing these lines, I have nothing against you in my heart, beyond the deep sorrow which I long have known for the irrevocable past. Andrew Jackson, who feels and reads men more clearly than any book (and this no one doubts who knows him), said to me on this matter just the following highly significant words: "I know you as *you are* now, and I *feel* you; I cannot and will not touch your past; I shall write to Mr. Aksakoff that he *does not know* you personally, while *I* know you." These words of A. J. Davis will be sufficient for you, and I have no further need to try and assure you that the Madame Blavatsky of twenty years ago, and of today, when she is over 40, *are two different persons*. I am a "spiritist" and "spiritualist" in the full significance of these two terms. . . . I was a "materialist" till I was 30, and both believed and did not believe in spiritism. As I did not believe in God, I could not believe in a future life. Morality and virtue I regarded as a social garment, for the sake of propriety; a social mask to be worn on one's figure in order not to shock the ethics of one's neighbor, much as one would place English taffeta over an ugly wound. I hated "society" and the so-called world, as I hated *hypocrisy* in whatever form it showed itself; *ergo*, I ran amuck against society and established proprieties. Result: three lines in your letter which have awakened all the past within me and torn open all the old wounds. I have now been a *spiritist* for more than 10 years, *and now all my life is devoted to this doctrine*. I am struggling for it, and try to consecrate to it every moment of my life. Were I rich, I would spend all my money, to the last farthing, for the propaganda of that divine truth. But my means are very small, and I am obliged to live by my work, translating and writing in the papers.

This is why I have approached you with the proposition to translate into Russian everything about spiritualism that comes out here. I have translated *Edwin Drood*, and it has long been ready, and now I am translating some letters (Colonel H. S. Olcott's) which are creating at the present moment such a revolution in the minds of materialists.

He *investigated* for eight weeks the materializations of spirits at the Eddy brothers in Vermont, and I went there and lived two weeks at their farm, where I got to know him. His letters and writings are worthy rivals of the books of

Robert Dale Owen, Epes Sargent, and other champions. But now that I know your just, though harsh, judgment of me, I see that there is no salvation for me but death. I shall have to drag to the grave the chain and ball of a social galley-slave. It is clear that neither repentance nor voluntary exile from my country, where I have brothers and sisters and beloved relatives, whom I shall never see again on Earth—nothing will pacify the wrath of this furious wild beast whose name is Public Opinion.

I have one request to make of you: do not deprive me of the good opinion of Andrew J. Davis. Do not reveal to him that which, if he knew it and were convinced, would force me to escape to the ends of the Earth. I have only one refuge left in the world—it is the respect of the spiritualists of America who despise nothing so much as "free love."

Does it give you any satisfaction morally to destroy forever a woman who has already been killed by circumstances? Pardon this long letter, and accept the assurance of the deep respect and devotion of your obedient servant.

Helena Blavatsky

NOTE:

1. The earlier letter is dated October 28 by Solovyov, and this one November 14; if those dates are correct, nearly two and a half weeks separated them.

SOURCE: Russian original unavailable. Translated by Boris de Zirkoff from Solovyov's *Sovremennaya* 256–8. Another English translation by Walter Leaf in *Modern Priestess* 227–30.

Introduction to Letter 12

Sometime after the middle of November, a new figure entered HPB's life. Michael C. Betanelly had read Olcott's accounts of the Chittenden phenomena and came to New York from Philadelphia to meet HPB. Olcott (*ODL* 1:55) describes the result:

It turned out that he fell at once into a state of profound admiration, which he expressed verbally, and later, by letter, to her and to me. She persistently rebuffed him when she saw that he was matrimonially inclined, and grew very angry at his persistence. The only effect was to deepen his devotion.

Toward the end of November, HPB went to Philadelphia to investigate the séances being held by a husband and wife team of mediums, Nelson and Jennifer Holmes. After several weeks there, she and Olcott went for a few days to Hartford, Connecticut, where Olcott's book, *People from the Other World*, was being published. It was during that brief stay in Hartford that the following letter was written:

Letter 12

To A. N. Aksakoff   *December 13, 1874*
                                       Hartford, Connecticut

I do not know how to thank you for your immeasurable goodness. Though you have the right, like any honorable man, to despise me for my sad reputation in the past, you are so condescending and magnanimous as to write to me. . . . If I have any hope for the future, it is only beyond the grave, when bright spirits shall help me to free myself from my sinful and impure envelope. Pardon me and forgive me for having, in a moment of despair, written you my foolish second letter. I did not understand you, and thought that you, like the rest, judged me only from the outside. When I had read your letter, I saw how I had been mistaken in you, and that you were ready to stretch out a helping hand even to a sinner like myself. I received your letter by a sort of miracle, which I really do not understand. . . .

. . . I am here in Hartford for a couple of days on business. I came to confer with Colonel Olcott about certain alterations in his letters and supplements. He is now publishing a book [*People from the Other World*] on the subject of his letters to the *Graphic*; the book is so complete that it forms two parts, 600 pages. The first part will consist of original letters, and the second will deal with public opinion about Spiritualism, and the antagonism between science, religion, and the phenomena of Spiritualism; the latter in the form in which it has manifested itself for the last 40 years in a community of the Shakers, etc. The book is too lengthy to translate. . . . It will be better if I send a translation of the letters as they were published in the *Daily Graphic*. All the sketches and illustrations of the spirits I will attach to the sheets of the translations—the portrait of a certain Hassan Aga as he appeared to me *materialized* at Chittenden, in the presence of 40 people, and talked to me half in Russian and half in Georgian, and the portrait of my grandfather Gustav Alexeyevich von Hahn, who also appeared twice. Generally speaking I play a considerable part in Olcott's letters, as all the seven spirits which appeared to me at the farm in Vermont resulted in a great triumph for the cause of Spiritualism. As long as the spirits only talked English and French there were reasons perhaps to doubt, as it was *possible* to suspect some play of prestige. But when seven *materialized* spirits, in flesh and bone, all differently dressed, according to their nationality, and talking six different languages, Russian, Turkish, Georgian, Hungarian, and Italian, appeared every evening and were heard by everybody talking like living people, the aspect of things changed. The country is all stirred up. I am getting letters from various countries, and from different editors. A doctor named Beard, who spent only one day at Chittenden, has allowed himself to insult all the spirits, calling them in the newspapers "weak-minded fools and idiots," and I have answered him twice in the papers. It appears that even without my realizing it I had struck right. The most eminent Spiritualists, such as Robert Dale Owen, Dr. Child, and others have written me letters, and the editors of the largest publishing company in America, here at Hartford, have written me asking me to get together a volume of letters concerning different phases of Spiritualism and of the *physical* manifestations of the spirits that I had seen in India, in Africa, and elsewhere. They are desirous of buying such a work. I would have my fortune secured if I wasn't carrying unfortunately my accursed name of Blavatsky. I do not dare to risk signing my name to any book. It might raise reminiscences too dangerous for me. I prefer to lose $12,000 which is what is offered me—the editors offer me 12 cents per copy, and they guarantee to sell 100,000 copies. These are the bitter fruits of my youth devoted to Satan, his pomps and works! I will send you, my dear Sir, at the end of this week, a package of data and articles cut from the most respectable newspapers of the country. I will also send you my two printed letters, as this will give you an idea ahead of time of the widespread interest that will be aroused by a book like Colonel Olcott's. Imagine, Sir, materialized spirits of Russian nurses speaking their language, of Georgian boys, of Kurd men, of Hungarian and Italian Garibaldians, and finally *my* uncle,[1] the Russian President of the Civil Court at Grodno with the cross of the Order of St. Anna on his neck, appearing at 6,000 miles from our place, in America, in an isolated farm, lost among the mountains of Vermont, with rather commonplace farmer-*mediums*, who couldn't speak well their own native tongue—and appearing *to me*, whom they did not know from Adam or Eve, in front of 40 people among whom were skeptical reporters, physicians, clergymen, distinguished men like Olcott, and many others! And to crown it *all*, at a *séance* separate from the "dark circle" a spirit bringing me the medal of my father for the 1828 war with Turkey, and telling me in the hearing of everybody else: "I bring you, Helena Blavatsky, the badge of honor, received by your father for the war of 1828. We took this medal through *the influence of your uncle* who appeared to you this night—from your *father's grave at Stavropol*, and bring it to you as a remembrance of us in whom you believe and have faith."[2]

I know this medal, I have seen it on my father and *I know* that it was buried *with him*, together with his other decorations. It has been sketched for the *Graphic*, and I have it! Understand it as you like! My father died last year at *Stavropol*.[3] How could the spirits know this? How could the mediums know that my father was a soldier and took part in the battles with the Turks? It is a mystery, a great mystery! In Russia, of course, it will not be believed. They will say that Blavatsky has either gone out of her mind, or perhaps something worse. Fortunately there were 40 witnesses. You cannot imagine what an impression it produced on everyone. I will write when I send the letters; I'm afraid of wearying you. Once more I thank you, and remain with sincere respect and devotion,

Yours obediently,
H. Blavatsky.

P.S.: Colonel Olcott desires to be respectfully remembered to you, and is sending you his photograph. From a furious skeptic he has become an ardent Spiritualist after spending 13 weeks with the Eddy brothers at Chittenden. . . . If you permit me, I will send you my portrait lithographed as an illustration in the *Daily Graphic*, with an account of my travels in Africa and the Sudan.[4] I do not know why they have done me such an honor as to set me beside Ida Pfeiffer and Livingstone. . . .

NOTES:

1. According to Olcott's *People from the Other World* (360), this was "Gustave H. Hahn, late President of the Criminal Court at Grodno, Russia, . . . who died in 1861."

2. Olcott (*People* 355–9) describes this event of the evening of October 24 in some detail, beginning:

> In the dark-circle, as soon as the light was extinguished, "George Dix," addressing Mme. de Blavatsky, said: "Madame, I am now about to give you a test of the genuineness of the manifestations in this circle, which I think will satisfy not only you, but a skeptical world beside. I shall place in your hands the buckle of a medal of honor worn in life by your brave father, and buried with his body in Russia. This has been brought to you by your uncle, whom you have seen materialized this evening." Presently I heard the lady utter an exclamation, and, a light being struck, we all saw Mme. de B. holding in her hand a silver buckle of a most curious shape, which she regarded with speechless wonder.

The "buckle," as appears from a drawing of it (*People* 357), is what today would be called a pin, to which a medal could be attached by a ribbon. The *Oxford English Dictionary* defines "buckle" as "a rim of metal, with a hinged tongue carrying one or more spikes, for securing a belt, strap, or ribbon, which passes through the rim and is pierced by the spike or spikes," a definition that describes the object in the drawing, a roughly heart-shaped, crowned piece of jewelry with a spike-pin attached to its back, which would have both pierced a ribbon to which the medal was attached and secured the pin or buckle to the wearer's garment. Olcott (356) cites HPB's authentication of the object by reporting that "she identified this particular article by the fact that the point of the pin had been carelessly broken off by herself many years ago"; he also says: "As to the authenticity of this present, so mysteriously received, she possessed ample proof, in a photographic copy of her father's oil portrait, in which this very buckle appears, attached to its own ribbon and medal." Olcott's account (357) includes a drawing also of the buckle with ribbon and medal attached, of which he says (356): "I now am able to present to the reader sketches of the spirit's present, and the whole decoration; the former copied from life, the latter from the photograph." Olcott clearly says that the "spirit's present" was the buckle or pin; in the letter above, HPB says that it was the medal. The discrepancy is perhaps explained as a trick of her memory by which her recollection of the buckle and medal were fused, reinforced by the sketch in the *Graphic*, depicting both the pin ("copied from life") and the medal ("from the photograph").

3. HPB's father died on July 27, 1873, or July 15 by the Julian calendar (*People* 356).

4. An interview with HPB was published as "About Spiritualism: Mme. Blavatsky's Visit to *The Daily Graphic* Office" in the November 13 issue of the newspaper (see also the introduction and endnote to letter 10).

SOURCE: Russian original unavailable. Translated by Boris de Zirkoff from Solovyov's *Sovremennaya* 258-62. Another English translation by Walter Leaf in *Modern Priestess* 231–5.

~

Introduction to Letter 13

When HPB wrote to the Russian Spiritualist, A. N. Aksakoff, she did so as a true believer in conventional Spiritualism, doubtless because she hoped to enlist his interest and perhaps because she expected his scientific curiosity to lead to a thorough investigation of the phenomena. Moreover, if his fellow Russians knew her real views, they could be expected to "say that Blavatsky has either gone out of her mind, or perhaps something worse." In her letters to her family, however, while not denying the reality of some Spiritualist phenomena, she presents quite a different view of their cause and value.

Letter 13

To her relatives [1874]

The more I see of Spiritualistic *séances* in this cradle and hotbed of Spiritualism and mediums, the more clearly I realize how dangerous they are for humanity. Poets speak of the *thin partition* between the two worlds—there is *no* partition whatever! Blind people have imagined some sort of barriers, because our gross organs of hearing, sight, and feeling do not allow the majority of people to penetrate the difference of being. Mother Nature, by the way, has done well in endowing us with *gross* senses, for otherwise the *individuality* and *personality* of man would become impossible, because then the dead would be constantly blending with the living and the living would assimilate themselves with the dead. . . . It would be possible to submit to the inevitable, however, were we surrounded by spirits similar to us, semi-spiritual reliquiae of mortals, who passed away without having reconciled themselves to the great necessity of death. One way or another, we cannot help assimilating ourselves physically and quite unconsciously with the dead, absorbing the component atoms of that which lived before us; with every breath we inhale them, and breathe out that which nourishes the formless beings, elementals hovering in the atmosphere in the expectation of being transformed into living beings. This is not only a physical process, but partly a spiritual one. Gradually absorbing their brain molecules, and exchanging our intellectual *auras*, which means thoughts, desires, yearnings, we assimilate those who preceded us.

This transformation is common to mankind and to all that lives, a natural process, the outcome of the laws of nature's economy. . . . It explains both external and moral similarities. . . . However, there exists another and exceptional law which manifests itself periodically and sporadically: this is a law, as it were, of artificial and compulsory assimilation. During epidemics of this kind the kingdom of the dead invades the domain of the living; fortunately, however, its dregs are bound by the ties of their former surroundings, and, when evoked by mediums, cannot trespass the boundaries and limits within which they acted and lived. . . . And the wider the doors are opened to them, and the further is this necromantic contagion spread, and the more concerted are the desires of the mediums and Spiritualists to spread the magnetic fluid of their evocations—the more power and vitality are acquired by the obsession.

For these are only such earthly dregs, irresistibly pulled, as they are, towards the earth, that could not follow the liberated soul and spirit, the higher principles of man's being, and are left for a second death in the terrestrial atmosphere. I have often observed with repugnance how such a revived shade separated itself from within the medium; how, oozing out of his astral body, it took a stranger's integument and impersonated some *dear one*, moving them to rapture, making them open their hearts and embraces wide to these shades, which they sincerely mistook for their beloved fathers and brothers, resuscitated to convince them of life eternal and of their eventual meeting. . . . If only they knew the truth! If only they could believe it! . . . If only they could see what I have often seen, how an ugly, bodiless creature pounces at times upon one of those present at these Spiritualistic enchantments. It envelops the man as if in a dark pall and slowly disappears within him, as if sucked into his body through every living pore.[1]

NOTE:

1. A slightly different translation of the final paragraph was published in the *Path* (NY) 9 (Feb. 1895): 380–1: "It stands to reason that this mere earthly refuse, irresistibly drawn to the earth, cannot follow the soul and spirit—these highest principles of man's being. With horror and disgust I often observed how a reanimated shadow of this kind separated itself from the inside of the medium; how, separating itself from his astral body and clad in someone else's vesture, it pretended to be someone's relation, causing the person to go into ecstasies and making people open wide their hearts and their embraces to these shadows whom they sincerely believed to be their dear fathers and brothers, resuscitated to convince them of life eternal, as well as to see them. . . . Oh, if they only knew the truth, if they only believed! If they saw, as I have often seen, a monstrous, bodiless creature seizing hold of someone present at these spiritistic sorceries! It wraps the man as if with a black shroud, and slowly disappears in him as if drawn into his body by each of his living pores."

DATE: As in "Mystical History"; in *Incidents*, the letter is dated 1875.

SOURCE: Russian original unavailable. Translated by Boris de Zirkoff from *Russkoye Obozreniye* 2 (Nov. 1891): 253–5. A different, but generally similar translation (except that the last paragraph is more divergent, as indicated in the note above) in *Path* (NY) 9 (Feb. 1895): 379–81. A wholly different translation in *Path* (London) 3 (Dec. 1912): 214–5.

In addition to the original version of this letter, HPB translated, edited, and augmented it in 1886 for use by A. P. Sinnett in *Incidents in the Life of Madame Blavatsky*. HPB's English revision of her own earlier Russian letter is as follows:

1886 Revision

The more I see of mediums—for the United States are a true nursery, the most prolific hot-bed for mediums and sensitives of all kinds, genuine and artificial—the more I see the danger humanity is surrounded with. Poets speak of the thin partition between this world and the other. They are blind: there is no partition at all, except the difference of states in which the dead and the living exist and the grossness of the physical senses of the majority of mankind. Yet—these senses are our salvation. They were given to us by a wise and sagacious mother and nurse—Nature; for otherwise *individuality* and even *personality* would have become impossible: the dead would be ever merging into the living and the latter assimilating the former. Were there around us but one variety of 'spirits'—as well call the dregs of wine, spirits—the reliquiae of those mortals who are dead and gone, one could reconcile oneself with it. We cannot avoid in some way or the other to assimilate our dead, and little by little and unconsciously to ourselves we become *they*—even physically, especially in the unwise West where cremation is unknown. *We breathe and eat, and devour the dead*—men and animals—with every breath we draw in; as every human breath that goes out makes up the bodies and feeds the formless creatures in the air that will be men some day. So much for the physical process; for the mental and the intellectual and also the spiritual it is just the same: we interchange gradually our brain-molecules, our intellectual and even spiritual auras, hence—our thoughts, desires, and aspirations with those who preceded us. This process—rather novel in its ultimate views to physiology and biology—is one for humanity in general. It is a *natural* one and one in the economy and laws of nature, owing to which one's son may become gradually his own grandfather and one's aunt to boot, imbibing their combined atoms and thus accounting for the possible resemblance (atavism?!)—but also one in which the latter could never become their grandson or nephew. But there is another law, an exceptional one and which manifests itself among mankind sporadically and periodically: the law of *forced* post-mortem assimilation; during the prevalence of which epidemic, the dead invade from their respective spheres the domain of the living—only within the limits of the regions they lived, very luckily, *and in which they are buried.*[1] In such cases the duration and intensity of this epidemic depends upon the welcome they receive, upon whether they find the doors opening widely to receive them or not, and whether the necromantic plague will be increased by magnetic attraction, the desire of the mediums, sensitives, and the curious themselves, or whether again, the danger being signalled, the epidemic will be wisely repressed.

Such a periodical visitation occurs now in America. It began with innocent children—the little Misses Fox—playing unconsciously with this terrible weapon, and, welcomed and passionately invited to "come in", the whole of the dead community seemed to rush in, and get a more or less stronger hold of the living. I went on purpose to a family of strong mediums—the Eddys—and watched for over a fortnight, making experiments, which, of course, I kept to myself. . . . You remember, Vera, how I made experiments for you at Rougodevo, how often I saw the ghosts of those who had been living in the house and described them to you—for you could never see them. Well it was the same daily and nightly in Vermont. I saw and watched them, these soulless creatures, the shadows of their terrestrial bodies, from which in most cases soul and spirit had fled long ago but which thrived and preserved their semi-material shadows, at the expense of the hundreds of visitors that came and went as well as of the mediums. And I remarked under the advice of my Master that (1) those apparitions which were genuine were produced by the "ghosts" of those who had lived and died within a certain area of those mountains; (2) those who had died far away were less entire—a mixture of *the* real shadow and of that which lingered in the personal aura of the visitor for whom it purported to come; and (3) the purely fictitious ones or as I call them, the reflections of genuine ghosts or shadows of the deceased personality. To explain myself clearer, it was not the spooks that assimilated the medium, but the medium—W. Eddy—who assimilated unconsciously to himself the picture of the dead relatives and friends from the aura of the sitters. . . .

It was horrid, ghastly, to watch the process! It made me often sick and giddy, but I had to look at it, and the most I could do was to hold the disgusting creatures at arm's length. But it *was* a sight to see the welcome given these *umbrae* by the Spiritualists! They wept and rejoiced around the medium clothed in these empty materialized shadows; rejoiced and wept again, sometimes broken down with an emotion, a sincere joy and happiness that made my heart bleed for them! "*If* they could but see *what I see*" I often wished. If they only knew that these *simulacra* of men [and] women are made up wholly of the terrestrial passions, vices and worldly thoughts of the residuum, of the personality that was, for these are only such dregs that could not follow the liberated soul and spirit and are left for a second death in the terrestrial atmosphere[2] that can be seen by the average mediums and public. At times I used to see one of such phantoms, quitting the medium's astral body pouncing upon one of the sitters, expanding so as to envelop him or her entirely and then slowly disappearing within the living body as though sucked in by its every pore.

NOTES:

1. [HPB's note:] Therefore when for example a medium in America personates a Russian (Sophie Perovsky, the regicide for instance), fraud or a monomaniacal hallucination is invariably the real cause of it, for what we call "shells" cannot emerge out of a certain area of *Kama loka*; whereas if the same spook obsessed a medium at St Petersburg or the vicinity, we might easily admit the genuineness of the phenomena. Luckily few shells prevail longer than the term of a natural life. *Translator*.

2. [HPB's note:] In the *shell* of the Earth for its (to us) invisible astral form is the region in which the *umbrae* linger after death, a grand truth given out in the *exoteric* doctrine of Hades of the ancient Latins.

SOURCE: "Mystical History" 29–31. Printed also in *Incidents* 175–9 (2nd ed. 137–9) with minor variations; cf *CW* 14:489–92.

BACKGROUND ESSAY D

HPB's Leg Injury

In January 1875, while HPB was staying in Philadelphia, Olcott returned there periodically during the month to begin his formal investigation of the Holmeses' séances (see background essay E, "The Katie King Affair"), which continued intermittently through much of the month, sometimes daily.

Toward the end of the month (on approximately January 30, if the phrase "about ten days ago" in letter 15 is accurate), HPB suffered an injury to one of her legs, which is referred to in several of the following letters as a source of great inconvenience and pain: 15, 20, 22, 23 introduction, 25, 28, 33, 38, 39, 40, 42, 43, 44, 46, 47 and introduction, and 49. HPB describes herself as "having nearly broken my leg by falling down under a heavy bedstead I was trying to move and that fell on me" (letter 20, written on or slightly before February 13).

Olcott (*ODL* 1:57) gives a different account, namely that the original injury was "a bruise on one knee caused by a fall the previous winter [*i.e.,* January 1875] in New York upon the stone flagging of a sidewalk, which ended in violent inflammation of the periosteum and partial mortification of the leg." Olcott's account is supported by an announcement in the *Spiritual Scientist* of June 3, 1875 (quoted in the introduction to letter 47), although it is possible that both events occurred.

In either case, the membrane at the knee became severely inflamed, with subsequent death of the tissue and partial paralysis by April. By mid May, her physician recommended that the leg be amputated to prevent the spread of gangrene. Amputation was still being considered as late as June 2 (letter 46), but a remarkable cure occurred in early June, described in letter 47: "The mortification had gone all round the knee, but two days of cold water *poultices*, and a white *pup*, a dog by night laid across the leg—cured all in no time." The story of the white dog gave rise to a legend that is still current in Philadelphia (letters 47 note 2, and 92).

Letter 14

To F. J. Lippitt   *January 30, 1875*

My dear General,

I have your letter dated Cambridge just now, and hasten to answer it. All the seemingly-signifying-nothing letters, dictated to you by spirits through your stand, are but so many instructions to your spiritualists in America, written out in cyphered alphabet (the Kabalistic employed by Rosicrucians and other Brotherhoods of the occult sciences). I am not at liberty to read them out to you *until allowed*. Do not take these words for a dodge. I give you my word of honor it is so. John King knew how to write that way of course, for he belonged as you know to one of the Orders. Preserve all you may receive in such a way *carefully*. Who knows what may yet be in store for blind America. One thing I *can* tell you though—the last words you ask about mean that until Spiritualism, or rather Philosophy and mysteries are solved in America in the *right way*, no help can be given by higher spirits, for the elementary ones and unprogressed ones would only give occasion—by making themselves erroneously understood—to the greatest misrepresentations of the science of sciences, which misunderstanding of the Divine Truth could but bring harm to mankind. *That's the reason why.* John has done all the [that he?] could do towards helping you with your stand, but the poor fellow is not allowed to do more. As it is, he is not even permitted to manifest himself any more, except by letters he writes or words he spells—unless I am alone with him. The time is close, my dear General, when Spiritualism *must* be cleansed of its erroneous misinterpretations, superstitions, and ignorant notions, all of which only make sceptics and unbelievers laugh at us. Deny Spiritualism and stop the progress of the Cause? It must be shown as it is—a science, a law of nature, an existing fact, without the existence of which all the Macrocosmos would soon go topsy-turvy, as a thing that popped out without any fundamental basis under it—a result without any reasonable cause for it—or a frolic of blind force and matter, the materialistic and crazy ideas of Büchner, etc.

I am glad you pass through Philadelphia—I shall be happy to see you and your dear daughter. But you must hurry, for I have to go away, lame as I am, on business which I cannot properly postpone. My way is to Boston and its vicinities, in a radius of about fifty miles around. I shall not be able to go to the charming place you speak about. It is not on my way, and my health, lame leg[1] and the rest of it, is all fiddle-sticks, and comes in secondary in my trip. *I am obliged to go*, my dear friend, and there is no saying "nay" to it, whether I am dead or alive. Duty is duty.

Olcott has gone to Boston for a few days; he is sent there on business. I don't know if you had time to see him.

My health is progressing very poorly but I don't care a sugar plum.

I have just received a letter from Prof. B . . .[2] with whom I am in constant correspondence. With his last letter he sent me two bits of autographs to put on my forehead to try to *pretend* I am a psychometrist. I saw all sorts of sights the moment I took up his letter—without knowing what was in it, and though I thought it was only idle fancies, I described him minutely what I saw, laughing at it as I did. What do you think? B . . . writes me that never was there given a more correct delineation of things and character! It seems I put my finger in the pie, without knowing it, for this psychometrical business is a new thing to me, and I never tried it in my life. I shall beg of our friend G. G. Brown[3] to advertise me in his paper as a psychometrist at 25 cents an hour. Is it too much, you think? 'Pon my word, I did laugh at myself at this new psychical discovery in myself. Ain't I a *well* of hidden treasures, General? "A regular one," John would say.

Do come quick, hurry up, and I may go with you to New Haven or Springfield.

I now close my letter for you to receive it sooner. God bless you, my dear friend: I have some good friends in America it seems—that's new business for me too, for I am not much spoiled with that sort of luxury as sincere friendship.

Truly yours,
H. P. Blavatsky

NOTES:

1. This is the earliest reference to the leg injury.

2. Perhaps Joseph Rhodes Buchanan, who is mentioned elsewhere in HPB's letters (letters 49 and 64), although correspondence with him has not survived.

3. Elbridge Gerry Brown.

SOURCE: Original unavailable. Copied from *Theosophist* 30 (Jan. 1909): 366–8.

BACKGROUND ESSAY E

The Katie King Affair

A principal reason for the attendance by HPB and Olcott at the séances of the Holmeses was to investigate the "Katie King" phenomena there. The "Katie King mystery" is first mentioned in letter 15, but was an American extension of phenomena that began in England.

"Katie King" was the spirit guide or control of an English medium named Florence Cook, who specialized in materializations (*EOP* 1:262–4, 712–3). From the time she was a child, Cook had seen and heard otherwise invisible spirits. By the time she was fifteen, she was attending séances and reportedly being levitated at some of them.

Shortly thereafter, Cook began to manifest an alternate personality named "Katie King," said to be the daughter of "John King" (an alias for Sir Henry Morgan, 1635–88). Morgan was a Welsh buccaneer who, with the connivance of the English government, preyed upon Spanish settlements in the Caribbean, as a result of which he was knighted and made deputy governor of Jamaica, where he lived in comfort and honor until his death. One of his crew wrote a sensationalized account of his exploits, which became the basis of the popular legend of Morgan, the pirate.

Materializations of "Katie" began in April 1872 and continued with increasing clarity for a few years. The medium and her materialized guide were extensively studied by Sir William Crookes, who took photographs of the materialized form and published a defense of the honesty of the medium and the reality of the materialization. The final materialization of "Katie King" by Florence Cook took place on May 21, 1874. In 1880, however, Cook was caught in the act of fraudulently impersonating another spirit guide, "Marie," and, despite Crookes's conviction, the genuineness of all the phenomena is in doubt.

Other spirit guides named "Katie" also appeared, although their identity with Florence Cook's "Katie" is unclear. One of those was a "Katie King" who, along with her father, "John King," manifested through the mediumship of Mr. and Mrs. Nelson Holmes of Philadelphia (in phenomena reported at length by Olcott in *People* 425–78, on which the following account is primarily based; a readable account of the events is Gomes, *Dawning* 45–61).

Henry T. Child, another Philadelphia Spiritualist, reported having seen a materialization of "Katie King" by the Holmeses in May 1874 and having himself subsequently had visitations from "Katie" and her father, "John King." General Francis J. Lippitt, a Civil War officer, and Robert Dale Owen, a prominent Congressman, publicized the materializations respectively in *Galaxy* magazine of December 1874 and the *Atlantic Monthly* of January 1875. Henry S. Olcott was interested in the Philadelphia manifestations of "Katie King" as potentially supporting the genuineness of the phenomena he had reported from the Eddy farm, so when invited by a letter from the Holmeses dated December 28, 1874, to investigate their mediumship under test conditions, he readily accepted.

On January 5, 1875, however, Owen and Child published statements withdrawing their former endorsements of the genuineness of the Holmeses' materializations. The landlady of the Holmeses, Eliza White, had signed a confession that they had employed her to impersonate the spirit of "Katie King" at their séances, beginning on May 12, 1874. She also held a mock séance for Owen, Child, and others, at which she demonstrated how the tricks of the "materialization" were worked. The affair consequently became a cause célèbre in the news media. It was in this climate that Olcott began his investigation on January 5, 1875, by examining documents and interviewing participants.

In his investigation into the reliability of Eliza White's testimony, Olcott found significant differences between her autobiographical statements and corroborative evidence, immorality in her past life, duplicitous statements, and attempted extortion of the Holmeses by an implicit threat to charge them with fraud. Moreover, he uncovered evidence that Eliza White's account of how she had performed the impersonation did not accord with attested physical facts, as well as documented appearances of the "Katie King" materialization when Eliza White was elsewhere. The affair was complicated by the fact that the Holmeses had apparently employed Eliza to pose for a photograph supposed to be of "Katie King." Olcott, however, found the representation in that photograph to be markedly different from other portraits of the spirit.

Olcott then arranged a series of séances at the Holmeses' and at his own quarters, at which he employed a variety of test conditions in an effort to eliminate the possibility of imposture or fraud. As a result of those tests, Olcott declared his belief in the genuineness of Mrs. Holmeses' mediumship, an opinion shared by General Lippitt. HPB was, however, present at many of those séances and later reported that she was the cause of the phenomena apparently originating from the Holmeses (*CW* 1:73):

> I went to the Holmeses and helped by M ∴ and *his power*, brought out the face of John King and Katie King in the astral light, produced the phenomena of materialization

and—allowed the Spiritualists at large to believe it was done thro' the mediumship of Mrs. Holmes. She was terribly frightened herself, for she knew that *this once* the apparition was real.

Despite Olcott's conviction of the genuineness of the Holmeses' mediumship and the reality of the "Katie King" materializations, HPB regarded them as frauds, although not alone in their fraudulency (*CW* 1:56-72, 73, 75-83; letter 15). In her scrapbook (1:47), on a clipping of an article entitled "Mrs. Holmes Caught Cheating" from the *Spiritual Scientist* of July 22, 1875, HPB (*CW* 1:120, transcribed here from the original) wrote:

> She swore to me in Philadelphia that if I only saved her that once she would NEVER resort to cheating & trickery again. I *saved* her but upon receiving her solemn oath.—And now she went out of greed for money to produce her *bogus* manifestations again! M ∴ forbid me to help her. Let her receive her *fate*—the vile, fraudulent liar! H. P B.

The affair was complicated by the question of Henry Child's involvement with it. In an article published in the Spiritualist journal *Banner of Light* on "The Philadelphia 'Fiasco,' or Who Is Who?" (*CW* 1:56-72), HPB charged Child with complicity and peculation on the Holmeses' seances and with collusion with Eliza White in falsely exposing the Holmeses, although she left open the question of their genuineness or fraud. She also defended Owen as an innocent victim in Child's machinations. Child responded to HPB's article with one of his own entitled "After the Storm Comes the Sunshine," in which he labels HPB's charge of his acquaintance with Eliza White as a fabrication. That evoked HPB's response in "Who Fabricates?" (*CW* 1:75-83), in which she cited contradictory statements by Child. HPB's antagonism toward Child continued through many letters (15, 17, 20, 22, 24, 25, 27, 28, 30, 31, 34, 36, 37, 40, 44, 45, 52, 64, and 67). She was particularly concerned about the effect of the dishonesty she attributed to Child on Robert Dale Owen, whom she admired and felt affection for.

Introduction to Letter 15

The several following letters give HPB's view of the "Katie King" affair. Letter 15 is a response to Professor Hiram P. Corson, of Cornell University, who wrote to HPB about her article "The Philadelphia 'Fiasco' or Who Is Who?" (*CW* 1:56–72) published in the *Banner of Light* on January 30, 1875. His letter (in the Archives of the Theosophical Society, Adyar) was written the day after the date of the issue and expressed a sentiment that supported HPB's view of the Philadelphia "Katie King" affair:

> The Cornell University
> Department of Anglo-Saxon and English Literature
> Ithaca, N.Y.
> January 31, 1875

> My dear Madame:
> Pardon the liberty I take in writing you to express my thanks for your noble letter in the "Banner of Light." It is a deep satisfaction to me, to find therein my own feelings in regard to the Holmes muddle, so mirrored, as they are, and *filled out*, especially those feelings that have been gradually developing and gaining strength, in regard to Dr. Child, whose visual nerve, it seemed to me, when I first read of his endorsement of the "Autobiography" of "Katie King," must have been purged with euphrasy[1] and rue,[2] to enable him, all of a sudden, to see so clearly what he had so long been stone-blind to.
> The seven mysteries which you wheel out, for solution, are sufficiently threatening in their aspect, to cause the laughers to look grave in *their* turn.

> Most respectfully,
> your obedient Servant,
> Hiram Corson

NOTES:

1. An herb also known as "eyebright" and used to cure eye ailments.

2. An herb with a bitter taste, but here also a pun on rue "regret, repentance."

HPB responded to Corson's letter with an apology for her delay and comments about the current Spiritualist controversy:

Letter 15

To H. P. Corson   *February 9, 1875*
                    825 North 10th Street, Philadelphia

Dear Sir

Pardon me if, to all appearance I have neglected to answer your very kind letter, received about a week ago. The fault is not mine as you will see, but ought to be laid right to the door of my "malchance" [*Fr.* bad luck] as the french Canadian say. I have nearly broken my leg about ten days ago and, cannot leave my bed as yet; otherwise, most assuredly, I would not have risked—even for awhile—to be thought so illmannered as that.

I have received many letters of thanks for my article, many undeserved compliments and—very little practical help in the way of published statements supporting my theory, which is certainly built upon evident proofs. As an illustration of the moral cowardice prevailing amongst Spiritualists, I take the liberty of sending you a letter just received by me, from General Lippitt, the commissioner sent by the "Banner of Light" to this city, with the special purpose of investigating thoroughly the Katie King mystery. He has done so, and he has discovered beyond any doubt the culpability of Dʳ Child.—He has in his possession the testimony of two well known photographers, whom the honorable "Father Confessor" has bribed, for the speculating purpose of obtaining Katie's portrait, by taking it from this creature *White*. The "Banner has refused as you see, point blank, to publish anything against Dr Child.

Talk after that of the wisdom of old mottos and proverbs and let us repeat if we dare, about innocence and virtue being rewarded and vice punished! Well, I *do* think that old dame Truth, has deserted for ever your beautiful shores. At least, by what I can judge from my own experience of over 18 months residence in your country, the old lady must be resting in undisturbed repose or in a state of deep trance, at the bottom of her native well.

There I am, unable to move, in the perfect impossibility of leaving my room and my articles sure to be henceforth refused.

I possess several valuable documents against our Philadelphian prophet, among others the sworn statement of a voluntary witness, which would kill Dr Child if ever it was brought against him in a Court of Justice. But—it never will; for the Doctor who is as cautious as he is peculating, declines answering me, even in print it seems. And to think, that I was simple minded enough to hope that he would try and sue me for libel, for it was the only way, to force him into a Court of Justice.

My dear sir, would it be impossible for you to publish a few words stating your opinion as to the matter? A few lines *from you* that the "Banner" is sensible enough to appreciate and would never dare refuse, would go far against our fraudulent prophet. The Editors will print nothing more from me, for they say, "there is no knowing where my literary *Russian bombs* may explode." The only good result that has been brought about by my article, as soon as it appeared, was the immediate resignation of Dr Child, from his office of President of the Spiritual Association of

Philad. otherwise, he plays at "dummy" and is to be seen or heard nowhere.

I came to this Country only on account of *Truth* in Spiritualism, but I am afraid I will have to give it up. We shall never be able to draw the line of demarcation between the true and the false, as long as the so called pillars of Spiritualism will, notwithstanding their half rotten and unreliable condition, be supported and helped out to the last, by the too *leniant* backs of the cowardly Spiritualists. Would the Holmese ever dare fool and swindle the public as they did, if they had not been backed and screened by Dr Child untill $3,000 offered him by the Y. M. Ch^n *Ass.* proved too much for his tender soul, and he had to turn a modern spiritual Judas and sell out his Christ to the highest bidder. Now, the Holmes, frauds as they partly are, are still genuine mediums, and no mistake, and if there is some excuse for them for the perpertration of such a swindle it lies in the "circonstance atténuante" [*Fr.* extenuating circumstance] of the perpetual danger of starvation, as in the case of most of the public mediums. As for Dr Child, a gentleman and a man known to be wealthy, there is no excuse for him, and such a character as that ought to be horsewhiped. His participation—in my eyes at least—in this fraud is worse than robbery, worse than the murder of a human being; it is a nameless crime, one of blasphemy, sacrilegious derision and pollution of the most holy sacred feelings treasured in the Souls of all Spiritualists.

He has done his work: for one of us at least. Poor, old Robert D. Owen will not recover from the shock he's experienced by the same hand that led him into the belief of the pure "spirit. He is 73 y. of age and does not leave his sick bed from the moment of the "exposure." *I know* it is his death blow.

That's why I hate Child so bitterly.

Excuse my long letter, dear Sir, in favor of the sincerity of my feelings, strong and too impetuous as they may seem [to] you perhaps.

With sincere regards of esteem dear Sir.

truly yours
H. P. Blavatsky

The Holmes have vanished from town and I took the house they used to live in, *for purposes you may guess.*

SOURCE: Transcribed from a microfilm and a photocopy of the original in the HPB Library. Published in *Unpublished Letters* 123–6.

Letter 16

To H. P. Corson?   *[early February 1875]*

The witnesses that were present besides Lippit at the delivery to me of the statement now in your possession were, Dʳ Felger,[1] Mʳ W. Wescott, leader of the Choir at the Spirit: Hall, Mʳ Betanelly and the two Holmeses besides myself, which in all are *seven* witnesses. I have written to Colby and told him what I had to say, giving him a bit of wholesome, sound truth.

NOTE:

1. Adolphus Fellger.

DATE: Although this fragment is undated, HPB's reference in letter 15 to "several valuable documents against our Philadelphia prophet [Child]" implies a probable date for this letter.

SOURCE: Transcribed from a microfilm and a photocopy of a fragment in HPB's handwriting in the HPB Library.

⌒

Letter 17

To A. N. Aksakoff   *February 11, 1875*
                                                Philadelphia

I have omitted from Olcott's letters[1] all that concerns
me *personally*, leaving only that which deals with the spirits
and my relation to them. His friendship has carried him
too far in boundless praise, and I cannot get into his head
that in elevating me to the rank of "Countess" he is only
giving the Russians who know me an occasion to laugh at
me. . . . I have written an article[2] (it has been republished in
the *Banner of Light*) against Doctor Child, as I felt myself
morally *bound* as a Spiritualist and a "crusader of the Spiritual Army," to tell the truth, to defend the innocent, and to
bring into the light of day the *guilty* and criminal. The story
about Katie King and the scandal have given such a setback
to "materialization," that a veritable tempest has been
raised in the land. It turns out that the mediums Holmes
are not the only guilty ones. The chief criminal is Doctor
Child, who, as a *speculation*, hired a certain Mrs. White to
allow her portrait to be taken as that of the Spirit Katie
King, who for some reason or other would not pose for her
own portrait. General Lippitt, Olcott, Roberts the lawyer,
and myself have set to work to carry out an inquiry. Olcott
has proved "the real mediumship" of Holmes and we have
discovered by the admission of the photographer and of
the mediums, that Doctor Child thought fit to bribe both
them and this Mrs. White in order to take in the public
by the sale of the photographs. That is why I wrote this
article, as I knew, or rather supposed, that we should never
get at the truth except by publicly accusing Doctor Child. I
hoped that if he had the least trace of conscience left, he
would sue me and even have me arrested for libel. I wanted

this, because I have already sacrificed myself for Spiritualism, and am ready at any moment to lay my head on the block, in defense of *my faith* and the *truth*; and in the court, before the Grand Jury, I would have shown who is innocent and who is guilty in this unparalleled swindle of Spiritualism, in this rascality, where no one sees what is truth and what is lies, and which is bringing despondency and confusion to the whole Spiritualistic world of America and Europe, and giving the skeptics the right to laugh at us. Poor Robert Dale Owen is *dying*. He is seventy-three years old and all his life has been bound up with the spirit of Katie King. This blow has been too heavy for the old man; and though after this *soi-disant exposé* he has twice seen at the Holmes' the Katie King whom he had previously recognized more than eighty evenings on end, and who proved to us at the investigation *séances* that she was a real spirit, and not a mortal substitute, and though she comforted Owen, yet he has fallen ill, and it appears may not recover. All his reputation as an author has gone; people are now doubting everything he ever wrote. And all this on account of Doctor Child, a swindler and speculator. You will see by my article that I do not spare him. I kept expecting, that he would send and have me arrested. . . . To my surprise Doctor Child has not even answered in the papers, but since that day has simply hidden himself in his own house, and dreads more than anything else that somebody may drag him into court. . . . He was president at the "Spiritual Hall" here, and resigned at once himself, just when we were on the point of requesting him to make himself scarce. I am receiving letters of gratitude from every side, from Spiritualists and *non*-Spiritualists, among others from Professor Draper[3] and Professor Corson. If you hear that the Blavatsky of many sins has perished, *not* in the bloom of years and beauty, by some curious death, and that she has dematerialized forever, you may know that it is for Spiritualism. In the Lord do we put our trust, nor shall we be shamed forever. . . .

John King has sent Olcott to Havana[4] for a few days. . . . I have ceased getting any letters from my aunts and sister; they have evidently all forgotten me, and so much the better for them. I am no credit to them, to tell the truth. I shall now *never* go back to Russia again. My father is dead, I am of no use to anyone, and am altogether superfluous in the world. Here I am at least a human being; while there, I am—*Blavatsky*. I know that everybody respects me here, and Spiritualism needs me. The spirits are now my brothers and sisters, my father and mother. My John King alone can substitute for all of them; he stands as a rock for me. And yet they call him and Crookes' Katie King the double of the medium! What sort of double can he be, when the medium Williams is not here at all, while John King in his own person, with his own black beard and his white Chinese upside-down-saucer cap, is going from one medium to another here in America, and is doing me the honor of visiting me incessantly, though he has not the least resemblance to me? No, John King is a personality, a separate, living spiritual personality. Whether a "diakka" or a pure spirit, he is at all events a spirit, and not the medium's prototype. But this is not the place, after all, to argue, and I must have already tired you out anyway. . . .

NOTES:

1. H. S. Olcott's New York *Daily Graphic* articles on the phenomena at the Eddy farm.

2. "The Philadelphia 'Fiasco,' or Who Is Who?" (*CW* 1: 56–72).

3. Possibly John William Draper, author of *History of the Conflict between Religion and Science*.

4. Olcott traveled to the village of Havana, Schuyler County, New York, in order to investigate the mediumship of Mrs. Elizabeth J. Compton. See *People* 479–88 and *EOP* 256.

SOURCE: Russian original unavailable. Translated by Boris de Zirkoff from Solovyov's *Sovremennaya* 265–7. Another English translation by Walter Leaf in *Modern Priestess* 240–3.

$\smile\!\!\!\longrightarrow$

Letter 18

To A. N. Aksakoff   *[February 1875]*
                                       Philadelphia

All this silly story is neither more nor less than a plot (now almost proved) of the Protestant Jesuitical Society called the "Young Men's Christian Association," a huge society scattered through all the cities of America. He (R. D. Owen) has morally killed himself in public opinion by his action and all the papers hold him up to ridicule. Here is a specimen: "The accomplice of Leslie (a well-known scoundrel and thief who has stolen millions in railroads) dressed herself up in the costume of the spirit Katie, and in a room and 'cabinet' prepared for the purpose showed in the presence of Robert Owen and others how she *personated* a spirit. The very same evening at the same hour the real Katie King appeared to 20 witnesses at a *séance* with the calumniated mediums, the Holmes." All the papers are full of *pros* and *cons*. It doesn't matter; we must console ourselves with the proverb, for the vulgarity of which I ask to be excused: "If God does not permit, the pig won't eat it." I have never heard of a cleverer swindle than this whole story. Poor Robert Dale Owen! If his eyes are ever opened, I'm afraid the poor old man will not survive the shock. At the present moment I am proud to say that I am making converts fast. . . . For spiritualism I am ready to work night and day as long as I have a morsel of bread, and that only because it is hard to work when one is hungry. . . .

DATE: The references to the "Katie King" affair date the letter approximately.

SOURCE: Russian original unavailable. Translated by Boris de Zirkoff from Solovyov's *Sovremennaya* 264–5. Another English translation by Walter Leaf in *Modern Priestess* 239–40.

⌒

Letter 19

To ??   *[ca. February 1875]*

[indecipherable fragmentary character] Poor old Robert Dale Owen! Mrs Holmes *did cheat*, & I held my tongue from the first out of regard to the feelings of the old man. Katie King's body "evaporated while her feet were still visible" because the *woman* representing the "Spirit" was in a DARK cabinet. While standing all clad in white a black curtain was slowly unrolled in front of her, descending from the ceiling of the "*cabinet* for apparitions" and so, in this more than half gloom first her head seemed to dissolve & disappear then her body, till the *feet alone remained visible*. Mrs Holmes is the biggest fraud of the age & Spiritualists.

H.P.B.

DATE: The subject of the Holmes fraud implies the approximate date.

SOURCE: Transcribed from a photocopy of the original in the Archives of the Philosophical Research Society, Los Angeles. The text, in HPB's handwriting, is on a fragmentary sheet with a ragged left edge, affixed to another sheet, marked in a different hand "Précieux autographe de Madame Blavatsky/vient d'un Scrap.book d'Adyar" [Precious autograph of Madame Blavatsky/comes from an Adyar scrapbook].

Letter 20

To F. J. Lippitt   [ca. February 13, 1875]

Francis J. Lippitt Esqr

My dear General,

Do not think me rude or impertinent, for not answering you immediately. When I received your letter I was *in bed* having nearly broken my leg by falling down under a heavy bedstead I was trying to move and that fell on me.[1] I keep to my room yet, being unable to move or walk but very little, and it is the first time I take a pen in hand.

I am surprised and shocked at what you write me about the "Banner of Light." Are they such cowards as that? Why in the name of truth do they intend crushing the Holmes and let Child go unmolested? Now it is not fair or just. Spiritualism will never be able to crawl out from the clutches of suspicion and ostracism unless we Spiritualists help ourselves to extricate the *genuine* facts from under the weeds of falsehood and lies that suffocate the former. Let the Editors of the Banner understand that the world is not to be deceived. The public at large judges Child by what he has done and there is not a man or woman or child, but thinks him more guilty than the Holmes for they judge him by his actions and those actions speak *for themselves*. What will people say, when they come to find out that the chief pillar of Spiritualism, the principal organ and propagator *of the truth*, turns over to the judgment and punishment of the world such petty larceny as made by the Holmes and shields in the same time a burglar like Dr Child? In what is the justice of the Supreme Court of Spiritualism any better in such a case than the bribed decisions of a jury acquitting a Jay Cook—and sentencing to prison a miserable wretch who steals 25 c. to bye[2] himself a loaf of bread? I have seen today Mr Roberts, who visited me, and *he* at least will do everything in his power to show the *truth* of this case and drag out Child in his true character. I have received a letter from Professor Hiram Corson of Cornell University and he agrees with me entirely, thanks me for my article and says, that his own feelings and opinion of Dr Child are *mirrored* in my article. I have received scores of letters from Spiritualists and I can prove that they all agree with me. I will say more, and please let it be known to the Edit. of "Banner." I received a letter from a very prominent person, who encloses therein a sum of money, as the beginning for a fund of money and sums to be spent for the expenses to arrive at the truth about Dr Child. Cette personne est decidée a commencer ou plutôt instituer *une bourse*, et promet de m'envoyer d'autres contributions afin de commencer de suite[3] et sans delai un proces contre Child. Comment trouvez-Vous le bouillon, general? [*Fr.* This person has decided to begin, or rather institute a fund, and promises to send me other contributions in order to begin without delay an urgent suit against Child. What do you think of how things are going,[4] General?]

I am sorry to feel so weak as to find myself unable to write any longer. Please let me know the present opinion and decision of the "Banner." I must have it. Did you read the "New solution of an old puzzle" in the *Scribners* for January and February? Now, this looks like something rational, though I do not agree with the writer. You ought to read it by all means. Dont you allow Beard to write if you can help it. I wrote to Wigttgenstein.[5] You can find his address in the "Banner." It is Nieder Walluf on the Rhine. I do not know any other address. God bless you General and good speed to you in your work. Compliments of John

[King] and Bettanelly. I will write you something wonderful next time. John begins his portrait for you on satin.

Yours truly

H. P. Blavatsky

NOTES:

1. The injury to HPB's leg, which happened in late January, grew worse and eventually threatened the need for amputation. It is a recurring subject in the letters over the next several months.

2. "Bye" is an archaic spelling variant for "buy," not much used since the sixteenth century, but it is HPB's regular use in the letters through 1880, where it occurs seven times in autograph letters 20, 38 (twice), 40, 41, 64, and 68. "Buy," on the other hand, occurs only in letters translated by others into English or available only in published form and so does not represent HPB's usage.

3. Earlier transcriptions of this letter (the handwriting of which is difficult) read this phrase, which is interlined, as "de stricte," which has no meaning in French. Jean-Louis Siémons (private communication) suggested that it should be "de suite," that is, "at once, immediately." A more careful inspection of the original showed that to be in fact the correct reading.

4. The last sentence is literally "What do you think of the broth, General?" Jean-Louis Siémons (private communication) observes that this recalls a catchphrase popular in Army use. When a general, on a tour of inspection, visited the kitchen and sampled the soup, he would be asked, "La soupe est bonne, mon Général?" HPB's use may echo that, with a substitution of *bouillon* "broth" for *soupe* "soup." She is asking for General Lippitt's agreement with her plans and procedures.

5. Prince Emil-Karl-Ludwig von Sayn-Wittgenstein.

DATE: Endorsed "From Mme. Blavatsky, Feb. 13, '75" (*HPB Speaks* 2:166).

SOURCE: Transcribed from the original in the Archives of the Theosophical Society, Adyar. Published in *HPB Speaks* 2:163–6.

BACKGROUND ESSAY F

The John King Portrait

The final sentence of the preceding letter 20 ("John begins his portrait for you on satin") refers to a phenomenally produced portrait of and by "John King." This portrait is referred to also in a number of other letters (25, 32, 35, 36, 39, 53). There are several first-hand accounts of the painting and the process of its making; one is by H. S. Olcott, who was present part of the time when the picture was being made, and the other by F. J. Lippitt, for whom the picture was painted.

On April 20, 1875, Olcott writing from 3420 Sansom Street, Philadelphia, sent a letter (original in the Archives of the Theosophical Society, Adyar, published in *HPB Speaks* 1:77–80) to General Lippitt, apparently responding to questions of his about the production of the painting:

Dear General.

In reply to your postal-card,[1] as well as to your letters to Mme de B, which she has shown me, I give you the following explanation of the way in which the John King picture was done:

By John King's request, Mme de B bought some fine satin, and a piece of the required size was tacked on a drawing-board. Dry colors, water, and an assortment of brushes were provided and placed in the room devoted to the spirits, and the whole left there over night, covered with a cloth. In the morning the whole upper portion of the picture and John's face were found traced in faint outline; the spirit figures were surrounded with a faint body of color, which formed the outlines as you see them now, without the usual single sharp lines of the pencil. When Mme de B sat down at the table John told her to begin the wreath of flowers and the vines which form the perpendicular supports of what may be called the central panel. Dissatisfied with her work, he bid her go away, after covering the satin, and when he called her back, she found that he had laid in the outlines of the perpendicular foliage, and the marble balcony upon which he stands. She then went to work upon the large wreath below the latter, and thereafter confined herself exclusively to that; John doing everything else himself— piecemeal, sometimes by day and sometimes by night. I was in the house most of this time, and on more than one occasion sat near her while painting, and with her stepped out for a few minutes while the spirit artist drew some portion of the picture, beneath the cloth that was spread over its face. The Greek and Hebrew words, and the cabalistic signs were put in last of all. You have correctly read the former, but must not suppose they are anything exceptional, for they are known to every student of the Kabbala. They and the signs and the jewel John King wears upon his breast are all Rosicrucian symbols, he having been a brother of the Order, and this being the tie which binds him to our gifted friend Mme de B You may properly estimate the favor done you when I tell you that the Madame has vainly begged John to do something like this for her, for years past, and I hope that if any other inducement lacked to enlist your sympathies and help for the proposed newspaper organ, through which we are promised the knowledge that we old Spiritualists have been so many years waiting and praying for, this may serve to that end.

I was unable to secure from my Publishers enough copies of my book[2] for my friends until now; but you may expect one in a few days, which I hope you will accept in token of my warm regard.

When I was at Chittenden, Mme de B tried to sketch some Oriental figures for Mr Kappes the artist, but made a wretched attempt at it; so she did in Hartford when she wished to show Mr Williams the artist of the Am Pub Co[3] how to correct certain errors in the costumes of the materialized spirits who appeared to her at C. I can certify, therefore, to the impossibility of her having drawn the charming figures which appear in the JK picture.

Yours truly,

H. S. Olcott

NOTES:

1. *Postal card* was originally the American term for what is now called a *postcard*. The latter term, along with the thing both terms name, was introduced in England in 1870.

2. H. S. Olcott's *People from the Other World*. In the copy that Olcott presented to HPB he wrote, "From Henry Steel Olcott (the author) to Helena Petrowna Blavatsky, whom he respects for her virtues, admires for her talents, pays homage to for her lofty courage, and loves for her noble self-sacrifice. The good regard her as a sister and benefactress; the bad dread her as one sent to punish and scourge. New York, March, 1875" (*HPB Speaks* 1:91–2).

3. American Publishing Company, the publisher of Olcott's book, which included drawings depicting the places and events at the Eddy farm in Chittenden.

General F. J. Lippitt, for whom the picture was painted, described it and its painter in a letter to the editor of the *Spiritual Scientist* 4 (Apr. 29, 1875): 90–1, which was published nine days after Olcott wrote the preceding letter (and reprinted with minor differences in *Harbinger of Light* 5 [Aug. 1875]: 866–7):

A REMARKABLE PICTURE.

To the Editor of The Spiritual Scientist:

Our friends in the other world seem to be using every method they can devise to demonstrate to us the scriptural truth that besides the natural body "there is a spiritual body." The manifestations are thus daily taking on new phases. One of the newest is the painting of pictures directly by disembodied spirits. A most beautiful one has just been painted expressly for me by the spirit known as "John King," and which has been forwarded to me from Philadelphia.

I will briefly state the evidence that has satisfied me that
THE PAINTER
was a disembodied spirit.

I. The positive testimony of Madame Helen P. Blavatsky, by whom the picture was sent to me, a Russian lady of rank and of high intelligence, now residing in Philadelphia; who, not only has no conceivable motive for deception in the matter, but is known by her friends to be the very soul of sincerity and honor. I know from her own lips that the spirit calling himself "John King" has been manifesting his presence to her in a variety of ways for a number of years; that she has had frequent communications from him, many of them by writings executed in her presence independently of all human agency; and that he has also repeatedly painted pictures for her, and performed various other acts obviously beyond the power of human beings in the flesh.

II. This testimony of Madame Blavatsky has been corroborated to me by the statements of Col. Henry S. Olcott and of Mr. M. C. Betanelly, an intelligent and honorable gentleman from Caucasian Georgia, who have been personally present when some of the most marvelous of these facts have occurred. Of one of them, moreover, I was myself a witness last January. The writing then executed in my presence by this same invisible agent, which was a reply to a remark just before made by Madame Blavatsky, I now have in my possession.

III. That it was by this identical spirit that the picture I have received was chiefly executed, is proved to me by the testimony of Madame Blavatsky, Col. Olcott and Mr. Betanelly. Moreover, that this was the same John King that Col. Olcott and I repeatedly saw, touched and spoke with last January at the Holmes's[1] will appear by the following facts, which also demonstrate that he was really a disembodied spirit.[2]

On one occasion, at the window of the Holmes' cabinet, to prove to Col. Olcott his identity, he gave him a certain sign which Col. Olcott had requested him to give when conversing with him that same day in Madame Blavatsky's apartments.

On another occasion, I myself heard him from within the cabinet speak to Col. Olcott about "his boy Morgan," in allusion to a promise made to him that day in Madame Blavatsky's presence.

On another occasion, I myself heard the same "John King" of the cabinet respond promptly and correctly to requests made to him in French, Spanish, German, Russian, Georgian, Latin and Greek; the mediums being notoriously ignorant of any language but their own.

On another occasion, the same "John King" at the Holmes's cabinet window borrowed from Col. Olcott his signet ring. At the close of the sitting, he not having returned it, the cabinet was searched for it in vain. Shortly afterwards, on retiring to rest at his lodgings, a mile or more distant from the Holmes's, Col. Olcott found his ring under his pillow.

One instance more; On the evening of January 24, 1875, at an improvised sitting in Col. Olcott's lodgings, at which I was present, the bed-room closet was made to serve as a cabinet, by a curtain hung before the door opening, in which a slit was cut for a window. The moment the medium had been seated in the closet, tied and sealed up in a bag, and the curtain had been let fall again, the same "John King" thrust his head through the aperture and spoke to us in his usual gruff voice. A few minutes afterwards he called up to him Mr. Betanelly, who, on returning to his seat, could not recover from his astonishment; John King, as he declared to me, having described to him, speaking in the Georgian language, an occurrence known to no human being but himself.

These statements will be found fully corroborated in that marvelous book, just published, of Col. Olcott's—but no more marvelous than truthful—People from the Other World.

So much for the painter, and now for

THE PICTURE;

my description of which, as I am not an artistic person, will be very imperfect.

It is painted on a piece of white satin, eighteen inches square. In the centre, on a tastefully carved marble balcony, (said by him to belong to his spirit home) stands John King himself; an exact likeness of the "John King" who appears in London, but better looking than our Philadelphia John, though, on the whole, the same face. With his white turban and long black beard, he looks like an Arab. The balcony is adorned by rich foliage, climbing round spear-headed rails of gold. Beneath, and forming the entire base of the picture, is a wreath of gorgeous flowers, among which are darting two humming birds, in their full brilliancy of plumage. The background is a lovely landscape, the most striking features of which are a silvery lake, temples and porticos, rather Oriental than Grecian, and a feudal castle in the distant perspective. Spirit forms are floating here and there through the blue ether, but all more or less veiled by a soft haze that pervades the atmosphere. Among them are a mother and child; and one, in a long, flowing white garment, is lifting up a torch towards one of the porticos bearing the inscription which will be presently mentioned. The only one of them whose face is distinctly seen, is that said to represent "Katie King." Several persons in Philadelphia by whom she was seen last summer recognized her, as I am informed, at once. I have not been so fortunate. The Katie I saw last May had the same style of face, but a shorter nose, and much more the look of an ordinary mortal. The Katie in the picture, loyalty to truth requires me to state, in the very ethereal drapery that veils her exquisitely graceful figure, might be taken for a beautiful houri, but never for a Scriptural angel.

On the frieze of one of the porticos is inscribed, in Greek:

$$\text{"πῦρ ἄσβεστον"}$$

(the unquenchable fire). The Hebrew word "Esh" on another front signifies "lightning" or "the fire of God," as Professor Sophocles, of Harvard University, informs me. John King holds in his hands a large, crimson-bound volume, on which are several inscriptions in gold:

$$\text{"A Ω"}$$

"To my best medium"[3]; something that Prof. Sophocles thinks to be the Hebrew word "Shem," "the name," (meaning "God.") Under this sign Libra; then what Prof. Sophocles supposes to be Egyptian hieroglyphics, of which he could decipher only the letter M; ending with the Hebrew letter S.

Standing against the balcony are the two pillars of Solomon's Temple, so familiar to the Masonic fraternity, on which Hebrew words ("Jachin" and "Boaz," no doubt) are inscribed. Between them are a double triangle, and a *croix cramponee* [*cramponée Fr.* swastika] (Solomon's seal and Thor's hammer, an ancient Scandinavian emblem, says Prof. Sophocles.)

From recent information, I have reason to believe that John King is dissatisfied with these partial explanations, declares that the whole of these mystic symbols, taken together, have a definite meaning, and invites me to "try and find it out," which I despair of doing, being no antiquarian or Orientalist.

Several artists who have examined the picture have expressed themselves as puzzled to know by what process it could have been painted on the satin.

The circumstances under which the picture was executed are stated in a letter to me from Col. Olcott, from which I take the liberty of extracting the following: [Here follows the greater part of the letter of April 20, given above.]

Col. O. adds some particulars within his own personal knowledge, which enable him to "certify to the impossibility of Madame B.'s having drawn the charming figures which appear on the John King picture."

And Madame B. writes me herself that, "except the flowers below, and some leaves round the balcony, I did not paint or touch one inch of the picture."

Why the spirit "John King" should have bestowed so much time and labor upon this picture, and then present it to one who is a stranger to him and to whom he can be under no personal obligation, I cannot explain except by supposing that an association of spirits is trying, as Katie King expressed it in a note to Robert Dale Owen (People from the Other World, p. 468), "to teach the people of this world they still live after death;" that John King, on account of his exceptional power over matter, coupled with a strong will and an untiring energy, is employed as an apostle, perhaps the chief apostle of this new dispensation; and that I happened to be selected as the recipient of the beautiful gift as being believed to be one of those persons who would not be likely to "hide it under a bushel."

F. J. Lippitt

NOTES:

1. HPB annotated a copy of this article in her scrapbook. She underlined "at the Holmes's" and put a question mark by it.

2. HPB added a note by "really a disembodied spirit": "Oh human delusion!!"

3. HPB underlined the word "medium" and noted: "of course."

Letter 21

To H. P. Corson   *Tuesday [February 16, 1875]*
825 North 10th Street, Philadelphia

Dear Sir

Just received yours, and many thanks for the readiness with which you undertake the defence of *Truth*. With my letter, you may do as you please; use my name, bring me out as a witness, just, whatever you may think proper—. I can as readily answer for Gen: Lippitts consent, though— not having his permission for it, I suppose it more advisable to lay it all to my door, and state that you learned the particulars about the cowardice of the "Banner of Light" through me, for I do not care if the Editors get a grudge against me, I am perfectly independant from them, but Lippitt is *employed* by them and his means are very limited. Just say that I wrote you *copying textually his letter*. I send you at the same time a very precious document, copied by the writer himself (from an original letter that he sent me) in the presence of Gen: Lippitt, whose signature you will find at the bottom, as a witness to the transaction. I have five more witnesses.

I am here, in this country sent by my Lodge, on behalf of *Truth* in modern Spiritualism, and it is my most sacred duty to *unveil what is*, and expose *what is not*. Perhaps, did I arrive here 100 years *too soon*. May be, (and I am afraid it is so) that in this present state of mental confusion, of doubt, of the endless and fruitless conflicts between the Tyndals and Wallaces, the issue of which are arrested by the almighty power of the dollar, for people seem to care every day less for truth and every hour more for gold,—my feeble protest and endeavors will be of no avail,—nevertheless, I am ever ready for the grand battle and perfectly prepared to bear any consequinces that may fall to my lot.

I pray you, do not take me to be a "blind fanatic" for, if *I am* the latter, *I am not* the former. When I became a Spiritualist, it was not through the agency of the ever lying, cheating mediums, miserable instruments of the undeveloped Spirits of the lower Sphere, the ancient *Hades*. My belief is based, on something older than the Rochester Knockings, and spring out from the same source of information, that was used by Raymond Lully, Picus of Mirandola,[1] Cornelius Agrippa, Robert Fludd Henry More etc etc all of whom have ever been searching for a system, that should disclose to them the "*deepest depths*" of the Divine nature and show them the *real tie which binds all things together*. I found at last—and many years ago—the cravings of my mind satisfied by this theosophy[2] taught by the Angels and communicated by them, that the protoplast might know it for the aid of the human destiny. The practical—however small knowledge of the Principle the *Ain Soph* or the Endless and the Boundless, with its *ten Sephiroths* or Emanations goes more towards opening your eyes than all the hypothetic teachings of the leaders of Spiritualism, let them be American or European. In my eyes, Allan Kardec and Flammarion, And. Jack. Davis and Judge Edmonds are but school boys just trying to spell their *A B. C.* and sorely blundering sometimes. The relation between the two is in just proportion what were in the ancient ages the book called *"Sohar"* based on the perfect knowledge of the *Cabala* handed down by oral tradition from David and Solomon to "Simon ben Jochai" the first man who dared *write it down* and—the *Massorah*, a book based on *outside*, not direct tradition and which never vouchsafed the truth of what it taught.

I do not know, why I write you all this. Perhaps, it does not interest you in the least; perhaps you will find me presumptious, conceited, boasting and—a *bore*. I must beg of you to account for it in one way at least, viz. the great desire I have to hear *responding echos*, to seek for them, whenever and wherever I can, in the only hope of being occasionally answered. If the Doctrine of the "Aged of the Aged" of *Sephira* its first born, the *Macroprosopros*[3] and so forth is a thing you never troubled yourself of investigating, then let it drop at once and consigning me for ever in the annals of your memory with the demented and crazy dreamers of the age; believe me only

gratefully and truly yours
H. P. Blavatsky.

NOTES:

1. Pico della Mirandola.

2. This is the earliest known use of the term "theosophy" by HPB.

3. Macroprosopus.

DATE: The envelope has a cancellation mark of February 16. February 16, 1875, was a Tuesday, so the letter was presumably written and mailed the same day.

SOURCE: Transcribed from a microfilm and a photocopy of the original in the HPB Library. Published in *Unpublished Letters* 127-9.

Letter 22

To F. J. Lippitt   *[ca. February 22, 1875]*
Philadelphia

Dear Sir,

Your two last letters actually force me, quoting a *Persian* expression to "stick a finger of surprise in a mouth of amazement." What in the name of Dickens do you mean by Mrs Whites seance? I live in the heart of this God forsaken and *Child* inhabited city, and see three score of gossips every day of my life, but *never*, notwithstanding all my inquiries and trouble—never did I hear of the black hearted *White turning up again to* sight or hearing. You are the first who astounded me with this piece of news. What seance, what for? I know Mrs Holmes is here, humbuging Evans and C^o with her own materialized arms and elbows, though I declined to see her myself, not feeling over anxious to *seek for pearls* in such a formidable amount of *rotten manure*, but of White or Leslie or Child giving seances never heard a word. If its a fact Lord help old Robert D. Owen for he is more crazy than ever it seems if he still credits Child's lies and fibs.

My leg is very little better and I am afraid I will remain lame for some time.

I sent for Roberts and I guess I will see him to morrow, and talk with him about Mr Hegards proposal. He has been to see me and is as anxious as ever to swallow Dr Child alive. "De gustibus non disputandum est" [*Ln.* There is no disputing about tastes]. For my part I would rather prefer swallowing a dead cat's tail, roasted in fresh bugs blood. Anything but Child—You shall be surprised at *Johny's present*. Have patience only for he is very whimsical and disappeared *again* a few days ago.

Pay my sincerest compliments to dear Mr Colby and tell him that henceforth I shall hang his portrait in company with "Bayard" the Chevalier sans peur et sans reproche [*Fr.* fearless and blameless knight], and Godeffroi *de Bouillon*, le capitaine le plus *consommé* de son siecle [*Fr.* the most consumate captain of his century].[1] I mean to put him to trial again, him and his pluck. He must—and tell him so,—as a true Spiritualist adopt the war cry of our Cossack Volunteers and print at the heading of his Banner the following "On thee o Lord of the Host we rely, and dont allow us to turn our faces on Eternal Shame." If its not quite good English, you must arrange it yourself. "La plus jolie fille du monde ne peut donner que ce qu'elle a" [*Fr.* The prettiest girl in the world can only give what she has]. *My* correspondents must accept me with my English or go without both.

Dont blow me up,[2] my dear General but for purposes known better to my own *vile black* heart I have copied your letter, (the one you spoke of the cowardice of the Editor of the Ban[ner)] and sent it to Professor Hiram CORSON for an article of his.

Betanelly's love and respect and Johnys too,

truly yours
H P Blavatsky

NOTES:

1. Bayard's traditional epithet was "chevalier sans peur et sans reproche" (see his entry in the glossary). Godfrey of Bouillon was another ideal knight, on whose name HPB is punning: *Bouillon* is both the name of an ancient French town from which Godfrey came and a common noun meaning "broth, soup"; *consommé* means both "accomplished, consummate" and "clear soup, broth."

2. *Blow up (at)* "to lose one's temper (with), explode emotionally" is usually an intransitive verb. HPB uses it transitively, *blow somebody up*, here and in letters 38, 39, and 40.

DATE: Endorsed by General Lippitt: "Mme. Blavatsky, 22 Feb., '75."

SOURCE: Transcribed from the original in the Archives of the Theosophical Society, Adyar. Published in *HPB Speaks* 2:167–9.

$$\smile$$

Introduction to Letter 23

Louisa Andrews corresponded with both Hiram Corson and HPB. The Blavatsky-Andrews correspondence has not survived directly, but in her letters to Corson, Andrews refers to HPB and quotes short passages of letters from her. In a letter to Corson dated February 26, 1875, she recounts the beginning of her correspondence with HPB:

> Feeling real genuine admiration for Md B, & being assured that she was not one to get much sympathy & encouragement from her own sex, I wrote to her last week and received a characteristic &, to me, delightful letter in reply. She seems really grateful to me for my kindly sympathy, & says that I am the "first woman in this country" who has shown any such feeling towards her, although from men she gets any quantity of letters. There is a tender womanly yearning in her letter which, in one like her, touched me deeply. She wants to meet me at the Cascade next summer, but I fear that is not on the cards. . . .
>
> . . . Md B is going to Boston as soon as her "best leg" is well enough, & purposes delivering a "Russian Speech" to old Colby. How I should like to hear it! He is a very cantankerous old chap, I hear, & I should like to be present to see how he stands the fire of the Russian batteries. It would be as good as a play. Do you know that she fought under Garibaldi—slept for weeks in the Pontine Marshes with the common soldiers & has now six bullet wounds in her body? She is also (I do not know whether this is to be repeated or not) a most powerful medium. Places a paper & pencil under the table, or in a drawer, & gets it covered with spirit writing. While in Phil she wanted a letter written by Mrs White which was locked in one of the Holmes's trunks in Vineland, & to the unspeakable amaze of the latter, John King brought it

& laid it upon the table before her. This last information comes through Gen Lippitt & I do not wish you to speak of it out of your own family. In her letter to me she says (I spoke of you in mine to her) [the quotation from HPB's letter to Andrews follows:]

Letter 23

To L. Andrews   [*ca. February 23, 1875*]

I am glad you know Prof Corson, with whom I am now corresponding. I am glad of it, for—judging you by him, & him by you, I can follow, this once, the first impression of my soul & admit both of you through the ironclad, securely bolted doors of my heart, right into its centre, if it is not quite dried up & mummified by this time. Pascal, I think, said that the style of writing was the person "Le style c'est l'homme" (a dangerous quotation by the way for myself!)— his first letter, Prof C's I mean—and your first letter recalled these words to my memory, and settled the matter at once. I scarcely ever answer letters, for in my way I am an Epicurean in all things, and, besides, not unlike "pur sang"[1] painters, I possess a—nose, and my scent is sure never to lead me wrong in the appreciation of human beings, if I trust to my instinct, only, pushing unceremoniously aside all reasoning or intellectual labor.

Louisa Andrews's letter continues:

She calls Dr C[hild] a "sacrilegious, blasphemous imp"! and Mr Owen "the poor old babe", although of the latter, too, she speaks with real respect & appreciation.

I have answered her letter & mean to keep up the correspondence unless she drops it. She is like a breath of invigorating mountain air, & if it be a little flavored by the scent of a cigarette, I shall not be in the least incommoded or alarmed. I am not only "half sick" (as the Lady of Shalott was of "shadows")[2] of commonplace people, but *wholly, thoroughly* sick, & if Md B will have me for a friend, "Barkis is willin'".[3] I however, being, as compared with her, a very commonplace little woman myself, I do not know that she will respond to the interest I feel in her. Time will show.

NOTES:

1. French, literally "pure blood." The sense, according to Jean-Louis Siémons, is that "such painters are real artists who, like poets, feel and perceive the true and the beautiful, beyond the appearance of outer things, with their sure instinct more than with their intellect."

2. Alfred, Lord Tennyson, wrote a poem entitled "The Lady of Shalott," whose central character was confined to a tower and was under a curse that destined her, if she looked directly out at the world, to suffer an unnamed fate. Because she could see the world only as it was reflected in a magic mirror, she complained, "I am half sick of shadows."

3. A popular catchphrase from *David Copperfield*, by Charles Dickens. Letter 43, note 2, comments further on it.

DATE: In Andrews's letter, dated February 26, 1875, she says she wrote to HPB "last week," and quotes from HPB's response to that letter. It is therefore likely that HPB's letter to Andrews was written only a few days before Andrews wrote to Corson.

SOURCE: Original unavailable. Transcribed from a photocopy of a letter from Louisa Andrews to Hiram Corson, in the Division of Rare and Manuscript Collections, Carl A. Kroch Library, Cornell University, Ithaca, New York. Published in *Canadian Theosophist* 70 (May-June 1989): 31.

⌒

Letter 24

To H. P. Corson   *March 6 [1875]*
                                                     Philadelphia

Dear Sir,

Will you kindly forgive me for intruding once more—unwelcome this time may be—on your valuable time. *I know* that I ought not be disturbing you *now*, for some how or other I feel that as the french say: "Vous avez d'autres chats à fouetter en ce moment" [*Fr.* You have other cats to whip (*i.e.,* fish to fry) at the moment] and my new message risks to become an unasked guest. But at the same time, I feel assured that you are not one of those that begin a job and leave it of[f] unfinished. Your article has appeared and I am glad of it, I knew Colby would never dare refuse *you*. My article has been sent ten days ago,[1] and—will never appear I am afraid, and so, I take the liberty of forwarding it to you for perusal when you have a moment to spare for it. As you will see, it's a new proof against Dr Child. I enclose together with it the statement of a man named Wescott, who was present when the bargain between the "Father Confessor" and Mrs Holmes for $10 a seance was made. In his "Sunshine"[2] that Colby wants to pass off as an answer for *my* questions Child dares not deny as you see; he only tries his best to *move* his readers hearts, and says I "fabricate stories."

I hope and pray for truth's and justice sake that you will be able to finish what Colby is determined not to let me do—to wit: unmask the lying villain.

With profound esteem and regard

Yours Truly
Hel. P. Blavatsky.

When you have done with my article, please forward it to Mrs L. Andrews [in] Spring field when you write her—I wonder if I could not have it published in the "Springfield Republican" by paying for it? I am ready to pay any sum of money for it.

Please find enclosed a letter from Gen Lippitt that will show you how our *leading* Spiritual paper is ready to die for truth.

NOTES:

1. Mary K. Neff (marginalia in her copy of *Unpublished Letters* now in the Archives of the Theosophical Society in America, Wheaton, Illinois) points out that HPB cannot have written the article before

February 27, when the Child article to which she was responding was published.

2. Henry T. Child published an article entitled "After the Storm Comes the Sunshine" in the *Religio-Philosophical Journal*, February 27, 1875, in which he says, "The stories of my acquaintance with Mrs. White are all fabrications." HPB took the retort as directed against her and replied with an article entitled "Who Fabricates?" (*CW* 1:75-83), which she submitted to Luther Colby, editor of the Boston *Banner of Light*. When he did not print her article, she sent it instead to Elbridge Gerry Brown, editor of the *Spiritual Scientist*, in which it appeared in April 1875. In her article, HPB mentions the "sunshine" of Child's title several times.

DATE: The year 1875 is evident from the references to the articles by Child and HPB.

SOURCE: Transcribed from a microfilm and a photocopy of the original in the HPB Library. Published in *Unpublished Letters* 130-1.

~~~~~~~~

Letter 25

To F. J. Lippitt   *Sunday [March 7, 1875]*
                                                Philadelphia

My dear Sir,

  Did I discover any fraud in the materialization of the Holmes? Allah is one and Mahomet is surely *his* prophet! Why, my best beloved General, did you not discover it yourself, the first time you saw Katie's face and recognized Mrs Holmes' *phyz* instead? They are mediums no mistake about it, but neither Mrs Jennie Holmes nor her spouse Nelson Holmes will ever offer you a *genuine* materialization in a bag, basket or wash-tub, unless they are in a *genuine, deep* trance—one or the other of them. Fraud is their nature, both of them were surely conceived in a moment of some cheating or some humbug as Mr Sterne in his "Voyage Sentimental;"[1] they are two incarnated *bipede* lies, and the less you have got to do with them the better for you. I have never believed *them*. I believed, *my eyes my senses* and *John*; and know *for a certainty* that Katie has materialized through them, when Nelson Holmes was in the cabinet in deep trance, and *four* times in all when he was outside. The balance of those *Katies* was Mʳˢ White, Child's confederate and—a young medium, now out of town. I have said. Believe me or not as you like it "ad libitum."

Mʳ Colby is very unjust, very unfair and—God help him, but I think him controlled for the present by some Diakka, extending his fatherly protection to Dʳ Child. Did you read his "Sunshine"?[2] There's an energetic answer for you. I sent a reply to Colby, if he does not print it and that immediately as I have a right to claim it for Child accuses me of fabricating stories, I will have it printed in the Springfield Republican or somewhere else and pay for it *anything they like*, but I am determined to show the public who fabricates stories, I or Child.[3] Please let Colby know it, let him know that if I had to give $100 for it I will have it published, *but* in such a case I will add something to it, to show *why* a *leading Spiritual[ist] paper* declines to publish the truth and nothing but the truth. For the Lords sake, do not lead your unfortunate Cambridge investigators into such a company as the Holmeses. Why do you want them to throw their money for? My advice to them if they are so rich and generous as that, to have an "Artemus Ward" with *his* show,[4] if the said gentleman is to be found somewheres in flesh and bones in preference to such *unreliable* mediums. They are sure to play tricks and if they are caught, all that is genuine in them will go to the four winds and their trickery will harm Spiritualism once more and hurt the cause and *yourself*.

John says: *"Either of them "I will try."* I suppose he means by that that you can go to Mumler or Hezelton and he will do his best. I will send you his picture on *his balcony*, in *Summerland* next week. He has finished it at one sitting but he ordered me to paint some nice flowers round it like a frame and I work very slow when he does not help me or do it himself. I feel very sick and miserable; why, I know it not myself. I find but one reason or cause for it: I wish I *were, home* up *stairs*,[5] and Spirits do not want me.

How can you think the Holmeses have lied about the photograph? The only time they spoke truth it was when they told you of it; they were very reluctant about it, for truth scratches and tears their throats like *lies* with some honest people. Have not you the testimony of [name indecipherable] and others besides that?

Believe me dear General that what *I* tell you about them is TRUTH: It's only when they speak true that they are under psychological influence.

I read Mr Epes Sargents "Proof Palpable" and I fell in love with him, he writes so very cleverly and so well. His book has interested me more than any other book in Spiritualism in America. You may tell him so if you see him and say to him, that he has perfectly psychologized a true born Cossack and made her fall in love with him. My best leg *wont* heal and seems determined to remain lame.

Write a little more than you do dont be so stingy with your letters.

Yours truly
H P Blavatsky

NOTES:

1. *A Sentimental Journey through France and Italy* (1768) by English satirist Laurence Sterne.

2. "After the Storm Comes the Sunshine," *Religio-Philosophical Journal* (February 27, 1875), a self-defense by Child.

3. HPB's reply was published as "Who Fabricates?" *Spiritual Scientist* 2 (April 1875): 44–5.

4. Artemus Ward was a comic literary character who managed a traveling sideshow.

5. HPB also uses *up stairs* or *upstairs* for "after death" or "in or to the afterlife" elsewhere (letters 27, 38, 44, 47, and 52).

DATE: Endorsed by General Lippitt as received on March 9, 1875, which was a Tuesday; since the letter was dated Sunday, it was probably written on March 7, 1875.

SOURCE: Transcribed from the original in the Archives of the Theosophical Society, Adyar. Published in *HPB Speaks* 1:55–8.

Introduction to Letter 26

In a letter written to Hiram Corson on March 23, 1875, a month after letter 23, Louisa Andrews continued the account of her correspondence with HPB:

> I have had two long letters from Md B during the last week & have sent her the article, which she thinks of getting into the Chicago Times. Her letters do me a world of good. They blow through me like a fresh, but not *cold*, wind and seem to bring strength with them. I certainly should never think of mentioning to her that you have quoted her far too enthusiastic praise of me, though I am quite certain that, if she did know it (through John for instance—who tells her many things) she would not care at all. She will know some day, if we should ever see much of each other, that she has overestimated my virtues: but I *am* at least sincere (I hope) and, for the rest, when she finds that I can be a true & tender friend, she will bear with the many imperfections & the *real* will displace the too highly colored *Ideal*, without a fatal shade, *I hope*. She idealises her friends because it is her "nature to" but is not one, I am sure, to be hard on faults & shortcomings which she failed to see at first. I feel that I can trust her as a friend, & I am sure, that, as such, she can trust me, & *that*, I hope, will suffice to draw us together. . . .
>
> I think, in Md B, there is a strong sense of *justice*, & if her terrible experience has embittered her it is no wonder. . . .
>
> Did Md B tell you about the writing that came out on the photo while she was buying the frame! No wonder the

shopkeeper broke out into a perspiration & absconded! *What a medium she is!* She says she has heard my voice so distinctly that now, she always reads my letters in it, & should recognize it directly! . . .

I wish you were here. I would show you Md B's last letter if you were, though I do not like to lend it. All that she tells me about "John", & about the higher powers & laws, & their action, is *very* interesting to me, & though, as to particulars, it has a very bewildering & mysterious seeming, tale, largely, it does not contradict any preconceived ideas of Deity or retribution.

John has been with her all her life—nearly—watching over & protecting her—her "dear brother & companion" as she says. He has been freed (as she tells me) after great torture, & years of suffering, to reenter the state in which he was before his evil deeds were done and must go on developing again from that period & *if* he falls again into his besetting sins, his probation will be more severe than before, because more interior & spiritual, as he *now* has great spiritual knowledge & power, though, in many respects, like a boy of fifteen. All she says is very wonderful & seems indeed like a part of the ancient mysteries—& yet of course it is but little that she is at liberty to divulge.

What a woman she is! Alluding to a man of whom I expressed some dread—she says:

Letter 26

To L. Andrews   *[mid March 1875]*

Fiddle dee stick! Milady—darling—I defy spirit or mortal, God or Demon to become dangerous to *me*. I was never controlled & never will be. I don't know a will on earth that would not break like glass in contact or conflict with mine.

Louisa Andrews continues:

She is a 'double natural' woman, I am sure—& both the natures are strong too. Surely she is a revelation to us common mortals! The last long letter is written at 4 a.m. & she thinks it is time to go to bed! I feel like a poor little fly, or something as weak & slight, when compared with her, & I only wonder that she cares for me or to write to me at all.

DATE: In Andrews's letter, dated March 23, 1875, she says she has received two letters from HPB "during the last week," from one of which the fragment of letter 26 is presumably quoted. It is therefore likely that the quoted letter was written between the middle of the month and March 22.

SOURCE: Original unavailable. Transcribed from a photocopy of a letter from Louisa Andrews to Hiram Corson, in the Division of Rare and Manuscript Collections, Carl A. Kroch Library, Cornell University, Ithaca, New York. Printed with some variations in *Canadian Theosophist* 70 (May-June 1989): 31.

Letter 27

To H. P. Corson   *Monday [March 15, 1875]*
                                          Philadelphia

Dear Sir,

Having received your letter on friday evening I post-poned answering it, wishing first to ascertain if my article[1] be printed in the last "Banner." I knew it would not and my prevision turned out to be true. Henceforth, if I do not promptly act I will have to follow the example of Blue Beards wife with her "Soeur Anne, ne vois tu rien venir?" [*Fr.* Sister Anne, don't you see anything coming?][2] Its use-less, Colby will *not* publish it, for some causes as unfath-omable as Spiritualism itself in certain minds: if it would not be giving you too much trouble I would beg of you to let Colby know that *you have* read a copy of my article as I tell him that I have sent it all over the country to all my acquaintances and correspondents. I am determined to see it published, whatever the cost may be. I write to Mrs

Andrews to day, asking her to try if she cannot manage to get it in the Springfield Republican; if she succeeds—so much the better for truth and the worse for Colby's impartiality. Have you read in the Boston "Spiritual Scientist" an extract from the "London Spiritualist"?[3] Even in London, they know, that out of the 11 mill: of Spiritualists, claiming to exist in this country, I, a foreigner a woman, am the only one to fight for truth. They are very complimentary to me, but Colby will take care *not to* quote from it in his paper.

Mrs Andrews has sent me a beautiful portrait of yours and I am very much obliged to her. I did not dare trouble *you* for it, being such an utter stranger to you. I *do* take her to be one of the brightest, purest spirits ever created *here* in this dirty swamp called Earth. She seems to be the incarnated kindness and gentleness. So sincere, so truthful, so ever ready to forgive and so unwilling to believe in evil, that, no wonder that she can never feel happy *here*. I am next to afraid of corresponding *too much* with her, lest I should inadvertently show her a glimpse of the "horns and hoofed heel" of my real true nature, for *I, cannot* and will not forgive as long as I can help it. I have taken to task to scourge and whip vice wherever I find it and in myself more than in others. You will surely blame me for it as many others did, but I cannot help it. I sooner will forgive murder or worse than that—*theft*, than *a lie*; and Dr Child is a bipede [*Fr. bipède* biped] lie, as you know it yourself. I have promised myself, and proclaimed to the world my indomitable resolution to take this Philadelphia hydra with her seven lying heads by the teeth and claws and not to relinquish my hold, until I strangle it fairly on the spot, though I may be bitten and wounded by it. Lies and untruthfulness or cheating, must be considered the greatest crimes in our sacred cause, for they are the more dangerous in a belief that allows so much margin for deception and self illusion, and ought to be persecuted above everything else. What the "pious frauds" of the "Fathers" of the Church in the early days of Christianity combined with the deliberate cheating of the Catholic priesthood have brought to the poor deluded humanity (or at least a portion of it) *must be* avoided for Spiritualism in the future ages. Humanity as a mass is worse than ever now; having sined through ignorance and frailty of our imperfect nature *then*, *now* they sin through the so called civilization and knowing perfectly what they are about. The prevailing, miserable tendency to materialism in our age, brought about by the never ending exposures by the Science of all manner of religious frauds can be cured by *Truth* alone and *only* by it, for humanity in general is certainly too much advanced to accept *one lie* for *another;* and on the whole, confessing to ourselves how things stand just now, we Spiritualists cannot certainly wonder at the evident reluctance of the majority of people to barter one erroneous belief which notwithstanding its numerous fabricated dogmas has still won its right of citizenship and respectability throughout ages—for another one, that *seemingly* fabricates his under the very eyes of the growing generations. How very careful must we be then in accepting phenomena and revelations purporting to come from Spirits. What dreadful consequences can bring about one *deliberate* lie found out beyond doubt in the mouth of a Spiritualist! Like one drop of gall in a bucket full of pure water it is ever liable to poison the whole of the truth. I know that what I undertake is perhaps, beyond my power but never beyond *my will*; for like a "sentinelle perdue" [*Fr.* forlorn outpost sentry] I will die at my post firm and unflinching, *trying to set* if not setting all facts in their *true light*. Those that seek to overturn the truth of Spiritualism will find a furious Dragon in me and a merciless exposer whoever they are. I see the arduousness and barrenness of the journey laying before me, the impassable thorns my path is covered with, but I do not fear or feel discouraged. I have received anonymous letters, threatening messages and insulting warnings but only feel as laughing at them. My reward is not *here* and I do not expect it here, its at home *up stairs* and I know well, that were *I to fail* or *succeed*, in either case I will be but laughed at, diffamed, slandered and blackmailed, and even should events subsequently vindicate fully the *whys* and *whatfors* of my mode of proceeding, I feel that not *one Dog* of the villifiers of our cause and scoffers of myself—will wag his tongue to acknowledge that at least *one* of the fanatical, *crazy* believers in Spiritualism has been truthful in every way. But what I do feel sometimes sorely, its—that I am but a *woman* after all, and that all the moral courage and physical too I guess, cannot carry me through, if some one does not help me and back an individual of my poor *weak* sex. Will you be one of your strong sex to help me in *the Truth*? When I look at your portrait though I see you but in profile it seems to me that you are one that accomplishes more than he promises and acts more than he speaks. Most probably you will never see me (and that's lucky, for my shocking Russian manners would terrify you) but will you allow me to write you and ask your advice and help for the forthcoming fight between *Truth* and Blind fanaticism in Spiritualism? I have secured the help of Col. Olcott, Gen: Lippitt, of Dr Taylor in the west,[4] Aksakoff in Petersburg and a dozen of others. Spiritualism as *it is* must be stoped in its progress and given another direction. The delusions and insane theories of some Spiritualists are pitiful and shameful in our Century. I have some *very rich* friends here in Philadelphia and the female portion of them are all ready to come out with their money and influence on behalf of the Cause. So, what we need the most its *brains* and fearless indomitable minds to work up in the mental Dep^r, for if we have plenty of money at our command, we have but very, very few *scholars*. Do not be frightened, dear Sir, for I will never take advantage of your kind permission (if you do give it) and become a bore; what I ask you is simply to contribute a few times a year some article like the one you sent in to the Banner, your last letter I mean,[5] and let Colby and his like know that there is behind the screen a small party of Spiritualists who are after truth *alone* and will never allow a lie or an exaggerated fact to spread abroad without trying to rectify it, as they will never allow *him*, the truthful Colby to withhold truth and help falsehood.

Well, I think that notwithstanding my fine promise for the future I *did* become a bore in my present letter which is undoubtedly too long for any mortals patience. So please, accept my sincere thanks and excuses and [last words and signature cut off]

NOTES:

1. "Who Fabricates?" (*CW* 1:75–83) responds to an implicit charge by H. T. Child that HPB had fabricated charges of his acquaintance with Eliza White. In the article, HPB specifies inconsistencies in his statements, hence the following references to Child as "a biped lie."

2. The allusion, as explained by Jean-Louis Siémons (private communication), is to a passage in Charles Perrault's famous tale "Barbe Bleue" ("Bluebeard"). Bluebeard's last wife discovers the remains of her murdered predecessors in a cupboard to which she was forbidden access and is therefore condemned to death by her husband. As the moment of her execution approaches, she asks her sister, Anne, to climb up in a tower to watch for the arrival of any help. French children learn a song with these words: "Anne, ma sœur Anne, ne vois-tu rien venir au loin?" (Anne, my sister Anne, don't you see anything coming from afar?). HPB is likewise hoping for some unknown assistance in getting her article published.

3. The weekly *Spiritualist Newspaper*.

4. Probably Timothy B. Taylor of Fort Scott, Kansas.

5. *Banner of Light* 36 (Mar. 6, 1875): 3. Corson's letter to the Editor supports HPB's attack on Henry T. Child in connection with the controversy surrounding the Holmeses (*CW* 1:56–72).

DATE: By Mary K. Neff (marginalia in her copy of *Unpublished Letters* now in the Archives of the Theosophical Society in America, Wheaton, Illinois), who observes that HPB's next letter to Corson (30), dated March 20, was written in response to a letter from him dated March 18, in which he says that her preceding letter arrived "last evening." That was March 17, making a probable date for the writing of this letter Monday, March 15.

SOURCE: Transcribed from a microfilm and a photocopy of the original in the HPB Library. Published in *Unpublished Letters* 162–6.

Letter 28

To H. S. Olcott   *[late March 1875]*

My answer to your letter *just received.*

Got it this very moment. I had a right and *dared* withhold for a few hours the letter sent you by Tuitit Bey,[1] for *I* alone am answerable for the effects & results of my chiefs orders. I am one of those who know *when* and *how*, and that for long years I guess and *you*—you are but a baby inclined to be capricious and selfwilled. The message was ordered at *Luxor* a little after midnight between Monday & Tuesday. Written out [at] Ellora in the dawn by one of the secretaries [or] neophytes and written very badly. I wanted to ascertain from T.B. [Tuitit Bey] if it was still *his* wish to have it sent in such a state of *human* scribbling, as it was intended for one who received such a thing for the first time. My suggestion was to let you have one of our parchments on which the contents appear (materialized) *whenever you cast your eyes on it to read it*, and disappear every time as soon as you have done, for, as I respectfully inferred you had been just puzzled by Johns[2] tricks, and that perhaps your mind notwithstanding your sincere belief would need strengthening by some more substantial proof. To this, T.B. answered me entre autre[s] [*Fr.* among other things] *thus*. "// b m 2 o w j k l m. (now I am getting crazy again and write you in a language you cannot understand). I translate verbatim "A mind that seeks the proofs of Wisdom & Knowledge in outward appearance as material proofs—is unworthy of being let in unto the Grand Secrets of the "Book of Holy Sophia." One who denies the Spirit and questions him on the ground of its material clothing—*a priori* will never be able to—"Try." —So you see there a rebuke again. Perhaps the physical suffering I am doomed to with my leg make me unfit for reasoning, but I have yet brains enough left in me to answer your questions *point blank*. You say *I want* all my messages from them *verbatim et literatim*. You want too many things at once my dear. *Whenever they write to you* and I have orders to give the letter to *you* I will do so, for you would be the first to teach me how to obey their orders. But when *I* receive orders written or spoken by "Messengers, surely you do not expect me to send them you. I will do so once for fun, and see what *you* will be able to make out of them without *my translation*. Now my advice to you Henry [is] a friendly one. Don't you *fly to[o] high*, and poke your nose on the forbidden paths of the Golden Gate without some one to pilot you; for John wont be there always to collar you in time and bring you safe home. The little they do for you is wonderful to me, for I never saw them so *generous* from the first. The message about Child is written to me, and I can but translate it, if you dont believe me that *they* want you to do it, as you please. If you do not believe me you wont believe them, and I dont think it *T.B.*'s principle to be too explicit. I am an *initiated* wretch, and I know what a curse the word "*Try* has proved to me in my life, and how often I trembled and feared to misunderstand their orders and bring on myself punishment for carrying them *too far* or not far enough.

You seem to take the whole concern for a childs play. Beware Henry, before you pitch headlong into it. Remember what you wrote *inspirationally* for me to *Alden*[3] in Girards St.[4] There is time yet, and you can decline the connexion as yet. But if you *keep* the letter I send you and *agree* to the word *Neophyte* you are cooked my boy and there is no return from it. Trials and temptations to your faith will shower on you first of all. (Remember *my* 7 years preliminary initiation, trials, dangers and fighting with all the Incarnated Evils and legions of Devils and think before you accept.) There are mysterious dreadful invocations in the letter sent you *human* and *made up* as it may appear [to] you perhaps. On the other hand if you are *decided*, remember my advice if you want to come out victorious of the affray. *Patience, faith, no questioning*, thorough *obedience* and *Silence*.

NOTES:

1. "The letter sent you by Tuitit Bey . . . The message was ordered at Luxor" doubtless refers to the undated letter 3 in *Letters from the Masters of the Wisdom*, Second Series. That letter is headed "From the Brotherhood of Luxor, Section the Vth to Henry S. Olcott" and ends "Tuitit Bey / Observatory of Luxor. Tuesday Morning." At the beginning of her letter she says the "message was ordered at Luxor a little after midnight between Monday and Tuesday."

2. "John King."

3. C. Jinarajadasa identifies "Alden" as presumably William L. Alden, one of the formers of the Theosophical Society.

4. C. Jinarajadasa (*Theosophist* 43 [March 1922]: 612) notes: "From a signed article of H.P.B.'s, we get her address in Girard Street as No. 1111."

DATE: The references to Henry T. Child, in both this letter and that to Olcott from Tuitit Bey, place this letter at the end of the "Katie King" affair. See also the note on the date of the next letter, 29.

SOURCE: Transcribed from the original in the Archives of the Theosophical Society, Adyar. The text is now completely illegible in some places, and earlier transcriptions have necessarily been relied on for those parts of the letter. Published in *HPB Speaks* 1:1–5.

Letter 29

To H. S. Olcott?[1]   *[late March 1875]*

I open the letter to enclose you something very original in its way. Its the portrait of Mr Betanelly with a white towel behind him purporting to be his grand aunt. We have in Philadelphia a young lady a *private* medium that pretends to paint photographs better than any artist. So I gave her mine and Betanelly's. See what came out of it. Poor B. is represented as a *tenor leger* [*It. tenore leggiero* "light tenor"[2]] in some Opera Bouffe, resting in a green bower. The young lady *artist* carried off by her mediumistic zeal painted even his grand aunt!! [*a few words now illegible*] she must be a medium for "copal varnish."[3]

Yours—
H P Blavatsky

Tear Beta: [Betanelly] photo he would be in despair were he to know that *I* sent you this caricature. I mean to play him a trick. But if you *do* find it resembling then keep it.

NOTES:

1. This note is written on paper of the same kind and width as the preceding letter (28) and generally resembles it. Although there is no internal evidence of the addressee or date, the physical similarity suggests that the letter referred to at the beginning of this note may be the preceding one.

2. A *tenore leggiero* is a lyric artist endowed with a voice of a particularly high register and characterized by notable agility, especially suitable for brilliant, vivacious comic roles (Salvatore Battaglia, *Grande dizionario della lingua italiana* 8:912 [Torino: Unione Tipografico-Editrice Torinese, n.d.]).

3. According to Jean-Louis Siémons (private communication), in order to increase the transparency of their colors, painters add substances

such as copal resin varnish to oil pigments. Such an additive is called a "medium," for example, "un medium au copal" (a copal varnish medium). HPB is punning sarcastically on the meanings of "medium" as both a painter's additive and a Spiritualistic channel to the other world.

DATE: By late March, HPB was living at 3420 Sansom Street, Philadelphia, which was also Betanelly's address.

SOURCE: Transcribed from the original in the Archives of the Theosophical Society, Adyar.

Letter 30

To H. P. Corson   *March 20 [1875]*
Philadelphia

My dear Sir,

I am all swollen up, my face as big as a pumpkin and I feel quite *dematerializing*, dissolving, but I feel so glad at the same time of having received such a kind friendly letter from you, that I forget all my ailings and sit down write away for the purpose of only telling you that I appreciate deeply, *very* deeply indeed all your kindness to a woman, a stranger that I am afraid you will find—when you know her better, not to deserve this *kindness* so much as you think perhaps. Alas, my dear Sir, I am really, very, very vicious in my own way, and impardonably so in the eyes of every true American. My only hope for future is, that you may turn out to be more of a man, a true hearted, noble minded *man* than of an American, for then perhaps you may forgive me my russian vices and put up with them for the sake of charity. I feel so happy to think that I may have a chance of passing a week or two in the society of my two correspondents and—may I add friends?—you and Mrs Louisa Andrews, and I am so scared at the same time when I come to think, how utterly *disenchanted* you may both of you feel, and how shocked Mrs Corson may feel though she is not an American but a french lady, who knows better than your own nation does, what we Russians are. You invite me so kindly to the Cascade[1] but what shall you say, when you see your guest stealing away from the room every 15 minutes, to go and hide behind the doors and in the yards and basements to—*smoke* her cigarette? For I am obliged here to confess that I, who together with all the *female* portion of Russia smoked in my drawing room as in the drawing rooms of every respectable lady to begin from an aristocratical Princess and down to the wife of an "employé"; who smoked according to our national custom in my carriage and in the "foyers" of the theatres, I am actually obliged to *hide* myself like a thief, for the Americans have insulted me and stared me out of countenance and published about me in the papers, ornamenting my poor self with the most wonderful names and inventing about me stories and so forth, till, unable to give up an innocent habit of more than twenty years standing, I was finally driven, to what I consider a mean act of cowardice; doing what I am ashamed (*here* in America) to proclaim to the face of the world. But if you can forgive me my national sins, then of course I will be most happy to avail myself of your kind invitation for which I thank a thousand times yourself and Mrs Corson, to whom, I beg you will present my most sincere compliments and ask her beforehand some indulgence and charity for a poor barbarian, that fell down from her Cosack-land in your civilized country like some ill shaped aerolithe [*Fr. aérolithe*, aerolite, aerolith, stony meteorite] from the moon. Tell her, I promise her *never* to smoke in her drawing room if—after my confession mrs Corson is still brave enough to reiterate her invitation—but to go and seek out for the purpose the company of the hamadryads in the silent woods. With the dear, sincere truthful Mrs Andrews I was more sincere still, if

I remember right: Heavens be merciful unto me, but I do think that to her friendly invitation to come and visit her one of these days at Springfield, I actually confessed her that I very often swore—in *Russian*. I do not know as yet, how she bore the shock, but I do hope that this fatal revelation did not kill her on the spot.

Oh dear me, you will have a nice idea of your correspondent *now*, that I have devoted nearly four pages to confess my two most disgusting vices but I like always to have people see my worst side at first, so that if they happen to find out some particle of genuine gold in a heavy, bad penny, so much the better for the penny.

I have not changed my residence, but it's always safer to send the letters to my P. O. Box 2828, as I am obliged to absent myself from town every now and then, on Spiritualistic business,—for as I told you I was sent to this country by our Society—and the letters may be mislaid sometimes.

It is sad indeed as you say that Truth has to beg and pray and humble herself to be admitted in the leading organ of the Spiritualists of this country, when *lies* have only to send in their cards to be received with outstretched arms. For instance, there is in the last "Banner" an account of one Mᵣ Wood, who pretends he saw his wife, at a seance given by Mrs Holmes. Now, I know it to be a falsehood. In the first place *never* no respectable wife dead or alive will ever materialize through such a source of vile impurity as this Mrs Holmes happens to be for the greatest disgrace of us Spiritualists. Then, a certain old lady, Mrs Lippincott in whose house the seance took place, assured me most emphatically that on that same evening the medium was found out tricksting[2] and cheating, but the old gentleman who wrote this *wonderful* account is a half crazy lunatic who happens to see his wife in every corner, under the chairs and in each glass of whiskey he swallows. "Et c'est ainsi que l'on écrit l'histoire!" [*Fr.* And that's the way history gets written.] Poor Spiritualism.

Most certainly, I am ready to do anything you or Mrs Andrews think proper.[3] You may curtail the article, and trim it, and even crop it in a Sing-Sing fashion[4] if you think it will do any good, but I really think, that for the sake of the cause, we Spiritualists ought not to humble ourselves when *we know we are right.* Don't think for a moment my dear Mr Corson, that it is vanity or author's pride that speaks in me. If I write well enough in other languages, and I know I do, I know well at the same time that I have nothing to boast of in my *English* articles, and if it was not for the thought and moral certitude that "however badly dressed "Truth" must always conquer, I would have never dared come out in polemic fights on the arena of English Literature. I guess you, a Professor of English Philology and Literature you have often laughed at my *moscovite* expressions. And I wish to goodness, *I could* make you laugh heartily, for it seems to me you sadly want it. I can't say more, and could not if I would, for I can never somehow or other express what I feel, unless I can fight for it. I am a poor hand—for any *outward* show of sympathy or compliments, and there are many things I would never dare touch for those wounds are so deep that they cut through the very centre of the heart, and my hands are so rough that I dare not trust to them.[5] One thing I must say though, for I can't help it. I am sorry to see that you a Spiritualist, and knowing yourself, that you use a wrong expression you still pronounce the word *lost* or "*dead.*" Now, it seems to me that it sounds like a profanation. We insult our beloved ones, our so far gone but still nearer to us than ever travelers, when we say: We *have lost them,* for they are dead." There is but one death in Nature, and it is the *moral death* of a person in our hearts, when the bad actions and deeds of this person compel us to bury him or her for ever in our souls memory, and when we feel obliged to make—even the remembrance of him vanish to the last particle. How can your beautiful, pure, innocent child be dead? Did not she, apparently to us, suffer *unjustly* the penalty of her living in this world and being confined in her prison of clay? This same apparent injustice ought to be to us Spiritualists the most apparent, convincing proof of the immortality of our spirit, that's to say to every one who firmly believes in a just omnipotent god as a principle of every thing. What harm did she ever do, what sin could she have committed to be made to suffer bodily as she did? Her physical death was but a proof that she *was ready*, ready before her natural term of years in Spirit, to live henceforth in a better world. As I once wrote before to Mrs Andrews about the loss of her young son Harold—I have yet enough left in me of love for the poor humanity, to rejoice when I see children and pure young people die or pass away, I should say. "Too good to live *in this world*," is not an idle saying. It is a profoundly philosophical verity. What really devoted father or mother would not consent to become *blind* for the sake of securing eternal bliss and felicity for their beloved children? Would not you? Well, is not cecity [blindness] worse in such a case? for it makes all and every thing vanish out of your sight for ever, whereas now, you cannot see only one dear one: to this you may object that a blind man can at least *feel* or *hear* the voice of the one the sight of whom he lost. But cannot you *feel* and *hear* her the same as ever. Did you ever *try?* Oh, how I wish I could teach you some things you seem to know nothing of as yet. How happy you could be then. American Spiritualism is dreadful in some things, it's *killing*, for it really brushes close Materialism sometimes. Why should you go and profanate the names of your best beloved, your departed ones, the holy Spirits inhabiting regions with atmospheres as pure and holy as themselves, by breathing these names to dirty, venal paid mediums, when you have all the means *within yourselves* to communicate and visit and receive visits from your departed! How willingly would I devote all my life, nay, sacrifice it even if I could only impart to some bereaved fathers & mothers, sons and orphan daughters, the grandest Truth that ever was, a Truth so easily learned and practised for whoever is endowed with a powerful will and—*faith*. I have said or too little or—too much I know not which. By the fruit shall we judge of the seed. —Amen.

You want to know about the "Revue Spirite."[6] I comply with your request the more willingly, for I know well and consider Mr Leymarie the Editor of it—my friend. This journal or periodical is the best in France. It's highly moral and truthful and—interesting. Of course the direction of it is purely Kardec-like, for the book was the creation of the "Maitre" himself as french Spiritists the *Reincarnationists* call Allan Kardec and was left furthermore a heirloom by the latter to Leymarie. The widow, madame A. Kardec is one of the noblest and purest women living. The *Spiritists* have a slight tendency to ritualism and dogmas but this is but a slight shadow of their Catholic education, a habit innate in this people that jumps so quick from Popish slavery whether to Materialism or Spiritualism. Mrs Corson will not repent if she subscribes for it. I find fault with them but for one thing—not with the "Revue Spirite" but with the teaching itself; it is, that they are *reincarnationists* and zealous missionaries for the same. They could never do anything with me in that way, so they gave me up in disgust. But we still are friends with M^r and Madame Leymarie who are both of them highly cultured people and—truthful and sincere as gold. For you dear Sir, if I can make so bold as to give you an advice would be to subscribe to the Boston "Spiritual Scientist." It is a worthy little paper and the tendency is good, though they are as poor as poverty itself. I have a good mind of sending my article to be published in that paper; they have very good articles sometimes, and moreover, print all they find of interesting in foreign Spiritualistic journals. I send you two copies; in both you will find marked with red pencil flattering notices about my fathers best daughter. Prince Wittgenstein is an old friend of my youth, but has become a *reincarnationist*, so we had a fight, or two for it and parted half friends and half enemies. He is the one that *feels sure* that the London Katie King was in a previous life *his wife*, when he was some Turkish Sultan or other. Theres the fruit of the reincarnational teaching.

As soon as my noble profile and classic nose reincarnate themselves in their previous normal state, I will have my portrait taken for you and Mrs Andrews,[7] but not in *profile* though, as by some mysterious and unfair decree of Providence, my nose presents in that way, the appearance of an upturned old slipper, a little the worse for the wear. I met Dr Child a few days ago at Lincoln Hall, *face to face*. He did not look at all, as if he saw the "Sunshine" this once, after a Storm,[8] but looked on the contrary when meeting *my gaze* the very picture of a venomous mushroom after a heavy shower and—cleared out.

My best compliments to Mrs Corson and to you my *sincerest, deepest wishes* for a genuine warm "Sunshine" to thaw the icicles from every place of your inner Self. —With sincere esteem and regard

truly yours
H P Blavatsky

NOTES:

1. A resort in New York State. Mary K. Neff (marginalia in her copy of *Unpublished Letters* now in the Archives of the Theosophical Society in America, Wheaton, Illinois) observes that in his letter of March 18, to which this is an answer, Corson wrote:

   I have understood through Mrs. Andrews of Springfield that you purpose visiting the Cascade next summer. I *do* hope you will. I shall spend a part of my summer vacation there, with my wife and our son, who graduates at the University in June, and will leave us after the vacation, to pursue his medical studies in N.Y. Mrs. Corson joins me in welcoming you to our home next summer. We are but an hour's ride, or perhaps 1½ hrs. from "The Cascade." We have a very large house and nobody in it but ourselves. The situation is beautiful, overlooking Cayuga Lake and a country that for natural scenery is not surpassed, or hardly equaled, anywhere. It is a region of cataracts and wild ravines. I am sure you could spend 2 or 3 wks. with us very pleasantly. It may be an additional inducement to say that Mrs. C. is a French woman, born and educated in Paris; but altho' I have lived with her over 20 yrs. I am a very poor Frenchman. My tastes are English, and my prof'ship confines my studies largely to Anglo-Saxon & English philology and literature.

2. "Tricksting" appears to be a nonce blending of *tricksing* "tricking, cheating" and the stem of *trickster* "one who practices trickery." *Unpublished Letters* has "tricking."

3. Mary K. Neff (marginalia) observes that in his letter of March 18, Corson wrote HPB that Mrs. Andrews thought the article "Who Fabricates?" (*CW* 1:75–83) should be published in a Spiritualist journal and suggested that, if HPB permitted it to be curtailed by omitting the part that showed personal feeling, it might be printed in the *Banner of Light*.

4. The hair of prisoners was cropped as a health precaution. Sing Sing State Prison, New York, is proverbial as a place of incarceration.

5. Mary K. Neff (marginalia) observes that in his letter of March 18, Corson had told of the loss in July 1874 of his only daughter, at the age of seventeen. Her health had been feeble, but she had borne it with patience and resolution.

6. Mary K. Neff (marginalia) observes that in his letter of March 18, Corson wrote that Mrs. Corson wished to subscribe to a "foreign spiritual paper" and inquired whether HPB knew anything about the character of the *Revue Spirite*.

7. In her letter (27) to Corson dated March 15, HPB wrote: "Mrs. Andrews has sent me a beautiful portrait of yours and I am very much obliged to her." Mary K. Neff (marginalia) observes that in his letter of March 18, Corson wrote:

Now that you have my picture, I think it would be no more than fair that I should have yours. I trust it is not making too free to beg the favor. I should prize it most highly and so would Mrs. Corson. I don't know what picture it was that Mrs. Andrews sent you. A Professor here has to have so many taken for the different classes that he loses the run of them all.

8. An allusion to the title of H. T. Child's article "After the Storm Comes the Sunshine," to which HPB was responding in her article "Who Fabricates?"

SOURCE: Transcribed from a microfilm and a photocopy of the original in the HPB Library. Published in *Unpublished Letters* 132–9.

Letter 31

To H. P. Corson   *[ca. March 24, 1875]*

My dear Sir,

Truly Spirits do bring on sometimes wonderful things! Hardly have I mailed you a letter,[1] three times too long perhaps for an ordinary man's patience when your own last favor has proved to be a real god send; first for a poor worthy fellow, and—then,—if Spirits help me—it may prove to be the *little first cause of great results*. You never thought I am sure, when writing as you did in your last,[2] and giving vent to an honest indignation that ought to be felt and shared by every Spiritualist, about the disgusting publication of "Duff M Duff" in the Ireligio-Unphilosophical,[3] as it ought to be called—that your indignation catching hold of me, would make me lay awake all night; and when I lay awake I think, and after thinking, I generally *act*. The same morning, brought me back my article from Colby, which, without further comments he "*respectfully declined*" on a bit of a dirty printed slip of paper. Very well; so I began thinking, and ploting and scheming and took the "Spiritual Scientist" to which little paper I had never paid much attention before, somehow or other; and finding there another mention of my name, from the "Revue Spirite (I sent it you, did you receive it? Not the *Revue* but the Scientist?) I took up some back numbers and read them through attentively, and the more I read, the less I found therein such like trash as found more or less in the *Religio*, and even in the great sublime "Banner," but on the contrary remarked in it a decided tendency, as I wrote you, to help our cause, and an earnest endeavor to follow the steps of the "London Spiritualist" and other such respectable foreign papers. Are you of my opinion? To be sure it is rather difficult for you to judge from two solitary copies; but I liked it so well myself, that I subscribed for it immediately. Then came in a gentleman from Boston to visit me and I learned from him that the Editor of the Scientist was a very well educated young man, well connected enough, but *poor as poverty itself"* for to become a Spiritualist and an Editor of a Spiritual paper, he had quarreled with all his family and the consequences were, that he had quite ruined himself; for the opposition on the part of the *Banner*—whose policy is to praise and puff up all Spiritual manifestations even fraudulous and spurious ones, and *never* to expose anything or any one—was untiring and *their* persecution of this poor Gerry Brown who took from the first quite a contrary course—was *merciless.* Thats what I learned from Mr Giles, of Boston. Of course I felt fired up like a dry match immediately, got several subscribers for him the same day and— sent him my article, adding in my letter that I begged him not to look on the subscription money in the light of a "bribery" for, if he were not to print my article at all for some cause or other—I thought it too long for the "Scientist"—I should try to find him subscribers all the same. Then I received a letter from Olcott, talking with me at length about the immediate necessity of having in this country a respectable Spiritualistic paper and that I must try and work for it, if I have the Cause at heart. So, I went and talked to my friends & acquaintances, and the idea struck me, that if we could secure the "Scientist" for the class of Spiritualists that I can name at once the "opposition party" we might do a vast deal of good for the cause. We have got *no antidote* as yet, for the poisonous stuff we are served, in the shape of all manner of bogus communications, and the peoples mind (the Spiritualists) is turning more and more bewildered and is actually getting benumbed and paralyzed by the pressure on their brains of *what they do not understand*, though believing it all the time *sur parole* [*Fr.* on someone's word], only because the "Banner," or the *dear old* Relig: Philosophical said so and endorses it. Such a state of mind is more than dangerous and does require an antidote. My idea was to raise up a subscription between the richer Spiritualists, at $100 p. share say. Spin a stock, or how, do they call it, and have a paper of our own, but then an Editor, an able one at least would be very difficult to select, for if he answered well enough one way, he might fail in something else. Col. Olcott is ready enough, but then he asks right away $700 per month and I find the nut too hard to crack—from a *fervent Spiritualist*. Would not you think that if we tried to help that poor Gerry Brown, something good might come of it? If we only help him, by inducing prominent Spiritualists and prominent well known men to write for his paper occasionally and help him in the way of finding for him subscribers (as the Banner acts so mean and ugly with him) dont you think, we would do fair for the Cause and act charitably towards a poor struggling fellow creature & a brother Spiritualist? I am not generally speaking very tender hearted, but my heart aches for that man after the letter I received this morning from him, and that I forward you for perusal.[4] Don't you think his very soul speaks in this simple, truthful narrative of his trials and his sufferings, and I know, he does not say, half of what really is. I know, his position is worse even than he admits it to me. He might always as a *printer*, a compositor or type setter get his $35 per week, and still he clings *to the truth* and struggles and works like a slave, to get but the half, with a weekly regular *deficit*, that slowly, but as surely drags him into the abyss! Isn't it meritorious in him? I do respect & honor him for that, and will do every thing in my power to help him through. If you could only write something serious for his paper, something that would attract attention and your name alone would be sufficient to raise up his paper. And then perhaps you might find him a few subscribers in Ithaca. If you can not, which I am afraid *is the case*, for I know more than you think about you, then *do* write something for his paper. See how freely and *unceremoniously* I act with you; thats the usual effect of *too much* kindness. But *I know* you are a kind, good noble heart and will not think me too daring or indiscreet, to claim such a service from you, for you are a Spiritualist and a true one. When you have read Gerry Browns letter in response to my second one, in which I ask him to tell me what I can do for him, and if a subscription would be of any good to him— please send it to Mrs Louisa Andrews. I know she will *cry* over it, that she will, and her *Buff* will howl with sympathy, for dogs are in our days more honest, and noble hearted than men are, and more truthful than Spiritualists of the class of *Colby*. Fancy *Rich* the proprietor of the Banner, in partnership with a low variety Theatre. *Spiritualism*, & *variety show!!* O Century, XIX of thy name, what a pretty fellow you are!

I will write to Flammarion the astronomer in Paris and ask him to write something for the "Scientist" and then I will get Mrs Andrews and—do you think if Longfellow would write a piece of poetry for him, it would do him any good?—with all this, I forgot my article. It will appear in the next N° of the Scientist, and I'm going to take several hundred copies with my article and send them all over the country. I guess Childs "Sunshine" will be eclipsed for a few days.

Excuse my "style echevelé" [*Fr. style échevelé* disheveled, disorderly style] and innumerable mistakes. But no one can reasonably expect a woman with her nerves all stretched out, like strings in an old fiddle, ready to burst, to write good English. I feel so excited, that I wonder how I didn't write my letter in Russian.

I enclose a very curious letter from a *prisoner*, published by the Hartford Times and sent me by Col. Olcott. Perhaps, it will make you smile. Please present my sincere compliments to Mrs Corson and keep on believing me,

Most truly and respectfully yours
H P. Blavatsky.

Thursday.

P.S. Could not you bring out our statements against Child in the "Scientist" and give it to Colby.

Will you kindly allow me, dear Sir one more question; if my inquisitiveness is rude or unwelcome, *dont answer me a word* and I will understand and feel the eloquent hint. I wanted to ask you that question from the first, but did not feel quite, I had the right to offer it to you.

Why, instead of the original sign of the "Labarum"[5] which stands thus: ˣ⚥ᴾ and is the one that is said to have appeared to the Emperor Constantine on the Heavens one fine morning, you have adopted a little change to it, at each side of the Labarum: A & Ω —? The latter characters *as far as I know* (and I judge in my own Rosecrucian way by the second table of stone in the *Double Lithoi*) mean— A which was given or delivered by ǀ (male Principle) and Ω because it passed or came *through*——(the female Principle Right & Left). But then, on *your* seal are lacking both on A & Ω the surrounding signs of Ꙩ .

It ought to stand if I understand right thus:

Can you tell me why?

Well, perhaps I am a fool after all and an inquisitive one too, and you are right and know better.

God bless you, and forgive me my indiscretion—if it is one.

Yours truly again

H P Blavatsky

NOTES:

1. HPB's letter (30) of March 20.

2. Mary K. Neff (marginalia in her copy of *Unpublished Letters* now in the Archives of the Theosophical Society in America, Wheaton, Illinois) observes that in his letter of March 18, Corson discussed the poor quality of the *Religio-Philosophical Journal* and the *Banner of Light* and expressed the wish that

   > a fund could be raised to support a high-toned, scholarly Spiritual paper, that would merit respect and that could speak the truth with all soberness irrespective of individual interests. There are now too many ignorant writers in the field, and there is accordingly too much trash published. Every ass that attends a seance and witnesses manifestations of any kind, thinks he must enlighten the public thereupon. Take your own case. You write an article that would help to raise the soiled robes of Truth out of the dirt and it is rejected by a dull-souled editor out of consideration for a Judas to the cause of Spiritualism, Dr. Child, who has stabbed it almost to the heart.

3. The *Religio-Philosophical Journal* printed several irreverent articles by "Duff M'Duff" or "Duff McDuff," satirizing the Bible and Christian churchmen. One such article in the issue for March 6, 1875 (17.25:9), "Comments: The Plan of Salvation, according to the Bible, Translated into Plain Modern Speech," was a comic retelling of the Genesis creation story, the Flood, and the Incarnation. It is probably this article that offended Hiram Corson, perhaps because of its flippant tone and lack of relevance to Spiritualism. Another

such article in the issue for May 22, 1875 (18.10:73) was entitled "A Story about One of God's Own—Thoughts," which was a retelling of the story of David, who sent Uriah into certain death in battle so that he could satisfy his passion for Uriah's wife, Bathsheba. The article ends with comments on sexually immoral clergymen, with possible reference to Henry Ward Beecher's extramarital affair with the wife of a colleague of his, which HPB also alludes to in letter 39. "Ireligio-Unphilosophical" (*Ln. irreligio* "false religion") is a satiric version of the journal's name *Religio-Philosophical Journal*.

4. HPB sent the same or a similar letter from Brown to Olcott (letter 44, May 21).

5. The Labarum is a continued subject of correspondence in letter 34.

DATE: Mary K. Neff (marginalia in her copy of *Unpublished Letters* now in the Archives of the Theosophical Society in America, Wheaton, Illinois) points to the fact that HPB says "Hardly have I mailed you a letter," presumably letter 30 of March 20 (a Saturday), "when your own last favor proved to be a real god send," referring to a letter from Hiram Corson that may have arrived the same day or possibly the following Monday (March 22). HPB then speaks of lying awake all night and acting the next day. This letter, part of her active response, would then be only a few days after the preceding one; the dating of the p.s. as "Thursday" would be March 25 and implies that the body of the letter might have been written on the preceding day, Wednesday, March 24. An envelope addressed to Corson is postmarked March 26.

SOURCE: Transcribed from a microfilm and a photocopy of the original in the HPB Library. Published in *Unpublished Letters* 156–61.

～

Introduction to Letter 32

The "John King" portrait was proceeding apace. The following letter from Michael Betanelly to General Lippitt of March 22, 1875 (*HPB Speaks* 1:59–60), gives some account of its painting, as well as a view of Betanelly's life with HPB and "John King" at this time and of Betanelly's personality:

My dear General,

Your's with pictures received. Accept my thanks for helping our business. I have not the slightest doubt, that in a few years I will be able to open a large trade between Russia and America.

John told us, that Colby is sick in bed. Is it true? John said, he made him sick, because he was mad with him.

John is making a splendid picture for you on Satin. I have not seen it yet, and he don't wish anybody see it, before he is through with it. He is making most mysterious and remarkable manifestations with us almost every day. This evening I forgot to deliver a letter to Mme. I brought from P. Office, and, when we were sitting at the dinner table, John went on rapping and telling, and abusing my bad memory, how and why I did not give the letter to her, etc., etc.

Since we came to this house, John took away his own picture from the frame twice, kept it several days and brought back—and all this as quick as lightning. There is no end of these wonders. Although a spiritualist of only 5 months standing, I have seen and witnessed more spirit manifestations, and see it more every day, than a great many others have seen in their long lives.

I have neither space nor time to tell you all what, J. K. does with us but, if told, it will make the most remarkable story ever written on spirit manifestations.

I want to try a spirit picture, taking if I could get some of my spirit friends. Suppose, I send a photograph picture of mine, could Mumler take spirit picture from it? Please write particulars, and also how much Mumler or Hezleton charge for it? Also, who is the best of them for spirit photographs?

With great esteem and respect,

I remain, Yours truly,

M. C. B.

The following letter from HPB to the General gives additional information:

Letter 32

To F. J. Lippitt   [*ca. March 24, 1875*]
                                      Philadelphia

My dear General,

John sends you the following wise answer that I copy "verbatim" (I asked him if he could tell you who the spirits were on your picture).

"Tell him that John never keeps bad companie. Those are ungodly sprites. Let him wait and see if he recognizes some of the spirits on my picture."

He means I suppose the picture he is about finishing for you. It's *one yard square* on white satin and all full of very funny things. His own portrait in the centre; on his balcony, surrounded by verdure and so forth. I only am perplexed how to send it without spoiling it. I suppose the best will be to roll it on a round stick and sew it up in oil cloth. Only please do not *let every one know* it was done *through me*. I do not want at all to be considered a Medium which *title* is synonymous to *"fraud"* in our days. Besides, I am not a medium at all and never was, at least a medium as you understand it, all of you mortals. Basta [*It.* enough].

Now my sweetest of generals, you must do me *one* favor. Notwithstanding my efforts and the combined efforts of Professor Corson, Mrs Andrews, Col Olcott and many others, *Colby* has sent me back my MSS. John told me he would not publish it, John was very mad with him and even (I did not verify if he said truth or not) went so far as to tell me a few days ago that he knocked down "that ungodly Colby" and *made him sick*, because "he made my labour *slake*."[1] What does John mean by the expression "slake" I do not know, but he has expressed of late some very funny words, which Col Olcott tells me are old saxon words. Well, *en desespoir de cause* [*Fr.* as a desperate shift, as a last resort] I sent my MSS.² to Mᵣ Gerry Brown Editor of the "Spiritual Scientist." His is a nice paper and beginning to be quite worthy of consideration of late for he tries evidently all he can to give it a serious direction. You find therein some very good articles and I mean *even if he cannot publish my articles*—for some reasons, to protect him and find him as many subscribers as I can. I found him *four* already, amongst others John Morton my friend, who is going to be elected Governor of Philadel. Well my darling General, you just run will you to, 18 Exchange St. to the aforesaid Mᵣ Gerry Brown shake hands with him and *do* ask him if he can print that blessed article or not. If not, upon my word I write the whole thing up and send it to the London Spiritᴵ [*i.e.,* Spiritualist] Papers. Wont I give it to Colby then, and to other cowards too! Will you do that for me, my dear General? You will oblige me ever so much, for I am sick of that article and sick of fighting, and want to get rid of it. (Read it please and tell me how you like it.)

Did you hear the trick John has played with Olcott? He actually wrote him a long letter, posted it himself it appears, and told him in it some wonderful secrets. He is a trump my John. Well you will be surprised at *his* picture. Wait and see, I think I will be able to forward it at the end of the week, if my *under-standing* is to be relied upon.

God bless you for ever and may you never see your shadow diminish in size—as the Persians say.

Yours truly

H P. Blavatsky

P. S.—So you are determined not to give up your Holmes? are you? Well, let me tell you that your bag and seal and crucial tests will prove of no avail and that they shall both of *them cheat better than ever.* I stake my head, she will. Just you catch the first materialized face by the nose, and see what will come of it. Its no use General. They *are* cheats and you will only hurt the cause.

NOTES:

1. *Slake*, "to diminish or lessen, to fall apart," used continuously in English since Anglo-Saxon times, today especially of thirst or curiosity "to quench."

2. "Who Fabricates" (*CW* 1:75–83), written on March 16, 1875 (*CW* 1:83n), and published in the *Spiritual Scientist* 2 (April 1875).

DATE: C. Jinarajadasa (*HPB Speaks* 1:70) says, "Received by General Lippitt, March 24, 1875," so written then or shortly before.

SOURCE: Transcribed from the original in the Archives of the Theosophical Society, Adyar, which is now barely legible, the ink having faded and the paper darkened with age; parts are completely illegible, and for them earlier transcriptions were relied upon. Published in *HPB Speaks* 1:61–4.

<hr />

Letter 33

To A. N. Aksakoff   *March 24, 1875*
                                                 Philadelphia

Olcott's book[1] is producing an enormous *furore*. . . . In this book he has made many changes from his letters, both by additions and omission. . . . and still the Lord only knows how many things he has mixed up in my biography: princes, boyards,[2] and imaginary governors-general—whatever they chose to tell him at the Consulate. It's really a pity; people will only laugh at me; they'll suppose that I have been throwing dust in people's eyes in America, like a fool; and yet, there is only one thing I am seeking and struggling for—that people should forget the former Blavatsky, and leave the *new* one alone. But it seems hard to achieve. I write so much in all the papers that there is no concealing my name. Not a day passes that some new story does not come out in the papers. Blavatsky was in Africa, and went up in a balloon with Livingstone. Blavatsky dined with the King of the Sandwich Islands. Blavatsky converted the Pope of Rome to Spiritualism; she predicted his death to Napoleon; she cured the Queen of Spain's face of warts with the aid of the spirits, and so on. Lord, what they can imagine! It is two months now since I went out of my room, with my *injured leg*,[3] yet according to the papers it appears that during this time I have sailed five times round the world! They won't leave me alone even with the Mormons. They say that I have spent several days at Salt Lake City and have induced Brigham Young to renounce polygamy. One good thing, I have frightened them so with my "thundering articles," as they call them, that all the papers are beginning to treat me with a good deal of respect. They are apparently cowards. In London, however, they extole me, thanks be to them, as the only champion of Spiritualism in America.

NOTES:

1. *People from the Other World*, which was published March 11.

2. Boyar, "a member of a peculiar order of the old Russian aristocracy, next in rank to a knyaz or 'prince', who enjoyed many exclusive privileges, and held all the highest military and civil offices: the order was abolished by Peter the Great, and the word is in Russia only a historical term, though still often erroneously applied by English newspaper writers to Russian landed proprietors" (*OED*). From Russian *boyárin*, pl. *boyáre* 'grandee, lord'; *boyard* is an erroneous French spelling adopted into English.

3. She sustained the injury in late January.

SOURCE: Russian original unavailable. Translated by Boris de Zirkoff from Solovyov's *Sovremennaya* 267-8. Another English translation by Walter Leaf in *Modern Priestess* 244-5.

⌣‾‾⟩

Letter 34

To H. P. Corson　　　　　　*Tuesday* night *[March 30 1875]*
3420 Sansom Street
West Philadelphia

My dear Sir,

I am doubly fortunate to day, in receiving letters from both yourself and Madame, but time permits my acknowledging only your own to night; to morrow I will answer Mrs Corson.

Your criticisms upon the literary aspirations of callow youth[1] is generally correct, but I am persuaded that it does not apply to the case in point. Epes Sargent has called upon Mʳ Brown by my request and makes a favorable report as to his industry and worthiness. His paper is selected for assistance, because it is already established, is on a very economical basis, has a clean record and presents itself to us as a "tabola rasa."[2] By degrees, the favor of such men as yourself, Epes Sargent, Gen. Lippitt, Col. Olcott, and others I might name, is being enlisted, and it is my desire that at a time not distant, the survival of the paper being assured a list of these eminent writers will be announced as thereafter contributing exclusively to its columns. My idea is, by no means to depend upon Mʳ G. Brown—*alone* for the direction of our campaign; however, more of this anon. I thank you in advance for your hearty and kind promise of valuable help. I have so much confidence in the future that, I have sent Mʳ G. Brown to day $50, scraped off the bottom of an empty purse and only regret my present inability to do more at a moment when, he requires at least $250, to tide him over deep water. He wrote me a desperate letter and I have put the matter in the hands of Mʳ Epes Sargent, who will go to him immediately on receit of my message, and handing him the sum, ascertain what more can be done (or ought to be done) for the paper.

Do not undervalue the importance of Spirit[u] [Spiritualist] phenomena; instead of regarding them as the letter "which kills" you should consider them as constituting the broad & deep foundations upon which alone intelligent belief in man's immortality can be safely reared. They heralded the birth of the Christian religion, clustered about its infancy, comforted, consoled and armed its patristic propagandists, and the decadence of the Church dates from the time when they were ignored entirely by one branch and misdirected by the other. If you will simply say that, the phenomena of the past twenty seven years, have mainly served to startle, amuse or terrify the public I will not contradict you; but, in beginning our work of expounding the laws by which they are produced, and inculcating the moral principles they suggest, our purpose would be fatally defeated, for we should soon come into the present extremity of the denominational churches, and propound dogmas as unsupported by vital proofs. He who attains to the sublime heights of Wisdom and Intuition, no more requires the buoyant support of these phenomena, than does the Eaglet needs to rest on its mothers back after his pinions are fairly spread; but the Eagles of mind are few, and the twittering sparrows multitudinous, and it is not for those who can mount above the clouds of doubt to despise the needs of their weaker fellows. The mighty Supernal Intelligences who are directing this Spiritual Movement, so far from sharing in your view of the manifestations, have already begun to produce phenomena of a still higher order such as transfigurations (n'en deplaise Professor Anthony [*Fr*. Professor Anthony notwithstanding]) direct writings, the photographing of the *wandering souls* of living persons, and the evocation of the latter (in spirit) while, their individual bodies are asleep. The occurrence of these marvels was foretold to me and *by me* to others, long before their advent, and if you will attentively watch the English, French and American papers, during the next three months, you will see more and more cause for astonishment. I do not need to go to the Franklin library or search in the annals of Baronius, Gibbon or other authors for the facts about the "Labarum," if it only interests you I can tell you all about it without ever reading one single of those books, for in the records to which I have had access, I find that this sign was known *ages* before Constantines birth, that it was flashed in the sky obediently to a purpose long before entertained, to furnish a sign and a convenient symbol to arouse the enthusiasm and stimulate the fervor of the hosts *to whom the execution of a great design was committed*. The books extant have only served to mislead men, whose minds were not prepared to receive the truth by reason of their extraordinary self sufficiency and conceit. The indications are, that we are about at the threshold of an epoch when, a thousand mysteries shall be revealed and it depends—at least in some degree upon such very feeble mortal agencies as your pen and mine and those of other zealous workers, how soon the world shall be enlightened.

Can you doubt what I meant by the language you quote from a former letter of mine?[3] Has your observation of Spirit^m [Spiritualism] been to such little purpose that you do not know that there are ways of talking to your departed ones, of seeing them, of feeling the clasp of their hands, the pressure of their lips, without going to *paid* mediums, whose moral depravity is so often the means of surrounding them with a foetid and polluting atmosphere, habitable only by lying, mischievous and vicious spirits, *such, as will be Child?* If you would learn the Secret of secrets, by which the highest Heavens can be brought within easy reach of your souls vision and grasp, you *must go* to those sources of knowledge which have been long closed except to the INITIATE. I cannot even name to you the Body which has these secrets in charge, much less impart to you any of those I have learned, unless I find your mind after longer acquaintance in such a stable mood as to indicate its *receptivity*. I have watched you through your moods of seclusion and can only say that if, with such abstraction, light has not at least glimmered upon your soul, you are not *now*, in a state that would warrant my doing what you desire. Instead of thanking me you would doubt me "even though one should rise from the dead"[4] to corroborate my statements. Oh, my dear Sir, why should poor humanity doubt so bitterly and repulse the divine hand stretched forth to every suffering mortal! Why is it that the more enlightened seems a man, the more his brains become thickly inlaid with a double crust of conceit and vanity which get so incrustated in the "seat of thought" that they actually shut out every glimpse of divine light leaving him a voluntary victim to the illusions of his self constituted gods, in the shape of precise ciphers, mathematical deductions & so forth?[5] Poor, poor humanity! Verily said Christ, that pure Spirit that will for ever remain in the heart of every noble man or woman the very ideal of perfection on this dirty Earth, that "the Kingdom of Heaven will be taken away from the wise men and revealed unto babes (if I quote erroneously forgive my ignorance of the precise words).[6] If my poor explanation and still poorer knowledge can be of any use to you I will explain you, *why* I asked the question about what you call "the monogram of Christ," the ☧. The question came after I had read your description of the suffering, the patience in illness and moral fortitude of that pure child that was your daughter on this Earth, and is now your daughter (and *thousand times* more so) in the Land of Light and Love. You seemed to feel the loss (!?) so bitterly, your agony appeared so intense to me, that I asked myself with a surprise (that will be justified in the hereafter *even in your eyes*) how it came to pass that you, who have selected the mysterious symbol of ☥ for your seal not only used black sealing wax for it (*the black*, emblem of darkness and irretrievable loss) but actually used in one breath 'if I am permitted this expression—the expressions of your sorrow and the exhibition of the symbol over the whole? I saw at once that you did not fully realize its secret meaning, that, standing before an opened door, that you had but to touch with your finger if you wanted to behold the "one that stood behind it" you lamented, believing the door shut if not for ever,—locked at least for the time of your earthly life and that perhaps you did not even know that you stood at the very door. I employed a little diplomatic subterfuge—pardon me, for I was afraid of becoming guilty of an indiscretion, and put you the question about the symbol in another shape, expecting to understand from your answer how far you knew its meaning and *properties*. I now see all. You are acquainted with the "Labarum but as many others are. You take it to be a monogram of Christ, for the books you allude to, never thought (or perhaps did not know themselves) that, because the shape of the (☥) happened to resemble the greek letters of X and P. it was not proof at all that the "Labarum" had been formed of the letters belonging to the greek alphabet. Why should not the greek alphabet be as likely composed partially of the most ancient symbols and signs? Such *is* the case I assure you. I defy all the scientists of the world as all the antiquaries, phylologists and all the *Champollion* Senior & Junior to prove me that this symbol of ☥ does not exist as much as 16,000 years previous to the birth of Christ. You can trace it from our modern Cathedrals down to the Temple of Solomon, to the Egyptian Karnac 1600 A.C. the Theba,[7] find it in the oldest Coptic records of Symbols preserved on tablets *of stone*, and recognize it, varying its multitudinous forms with every epoch, every people, creed or worship. It is a Rosecrucian symbol, one of the most ancient and the most mysterious. As the Egyptian *Crux ansata*,[8] ♀, or ⚥ that traveled from India where it was considered as belonging to the Indian symbolism of the most early ages, its lines and curves could be suited to answer the purpose of many symbols in every age and fitted up for every worship. But the *real*, genuine meaning very few know, and when they *do* know it, they are afraid to use through moral cowardice and—stubborn doubt. The *Crux ansata* meant the "time that was *to come*, the "Labarum" when it went under another "alias" meant "The time *is* come." As God looks down upon the passing ages and remains for ever the same unchangeable A & Ω the Alpha & Omega, so is with this symbol and powerful sign. You may alter its shape and adapt its form to suit any period or fancy, call it whatever name you like, it will notwithstanding all its metamorphoses remain the same, with the identical power it possesses and will always help the *initiated* to unlock as a genuine *key* the door of the "Mystery of Mysteries." its origin belongs to the greatest of *light suns* in history; for it is born from the central "intolerable ring of brilliancy" to quote the words of Flammel—the original gods revelation, it retains its power up to our days, belongs to the eldest of Religions, or *Knowledge* I should rather say and is ever ready to usher us—through its potency in the presence of our beloved, living in a brighter world. Even the famous "Sesame, ouvres toi" [*Fr.* Open, Sesame] refers to the "Labarum" "*Omnia ex uno, omnia in uno, omnia ad unum, omnia per Medium, et omnia in omnibus*" [*Ln.* All things from one, all things in one, all things toward one, all things through the Center, and all things in all] is a Hermetic axiom and can be applied to the so called "Labarum." The two lines of \ / or X *do not* represent the greek letter (the Russian or Slavonian too) X or guttural *ch*. in the Rosecrucian teaching both of those lines united or separated have special

133

magic or Spiritual, powers according to where they stand to the supernatural extra forces that help them through the operations of those *"who know how* and *when* to direct the weird power"* says Robertus di Fluctibus[9] "the great English Rosecrucian or Alchemist in his learned work called "Examen in quâ Principia Philosophiae, Roberti Fluddi, Medici." I wish you could read it. *He* would teach you all you may expect to know.

Forgive me my long letter.

Truly yours with the greatest esteem
H P Blavatsky

My dear sir, please note the letters I write you at *night time* and put more faith in them than in those scribbled in day light. I will explain when I have the honor and pleasure of seeing you personally.

NOTES:

1. Gerry Brown.

2. *Tabula rasa,* Latin for "erased tablet" or "blank slate." HPB's spelling of the first word was perhaps influenced by the Italian development of the Latin word, *tavola.*

3. Letter 30, March 20.

4. Luke 16.31.

5. Although "forth" is what makes the best sense and appears to be what was originally written, the word looks as though it was over-written to change it to "faith."

6. Cf. Matthew 11.25 and 21.43 and Luke 10.21.

7. Karnak was the northern part of ancient Thebes, a center of Egyptian civilization; Luxor (letters 28, 59) was the southern part of Thebes. Both were associated with Egyptian esotericism.

8. The crux ansata [*Ln.* cross with a handle], an Egyptian symbol of immortality (*Theosophical Glossary* 91), later incorporated into the seal of the Theosophical Society as its central element. The second drawing of the symbol in the letter is heavier and resembles a stylized human or angelic figure with outstretched arms.

9. The Latin form of the name of Robert Fludd.

DATE: March 30 by Mary K. Neff (marginalia in her copy of *Unpublished Letters* now in the Archives of the Theosophical Society in America, Wheaton, Illinois); sometime during the summer by Boris de Zirkoff. The letter's discussion of Gerry Brown and the funding of the *Spiritual Scientist*, following shortly after letter 31 of March 21, makes the earlier date reasonable.

SOURCE: Transcribed from a microfilm and a photocopy of the original in the HPB Library. Published in *Unpublished Letters* 148–55.

⌒

BACKGROUND ESSAY G

HPB's Marriage in Philadelphia

On April 3, 1875, HPB married Michael C. Betanelly, a Caucasian Georgian in the import and export business. He had met HPB some four or five months earlier and persistently wooed her. Olcott (*ODL* 1:55–7) describes the upshot:

> He finally threatened to take his life unless she would accept his hand. Meanwhile, before this crisis arrived, she had gone to Philadelphia, put up at the same hotel, and received his daily visits. He declared that he would ask nothing but the privilege of watching over her, that his feeling was one of unselfish adoration for her intellectual grandeur, and that he would make no claim to any of the privileges of wedded life. He so besieged her that—in what seemed to me a freak of madness—she finally consented to take him at his word and be nominally his wife: but with the stipulation that she should retain her own name, and be as free and independent of all disciplinary restraint as she then was. So they were lawfully married by a most respectable Unitarian clergyman of Philadelphia [the Rev. William H. Furness], and set up their *lares* and *penates* in a small house in Sansom Street, where they entertained me as guest on my second visit to that city—

135

after my book was finished and brought out. The ceremony took place, in fact, while I was stopping in the house, although I was not present as a witness. But I saw them when they returned from the clergyman's residence after the celebration of the rite.

When I privately expressed to her my amazement at what I conceived to be her act of folly in marrying a man younger than herself, and inexpressibly her inferior in mental capacity; one, moreover, who could never be even an agreeable companion to her, and with very little means—his mercantile business not being as yet established—she said it was a misfortune that she could not escape. Her fate and his were temporarily linked together by an inexorable Karma, and the union was to her in the nature of a punishment for her awful pride and combativeness, which impeded her spiritual evolution, while no lasting harm would result to the young man. The inevitable result was that this ill-starred couple dwelt together but a few months. The husband forgot his vows of unselfishness, and, to her ineffable disgust, became an importunate lover. She fell dangerously ill in June from a bruise on one knee caused by a fall the previous winter in New York upon the stone flagging of a sidewalk, which ended in violent inflammation of the periosteum and partial mortification of the leg; and as soon as she got better (which she did in one night, by one of her quasi-miraculous cures, after an eminent surgeon had declared that she would die unless the leg was instantly amputated), she left him and would not go back. When, after many months of separation, he saw her determination unchangeable, and that his business, through his mismanagement, was going to the dogs, he engaged counsel and sued for a divorce on the ground of desertion. The summonses were served upon her in New York, Mr. Judge acted as her counsel, and on the 25th May, 1878, the divorce was granted.

It is noteworthy that HPB makes little reference in her surviving correspondence to this marriage. In letter 35, written the day of her marriage, she promises General Lippitt only that she will explain why she "changed house," to 3420 Sansom Street, the residence she shared with Betanelly. HPB wrote Gen. Lippitt (letter 47) that she sent Betanelly away about May 26, 1875, though he returned briefly by mid June.

On the other hand, a good many letters over the following months allude to her injured leg, the threat of its amputation, and its eventual marvelous cure.

Letter 35

To F. J. Lippitt   *[April 3, 1875]*

[postcard addressed to]
General Francis G. Lippitt.
13 Pemberton Square (Room 13)
Boston Mass:

Picture ready and sent by Adams Express C°. Was as clear and pure as a newly fallen snow. Betanelly carried it to his office to show to some artists and it passed through so many uncleanly hands that it lost partially its virgin purity. John asks you to give your attention to the flying figure of the Spirit *above*—"mother & child. Says you will recognize her. I do not. Johny wants you to *try* & understand all the symbols & masonic signs. He begs you will *never* part with this picture and must not let too many persons touch it, not even *approach* it too close. I will explain why I changed house. Sansom Street 3420 West Phil:

yours truly
H. P Blavatsky.

DATE: The card is postmarked "Apr. 3" and endorsed "Mme Blavatsky Apl 3ᵈ /75".

SOURCE: Transcribed from the original in the Archives of the Theosophical Society, Adyar. Published in *HPB Speaks* 1:64–5.

Letter 36

To F. J. Lippitt   *[early to mid April 1875]*
3420 Sansom Street, West Philadelphia

General Lippitt.

My dear General,

I am glad you like Johny's picture, but you must not call him a Turk, for he is a noble dear Sprite and loves you much. It's nobodys fault, if you did not see him till now, *as he is in reality*, and always thought him to be like the old Jewish half materialized phyz. you were generally treated to at the Holmes. In London *only*, he appears as he is; but bearing still on his dear countenance some likeness to his respective mediums, for its hard for him to change completely the particles drawn by him from various vital powers. How is it you *do not* recognize your Katie King of last May? John says its herself as she *is now* and several persons have recognized her *immediately* upon seeing the picture at the time. I did not know of it myself for John told me but afterward. Evans and M^r & Mrs Ames and Morton and others exclaimed right away It's Katie King! I did not see her so I cant tell. The mother & child are not *likenesses* and of course you cannot, no more than any one else recognize spirits you *do not know*. Now my dear General whats that about the fortune we are to make? Its your tipping machine your invention I have no doubt, for *I am told so*. I wish I could go to Boston now, but its impossible for my law suit[1] is coming off, on the 26th day of April Monday and I have to go to Riverhead Long Island with my lawyers. So that before the beginning of May it will be impossible for me to go to Boston. Try and keep off the job till then if you can.

My dear, very dear General, do come in with us for the "Scientist." See now, you have fallen out with that old, over boiled pumpkin of Colby, and the Galaxy is a heartless paper that will print nothing but sensational lies, [indecipherable, possibly "with" or "and"] all the rest of them. We must have your articles published. See what Stainton Moses says about them in his letter to Mr Epes Sargent. I am determined to lift up the "Sp^l Scientist" and to keep it afloat till the people find out for themselves what an ably conducted little paper it is. If Mr Epes Sargent and Col. Olcott and yourself and Prof. Corson of Cornell U. and Mrs Andrews, will all write or begin writing for this paper so as to make of it our special *truthful* organ what a blessing it will prove to Spirit^m in general and the cause in America in particular. *Now*, as the case stands with only the "Banner" and the filthy Relig. Phil:, the leaders of the Sp^l cause may be assimilated to the "les aveugles conduisant les borgnes" [*Fr*. the blind leading the one-eyed]. *Then* if my plan succeeds, *we* shall get the lead, and direct the world in the true path, showing the skeptics and infidels the *cause* of the results, while now they have but doubtful and ever doubted effects thrust in their throats without so much as a word of rational explanation, or trustworthy evidence. What can we expect from the outsiders? How can we hope of their ever drop[p]ing off their Christian notions and membership of diverse Churches that furnish them with a certain light—false as it may be—of respectability, to pitch headlong in a belief that is unpopular, full of illusions as long as facts are disputed, and the chief leaders of which, as Eusebius of old, that pious old fraud of the first Christians—not only interlope fancy fairy tales but actually withhold from the knowledge of the world at large the crimes of certain parties that happen to be for certain mysterious reasons the "beloved ones" and the favorized of those leaders and "en odeur de saintete" [*Fr*. in the odor of sanctity, *i.e.*, in good grace] with the organs. You call my article against Child ferocious! Why, if you had in hand the proofs I *have*, with all your inborn mildness and sweet temper you would be the first to confess that the "Father Confessor" richly deserves a cow hiding. Do give a helping hand to the poor Gerry Brown—not for *his sake*—I know very little of him beyond that John says he is a true, honest worthy, untiring worker and will and can do much for the cause if properly helped—but for our own, for the benefit of Spirit^m and humanity. Olcott is writing an article for the Sp^l Scientist." I understand that Mr Epes Sargent does the same. Professor Corson is going to send one next week. Why should not you contribute the same and have your articles printed in that paper. I wrote to Wittgenstein and asked him to write every month—something for the "Scientist, relating to phenomena occurring in Germany and elsewhere. I am sure he will do so. John says he heard your daughter the other day "flourish on the harpsichord" and that she "flourished mighty sweet." When I told him that his expressions were very queer and that I did not well understand what he meant by "harpsichord" he got mad at me and abused me adding that other people would prove to be *less fools* than I was, and would certainly understand his meaning. I send it you "verbatim." Well God bless you and may your life pass in the sunshine for ever till the last.

Yours sincerely & truly
H P. Blavatsky

NOTE:

1. The lawsuit was over a farm that HPB had bought. See background essay H: "HPB's Lawsuit in America," before letter 41.

DATE: By Boris de Zirkoff. The letter was written between Lippitt's receiving the picture, which HPB's letter 35 said had been sent as of April 3, and April 26, mentioned in this letter as in the future.

SOURCE: Transcribed from the original in the Archives of the Theosophical Society, Adyar. Published in *HPB Speaks* 1:65–9.

Letter 37

To A. N. Aksakoff   *April 12, 1875*

In a detailed account of the story of Katie King,[1] Olcott makes of me something mysteriously terrible, and almost leads the public to suspect that I have either sold my soul to the devil or am the direct heiress of Count de Saint-Germain and Cagliostro. Do not believe it; I have merely learned in Egypt and Africa, in India and in the East generally, a great deal of what other people do not know. I have made friends with dervishes, and it is true that I do belong to one mystic society, but it does not follow that I have become an Apollonius of Tyana in petticoats. Moreover the spirit of John King is very fond of me, and I am fonder of him than of anything on earth. He is my only friend, and if I am indebted to anyone for the radical change in my ideas of life, my yearnings, and so forth, it is to him alone. He has made me over, and, when I shall depart for the "attic," I shall be indebted to him for not having to dwell for maybe whole centuries in darkness and gloom. John and I were acquainted from olden times, long before he began to materialize in London and take walks in the medium's house with a lamp in his hand. But all this does not interest you, I imagine.

. . . Since I have been in America I have devoted myself entirely to Spiritualism, not to the phenomenal, material side of it, but to spiritual Spiritualism, the propaganda of its sacred truths. All my efforts tend to one thing: to purify the new religion from all its weeds, which grow so fast that they threaten utterly to stifle with their dead letter the spirit of truth. In this desire and effort I have been hitherto *alone*. I am only now beginning to collect adepts; I have collected half a dozen and, I say boldly, the best and brightest minds in America. Later on I will enumerate them for you. Every day I grow more and more convinced that so long as people, even the most Crookes-like of all the Crookeses, will stand up for nothing but the mere facts, *i.e.*,—the phenomenal side of Spiritualistic manifestations—so long will furious opponents appear, beginning with Tyndall and ending with the miserable Dr. Beard; and that the public, who have hitherto been treated only to stories and facts about the materialized bust of somebody's great grandmother, and the legs in top-boots of an imperfectly materialized Washington, or the appearance of your baker's deceased cook, will of course always prefer to take the side of science "for respectability's sake," rather than to befriend us, whom they regard as half-wits and idiots. I have learned that there is no convincing people with suspicious facts only, and that even every genuine fact always presents some weak side or other on which it is easy for opponents to fasten. This is why I have laid down the rule never in any case to permit outsiders to utilize my mediumistic powers. Except Olcott and two or three very intimate friends, no one has seen *what* happens around me, and when my John or the other *diakka* go too far, I immediately put a stop to *everything*. I have decided to devote myself to Spiritualism from the point of view of Andrew Jackson Davis and Allan Kardec (though I do not believe in reincarnation in the same sense as the French spiritists do)[2]; and though I always stand up for *real* phenomena such as the Eddy's, no one can more violently attack the forgeries of the mediums and the credulity of some of the spiritists, and that is why I have conceived the idea of setting about a serious business.

I have lost no time in setting to work in another direction. I have prepared the mind of the most influential spiritists and brought them over to my side, and now, as I am convinced that there is no getting at the truth through the *Banner*, we have all joined forces, and have chosen a small paper, the *Spiritual Scientist*, to become our own special organ. I have published in it my last article[3] in answer to the feeble and idiotic defense of Dr. Child in the *Banner*. I am sending you this issue of the journal, and two others which have reprinted an article about me from the London *Spiritualist*. This paper, the *Spiritual Scientist*, was perishing, though its policy was always more honorable and sincere than that of the *Banner*, which is one-sided, and gives nothing but the facts, without explaining the causes of the manifestations. I have got as many as a hundred subscribers for it in these three weeks; I have urged others to donate some little money, and I have myself given $50.00 (my last, God knows), in order only to shame the *rich* spiritists, and to force them to open their pockets. I have persuaded Olcott, Epes Sargent, Prof. Corson, Lippitt, Mrs. Andrews, the authoress, Owen (who has gone into hiding and cannot bring himself to believe in the criminality of his friend Child) and others to write exclusively for the *Scientist*. I am printing circulars at my own expense.

I am ready to give my life for the spread of the sacred truth. Olcott is helping me as much as he can, both with his pen and with pecuniary sacrifices *for the cause*. He is as passionately devoted to spiritism as I am; but he is far from rich and has nothing to live on but his literary labors, and he has to keep a wife and heap of children.

NOTES:

1. In *People from the Other World* (425–78).

2. HPB's statement about reincarnation is noteworthy, especially its qualifying phrase: "I do not believe in reincarnation in the same sense as the French spiritists do." It has sometimes been said that HPB did not know about or did not accept reincarnation when she wrote *Isis Unveiled* and that she adopted the concept only after she moved to India. This letter clearly indicates that she was familiar with more than one interpretation of reincarnation and rejected

that of Kardec and his followers; it implies that she believed in a different view of reincarnation.

3. "Who Fabricates" (*CW* 1:75–83), published in the *Spiritual Scientist* 2 (April 1875); see letter 32, note 1.

SOURCE: Russian original unavailable. Four excerpts are given here, probably from the same letter. Translated by Boris de Zirkoff from Solovyov's *Sovremennaya* 268–9, 269–70, and 270–1. Another English translation by Walter Leaf in *Modern Priestess* 246–7, 247–9, and 249–50.

⌒

Letter 38

To F. J. Lippitt   *Wednesday [April 14, 1875]*
                         3420 [Sansom Street,] W. Philade—

My dear General.

Do not blow me up,[1] pray do not, I beg you should not take me a "priori" for a heartless, wicked, coldblooded wretch—"Frappes mais écoutes" [*Fr.* strike but listen] hollowed out Epictetus, to his master while the latter was thrashing him with a heavy stick, some thousand years ago, and so do *I*, hollow now to you, for I'm *obliged*, morally obliged to do my duty, and warn you by telling you what you *do not* know, but *can* and *must* know by writing a few words one question, to John Morton Esqr President of the Market St Railroad, who will endorse what I say to you now and prove you how easily, can a noble minded, kind hearted, thoroughly good man, such one as you are be imposed upon by cunning impostors at some 200 miles distance.

You are *losing your time dear* General, running about and *begging for people that have more money than you have yourself.*

One word more and I will be silent.

The Holmeses couple are at this very moment bargaining to bye *a good horse and buggy* to ride at their country seat, *Vineland.* They have opened the negotiations for this purchase—which perhaps you *yourself* could not afford—about a month ago, and as they could not get the horse as they wanted it *on credit* from Mr John Morton President as I said of the Market St Railroad they are bying it now from another party, boasting that they have friends enough to pay for 10 horses. Can people doing such a thing be in great need, and starving as they pretend. No! thousand times no! Mrs Holmes cannot give seances now, for no one will have her on account of her tricks, and not willing to lose her time, taking advantage of the stupid endorsement of some *crazy idiots*, who gave her all the chance in the world to cheat them, and puffed her up in the bargain in the "Banner," she now, with an impudence really worthy of admiration comes out imposing on Spiritualists and trying to snatch the bread from really *needy starving* Sp^l mediums and lecturers to—bye *horses* with!

Do you know, that I *know* for a certainty that the $18 swindled of me by the soi disant "detective" Holmes[2] went every cent of it in the pocket of *Nelson Holmes* the *medium*, for the former owed the latter this money and was put up to that trick by Nel. Holmes himself. I will *prove it you* when I see you. If you do not believe me theres an end of it. I give you *facts*. I will find out for a certainty how many 100, or perhaps thousands they have in the Bank. I have letters from London and from the West, and then I will prove you that kind heart can sometimes do more mischief by help-ing impostors to impose upon the good faith of truly hon-est people than such cold hearted wicked wretches as I may seem to you to day.

Pray, dear General, do not judge me harshly and before you have ascertained that *I lie*. I have so few true friends in this world and have been lately so cruelly misunderstood, doubted and *branded*—aye, branded with vile suspicion when all my life is devoted to truth and only to *Truth* that I write you this with fear and as its only because I deem it my duty. My leg is getting *paralyzed*. So there's an end of it. God grant me I may follow it "upstairs" as soon as possible.

Sincerely yours,
H. P Blavatsky

NOTE:

1. "Blow up at me." See letter 22, note 2.

2. The identity of "the soi disant [self-styled] 'detective' Holmes" is unknown, as is the allusion to an $18 swindle.

DATE: C. Jinarajadasa (*HPB Speaks* 2:173) says, "Endorsed 'Mme. Blavatsky, Apr, 1875.'" A date in the middle of the month would fit with other letters to Lippitt.

SOURCE: Transcribed from the original in the Archives of the Theosophical Society, Adyar. Published in *HPB Speaks* 2:170–3.

⌒

Letter 39

To F. J. Lippitt   *3:00 a.m., Tuesday [April 20, 1875]*
                          3420 Sansom Street, Philadelphia

Mon General,

Received yours this afternoon. Politeness required an answer but I felt so cross and so sick—(or perhaps I better say—felt so sick and *therefore* so cross) that I blew up[1] Olcott, tried to set on a pillory Betanelly, had a fight with *John*, threw the cook into a fit and the canary bird in regular convulsions, and having made myself agreeable in such a general way went to bed and—dreamt of old *Blavatsky*; this last occurrence, I took positively for a premeditated insult on the part of Providence and so, prefering anything to such a nightmare as that one, there I am, at 3 A.M., swallowing Brown's lozenges, which make me sneeze, if they *do* prevent me from coughing, and—trying to write you something in the shape of a reasonable sober answer; if the present does not positively answer the latter "adjectives" lay it boldly on the bill to the said old *Sire*, and send it with the first opportunity to the Summer land with John King, to be settled by his late Excellency.

Your Prof. Sophocles, has proved himself a pretty good scholar and Orientalist, but—the best of the latter are but mere school boys in comparison to the dirtiest of the Jews born and bred in—well never mind where. It's all very fine and looks mighty wise to be able to name separately every rib and bone and sinew of a dead cow's carcass, but, if after having performed this *nomenclature* of names of the various portions of the body, you cannot tell "à la Cuvier" who the whole animal was, and mistake it perhaps for a dog, you are none the wiser for it. M Sophocles has named separate symbols[2] and bits of Hebrew & Greek words—he found out the two pillars of Jachin and Boaz (they mean something else besides an architectural idea of this old mormon[3] of Solomon, who *prigged* [stole] them for his Temple from the masters of his masters, who knew it some thousands of years before his mormonic Majesty) and furthermore M Sophocles unmasked right away Solomon's seal, (so did Bulwer—before him) but why, does not M Sophocles tell you the *whole* meaning of the symbols put together? For *they have* a meaning; and believe me, that in drawing them John made a sad satire on the ignorance of the "soi-disant" [*Fr.* so-called] savan[t]s of the present generation, who boast so much of their knowledge and wonderful progress in unriddling the mysteries of the past, and who cannot even be certain of finding out the difference between an "ancient Scandinavian symbol" and the key to the "Golden Gate," and who mistake the most potent of the gnostic talismans for a "distant arrière petit cousin" [*Fr.* very distant cousin, cousin many times removed] and call it *Thors Hammer!!*

Until the *whole* of the meaning of the symbols on Johns picture is found out, John cannot teach people and—declines to make them wiser. "Try" and find it out, if you can. Let the immense and profound wisdom of your scientists, who have on the basis of their *positive knowledge* created so many Büchners, Molechotes,[4] and Fogts[5] and Richters and other atheists,—find the solution *to this one* mystery of the picture, now in your possession and—the world may close his study books for some time and take a slight recreation; for they will have learned what hundreds of generations and centuries have tried to find out for a certainty, and never did; for in their proud and impatient hurry that made them ever mistake some "croix cramponnée" [*Fr.* hooked cross, swastika] for a "croix chiffonnée" [*Fr. literally* crumpled cross][6] they generally howled out "Eureka, when they ought to remember that even the Alpha, did not hold quite secure in their empty heads.

My darling General, please tell *everybody*, who honors and flatters me by insisting on the idea that the picture is the work of my own mortal hands—that my fathers daughter never acted the part of a "plagiaire" [*Fr.* plagiarist]. The picture is good enough, I guess to give the right to anyone to feel proud of it if *he had* done it himself, but as except the flowers *below* and some leaves round the balcony, I did not touch or paint one inch of the rest of the picture, I do not see, why I should say I did. *Everybody* is welcome to believe what he or she likes. Let skeptics say—*I did it;* half-Spiritualists—that it was done *under spirit inspiration,* orthodox members of the churches—*that old Nick has a share in it* and Episcopalian Clergymen (a fact that just happened here) that no respectable man or woman ought to read Olcott's book or look at those "*Satan's* pictures of Mme Blavatsky as the latter *smokes* and swears (!) and Olcott admires her and speaks of her in his book. —The first time I meet this very respectable party of the "Beecher School for Scandal"[7] I mean to go and shake hands with him, after which I will force him to confess *publicly* that *my swearing* stinks less to the nostrils of God than his *praying* you see, if I dont do it.

My lovely General I am sadly afraid I will not be able to go to Washington with you. My leg is worse than ever. John had completely cured it, and ordered me *rest* for three days. I neglected it and from that day feel it getting worse and worse. It's under regular treatment now. Then my law suit comes off at Riverhead on the 11th of May I think.[8] I shall have to attend to it and so etc: etc: I would be so happy to be of any service to you but I am afraid it will prove impossible.

Then, I am not so sure as that of John. He never taps with any one but me and that quite different from what your mediums do. If he could promise me faithfully to do the thing I might risk but *he does not* and furthermore he is vicious enough never to do what he is asked, unless he proposes it himself. Dont you remember, how independent he is? I cannot consent, without he tells me to do so. And so we must wait. But I would strongly advise you to look out for some private medium for really and indeed *I am not* a medium myself.

I send you a strange and weird Circular.[9] Read it, and tell me how it sounds to you. Ask the *Brotherhood* to help you. John dares not disobey their orders. Employ the *will-power* in order they should hear you and notice your application. Do, please do write something *over your own signature* for the "Scientist," this is the only way to please John and perhaps then he will serve you. I cannot say more. Speak about it with Mr Epes Sargent.

I feel very sick and must close. I have thousands of things to tell you. I wish *I could* help you, for your patent— but believe me on my word of *honor*, I am but a slave, an obedient instrument in the hands of *my masters*. I cannot even write good English, unless they dictate me every word.

See what a long stupid letter, what an ungrammatical ignorant message is the present; for I *am alone* at this moment and utterly helpless.

Sincerely & truly yours

H. P Blavatsky

NOTES:

1. "Blew up at Olcott." See letter 22, note 2.

2. The references are to symbols on the painting of "John King." The figure of "John King" is behind a balcony, at one end of which is a column or perhaps altar on which are depicted two sphere-topped pillars standing for the entrance pillars of King Solomon's Temple, which were called Jachin and Boaz (1 Kings 7.21, 2 Chron. 3.17). Between them, midway up the column is a swastika, popularly called "Thor's hammer." Between the tops of the pillars is a pair of interlaced triangles or "Solomon's seal." John holds in his hand a book, at the top of whose cover is the letter A or alpha.

3. The allusion is apparently to both Mormons and Solomon as polygamists.

4. Jacob Moleschott.

5. Karl C. Vogt.

6. *Croix chiffonnée* is not a usual term in French. Jean-Louis Siémons (private communication) suggests that HPB may have invented the term in derision, to ridicule the ignorant "savants" of her time.

7. Henry Ward Beecher, a popular Protestant clergyman, in 1874 was sued by a former friend and protégé for adultery with the latter's wife. *The School for Scandal* is the best known play of Richard Brinsley Sheridan (1751–1816); it is a comedy of manners satirizing sexual license and hypocrisy.

8. The lawsuit was heard by jury on April 26. See the account "HPB's Lawsuit in America" before letter 41.

9. The circular, "Important to Spiritualists" (reproduced and described in *CW* 1:85–8) was published in the *Spiritual Scientist*, April 29, 1875, page 1. It is a promotional statement for the journal, advancing HPB's view that Spiritualism should be concerned with philosophy rather than phenomena. The circular, which is signed "*For the Committee of Seven*, BROTHERHOOD OF LUXOR," was written by Olcott (*Old Diary Leaves* 1:73–6).

DATE: Boris de Zirkoff (notes on his copy of the letter) believed it to have been "written most likely either April 20 or 27, 1875." The date cannot be April 27 because HPB was in Riverhead, Long Island, on April 26 for the trial of her case, which she won and commented upon in some detail in another letter (41), whereas in the fifth paragraph from the end of this letter, she says she thinks the Riverhead case is on May 11. The date of the letter must therefore be April 20 or perhaps as early as April 13, though the reference to the circular published on April 29 makes April 20 probable.

SOURCE: Transcribed from the original in the Archives of the Theosophical Society, Adyar. Published in *HPB Speaks* 1:71–7.

<hr />

Letter 40

To H. P. Corson   *Sunday [mid April to early May 1875]*
                Philadelphia

My dear Sir,

Really it's very, *very* kind of you to care so much about such a poor lame creature as I have become lately, and how gladly would I avail myself of the opportunity you offer me so amiably, were I able to do so at present! But, as I can hardly travel from my bed, to the other end of the room without help, how can I travel by railway to Ithaca? And how can I risk to encumber you, with such a sad, cross, limping, disagreeable thing as I feel myself to be at present? As soon as I feel better and able to walk—if it be on a crutch, I will come to Ithaca and then—we will *talk*. Just prepare me a little corner, where I can safely surround myself with clouds of smoke and change the spot into a miniature valley at the foot of a mount Vesuvius, without shocking too much poor Mrs Corson, and I will soon appear in it like some weird, monstrous *she* goblin or spook, peeping out from this dense smoky atmosphere only to force you to follow me into realms and regions far more dense and foggy and impenetrable at first sight than the former. But with a sufficient stock of will power and earnest desire to impart to others what I happen to know myself, and a good dose of introductory knowledge on your part, as you happened to study so seriously Howitt's "Ennemoser" and others, let us hope that this mutual introreception[1] will not be followed (as in some cases I experienced lately) by a violent commotion of conflicting, adverse elements, causing a wide breach to form between the interlocutors for want of calm reasoning or too much fanaticism on either side.

Yes, I wrote to Mr Sargent, and blamed him for having allowed the "Scientist" to go on with his idiotical *Diogenes* whom Brown has certainly fished out from some *wash-tub*— in Boston.[2] Of course I excuse the poor man in one sense (Brown not Diogenes, who is no man but an *ass*) for he had to fill up his paper *quand même* [*Fr.* in one way or another], and perhaps was driven by necessity to ornament it with such impudent and occasionally *indecent* stuff. But previously to that, I had blown up[3] Mr Brown himself and told him what I thought of him and his Diogenes. He *will not* publish it any more I bet you. So you can contribute something to it occasionally, and receive for it the thanks of Spiritualists in general and mine in particular. You are right, and the wickedest traitors are mostly to be found in ones own family. Such is the wolf like propensity of human nature. I do not know Brown personally, nor do I care much for such an honor, but I *do* think him more foolish and young and inexperienced than conceited or stupid. He seems perfectly willing to take any advice, and has never accepted it from me or Mr Sargent, but with real gratitude and readiness to submit most humbly to our *sine qua non*'s and decrees. So dont be *too* hard on him. Poor Mr Owen, between the cruel Truth staring him in the face, his long friendship for the Judas-Child and his own Spiritual *fluctuations*, he is sadly situated the dear old Patriarch. I do not think *him fair* in what he wrote so far as he consented to write anything at all, and *vis a vis* Olcott, but he speaks truly and sincerely when he says that he better abstain from giving his opinions about the Holmeses, who *are* mediums and for all that frauds and so they are. I will explain you many things when I see you (if I ever do.) Now look at poor General Lippitt and his efforts to save *them* from starvation and want! Why, he does not know of course what all of us know in Philadelphia, namely, that Mrs Holmes's appeal to Spiritualists, was chiefly made for the purchase of a buggy and horse. *They just bought one*, and paid between $150 to 200 for this apparel of luxury. What people who are in *real* want, will ever think of bying horses and buggies? Now this is mere imposition, and I call it robbing the really needy ones from their last piece of bread to satisfy cheating, wicked, lying impostors! Do not write this to Mrs Andrews, she will *never* believe it, any more than she believes about Slade, but if you want to ascertain the fact, have some one ask Mr John Morton, a Philad gentleman of high standing, President of the Market St. railroad, to whom Mrs Holmes applied for this same horse. I never give to the world anything but *true facts* and I will never allow myself to throw discredit on no one, not even on Child that I despise and loathe unless I am *perfectly sure* of the fact.

Child never answered my last letter.[4] He never attempted to by printed word or a spoken one, except once, the day I had 200 copies of my article distributed by my order on a Sunday at Lincoln Spirit[1] [*i.e.,* Spiritual] Hall: the agent by an act of ironical politeness offered him one (as they were given away *gratis*), and a gentleman who knew Child asked him before quite a number of people what he was going to say in answer to that article: to which Child with an unparraleled coolness, a *nee plus ultra* of sublime impudence said aloud: "Oh pshaw! I know what it is all about. Some *lying* information furnished to this *Russian*, by *Leslie* no doubt." And that was all. Orestus turning back on

Pylades, *Castor* accusing his bosom friend *Pollux*[5] of lying information! Rich and sublime, wasn't it? for this Leslie is the same "amateur detective" that played such a conspicuous part in the detection of the false *she-spirit*,[6] together with Child. Some time ago, Child tried to *creep* in as secretary to the International Committee of Spirit[sts] for the Centenial. I knew of it an hour after, and went to work; the result of my labor was that he was *pitched* out of that place, obliged by Spiritualists themselves *to resign* as he resigned his Presidency three months ago. He is an honorary member and correspondent of the "London Spiritualist" his name is on the list as you can see, if you get the "Lond Spirit:" elbowing the names of the Prince Emile de Wittgenstein, Aksakoff, Epes Sargent Eugene Crowell and such like *earnest, honest* Spiritualists: *I am at work* and need say no more. From the deepest recess of my sick bed, with my lame leg compelling me to an utter inactivity and obliging me to withdraw from many *public works*, (?) I have yet a few ressources left in me, as you can see to protect my cowardly, timid, silently suffering brother Spiritualists from the sham and degradation of such an association as this one. If I live, his name will disappear from the list, and vanish in oblivion. Like some *unlicensed*, self constituted Nemesis, I work silently but surely for all that—I am bed ridden and a helpless cripple to be perhaps. If my leg is paralyzed, my brains *are not* paralyzed thats sure, and *Will-Power* my dear M[r] Corson goes far when well applied by those "who know *how* and *when*."

Excuse me for this long, very long letter Somehow or rather, all my letters, especially if addressed to those that I believe and hope will *understand* me, become too long.

I thank you most sincerely for all the sympathy you show for the afore mentioned luckless leg of mine but, as it is a *cloven hoofed* one in the mystical sense of the word, it will be no great loss to humanity to see it disappear before its unworthy mistress. I guess there are more than one of my *true friends* who are secretly hoping—and praying—for both of us—leg and myself—that we might vanish in the space on the traditional broom stick and be seen—no more. But fate is fate, and we are but its helpless toys.

Now, I will deliver you of myself and letter, and close, by calling on your head all the lights and blessings of the *Empyraeum* and its host of *Teraphims*, if you are acquainted with the latter mysterious gentlemen.

"May your shadow never decrease and may it screen you for ever from your ennemies." (Thats a Chaldeo-Persian compliment, I learned in its native land).

With Sincere regard and esteem
very truly yours
H P. Blavatsky

NOTES:

1. The word "introreception" is rare, with only two examples in the *Oxford English Dictionary*, both from the later seventeenth century. The *OED* defines it as "the action of receiving within."

2. A series of articles by "Diogenes," entitled "The Mediums of Boston," was published in issues of the *Spiritual Scientist* for December 10, 17, 24, 31, 1874, January 7, 28, February 4, 11, 18, 25, March 4, 11, 18, April 23, and May 13, 1875.

3. "Blown up at Mr Brown." See letter 22, note 2.

4. "Who Fabricates?" *Spiritual Scientist*, April 1875 (*CW* 1:75–83).

5. Pylades and Orestes are types of the loyal friend; Castor and Pollux are symbols of devoted brothers.

6. Eliza White.

DATE: In April (letter 38), HPB was scolding Lippitt for raising money in support of the Holmses, who, she wrote, "are at this very moment bargaining to bye *a good horse and buggy*," whereas in this letter she writes, "Now look at poor General Lippitt and his efforts to save *them* from starvation and want! Why, he does not know of course what all of us know in Philadelphia, namely, that Mrs. Holmes's appeal to Spiritualists, was chiefly made for the purchase of a buggy and horse. *They just bought one*, and paid between $150 to 200 for this apparel of luxury." The two statements suggest that this letter was written not long after letter 38. In addition, the last installments of the series by "Diogenes" (note 2) were published on April 23 and May 13.

SOURCE: Transcribed from a microfilm and a photocopy of the original in the HPB Library. Published in *Unpublished Letters* 143–7.

⁓

BACKGROUND ESSAY H

HPB's Lawsuit in America

[Adapted from the account by Boris de Zirkoff, *CW* 1:83–5]

HPB lived for a time in Brooklyn, NY, with some French people who came to the United States at the same time she did. Her father died on July 27, 1873, and the following fall she received a sum of money as part of her inheritance. She was apparently induced to invest that money in two parcels of land at the east end of Long Island. One of those tracts was in the northern part of Huntington township, in Suffolk County on the north shore of Long Island, and the other was a farm near the village of Northport, also in that township. Court records show this land to have been purchased by a certain Clementine Gerebko on June 2, 1873, the month before HPB's arrival in the United States on July 7, 1873.

On June 22, 1874, HPB entered into partnership with Clementine Gerebko for the purpose of working the land at Northport. The partnership was to begin July 1, 1874, and continue for three years. Their agreement specified that Clementine Gerebko was to put the use of the farm into the partnership in return for the sum of one thousand dollars paid by HPB and further that "all proceeds for crops, poultry, produce, and other products raised on the said farm shall be divided equally, and all expenses" equally shared. The title of the land was reserved to Clementine Gerebko.

HPB went to live on the farm, but soon found herself in litigation with Clementine Gerebko as to the validity of their agreement about a mortgage, and so returned to New York.

The Brooklyn law firm of Bergen, Jacobs, and Ivins represented HPB. Her case was tried by a jury on Monday, April 26, 1875, before Judge Calvin E. Pratt, in the Supreme Court of Suffolk County, at Riverhead. She won the suit and recovered the sum of $1146 and costs of the action. The judgment, dated June 1, 1875, was filed on June 15 in the Office of the Clerk of Suffolk County, N.Y.

From the recollections of William M. Ivins, Attorney-at-Law, who became a very good friend of HPB's, we learn some of the circumstances of this curious trial. He wrote:

> Long Island in those days was a long ways from Brooklyn, for travelling facilities were limited. The calendar of this particular term was very slow, and all the parties were kept there waiting their turn to be heard. As many of the documents and witnesses were French, and there was no interpreter to the court, William S. Fales, a student in the law firm of General Benjamin Tracy, was made special interpreter, and he reported HPB's testimony which was given in French. For two weeks[1] the Judge, the lawyers, clerks, clients and interpreter were guests in a dull country hotel.

Ivins, in addition to being a brilliant lawyer, was a bookworm with a phenomenal memory. More as a joke than in earnest, he deluged his client with talk of occultism, Gnosticism, Kabbalism, and white and black magic. Fales, taking his key from Ivins, gave long dissertations on mystical arithmetic, astrology, alchemy, medieval symbolism, Neoplatonism, Rosicrucianism, and quaternions. It is a great pity that none of this was apparently recorded, and therefore cannot be recovered from the court records. Another sidelight on this interesting episode is in a work by Charles R. Flint entitled *Memories of an Active Life* (New York: Putnam's, 1923). He writes:

> The circumstances of the trial were interesting, for Madame, who was her own principal witness, testified quite contrary to the way in which her attorneys assumed she would testify. Ivins had associated with him in the trial Fales, who

was then a law student. As cautious lawyers, they had gone over the testimony with Madame before the trial, and had advised her as to what points she should emphasize; but, to their great discomfiture, on the witness stand she took the bit in her teeth and galloped along lines of evidence quite opposed to their instructions, giving as a reason, when they complained of her testimony, that her "familiar," whom she called Tom [John] King, stood at her side (invisible to everyone but her), and prompted her in her testimony. After the court had taken the matter under advisement, Madame left the city, but wrote several letters to Ivins asking him as to the progress of the suit, and finally astonished him by a letter giving an outline of an opinion which she said the court would render in the course of a few days, in connection with a decision in her favor. In accordance with her prediction, the court handed down a decision sustaining her claim upon grounds similar to those which she had outlined in her letter.

NOTE:

1. The trial was held on a single day, April 26, according to contemporary testimony. However, the judge's ruling was not handed down until June 1. In addition, HPB writes in the following letter (41) that there was a threat of further litigation on a charge of forgery and possibly an assault charge because HPB's lawyer struck the opposing lawyer. Although there is no evidence of additional litigation in the matter, those factors may have prolonged for two weeks the stay in the area by the judge, lawyers, and others, as Ivins's recollections state.

Introduction to Letter 41

The following letter was apparently written two days after HPB's case was tried on Long Island when she was on her way back to Philadelphia.

Letter 41

My dear General.

Writing from New York, I will receive your answer at Philadelphia, for I must return there tomorrow.

I am full of sickness and—botheration, and hope to goodness you will be kind enough not to refuse me a little *service obligeant* [*Fr.* kind service]. I mean to ask you; its a very serious matter for me and if you succeed you will help me out of a great trouble.

Can you get some information in Boston about an old maid, named J Loraine Raymond, or Lulu Loraine Raymond as she calls herself. Her attorney is *H. L. Newton* Nº 27 Pemberton Square, Boston, but you must not try to get the information I want from him, for he is her counsellor. The only thing you could get from him would be her present *whereabouts*, the last will be very useful, but what I will ask you to do is to ascertain what law suit [it] was she had which has been on the calendar for some time and is supposed to have terminated October, 1874.

Can you do so? If you find out, that it was a suit for *blackmailing* on her part then, I am all right.

I just come from Riverhead where my case was tried on Monday the 26ᵗʰ of April. I have won it. I proved fraud and conspiracy between the woman that swindled me and her lawyer Marks. The jury found a full verdict for me for the amount claimed, damages and costs, but—Mʳ John in his ardent desire to help me has carried his zeal too far. Hear what happened. After the verdict, Marks the defendants lawyer, insulted me by saying that I won the case through a *forgery* of certain documents. If I had scorned the insult all should have been right but I did not, and called my lawyer to witness the insult. My lawyer, called Marks a d—— perjurer and Jew and a liar. The latter returned the compliment and my lawyer prompted by John (for he says he cannot understand *how* he did it) throttled Marks and throwing him on the ground gave him the most magnificent *thrashing* to the delight of the audience and jurymen, for it was in the Court Room right before the Judge's nose. So that Marks, beaten in the law suit and beaten *physiquement parlant* [*Fr.* physically speaking] after the law suit grew as desperate as a wild boar and now brings out as a last annoyance, an indictment against me and my lawyers, before the great jury for *forgery* of certain documents!! Of course the scoundrel can do nothing by it, for the woman herself has run away to London, and I can prove that she had on a previous occasion denied her signature in a contract under oath, but still he can create me much annoyance, and he did already for he succeeded in getting from the Judge *Pratt* a brief, till the 1st of June, and I cannot get my money for months to come yet notwithstanding I won the law suit. Now this Marks is known to be the greatest scoundrel in New York he is known to be a thief by the judges and bench and a disgrace to the profession by the lawyers. Still he has the right *to accuse* even if he does not prove the crime. You can judge of him by one solitary fact, namely, that after I had obtained full verdict by the jury in my favor at six o'clock in the afternoon of Monday, he actually knowing that the case would not be put on record till 10, the following morning, went and making a deed of the property sold it at 8 A.M. to another scoundrel as himself, defying the court and showing his contempt for it.

Now he is just the man to bye as many false witnesses as he can. He says that this Raymond will be his witness to prove that she had seen on my table the memorandum book where the document was and will swear that she did not see it at the time inside of it. —Now, its a falsehood, for this Raymond never entered my room to my knowledge, but still the law is the law and unless we can prove that this witness is an unreliable drunken woman who has blackmailed others before me, her oath and evidence may wrong me a good deal.

Please dear General do me the favor I ask you. C'est a titre de revanche [*Fr.* I will return the favor or service], whenever I can.

truly yours
H P. Blavatsky

Johns compliments and best love.

DATE: C. Jinarajadasa (*HPB Speaks* 2:178) says, "Endorsed: 'From Mme. Blavatsky around May 1st and 3rd, '75.'" As the letter is dated "Wednesday" and the case was heard on Monday, April 26, the letter must have been written on April 28.

SOURCE: Transcribed from the original in the Archives of the Theosophical Society, Adyar. Published in *HPB Speaks* 2:174–7.

Letter 42

To H. P. Corson

May 20, 1875
Philadelphia

My dear Sir,

As you will learn in my letter addressed to Mrs. Corson, if you ever do see me you will never have the pleasure of admiring but one of my legs, I am afraid. Fate is fate, and the less we talk about it the better it may be.

I agree with you that any talk about such an abstruse subject as spiritualism can be a great deal better done in conversation than through letters. I will "try" and come to see you if it were only for that; for I know you could be in great need of spiritual truths, and the sooner you will get convinced of the simple facts the less you will have chances of pondering over this subject as well as over others that may preoccupy you as I often saw you do, rubbing slowly your hands in your meditative mood, in the meanwhile, and asking yourself thousands of questions, all of them unanswered.[1] Is it so? Or is it but the vicious images sent forth by the emanations of my own perverse imagination? It's for you to agree, and for me to submit to your decision.

I have an article by Professor Wagner, Professor of Zoölogy, and a very eminent scientist, a friend of the late A. Humbolt. Wagner has been battling and kicking and fighting for years against spiritualism. Now he has found out at last that he has been "kicking against the pricks," as they say, shows his sores to the public, and admitting in a very lengthy article the truth of the phenomena, begs his brother scientists of Europe and America not to make asses of themselves any longer but decide once for all and go and investigate spiritualism earnestly and very seriously. Alas! Alas! I am afraid his voice will be one in a wilderness here in this country. Too many Dr. Beards and Professor Anthonys for that in America. As soon as I feel better I will translate this article for the *Scientist*.

Now you must excuse even this bit of a letter, for I write it from the deep recess of my bed, which is far from being a bed of roses, suffering as I do. You may think me perhaps a cheat if you did not forget that I promised you my portrait and that you have to see it yet. But I am not to be blamed. I seldom allow my noble countenance to get immortalized in portraits. I have none, and passing through New York had some taken at a spirit photographers. There I am, represented on it looking like some elderly idiot staring disconsolately at a she spirit with a rooster crest on its head, making faces at me.[2] Really, putting all vanity aside, how can I send you such an awful caricature? So I gave two of those libel pictures to two persons I do not care about; but neither you nor Mrs. Andrews, nor Mr. Sargent, or even Olcott got one, and have to wait.[3]

I feel very faint, and therefore, begging you will excuse my blots and scratchings out, and the general unclean appearance of my poor epistle, I hope you will still believe in the sincerity with which I sign myself,

Truly yours,
H. P. Blavatsky.

My constant address is P. O. Box 2828, Philadelphia.

NOTES:

1. Compare letter 34, March 30 or April, in which HPB writes, "I have watched you through your moods of seclusion."

2. The portrait, a "spirit photograph," shows HPB in a typical pose, the back of her right hand supporting her chin, but to the front of her face and slightly above her in the background is a cloudy and indistinct image.

3. Despite what HPB writes here, as the next letter 43 makes clear, she did send Corson a copy of the "spirit photograph." Mary K. Neff (marginalia in her copy of *Unpublished Letters* now in the Archives of the Theosophical Society in America, Wheaton, Illinois) observes that in a letter of May 30, Corson thanks HPB for her photograph and says of it:

> The photo has impressed me deeply. But how should I have conceived so accurately of your face in advance of the picture and without anyone's description of it? The energy and the will-power exhibited, he who runs may read. But he who has any skill in reading *soul* lines, can read out of the face more than energy and will-power. And that I do. Pray excuse the freedom with which I write. Allow me only to add that I find myself again and again pensively musing upon it. Whose is the other face dimly revealed in the background? I shall always value the picture most highly.

SOURCE: Original unavailable. Copied from *Unpublished Letters* 140–2.

⌒

Letter 43

To H. P. Corson

[May 21, 1875]
Philadelphia

My dear Sir,

Just sent you a letter yesterday for I felt better, and for this last reason did not like sending you such a horrid portrait.

But—to day I feel *worse*, and as I want you to recognize *me* whenever I peep out from "under the veil of Isis" to come down and have—a bit of friendly chat with you in your scientific Ithaca, I send you *this one*. Dont get too scared and try to keep away the nightmare from you. *They want me to part with my leg to morrow.*[1] "Barkis is willing"[2] I will do to night, what I would not have done a month ago to save my life (had it been dear to me which *it is not*) and ask those I dread and fear but who alone can save it from amputation to come and help me, for I am afraid I am so strong that *I may* survive this horrid leg, and above all I dread such a prospect.

I would have sent another picture of mine to Mrs Corson, but this is the *last* I have, except one that I am sending to Mrs Andrews.

Good bye, and God bless you both of my dear unknown correspondents.

I WILL COME.

Yours truly *here* and *there*
H P. Blavatsky.

NOTES:

1. This indicates a date of May 22 for the proposed amputation of HPB's leg, but references to amputation still occur as late as June 2 (letter 46).

2. A catchphrase from *David Copperfield* (1850, ch. 5), by Charles Dickens, in which Barkis is a character who sends the message

"Barkis is willin'" in Copperfield's letter to another character, Peggotty, indicating his desire to marry her. The expression quickly became proverbial and was also used elsewhere by HPB (*e.g.*, *LBS* 109). Louisa Andrews used it in a letter about HPB (23, note 2), and HPB used it in a letter of 1887 that was printed in the *Irish Theosophist* 3 (Feb. 1895): 76–7, to which the editor of that journal, D. N. Dunlop, added a note: "The expression 'Barkis is willing,' H. P. B. said once was a mantram unconsciously made by Dickens. She used it upon occasion to certain persons on meeting (or writing) them for the first time. Spoken, it had such peculiar force as to alarm one who thus heard it from her lips and as she used it" (77).

DATE: The reference to "a letter yesterday" and the statement that she is sending "this one" (apparently an enclosed copy of the "spirit photograph" described in the letter of May 20), indicates a date of May 21 for this letter.

SOURCE: Transcribed from a photocopy of the original in the HPB Library. Published in *Unpublished Letters* 169.

⌒

Letter 44

To H. S. Olcott   *Friday, May 21, 1875*
                                                  Philadelphia

Dear Henry.— The paralysis *has set in*.[1] I had the surgeon Pancoast and Mrs Michener the Clairvoyant. The former says its too late, the latter promises recovery if I do as *she* tells me. I have taken her again.

The Lodge[2] will send an article this week, N° 1° of the series of articles to come from *Luxor*.[3] It is a sort of rudimental insight given by them to the world. It treats of what *is* a man on Earth and of the object of his life here or what it should be. It goes to prove that the first seven of our past, present and subsequent existences in different spheres are but a sort of Embryonical Essays, modelings of Nature (so much dreaded by the Rosicrucians for that reason)—herself, who tries her hand for the final formation of the *real, complete man*, who can become only on the Seventh

Sphere a perfect *microcosmos* or a miniature store house of samples of everything from the Alpha down to the Omega of the great *Macrososmos*, whom he must represent to perfection before he steps *beyond* the Seventh Sphere. A man who has not succeeded in perfecting himself finally when arrived to the Seventh Sphere cannot become a microcosm and at the end of his natural existence in the last sphere allowed to him for final perfection, the punishment is awaiting him. Its the ultimate *irretrievable* and *irrepealable* sentence that is passed on him. His immortal spirit loses its individuality and sinks for *eternities* (as conceived by our limited human brain) in the ocean of Spiritual Light and Cosmical matter combined, in order that returning once more to its primal source it might remingle with it, like a drop of water thrown back into the ocean loses its *whole* (which dissolves for the cohesion of the particles exists no more) but still exists in those scattered particles to be used perhaps again in *ages* to come; *r*ebecome again a new individuality (not the same) and begin again a mans life on the first sphere. But his chances for it do not depend any more on the intelligent selections of the wise Sephiroths, but on the blind work of the *Material* Light (not the Celestial) which is the producer, the god of the *Material* worlds, though it is still proceeding from God—the *Spiritual Light*, the Enlightening Light, the Ain Soph, for He is all. The articles have to show then, that as the future gifts qualities, homeliness or beauty, vice or virtue of the man that has to be developed from the *foetus* depends wholy on how the mother carries it and cares for it for the nine months of its embryonic formation (nine *months* represent nine *tens* of years, the letter ‏שׁ‎ Shin, the natural term for life), for the mental and physical formation of her child will be what *she* does [for] him—not his father who is but the generative male potency—so the progress of every one of us mortals in our future life (first sphere) in what we term *Spirit* (?) life depends on how we moulded here on Earth our *Embryonic mental* life and how far we progressed in this Existence. For if your mother has to answer and bear the punishment (in as much [as] she has sinned through carelessness willingly and knowingly) for what she has made you while in her *womb*, you being in a state of Embryonic physical life, *her* offspring and her creation, so you shall have to answer for the sins of your *mental* offspring,—mind, for it remains with you to develop it give it the proper direction and use your souls suggestions which is *conscience*, while you are here on Earth, and find yourself in a Embryonic *mental* life in relation to the Spirit Life; for the *mental* development of the man *here* in relation to the mental spiritual life of the man *there* (*beyond* the first river) is just in proportion and relation what the mental man *here* is to the *foetus* in the womb. All the seven spheres one after the other present the man in a state of more or less developed *embryo*, according to his own exertions. Judge yourself, by remembering how many degrees of development present different Spirits from *one and the same Sphere*. You know it. I have been intrusted with an arduous and dangerous task Harry to "try" and teach you, having to rely solely on my poor, lame English. They *must* have tremendous hopes in your *intuitional* gifts, for 'pon my word I put very little hope myself in my powers of elocution and *clear*, definite explanations. *Do you* understand friend? Well I proceed as I can, limping in my English as I limp on my leg. I wish *More*[4] would undertake you, I wish he was appointed instead of poor me. . . Well to the task. As it is difficult and next to impossible sometimes to correct subsequently a short leg or crooked hand or some *physical* defect or monstrosity that exists from birth, having been formed in the development of the *foetus* so it is as difficult and next to impossible to correct at once in Spirit life the *mental* monstrosities and defects of our morality and intellect we carry "up stairs," *just as they are* at the time when we part with our mortal envelope. Its for the *man* of the first Sphere to correct all the imperfections he has endowed himself with, in his Embryonic state *here* "down stairs" .., and for the *man* of the second (third, fourth and so on up to the seventh sphere) to redress what he might have done so much more easier in his former existence. See, if *John* if he does not look out, wont have to toil and despair and work after he comes out *of his sleep* for what he might very easily *not* have done at all in the sphere he is now. It does *not* prevent him passing into a higher sphere, for *laws* are *laws* and are created for all good or bad and they do not depend on the state of the individual at all. How many men *here die unprepared*, so much the worse for them; and death will *not* wait for them to amend. They prepare themselves double work for the future, thats all. To show you with what scornful pity people are looked at by the Lodge, I'm at liberty [page break] at liberty to tell you that the articles in question have been ordered to be written by *mere* children of the Science, by the *neophytes* (of course they will be carefully revised), and such as they are, *Tuitit* thinks them *too good* for the green Americans, he says *few* will understand and many of the *omniscient* Spirit^sts will pitch into them and feel *shocked*.

Now to the five coloured star and the *red* thing. There are *seven* spheres as you know, *seven* vowels, *seven* (?) it will be explained prismatic colours, *seven* notes or *chromatic* scale in music, (Music of the Spheres).

Every man or person living on this Earth lives in the *fourth* sphere properly speaking. We reckon 7 spheres from the 1st sphere we go to from here, but it's an incorrect word. For every sphere has seven subdivisions or sections or regions; and when we say "the spirit passed to the second or third sphere" we ought properly to say that he passed to the 2nd or 3rd *region* of the 5th sphere (our Earth is the last region of the 4th). Do you understand. Well the star was an emblem of your mind and meant to throw a beneficent influence on you. It had but *five* colours for you only *begin* to get an insight of the fifth sphere and meant:

1° Red-*violet-bluish* (gradations.) *Matter* (yours) spiritualized by *Light*

2° *Blue*: *pure matter belonging to Elements* (baptism for your carnal purification).

3° *Purple* Amethyst Mercurean Color the ☿.[5] (gradation of *indigo*) and *Red* meant when *more* blue the deep the Ruling *Feminine Principle*. When more of an indigo blue, colour of the seas, meaning *Aphrodite*,[6] when tinted with *red* makes it (sexless). The *spiritual* material world made manifest to you. "PATIENCE" also the note of the chromatic scale that sounds the longest. the C answering to *Purple*, the *high treble* vibration to produce which requires a vibration of 699 millions of millions in *one* second, means be *patient active* and *enduring* (you can verify the above with chemists and for music with Mʳ Bowman).

4° *Green* (gradation yellow & blue) meaning that *living* forms and their spirits will be shown to you, for they will be disclosed, by the virtue of the *seeming* colour of vegetation products of *material* nature. Colour of the "Fairy races" the Elementary Queen of genii "*Smaragda*."[7] Your material bodily sight will open and by the baptism of Spˡ Light "you will see."

5° *Yellow*, "Elementum Ignis" [*Ln.* element of fire]. First results of the Baptism of the *Red*, for the yellow *fire beginning to glow* or *flower*, will gradually become the *Producing Spiritual* Power or Red, colour of the Spirˡ *Sun* (our material one is yellow) *Sexless*, or *Triumph of Spirit over matter*. "*Try*," and from the red of *Elementary Region*—of Cherubim, progress towards the *Osiris* the highest *Ethereal One*, the "Empyraeum"—Sphere of *Teraphim*.[8]

That will do I guess for lesson the 1ˢᵗ. I send you a letter from the unfortunate Brown this *malchanceux* [*Fr.* unfavored one] of Fate.[9] What am I to do with him. What advice *can* I give him? Write me please to say what's the best course for him, for I be switched if I know. John has disappeared . . not to be seen or heard. I'm afraid if something can't be done for him he will go down to the Devil. Can't you find him subscribers? For God's sake do if you can. Why, they say the Lotus Club and all your numberless acquaintances can furnish hundreds and hundreds. Could not we take it on shares and make up the money, how do you think. I wont stir one step without your advice. Child has *been turned* out as secretary for the International Committee of Spiritualists for the *Centenial*. He has cut his hand at a post mortem examination with a half putrified corpse and is beginning to rot, but he will not die for *he has to be punished by those he has wronged.*

Good bye—God bless you. I'm too tired to write more. I send you the 1st part of Wagners article.[10] You will receive the 2nd next week. I send you too a *german* pamphlet, articles in favor of Spiritualism by Prof. Boutleroff and Aksakoffs newspaper. Cant you translate it, or have it translated?

Yours truly
HPB

Approved
Tuitit Bey.

NOTES:

1. The paralysis was of her leg, injured in late January.

2. The Egyptian Lodge, under the direction of the Master Serapis.

3. C. Jinarajadasa (*Theosophist* 44 [Apr. 1923]: 97) believes that this probably refers to "A Few Questions to 'Hiraf'" (*CW* 1:101–18). At the end of that article in her scrapbook (1:45), HPB wrote, "Shot No. 1—Written by H.P.B. by express orders from S *** " (*CW* 1:119).

4. Robert More, mentioned in a letter from Tuitit Bey to Olcott (*LMW2*, letter 3, p. 12).

5. The astrological symbol of the planet Mercury.

6. Aphrodite, a Greek goddess, was said to have been born from the foam of the sea.

7. *Smaragda,* feminine form of Latin *smaragdus* "emerald," hence "green."

8. Teraphim. In *HPB Speaks* 1:45, the reading is *Seraphim,* the highest of the nine orders of angels, which makes better sense, but elsewhere also (letter 40) HPB associates the teraphim with the empyrean, so the reading "teraphim" is probably correct.

9. HPB sent the same or a similar letter from Gerry Brown to Hiram Corson (letter 31).

10. Boris de Zirkoff notes, "H. P. B. translated into English Wagner's articles concerning séances with French medium Brédif (*Vide* the short-lived *Spiritual Scientist,* Boston, Mass., June 3, 10, and 17, 1875)" (*CW* 6:449).

SOURCE: Transcribed from the original in the Archives of the Theosophical Society, Adyar. Parts of the original have decomposed or are no longer legible; for these parts, earlier transcriptions have necessarily been relied upon. Published in *Theosophist* 44 (Apr. 1923): 96–102; *HPB Speaks* 1:37–46.

⌒

Letter 45

To A. N. Aksakoff　　　　　　　　　　　　*May 24, 1875*

Have you received the issues of the *Spiritual Scientist* which contain my latest article, "Who Fabricates"? I have sent you several numbers, *faute de mieux* [*Fr.* for lack of anything better], as in the so-called *respectable* newspapers there is nothing whatever about Spiritualism, and after the Katie King scandal, the *Banner of Light,* the *Religio-Philosophical Journal,* and the *Spiritual Scientist* are foundering, and are crying for help from sheer starvation. Disaster has come upon us. Dr. Child has appeared in the character of a spiritist Anti-Christ, and, as the Judas of the seven councils, has destroyed Spiritualism. Even the most advanced Spiritualists begin to fear public opinion and their "high respectability" induces many to continue to secretly and privately believe in spirits. Of trusty soldiers ready to die for the truth, there remains only my own little army. Like unrelieved sentinels we stand at our posts, we fight and struggle, we write and spend our last coins; but it seems as though we are petrified in our places like so many spiritist mummies, quite useless. . . . In order to support the sinking *Spiritual Scientist*, the only conscientious, honest and fearless paper (and that, thanks to our efforts), I have spent my last $200. I am the poorest, except Professor Britten,[1] and yet I have more than anyone. La plus jolie fille du monde ne peut donner que ce qu'elle a [*Fr.* The prettiest girl in the world can give only what she has]! Ask Olcott whether I would spare my very life for the sake of Spiritualism, in other words of the Divine Truth which is the only consolation of humanity and its last hope. This year I have earned as much as $6,000 by my articles and other work, and all, *all* has gone for Spiritualism. And now, in the present attitude of *negation*, doubt and blindness, after the Katie King business, everything seems to have come to an end.

Hitherto when I had written a sensational article, I had it reprinted in the form of a pamphlet and sold several thousand at 10 cents a copy, but what can I reprint now? One cannot even get into a quarrel with anyone. Previously opponents appeared by the hundred and wrote against me. I then would attack them directly and break them into smithereens. You can judge from my article, "Reply to Dr. Beard."[2] My portrait used to be printed, and the *Graphic* was to have published a picture of my militant person. Katie King appeared, and in an instant everything fell apart. Look at poor A. J. Davis; he can barely keep body and soul together, and his books are not selling at all. The *Banner* has fallen from 25,000 subscribers to 12,000. Olcott is sitting on a heap of his *People from the Other World*, like Marius on the ruins of Carthage,[3] and thinking bitter things. Not a thousand copies of his book have been sold in five months. Epes Sargent, the favorite and most learned of the American authors, the only spiritist whom everyone respects and who has hitherto been regarded as an authority, is lighting his stove with his *Proof Palpable of Immortality*, his last work. Robert Dale Owen has hidden himself and vanished from the face of the earth, and so on and so on. An *earthquake* is needed in order to rouse the American public from this apathy. And the financial situation has fallen frightfully low also. Failure succeeds failure. There is a terrible panic; those who have money hide it, and those who have not are dying of hunger. Still Olcott does not lose heart; with the sense of a thoroughbred Yankee he has invented a "Miracle Club"; we shall see what will come of that. I can answer for myself; so long as my soul remains in my body I shall stand up and fight for the truth.

NOTES:

1. Possibly Dr. W. Britten.

2. "Reply to Dr Beard" is probably either "About Spiritualism," *Daily Graphic* 6 (November 13, 1874): 90–1 (*CW* 1:36–44), or "Madame Blavatsky: Her Experience—Her Opinion of American Spiritualism and American Society," *Spiritual Scientist* 1 (December 3, 1874): 148–9 (*CW* 1:46–9).

3. Gaius Marius (ca. 157–86 B.C.), a Roman general. The allusion is probably to a play, *Caius Marius: A Tragedy*, by Richard Penn Smith, premiered in Philadelphia in 1831 and revived there in 1858. It is possible that HPB saw the play in a later revival while she was living in Philadelphia when she wrote this letter. Act 4, scene 7, has this setting: "The ruins of Carthage. Marius discovered sitting on the prostrate pillar of a temple, in deep thought." A centurion arrives, bringing Marius a command from the governor, Sextilius, that he should depart from the province. The following exchange ends their dialog (109–10):

   CENTURION What answer shall I bear Sextilius?
   MARIUS Go—Go and tell him
   That thou hast seen the exiled Marius
   Sitting upon the ruins of Carthage.

SOURCE: Russian original unavailable. Translated by Boris de Zirkoff from Solovyov's *Sovremennaya* 271–2. Another English translation by Walter Leaf in *Modern Priestess* 250–3.

〜

Letter 46

To H. P. Corson   *Wednesday [June 9, 1875]*
                                                      Philadelphia

My dear Sir—How can I ever thank you for your kind remembrance and friendly wishes to me?—Really and in deed, this fearful sickness has opened my blind eyes and perhaps—cured me of my injust and bitter suspicions—towards many of my friends. I never believed in the possibility for myself to find any other but indifferent acquaintances and correspondents. I have found out my mistake with some and will profit by it.

The danger is far—*unfortunately:* but at least, I will not be obliged to add to the list of my natural accomplishments and charms the one of a wooden leg, once that I am doomed to live.

I am really glad and proud to see that you are able to discern in my face something else—besides a pug nose. It rekindles my hopes for the future times to come—when we shall be sitting both of us smoking and talking—and I expect that having been able to find out *something* behind the veil of flesh *on the portrait*—you may perhaps find out too, behind or rather *inside* that clumsy Russian form of mine something too, worthy of your attention. You know I am *a missionary*, and a fanatic too—by the way. You *must* believe in something else besides your "Ennemosers—Howitt." Magnetism is all very fine and a very appropriate word sometimes, but it does not cover all the ground and there is most assuredly something yet at the back of it which Ennemoser failed to perceive, for nothing blinds so much your intuitional perceptions and prevents you from hearing the whisperings of your spirit as *too much* study and pondering over books. "The dead letter that killeth." Read more on the *pages of your Soul* if you can, and leave the idle speculations of others—*outwardly* scientific as they may appear—to the stony Tindalls[1] and the skeptical book worms, who live and die believing only in other peoples authorities though in their pride they may fancy them their own.

I am afraid my scribbling will be a sad strain on your nerves. Excuse me and believe in the sincere and true feelings of your very grateful—

H P. Blavatsky.

NOTE:

1. John Tyndall, a British physicist.

DATE: This letter, responding to Corson's acknowledgment of and comments about HPB's portrait in his letter of May 30 (cited in note 4 of letter 42), was presumably written not long after Corson's, hence early June. An envelope addressed to Corson is postmarked June 9, so that date is adopted for this letter.

SOURCE: Transcribed from a microfilm and a photocopy of the original in the HPB Library. Published in *Unpublished Letters* 167–8.

Introduction to Letter 47

The *Spiritual Scientist* 2 (June 3, 1875): 151 carried a personal announcement of HPB's leg injury:

> WE REGRET to announce that Madame Blavatsky is seriously ill, and her life has been in great danger. Last winter she fell with great force upon one of her knees, on the sidewalk, and the result was an inflamation of the *periosteum*, or covering of the bone, which has progressed so far that it is now uncertain if the limb will mortify and be amputated, or become paralyzed. It would be a great loss to the cause of

Spiritualism if this distinguished lady should die, for her devotion, learning, and enthusiasm are unsurpassed, while in "spiritual gifts" she has scarcely an equal.

Later, the *Spiritual Scientist* 2 (June 10, 1875): 166 reported that the crisis had been reached at midnight on June 3, and that HPB was recovering.

Letter 47

To F. J. Lippitt   *Thursday [June 10, 1875]*
                                              Philadelphia

My Sweet General—
    You must thank "John King" if your last is answered at all—for Mʳ Betanelly is West. I sent him away about the 26th of May—when I was taken so sick, and the doctors began thinking about depriving me of my *best* leg.—for I thought at that time that I was going "upstairs" *pour de bon* [*Fr.* for good], and as I hate seeing long faces *whiners* and *weepers* and such like things when I am sick, I made him clear out. I have in many things *cat*-like propensities and one of them is to be ever on the look out and try *"to die"* alone if I can. So I told him to be ready to come back when I write him that I am better, or when somebody else writes him that I am gone *home*, or "kicked the bucket" as *"John"* very kindly learned me to say. Well, I did not die quite *yet*, for again, like the cats I have *nine* lives in me it appears—and because I am not wanted yet in the bosom of Abraham I suppose—but as I am still in bed, very weak, cross and generally feel *mad* from 12 AM. to 12 PM, so I keep the chap away yet—for his own benefit and my own comfort. My leg was going to be chopped off clean, but I said "mortification or sugar plums I wont have it!" and I kept my word good. Fancy my fathers daughter—on a wooden leg—fancy my leg going

in the spirit land before me! pour le coup [*Fr.* really! just imagine that!]—George Wash: Childs[1] would have a nice chance to compose *un quatrain* [*Fr.* a quatrain], pretty obituary *poekry* as Mr Artemus Ward[2] used to say, closing the verses with the usual refrain of his immortal "Philadelphia Ledger" Gone to meet her leg! Indeed! So I summoned my best *will power* (my Sunday one) and begged of the doctors and surgeons to go and look for my leg on the Centenial Grounds. . . .

After they had vanished like so many unclean goblins or *Kakodemons* [cacodemon "evil spirit"] I called in Mrs *Michener clairvoyante*, and had a talk with her. . . . In short I had prepared myself to die—didn't care—but decided to die with both legs. The mortification had gone all round the knee, but two days of cold water *poultices*, and a white *pup*, a dog by night laid across the leg[3]—cured all in no time. Nerves and muscles weak, cant walk but all danger is far. I had two or three other *maladies*, showing an ambitious design to ornament themselves with *latin names*,—but I stopped it all short. A bit of will power, a nice crisis—tried hard the latter to have the best of me—a healthy tug with the "pug-nosed messenger" and there I am. Betanelly is a soft *ninny*—he would have never described you my *sufferings* so poetically as I did. Would he—"mon General"?

Now to John King—that *King* of mischievous reprobates. What he did about the house, while I was sick, in bed, on the point of dying—three volumes could not express! Ask only Mr Dana and Mme Magnon a french lady friend of mine who are visiting me and live in my house now. The fact is, there is no knowing what he may do next. When they brought the letters to day, he had opened every one of them before the postman had time to hand them. My servant maid, who is a wonderfully mediumistic—as much perhaps as she is stupid—and who is all day entranced, *dematerialising* everything in the kitchen—came running in my bedroom, half crying and so scared that she looked quite pale telling me that "that big fellow spirit with the black beard had torn open the envelopes right in her hands—and so I read your letter.

Now let me tell you something my dear General a good advice—unless you know *thoroughly* well *John*, dont trust him, more than needed. He is kind hearted obliging, ready to do anything for you—(ask Olcott)—if he takes a fancy to you, he is a powerful, noble hearted spirit and *I love him dearly*, before God Almighty I swear to the truth of what I say—*but*—he has his vices and considerably *vicious vices* too. He is spiteful, and revengeful sometimes; *lies* occasionally like the most notorious of french dentists,[4] and delights in *humbuging* people. Now, I wont undertake to say and testify in a Court of Justice that *my John*, is *the* John of the London seances John of the "phosphorus lamp"[5] though I am pretty sure he is, and he says so. But the mysteries of the Spirit world are so mixed up, they present such a wonderful inextricable labyrinthe [*Fr.* labyrinth] that—who can tell? NOT COLBY; of this I am most positively sure.

Look at *me*. I know John for 14 years. Not a day but he is with me, he made acquaintance with all Petersburg and half of Russia under the name of *Yanka*, "or Johny"; he travelled with me all over the world. Saved my life *three* times, at Mentana, in a shipwreck, and the last time near *Spezia* when our steamer was blown in the air, to atoms and out of 400 passengers remained but *16* . . in 1871, 21 of June.[6] He loves me, I know it and would do for no one more than for myself—See what tricks he plays with me! at the least *contrarieté* [*Fr.* opposition (to his wishes)], the least thing I wont do as he would like me to, he begins playing the old Harry,[7] making mischief—and what mischief!—He abuses me dreadfully, calls me the most wonderful, "never heard before" names, goes to mediums and *tale tells* them, about me, saying to them I hurt his feelings, that I am a vicious liar, an ungrateful so and so: he becomes so powerful that he actually writes letters himself, without any mediums help, he corresponds with Olcott, with Adams with three or four ladies that I dont even know, comes and tells me "What a goodly fun he had with them," and how he humbuged them. I can name you ten persons he corresponds with: He steals everything in the house, brought to Dana $10, the other day, when I was so sick, for Dana, had written him in the morning *secretly* in his room asking him for it (Dana knows him for 29 years) brought $10 for Mr Brown, brought Mme Magnon a ruby ring, she had lost 8 months ago (lost or had it stolen I dont know which) "to reward her" he said, for she took care of "his lass Ellie" (poor *ego*) she had written him too, two hours previous to that, at 9 o'clock in the evening and found her ring under her bed clothes at 11 o'clock, with a note from *him*. He forges peoples handwritings and makes mischief in the families—he pops off and pops in" like some infernal *Deus [ex] machina*, he is everywhere at the same time and pokes his nose in every ones business. He plays me the most unexpected tricks—*dangerous* tricks sometimes—quarrels me with people and then comes laughing and tells us all he has done, boasting of it and teasing me.

A few days ago he wanted me to do something I *did not* wish to do—for I was sick and did not think it right—he threw at me a *caustic*, un morceau de pierre infernale [*Fr. literally* a piece of infernal rock[8]] that was *under lock* in a casket in the drawers and—burned my right eyebrow and cheek—and when on the following morning my eye brow had become black as jet he laughed and said I looked like "a *fine Spanish wench*." I will now be marked for a month at least. I know he loves me, *I know it*, he is devotedly attached to me, and he abuses me most shamefully, the wicked wretch. He writes long letters to people about *me*, makes them believe the most horrid things and then—boasts of it! Your ideas about the Spirit world and *mine* are two different things. *My lord*, you will think perhaps—"John is a diakka." John is a *bad* spirit un esprit farfadet et malin" [*Fr.* a hob-goblin and malicious spirit]. Not a bit of it. He is as good as any of us any day, but why I tell and warn you it is because I want you to know him, before you keep company with him. Now, for instance, nature has endowed me pretty generously with the *Second Sight*, or clairvoyant gifts—and I generally *can* see what I am anxious to see but I can never *present* [*Fr.* foresee, anticipate] his tricks or know of them, unless he comes and tells them himself. Now, last night, I had three persons come visiting me and *Dana* and Mme Magnon were in my room. John began rapping and talk-ing—I felt very sick and didn't feel like talking, but John insisted. By the way, I have arranged a *dark cabinet* in my spirit room near my bedroom and Dana of the "Miracle Club," sets there every night. John made his appearance. "I say, Ellie," (he always begins like that[)]. "Well? said I what are you up to again, you villain?" I wrote a letter my lass"—says he, "a *love* letter." For God's sake to whom?" exclaimed I in utter distress, for I know him well, and feared some new mischief. "—You did not receive a letter to day, from Gerry Brown, Ellie?—did you?—No, I did not. What about Mr Brown?"—"Well, answers John, "it's because he wont write you no more, he is *mad* with you, for I described you and drew out your portrait—first rate to him.—What did you tell him, John, you mischievous devil, I want to know it!—and I became so excited, that my visitors began all laughing at me—"Why, answers John very coolly—"I didn't tell him much; I only just gave him a friendly hint or two—told him about you being such a sweet tempered *she-cat*. I called you a (mondy or) pondy-legged[9] *something.*" (I forget his expression) "explained him how you *swear* at me in dif-ferent languages, and assured him on my honor, that you abused him (Mr Brown) fearfully, to every one who comes to visit you, furthermore, I told him you looked like a *fancy she dumpling* sitting up in your bed, as solemn as *a Cathedral* and as cross as a *butchers bull-dog*. He is disgusted with you, now Mr Brown is, and is going *to shut you out* from his "Scientist" altogether."—When I answered him, that Mr Brown would not believe him, and that I would write him asking him to send me his letter—John said— "No he wont send it you; for now, we are fast friends with him, and he knows, I will be more useful for his "Scientist" than you ever will—*for I promised to write an article* for him, I did, and he accepted it with thanks, and said,—"I give her up—the *cross Russian Devil!* and *many thanks* to you Mr King for having posted me so well."

Now, fancy people listening to that, and I not knowing what to do—to laugh, or feel mad with this mischief making goblin! I dont know if he invented the whole story just to tease me as he generally does, or if he has *really* written to Mr Brown. It would be ridiculous for me to write about this to the latter—on the faith of only of what John told me. Please dear Mr Lippitt, go to Mr Brown, if you have a moment to spare, and ask him to tell you if he has *really* received something from John. Read him all this letter concerning John, for if he *has* received it (of course I do not believe the wicked imp, when he says, that Mr Brown *said so* and *so* about me,) but he will perhaps tell you of it. *If he does not like* telling you anything of it, please do not insist, for may be *John* has written him something else, *about business*— I know he took a fancy to Mr Brown about a month ago—and helped me much in different things, (to persuade people to write for the *Scientist* for instance) and told this story just to bother me, as he generally delights making himself agreeable in this direction—and then John would not like Mr Brown or any one else showing his letters to people—but you just try. You may let him see all this letter if you like.

And now, I begin feeling very tired, for I am very, yet. I won another law suit, and may perhaps save $5 000, out of what I lost: John has helped me in my law suits thats certain, but—he did a *very* bad thing, though—not from the standpoint of the Summer Land—but according to the human, earthly code of honor. I'll tell you someday—God bl[*remainer of word unclear, perhaps* bless]. Write me to tell about it & I think I will go in about a fort night or three weeks if better to Prof. Corson—Ithaca—for a month or so, and then I shall have to go on the *sea shore* somewhere till October. I am ordered, but I must find some *isolated spot* on this globe.

Sincerely yours
H P. Blavatsky

PS. Oh, the words you wrote as given by John are *Slavonian.* I can make out but half of them. They mean [following are six words that look somewhat like the following: URSLH TOLK TSH BOG TIS VVLIKISI] Better than argue pray to God the Great—or Powerful. I will write you more.

H—

[H *followed by an indecipherable trailing-off, presumably* HPB]

[Across the bottom of the last sheet of the letter, in red printed letters, overwriting the text of HPB's postscript and extending slightly below it, is the following message:]

Now whats the use abusing a poor ᴐ innocent sprite that way ᴗ Tell Ellie •/ "—Yglie—// General I did write Gery Brown—a love letter for I love the chap and my heart is opened to him—my business isnt it—?
I say, Frankie [*i.e.,* Francis (Lippitt)]—isnt she a brick my lass ≑ has a reglar foregn popgun isnt she thats why I love her—your benevolent.

John King

NOTES:

1. An article in the *New York Sun* (March 28, 1877) elicited a response from HPB (*CW* 1:241–5), in which she wrote, "No doubt it is a great honor for an unpretentious foreigner to be thus crucified between the two greatest celebrities of your chivalrous country—the truly good Deacon Richard Smith, of the blue gauze trousers, and the nightingale of the willow and the cypress, G. Washington Childs, A.M." That and the mention in this letter are the only references in HPB's writings to a putative poet George Washington Childs. No such person, however, has been identified. George William Childs was, however, the editor of the Philadelphia newspaper, the *Public Ledger*, presumably the "Philadelphia Ledger" of this letter. A common euphemism for dying was "gone to meet his or her maker."

2. Artemus Ward was a comic literary character noted for his misspellings and mispronunciations.

3. The story of the white dog has entered into Philadelphia lore, with a restaurant named "The White Dog" now in the building where HPB lived.

4. The French have a saying about dentists: "Il ment (or Il est menteur) comme un arracheur de dents," literally "He lies (or is a liar) like a tooth-puller," doubtless because dentists tell their patients, "This won't hurt a bit." Hence "to lie like a dentist" is to be a barefaced liar (as pointed out by Leonard Zwilling in a personal communication). It is not that French dentists are more mendacious than others, but rather that the French have a phrase about dentists as liars. Jean-Louis Siémons (personal communication) points out that the tooth-puller or dentist "is represented in old pictures as a man established on the market-place, or in a street, pretending to be an expert dentist, and attracting his practice by a fine quack's patter, vaunting his skill in curing dental ailments and extracting teeth without pain."

5. "He [John King] was usually seen in the light of a peculiar lamp that he carried and that illuminated his face and sometimes the room" (*EOP* 711).

6. Boris de Zirkoff (*CW* 1:xlix) gives the date of the steamer *Eunomia*'s explosion as July 4, 1871, near the island of Spetsai. If HPB's date given here as June 21 was according to the Julian calendar, the corresponding Gregorian date would be July 3. HPB's recall of details was often imperfect; in a later letter to A. P. Sinnett (*LBS* 215), she says, "in April, I think, got blown up in *Eumonia* [sic]."

7. Playing the devil, being vexatious.

8. *Pierre infernale* is silver nitrate in the form of a rock or pencil, used to cauterize wounds. *Merriam-Webster's Collegiate Dictionary*, 10th ed., explains that silver nitrate is "an irritant compound $AgNO_3$ that in contact with organic matter turns black and is used as a chemical reagent . . . in medicine esp. as an antiseptic and caustic."

9. Neither "mondy" (the spelling may be "mandy") nor "pondy-legged" has been found in dictionaries. As HPB added, "I forget his expression," it may be "bandy-legged," that is, "bowlegged."

DATE: A list of envelopes in the Archives of the Theosophical Society, Adyar, says the one for this letter was postmarked June 10 and endorsed as received June 12.

SOURCE: Transcribed from the original in the Archives of the Theosophical Society, Adyar. Published in *HPB Speaks* 1:80–91.

Letter 48

To F. J. Lippitt   *[June 19, 1875]*

To General F. J. Lippitt
13 Pemberton Square
(Room 13)
Boston Mass.

Mon cher General

"Le petit bon homme n'est pas mort encore." [*Fr.* The nice little fellow isn't dead yet.] Lo! how I *am* tired with all this *dying* business. I wish I could die once for all and *for good* as John says, for really it becomes a comedy.

As soon as I am better I will write many interesting details. I am too weak now. Wrote to Petersb[urg] and many others.

Betanelly writes Isn't my *John* a *brick*? He is invited to St Petersburg by the Committee. Ask Mr Sargent he'll tell you all.

friendly and with thank you,

H. P Blavatsky

DATE: This postcard has a cancellation date of 19 June and is endorsed "Mme. Blavatsky, June 19, '75."

SOURCE: Transcribed from the original in the Archives of the Theosophical Society, Adyar. Published in *HPB Speaks* 2:179.

———————

On June 23, 1875, Lippitt wrote from Boston, in reply to the foregoing letter (47) and postcard (48), expressing concern for HPB's health, commenting on the message from "John King" written in blue overscript, and describing several Spiritualist sittings that involved "John King" (here transcribed from the original in the Archives of the Theosophical Society, Adyar):

Madame H P Blavatsky

My dear friend,

I have not ventured to write you for the last two weeks, for fear of exciting and thus harming you in your weak state; but, from all accounts you are so much better, it is time that I should inform you of the intense anxiety your illness has caused not only myself, but other friends of yours who have never yet seen you, and the great pleasure given us by the news of *both* your convalescences. Mr Betanely's letter of the 18th and your welcome postal I read with great interest. Mr Brown read them to day. I could not find him before. He will no doubt inform you what use J K made of the $50. Wonderful indeed!

On opening your most interesting eight page letter of Thursday (the 10th?) I found the following written over your postscript and the rest of the page in red pencil in J K's hand.

"Now what's the use abusing a poor innocent sprite that way? Tell Ellie (', "—Yglie) (?) General I did write Gery Brown a long letter, for I love the chap and my heart is opened to him—*my* business isn't it?

"I say Frankie, isnt she a brick? my lass? a reglar foreign popgun, isnt she? That is why I love her. Your benevolent

John King"

This was probably written by J.K. after your letter was sealed. Mr Betanelly's last letter had a postscript in blue pencil, as follows,
    "True,

            J.K."

At the sitting with my Psychic Stand (which has already given us communications in five languages, English French, Latin, Sclavonian and Wallachian) June 19th, the following was spelled out the moment Mrs French put her hands upon it:

"Letmon. [*1st letter unclear:* H?] I am sent by John King to give this message. She is better. All right. We wish to give you our thanks for lending your help. John thinks she will live to render you much good". (She has already done so by getting better)

Among other things, at the end of quite a long communication from Katie King, came "Mein diest—Mond dieu—Laffset, counstivo—"
(In what language are the last two words?)
    "Sclavonian".

And afterwards, "Discoloff [*4th letter unclear*] is with you".

On the 21st came on my invitation to see the Stand Lee & Shepard, the publishers. Mr Lee a doubter, Mr Shepard an obstinate disbeliever. After a long sitting, Mr Lee went away firmly convinced, and Mr Shepard has to day admitted to me that the Stand has convinced him it was moved by *an unseen agency that is intelligent.* (in other words, *a spirit*).

Katie came at the same sitting and said (*inter alia*) "I go with father to Philadelphia."

Evening sitting on the 21st at Mrs Boothby's, where the materialisations are as good as through the Holmes, excepting that most of the spirits appear only for an instant (the medium having had but a few months' development). Dr Webster (the murderer of twenty six years ago) is the conducting spirit. I had from him the Monday before one or two strong tests of identity. Though visible only at times and for an instant, he talks to us from behind the curtain. I asked him if John King had made his appearance there. He said No indeed; he would sooner have the devil. He then gave us a graphic account of John's character, agreeing exactly with all your accounts of him, acknowledging that he is a very powerful spirit, and doing, after all, a great deal of good. He spoke *spontaneously* of his "beautiful talent for painting." In reply to questions from me he said he *is* the John King of London, that, to the best of his belief, he was formerly Sir Henry de Morgan, and that the Katie King of Philadelphia is his daughter; that Katie is a beautiful and a truthful spirit, whose father "only furnished the house in which she dwells"; and that she is beyond doubt, the London Katie also.

At the sitting yesterday afternoon about 4.30 P.M. John spelt out "I am King John."

Also, "Omniloff is now with Madam".

(How is she?) "Better, but very weak".

(Do you know what Prof. Webster said about you last night at Mrs Boothby's?) "Some of it". (Was it truthful?) "I suppose he did not tell any lies".

I leave next Monday to take my daughter from her school. On our return we shall stop several days (possibly a week) in Washington and two or three days in Philadelphia, when I shall bring her to see you. I shall then tell you all about that lovely, secluded seaside at Tiverton [Rhode Island] on Narragansett Bay, not far from Newport, hoping you will go there to recourt [? recouperate]. My sister and mother in law (*charming people*) with their families live there. Till then, adieu. Hope to see you by July 10th at latest. F. J. Lippitt

Letter 49

To F. J. Lippitt   *June 30 [1875]*
                                                        Philadelphia

General F J. Lippitt.

My dear General,

I had your letter dated Cambridge just now, and hasten to answer it. —All the *seemingly* signifying *nothing* letters dictated to you by spirits through your stand are but so many instructions to your Spiritualists of America, written out in ciphered alphabet (the Cabalistic, employed by *Rosecrucians* and other Brotherhoods of the Occult Sciences. I *am not* at liberty to read them out to you, *untill allowed*. Do not take these words for a dodge. I give you *my word of honor*, it is so. John knows to write that way of course for he belonged as you know to one of the orders. Preserve all you may receive in such a way *carefully*. Who knows, what may be yet in store for blind America.—One thing I can tell you though— the last words you ask about mean that untill Spiritualism, or rather the Philosophy and Mysteries are solved in America in the *right way*, no help can be given by higher Spirits, for the Elementary ones and the unprogressed ones would only give occasion—by making themselves understood erroneously—to the greatest misrepresentations of the Science of Sciences which misunderstanding of the Divine Truths could but bring harm to mankind. *That's the reason why*. John has done all he could do, towards helping you with your stand—but he *is not* allowed the poor fellow to do more. As it is, he is not even permitted to manifest him self any more or through me, except occasionally by letters he writes or words he spekes,[1]—unless I am perfectly *alone* with him. The time is close my dear General, when Spiritualism *must* be cleansed of its erroneous interpretations, superstitions, and ignorant notions, all of which only make skeptics and unbelievers laugh at us, deny Spiritualᵐ and stop the progress of the Cause, it must be shown as it is—a Science, a law of Nature an existing fact, without the existence of which all the *Macrocosmos*, would soon go topsy turvy, as a thing that popped out without any fundamental basis under it—a result without any reasonable cause for it— or a frolic of blind Force and Matter, the Büchner's materialistic and crazy ideas of the *Kraft* und *Stoff* etc.[2]

I am glad you pass through Philadelphia. I will be happy to see you and your dear daughter. But you must hurry—for I have to go away, lame as I am, on business which I can not possibly postpone. My way is to Boston and its vicinities, on a radius of about 50 miles around. I wont be able to go in the charming place you speak about. It is not on my way and my health, leg and the rest of it, is all fiddlesticks, and comes in secondary in my trip. *I am obliged to go* my dear friend and there's no saying "nay" to it, whether I am dead or alive. *Duty is duty*.

Olcott is gone to Boston, for a few days, he is sent there on business. I dont know if you had time to see him.

My health is progressing very poorly, but—I dont care a sugar plum.

I have just received a letter from Prof. Buchanan with whom I am in constant correspondence. With his last letter he sent me two bits of autograph to put on my forehead and *try* to *pretend* I am a psychometrist. I saw all sorts of sights the moment I took up his letter—with out knowing what was in it, and though I thought it was but idle fancies, described him minutely what I saw, laughing at it, as I did. —What do you think? Buchanan writes me that never was there given a more correct delineation of things and characters! —It seems I put the finger in the pie, without knowing it for this psychometrical business is a new thing to me, and I never tried it in my life. I shall beg of our friend E. Gerry Brown to advertise me in his paper as a psychometrical reader at 25 cents per hour. Is it too much you think? 'Pon my word, I did laugh at myself at this new psychal discovery in myself. Aint I a *well* of hidden treasures, General? A *reglar* one, John would say.

Do come quick, hurry up, and I may go with you till New Haven or Springfield.

I now close my letter for you to receive it sooner. God bless you my dear friend, and General, I have some good friends in America it appears—that's new business for me too, for I am not much spoiled with such a sort of luxury as sincere friendship.

My love, to your dear daughter, and I hope she wont abuse TOO much my poor John, or laugh at the poor fellow, for he really seems to like her, and is often talking of her sweetness on the "harpsichords."

What funny spirit he is. Why he makes use of the funniest words you ever heard in your life. I dont know where he takes them from. Didn't he ask me, the other day, to put on my white *trollopee*,[3] and be less *trouncing*[4] with him, for that, I really treated him sometimes *worser*[5] than an *unbreeched truant*.[6] Now, did you ever hear of such words! Perhaps *you* have, but I cant say *idem* [*Ln.* the same]. —I had to hunt all the dictionary before I found out the meaning of the word—*trollopee*, which seems to signify a *wrapper*, robe de chambre [*Fr.* dressing gown].

truly yours
H P Blavatsky

Enclosed find a facsimile of what spirits give you.

NOTES:

1. This word is unclear; it looks like "spekes," *i.e.,* "speaks," but might be "spells."

2. An allusion to Ludwig Büchner's major work, *Kraft und Stoff* (*Force and Matter,* 1855).

3. An obsolete term for "a loose dress worn by women in the 18th century" (*OED*), from *trollop* "an untidy or slovenly woman; a slattern, slut."

4. From *trounce* "to harass, beat as punishment, chastise, scold severely."

5. A double-comparative variant of *worse,* common in the sixteenth and seventeenth centuries, used in current English as a literary form ("the worser part") or as a vulgarism (*OED*).

6. Probably an allusion to the practice of punishing truant schoolboys by making them lower their trousers (making them "unbreeched") and switching or caning them on the bare buttocks.

DATE: In this letter, dated June 30, HPB writes of being on her way to Boston, where she in fact was in July 1875, so that is almost certainly the year of the letter.

SOURCE: Transcribed from the original in the Archives of the Theosophical Society, Adyar. Published in *HPB Speaks* 1:97–101.

~

Letter 50

To V. de Zhelihovsky   *[June 1875]*

I see this Hindu every day, just as I might see any other living person, with the only difference that he looks to me more ethereal and more transparent. Formerly I kept silent about these appearances, thinking that they were hallucinations. But now they have become visible to other people as well. He (the Hindu) appears and advises us as to our conduct and our writing. He evidently knows *everything* that is going on, even to the thoughts of other people, and makes me express his knowledge. Sometimes it seems to me that he overshadows the whole of me, simply entering me like a kind of volatile essence penetrating all my pores and dissolving in me. Then we two are able to speak to other people, and then I begin to understand and remember sciences and languages—everything he instructs me in, even when he is not with me any more.

DATE: The date of this letter is uncertain, but a general similarity of its subject matter with that of the following letter suggests that they are of approximately the same time.

SOURCE: Russian original unavailable. Copied from a translation in *Path* (NY) 9 (Jan. 1895): 297. Another English translation in *Path* (London) 3 (Dec. 1912): 211.

Letter 51

He has cured me entirely. And just about this time I have begun to feel a very strange duality. Several times a day I feel that besides me there is someone else, quite separable from me, present in my body. I never lose the consciousness of my own personality; what I feel is as if I were keeping silent and the other one—the lodger who is in me—were speaking with my tongue. For instance, I know that I have never been in the places which are described by my "other me", but this other one—the second me—does not lie when he tells about places and things unknown to me, because he has actually seen them and knows them well. I have given it up: let my fate conduct me at its own sweet will; and besides, what am I to do? It would be perfectly ridiculous if I were to deny the possession of knowledge avowed by my No. 2, giving occasion to the people around me to imagine that I keep them in the dark for modesty's sake. In the night, when I am alone in my bed, the whole life of my No. 2 passes before my eyes, and I do not see myself at all, but quite a different person—different in race and different in feelings. But what's the use of talking about it? It's enough to drive one mad. I try to throw myself into the part and to forget the strangeness of my situation. This is no mediumship, and by no means an impure power; for that, it has too strong an ascendency over us all, leading us into better ways. No devil would act like that. "Spirits", maybe? But if it comes to that, my ancient "spooks" dare not approach me any more. It's enough for me to enter the room where a *séance* is being held to stop all kinds of phenomena at once, especially materializations. Ah no, this is altogether of a higher order! But phenomena of another sort take place more and more frequently under the direction of my No. 2. One of these days I will send you an article about them. It is interesting.

DATE: The date of this letter is uncertain, but if the statement in the first sentence about being cured refers to HPB's leg, the letter may have been written in June 1875, when she recovered from that injury.

SOURCE: Russian original unavailable. Copied from a translation in *Path* (NY) 9 (Dec. 1894): 269–70. A different translation in *Path* (London) 3 (Nov. 1912): 170–1.

Letter 52

To F. J. Lippitt   *[July 6, 1875]*

General F J. Lippitt
Washington—DC.
1200. K Street

Dear General[1]
Unfortunately "man proposes and God disposes." I am unable to have the pleasure of seeing you in Philadelphia. I am leaving tomorrow, *Wednesday*, evening—or during the night. I am going on a *mission* to repair the wrong done to the cause of Spiritualism by that rascal Dr. Child in making poor old Owen mad. They will have a fine account to render "up stairs," those rascals the Holmes and their *Barnum*[2] show. I shall see you in Boston, where Olcott is at the moment. My love to your dear daughter.

Yours truly
H P Blavatsky

NOTES:

1. Except for its last sentence and a few other words, which are in English, the body of this postcard is in French.

2. HPB refers elsewhere (*CW* 1:68) to Child as "the Barnum of this spiritual show." The allusion is to P. T. Barnum, whose circuses and sideshows were noted for their sensationalism and fakery.

DATE: This postcard was endorsed by General Lippitt as received on July 7, which was a Wednesday in 1875. As HPB refers to "tomorrow, *Wednesday*," the postcard was probably written on Tuesday, July 6.

SOURCE: Translated and transcribed from the original in the Archives of the Theosophical Society, Adyar. Published in *HPB Speaks* 2:180-1.

Letter 53

To A. N. Aksakoff   *July 18, 1875*

I am ready to sell my soul for spiritualism, but nobody will buy it, and I am living from hand to mouth and earning from \$10 to \$15 when necessity arises.

SOURCE: Russian original unavailable. Translated by Boris de Zirkoff from Solovyov's *Sovremennaya* 273. Another English translation by Walter Leaf in *Modern Priestess* 253.

Letter 54

To A. N. Aksakoff   *September 10, 1875*

John is distinguishing himself by wise silence. He is in bad humor with me, and for the last three weeks and more he only appears to me to talk nonsense and even unkindly. Everything is not perfect in Summerland, as I see it. . . . There are such attacks upon us that we do not know what will come. The Spiritualists are furious because we do not share many of their opinions and do not regard all their mediums' lies as gospel truth. The mediums are wild because we (that is Olcott and I) observe them too closely and do not believe in their honesty. The anti-Spiritualists deride us as usual, and the church members fill the clerical papers with abuse, and seriously assure the public that we have sold our souls to the devil.... "You can't say 'God bless you' to every one who sneezes," as they say. In any case the *Banner of Light* and the *Religio-Philosophical Journal* are full of insinuations and malignities about us.

SOURCE: Russian original unavailable. Translated by Boris de Zirkoff from Solovyov's *Sovremennaya* 273. Another English translation by Walter Leaf in *Modern Priestess* 254.

Introduction to Letter 55

Between mid September and mid October 1875 (the exact dates are not known), HPB visited Hiram Corson and his wife in Ithaca, New York. During this visit she worked doggedly on the manuscript of the future *Isis Unveiled* and produced her article on "The Science of Magic" (*CW* 1:134–43) in response to an editorial in the Spiritualist journal *Banner of Light*. While there, she also wrote several letters (55 and probably 56), referring to her work on the manuscript of the book as well as other matters.

Letter 55

To A. N. Aksakoff   *September 20, 1875*

Oh, if only no one knew me in St. Petersburg! We would have shown your professors—John King and I—how pots are made by us in the Summerland. John promises to come to St. Petersburg, but perhaps he is only lying and deceiving; it is hard to rely on him. . . .

. . . Olcott is now organizing the Theosophical Society in New York. It will be composed of learned occultists and Kabbalists, of Hermetic philosophers of the 19th century, and of passionate antiquarians and Egyptologists in general. We want to do experiments comparing spiritualism and the magic of the ancients by following literally the instructions of old Kabbalahs, both Jewish and Egyptian.

For many years I have been studying the Hermetic philosophy in theory and practice, and day by day I am coming to the conclusion that spiritualism in its physical manifestations is nothing else but the python[1] of the ancients or the astral or sidereal light of Paracelsus, i.e., that intangible ether that Reichenbach calls *Od*. The Pythonesses of the ancients used to magnetize themselves—read Plutarch and his account of the oracular currents, read Cornelius Agrippa, Paracelsus, the *Magia Adamica* of Eugenius Philalethes, and others. You would always see better and communicate with the spirits by this means—self-magnetization.

I am now writing a big book, which, on John's advice, I call *Skeleton Key to Mysterious Gates*.[2] I am going after your European and American men of science, Papists, Jesuits, and that race of the half-learned, *les chatrés de la science* [Fr. the eunuchs of science], who destroy everything without creating anything and are incapable of creating.

NOTES:

1. Gk. *pythōn* "spirit of divination."

2. *Skeleton Key to Mysterious Gates*, an early working title for *Isis Unveiled*.

SOURCE: Russian original unavailable. Translated by Boris de Zirkoff from Solovyov's *Sovremennaya* 273. Another English translation by Walter Leaf in *Modern Priestess* 254, 256–7.

Letter 56

To V. de Zhelihovsky   *[latter half of 1875]*

I am embarked on a great work treating of theology, ancient beliefs and the secrets of the occult sciences, but fear nothing for me; I am sure of my facts, more or less. I should not, perhaps, know well how to talk of these abstract things, but all essential matter is dictated to me. . . . All that I shall write will not be my own; I shall be nothing more than the pen, the head which will think for me will be that of one who knows all. . . .

DATE: Vera de Zhelihovsky says that the letter from which this fragment comes was written in 1874; but the "great work" referred to is probably *Isis Unveiled*, and there is no evidence of HPB's working on it before summer 1875. HPB's letters to her family were often without dates; as her sister notes (*Lucifer* 15:473), "I have one [letter] before me, unluckily undated, as it was her habit in writing to us—her aunt and myself—not to trouble about the day of the month." Consequently the dates assigned to HPB's correspondence by Vera are often conjectural and unreliable. Boris de Zirkoff tentatively dates the letter sometime in 1876. However, because in this letter HPB says she has "embarked" on the work, the letter may be from the latter half of 1875.

SOURCE: Russian original unavailable. Copied from a translation in *Lucifer* 15 (Dec. 1894): 276.

Letter 57

To H. P. Corson   *[October 13–16, 1875]*

My dear Professor—

Lord love you, my best friend, is your wifes sisters nieces child dead,[1] or what, that neither yourself or your dear *épouse* [*Fr.* spouse], can write a line to a poor she traveller? This is the *third* letter I write you and not a word in response. Are you angry? Are you mad with me for any thing. Think not, for I feel as innocent of any wrong done to you as an unborn kitten.

The boots are here, but I would prefer a letter.[2]

I am nailed up like a slave to my chair writing all day as I did in your place. I have found some very precious rare works at Mr Ditson,[3] like B.[4] Higgin's *Anacalypsis* for instance, and its very useful to me. And what do *you* do, and pussy and the books and the apple trees? I feel as if I had left a home where I lived for twenty years. God bless you. Is my dear Mrs Corson translating hard?[5] 'Pon my word *I feel* as if all was *not* right, as if she was kind angry with me for something. Olcott wants me to go *home* (?!!) and does not even say where is this home. I like his impudence.

I send you the World, with an interesting letter in it addressed to Olcott, from un temoin oculaire [*Fr.* an eyewitness].[6] I will send you hereafter all the interesting things that might chance to come out, and the bye laws of our Society.

Did you read the true *pro* and *con* in the last Banner?[7] Brittain versus Britten, one stating that she has seen herself the Elementary, and the other denying that ever such a thing existed at all.

Well, we have lit a "goodly bonfire" as John says it, and I guess we will have to fight out our way pretty nice this winter for our Spiritual heresy.

Do, tell me please *in a letter* the words you told me about the Koran. "Every word of it is true" is it? I forgot them, and want really with my usual impudence to place them at the beginning.

I enclose fifty c. for Mary. I forgot to pay her for her last washing and she must think me mean.

God bless both of you Do let us hear if it were but one word in answer. —When will Beardsley send me the rest of my portraits? Please order him two dozens more of those with the cigarette in the hand, only bigger if he can do them. I will enclose you a post office order for $8-.50 in my next, if you answer me that he is on work at them. I suppose by the $13 he has charged me for the three dozens that every extra dozen will be $4–25. Will you enquire please.

God *re*bless you.

Sincerely and truly yours
H P Blavatsky

NOTES:

1. From the punchline of a shaggy-dog story Hiram Corson told HPB (*Unpublished Letters* 237–8), which she enjoyed, repeated, and allud-

ed to several time in her correspondence with the Corsons. The Corson son, Eugene, recounts it thus:

> The story goes back to my youth and shows H.P.B.'s sense of humour. The story as told by my father was something like this. The incident occurred in a large establishment in Philadelphia. The place was about to be closed up for the day, and my father with several others were discussing omens and perhaps other mysterious subjects. The Irish janitor was standing by evidently much interested. Suddenly he made bold to interrupt the talk, and this is what he said: "Gentlemen, pardon me for interrupting you, but I can tell you about a wonderful omen that happened to me. I was living in the city of Limerick with my wife's sister's niece, when my wife's sister's niece's child was taken very ill in the night, and I was sent out to get a doctor, and while on my way to the doctor's, I saw a man on the opposite side of the street enter a chemist's shop; *and that night my wife's sister's niece's child died!*"

2. Mary K. Neff (marginalia in her copy of *Unpublished Letters* now in the Archives of the Theosophical Society in America, Wheaton, Illinois) observes that on October 12, Mrs. Corson wrote to HPB, complaining of the weather, which was snowing and raining, so they could not go out to give HPB's order to Beardsley, but they had mailed HPB's boots to her. Mrs. Corson also wrote: "My husband does homage to your memory by smoking cigarettes—it's true!"

3. The reference to finding books at Mr. Ditson's and the following remark "Olcott wants me to go *home*" both suggest that HPB did not return directly from the Corson's to her New York residence, but stopped on the way to visit George Leighton Ditson. That suggestion is reinforced by the following remark from Mrs. Corson's October 12 letter to HPB: "When you are back in N.Y. I'll write you a long letter." Nothing else is known about a visit of HPB to G. L. Ditson, but on the basis of this evidence, Mary K. Neff (marginalia) believes this letter was written from Ditson's house.

4. Handwriting unclear; possibly "R." Higgins's first name, however, was Godfrey.

5. Mary K. Neff (marginalia) reports that Mrs. Corson writes in her October 12 letter: "I've finished my part of the translation. . . . If you have too much to do, I am quite willing to translate your part too, or part of it."

6. The letter, dated October 8, 1875, from Edwin Wyndham Lawry, describes an event he witnessed in India, which was the interment for four weeks followed by the resuscitation of a magician named Meechum Doss. The letter headed "Buried for a Month: A Trance Medium among the Indian Jugglers" (*New York World*, October 13, 1875, 6/3-4) has this introduction: "A dispute has arisen in Spiritual and Theosophic circles as to the possible duration of a 'mediumistic trance,' or coma. The account which follows was written for the information of Col. H. S. Olcott, one of the disputants, in the form of a private letter, by a gentleman who, at the time of the occurrence described, was a major on the general staff in the British Army."

7. The *Banner of Light* 38 (October 9, 1875) contained two articles on the question of the nature of the spiritual intelligences communicating through mediums and otherwise: Emma Hardinge Britten's article "What Spirits Are Amongst Us?" (page 1) and S. B. Brittan's article "Colonel Olcott and Spiritualism" (page 8), both of which commented on two letters by Olcott in the *New York Tribune* (August 30 and September 17). In the second of Olcott's letters, "Spiritualism Rampant," which is reprinted immediately before S. B. Brittan's response, Olcott states his belief that some spirit communications are genuinely from disembodied human beings but that most of them are due to elementals. Emma Hardinge Britten, while speaking with high regard of Olcott, expresses her opinion that all mediumistic communications and materializations in human form are in origin human, either deceased or living. The bulk of her article, however, is testimony to the reality of elemental spirits, with a number of personal accounts of her contacts with them. S. B. Brittan's communication is a wide-ranging, often ad hominem attack on Olcott; its treatment of the subject of elementals is dismissive, tracing them "through the dismal superstition of the past, to the demonologists of the Mediæval Ages."

DATE: HPB left the Corsons in Ithaca by October 11, 1875, or somewhat earlier, and she refers to two earlier letters written presumably after her visit there, so this letter is likely to have been written no earlier than mid October. The statement that "the boots are here" suggests this letter was after Mrs. Corson's October 12 letter saying they had mailed HPB's boots to her (note 2). The Society's bylaws were considered at a meeting on October 16 and adopted on October 30, so HPB's promise to send them to Corson also suggests a date of mid October. HPB refers to a letter by Corson in the *New York World* (note 6), published on October 13 and to articles in "the last" issue of the *Banner of Light* published on October 9 (note 7). As the *Banner* was at the time a weekly publication, this letter must have been written between October 13 and October 16.

SOURCE: Transcribed from a microfilm and a photocopy of the original in the HPB Library. Published in *Unpublished Letters* 170–1.

Letter 58

To V. de Zhelihovsky   *[late 1875 or thereafter]*

Humanity has lost its faith and its higher ideals; materialism and pseudo-science have slain them. The children of this age have no longer faith; they demand proof, proof founded on a scientific basis—and they shall have it. Theosophy, the source of all human religions, will give it to them.

DATE: Although HPB used the term "theosophy" in a general sense as early as February 16, 1875 (letter 21), its use here in connection with "proof founded on a scientific basis" suggests the activities that gave rise to the founding of the Theosophical Society and so suggests a date of the final months of 1875 or later.

SOURCE: Russian original unavailable. Copied from a translation in *Lucifer* 15 (Dec. 1894): 274.

Introduction to Letter 59

The following letter to the English clergyman and Spiritualist Stainton Moses survives only as a transcription in a manuscript commonplace book (see the source note following the letter). The handwriting is sometimes difficult to decipher; capitalization and punctuation are erratic. Many such anomalies, as well as the misspellings, are doubtless attributable to the transcriber because other entries in the commonplace book have the same characteristics, which are not typical of HPB's autograph letters. The general tenor of the text can be accepted as HPB's but the formal oddities are likely to be the transcriber's rather than hers. Since, however, there is no way to know certainly what can be attributed to HPB and what to the transcriber, the text below aims at a faithful reproduction of that in the commonplace book, although its text is obviously corrupt.

Letter 59

To S. Moses   *November 16, 1875*
                                                                          New York

My dear Sir

I feel guilty indeed towards you. I have received your first letters, on a visit to Prof Corson & wife at Ithica Connelt [*i.e.,* Ithaca, Cornell] University, and was so busy at the time that I had actually no time to acknowledge your favor—I did not wish to make of it merely an interchange of polite ceremonies, for my object in writing you, was to give you all the information that was in my power, and having my book to attend to at the time busy in the university library I felt unable to collect two ideas—now I just received your second letter and the pangs of smitten conscience proved so powerful that I intend to devote you this day and so will give all I *can*—There are certain subjects which I am not at liberty to mention—neither will you ask me to give you on them any information

Before I begin answering your questions I beg leave to take—Sir Lt Bulwers [*i.e.,* Bulwer-Lytton's] part—He was an *adept* and kept it secret—first for fear [of] ridicule—for it seems that [is] the most dreaded weapon in your 19th century—and then because his vows would not allow him to express himself plainer than he did—he might have supped on pork chops for all I know—and perhaps they were under-done—but no chops either raw or reduced to cinders will prevent you if ever you are initiated to see the *Dweller of the T[h]reshold*—and the Dweller is far from being a welcome or agreeable visitor I can assure you—

You offer me a good many questions—and if necessary I will answer them all—but will you understand me? not that I doubt your intelligence but I doubt two things first my ability to express them—and second the aptitude of any one in this world to understand tail when he has no idea of a head—learning must come gradually—you have to learn the A.B.C before you can spell, and spell before you can read fluently—and though you may read fluently you may understand what you read in the wrong way—and be worse off than ever—

I am ready to stake my life—though it is not worth much for me—that the most illiterate of our fakeers knows *practically* more than all your Tyndal's and Huxleys put together—he will not be able to give a theoretical description of a fire mist—as the former does but he may teach Mr Tyndal what things were created out of the fire mist—what it is good for—and how he could produce it perhaps on a small scale—without any paraphernalia of science and useless apparatus—a Brahim yoggi will not loose his time by splitting his brains over the probable evolution of our race—but he will take you to an aperture in a dark room and tell you "see for yourself"—

Then Mr Darwin or Wallace may perhaps *see* how at the beginning of time "the Spirit moved upon the face of the waters" in total darkness *for us*—in Divine self-radiancy for Himself—Mr Darwin might discern perhaps the chaos of the ancients—our modern ether *the first matter*—For it was existent before man—

This is the En soph—from his outward aspect the *darkness* before the *light*—the Orphic night "O Night thou blackness of the golden stars [*or* stairs]"[1] out of this darkness the Invisible remote Maker or Chaos, all things that are in this world came out as of a primal source, the Matrix as the Caballists call it—

Nature has two extremes between the two there is a middle substance or nature—man in his natural state is in this middle nature—where lurk the elementary future men of the Earths (plural if you please) rude sketches of men from different planets—you do not suppose we are the only inhabitants on an inhabited planet do you?

From this elementary state man must recede to one extreme or the other either corruption in his grave where he rots away, or to a spiritual glorious condition Now listen well—the human earthly body must change i.e die, for death is the transformation of the body to a more perfected shape materially and the man properly has nothing to do with it—towards the end of his life—but the inner man— the real one (not his mask) is not so well off as his body— for whilst the latter is an irresponsible matter or substance— gets through various transformations always becoming more perfect—the spiritual man is either translated like Enoch and Elias to the higher state, or falls down lower than an elementary again—

There is an evolution and Darwin is right but not as he understands it—if science searched *both ways* as the Chaldean primeval sages did, she would be better off— there's an evolution for spiritual nature as for the material one—when professor Draper says in his "Conflict" "theres no such thing as a sudden creation"—a sudden strange appearance, but there is a slow Metamorphosis a slow development from a pre-existent form"—this great scientist only repeats what Hermes Trismegistus (or Enoch or Abraham for the[y] are all one) said many thousand years before him—and he learned it from the lips of nature herself—for "He walked with God"[2]

Remember what Orpheus "De verbo sacro"[3] nemo illus [*i.e.*, illud], nisi chaldaeo de sanguine quiddam [*i.e.*, quidam] progenitus vidit" [*Ln.* "Concerning the holy word," no one has seen that, except someone born of Chaldean blood], and this man descended of the Chaldean blood was Abraham, or Brahma, or Enoch, or Hermes Trismegistus, or Thaut or Thutii[4]—take Higgin's Anacalypsis—see what he says of Abraham being Brahma[5]—and he is right so far but not further.

The Bible the old Testament is a real Cabala and the Apocalypse gives the key of it—the same with the Vedas—and the numbers of Pythagoras the same with Appollinus of Tyane [i.e., Apollonius of Tyana] and the Apocrypha (sun [i.e., some] of them at least, Christianity is a hideous skeleton of paganism and Judaism, with the spirit having fled from it from the first century—this spirit of truth is now manifesting itself in the spiritual phenomena again, but it can never reenter the once abandoned skeleton—

It remains for us to build for him a new Temple—we must first understand the great magical axiom which says "Ex invisibili factum est visibili" [Ln. From the invisible, the visible has been made]

The Spirit moving upon the face of the water Is the one that none of us will ever know before we get so purified as to be able to behold her—the Adonai themselves never saw him—and Hermes, or Brahma, or Enoch saw him but through the Adonai—who was himself but a cloud of fire—

The Fire worshippers were no fools they adored the spirit in its only visible form—the Chaos or Ether—science goes against theology—for the latter repeating like a parrot a word the meaning of which the clergy do not understand and so take it literally—theology says that God created all out of nothing—

Does science know better than Theology from whom and how that seed which we call first matter for want of a better name proceeded—"God created out of nothing something" and science grins—yes but that something which proceeded from nothing was created one thing in which all things were contained—every being celestial and

Terrestrial, and this first something was but a cloud or
darkness—for the latter is matter to—which condensed
into matter—and this water or chaos or Ether—is the store-
house of everything in the universe—but you ask science or
theology, what was that nothing out of which the first
principle the Creator of all and everything was made—It is
indeed as the Rosicrucians say with "Robertus Fluctibus"
[*i.e.*, Robert Fludd] ["]nihil quo ad nos" [*Ln.* nothingness by
which to us].[6]

Will then let us leave it alone—and not quarrel over it
Dionysius expressed it perfectly when he said it is nothing
that was created or of those things that are and nothing of
that which thou dost call nothing, that is of those things
which are not—in thy empty destructive sense. "But by
your leave it is a *true thing*—it is that transcendant essence
whose *theology* is *negative*, as says Eugenius Philalithes—and
was known to the primitive Church, and to Christ or Jesus
rather—but is now lost "to know nothing is the happiest
life" said Cornelius Agrippa for to know this nothing is
life eternal—

This nothing is a Cabalistical name for God—and so far
church is right unconsciously when she says that everything was created out of nothing—for the universe cannot
certainly be an offspring of blind chance all this does not
answer your questions—

I did not mean to say to you that Spirits (Elementary)
were created out of or by the perpetual and universal motion of cosmic matter—as this used is understood by science
but of what might be called the essence of it—Their creation
is like our Creation to science a mystery—when you become
an adept you will learn it without me teaching you

Enough that they do exist and are created and can communicate with us a great deal easier than the disembodied
men and women or immortal spirits it is easy to understand why the like attracts like ethereal as they are and

invisible they are more matter than ourselves—the more terrestrial the more sinful we are—the more we attract these material beings created out of this cosmic matter—but over which substance "the Spirit who moved on the face of the water" did not spread his Divine Ether as yet—thus conferring on them immortality the Adonai and Elohim—did not present them to Him to breathe in their nostrils the breath of Immortal Life—they are of the middle nature of which I spoke above—

A man is a Trinity like the essence of God when man dies, as soon as he dropped off his body which must decay and so become more perfect his Spiritual or sideral body takes place of his old Terrestrial body—and a new still more Ethereal envelope is given him—to cover the Divine ray of his *Augoeides* his soul or the real self—who waits during his endless transmigrations until he becomes absorbed in God or nothing—

This part of himself the Augoeides is the Cabalistic nothing, or a particle of God—for being a particle and not the whole (for how can the endless and boundless be a whole)? It is not the less divine for it—it is not the less God—as a flame borrowed from a light or candle if you like will not diminish if you ignite at this mother flame, millions and myriads of other flames—

The sublime Hindoo doctrine of Emanation and absorption was never rightly understood Budhism is an Esoteric religion and only give it vital life—or rather resurrect it in the Elementary foetus and endow sometimes with much of their vices—the astral body of the child—the second person of the Trinity—but with his soul neither elementary or Father or Mother have aught to do—

His Augoeides is a spark of the great fire, the En soph—the invisible nothing—it is this Trinity in man which puzzles so much the scientist for they can hardly admit of a duality in man—the poor psychologists let alone the

Trinity—and thus physiologists and psychologists, and anthropologists—all scream annihilation and incomprehensible—and come to a dead stop—whereas if they only studied the chaldean Book of numbers the analogies and numbers of Pythagoras, the Books of Hermes and so forth they would learn the value of the Hermetic axiom "quod est superius, est sicut ad quod est inferius" as above so is it beneath and vice versa—

I see you ask a good many questions which I cannot answer you—not because as I told you—you would not understand me bye and bye—but it would be useless for you—you would not realise it—I make an experiment if you show me candidly and honestly that you understood all I wrote above—I will tell you more—but I cannot begin by the end—now in schin [the Hebrew letter shin] שׁ is contained *all* the astral light is the alpha and omega—I can tell you so much not more, what you received about elementary spirits, was not intended for you at first, but for some one who studies already for several years Col: Oldcott asked me to send it to you and I did—copying it as it was from the Treatise or M.S.S—you are a clairvoyant and have direct communications with spirits—perhaps you may see some of the Brotherhood—I mean the one I belong to—not of Luxor—for Luxor is but an adopted name for the committee.

I think in your first letter which I cannot find at the present moment you tell me something of a certain gentleman who wants to know to what lodge I belong—it is certainly not to the Rosicrucians—as I said to every one on the article to Hiram[7]—It is a secret Lodge in the East perhaps they are the Brotherhood Mejnour speaks about in Zannoni—

Believe me dear Sir that if I do not say more it is not because I do not want to tell you. Col Oldcott knows as little as you do—but he has faith and knows me—he knows I am incapable of deceit or deliberate falsehood—Except receiving a few letters from the Brothers and meeting one or two occasionally—he is utterly in the dark—Judge me by the works I do not by my words.

To night is the inaugration meeting of our Theosophical society[8] and Olcott is busy with his address for he is elected President and poor me corresponding secretary of the society time will show you can always write me to the p.o. box of the society 4335—

I wish you would do me the favour of asking one of your best *spirits* to answer me two or three mental questions—I have stored for him in my head he knows—then I will tell you something very interesting for you

Believe me
truly and faithfully yours
M. P. Blavatsky

[The following is a continuation on the same page of the manuscript commonplace book. It may be a postscript to this letter, or it may be a different communication. Since it is in the section of the manuscript book identified as "Corpus of letters from Col Olcott and Madame Blavatsky," it is presumably by HPB.]

What did you think of seeing when you looked so hard out of the opened window in the country. I think it was a friday or a Saturday evening it was the emanation of the water—did you remark anything

You will find much of what I write in Magie [*i.e.,* Magia] Adamica by Eugenius Philalethes. I see you do not understand it rightly—he did not even finish it I explained several passages of it—of the astral light—

[The foregoing text ends on about the top third of manuscript page 102, the remainder of the page being blank. The following text begins at the top of manuscript page 103, but appears to be a continuation or perhaps from subsequent communications:]

The astral light? yes it is the spirit world in one sense, or rather a picture gallery it is, where all that [blank space], is and will be imbeded [sic] for ever and cannot be erased until the density of your good actions overpowers by the impressable law of compensation the colours with which your evil actions are pictured, and the picture of the good takes the place of the picture of the evil—but you yourself can never disappear from the astral light—for there is your future eternity—as there was your past eternity—for you ever were and ever will be—the astral Light is the Book of Life, in Sr John's apocalypse, it is the memory of God—or first primal cause (the nothing?) the rediculous [sic] supposition of science that the first cause ever creating new souls—since soul is an active principle, is thereby always augmenting or increasing the totality of force, has nothing to do with truth—when science gets a true conception, of what is this first matter, then they may speak and give their opinions, 'till then let them play at hide and seek with physiology and leave psychology alone. Read the "unseen universe" and what the author says of the future "may be" and "perhaps" and possibilities contained in the Ether they the scientists discovered? take all for granted and thousand times more, you will be on the path of truth on the treshold of it. Did you see Mr Massey I gave him a portrait for you—he will tell you about a book I am writing perhaps you may learn something in it perhaps not—you cannot conceive you say of the union of an elementary with an infants unborn body—why not?—how do you conceive of the death of a man here and his immediate birth in the spirit world? an elementary spirit dies and his matter which looks spiritual to us is absorbed by the foetus which attracts him—these elementary [sic] once disembodied in their way are attracted within the current of human terrestrial world—as our spiritual bodies are attracted towards the spiritual world as you call it—in a higher sphere—I say *higher* only in the sense of that it is more ethereal and less material sometimes it is a great deal lower) [sic] all is evolution in the universe[.] The elementary furnish the primeval cosmic matter the Father and Mother fashion it unconsciously if they were [blank space] they would give it the form they like—and so pass to the foetus their defects or their perfections, depends on chance and under the influence of what star you are born dont laugh you will learn some day of the truth of it.

[The foregoing text ends at the top quarter of manuscript page 105, the remainder of the page being blank. The following, beginning at the top of page 106, may be from a different communication:]

Not even Max Muller is able to understand it, alone the adepts have the secret key to it—that is why Brahmins and faquirs will produce seeming miracles—which no one will think but supernatural, while it is the oriente essence of the natural man is called the microcosm of the macrocosm—and so he is—his body—his spirit and his soul—the Trinity of the Great first trinity—the Terrestrial log ignited and flaming away, the cabalistic fire within it—abode of the Salamanders and the pure divine ethereal fire the essence to be sought still deeper and still more invisible incomprehensible regions why wonder and deny that man possesses within himself the attributes of God the first cause? read Paracelsus and Van Helmont—read Cornelius Agrippa and the Alchymists if do not understand the terms therein I will explain you as far as possible—as much as I will be allowed to only remember that you being immortal are a God and the more you absorb within yourself of your Augoeides the more will you feel your God like power developed remember [? handwriting unclear] Socrates who said Man know thyself there are no miracles in the world they do not exist, and cannot be for it would destroy in one second the universe which exists in harmony alone, it is as if you destroyed the movement within a watch it will stop, the centripetal force must not outweigh for the weight of one hair, or depress by one line the centrifugal one, or the world would be destroyed—how is it then that for over 4000 years we have the constant testimony of witnesses of Miracles having been performed, why is it that one man produces them either consciously or otherwise—and another one denies them and is unable to move a straw from its place—

The greatest caballist of the world (for he was the purest) taught you well; how is it you do not understand his words for 19 cent you are quarrelling over them—Faith and will power that's all—every man is a naturally born magician, a divine one too: comes the devil the sin [one word is unclear] ne[s]cience of matter not the horny gentleman—and blinds that man to his own powers once the communication between yourself the Augoeides, above and you the body interrupted or so dark[e]ned that its rays are unable to reach your reasoning powers you become at once a poor helpless mortal

Now can you doubt but we preserve our individuality through the whole of the endless series of evolution from one sphere to another—do not believe in the Exoteric religion, seek truth in the Esoteric one except christianity they are all Esoteric—

[In the manuscript commonplace book, there follows, beginning at the top of page 109, an essay on "Elementary Spirits," which is not attributed to HPB in the index (*i.e.,* table of contents) of the commonplace book. It is based on Éliphas Lévi's *Rituel de la haute magie* (1856), first translated into English by A. E. Waite in 1898, in which the source of the essay corresponds to part 2, chapter 4, "The Conjuration of the Four." The essay was placed after the foregoing material in the commonplace book perhaps because its subject continues the reference to "elementary spirits" in HPB's letter.]

NOTES:

1. The source of this quotation is unidentified.

2. "And Enoch lived sixty and five years, and begat Methuselah: and Enoch walked with God after he begat Methuselah three hundred years, and begat sons and daughters: and the days of Enoch were three hundred sixty and five years: and Enoch walked with God: and he was not: for God took him." (Genesis 5.21–4)

3. The sense is perhaps something like "Remember what Orpheus [said in] 'De verbo sacro':" but the source is unidentified.

4. Tehuti or Thoth, the Egyptian God of Wisdom.

5. In his *Anacalypsis* (2:139, 257), Godfrey Higgins avers that Abraham was a Brahmin and that Ur of the Chaldees was in India.

6. The subject and verb of the quotation are lacking. It may be something like "The nothingness from which (the first principle comes) to us," but any such expansion is speculative.

7. "A Few Questions to 'Hiraf'," *Spiritual Scientist*, July 15 and 22, 1875 (*CW* 1:101–8).

8. The inaugural meeting of the Society was November 17, 1875. HPB may have been writing the letter late at night or for some other reason anticipated the following day, or else the letter was misdated either by her or by the commonplace-book copier.

SOURCE: Original unavailable. Copied from a transcription in the Francis G. Irwin and Herbert Irwin manuscript commonplace book *Rosicrucian Miscellanea* (1878), pp. 88–108, in the United Grand Lodge of England Library, Freemason's Hall, London. Pages 68–108 of the manuscript are identified in its index (*i.e.,* table of contents) as "Corpus of letters from Col Olcott and Madame Blavatsky." Reproduced with permission from The Library and Museum Charitable Trust, United Grand Lodge of England.

⌒

Letter 60

To A. N. Aksakoff   *December 1, 1875*

All phenomena are produced by currents of the astral light or the ether of the chemists. Remember Plutarch, high priest of the temple of Apollo, and his *oracular* subterranean exhalations, under the intoxication of which the priestesses prophesied. The atmosphere around us is full of spirits of various kinds. There is not a single empty spot in the world, for nature abhors vacuum and nonbeing, as Hermes says. It is possible to understand the phenomena of the present day only by studying the ancient theurgists such as Iamblichus, Porphyry, Plotinus, and others.

SOURCE: Russian original unavailable. Translated by Boris de Zirkoff from Solovyov's *Sovremennaya* 276. Another English translation by Walter Leaf in *Modern Priestess* 260.

〜

Letter 61

To A. N. Aksakoff   *December 6, 1875*

All the spiritists even in England are disturbed now about this Theosophical Society, because they know that I hatched it; but, if we had not started it, we should never in our lives have thought of interesting ourselves in spiritism or studying it. And we already have two learned professors from Boston as members. Several reverend clergymen of diverse colors and many notables. It is the same spiritualism, but under another name. Now you will see we shall start the most learned investigations. Our Vice Treasurer, Newton, is a millionaire and President of the New York Spiritualists. But the spiritists do not understand what is for their own good. I have talked to them as much as I can—but nothing came of it. It is a heresy. And there is another thing for which the public bears us a grudge: the rules of the Society are so strict that it is impossible for a man who has been associated in any disreputable matter to become a member. No free lovers or atheists or positivists are admitted to the Society.

SOURCE: Russian original unavailable. Translated by Boris de Zirkoff from Solovyov's *Sovremennaya* 280. Another English translation by Walter Leaf in *Modern Priestess* 265.

⌒

Letter 62

To V. de Zhelihovsky [late 1875 or early 1876]

Well, Vera, believe it or not, some enchantment is upon me. You can hardly imagine in what a charmed world of pictures I live! . . . I am writing *Isis;* not writing, rather copying out and drawing that which *she personally* is showing me. Really, it seems to me as if the ancient Goddess of Beauty in person leads me through all the lands of bygone centuries which I have to describe. I am sitting with my eyes open and, to all appearances, see and hear everything real and actual around me; and yet at the same time I see and hear *that which I write*. I feel short of breath; I am afraid to make the slightest movement, for fear the spell might be broken. . . . Slowly century after century, image after image, float out of nowhere and pass before me as if in a magic panorama; and meanwhile I put them together in my mind, fitting in epochs and dates, and know *positively* there *can be no mistake*. Races and nations, countries and cities, long vanished in the darkness of the pre-historic past, emerge and disappear, giving place to others; and then I am told the consecutive dates. Hoary antiquity gives room to historical periods; myths are explained to me by means of events and people who actually existed, and every event which is at all remarkable, every newly-turned leaf of this many-colored book of life, impresses itself on my brain with photographic accuracy. My own conceptions and calculations appear to me later on as the separate colored pieces of different shapes in the game which is called *casse-tête* [*Fr.* brain teaser, puzzle]. I too gather them together and try to match them one with the other, and in the end there always comes out something geometrically correct. . . . It stands to reason, it is not I who do it all, but my *Ego*, the highest principles that live in me; and even then with the help of my *Guru*, my teacher, who helps me in everything. If I happen to forget something, all I have to do is to address him, or another one like him, in thought, and what I had forgotten emerges once more before my eyes, sometimes whole tables of numbers and long inventories of events passing before me. *They remember everything. They know everything.* . . . Without them, whence would my knowledge come?

. . . Both in my waking state and, it seems, in my sleep, I am occupied with my Isis! I look and observe, and am filled with delight over that which I see, as her veil becomes thinner and thinner and falls away before my very eyes! . . . It is already almost three years since pictures of the past, daily and nightly, have hovered around me. . . .

DATE: On September 20, 1875 (letter 55), the working title of the manuscript that was to become *Isis Unveiled* was *Skeleton Key to Mysterious Gates*, so this letter must postdate that one. However, the enthusiasm it expresses suggests an early stage in the composition, so sometime in late 1875 or early 1876 seems likely.

SOURCE: Russian original unavailable. Translated by Boris de Zirkoff from the *Russkoye Obozreniye* 6 (Nov. 1891): 274 and *Rebus* 2 (Dec. 4, 1883): 430. The *Rebus* text has a few lines that differ from the version in *Russkoye Obozreniye*. Other quite different English translations in *Incidents* 206–8; *Path* (NY) 9 (Jan. 1895): 300–1; *Path* (London) 3 (Dec. 1912): 213–4; and "Mystical History" 63–4.

Letter 63

To V. de Zhelihovsky   *[late 1875 or early 1876]*

See, how cleverly he[1] proves that people are mistaken when they say that we disseminate old superstitions and prejudices, and that a body of people who are teaching the study of human nature by means of an investigation of its moral and spiritual forces, and are showing how to attain enduring bliss as a result of the fullest unfoldment of these forces, is the chief enemy, not only of gross materialism, but also of every foolish prejudice and myth worship. . . . Spiritualism is an experimental science. Its development, which is the aim of the Theosophical Society, will make it possible at long last to find the foundation of a true philosophy. Truth is one and is higher than all else! Theosophy is bound to wipe out such meaningless expressions, as "miracle" or the "supernatural"! . . . Everything in nature is natural, but not everything is known. And there is nothing more wonderful than its powers, whether hidden or revealed. Spiritualism—i.e., the spiritual powers of humanity and a deeper knowledge of the psychical aspects of being, which we Theosophists teach, will cure the centuries-old evils of religious strifes, owing to which the faith of men in the sacred and immemorial truths of immortality and the reward for merit is disappearing. Wallace speaks the truth when he says that spiritualism will deserve the sympathy of moralists, philosophers, and even politicians, and of everyone who desires the perfecting of our society and our life.

NOTE:

1. Presumably Alfred Russel Wallace, to whose book *On Miracles and Modern Spiritualism* HPB is probably referring.

DATE: Although Wallace published periodical articles earlier, the appearance of his book *On Miracles and Modern Spiritualism* in 1875 attracted wide attention. It is likely that this letter was written shortly thereafter, hence in late 1875 or early 1876.

SOURCE: Russian original unavailable. Translated by Boris de Zirkoff from *Russkoye Obozreniye* 2 (Nov. 1891): 259. Another English translation in *Path* (NY) 9 (Feb. 1895): 381.

⌒

The Founding of the Theosophical Society and Controversy over the Inaugural Address

An early effort to establish an organization for the investigation of Spiritualistic phenomena did not succeed. Olcott (*ODL* 1:25–26, 34) writes of his and HPB's attempt:

> In May, 1875, I was engaged in trying to organise at New York with her concurrence a private investigating committee under the title of the "Miracle Club." In the *Scrap-book* (Vol. I.) she writes about it:
>
> "An attempt is consequence of orders received from T* B* (a Master) through P. (an Elemental) personating John King. Ordered to begin telling the public the truth about the phenomena and their mediums. And now my martyrdom will begin! I shall have all the Spiritualists against me, in addition to the Christians and the Sceptics. Thy will, oh M., be done. H. P. B."
>
> The plan was to keep closed doors to all save the members of the Club, who were forbidden to divulge even the place of meeting. "All the manifestations, including materisations, to occur in the light, and without a cabinet." [*Spiritual Scientist*, May 19, 1876.] ... [But] her intended medium for the Miracle Club ... utterly failed us and so precluded my completing the organisation. ...
>
> ... The intended medium belonged to a most respectable family, and talked so honestly that we thought we had secured a prize. He proved to be penniless, and as H. P. B. in his hour of greatest need had no money to spare, she pawned her long gold chain and gave him the proceeds. That wretch not only failed utterly as a medium, but was also

reported to us as having spread calumnies against the one who had done him kindness. And such was her experience to the end of her life.

In August 1875, HPB moved to 46 Irving Place in New York City, where she held soirees attended by "numbers of bright, clever people of occult leanings . . . scientific men, philologists, authors, antiquarians, broad-minded clergymen, lawyers, and doctors, some very well known Spiritualists, and one or two gentlemen journalists attached to metropolitan papers, only too eager to make good 'copy' out of the business" (*ODL* 114). Among those in attendance were Henry S. Olcott, Charles Sotheran, and William Quan Judge. The subjects discussed, according to another participant, Unitarian clergyman J. H. Wiggin, ranged over such diverse topics as "the phallic element in religions; recent wonders among the mediums; history; the souls of flowers; Italian character; the strangeness of travel; chemistry; poetry; Nature's trinity; Romanism; gravitation; the Carbonari; jugglery; Crookes's new discoveries about the force of light; the literature of Magic . . . topics of animated discussion lasting until after midnight" (quoted in *ODL* 115).

It was at one of those soirees that the idea of starting the Theosophical Society was brought forward. On September 7, George H. Felt, an architect and engineer, gave a talk on "The Lost Canon of Proportion of the Egyptians, Greeks, and Romans." Felt presented a diagram consisting of a circle, squares, triangles, and a pentagon, which he said defined the architectural proportions of the Egyptian and Classical worlds. He also claimed to be able to duplicate the feats of ancient Egyptian priests in evoking elemental spirits and offered to demonstrate the process and instruct others in it.

In the discussion that followed, Olcott proposed the formation of a society for such study and more particularly "for the collection and diffusion of knowledge; for occult research, and the study and dissemination of ancient philosophical and theosophical ideas; one of the first steps was to collect a library" (*ODL* 120). The company—which included, in addition to HPB and Olcott, also the visiting Englishman C. C. Massey, Emma Hardinge Britten, William Quan Judge, and others—chose Olcott as chairman. The meeting continued the following evening, when Olcott appointed a committee to draw up rules for the new organization.

On September 13, the company met again in HPB's rooms and agreed upon the name "Theosophical Society" for the organization. A month later, on October 16, another meeting was held at the home of Emma Hardinge Britten, 206 West 38 Street, when bylaws were presented. On October 30, they met again at the Britten house to adopt the bylaws and elect officers, including Olcott as President and HPB as Corresponding Secretary. Meeting space having been rented at Mott Memorial Hall, 64 Madison Avenue, on November 17 the members assembled there to hear Olcott read his inaugural address.

The address did what is expected on such occasions: it viewed with alarm, pointed with pride, and issued a clarion call. Its clarion presented a vision of the role of the Theosophical Society in contemporary culture (Olcott, "Inaugural Address" 502–4):

> In future times, when the impartial historian shall write an account of the progress of religious ideas in the present century, the formation of the Theosophical Society, whose first meeting under its formal declaration of principles we are now attending, will not pass unnoticed. . . . It has sounded in the ears of some of the leaders of the contending forces of theology and science, like the distant blast of a trumpet to the struggling armies in a battle. . . .
>
> The present small number of its members is not to be considered at all in judging of its probable career. Eighteen hundred and seventy odd years ago, the whole Christian Church could be contained within a Galilean fisherman's hut . . . .
>
> No, it is not a question of numbers how great an effect this Society will have upon religious thought—I will go further, and say, upon the science and philosophy of the age: great events sometimes come from far more modest beginnings.

Olcott's enthusiasm in carrying out all three of those functions of issuing a clarion call, pointing with pride, and viewing with alarm generated, however, some problems. In particular, Olcott's alarmed view was strongly critical of Spiritualism, as the following extracts (503, 506–7) show:

The spiritualists began, a few weeks ago, with voluminous and angry protests against its [the Theosophical Society's] promoters, as seeking to supplant the prevalent democratic relations with the other world by an aristocratic esoterism, and even now, while they seem to be watching our next move with the greatest interest, their press teems with defamatory criticisms. . . .

But when they ["people struggling blindly to emancipate their thought from ecclesiastical despotism"] turn to Spiritualism for comfort and conviction, they encounter such a barrier of imposture, tricky mediums, lying spirits, and revolting social theories, that they recoil with loathing; secretly lamenting the necessity which compels them to do it. . . . so many immoral people have fastened upon the cause, and mediums are being so constantly detected in trickery, that it is almost disreputable to be an open and avowed Spiritualist. The organs of the class apologize for cheating mediums, demanding that skeptics shall overlook the nine instances of fraud and consider the one genuine phenomenon; forgetting that it requires blunt nerves and a strong purpose to dig to the bottom of a muck-heap for the chance of finding something of value there.

Such viewing with alarm did not endear Olcott or his inaugural address to the many Spiritualists who were potential members or at least friends of the new Society. In addition, Olcott pointed with pride in an unfortunate direction. He chose to highlight the promise of George H. Felt to perform an experiment that was to demonstrate the existence of elemental beings—a promise never kept. The address ends with the following peroration, which Olcott lived to regret (516):

The day of reckoning is close at hand, and the name of the Theosophical Society will, if Mr. Felt's experiments result favorably, hold its place in history as that of the body which first exhibited the "Elementary Spirits" in this nineteenth century of conceit and infidelity, even if it be never mentioned for any other reason.

Josephine Ransom (83) comments, "Written in the Scrapbook is one of H. P. B.'s shrewd comments to the effect that these were rash statements—it was 'counting the price of the bear's skin before the beast is slain.'" And Olcott acknowledged in *Old Diary Leaves* (1:137–8) that, in part at least, the address "reads a bit foolish after seventeen years of hard experience," and in particular he observed of the passage on Felt: "Luckily for me, I put in the 'if'; and it might have been better if it had been printed thus—IF."

Among the practicing Spiritualists who took umbrage at Olcott's critical remarks in the inaugural address was Hiram Corson, with whom HPB had been corresponding. He responded with the following letter in the *Banner of Light* 50 (Jan. 8, 1876): 2.

THE THEOSOPHICAL SOCIETY AND
ITS PRESIDENT'S INAUGURAL ADDRESS.

To the Editor of the Banner of Light:

I have recently read the Preamble and By-Laws of the Theosophical Society, organized in the city of New York, October 30th, 1875, and the Inaugural Address of the President of said Society, Col. Henry S. Olcott, delivered at Mott Memorial Hall, in the city of New York, at the first regular meeting of the Society, November 17th, 1875; and, as a believer in Spiritualism as the sheet-anchor of man's belief in immortality, and as the destined fusing and harmonizing principle of the now conflicting elements of the religious and scientific worlds, I beg leave to make a few remarks on the above productions, through the columns of your valuable paper.

And, first, please allow me to say, in a general way, that so much assumption and pretension as are contained within these two small documents, it has not been my fortune to meet with for many a day, in "this nineteenth century of conceit," as President Olcott characterizes it, not withstanding that my reading, outside of my regular line of study, has been very extensive and varied. In the course of their perusal, an ominous threat of one of the witches in Shakespeare's tragedy of Macbeth, kept constantly obtruding itself upon my mind

"But in a sieve I'll thither sail,
And like a rat without a tail,
I'll do, I'll do, and I'll do."

A certain Frenchman of an inquiring turn of mind, was sorely exercised as to *what* the witch was going to do: "vell, *vat vill she do?*" and every reader of an equally inquiring turn of mind must also be sorely exercised, after reading the Preamble and By-Laws of the Theosophical Society, and its President's address, as to what astounding and earth-shaking things are to be done; for there is not the least intimation given of their character nor of the means to be employed, further than that "we'll do, "we'll do, and we'll do."

Once I suspected that the whole thing might be an ironical hoax, and I gave said documents a second reading to ascertain whether such a suspicion could be legitimately supported; but I finally came to the conclusion, having had, besides, the opportunity of frequent conversations, previous to its organization, with one of the leading members of the Society, that it was a *bona fide* movement for the dispersion of the black and ugly clouds of ignorance, error and degrading superstition that have been hanging over the human race ever since "the days when the neoplatonists and the last theurgists of Alexandria were scattered by the murderous hand of Christianity." [Inaugural Address, p. 15.]

Turning first to the "Preamble," we read that the founders of the Theosophical Society "hope, that by going deeper than modern science has hither to done, into the esoteric philosophies of ancient times, they may be enabled to obtain, for themselves and other investigators, proof of the existence of an 'Unseen Universe,' the nature of its inhabitants, if such there be, and the laws which govern them and their relations with mankind."

Now it is hardly necessary to state that the age of "Authority" has gone by, never, it is to be hoped, to return, as it has been fruitful of untold evils to humanity. Science has trained the general mind not to accept anything on "authority;" and however deeply we may study "the esoteric philosophies of ancient times," their doctrines can be accepted only

to the degree that they bear the tests of the modern processes of induction from known and established facts. Outside
of such induction (whatever may be claimed for the faculty
of intuition, and I myself claim a great deal for it), the scientific mind, at least, will accept nothing. If those "esoteric
philosophies" tell us anything of the nature of the inhabitants
of the Unseen Universe, of the laws which govern them, and
of their relations with mankind, said philosophies will be
required to produce and to establish such facts as are cog-
nizable by the human mind, and to confirm the legitimacy
of the inductions leading up therefrom to the principles and
laws which they set forth. The fairness of such a requisition
will be admitted by all enlightened truth-seekers of the present day; by all who are acquainted with the conditions of
positive knowledge.

Further on we read: "The Spiritualists, who professed to
be in constant relations with the departed, are unable to agree
upon a system of philosophy." This is an altogether gratuitous assertion. Spiritualists have not yet *aimed* after the
establishment of a system of philosophy, and, consequently,
it cannot be said that they "are unable to agree." They
haven't tried nor cared to agree. At the same time it should,
in justice, be said, that the teachings of Modern Spiritualism,
disorganized as they are, involve the most beautiful philosophy that the world has ever known. There is material enough
in the last ten numbers of "The Banner of Light," and I don't
name these particular numbers at random, but because they
possess a peculiar and transcendent value—material with at
least as good a claim to authenticity as any, no doubt, that
may be found in the "esoteric philosophies of ancient
times," for the establishment of the soundest philosophy of
life both as to its present and its eternal relations.

Again we read:

"In the United States, the rebellion of the public mind
against ecclesiastical authority has been comparatively more
general than in the parent country, and at the present time,
so inconsiderable has the influence of the Protestant Church
become, that it may almost be said that the conflict is

between the Romanists and the Spiritualists—the former representing the idea of ultramontanism and intolerance; the latter *that of the absolute sovereignty of the individual in the matter of belief as regards their assumed intercourse with a spirit world, and, with many, that of unbridled license in the relations of the sexes.*"

The italics in the above quotation are mine. It is true, indeed, that the Protestant church has become a comparatively insignificant factor in the great product which we call "the age;" and the decline of Protestantism, and the causes of that decline, have been very clearly set forth by the Hon. Robert Dale Owen, in the Address to the Protestant Clergy, with which he prefaces "The Debatable Land," pages 23–181. Every representative of this clergy should read, "not to contradict and confute, but to weigh and consider," this able and dispassionate appeal. But my present business is with the italicized portion of the above extract.

The Spiritualists, it is stated, represent the idea of the absolute sovereignty of the individual in the matter of belief as regards their assumed intercourse with a spirit world, etc.

Now the idea of the absolute sovereignty of the individual, in all matters whatsoever, is implied in the general rejection of "authority," which is, at this day, by all enlightened investigators, mental philosophers, and logicians, claimed to be one of the indispensable conditions under which the mind can free itself from error and work toward truth. And it doth not appear why mere "authority," whether in the form of alleged inspiration, of a decree of an ecclesiastical council, of a papal bull, of an occult philosopher's *ipse dixit*, or in any other form, should be a factor, even the smallest, in the investigation of spiritual things, anymore than in other kinds of truth-seeking, and that without it, "intercourse with a spirit-world" would have to be "assumed." I very much suspect that when that sentence was first penned, it was without the word "assumed." On revising the rough draft, the writer said to himself, with "elementary spirits" in his mind, (and it doesn't matter whether this latter expression be taken literally or metaphorically,) "I'll not give the

wretches credit for *actual* intercourse with the spirit world—
that is the exclusive prerogative of the favored few who have
been initiated into the mysteries of the occult philosophy—
and I'll stick in the word "assumed." It can easily be seen that
this word doesn't come naturally into the current of the
thought: it has been dropped in, manifestly by one who has
just kicked aside a belief in which he had professed himself
well grounded, and become an enthusiastic convert to the
doctrine of elementary spirits. Such a convert, in the first
gush of his enthusiasm, could not believe that common mortals could possibly have anything to do with people from the
other world.[1] Oh, no! what they in their idiocy have believed
to be the spirits of their dear departed, have been nothing
but a set of tricksy Pucks, that inhabit earth's atmosphere

"As thick and numberless
As the gay motes that people the sunbeams."[2]

I come now to consider the last clause of the above extract,
which charges Spiritualists with the doctrine of "unbridled
license in the relations of the sexes." Such a charge should
arouse a burning indignation in the breast of every true
Spiritualist. You, Mr. Editor, in common with all enlightened representatives of Spiritualism, know that it is a base
and wicked lie, a foul slander cast upon a cause that is doing
more than any other agency of the day to bring about purity of sexual relation. It is of a piece with the charge of "intellectual whoredom," advanced by Prof. Tyndall, and which
has recently been so triumphantly refuted by Mr. Epes
Sargent.

I do not consider myself obliged to take into account the
few who, having identified themselves with Spiritualism,
have been carrying on a sort of guerrilla warfare against the
institutions of society. SPIRITUALISM IS IN NO WISE RESPONSIBLE
FOR WHAT SUCH SAY AND DO, ANYMORE THAN GENUINE CHRIS-
TIANITY IS RESPONSIBLE FOR ALL THAT HAS BEEN SAID AND DONE
IN ITS NAME. I deem it sufficient to refer anyone who is disposed to believe the charges that have been made, of "intellectual whoredom" and of "unbridled license in the relations
of the sexes," to that portion of the already vast literature of

Spiritualism which is regarded as best representing its doctrines; or I should be content to refer such an one merely to the numerous weekly organs of the cause that are now published in this country, and in England, France and Germany, and in other parts of the civilized world—organs that are under the necessity even of publishing much that their editors do not approve of. He could not find in them, peer he ever so closely, anything substantiating the charge of "unbridled license." If he were to turn to that paper which, of all, is, perhaps, the most free-spoken, namely, The Religio-Philosophical Journal, instead of finding any teachings that would afford the slightest support to the charge, he would find the most emphatic denunciations of the doctrine of Free Love.

Please note the beautiful consistency of the unfounded and basely slanderous charge, with the high flown disavowal contained in the last paragraph of the Preamble:

"The Theosophical Society, disclaiming all pretension to the possession of unusual advantages, all selfish motives, *all disposition to foster deception of any sort, all intent to willfully and causelessly injure any established organization*, invites the fraternal cooperation of such as can realize the importance of its field of labor, and are in sympathy with the objects for which it has been organized."

In the third paragraph from the end we are informed that "the Theosophical Society has been organized in the interest of religion, science, and good morals; *to aid each according to its needs*." It must have a large fund of succor stored away somewhere, if it is going to aid, *according to its needs*, each outside institution that is struggling after life and truth. What a consolation it ought to be to such institution, to know that whenever it comes short of its ends, it can be helped "according to its needs," on application to the Theosophical Society, not withstanding that the society "disclaims all pretension to the possession of unusual advantages."

In the next paragraph we are informed that "the founders being baffled in every attempt to get the desired knowledge in other quarters, turn their faces toward the Orient, whence are derived all systems of religion and philosophy."

On reading this, the words of "Truthful James" came into my mind:

"Is our civilization a failure?

Or is the Caucasian played out?"[3]

Turning now to the President's Inaugural Address, I must say that it exhibits an inflation of paper currency far beyond the wildest dreams of certain financiers who fancy that a plentiful supply of money can be kept up by printing greenbacks. It really seems that the promises of the occult philosophy have turned his head. The Address is nothing but words, words, words. Even if Mr. Olcott were perfectly assured that the Society is destined to do all mighty things, it would be better to wait until it has something more substantial to show than prospective brags. The already, as I fear, too great length of this letter forbids me to site specimens of the sublimity of brag with which the Address abounds. But I cannot refrain from quoting what he says in the concluding paragraph, about the Vice President's promises, and the consequences of their realization:

"Without claiming to be a theurgist, a mesmerist, or a Spiritualist, our Vice President promises, by simple chemical appliances, to exhibit to us, as he has to others before, the races of beings which, invisible to our eyes, people the elements. Think for a moment of this astounding claim! Fancy the consequences of the practical demonstration of its truth, for which Mr. Felt is now preparing the requisite apparatus! What will the church say of a whole world of beings within her territory, but without her jurisdiction? What will the academy say of this crushing proof of an unseen universe given by the most unimaginative of its sciences? What will the Positivists say, who have been prating of the impossibility of their being any entity which cannot be weighed in scales, filtered through funnels, tested with litmus, or carved with a scalpel? What will the Spiritualists say, when through the column of saturated vapor flit the dreadful shapes of beings whom, in their blindness, they have in a thousand cases revered and babbled to as the returning shades of their relatives and friends? Alas! poor Spiritualists—editors and

228

correspondents—who have made themselves jocund over my impudence and apostasy. Alas! sleek scientists, overswollen with the wind of popular applause! The day of reckoning is close at hand, and the name of the Theosophical Society will, if Mr. Felt's experiments result favorably, hold its place in history as that of the body which first exhibited the 'Elementary Spirits' in this nineteenth century of conceit and infidelity, even if it be never mentioned for any other reason!"

How very droll, in the midst of all this swagger, is the conditional clause, "IF Mr. Felt's experiments result favorably"![4] There is, as Touchstone says, "much virtue in *If*."[5]

Hiram Corson
Ithaca, N.Y., 26 December, 1875

NOTES:

1. An allusion to Olcott's book *People from the Other World*.

2. John Milton, *Il Penseroso*, lines 7–8.

3. Francis Bret Harte, "Further Language from Truthful James" (1870).

4. HPB pasted into her Scrapbook 1:111 a clipping from the *Banner of Light* (January 15, 1876) quoting Olcott's Inaugural Address on Felt's promise to exhibit elementals by chemical means, and annotated it: "And Mr. Felt *has done it* in the presence of nine persons in all" (*CW* 1:192–3).

5. William Shakespeare, *As You Like It*, act 5, scene 4, line 108.

Introduction to Letter 64

Olcott replied to Corson in the *Banner of Light* of January 22 (38:1), defending the Theosophical Society and himself, ending with a ninefold statement of his personal beliefs intended to clarify his position with respect to some of Corson's criticisms:

First: I believe in the existence of a First Cause, the source of all things visible and invisible.

Second: I believe in the doctrine of Evolution, and believe that it applies to *both sides of the Universe*—spirit and matter.

It has produced man upon this sphere, and it follows him beyond the death of the body.

Third: I believe that in the course of this Evolution of man, successive forms of spiritual entities were brought into existence, just as there have been a countless succession of physical forms of plant and animal.

Fourth: I believe that, after the death of the physical body, man's spirit survives; and that, under favoring conditions, he can communicate with those whom he has left behind. This manifestation may be made either through mediums or in other ways.

Fifth: I believe, as the result of study and of personal observation of practical experiments, that the human mind can control the occult forces of Nature, and subjugate all spiritual beings lower than himself in the scale of Evolution, just as he has natural dominion over all the lower animals.

Sixth: I regard Modern Spiritualism, in its present form, as only a record of sporadic phenomena; which do not occur except under conditions not of our choosing; which cannot be controlled; and which are accompanied with so much that is contradictory and untruthful, that more investigation is necessary before we can be said to know anything definite about the laws of spiritual intercourse. But, still I believe that, even under such unfavorable conditions as are now furnished us by our uninstructed mediums, disembodied spirits are often drawn into communication with us by the attraction of our intense love for them.

Seventh: I regard Mesmerism and Spiritualism as portions of a broader and a demonstrable science—that of MAGIC. This science was known to the ancient, has been practiced for countless ages, and is now practiced, in the Orient.

Eighth: I believe that the forces known as Animal Magnetism, Odyle, the magnet, psychic force, and the spiritual force, are all various manifestations of the same force—the Astral Light. This is the medium of which our spiritual bodies, the astral bodies of animals, and the vital force of plants, are portions; and the varying vibrations of which (under the name of "Ether,") are severally designated as light, heat, electricity, and chemical action.

Ninth: While I believe that, often, human spirits have appeared to us in materialized form, more frequently a lower order of beings have appeared in the forms of persons who are called dead. Spiritualists have no means of distinguishing between these spiritual beings; Cabalists have, and need never make mistakes.

Before Olcott's defense and confession of belief were published, Blavatsky sought to clarify Olcott's intentions and to soothe Corson's offended response to the inaugural address in the following letter, which she wrote immediately after reading Corson's published letter:

Letter 64

To H. P. Corson   *January 8, 1876*
[letterhead] The Theosophical Society
Mott Memorial Hall
64 Madison Avenue
(P. O. Box 4335)
New York

Happy New Year to both of you!

My dear Mr Corson

Et tu Brute! Well you have given me a nice blow and a very unexpected one. You have obliged me to read over and over Olcotts Inaugural Address, and confess that you are *partially* right. I never read it before, and when he delivered it I was so preoccupied with my own thoughts that I only heard the "spirit" of it not the dead letter. But my dear, dear Mr Corson, believe me that greatly as I value your opinion and much as I know you to be unable of premeditated or conscious injustice you have been *too* hard and too unjust to him, for on my soul, he is the most *fervent* the most *unselfish* and fanatical Spiritualist that ever was.

What is there in his unfortunate English phraseology which makes *him*, an able writer, shape his words so as to be misunderstood by the two thirds of his opponents! My knowledge of the English is so superficial that most likely I do not well understand the value of words. But I am ready to stake my life, that Olcott neither wanted to insult Spiritualism nor mean what you think; for never was his indignation so great as when he learned about the insult offered us by Tyndall—it was greater than mine perhaps. Do not you agree with him in deploring that state of things in American Spiritualism? *You* are not a free lover; hundreds of well educated men and women Spiritualists are *not* free lovers, thousands of them *are*. I can tell you one thing Mʳ Corson, and I swear it to you *on my eternal soul*, that Olcott who was himself not of a very virtuous life as most men are in New York, and committed licentious actions before, since he became a Spiritualist—for *he is* a Spiritualist,—has began to lead the most *ascetic* life. Mʳ Corson, I write this to you as to a gentleman, if not as to a friend,—for now that you are so mad with Theosophists perhaps you do not wish to be any more *my* friend—therefore I write you this in strict confidence, and if you do not believe *me*, write to your old friend Monachesi who is a member of our Society and he will corroborate my words. Olcott *is a fanatic*, so much so, that I am afraid that this abrupt change from a comfortable life, well eating and drinking and indulging in all sort of worldly things, will either bring him to insanity or death. He is getting thinner with every day. He eats no more meat, renounced supper and wine, his only aim in life is to *become purified* as he says, of his *passed life*, of the stains he has inflicted on his soul. I can do nothing with him. I have evoked the spirit of fanaticism in him and now I cruelly repent for this man does nothing by halves; his only object in life he says is to purify American Spiritᵐ of the dirt of free love, to never proceed to hold séances except by making the greatest efforts to secure *pure* mediums of good morality, children or young innocent persons if possible, such selected priestesses vowed to chastity as in times of Theurgy. He is right there, for if we wish to commune with *pure* spirits, we must open them *clean* passages, and offer pure, chanels. You have Mary Andrews, a good, honest, virtuous woman, a mother of a family, but how many have you of such? Think of the New York mediums; ask people what they are, and how can you expect to have any other spirits but unprogressed, vile criminals like the murderer Webster, or Elementaries through those who are so impure. See Home, the best of all physical mediums in Europe. Why, he is positively obsessed by the seven devils! No slander, no diffamation, no lie is too much for him, and, because Olcott views Spiritualism perhaps too exultingly, and expresses himself in too strong terms,—for I agree with you in that—why should people misunderstand him, and accuse him of that, which never entered in his mind? Many and many times, day after day, I repeat to him that he must not brague of what is not done yet. For Felt, though he promised to all the Theosophists to clear the atmosphere chemically and show the *unseen* monsters around us, and though he has done so before a *dozen* witnesses at least, who traduced him and called him a sorcerer, —I do not know *whether* or *when* he will make his promise good. But Olcott is such a sanguine fanatic, so sure of the *other* world, so certain that if he leads a pure life he will be helped by genuine spirits, pure, disembodied men and women, that he speaks of it very foolishly as if it was already demonstrated and done.

My dear Mr Corson, will you doubt me being a Spiritualist? You know my ideas, I have shown you fully what I am and what I think. I told you that I did not think myself good and pure enough to evoke spirits, that I am so wicked that I cannot even control John and I have given him up.

The last evening I passed with you, Mrs Corson gave me a lesson which I will never forget in my life, and the mother, in whom the most sacred feelings were so aroused to indignation by the mere idea of seeing her departed angel mixed up with ex-pirats and unprogressed spirit—*was right*, and since that night she is constantly before my eyes, whenever I am about to fall to the temptation and allow John to speak to some distressed mother, father, brother or some other person who holds the spirit he wants to communicate with as sacred. Forgive my stupid English and *do try* to understand me if you can. Perhaps, I will never see you again, but the warm sincere friendship, the high respect and esteem I feel for both Mrs Corson and yourself will *never* change. You may reject me as unworthy of you; you may, perhaps believe all the calumnies circulated about me, you may become *my enemy*, but I will not change for all that. My book is finished,[1] and it is there you will find all I think. It is no more what it was, when I was writing it in your place than one chapter of twenty or thirty such. I take every phenomenon, every manifestation and try to show Science that not only it is possible, but that it is so and *must be so* in the Nature of things itself. I sent the introductory chapter to Buchanan, and he calls it "grand, gloomy and peculiar," but suggests few changes. I will send him Chapter after Chapter for I have no one in the world to help and show me, where I am wrong and where right, and I will feel grateful to any scientific unprejudiced Spiritualist who will help me in that. At least I am a Spiritualist, and bitter as my last letter[2] is (the Scientist) you can see by it that I *am* a true Spiritualist. Papers slander me, mediums defame me and Spiritualists misunderstand me. What can I do? There is no one in this wide world but hates me, who have never harmed no one knowingly. Well, such is my fate. All the slanders set about me afloat in London and here come from Dr Child and Catholic priests (two of them here). See what Algernon Joy writes about Child and the "London Spiritualist." Notwithstanding every one knows in the Country that the Holmes and he were frauds, he goes on selling in Philadelphia, his "biography of John King" dictated by the *mask* showed by the Holmeses! And Child is an honorary member of the "Lond: Spiritualist," he is one of the most eminent writers and supporters of the "Rel. Phil. Journal" *he* a proved fraud, a *mercenary* humbug! There's justice in Spiritual papers. He makes money by Spiritual frauds and is *honored*. I give my last cent to the Cause, and leave myself no means to bye boots with, and I am slandered and vilified, as if I were the "Mother of Harlots" in person. Did I invent Elementaries? Are they Olcott's and my creation? Such was the firmest belief of Theurgists and mediaeval Occultists. Aksakoff writes me that Prince Dolgorouky, the greatest mesmerizer now living except Dupotet, speaks from 30 years experience with Clairvoyants that they draw a large line of demarcation between *disembodied* genuine Spirits and Elementaries. That they see and describe them, and assure him (without knowing one word of occultism) that at seances the Gnomes and Sylphs—generally prevail, if the medium *is not pure;* they describe these beings, just as Paracelsus and others described them, these ignorant clairvoyants, most of them illiterate peasant girls. Charles Massey, our English member writes from England to Olcott, that he dined with Crookes and passed half a day in deep conversation with him, and that Crookes confessed to him, he was *an occultist*, a pupil of Eliphas Levi; that Crookes showed and explained him many things giving him as a reason of his *unbelief in Spiritualism*, his firm knowledge that Katie King was an *Elementary Spirit*. Now, you see, that the Magic half explained by Eliphas Levi, brings *to results*, and places you in contact with Elementaries only; for were Crookes an initiate of the East, he would know, how to drive away

Elementaries and commune but with *immortal* Spirits. Such Magic is Sorcery and is more than dangerous while White or Sacred Magic of the Theurgists is Spiritualism in its most *sublime, pure state*. If we talk of Elementaries it is not because we want to prove that all of the Spirits are such, but to warn people to discern between those and immortal Spirits, because for us Occultists, Spiritualism is the most sacred belief, that can be given to humanity, and that we consider the communication between disembodied Spirits and ourselves such a mysterious sacred affair as not to contaminate it through such channels as most mediums are. Iamblichus, Porphyry, Plutarch Apollonius, and all the Neo Platonists wrote hundreds of volumes, on the difference existing between bad demons or Elementaries, and good demons or the souls of the departed. See what Iamblichus, a practiced Theurgist writes. He deems it so sacred, that the least error he says—the least impurity during the evocation can bring Elementaries in the shape of monstrous animals, and so forth. The Spiritists of France never proceed to hold a seance without a fervent, harmonious prayer, and they are right.

Well, I have said enough. Time will show who is right and who is wrong.—I sent you two copies of the "Sun" of Deceb'- 26 and January 2^d with my two articles.[3] I have contracted with the Sun (or nearly done so) for an article every Sunday, for $30, it helps me to live; and that is why my book goes so slowly, for one cannot well write with an empty stomach.

I did not see Olcott, since I read your article in "Banner. I am sure it will be a sad blow to him, for he makes of you a good deal, and is never tiring[4] in praises of esteem about you.

We hold seances with every medium who consents to be tested. What we want is to kill fraud. We had three seances with Mary Thayer; the most beautiful they were. We were

16 Theosophists, *all skeptics* except Olcott and me, and 7 editors of different papers. She was baged,[5] the seance was held at Mr Newton's house (Presid: of N.Y Spirituals —no fraud possible, room searched, doors sealed and locked, our own pockets ransacked. In three minutes the enormous table was literally covered with flowers the most rare plants, two ring doves, a canary bird, shells, pieces of *wet coral* from the sea, etc. *That is* a test. God bless you, and Mrs Corson.

truly and sincerely yours,
H P Blavatsky

NOTES:

1. This remark must refer to *Isis Unveiled*, but later in this same letter, HPB writes, "my book goes so slowly." Boris de Zirkoff says of the first statement, "this is somewhat puzzling, and may refer to a first draft only" (*CW* 1:lix). Writing on *Isis* continued for more than a year.

2. "Madame Blavatsky Explains," *Spiritual Scientist* 3 (Jan. 6, 1876): 208-9 (*CW* 1:186-92).

3. "A Story of the Mystical," *New York Sun*, Dec. 26, 1875 (*CW* 1:163-73); and "The Luminous Circle," *New York Sun*, Jan. 2, 1876 (*CW* 1:177-86). A third story, "The Cave of the Echoes," was apparently submitted to the *Sun* but (HPB says in her scrapbook 1:119) "Killed on account of being too horrible!!" It was subsequently published in the *Banner of Light* 42 (Mar. 30, 1878): 2 (*CW* 1:338-53).

4. Approximately six letters that look like "toning" or "taning," here emended to "tiring."

5. *I.e.,* "bagged." The medium was enclosed in a bag to obviate suspicion of fraud.

SOURCE: Transcribed from a microfilm and partly from a photocopy of the original in the HPB Library. Published in *Unpublished Letters* 172-9.

⌐‾‾⌐

BACKGROUND ESSAY J

Further Controversy over the Inaugural Address

Another person, and indeed a founding member of the Theosophical Society, who was also offended by Olcott's address was Charles Sotheran. He, however, reacted not to Olcott's remarks about Spiritualism, for which he held no regard himself, but perhaps to the highlighting of George Felt's aborted demonstration or to the visionary future Olcott saw for the Society. In a letter to the Spiritualist publication *Banner of Light*, Sotheran announced his resignation from the Society, disassociated himself from Olcott's address, responded to HPB's criticism of him, and proffered an expression of backhanded sympathy to her by using her own words to point out the failings of mediums.

Boris de Zirkoff (*CW* 1:526) comments about Sotheran in general and this episode in particular:

> His rather fiery temperament kept him and his friends in a turmoil. He took active part in the founding of the Theosophical Society, but only three months later made some inflammatory speeches at a political street meeting, to which H.P.B. strongly objected. Sotheran resigned from the T.S. in a huff, but six months later apologized for various critical and unfriendly remarks he had made, and was reinstated.

The *Banner of Light* (38 [Jan. 15, 1876]: 5) announcement by Sotheran of his resignation, quoting an intemperate phrase from HPB's letter to him, was as follows:

To the Editor of the Banner of Light:

Sir—As I have been much annoyed by inquiries and statements concerning my connection with the Theosophical

Society, I wish it to be distinctly understood that I have no longer anything whatever to do with that organization. The Society accepted my resignation of fellowship at its last meeting, January 5th.

It has been asserted that I have left the Theosophical Society through "lack of moral courage." Those who know me well cannot but be aware that such a statement is utterly false, and that my real reasons for taking the step are because I am confident the pretensions of the Society are fallacious; further, that the position taken by the President in his inaugural address, and the expressions of other members, are of such a character as to only render the body ridiculous in the estimation of all thinking persons.

I would not thus trouble your readers with matters of a personal nature, but I consider it a duty to myself and friends to do so, because, in consequence of having recently recommended acquaintances and others not to join the Society, the Corresponding Secretary, Madame Blavatsky, has in a letter dated the 8th inst., and written on official paper—whether by order of the Society or not, it is immaterial—threatened me as "one who should be and will be proceeded against in such a way as to prevent his attempting or doing further harm."

Madame Blavatsky *may have* occult powers of an extraordinary character; but after intimate knowledge of her for a considerable period, I can affirm that in my humble opinion she possesses NONE WHATEVER, notwithstanding she may have psychologized herself and her companions into believing so, and therefore her threats fall on me with as little effect as

"The wind which passeth idly by."

I would advise her, instead of abusing those who, like myself, are struggling for the Highest Truth, and detest *imposture of any kind* to content herself with combating those with whom she has a real cause of grievance, as appears from the following extract in a communication from her to The Spiritual Scientist of January 6th:

"Whatever objection any one may have to me on account of country, religion, occult study, *rudeness of speech*, cigarette smoking, or any other peculiarity, my record in connection with Spiritualism for long years does not show me as making money by it, or gaining any other advantage direct or indirect. On the contrary, those who have met me in all parts of the world (which I have circumnavigated three times) will testify that I have given thousands of dollars, imperiled my life, defied the Catholic Church, where it required more courage to do so than the Spiritualists seem to show about encountering Elementaries, and in camp and court, on the sea, in the desert, in civilized and savage countries, I have been, from first to last, the friend and champion of mediums. I have done more. I have often taken the last dollar out of my pocket and even necessary clothes off my back to relieve their necessities.

"And how do you think I have been rewarded? By honors, emoluments, and social position? Have I charged a fee for imparting to the public or individuals what little knowledge I have gathered in my travels and studies? Let those who have patronized our principal mediums answer. I have been slandered in the most shameful way, and the most unblushing lies circulated about my character and antecedents by the very mediums whom I have been defending at the risk of being taken for their confederate when their tricks have been detected. What has happened in American cities is no worse nor different from what has befallen me in Europe, Asia, and Africa. I have been injured temporarily in the eyes of good and pure men and women, by the libels of mediums whom I never saw and who never were in the same city with me at the same time—of mediums who made me the heroine of shameful histories whose action was alleged to have occurred when I was in another part of the world, far away from the face of a white man. Ingratitude and injustice have been my portion since I had first to do with spiritual mediums. I have met here with few exceptions, but very, very few."[1]

I regret that any individual with the experience gained

from travel, and the literary capabilities which every one who knows Madame Blavatsky must acknowledge she has acquired, has so heavy a cross to bear. I trust she will successfully disprove these calumnies, and having done so, will learn to be less impulsive, and give credit for at least honesty of purpose to those who may disagree with herself or the Theosophical Society. Yours faithfully,

Charles Sotheran
Office of the "American Bibliopolist,"
84 Nassau street, New York, January 10, 1876.

NOTE:

1. The communication to the *Spiritual Scientist* from which this passage is quoted is published in full in *CW* 1:186–92.

Olcott's inaugural address was noticed also in England, and began a series of articles and letters in the *Spiritualist Newspaper* that culminated in a letter by HPB commenting on some aspects of the discussion. The series began with an anonymous article (Jan. 7, 1876, 8:4–5) that included the following observations:

WHAT IS MAGIC?

Recently a few American inquirers into Spiritualism have floated some rumours that a portion of the modern psychological phenomena are due to magic, but they have given no exact information what magic may be, nor clearly detailed a single experiment which it is possible to repeat. Notwithstanding the absence of any published evidence in support of their position, the "occultists," as they are called, have been enabled by the press to make quite a little breeze among Spiritualists in the United States, and have formed themselves into a "Theosophical Society," under the presidency of Colonel Olcott, with offices at the Mott Memorial Hall, 64, Madison Avenue, New York. Madame H. P. Blavatsky, a Russian lady, is the recording secretary. The object of the society, as set forth in its preamble, is "to obtain knowledge of the nature and attributes of the Supreme Power, and of the higher spirits, by the aid of physical processes." . . .

The presidential address contains nothing approaching the practical until its closing paragraphs are reached; in these much responsibility is thrown upon a Mr. Felt, who promises to raise spirits by magical arts. Would it not have been better had the promotors of the new organisation seen the experiments first, and formed their Association afterwards, for if Mr. Felt fails to raise spirits by the use of odoriferous chemical substances, what will be the fate of the Theosophical Society? . . .

In consequence of the rumours floated in America that ancient magic had some foundation of fact, a friend of ours examined some of the rich collection of ancient books on magic in the British Museum, but could find nothing definite of any value, or tending to throw light upon the phenomena of modern Spiritualism.

An old proverb speaks of—

> Much crie and little woo'
> As the de'il said when he sheared the soo.

Let us hope that after so much crying on this subject from the other side of the Atlantic, something real may reach these shores shortly in the shape of wool, but should the Theosophical Society find itself in a precarious condition, in consequence of being unable to prove that its assertions have any foundation in experimental facts, it might still do good work in Spiritualism, by undertaking historical research for the purpose of unveiling the many examples of misunderstood mediumship in the past, as we once did in the matter of the psychological experiences of Dr. Dee—the reputed astrologer of the days of Queen Elizabeth—and his medium Kelley. *The Spiritual Scientist*, of Boston, is about to publish the life of Cornelius Agrippa, as viewed by the light of modern Spiritualism, and his career no doubt presents many points of interest to Spiritualists. Several of the original necromantic books written by Cornelius Agrippa are in the British Museum Library, so are easily accessible. The mediumship of the Holy Maid of Kent should also be examined by the light of present experience. The Theosophical

Society might do much good by executing work of this kind, for no private individuals in this country have leisure enough to undertake it at present.

The next issue of the *Spiritualist Newspaper* (Jan. 14, 1876, 8:20) published a letter from C. C. Massey, writing as "An English Member of the Theosophical Society," in part replying to observations in the foregoing article:

THE THEOSOPHICAL SOCIETY OF NEW YORK.

Sir,—Without at all pretending to answer the question, "What is magic?" which is the title of your article on the Theosophical Society of New York, I venture to suggest that the subject is not one which Spiritualists, of all people in the world, should treat with levity, or in a disparaging and derisive tone. Nor can it be considered to have been adequately investigated and disposed of by a cursory examination of ancient books in the British Museum. We have to deal with a mass of testimony in every age, down to and including the present, which we shall find it equally difficult to reject as the records of charlatanism, or to explain upon any theory of "misunderstood mediumship."

The two main propositions of occultism seem to be:— 1. The existence in the universe of spirits other than those of human origin. 2. The power of human will, aided by knowledge and strengthened by discipline, to control and direct certain classes of these spirits. . . .

. . . Whether Mr. Felt will succeed in giving to the Theosophical Society ocular demonstration of the elementary spirits remains to be seen; but the language of the highest authorities on this mysterious subject would certainly not lead one to suppose that practical magic is as capable of verification by anybody who chooses to take a little trouble, as the phenomena of mediumship. The *raison d'être* of the Theosophical Society is independent of the success of any particular experiment. It is, as I understand it, an association of educated students, whose minds have been emancipated from materialism, and who propose to seek truth, knowledge, and perhaps power, in ancient sources, to which modern research has traced the germs of every religion and every spiritual philosophy. The name at first suggested for it was the Cabalistic Society. It may be that undue stress is laid in the preamble on the practical experiments in contemplation. Even if the latter are successful, it does not follow that the report of them will be believed. Experience shows that Spiritualists can be just as incredulous of facts which do not suit them, as are the world at large about the spiritual phenomena themselves. But, even in the event of failure, I cannot at all assent to your contemptuous suggestion that the society should stultify itself by an attempt to reduce every success recorded in the past to cases of "misunderstood mediumship." In like manner a scientific man, who has been present at a test *séance* which has proved a failure, may be supposed to recommend the British National Association of Spiritualists to apply itself in the future to the explanation of mediumship on the theory of undetected trickery.

AN ENGLISH MEMBER OF THE THEOSOPHICAL SOCIETY.

Two weeks later (*Spiritualist Newspaper*, Jan. 28, 1876, 8:44–5), another correspondent, writing under the nom de plume of "M. A. Cantab.," entered the fray with a letter that included these comments:

ELEMENTARY SPIRITS.

Sir,—A belief in the existence of elementary spirits has been held all along by the followers of Allan Kardec; and the question seems to me to be, not so much whether they are "spirits other than those of human origin," as laid down by the modern Occultists, according to your correspondent, an English member of the Theosophical Society; but whether they may not be in one of the phases of the origin of human beings? In other words, whether we may not have been, once upon a time, elementary spirits ourselves. The three questions, 1st, That of men being "sparks struck off from Deity itself," as alleged in 'Spirit Teachings,' and in other articles of *The Spiritualist;* 2nd, The question of elementary spirits; and 3rdly, That of the incarnation and reincarnation of spirits. These three questions have all cropped up lately in such quick succession, and in such intimate connection with each other as to give Spiritualists new sources for thought, and perhaps for guidance . . . .

The second proposition of the Occultists, as quoted by your correspondent, which alleges that "the human will has power to control certain classes of these spirits," shows the very close connection that exists between Spiritualism and magic; for that a magician may control and be assisted by spirits without his even believing in them, is more than probable, and that the movements of spirits are not confined to magic or to Spiritualism, as we understand the latter, we may rest assured.

There is, however, one sensible difference between a magician and a medium, as spoken of in modern terms. Whatever may be the advantages of the medium over the magician in many respects, in one the magician is the superior. The magician controls his familiar spirits, while the medium proper is generally controlled, though it is quite possible (since we find that certain conjurors have now turned mediums) that they were passive mediums all along, and were really the controlled when they were playing the part of the controllers, just as a servant in a comedy sometimes, by command of his master, takes his master's place. That spirits, to be controlled at all, must be of a low order, none can doubt; but that some magic men, even of the present day, have strong wills, combined with medium power, which in conjunction fit them for this work, we can hardly question.

<hr>

Introduction to Letter 65

The letter of "M. A. Cantab." caught the attention of HPB, who commented on it in a letter to C. C. Massey. On March 2, Massey wrote to the *Spiritualist Newspaper*, quoting HPB as "a very learned Occultist"; his letter was published in the issue of March 10, 1876. In a communication to that journal two years later, HPB identified herself as the "learned Occultist" in question (*CW* 1:326). Massey introduces his quotation from HPB's letter as follows:

SPECULATIONS ABOUT ELEMENTARY SPIRITS, SPIRITUAL
EVOLUTION, REINCARNATION, MAGICIANS, AND MEDIUMS.

Sir,—The letter of "M.A. (Cantab)" upon the above topics in your number of the 28th January, has just brought me a communication from a very learned Occultist, containing what appears to me a more than usually clear and definite statement of the doctrine of spiritual evolution. My correspondent deals also with the question of reincarnation and with the suggestion of "M.A. (Cantab)," that the magician's will must be associated with medial power. The letters which have appeared in *The Spiritualist*, testifying to a wide-spread interest in, and curiosity about, these subjects, I make no apology for sending you a long extract from this communication, although I am not at liberty to give the name of the writer. If the reader, unlearned in the terminology of the occult writers, will interpret the "astral light," to which allusion is more than once made, into the "universal ether" postulated by modern science, I think there is little else that requires explanation to be, at all events, intelligible.

Letter 65

To C. C. Massey   *[February 1876]*

He (M.A., Cantab) is right in holding that the elementary represents one of the phases of human beings. No one can understand the Hermetic philosophy without beginning *ab initio*. The astral light (universal ether) is our starting point. It is not to the purpose to go behind the operative activity of the law of evolution for its cause; that is a separate branch of metaphysics. Let us take the principle of cosmogony admitted by science, *viz.*, that the visible universe is the result of aggregations of molecules caused by evolution. Every molecule has its inherent energy, and is thereby forced into each successive relationship as it passes through the mineral, vegetable, and animal kingdoms. The Hermetist, who sees with both eyes, instead of with one only, observes that each atom, no matter where found, is imbued with that vital principle called spirit. Thus each grain of sand, equally with each minutest atom of the human body, has its inherent latent spark of the Divine light; and, as one law of evolution applies to the whole universe, so each of these grains of sand will assuredly one day go to make up the body of man. In the progress of these atoms, from the primitive rock to the human being, there is a constant giving off of astral emanations. These go into the common store-house of nature, the astral atmosphere of our planet. The same law following them here, these emanations have a tendency to assume concrete forms. Exactly as the fishes of different species represent the successive stages of nature's journey-work in her attempt to produce the most perfect piscatorial form, so the multifarious forms of the elementary mark her attempts to produce the perfect and concrete physical man. This implies an evolution of spirit keeping pace with the evolution of matter, and a constant tendency of the spirit to gain acendency over, or rather to escape from, the bondage of its encompassing matter. When this double evolution has reached a certain point, it is possible for the third principle to come into the union, that is, the immortal spirit [soul],[1] which makes of man the Triad. As these emanations were given off, so at the proper time they are drawn back again into the vortex of evolution, and the elementary, *dying* in the astral light, goes to make the human being—the fœtus— the grosser portions furnishing the *germ* of its body, and its finer ones its astral body, the *perisprit* of Kardec, or the spirit. Then, after the body of the fœtus is prepared to receive it, at the fourth hour (read the Nuetemeron[2] of El. Levi) comes in the influx of the Divine breath. You will doubtless observe the analogy between this giving off of astral emanations, their concentration into elementaries, and return to physical nature, and the evaporation of watery vapour, its condensation into clouds, and return to the earth as rain or snow. Modern scientific research demonstrates this ebb and flow of influences and matter to be going on throughout the whole cosmos, and, therefore, unless we were to admit the absurd theory of special creation and miracle, we must see that this philosophy of the evolution of species by flux and reflux from matter to spirit and back again is the only true one; . . . the whole trouble of Kardec, and other reincarnationists, lies in their misunderstanding the hermetic philosophy upon this point. While it is true that there is a reincarnation in one sense, in the other it is untrue. Nay, more, it is absurd and unphilosophical, doing violence to the law of evolution, which is constantly carrying matter and spirit upward towards perfection. When the elementary dies out of one state of existence he is born into a higher one, and when man dies out of the world of gross matter, he is born into one more ethereal; so on from sphere to sphere, man never losing his trinity, for at each birth a new and more perfect astral body is evolved out of elementaries of a correspondingly higher order, while his previous astral body takes the place of the antecedent, external earthly body. Man's soul (or Divine spirit, for you must not confound the Divine with the astral spirit) constantly entering into new astral bodies, there is an actual reincarnation; but that when it has once passed through any sphere into a higher one, it should re-enter the lower sphere and pass through other bodies similar to the one it has just quitted, is as unphilosophical as to fancy that the human fœtus could go back into the elementary condition, or the child after birth re-enter its mother's womb. The eastern Kabbalah embraces the Pythagorean philosophy; the western, or Rosicrucian, *did not*. But the metempsychosis of Pythagoras was an exoteric expression to cover the esoteric meaning, and his commentators, who had not the key, have misunderstood him as grossly as they have misunderstood everything else written by those of the Neo-Platonics, who, like Porphyry, Iamblicus, and Plotinus, have been adopting and elaborating his precepts. The spirits upon whose communications the reincarnationist school base their theory, have simply given back the opinions which they found in the heads or brains of their mediums and the circle about them. Reincarnationist spirits never insist upon their doctrines to any but reincarnationist mediums, and the troops of soldiers seen about Prince Wittgenstein are pretty pictures made in the astral light, for the delectation of those who are ready to gobble them. "Cantab" suggests that the controlling power of the magician cannot produce phenomena unless conjoined with medial power, and this is perhaps the view of Professor Perty. Now, the magician, when he evokes human spirits, furnishes them with such a condition in his own pure atmosphere—a spiritual atmosphere, untainted with gross matter—that they can approach and manifest themselves. The sorcerer, as well as the impure medium, are but *necromancers*. They are surrounded by such a fetid atmosphere, that only elementary and gross human spirits of their own class—whose very grossness keeps them closely attracted to the earth—can either approach them or be evoked to help them in their wicked designs. Both magician and sorcerer can produce phenomena by the power of their own will and their own spirit, unaided by any other either elementary or human; but the impure medium, who is but the football tossed from one influence to another, can do nothing but passively obey. Pure and sincere-minded people, who accept mediumship for the sake of instruction from superior spirits, keep the elementary at bay by virtue of their own purity, and the pure atmosphere of the spirits surrounding them. And still they cannot call them *at will*, until they have become adepts of the divine science, and learned to combine the Ineffable Name.

NOTES:

1. The word was bracketed in the original publication.

2. No work of this title has been identified. However, in her commentary on the *Pistis Sophia*, HPB notes: "In the second volume of the *Dogme et Rituel de la Haute Magie* (pp. 386 et seq.), Éliphas Lévi gives the *Nychthēmeron* of Appollonius of Tyana. *Nychthēmeron* means the space of a day and a night or twenty-four hours" (*CW* 13:7–8).

Massey ended his letter as follows:

I am far from laying these views before your readers as free from difficulty. But unless Spiritualists are prepared to deny or disregard the whole philosophy of evolution—in its development the greatest achievement of modern thought—it behoves us to establish relations with it, and to lend a willing ear to any exposition of the correspondence between the physical and spiritual kingdoms in the historical department.

AN ENGLISH MEMBER OF THE THEOSOPHICAL SOCIETY.

London, 2nd March.

DATE: Massey's letter quoting HPB's was dated March 2, 1876, and HPB was responding to a publication of January 28, 1876, so she doubtless wrote her letter sometime in February 1876.

SOURCE: Original unavailable. Copied from *Spiritualist Newspaper* 8 (Mar. 10, 1876): 117. Reprinted in *Canadian Theosophist* 64 (July-Aug. 1983): 50-3, with notes by Ted G. Davy.

Letter 66

To A. N. Aksakoff   *[ca. February 1876]*

As soon as he (the medium) is better—the spirits have been knocking him about—he will come to us and we will try to test him at our meetings of the Theosophical Society. Our Society is a *touchstone. For that it was founded.*

DATE: Boris de Zirkoff cites Solovyov's statement that the letter was written more than two months after the founding of the Theosophical Society.

SOURCE: Russian original unavailable. Translated by Boris de Zirkoff from Solovyov's *Sovremennaya* 279. Another English translation by Walter Leaf in *Modern Priestess* 264.

Letter 67

To C. R. Corson

March 12, 1876
[letterhead] The Theosophical Society
Mott Memorial Hall
64 Madison Avenue
(P. O. Box 4335.)
New York

My dear Madame Corson,

For more than a month I have been getting up every morning with the firm intention of writing you and—always held back in my plans; with the persistent idea that if I waited there would be more grounds day by day to support with glaring proofs what there is for me to tell you.

War is declared. All the dogs are aroused and baying at the moon. The Spiritualists have condemned me. Have they executed me? Not yet; and they will find it more difficult to do than to try.

And first—before I launch into some necessary explanations, in order to clarify the situation and leave no misunderstanding between us, I start by telling you, that I have known for nearly a month that for some reasons *inscrutable* as fate itself, without any more motive than when I was with you, M͏ʳ Corson has called me an "impostor," in speaking of me to a gentleman who makes up or tells tales—Clark I believe.

If the expression was gentler I thank him for it; if it was accompanied by anything stronger still, neither my opinion nor my esteem for him, nor the sincere friendship, esteem and even affection that I feel for you could be either changed or modified, or lessened in any way. I know too well the effects and *changes of scenery* produced before one's very eyes by skilful stagehands in this *angel*-girt world, to be astonished by the least thing, that these gentlemen and ladies of the invisible world are capable of producing on a nervous temperament like that of Mr Corson. Time is the best avenger Madame; one day perhaps Mr Corson will realize that this was a gratuitous insult, which I had not deserved from him, any more than I had expected it.

But let us pass over that, because if I speak of it *at all*, it is only to let you know that I know it, and that if it has cut me to the quick, and made me suffer, the blow was softened because I knew of it beforehand, I was expecting it, and it had to be so. As for me, it does not change me by one iota, and my feelings for you are the same as they were at the moment when we parted at the station.

They publish slander about me, they try to make me out *the confederate* of the Eddys, or indeed of Olcott; finding it impossible to find in me an adventuress, who gives herself names titles, relatives and a position in Russian society that she does not have, they do an about-face and they attack my reputation, *my honor*, by base and cowardly insinuations—for I defy anyone at all, to publish anything but insinuations and one single *good proof.*

Here now is the great moment! Mme Blavatsky although the daughter of her forefathers is an immoral woman, a woman who has had loads of lovers. While Dr Bloede *secretly* spreads the tale in Brooklyn that I have had a criminal liaison with the Pope and Bismarck, Mr Home, that *unstained* medium, pours his venom over me in Europe. More than that. I, who have worked 18 hours a day since last summer,

I am accused in anonymous letters sent to *my women friends*, who bring them to me indignantly (like Emma Har: Brittain[1] for example) of frequenting houses of assignation. They offer to lead Emma H. B. to these spots and to give her *proofs* that I was there the very same day and hour *that she spent an entire day with me!*

Very fortunately I have true women and men friends here. Olcott's sister,[2] an older lady and mother of six children whom everybody respects and knows, who has become such a good friend that she comes from Orange[3] two or three times a week, Emma H. Britten, Mrs Judge Miller and Westbrook[4] ladies who are all known here are my steadfast friends and are ready to go swear on the *stand* before the judges, that never has there been a woman more slandered more cravenly *traduced* than I! I have a packet of letters that come to me every morning, letters of sympathy and of esteem, and—I am proud of them, Madame.

If you were only a Spiritualist flapdoodle my dear Madame Corson I would not take the trouble of writing you all this. But, being one of the most virtuous and estimable women that I know, *an angel* as Monachesi constantly calls you—I am eager that one day,—the day of great justice, you will be able to say to yourself that you have shown some acts of friendship to a woman who was not altogether unworthy of your friendship, even though she smokes and even swears.

Truth comes to light slowly,—very slowly, but it is impossible to hide light under a bushel—and every shred of my reputation, every gob of poisonous venom like that with which Dr Bloede fills his syringe, is a hole made in the curtain lowered over the angel world—the Sweet Spirit-Land, whose inhabitants control the mediums [ostensibly] inspiring them with the spirit of *charity*, of *love*, of *faith* and *of justice*, [but actually] transforming them into incarnate devils who breathe only malice, falsehood, cowardly calumny and all the seven deadly sins!

By its fruits the tree will be known. I am quite happy if by losing my reputation I save millions who are now lost in the illusion that all the Spirits who communicate with them are Angels of purity, *disembodied Spirits*. I am ready to offer myself as a sacrifice for humanity. I am an old woman, and it is easy for me to prove that if I am accused now, in New York, when from morning till night I am under the eyes of my friends, of that of which I was not accused when I was young and alone in the world then as now. And notice that my most fervid enemies, those who will not stop at any cowardness any infamy, are Spiritualists and *mediums*. No! Neither Christ nor the Apostles have chased away all the demons, and they will never achieve that—for *legion* is their name! The Christs and the Apostles of our day are the mediums and the lechers;[5] the Spiritualists in a word, who preach reform, and announce to a blast of trumpets the new Gospel, the kingdom of God, now that the mortals are so mixed up with the Invisibles and the Immortals; now these Christs and these New Apostles being possessed themselves, of the seven Biblical demons, whom do they wish to reform and to what end? The ranks of the Spiritualists increase every day, and with each day one hears and feels more malice, more infernal spitefulness. The mediums tear each other apart like ferocious beasts,—Home writes a book,[6] in which he exposes all the mediums in America; he is seeking all the pamphlets which exposed mediums: M^r and Mrs Hardy, tear Mrs Thayer and others to pieces. The Holmes have become *greater mediums* than ever and flourish in Philadelphia metamorphosing their fists masked as grandmothers, angel-wives, and military uncles, and the Spiritualists gobble all that up! Dr Child has again started to sell his book on John and Katie King publicly, and Olcott has 19 letters written by *spirits* and addressed to him as well as to Gardener threatening to *kill* him and Dr Gardner if he dares to deliver his lecture in Boston against the Elementaries. He has delivered it—and even two, and is still alive.

And why this hate that nothing can assuage, this constant, malign, frenzied persecution which by itself would transform a criminal, a thief and a—*mother of Harlots* into a martyr? All this because our Society is composed at this time of 79 members all educated people, and almost all although skeptics ardently desire to be convinced of the Great Truth, of *Immortality*. By intercourse with spirits,[7] they work to separate the good grain from the heap of filth in order to assure themselves and to prove to others that there is a world of discarnate Spirits, composed of liberated souls, working to progress and to purify themselves in order to ascend always by drawing near to the great Divine Source—*God*, the great Principle pure and invisible,—but—that there are also invisible worlds that surround us full of unrepentant souls, *unprogressed!! and malign spirits*, the *demons* of Christendom, and creatures without any soul, elementary principles of matter without conscience, without responsibility as without light because still bereft of an immortal soul.

They think that all this is my invention when mountains of books have been written on this subject for 4000 years and more!

If I were killed today, the stones of the road would cry out the truth after me. So let them crush the Theosophical Society. May God keep you and bless you. May the *All Good and Wise* protect you. Such is the fervent desire of one who signs herself for the last time.

Your devoted,
H. P. Blavatsky.

NOTES:

1. Emma Hardinge Britten.

2. Olcott's sister, Isobel Buloid Mitchell.

3. Mrs. Mitchell lived in Orange, New Jersey.

4. The reference is probably to two wives of judges: Mrs. Miller and Mrs. Westbrook (the wife of Judge R. B. Westbrook), using the husband's professional title of "Judge" as part of the wife's social title.

5. The word in the French text is "lecherers," which is not French; it is, however, a rare and old-fashioned English variant of "lechers." HPB mixed English words into her French, and her English vocabulary was often of an antiquated sort.

6. The reference seems to be to *Lights and Shadows of Spiritualism*, which was, however, not published until 1877.

7. This part of the original letter was not available for examination. The text in *Unpublished Letters* begins this sentence with the two words "Spirits (intercourse)," which appear to be English rather than French. Their meaning and that of the sentence as a whole is unclear. The translation adopted here follows a suggestion of Boris de Zirkoff's that makes the sentence coherent.

SOURCE: Translated partly from a photocopy of the French original in the HPB Library and partly from the text in *Unpublished Letters*. Published in Corson, *Unpublished Letters* 184-9 (French original) and 189-94 (English translation).

❧

Letter 68

To H. P. Corson

March 22, 1876
[letterhead] The Theosophical Society,
Mott Memorial Hall,
64 Madison Avenue,
(P.O. Box 4335)
New York

My dear M\ Corson,

I need not tell you that your letter was a very agreeable surprise. It proved to me that the recent distrust in my own judgment which I have had in consequence of the abuse which has showered upon me from every nook and corner is not always warranted. I had got almost to believe that I was an *impostor* because every body said so. I could not blame you to be the echo of the great uproar of a thousand slanderous tongues. What little good opinion I had of myself was crushed out; and if they had accused me of having murdered President Lincoln or of being a reincarnation of Pope Joan, I would not have been surprised. But let us drop it. I never would have said a word, if the story had not been told to me in the presence of several of my friends, who expressed their indignation at this unmerited epithet. Your letter in the 'Banner' made me think that you had very hard feelings against occultists as a pack of assassins who were going to murder all the Spirits and mediums, instead of being as they are their most devoted friends. The difference between us is that the mediums *sell* Spirits and their phenomena for money, and Spiritualists bye them as they would sweet candy; while we occultists regard the subject as a *Religion* that should not be profaned.

Olcott blew a loud blast on the trumpet, because *he knew* that Felt's experiments would come right upon his heels, *and so they did*. Our society is now pledged to secrecy and we have a grip and a pass word.[1]

Spiritualism is based upon *blind faith*, that is the Spiritualist *cannot* demonstrate the reality of their Spirits—while the faith of the Occultists in God and the Spirits is firmly based upon a mathematical demonstration of both. Therefore the belief of the former is built upon sand but ours upon the firm rock. There can be no such undaunted believers as we Cabbalists are for no amount of fraud, lying, or exposures can shake a conviction based upon such a ground. With you all is hypothesis; with us Spiritualism is a geometrical theorem solved and proved ages ago, by philosophers who lived thousands of years before Pythagoras.

With Spiritualists 2 + 2 = five, and half a dozen in the bargain; and with us they can make nothing but four. We ask no Spiritualist to believe what we say, because we say it, we ask them to investigate and see for themselves. If Plato's philosophy—called a dreamy fiction by the Epicureans of our modern days—is accused of being the opposite of that of Aristotle; and if instead of proceeding like the latter from the particulars to the Universals, it adopts a vice-versa method and proceeds from the Universals to particulars; we have but one unanswerable argument to offer. Geometry, the only *exact* science among the many others; the only one which accepts *no hypothesis*, no *theories*, no *speculations* but whose decisions are irrevocable—proceeds also from Universals down to particulars. So that Spirit[u] who are so anxious to upset the Kabbalah as a Science must first prove Geometry and Euclid to be an error. Of course the manner in which this idea should be enforced upon the attention of Spiritualists, is far from being that which should have been employed by Olcott. But he is of a very combative disposition, and a crazy enthusiast, but his honesty no one can question. He kicked up a tremendous row on the two continents and *I* received all the return blows, as I am generally considered in the light of the *daemon* of Socrates towards him. He did no good to Spiritualism but a serious harm to the cause he represents as the President of our Society. But now he knows better, as you may judge by his recent letters. This seems to be a very critical time for Spiritualists and all of us who believe in genuine phenomena, may well afford to put aside minor differences to fight the common Enemy—That unmitigated blackguard Home, not content with spitting venom upon every one who is said to produce phenomena has attacked the pure and innocent Leymarie, the dead Eliphas Levi, and all the mediums of Christendom. The Editorial of Colby in last weeks Banner, will find echo all over Europe.

I understand and appreciate your fine Latin quotation from one of the hypocritical Fathers of the Early Church You surely do not want me to be canonized at such a price? Think only. Sᵗ Blavatsky—Impostor and Martyr. Pretty epitaph to be engraved on my tomb stone. That would surely beat "my wife's sister's niece's youngest child!"[2]

Well God bless you. I am glad we have settled. Thousand, sincere regards to Mʳˢ Corson, which—unless she takes me really to be an Antichrist in petticoats—she must accept as sincere

Yours truly and sincerely

H P Blavatsky

My love to Mʳ Beardsley—whose work is all over Europe now.

NOTES:

1. At a March 8 meeting of the Council of the Theosophical Society, it was resolved to adopt signs of recognition (*CW* 1:lx).

2. This catchphrase, a joke between HPB and Corson, is used also in letter 57 (note 1).

SOURCE: Transcribed from a microfilm and a photocopy of the original in the HPB Library. Published in *Unpublished Letters* 180–3.

Letter 69

To A. N. Aksakoff   *[? spring or summer 1876]*

I was not at my father's funeral. But at this moment the medal and clasp which were brought to me are hanging on my neck; and at the stake, on my deathbed, or on the rack, I could say only one thing—it is my father's *clasp*.[1] The medal I do not remember. I myself broke the end of the clasp at Rugodevo, and I have seen it a hundred times in my father's hands. If it is not his clasp, then it must be that the spirits are real *devils* and can materialize what they like and drive people out of their senses. But I know that, even if my father's principal decorations were not buried with him, still, as he always wore this *medal, which he had received for 25 years of service,* and the one he had for the Turkish War, even in his retirement and out of uniform, it is likely that they did not take it off him. After his death there was some talk about money that he bequeathed to me, and of which I never got half, and my younger sister never writes to me at all. But I shall write to Markoff, who was present at the funeral, and to my brother at Stavropol, because I want to know the truth. . . . Everyone heard the spirit's speech, 40 persons besides myself. So, then, it would seem that I had been in collusion with the mediums! Very well, let them think so. . . . How on earth do I interfere with Home? I'm not a medium, I never was and never will be a professional one. I have devoted my whole life to the study of the ancient Kabbalah and occultism, the "occult sciences." I really cannot, just because the devil got me into trouble in my youth, go and rip up my stomach now like a Japanese suicide in order to please the mediums. . . . My position is cheerless—simply helpless. There is nothing left but to start for Australia and change my name forever.

NOTE:

1. The medal and clasp or buckle are treated in letter 12 and the end-note to letter 10.

DATE: The date is implied by Solovyov.

SOURCE: Russian original unavailable. Translated by Boris de Zirkoff from Solovyov's *Sovremennaya* 281. Another English translation by Walter Leaf in *Modern Priestess* 267–8.

⌒

Introduction to Letter 70

Joseph Henry Louis, Baron de Palm, was an impecunious Austrian aristocrat resident in the United States at the end of his life. He was briefly a member of the Theosophical Society, but his role in the Society was marginal until his death, which catapulted him into some prominence. He had requested that his body be cremated, an uncommon form of disposal at that time and therefore an event that attracted a great deal of public attention. Olcott took charge of the proceedings and arranged a spectacular funeral at the Masonic Temple in New York City. Newspaper accounts of the funeral, held on May 28, 1876, headlined it as "Pagan," "Queer," or "Elaborate Egyptian," with "White Magic."

The greatest flurry of reporting, however, was about the cremation, more than six months later, on December 6. It was held in Washington, Pennsylvania, where Dr. Francis Julius Le Moyne had built the first crematory in the United States in 1876. Le Moyne was a social activist who advocated cremation but, because of local opposition, had to construct the building at night. He had intended it for the use of his own family, but Baron de Palm's body inaugurated its use. Boris de Zirkoff (*CW* 14:560) notes that the cremation was reported by more than 7000 journals in the United States and abroad.

The Baron had also been something of a confidence man, as the following letter (in the Archives of the Theosophical Society, Adyar), which he wrote to Olcott, suggests:

April 30, 1876
[letterhead] Lotos Club
Nº 2 Irving Place
New York

Colonel H. S. Olcott.

Dear Colonel

"Alea jacta est" [*Ln.* the die is cast] as Caesar exclaimed when he marched against Rome. À propos de quoi [*Fr.* concerning what]—you will enquire, this enigmatic commencement of my letter, and so I have to tell you, that it has always

261

been a puzzle to me, what I am placed in this world for, and being unable to solve it, I have only to deal with the fact, that I am here and must make the best of a very bad job. I am like an arrow shot out into the wide ocean, and all that is left to me is to try to drift into a safe harbor. Now the life I used to lead, a life of vanity, ambition and fashion was never destined to bring me nearer such a harbor and I look upon it as the working of a kind guardian or tutelar angel, which has worked upon me and [*page damaged: ?* by means] of privations, troubles & anxiety—forced upon me my salvation. This guardian angel made me strand here—compelled me to seek your acquaintance, and by means of my helpless condition, physically, mentally and financially utterly broken up, had to seek your hospitality and get instruction from the different works, with which you have surrounded yourself and the perusal of which is of infinite benefit to me, so it looks as if every thing tended finally to the best end; for certainly in the career of my early life, I would never have found the leisure or pleasure to reflect and stop for any future existence.

My health is improving *very*, very slowly, but still it is improving, and I am glad. I feel well enough to express to you my gratitude for your very kind hospitality, which calls to my mind the last will of your English protégé, which gives me a poor idea of his gentlemanly sentiments; he might and ought to have remembered also the definition of Louis XVI or XVIII who said: "la canaille se batte—la noblesse oblige" [*Fr.* the commons fight one another—nobility assists]—

Bye-the bye we had a big fire this morning (Saturday) right in the rear of our house, the laundry there was burnt out, but did no other damage.

My landlady of N° 60 E. 9th St was inconsolable to loose me, she told me she would trust me for my room rent, as long as I would stay with her, but if I left I had to pay her first—"if you choose to stay, I will not press you for the rent and you can stay as long as you have a mind to stay; but if you are going to leave me, you have to pay, before I let you go" The kind and affectionate creature. I had to raise the money and left her in peace and with a very good character. What a charm money has: a few dollars can stamp a man a villain, a scamp, a scoundrel, or to a very nice gentleman.

In regard to business transactions I have been offered a tract of land some 50 acres more or less in *New Hampshire*, containing very rich argentiferous galena; the assay shows value of SILVER per *ton* $ 32.

58 per cent lead	" 81.
31 per cent metall. zinc	" 49.
Total	$ 162.—

It has been offered to me one half interest for $100.000— and will only take $10.000 to secure the title; the balance can be paid out of the proceeds of the mine. If you should happen to come into contact with some wealthy capitalists, we might make some money in way of commission. You better not mention anything about the price yet, but sound your parties first, then we talk the matter up, when you return. My best regards to M^rs Bl.

very sincerely yours
Baron De Pal [*page damanged:* Palm]

433 W. 34th S^t.

HPB commented on the Baron, his funeral and his supposed legacy in a letter to Aksakoff:

Letter 70

To A. N. Aksakoff   *[July 1876]*

I am sending you some clippings about the funeral (heathen, almost ancient pagan) of our member Baron de Palm. He has left all his property to our society. Read what the papers say. Before the funeral they laughed and joked at us, but as soon as they saw it, they quieted down. There was nothing to laugh at, and they looked very silly.

DATE: Dated by Solovyov.

SOURCE: Russian original unavailable. Translated by Boris de Zirkoff from Solovyov's *Sovremennaya* 282. Another English translation by Walter Leaf in *Modern Priestess* 269.

Introduction to Letter 71

By the middle of 1876, Alexander Wilder was involved with HPB's writing of the book eventually published as *Isis Unveiled*. The details of his involvement are treated in the background essay K on "Writing and Publication of *Isis Unveiled*." That involvement was early and extensive, as the following letter and letter 75 show. These letters were published toward the end of Wilder's life with introductory comments on his exchanges with HPB while working on *Isis:*

> The understanding had been reached that Mr. Bouton should publish Madame Blavatsky's manuscript of *Isis Unveiled*. It was placed in my hands by him with instruction to abridge it all that I thought best. It was an undesirable task, but I did it with scrupulous regard to the interest of the publisher, and to what I esteemed to be just to the author. I was introduced to her about this time. She spoke of what I had done, with great courtesy, employing her favorite term to characterize what I had thrown out. She was about to begin a revision of the work, and asked me to indicate freely wherever I considered it at fault or not well expressed. It is hardly necessary to say that this was a delicate matter. Authors are sensitive even to morbidness, and prone to feel a criticism to be an exhibition of unfriendliness. Nevertheless, I faced the issue, and pointed out frankly what I considered fault of style, and also the importance of explaining her sources of information. She was frank to acknowledge her own shortcomings, but pleaded that she was not permitted to divulge the matters which I urged. We compared views, ethnic and historic, often not agreeing. I took the pains to embody many of these points in a letter, to which she made the following reply:

Letter 71

To A. Wilder   *August [1876]*

My dear Sir:—

Your kind favor at hand only to-day, for my friend Mr. Marquette[1] has proved an inaccurate postman, having some sun-struck patients to attend.

There are many parts in my Book *that I do not like* either, but the trouble is I do not know how to get rid of them without touching facts which are important, as arguments. You say that when I prove something, I prove it too much. There again you are right, but in such a work—(and the first one of some importance that I ever wrote, having limited myself to articles) in such a work when facts crowd and elbow each other in my brains, really one does not know sometimes where to stop. Your head is fresh, for your read it for the first time. Therefore you see all the faults and shortcomings, while my overworked brains and memory are all in a sad muddle, having read the manuscrips over and over again. I am really *very*, very thankful to you for your suggestions. I wish you made more of them.

Do you think the Phenicians[2] were an Ethiopian race? Why? They have certainly mingled much with them, but I do not see well how it can be. The Phenicians were the ancient Jews I think, whatever they have been before. Josephus admits as much, unless it is a hoax to escape other accusations. The biblical mode of worship and the bloody sacrifices in which the Patriarchs and other "chosen ones" delighted are of a Phenician origin, as they belonged in days of old to the Bacchic and Adonis Phenician worship. The Adonis is certainly the Jewish Adonai. All the Phenician deities can be found in Joshua as well as their temples. xxiii, 7. Herodotus traces the circumcision to them. The little bulls of the Jews—the Osiris-Bacchus-Adonis—is a Phenician custom. I think the Phenicians were the Canaanites. When settled in Jerusalem they appear to have become friends. The Sidonian Baal-Adonis-Bal is closely related to their Sabean worship of the "Queen of Heaven." Herodotus shows that the Syrians—the Jews of Palestine—lived earlier on the Red Sea and he calls them Phenicians. But what puzzles me is to reconcile the type. The Jews appear to have *never* intermarried among other nations—at least not to the extent to change their type. They have *nothing* Ethiopian about them. Will you tell me your reasons and oblige?

You told me in a previous letter that the Ethiopians have anciently dwelt in India. In Western India there is in a temple the statue of Chrishna and he is a splendid black Ethiopian with woolly hair, black lips and flat nose. I trace every or nearly every ancient religion to India because of the Sanscrit names of the gods of every other nation. If you trace them etymologically you are sure to find the root of every god (of the Aryan family) in Sanscrit, and many of the Semitic gods also, and that before the Aryans broke up towards the South and North. Every Slavonian Deity can be traced back to India, and yet the word *Bog*, the Russian word for God, a derivation from *Gosped*, gosped in Hospodar or gospodar, "the Lord" seems to come right from the Babylonian Bel, Baal, or Bal. In Slavonian and Russian *Bjeloybog* means literally White God, or the God of the Day,—Good. Deity, as Teherno-bog is Black God—the Evil, Night-Deity. The Tyrian god was Belus—Babylonian Bel, and *Bok* means Light and *Boga* the sun. I derive Bacchus from this—as a Sun god. I suppose we ought in the derivation of the names of all these gods, take in consideration the aspiration. The Semitic *S* generally softens to *Ah* in the Sanscrit. The Assyrian San becomes in Sanscrit Ahan; their Asuria is Ahura. *As* is the sun-god and Ar is a sun-god. Assur is a Syrian and Assyrian sun-god; Assurya is one of the names of the Sun, and Surya in Sanscrit is the Sun (see

M. Miller[3]). It was the rule of Bunsen to soften the S to u. Now *As* means life and *Asu* Spirit, and in India, even in Thibet, the life principle, the great agent of Magic, the Astral light by which the Lamas and Siamese priests produce their wonders is written *Akasa*, pronounced *Ahaha*. It is the life-principle, for it is the direct magnetism, the electric current proceeding from the Sun, which is certainly a great Magnet as the ancients said, and not as our modern scientists will have it.

I have studied some of the old Turanian words (beg pardon of philology and Science) in Samarkand with an old scholar, and he told me that he traced somehow the deities of every subsequent nation a great deal further back than the Aryan roots before the split of the nations. Now Max Muller does not concede, it seems to me, anything positive or exact as roots beyond the old Sanscrit, and *dares* not go further back. How do you account for that? You say that the Chaldeans were a tribe of the Akkadians, come from Armenia. This is Rawlinson's views. But did you trace the primitive Akkadians back? I have been living for a long time at the very foot of Mount Ararat, in Erivan, where my husband was governor for twenty-five years, and we have profound scholars among some Armenian Monks in the Monastery of Etchmiadjene,[4] the dwelling-place or See of the Armenian Patriarch (the Gregorian). It is but a few verstes from Erivan. Abieh,[5] the well-known geologist and archeologist of the Russian government, used to say that he got his most precious information from Nerses, the late Patriarch. In the garden of the very house we lived in was an enormous column, a ruin from the palace of Tyridates,[6] all covered with inscriptions, about which the Russian government did not care much. I had them all explained by a monk of Nerses. I have reasons to think the Akkadians came from India. The Bible *mandrakes* were never understood in their Cabbalistic meaning. There is a Kabbala older

267

than the Chaldean. Oannes has never been traced to his origin; but, of course, I cannot, at least *I must not*, give to the world its meaning. Your article on the Androgynes is splendid. I did not *dare* write it in my book. I think the Amazons were Androgynes and belong to one of the primitive cycles. You do not prove them *historically*, do you?

I will certainly adopt your suggestion as to *Job*. I see you have more of *Cabbalistic intuition* than I thought possible in one *not* initiated. As to the chapter of explanation about the Hierophants, the Florsedim and others, please suggest where it ought to come in and what it should cover. It seems to me that it will be difficult for me to explain what *I am not allowed to*, or say anything about the exoteric part what intelligent people do not already know. I am a Thibetian Buddhist, you know, and pledged myself to keep certain things secret. They have the original *book of Yasher*[7] and some of the lost manuscripts mentioned in the Bible, such as the *Book of War*, as you knew, perhaps, in the *old place*. I will write to General Kauffman one of these days to Teschkent,[8] where he is General Governor for the last ten years, and he can get me all the copies and translations from the old manuscripts I want. Isn't it extraordinary that the government (Russian) does not care more about them than it does? Whereto do you trace the lost tribes of Israel?

I suppose I gave you the headache by this time, so I close; I will forward you Saturday the last chapters of the Second Part if I can, but this part is not finished yet and I want your advice as to how to wind it up.

Truly and respectfully yours,
H. P. Blavatsky.

NOTES:

1. The reference seems to be to the physician Dr. Marquette, but she was a woman. It is likely that "Mr." is a typographical error for either "Dr." or "Mme.," the latter title being one HPB used for her elsewhere (*CW* 1:408).

2. Wilder followed the text of this letter with a note on the identity of the Phoenicians and other matters mentioned by HPB. The full note is as follows:

> Perhaps there should be some reply made here to these inquiries, though it seems hardly in keeping. It is true that Herodotus states that the Phoenicians came from the country of the Red or Erythrean Sea, which washes Arabia.
>
> Mr. J. D. Baldwin classifies them as "Cushites," in which race he includes the Arabians and the dominant dark people of India, but not the African tribes. The Cushites of Asia are the Ethiopians of classic times. Although the Phoenicians were styled Kaphts by the Egyptians, and the Philostians are said to have migrated from Kaphta, it has been quite common to identify the Phoenicians with the Canaanites of the Bible. Whether anciently the Jews were of the same people, there must have been a close relation, and we find in the Bible that no exception was taken to intermarriage till the time of Ezra and Nehemiah. Probably the type was established subsequent to that period. "Ephraim is a Canaanite," says the prophet; "deceitful balances are in his hand, and he loveth to oppress."
>
> I think that Godfrey Higgins and Moor in the "Pantheon" denominated the figure a "Buddha" and negro, that Mme. Blavatsky describes as Krishna. True, Krishna had another name, and this term signifies black. But when India is named, it is not definitely certain how far it extended, or differed from the Asiatic Ethiopia. The Akkadians may have come from that part of Asia; the term signifies Highlands. But the Chaldeans, their supposed successors, are called Kasdim. In the Bible Xenophon wrote of Chaldeans, natives of Armenia.

3. F. Max Müller.

4. Echmiadzin, Armenia.

5. Otto Hermann Wilhelm von Abich.

6. Tiridates.

7. Jasher.

8. Tashkent, Turkistan, now Uzbekistan.

DATE: In its 1908 published version, this letter is dated "August" without a year. *Isis Unveiled* was published on September 29, 1877, and Wilder worked on the index for it a month or so before that. HPB says in the letter that the second part (volume 2) is not yet finished, so August 1877 would be too late a date for the letter. In addition, Wilder comments that Baron de Palm had died during "the season previous," which establishes the year as 1876.

SOURCE: Original unavailable. Copied from *Word* 7 (June 1908): 148–51. Wilder's "Introduction" and "Note" appear on pp. 148 and 151–2 respectively.

~~~~~~

Introduction to Letter 72

The Baron de Palm's bequest to Olcott for the Theosophical Society mentioned in HPB's letter to Aksakoff (70) proved to be a chimera. The Baron's papers showed him to own "the castles of Old and New Wartensee, on Lake Constance, . . . 20,000 acres of land in Wisconsin, . . . and some seven or eight mining properties in Western States" (*ODL* 1:160). The reality Olcott describes was otherwise: "Our first shock came when we opened his trunk at the hospital: it contained two of my own shirts, *from which the stitched name-mark had been picked out.* This looked very cloudy indeed, a bad beginning toward the supposed great bequest" (*ODL* 1:159). Further investigation revealed that "the Wisconsin land had been sold for taxes years before, the mining shares were good only for papering walls, and the Swiss castles proved castles in the air; the whole estate would not yield even enough to reimburse Mr. Newton and myself for the moderate costs of the probate and funeral! The Baron was a broken-down noble, without means, credit, or expectations; a type of a large class who fly to republican America as a last resource when Europe will no longer support them" (*ODL* 1:160–1).

Nevertheless, rumors of a vast estate were rife and are reported in the following two fragments of another letter supposedly written by HPB to Aksakoff:

Letter 72

To A. N. Aksakoff   *October 5, 1876*

. . . considerable number of rich silver mines and 17,000 acres of land.[1]

. . . we are eight of us, and we plan to journey to Thibet, Siam, and Cambodia; however, half of us are archaeologists, and these want to go first to Yucatan and Central America in general, in order to compare American ruins with those of Egypt.[2]

NOTES:

1. According to Solovyov, HPB is referring to the estate of Baron de Palm, who died on May 20, 1876.

2. According to Solovyov, this is what members of the Society planned to do with the proceeds from the Baron's bequest. Such plans are otherwise unknown.

SOURCE: Russian original unavailable. Translated by Boris de Zirkoff from Solovyov's *Sovremennaya* 282. Another English translation by Walter Leaf in *Modern Priestess* 269.

Letter 73

To V. de Zhelihovsky   *[late October or early November 1876]*

I am sending you, my friends, one more article of mine,[1] which received by no means small honors here and was reprinted by several New York papers. You see, the London scientist Huxley has been here, "the progenitor of proto-plasm and highpriest of *psychophobia*," as I have christened him. He delivered three lectures. In the first, he made short work of Moses and abolished the whole of the Old Testament, declaring to the public that man is nothing but the great-grandson of a frog of the Silurian period. In the second, like another *Kit-Kitich*,[2] he insulted everyone. "You are all fools," he said, "you don't understand anything. . . . Here is the four-toed foot of Hipparion, the antediluvian horse, for you, from which it follows that we, five-toed men, are closely related to it as well, in respect to our origin." What an affront! At the third lecture, our very wise psychophobe overstepped all bounds and started telling fibs. "Listen to me," he said, "I have looked through telescopes, I have whistled under the clouds in balloons, looking everywhere for God with great zeal. And nowhere, in spite of all my seeking, have I either seen him or met him! . . . *Ergo*—there is no God and there never was any such!" Of what worth was it to pay him five thousand dollars for three lectures of this sort of logic? "Also," he says, "the human soul . . . Where is it? Show it to me as I can show you the heart and the other 'innards. Anima mundi—Aether, the Archon of Plato. Search as I may through spyglasses and microscopes, observing those about to die and dissecting the dead, nowhere," he says, "on my word of honor, is there a trace of it! . . . It is all a lot of hokum on the part of Spiritists and Spiritualists. Don't believe them!"

I was quite saddened over this! I even got angry, so I thought to myself, let me go and write an *editorial* about this conceited Kit-Kitich! Well, what do you know? I wrote it. And it didn't come out badly, as you can judge by the enclosed copy. Of course, I immediately took this article, sealed it, and sent it through our corresponding fellows to London, to Huxley, with my most earnest compliments.

NOTES:

1. "Huxley and Slade: Who Is More Guilty of 'False Pretences'?" *Banner of Light* 40 (Oct. 28, 1876): 1 (*CW* 1:226–33).

2. A note in the *Path* (NY) 9 (Feb. 1895): 384 explains:

> Kit Kitich, or in Academic Russian Tit Titich, is a stage character whose favorite saying is: "Who can beat Kit Kitich when Kit Kitich will beat everyone first?" He has long become the synonym of a bully, a petty, self-willed, domestic tyrant. The popular Russian dialect quite unconsciously transforms "Titus, the son of Titus" (Tit Titich) into "the Whale, the son of the Whale" ("Kit" means "whale" in Russian); and H.P.B. used this unconscious pun to make fun of the biological evolutionist who claimed to be, in some sense, the son of the whale, and whose doctrines she found to be "very like a whale", too.

The phrase "very like a whale" is an allusion to Shakespeare's *Hamlet* (3.2.400), in which the dotard Polonius humors Hamlet by seeing similarities where none exist:

[Hamlet:] Do you see yonder cloud that's almost in shape of a camel?
[Polonius:] By the mass, and 'tis like a camel, indeed.
[Hamlet:] Methinks it is like a weasel.
[Polonius:] It is backed like a weasel.
[Hamlet:] Or like a whale?
[Polonius:] Very like a whale.

DATE: Since HPB's article on Huxley was in the issue of the *Banner* for Oct. 28 and HPB says it was reprinted several times, this letter was probably written in late October or possibly early November.

SOURCE: Russian original unavailable. Translated by Boris de Zirkoff from *Russkoye Obozreniye* 2 (Nov. 1891): 261–2. Another English translation in *Path* (NY) 9 (Feb. 1895): 383–4.

Letter 74

To C. C. Massey   *[November 1876]*

Hail Son of the West,—(End), adept of the Athenaeum, Seer of the Saville;[1] may your shadow never diminish but dazzle the Elmo[2] with its unfailing brightness. So, you will persist in misunderstanding, and insulting my white hairs like our friend—the *Imperial* Cross Medium?[3] Formerly, you did not write to me because you were afraid that I had seven illegitimate children, and now, because you do not know how to call me.—"What the devil shall I call her"? you ask Olcott.[4] Meanwhile, I don't hear from you at all. Your silence is growing as monotonous as the shower of mules did through Mark Twain's mining cabin. For the Lord's sake, let us have a few of these graphic and highly sympathetic hieroglyphics of yours, which you write so well and others decipher with such pain. What you put in the papers is all well enough: "High-toned"—as our Emma H.

Britten says—and dignified but that is only an Occultist under a mask—I want to see what progress you really made. Now, that I have my infernal book off my hands my heart yearns after the trans Atlantic brace of Iamblicho-Apollonians, and Porphyritico-Hermetists.[5] Are they treading with stone-proof and fire-proof *sole* the rugged path of truth, or wandering in the enticing fields of sense and juvenile fancy?

Beware o young Böhmenist,[6] lest in grasping the shadow of the small shoemaker's enticing Eve, you lose the favors of the veiled Mother Isis! "—Is there a purgatorial state"? Alas! my young—neither single nor married friend, need you ask *me* the question? So long as you know that upon your tombstone can be inscribed: "Honest citizen, Well meaning father, reformed Belgravian,[7] etc. etc." Why need you fear? I am glad, my friend, Mme Kittary left London in a hurry and so removed the danger to the General's (Kittary) peace of mind. Her dreamy beauty might have proved à la longue [*Fr.* in the long run] too much for you two hungry, fasting and praying occultists. You can now judge by Slade's spooks,[8] what sort of a control you would have made if you had not reformed. But seriously, I am extremely glad that you and Cox and others have had this experience; for now you will appreciate and enable others to appreciate the character of (physical medium's) "angel" guides. If to convince doubters you require corroboration of that case, point them to what generally happened at Spiritual seances *twenty* years ago. From the great Medium Slade, pass to the now less glorious and *pure* Medium Home. See what des Mousseaux writes of *his Spirits*, at a certain seance with Madame Benajet (?) and some other ladies of the highest and most respectable Parisian society. Take the "Hauts Phenomènes de la Magie," and at Pag. 348, read of a seance which was commented upon by all Paris. The same happened at St Petersburg, with the old Princess

Troubetzkoy, who complained of it to the Emperor. No women's *crinolines* are safe from the explorations of these Elementary Livingstones.[9] The same thing happened here with Slade frequently, and some years ago, a Mrs Porter, a famous medium of her day, shocked while under control the most depraved of her visitors with her awful immorality and profanity of speech and action. These are only specimen-cases, to which an unlimited number might be added. The germinal vice of mediums sprouts, matures, and flowers under the control of the *eight* sphere spirits, (which are far worse than the poor fools called Elementary) like poisonous toad-stools after a summer shower. You would *do your duty*, and a SACRED duty it is Mr Massey, if you would publish something upon this point and translate what des Mousseaux says in the above indicated Chapter. You can use a pseudonym. Of course I make this suggestion as to one who is an Occultist; if the shoe does not fit you, do not wear it.

And now my dear camarade,[10] I am sorry to say, that you are an awful cheat. How many times did you promise me your picture? Is it noble, and fair and just, to deceive a poor, old, helpless creature like me, a weak woman, abandoned by the stern and puritan like, virtuous world to her solitary remorses? Do you wish to bring my white hairs in sorrow to the grave? No; then send me your portrait that you faithfully promised and so wickedly cheated me out of. Let me hang it between the dove-eyed, dear M. A. Oxon[11] and the shock-headed Judge, in company with our lion-hearted and brave President, H S. Olcott, who backs out and takes to his heels in no time before an angry astral *eel*, after having defied the whole city! Fancy, Olcott heels up on the floor and taking the said eel for the materialized shape of the "Dweller" in the skin of a boa constrictor 70 feet long. He tells me he described the scene to Oxon; but I doubt if he did full justice to the outrageously ridiculous sight that he presented at that moment. Alas! Alas! we are not quite ready yet to encounter the Dweller of the Thresh-hold!! Now look here, Milord, if you do not send a magnificent Imperial photo of yourself, Sunday shirt collar and sweet smile and the rest, I—well see what I will do with you. En attendant [*Fr.* meanwhile] may the Proarchē,[12] send you his materialized Paradigm for your edification.

Halloo—hold on! . . .

Olcott just read me your last letter. What the devil are you abusing me for when I am as innocent of all guilt towards you as an unborn Elementary? "Poor Massey" *indeed!*" you quote a *would be* phrase, or sentence of mine. Well, and if I did write "*poor* Massey", what of that? I like to stimulate occasionally well meaning Occult candidates. And I bet two pence ha'penny[13] that were it not for that slight impertinence on my part the world would not have seen the exhibition of moral courage that you have given it. But now, I *respect* you, I *admire* you, I stuck you snug at the very bottom of my tender, motherly heart; and every time I turn the prayer cylinder[14] I grind out eighteen Pater Nosters and forty two Aves[15] for the growth of your astral Soul. And when at the silent watches of the night I spread my bat's-wings and fly on my spiritual broom-stick to the head-waters of the Ganges, I take your dear Spirit upon one arm, Oxon's upon the other and with Olcott hooked to my back and Judge to my girdle I carry my newly hatched brood to the feet of the grand Lama and have their heads shampooed.[16]

Of all the flap-doodles Cora Tappan's last is the greatest. Did you read her masterly dissection of the word Occultism? or her Symbolism on the mother, the letter M and the religion of the ancients? Really the woman seems to have a Verbo-mania. She galops furiously through the Dictionaries clutching adjectives nouns and verbs with both hands as she passes and crams them into her mouth. It's a perfect

Niagara of Spiritual flap-doodle; enough to force any respectable shadow of a camp-meeting preacher let alone Demosthenes or Cicero [to] fly in terror for their lives. As she misrepresented Olcott in her speech he took up the challenge, and will comb her hair in the next "Banner."

The cremation of the old Baron [de Palm] will take place next month if nothing prevents. He must be a pretty boy to look at now. The Newspapers begin ringing the bells already, and when the thing comes off you will see the liveliest excitement that this country has ever produced: I have a good mind to cremate myself in the sight of the public together with him (or rather what remains of him, for he has turned into a Baronial broth by this time) and then resuscitate again phenix-like.

You never tell us what sort of phenomena takes place with Oxon, when you are alone with him. You are a bad boy altogether.

May the shadow of the Athenaeum and Saville Clubs keep you fresh and pure from the Universal pollution.

Sincerely and honestly
Votre tres humble et tres devouée
[*Fr.* Your very humble and very obedient]
H P Blavatsky

NOTES:

1. The envelope of the letter is addressed thus:

   C. Carlton Massey Esq.
   Athenaeum Club
   Pall-Mall
   LONDON
   England

   The Athenaeum and Saville are fashionable clubs in the West End of London, affording sociability, food, and temporary lodging to their members.

2. Perhaps St. Elmo's fire.

3. The *"Imperial* Cross Medium" is William Stainton Moses, whose chief control signed his written communications to Moses as "Imperator +."

4. Across the top of the first page, written upside down on either side of HPB's monogram, is the following:

> How shall you call me? Well suppose you call me, or rather address me as [there follow two groups of four symbols each] —or if you prefer as [there follow two groups of three symbols each, followed by a dash and on the next line two more groups of three symbols each and a period] This looks ancient, pretty and *truthful*, for this is one of my *true* names.

The symbols, each different, look like a form of writing but, given the banteringly jocular tone of the letter, were probably arbitrarily invented for this use and meaningless.

5. A playful allusion to nineteenth-century enthusiasts of Iamblichus, Apollonius, Porphyry, and Hermeticism.

6. "Young Böhmenist" refers to Massey as a disciple of Jakob Böhme, who was a shoemaker by trade. In this metaphorical warning, she may be advising Massey not to become exclusively committed to Böhme's Christian mysticism ("grasping the shadow of the small shoemaker's enticing Eve") and thereby missing what he can learn from Eastern occultism ("lest . . . you lose the favors of the veiled Mother Isis").

7. A resident of Belgravia, a very fashionable area of London near Hyde Park.

8. On October 1, 1876, the month before the probable date of this letter, the medium Henry Slade was tried in London and found guilty of obtaining money under false pretenses by faking writing by spirits on a slate. He was sentenced to three months of hard labor, but the conviction was nullified on technical grounds. The case was a cause celebre at the time HPB wrote this letter. (*EOP* 2:1185)

9. An allusion to missionary-explorer David Livingstone, whose explorations took him to parts of equatorial Africa not earlier discovered by Europeans.

10. French; in English, an obsolete form of *comrade*; cf. *camaraderie*.

11. An academic degree, Master of Arts, Oxonian (*i.e.*, from Oxford), used as a byname by Stainton Moses.

12. The demiurge or builder of the universe, who works according to a *paradigm* (Gk. *paradeigma*), a "pattern, model, architect's plan, sculptor's or painter's model."

13. Two and a half pennies, a British English expression for an inconsiderable amount; cf. "not give a twopenny damn" (not care at all), "not have two halfpennies to rub together" (not have a dime or a red cent), and American "a dime a dozen."

14. A reference to the popular Tibetan Buddhist practice of turning a handheld cylinder to which are attached written mantras (such as "Om Mani Padme Hum"), each revolution of the cylinder representing an utterance of the mantra, thus permitting a large number of mantras to be uttered quickly.

15. Pater Nosters (Our Fathers, or repetitions of the Lord's Prayer) and Aves (Ave Marias, repetitions of the prayer beginning "Hail Mary") are part of the Catholic recitation of the rosary, a devotional practice comparable to the use of Tibetan prayer cylinders. HPB's reference to 18 Pater Nosters and 42 Aves is unclear; the numbers may be unrelated to Catholic practice. In the traditional rosary prayer, attributed to St. Dominic, there are three cycles (devoted to respectively joyful, sorrowful, and glorious events in the lives of Mary and Jesus), each cycle consisting of five "mysteries." For each mystery, one Pater Noster, ten Aves, and one Gloria Patri ("Glory be to the Father, to the Son, and to the Holy Ghost") are recited, making 5 Pater Nosters and 50 Aves for each mystery, or 15 Pater Nosters and 150 Aves for the complete rosary. The recitation of these prayers was also often assigned as penance after the confession of sins; the number of recitations varying according to the Father Confessor's judgment of the seriousness of the offence.

16. A mocking reference to the manner in which witches were supposed to travel to their sabbat, or midnight assemblies to renew their allegiance to the devil.

DATE: Near the end of the letter, HPB says the cremation of Baron de Palm "will take place next month." The cremation was on December 6, 1876, which suggests that this letter was written in November. HPB's statement in the first paragraph, "Now, that I have my infernal book off my hands," must refer to *Isis Unveiled* and so suggests a date about a year later; however, she often anticipated the completion of writing projects well before she actually reached that point.

SOURCE: Transcribed from the original in the Archives of the College of Psychic Studies, London. Published in *Light* 113 (spring 1993): 21–4.

⌒

Introduction to Letter 75

Alexander Wilder continued his article in *Word* (see letter 71) with a second letter from HPB, which he introduced with the following explanation:

> The ensuing autumn and winter I delivered a course of lectures in a medical college in New York. This brought me from Newark several times each week and gave me an opportunity to call at the place on West Forty-seventh Street if there was occasion.
>
> During the season previous Baron de Palm had died in Roosevelt Hospital. He was on intimate terms with the family group in West Forty-seventh Street, and had received necessary attentions from them during his illness. Whatever he possessed of value he bestowed upon them, but with the pledge or condition that his body should be cremated. This was a novel, not to say a shocking idea, to people generally. There was but one place for such a purpose in the United States. Dr. Francis Le Moyne had constructed it at Washington, in Western Pennsylvania. He was an old-time abolitionist, when this meant social proscription, and in 1844 was the candidate for the Liberty Party for Vice-President. He had advanced views on the disposal of the dead and had built the crematory for himself and family. The arrangements were made for the cremation of the body of the deceased Baron, as soon as winter had come to permit its transportation from New York. Colonel Olcott had charge of the matter. Being a "newspaper man" and rather fond of display, he induced a large party to go with him to see the first cremation in America. This was the introduction of this practice into this country.
>
> During his absence I called at the house on Forty-seventh Street, but my ringing was not answered. I then wrote a note

stating my errand. Madame Blavatsky answered at once as follows:

Letter 75

To A. Wilder [ca. December 6, 1876]

My Dear Doctor:

Now, that's too bad, but I really think you must have rung the *wrong* bell. I did not go out of the house for the last two months, and the servant is always in the kitchen until half-past nine or ten. Why did you not pull all the bells one after the other? Well, you must come Monday—as you have to come to town, and stop over till Tuesday. You can attend your College and sleep here the same, can't you? And Olcott will be back to talk your law business with you; but if you want something particular, or have some law affairs which are pressing, why don't you go to Judge, to 71 Broadway, Olcott's and Judge's office. Judge will attend to anything you want. He is a smart lawyer, and a faithful true friend to all of us. But of course you know better yourself how to act in your own business. Olcott will be home by Friday night I think. I could *not* go, though they expect me there to-day. To tell you the truth, I do not see the fun of spending $40.00 or $50.00 for the pleasure of seeing a man burnt. I have seen burnings of dead and living bodies in India sufficiently.

Bouton is an extraordinary man. He says to Olcott that it is for you to decide whether it [*Isis Unveiled*] will be one or two volumes, etc., and you tell me he needs no estimate of yours! He told you "how to go to work." Can't you tell us what he told you? It is no curiosity, but business. As I am adding all kind of esoteric and other matter in Part II, I would like to know what I can write, and on what subjects I am to shut my mouth. It is useless for me to labor if it is all to be cut out. Will you please, dear doctor, tell me what

I have to do? I am of your opinion about Inman; but *facts are facts*. I do not go against Christianity, neither against Jesus of Nazareth. I simply go for the skulls of theologians. Theology is neither Christianity nor religion. It is human and blasphemous flapdoodle. I suppose any one understands it. But how can I make a parallel between heathen or pagan worship and the Christian unless I give facts? It is facts and scientific discovery which kills exoteric and fetish-worshiping Christianity, not what Inman or I can *say*. But laying Inman aside, read "Supernatural Religion"[1] which had in less than 18 months six editions in England. The book is written by a Bishop, one of the most learned Theologians of the Church of England. Why he kills divine *Revelation* and *dogmas* and *Gospels* and all that.

Believe me, Dr. Wilder, a little and cowardly abuse will kill a book; a courageous and sincere criticism of this hypocritical, lying, dirty crew—Catholic Clergy—will help sell the book. I leave the Protestants and other Christian religions nearly out of question. I only go for Catholics. A pope who calls himself the Viceregent of God on earth, and openly sympathizes with the Turks against the unfortunate Bulgarian Christians, is a Cain—a fiend; and if the French Liberal papers themselves publicly abuse him, Bouton must not fear that the book will be prevented in its sale because I advise the old Antichrist, who has compared himself for the last two years with all the Prophets of the Bible and with the "slain Lamb" himself—if I advise him moreover, to compare himself, while he is at work, to Saul; the Turkish *Bashi-Bazook*[2] to David; and the Bulgarians to the Philistines. Let him, the old cruel Devil promise the Bashi-Bazook (David) his daughter the Popish Church (Michal) in marriage if he brings him 100 foreskins of the Bulgarians.[3]

I have received letters from home. My aunt sends me a piece of poetry by the famous Russian author and poet—

J. Tourgeneff.[4] It was printed in all the Russian papers, and the Emperor has forbidden its publication from consideration (and politics I suppose) for old Victoria. My aunt wants me to translate it and have it published here in the American newspapers, and most earnestly she appeals for that[.] I cannot write poetry. God knows the trouble I have with my prose. But I have translated every line *word for word* (eleven quatrains in all). Can you put them in verses so as to preserve the rhyme and rhythm, too? It is a splendid and thrilling thing entitled "Crocket at Windsor," the idea being a vision of the Queen, who looks upon a crocket game and sees the balls chased by the mallet, transformed into rolling heads of women, girls and children tortured by the Turks. Goes home; sees her dress all covered with gore, calls on the British rivers and waters for help to wash out the stain, and hears a voice answered, "No, Majesty no, this innocent blood,"— "You can never wash out—nevermore," etc.[5]

My dear Doctor, can you do me a favor to write me half a page or so of a "Profession of faith," to insert in the first page or pages of Part II?[6] Just to say briefly and eloquently that it is not against Christ or the *Christ*-religion that I battle. Neither do I battle against any *sincere, true* religion, but against theology and Pagan Catholicism. If you write me this I will know how to make variations on this theme without becoming guilty of false notes in your eyes and the sight of Bouton. Please do; you can do it in three minutes. I see that none of your symbologists, neither Payne Knight, King, Dunlap, Inman, nor Higgins, knew anything about the *truths* of initiation. All is *exoteric* superficial guess work with them. 'Pon my word, without any compliment, there's Taylor[7] alone and yourself, who seem to grasp truth *intuitionally*. I have read with the greatest pleasure your edition of the "Eleusinian and Bacchic Mysteries!" You are right. Others know Greek better, but Taylor knew Plato thousand times better; and I have found in your short fragments much matter which for the life of me I do not know where you could have learned it. Your *guesses* are so many *hits* right on the true spot. Well, you ought to go East and get initiated.

Please come on Monday. I will have a bed ready for you Sunday, Monday, and Tuesday, and I will be expecting you to dinner all these days. If you cannot come until Monday, do tell me what instructions Bouton gave you, and what are the precise orders for *mutilations*, will you?

Esoterically yours in true Platonism,
H. P. Blavatsky.

NOTES:

1. By Walter Richard Cassels.

2. Bashi-bazouk, "a member of an irregular ill-disciplined auxiliary of the Ottoman Empire…a turbulent ill-disciplined person" (*Webster's Third*).

3. The Biblical allusion is to the scheme of Saul, who was jealous of David's popularity with the people, to force David into a battle with the Philistines in which he might be killed. To effect that, Saul offered his daughter Michal as David's wife, if David would bring Saul, in lieu of a bride price, one hundred foreskins from Philistines he had killed. The topical allusion is to what HPB considered an unholy alliance in which the Pope (as Saul), gave the sympathy of the Catholic Church (as Michal) to the Turkish forces (as David), in fighting against the Orthodox Christian Bulgarians (as the Philistines), which had begun on June 30, 1876. Other references to this war are in letters 77 and 81.

4. Ivan Sergeyevich Turgenev.

5. Turgenev's poem "Croquet at Windsor" appeared in an English translation in the New York *Illustrated Weekly* of June 2, 1877, in 10 quatrains (*CW* 1:253–4). This letter indicates that HPB made a literal translation of the Russian and Alexander Wilder put her version into poetry, the English poem thus having two authors.

6. The apologia that HPB asked Wilder to write for her is doubtless the "Preface to Part II" of volume 2 of *Isis Unveiled*, or at least the basis for it. The diction and style of that preface suggest that it is primarily Wilder's work.

7. Thomas Taylor, the classicist author of *Eleusinian and Bacchic Mysteries*, which Wilder edited.

DATE: HPB writes in the first paragraph that she was expected "today" for the cremation of Baron de Palm's body. It was cremated on December 6, 1876, so this undated letter must have been written on or just before that day.

SOURCE: Original unavailable. Copied from *Word* 7 (June 1908): 153-5. Wilder's introduction is on pp. 152-3.

Letter 76

To A. N. Aksakoff   *[late 1876]*

Last year when I wrote an article[1] on the identity of the ancient symbols and religions of Egypt and Assyria and the cults of the Aztecs and Quichés, as described by Brasseur de Bourbourg and Herrera, the Spanish historian, all the archaeologists attacked me and accused me of various fancies. But I have myself seen in Palenque and Uxmal vaults with triangular arches without keystone; this sort of architecture is to be found *only* in the oldest of the ancient temples of Egypt, in Nagkon Wat and Angkor, in Siam and Cambodia; the ruins of the latter country puzzle all the learned societies, who have all racked their brains with every sort of hypothesis but the right one, which is that in the archaic ages, how many thousands of years ago we do not know, but certainly before the Mosaic people, both the Aryan and Semitic tribes (in short, before the separation of these nations) belonged to one and the same religion, the same which only survives today among the adepts of the Occult Sciences. And now it is turning out as I said. Lord Dufferin, Governor General of Canada, discovered in British Columbia an Indian tribe hitherto almost unknown, who live in a village, several centuries old, built of the remains of the most magnificent temples, columns, porticoes, etc.

And what do you know? The sculpture is precisely the same as in the temples of Egypt, sphinxes, winged bulls as in Assyria, snakes, and finally the god Thoth or Tot (Hermes) with a hawk's head! I long ago pointed out the strange fact that the descendants of the Quichés in Mexico call themselves snakes. "We are snakes, sons of the wise serpents," they say. Other tribes call themselves that too, such as the Canaanites and Medians,[2] i.e., those who were initiated into the mysteries of the temples, the initiates of the high Theurgy, as the father of Moses' wife, for instance, Reuel, or Jethro the Medianite,[2] who instructed him in magic. "Snakes' holes" was the name given to the underground passages which served as the seat of the mysteries of the temple, and were known only to the initiated adepts; crypts of the snakes as Champollion-Figeac calls them. Hieroglyphics, pyramids, cynocephali,[3] sacred apes, crocodiles, rituals, adoration of the sun as the visible symbol of the invisible Godhead, all this Egyptian and Chaldean antiquity you will find in Central and North America, and much of it also in the esoteric rites of the Buddhist mystics. When Wrangel showed the world of science the possibility—or rather the probability—that the Indians and Mexicans found by Cortes in America are the descendants of emigrants from Europe and Asia, and of the Tartar tribes of Siberia who had crossed from one continent to the other by the Bering Straits, they actually laughed at him, but now it turns out that he was *partially* right. All popular legends point to this. But the Indians of British Columbia, the owners of the Egyptian sphinxes and other symbols, have yet another tradition. They positively say that their ancestors flew over the ocean on *Birds with wings* (ships with sails as I understand it), and that each of these birds had on its breast the face of the wife of the "Great Spirit," Dida, as they call her. How can we help recognizing in this Dida Dido, whose name was in different nations

Astarte, Venus, Didona, Elissa, Anaita, Artemis and Al-iza, now the Goddess of the Mohammedan Mecca? Dido was, as you know, not a living queen, but a mere myth, the idol of the Goddess Astarte, the unfailing attribute of every Phoenician ship; they usually fastened her head on the prow of the ship. And the Phoenicians were themselves the ancestors of the Jews of Palestine in the opinion of Herodotus and more modern historians. Finally, the Phoenicians are the same as the Canaanites who fled before the armies of Joshua, son of Nun, and passed through the Pillars of Hercules, on which according to the historians there was an inscription saying: "We are the sons of those who fled the brigand Jesus, son of Nave." This is stated by Procopius the historian (*De bello vandalico*), and St. Augustine. It means that those who fled and escaped to America are the Hivites or the Hiveens, descendants of Heth, son of Canaan.[4] However, all the above is *my own particular* speculation, while archaeologists are of a different opinion. I am writing you all this without knowing if it interests you. But you wish to know what we occupy ourselves with at our gatherings. As you see it is with archaeological investigations that explain the identity of symbols of all ancient peoples. From symbols it is not far to "medicine men" of all the Indian tribes, i.e., adepts in magic— though degenerated—as in ancient Egypt and modern India, with its Lamas and fakirs, whom Jaccoliot,[5] as well as *Art Magic*,[6] describes. We are getting at the roots of everything. A given symbol, for instance, means so and so, and belongs to such and such a divinity, Jupiter for example; Jupiter in each of his transformations, as the "descending" in the form of *rain*, must of necessity typify some one force of Nature, whether known to the science of today or *still unknown* (the latter is much more often the case). Every such force, a cosmic force or power, if it was once raised to a symbol by the ancients, shows that its nature or quality was known to them. The symbol in its exoteric sense was given over to the ignorant masses and is being looked upon in our era (so learned, God knows!) as *superstition*; but the initiates, the priests of the adytum and of the sanctuary knew its real value well; they knew what the physical and natural force contained within itself as far as the various combinations of the occult and the mysterious are concerned, something that the scholars of today ignore and consequently reject. . . .

. . . Good gracious, you are very likely wondering at this moment if I had gone entirely out of my mind! Yet so it is. I have explained this law—*a purely physical one*—to our members, and proved to them besides, by facts, that it is so. With an electric battery and a powerful current we first ascertained by a well-known process what sort of magnetism there was *on the carpet* of the room; we electrified a cat and it rose up several inches. In spite of my warnings, it was then electrified more powerfully, and of course the poor cat suddenly expired. . . .

NOTES:

1. No such published article has been identified. An article on somewhat similar themes, "A Land of Mystery," was published in the *Theosophist* in 1880 (*CW* 2:303–38). However, the second half of chapter 14 in volume 1 of *Isis Unveiled* covers the topics mentioned here. It is likely that the "article" was incorporated into *Isis*, which HPB was writing at the time.

2. Midians, Midianite.

3. Latin from Greek, literally "dog-headed ones," a fabulous race of humans with the heads of dogs or dog-faced baboons.

4. Hivite, Heth, Canaan: Genesis 10.15–7.

5. Louis Jacolliot.

6. By Emma Hardinge Britten.

DATE: Because the book *Art Magic* referred to in the letter was published in September or October 1876, this letter must have been written after that. If "our gatherings" mentioned by HPB toward the end of the letter are meetings of the Theosophical Society, a more precise date is possible. Boris de Zirkoff (*CW* 1:lx–lxi) cites Olcott as reporting that no meetings of the Society were held in New York between November 15, 1876, and July 16, 1877. That would date the letter probably in October or November 1876. However, if the "gatherings" were soirees at the "Lamasery," as the apartment on 47th Street was nicknamed, the terminus ad quem could be later.

SOURCE: Russian original unavailable. Translated by Boris de Zirkoff from Solovyov's *Sovremennaya* 283–6. Another English translation by Walter Leaf in *Modern Priestess* 271–5.

Letter 77

To V. de Zhelihovsky [*February 1877*]

I told him[1] that his efforts were in vain; that whatever I personally, as a Theosophist, believe, was none of his business! That the Orthodox faith of my Russian brethren was sacred to me! That I will *always* defend that faith and Russia, and shall challenge the attacks of the hypocritical Catholics upon them, as long as my hand can hold a pen, without fear of either the threats of their Pope or the wrath of the Roman Church—*la Grande Bête de l'Apocalypse* [*Fr.* the Great Beast of the Book of Revelation].

NOTE:

1. The Jesuit Secretary of Cardinal McCloskey, who according to Vera de Zhelihovsky was sent to HPB by the Cardinal as a result of her articles against the Pope's support of the Turks during the Serbo-Turkish War, which began June 30, 1876, ended with an armistice on October 31, 1876, and a treaty on March 1, 1877, but was resumed in December of that year after Russia declared war on Turkey on April 24, and eventually concluded with a treaty on March 3, 1878. Letter 75 contains another allusion to this war.

DATE: By Vera de Zhelihovsky.

SOURCE: Russian original unavailable. Translated by Boris de Zirkoff from *Russkoye Obozreniye* 2 (Nov. 1891): 260–1. Another English translation in *Path* (NY) 9 (Feb. 1895): 383.

Introduction to Letter 78

On January 23, 1877, the *New York World* (page 5) published an interview with HPB, which was reprinted in the *Banner of Light* on February 3, 1877 (page 2). The interview, of interest in its own right despite some errors, elicited some responses from HPB. The article was as follows:

A COMING BUDDHIST BOOK.
"THE VEIL OF ISIS" AND THE LADY WHO IS WRITING IT
A DOUBLE ATTACK UPON SCIENCE AND DOGMATIC THEOLOGY.

Mme. Blavatsky was found yesterday afternoon sitting by a blue window with rose-pink curtains at a large library-table which occupied all the available space that was not taken up by a desk almost as large, in her cosy work-room. She is an affable Russian lady, no longer very young and certainly not old, who is known all over the world as a scholar in various branches of occult knowledge. She was a member of the commission appointed some time since by the Russian Government to investigate spiritualism, and dissents decidedly from the report of that commission, which was adverse to the claims of Spiritualists. Piled up on the table and desk, and strewed thick upon the floor were hundreds upon hundreds of sheets of manuscript, and in the circumscribed space on the table, kept clear for reading and writing, were proof-sheets and more manuscripts and writing materials.

"Yes. I am writing a book," she said in reply to a question from the reporter. "It is to be called 'The Veil of Isis,' and is in two parts. In the first part I attack science, and in the second part dogmatic theology."

"Surely you do not attack science," said the startled reporter, wondering what would be left.

"No, not science as it is, but the teachings of modern scientists. Science is a true and beautiful thing, but these modern scientists have not found out what it is. They borrow theories from the ancients, and dress them up in beautiful, eloquent language, and pass them off for their own productions. The ideas that Huxley advanced while he was over here are all taken from the ancients, as I shall show in my book. But they don't any of them know what they talk about—Huxley, Tyndall and the rest. They refuse to investigate things which are absolutely demonstrated, and they break their noses over the origin of matter, which is a correlation of spirit, and they reach, for a conclusion, the annihilation of man."

"What is your religion?" asked the reporter.

"I am a Buddhist."

"But does not Buddhism hold out annihilation as the last best good?"

"Not at all. That is simply one of the misrepresentations of ignorant theologians. The Buddhists say that whatever is beyond the power of human language to describe, beyond the reach of human intellect to conceive—whatever is impossible in any measure to understand is, so far as man is concerned, non-existent, and what we term God is therefore non-existent. That is, that so far as the understanding of man is concerned, God can have no existence. You see it is merely a refinement of metaphysics. And they believe in the triple nature of man; they teach that we are a material body, an astral body and pure soul, or *nous*, as the Greek terms it. After the death of the material body we lead a dual existence, and finally, when purified, the soul enters *nirawana*, that is, it rejoins the Creator."

"But do Buddhists believe in spirits?"

"Most certainly. The lives of the fakirs illustrate that. A European or an American can hardly imagine the lives they lead. They remain in one attitude, in one spot, for years, absorbed in the contemplation of their souls. If you put food into the mouth of one of them, he will eat it. If you don't he will quietly sit and starve to death. Those men are possessed of pure spirits. And they apparently overcome the laws governing matter. You would not believe me if I should tell you what I have seen them do, and yet the whole world knows that the Prince of Wales saw one of them lift himself up and sit motionless in mid air a yard or more away from any support."

"But what is this astral body you speak of?"

"It is not spirit and yet not the matter with which we are familiar. It is imponderable matter, imperceptible to the senses."

"Believing in spirits, so you believe in what are called spiritual manifestations?"

"Certainly. The phenomena that are presented as such are perhaps often frauds. Perhaps only one in a hundred is a genuine communication of spirits, but the one cannot be judged by the others. It is entitled to scientific examination, and the reason the scientists don't examine it is because they are afraid. They explore in all directions till they come to shut doors, and they dare not open them for fear of returning to the superstitions of our ancestors, who knew far more than we do. But I believe in them because I have seen them. These mediums cannot deceive me. I know more about it than they do. I have lived for years in different parts of the East, and have seen far more wonderful things than they do.

"The day after I arrived in New York," she continued, "having left Paris suddenly (I did not think of starting until the evening before I started) I went to see Dr. Slade. He knew I was a foreigner by my accent, but he could not tell if I was German or French, or what. He wrote out a message in the Russian language from a friend of my childhood, who died years ago. Again, I have had Mrs. Thayer here over night. She went to bed, and I sat writing, as I often do, until three or four in the morning. I heard her trying to say something in her sleep. Probably (laughing heartily) her materialized grandfather was trying to appear. I went into her room and said, 'What is the matter?' On the instant, a shower of freshly cut flowers, with the night-dew on them, fell from the air, burying her up in the bed."

"But what purpose is served by spiritual manifestations?" was asked after Mme. Blavatsky had related several such incidents.

"It is proved that spirits do exist. And I have known good done in various ways by private mediums, and by mediums in the East," was the reply. "But it cannot be expected that pure spirits will communicate with us through such mediums as many of those are to whom you can go and pay 50 cents or $1, or $3 or $5. It is capable of demonstration by medical science that spirits do not communicate through healthy persons. In some way or another, mediums are all imperfect. The spirits which are forever seeking a body to inhabit seize on those which are defective, being unable to control those which are not. So in the East, insane persons are regarded with peculiar veneration, as being possessed of spirits."

"Possessed of a devil, the Scripture has it," suggested the reporter.

"No. *Daimon* is the word in the Scriptures. It does not necessarily mean a devil. It may mean a god. Socrates had a *daimon*, and he certainly was not possessed of a devil."

"A god? Then do you believe in gods?"

"According to the Scriptures, Jehovah said, 'Fear the gods,'" was the indirect reply. "And what do you think the theologians had the sublime impudence to do? They translated it, 'Fear the rulers.'[1] But, as to insane persons. Can any of the medico-scientists tell the reason for insanity? Can they explain it in any way? They stop when they come to anything that requires an explanation involving the so-called supernatural—so called because nothing can be supernatural. The whole universe is filled with spirits. It is nonsense to suppose that we are the only intelligent beings in the world. I believe there is latent spirit in all matter. I believe, almost, in the spirits of the elements. But all is governed by natural laws. Even in cases of apparent violation of these laws, the appearance comes from a misunderstanding of the laws. In cases of certain nervous diseases it is recorded of some patients that they have been raised from their beds by some undiscoverable power, and it has been impossible to force them down. In such cases it has been noticed that they float feet first with any current of air that may be passing through the room. The wonder of this ceases when you come to consider that there is no such thing as the law of gravitation as it is generally understood."

"I don't think I catch your meaning, exactly," said the reporter faintly.

"No. The law of gravitation is only to be rationally explained in accordance with magnetic laws, as Newton tried to explain it, but as the world would not accept it. If the earth is, magnetically speaking, positive, and you can make yourself positive, you are at once repelled. It is told in a fable of Simon Magus that he lay down on the earth, and giving her his breath took hers and visited the stars.

"The world is fast coming to know many things that were known centuries ago, and were discarded through the superstition of theologians," she continued, referring again to Spiritualism. "The church professes to reprobate divination, and yet they chose their four canonical gospels of Matthew, Mark, Luke and John by divination. They took some hundred or so of books at the Nicene Council and set them up, and those that fell down they threw aside as false, and those that stood, being those four, they accepted as true, being unable to decide the question in any other way. And out of the three hundred and eighteen members of the Council only two—Eusebius, the great forger, and the Emperor Constantine—were able to read. The rest were ignorant donkeys. And the theologians of to-day are as great donkeys as they were—greater than Balaam's, for he knew a spirit when he saw it, and owned up to it at once.

"Yes, I suppose there will be any quantity of mud thrown at me," she said, referring to the probable reception of her book by the public. "They have been throwing mud at me ever since I came here, but that has been nothing to what will come when the book appears." But she laughed heartily at the prospect, and seemed to think that the adverse criticisms which she expected from theologians and scientists would be the best compliments she could receive.

NOTE:

1. The reference is to Exodus 22.28: "Thou shalt not revile the gods, nor curse the ruler of thy people." HPB wrote the editor of the *World* a letter that was published on January 24 containing a correction (*CW* 1:237), which included the following:

> I find in his [the interviewer's] "report" a little error that is calculated to give my very esteemed antagonists, the theologians, a poor opinion of my Biblical scholarship. He makes me put into the mouth of Jehovah the injunction, "Fear the gods." What I did say was that in *Exodus*, xxii, 28, Jehovah commands, "Thou shalt not revile the gods"; and that, attempting to break its force, some commentators interpret the word to mean the "rulers."
>
> As I have had the opportunity of knowing many rulers, in many different countries, and never knew one to be "a god," I made so bold as to express my wonder at such an elastic interpretation.

The *Banner of Light* (40:8, Feb. 3, 1877) reprinted her letter to the *World* cited in the note above and added the following:

> The New York World says of Madame Blavatsky that she was first brought to the prominent notice of American Spiritualists by her investigations of the Eddy family in Vermont, and her replies to Dr. Beard on his theory in explanation of the manifestations occurring there. She was born in 1834 at Ekaterinoslar, a province of Russia, of which her father, Colonel Hahn-hahn, was Governor. He was a cousin of the Countess Ida Hahn-hahn, the authoress. Her father dying, she went to her grandfather, one of the three councillors of the Viceroy Woronzoff, in Tiflis, in Georgia. At sixteen she was married to M. Blavatsky, aged seventy-three, Governor of Erivan. At the end of a year they separated, since which time she has traveled all over the Eastern countries, and, in fact, the entire world.

HPB responded in the *Banner of Light* with the following letter, published under the heading "Corrections by Mad. Blavatsky":

Letter 78

To the Editor of the Banner of Light   *[early February 1877]*
302 West 47th street, New York

Sir: Please allow me to state:

1. That I was not born in 1834.

2. That Ekaterinoslaw cannot claim the illustrious honor of being my birth-place.[1]

3. That M. Blavatsky was *not seventy-three* when he capped the climax of my terrestrial felicity by placing his valetudinarian hand in mine. He might have been older, and he might have been younger; some men are.

4. My father's name was *not* Hahn-Hahn.

5. He was *not* Governor of Ekaterinoslaw.

6. I achieved *no* eminence (since such a thing was impossible) by plucking the electrical Beard of the plumes of his conceit.

7. As my grandfather died some twelve years *before* my father, I did *not* live with him two years after his decease.

8. My book, "The Veil of Isis," is not being published by J. W. Benton, but by the well-known house of J. W. Bouton.

And yet, with the reporters' permission, I *do* sign myself,

Yours faithfully,

H. P. Blavatsky

NOTE:

1. Ekaterinoslaw was her birthplace according to reliable accounts (*CW* 1:xxvi).

DATE: The letter, which was printed in the *Banner of Light* for February 17, 1877, would have been written after February 3, when the *Banner* article to which she was responding was published.

SOURCE: Original unavailable. Copied from *Banner of Light* 40 (Feb. 17, 1877): 5.

Letter 79

To N. de Fadeyev   *[March 1, 1877]*

Tell me, my dear, are you interested in physiologico-psychological mysteries? The following thing is certainly an astounding problem for any physiologist: we have in our Society some very learned members (Professor Wilder, for instance, an archaeologist and Orientalist), and all of them come to me with questions and assure me that I know better than they do Oriental languages, and positive as well as abstract sciences. That's a fact, and you can no more ignore a fact than you would a pitchfork! . . . Now then, tell me: how could it have happened that I, a perfect ignoramus up to my mature years, as you know, have suddenly become a phenomenon of learning in the eyes of people who are really learned? . . . This is an impenetrable mystery! I—a psychological enigma, a puzzle for future generations, a Sphinx! . . . Just fancy that I, who never studied anything in life; I, who did not have the least idea, either about chemistry or about physics, or about zoology, am now writing dissertations on all of these subjects. I enter into discussions with scholars and come out victorious. . . . I am not joking; I am speaking seriously. I am scared, because I do not understand how it all happens. . . . It is true that for nearly three years past I have been studying night and day, reading and thinking. Whatever I am reading now seems to me *familiar*. . . . I find errors in the articles of scholars, in the lectures of Tyndall, Herbert Spencer, Huxley and others. . . . If some archaeologist happens to call on me, on taking leave he is certain to assure me that I have made clear to him the meaning of various monuments, and pointed out things to him of which he had never dreamed. All the symbols of antiquity, and their secret meaning, come into my head and stand there before my eyes as soon as the conversation touches on them.

A pupil of Faraday's, a certain Professor H.,[1] who has been christened "the Father of experimental physics" by the voice of a thousand mouths, having spent last evening with me, now assures me that I am well qualified to "put Faraday in my pocket." Can it be that friends and enemies alike have leagued together to make of me a savant, if all that I do is to prove superficially certain wild theories of my own? And if it were only my own devoted Olcott and other Theosophists who had such a high opinion of me, it could be said: *"Dans le pays des aveugles les borgnes sont rois"* [*Fr.* In the land of the blind, the one-eyed are kings]. But I continually have a whole crowd from morning till night of all kinds of Professors, Doctors of Science, and Doctors of Divinity.... for instance, there are two Hebrew Rabbis here, Adler and Goldstein, who are both of them thought to be the greatest Talmudists. They know by heart both the *Quabalah* of Shimon ben Yohai and the *Codex Nazaraeus* of Bardesanes. They were brought to me by A., a protestant clergyman and commentator on the Bible, who hoped they would prove that I am mistaken on the subject of a certain statement in the Chaldean Bible of Onkelos. And with what result? I have beaten them. I quoted to them whole sentences in ancient Hebrew and proved to them that Onkelos is an authority of the Babylonian school.... When I tell these people that I have never been in Mongolia, that I don't understand either Sanskrit, Hebrew or the ancient European languages, they simply laugh at me and say "How does it come that you can describe everything so exactly, if you have never been there?" They believe that I have some secret reason for not admitting the truth, and I feel embarrassed when I must say that I have no knowledge of languages, while at the time everyone can hear me speaking different Indian dialects with a learned man, who has lived twenty years in India.[2] . . . I never tell anyone here about my experience with the Voice. Where does it all come from? Am I a changeling?

NOTES:

1. Professor H. is unidentified. The epithet "Father of experimental physics" probably refers to Michael Faraday, not to the unidentified professor.

2. Boris de Zirkoff notes that the two sentences beginning "When I tell these people . . ." and ending ". . . twenty years in India" are additional sentences that occur in the *Path* (London).

DATE: Boris de Zirkoff in his notebook of the letters dates this letter as most likely March 1, 1877.

SOURCE: Russian original unavailable. Translated by Boris de Zirkoff from *Blue Hills*, xii–xiii. Other English translations in *Path* (NY) 9 (Dec. 1894): 266–8; *Lucifer* 15 (Dec. 1894): 276–7; and *Path* (London) 3 (Nov. 1912): 168–9.

Letter 80

To V. de Zhelihovsky   *[ca. March 1, 1877]*

Would you believe that while I write it seems to me I am writing rubbish and nonsense, which no one will ever understand. Then it is printed and they all begin to rave over it. They reprint it and are in ecstasies! . . . I often wonder: can it be that they are all asses to be in such ecstasies? . . . Now, were I to write in Russian and be praised by my own people, I might, perhaps, believe that I am a credit to my ancestors, Counts Hahn-Hahn von der Rotter-Hahn of blessed memory.

DATE: According to Boris de Zirkoff, written most likely in the summer of 1877. As this letter is similar to letter 79, written to HPB's aunt, it is given a similar date.

SOURCE: Russian original unavailable. Translated by Boris de Zirkoff from *Russkoye Obozreniye* 2 (Nov. 1891): 269. Another English translation in *Path* (NY) 9 (Jan. 1895): 301, where it is combined with letter 87.

⟿

Letter 81

To V. de Zhelihovsky   *[ca. May or June 1877]*

. . . have prophesied that he will not come out of the war unscathed.[1] Wittgenstein writes me and asks what I think about it. . . . What can I think? . . . I inquired of the Master, asking him for an answer. He laughed and said: "Not only will your friend not be killed, but *he will not take part in any engagements of the least serious nature.*" I have written him to this effect.[2]

NOTES:

1. The Russo-Turkish War (1877–78), an extension of the Serbo-Turkish War (1876–78), which concluded by separating Serbia and Montenegro from Turkey as independent states. Other allusions to this war are in letters 75 and 77.

2. On June 18, 1878 (a few months after the war had ended on March 3, 1878), Prince Wittgenstein wrote the editor of the *Spiritualist* magazine about both the prophesy and the protection of the Brothers (reprinted in *Incidents* 209–11). In 1883, HPB wrote her account of the incident, "Comments on 'The "Blessing" of the Brothers'" in the *Theosophist* (CW 4:354–5).

DATE: On June 18, 1878, Wittgenstein wrote that he had received the death prophesies "A year and some months ago, while getting ready to join our army on the Danube." Russia declared war on Turkey on April 24, 1877, which was a year and nearly two months before the date Wittgenstein was writing. HPB's letter appears to have been written not long after the death prophesies, so a date around May or June 1877 is likely.

SOURCE: Russian original unavailable. Translated by Boris de Zirkoff from *Russkoye Obozreniye* 2 (Nov. 1891): 275.

Letter 82

To N. de Fadeyev   *June 8, 1877*

I have finished my article on Nirvana and the conceptions of the ancient Buddhists concerning God, the immortality of the soul, and cosmogony, as compared to the modern decadence of religious ideas.[1] The Editor seems to be very pleased. . . . To be sure, my Master helped me to write it, yet it took me only two evenings. I shall send it to you to look at; possibly someone will translate it for you. I wish Vera would translate it for the Russian press. The article is a good one. Its learning is so great that all the Orientalists will have tremblings in their legs. I also send you Turgenyeff's poem on "the game of croquet at Windsor."[2] I have translated it and received compliments for it. Note please that your relative is called "an accomplished lady" in the editorial note. . . . Life in this country is pleasant, just because you can abuse anybody with perfect immunity, not merely the Pope, but even the Editor of the Presidential organ, the New York Herald. Yet he is an untold power here. However, print will stand anything! . . .

Do not ask me, friend, what I experience, and how these things come about, for I cannot explain anything clearly to you. I do not understand it all myself. One thing I do know: that toward my old age, I have become a bric-a-brac store for the accumulation of various disused objects of antiquity. *Somebody* comes, winding around me like a misty cloud, and then, in one turn sends me out of my body, and I am no more Helena Petrovna, General Blavatsky's faithful spouse, but somebody else, born in a different part of the world, strong and mighty; as to me, it seems as if I were sleeping meanwhile, or at least dozed; not *in* my body, but *beside* it, as if there was some kind of a thread only binding

me to my body, and not letting me go more than two paces
from it. At other times I see clearly everything done by my
body and I understand and *remember* what it says: I see awe,
devotion, and fear in the faces of Olcott and others, and
observe how the Master looks condescendingly at them out
of my eyes, and speaks to them with my physical tongue,
yet not with my brain but his own, which enwraps my brain
like a cloud. I cannot tell you all, Nadya, and just because,
though you are the best, most honest, and noblest of human beings, you are very religious, and you hold to the
holy faith of your forefathers; as to me, though God sees
that in reality I believe in the same things that you do,—
yet I believe *in my* own way. You are accustomed to believe
in the interpretations accepted by the Church, and the
dogmas of orthodoxy, and though I feel that I *know* them
correctly, and firmly, *I do not* understand them from the
human point of view, but from the spiritual point of view,
metaphysically, so to speak. For me, all the symbols, great
and holy as they are in the eyes of the Christians, are still
merely symbols invented by erring humanity for the sake
of a surer and more universal comprehensibility. But I look
through them—not at them—at their very spiritual significance, and in order to come nearer to this meaning, I do
not even notice that often do I overturn the objective in
order to reach the subjective the sooner. In my ideal, Christ
has incarnated, not in Jesus only, but in humanity in its
totality; and as His flesh was crucified, so must all human
flesh be crucified, before man—the *inner* man, the Ego,—
gets a chance to become the *real* man, the Adam Kadmon,
the Heavenly man, of the Chaldean Kabbala. Christ is the
symbol of the highest spirit of man, not of the soul. The
soul is one thing, the spirit is another. There is a soul
(*anima*) in every animal, in every infusoria; but the human
spirit is a direct emanation of the Universal, Boundless,
Endless Spirit of God, about which we sinful creatures

ought not even to think, unless it be in the depth of our hearts, locking ourselves in solitude in the inner chamber, pronouncing His Name mentally, and by no means aloud. (Matthew VI, 5–23). The flesh is the devil, the only devil in the world. There can be no other objective devils of any kind; and the whole world—not our planet alone, but the universe,—is divided into three parts: first, pure spirit; second, half-spirit, half-matter; third, gross matter, our flesh. Every atom of matter (flesh) whether it is earthly, or belongs to the human body, every grain of dust, before it reached its present aspect, was pure spirit, its own essence, so to speak. It is not in the crude material evolution of the physical world, as Darwin teaches it, that I believe, but in the double evolution, the spiritual walking hand in hand, and having always so walked, with the physical. In this I believe completely, just because I believe in the one Universal God, and the immutable logic and necessarianism of His laws, established once for all. This is why I do not believe in the creation of the world *ex nihilo*, nor in miracles, as the foundation of which we have to accept a temporary stoppage of these immutable laws. Do not be angry, but understand me. I *believe* in the *miracles*, the so-called miracles of both Christ and the Apostles, but I do not believe that the Supreme Power in Its own person, brought natural laws to a stoppage for their sake. These laws I do not understand in the sense of our foolish learned folk; for they have not yet dreamed of a tenth part of them, and it is not of natural, physical law I am speaking, but of *spiritual laws* which become manifest in all their power only when man, having become like unto bodiless spirits, has reached, like some miracle-workers, the divine point of his individuality. It is because of this that their own spirit, rid of every trace of the flesh and the devil, acquires the faculty *apparently* to work miracles. Can't you see that the basis for the springing up of all kinds of heresies consisted exactly in the fact of the Fathers of the Church having anathematised the ancient philosophical conception of the triple individuality of man, and the emanation of the Spirit of man from the essence of Divinity itself. This triple individuality was upheld and believed in by Origen, for which he was exiled, and even Irenaeus, in 178 A.D. Perchance it may be said that Origen was once upon a time a Neo-platonist, but Irenaeus hated this school, and for him the philosophers and Eclectics of Alexandria were even worse than the Gnostics themselves, whom he so persistently fought. Yet what does he say?—"Carne, anima, spiritu, alteri quidam figurant, spiritu altero quod formatur, carne. Id vero quod inter haec *est duo est anima*, quae aliquando subsequens spiritum elevatur ab eo, aliquando autem consentiens carni in terrenos concupiscentias" (*Irenæus* V. I.) [*Ln*. There are three things out of which, as I have shown, the complete man is composed—flesh, soul, and spirit. One of these does indeed preserve and fashion (the man)—this is the spirit; while as to another it is united and formed—that is the flesh; then (comes) that which is between these two—that is the soul, which sometimes indeed, when it follows the spirit, is raised up by it, but sometimes it sympathizes with the flesh, and falls into carnal lusts.].[3] In other words, the altogether perfect man consists of body, soul and immortal spirit; the Soul stands as intermediary between them; 'Soul' in the Old Testament is *Nephesh*, which word, without either choice or sense is translated indifferently, 'Soul, life, blood' and various other terms; and when this soul, by the power of its own highest aspirations, holds more to its Supreme Spirit, well and good; but when it is more in sympathy with the flesh, the latter absorbs it in itself, and will ultimately bring it to perdition. *Per se*, the soul is not immortal. The soul outlives the man's body only for as long as is necessary for it to get rid of everything earthly and fleshly; then, as it is gradually purified, its essence comes into progressively closer union with the Spirit, which alone is immortal. The tie between them becomes more and more indissoluble. When the last atom of the earthly is evaporated, then this duality becomes a unity, and the Ego of the former man becomes forever immortal. But if whilst still in the flesh, the man has failed to prepare himself to part with joy from his perishable body, if the man has lived only his earthly life, and the fleshly thoughts have strangled all trace of spiritual life in him, he will not be born again; he will not see God (John iii, 3). Like a still-born child, he will leave the womb of earthly life, his mother, and after the death of his flesh he will be born not into a better world, but into the region of eternal death, because his *Soul* has ruined itself for ever, having destroyed its connection with the Spirit. The flesh has triumphed, and the soul is carried downward, not upward.

And so not all of us human beings are immortal. As Jesus expresses it, we must take the Kingdom of Heaven by violence. Alas, my dear Madam, there are not many of the great parables of Christ which have been understood. Read in Matt. xiii, the parable of the seed, some of which fell by the wayside and the birds devoured them, and some brought forth a hundredfold, because their roots struck deep into their own spirit. As to the grains that were lost forever, they are human souls. Have you never met people who have long ago parted with their souls—people who have nothing left but their animal souls, and of whose spirit there is no more trace? I have met such. When their bodies die, these people will die forever. No resurrection for them, no future life, and not the strongest mediums could call them back any more, because they are nowhere to be found any more. Origen says the same thing. Consequently we are all trinities. Plato, Pythagoras and Plutarch all taught this; but so far these philosophers have been so little understood, that all their terminology is dreadfully mixed up. Both *nous* (immortal spirit) and *psyche* (soul), have been rendered by the same word, "soul;" in the *Acts of the Apostles* you will find the same thing. St. Paul clearly speaks of two principles; the soul and the spirit, but the translators have distorted everything. Look up the epistle of James, Our Lord's brother (Ch. iii. 15).

I do not know how it is translated in Russian, but in the Greek text you will find that James points out directly the kind of thing our soul is, by the following words: this wisdom descendeth not from above, but is earthly, psychical, devilish. The human spirit (man's spiritual individuality) lights up the earthly man, the Adam of the second chapter of Genesis, from above, touching more or less his head only, and the soul (*Nephesh*) has its seat in the blood and bones, throughout the body[.] The soul is the spiritual man, merely in the physiological sense. When the soul is imprisoned in a sinning body, it is as if in jail, and in order to get rid of its chains, it has progressively to aspire upward toward its spirit. The soul is a chameleon. It becomes a copy either of the spirit or of the body. In the first case, it acquires the faculty of separating itself from the body with ease, and of setting forth, traveling all over the wide world, having left in the body a provision of vital forces, or animal, instinctive mental movements.

For it, there are no obstacles of either distance or matter. In the measure of its union with the spirit it becomes more or less clairvoyant. It may even become all-seeing and omniscient for a few earthly moments, or even hours. This is the secret of somnambulism and certain kinds of mediumism. But in the second case it is merely an animal soul. In it there is no clairvoyance, not even any glimpse of prescience; yet mediumism is by no means an indication of a man's holiness. It is merely a physiological phenomenon. Usually, the better the medium, the more delicate he is; yet it is not disease that comes as a result of mediumism, but the latter as the result of bodily weakness, of shattered nerves. The walls of the prison being down, the soul will find it easier to tear itself away and go forth into free space. A man may be a blackguard, like H——,[3] and be the greatest of mediums; but in this case his soul will be obsessed by other souls, more or less sinful, in accord with the quality of his own; as is the pastor, so is the parish. But there are thousands of shades of mediumism, and they cannot all be enumerated in a letter. All the ancient philosophers knew this, and shunned mediumism to such an extent that it was strictly forbidden to admit mediums to the Eleusinian and other Mysteries: those who had a "familiar spirit." Socrates was higher and purer than Plato; yet the latter was initiated into the Mysteries, while Socrates was rejected, and in the course of time he was even doomed to die, because, though not initiated into the Mysteries, he revealed a part of them to the world through the agency of his *daimonion*, of which he himself was not consciously aware.

The Egyptians also divided man in the same way, and gave the name of *Nut* to the one Spirit of God. It would seem that Anaxagoras was the first to borrow this name from them, and gave to the omnipotent spirit (Archê tês Kenêseôs [*Gk.* the Beginning of Creation]) the name of *Nous*, or as he puts it, Nous Autokrates [*Gk.* Sovereign (or Self-ruling) Mind]: "At the beginning of Creation," he says, "everything was in chaos; then appeared *Nous* and introduced order into this chaos." In his idea, *Nous* was the Spirit of God. The Logos was man, an emanation of *Nous*. The exterior senses could cognize phenomena, but *Nous* alone was capable of a mental contemplation of noumena, or subjective objects.

But you are probably tired of all this. I do not know how to write Russian, and cannot express everything I should like to, but, dear soul, please do not imagine that I have become even worse than I used to be in regard to religious matters. Now there is more religion in me than ever before. *Master is teaching me*, and I am irresistibly drawn to study, to know, to learn. . . .

NOTES:

1. No journal article has been identified to which this is likely to refer. The reference is perhaps to material published in *Isis Unveiled*, vol. 2, ch. 6.

2. "Croquet at Windsor" (*CW* 1:253–4); see also letter 75, in which the translation of the poem is mentioned.

3. Irenaeus, *Adversus Haereses* [Against Heresies], 5.9.1. The Latin quotation in the letter is corrupt. According to *Sancti Irenæi Libros quinque adversus Haereses*, ed. W. Wigan Harvey (Cambridge: Typis Academicis, 1857; reprint, Ridgewood, NJ: Gregg Press, 1965), the passage is as follows: ". . . carne anima et spiritu: et altero quidem salvante et figurante, que est Spiritus; altero quod unitur et formatur, quod est caro; id vero quod inter hæc est duo, quod est anima: quæ aliquando quidem subsequens spiritum, elevatur ab eo; aliquando autem consentiens carni, decidit in terrenas concupiscentias." The English translation is from a text at <http://ccel.org/fathers2/ANF-01/anf01-63.htm#P8900_2545577>. The quotation also appears in *Isis Unveiled* 2:285, which HPB was still working on at the time of this letter.

4. Probably D. D. Home.

SOURCE: Russian original unavailable. Copied from a translation in *Theosophical Quarterly* 5 (July 1907): 11–5.

Introduction to Letter 83

The following letter closely duplicates the first part of the second paragraph of the preceding letter. Several explanations can be offered for the close similarity of the two. HPB may have written both relatives, her aunt and her sister, about the same time and copied the text of one letter into the other. Or the following letter may actually be a part of the preceding letter that was separated from the rest of it. Or the preceding letter may actually be a combination of several different letters, including the following. Because we do not have the original texts of these letters, but only published versions whose provenience is unknown, there is no sure way to decide among these possibilities, and consequently the two letters are treated here as separate ones, although they are obviously closely related.

Letter 83

To V. de Zhelihovsky   *[June 1877]*

Do not be afraid that I am off my head. All that I can say is that someone positively *inspires me*— . . . more than this: someone enters me. It is not I who talk and write: it is something within me, my higher and luminous Self, that thinks and writes for me. Do not ask me, my friend, what I experience, because I could not explain it to you clearly. I do not know myself! The one thing I know is that now, when I am about to reach old age, I have become a sort of storehouse of somebody else's knowledge. . . . *Someone* comes and envelops me as a misty cloud and all at once pushes me out of myself, and then I am not "I" any more— Helena Petrovna Blavatsky—but someone else. Someone strong and powerful, born in a totally different region of the world; and as to myself it is almost as if I were asleep, or lying by not quite conscious—not in my own body but close by, held only by a thread which ties me to it. However, at times I see and hear everything quite clearly: I am perfectly conscious of what my body is saying and doing—or at least its new possessor. I even understand and remember it all so well that afterwards I can repeat it and even write down *his* words. . . . At such a time I see awe and fear on the faces of Olcott and others, and follow with interest the way in which *he* half-pityingly regards them out of my own eyes and teaches them with my physical tongue. Yet not with my mind but his own, which enwraps my brain like a cloud. . . . Ah, but really I cannot explain everything.

DATE: The similarity of this letter to part of letter 82 suggests that both were written about the same time if they are not in fact the same letter.

SOURCE: Russian original unavailable. Copied from a translation in *Path* (NY) 9 (Dec. 1894): 266. Another English translation in *Path* (London) 3 (Nov. 1912): 167–8.

Letter 84

To her relatives   *[June 1877]*

In our Society everyone must be a vegetarian, eating no flesh and drinking no wine. This is one of our first rules.[1] It is well known what an evil influence the evaporations of blood and alcohol have on the spiritual side of human nature, blowing the animal passions into a raging fire; and so one of these days I have resolved to fast more severely than hitherto. I ate only salad and did not even smoke for whole nine days, and slept on the floor, and this is what happened: I have suddenly caught a glimpse of one of the most disgusting scenes of my own life, and I felt as if I was out of my body, looking at it with repulsion whilst it was walking, talking, getting puffed up with fat and sinning. Pheugh, how I hated myself! Next night when I again lay down on the hard floor, I was so tired out that I soon fell asleep and then got surrounded with a heavy, impenetrable darkness. Then I saw a star appearing; it lit up high, high above me, and then fell, dropping straight upon me. It fell straight on my forehead and got transformed into a hand. Whilst this hand was resting on my forehead I was all ablaze to know whose hand it was. . . . I was concentrated into a single prayer, into an impulse of the will, to learn who it was, to whom did this luminous hand belong. . . . And I have learned it: there stood over it I myself. Suddenly this second me spoke to my body, "Look at me!" My body looked at it and saw that the half of this second me was as black as jet, the other half whitish-grey, and only the top of the head perfectly white, brilliant, and luminous. And again I myself spoke to my body: "When you become as bright as this small part of your head, you will be able to see what is seen by others, by the purified who have washed themselves clean. . . . And meanwhile, make yourself clean, make yourself clean, make yourself clean." And here I awoke.

NOTE:

1. William Quan Judge adds a footnote at this point in the New York *Path*: "This was a proposed rule. H.P.B. accepted a thing proposed as a thing done, and so spoke of it here. But she did not carry out that rule then proposed, and never then suggested its enforcement to me." But see also letter 85, for a similar statement. The rule specified here is, however, part of the rules of the later Esoteric School, which in a number of respects attempted to follow the principles of the early Society, even those that were not actually put into practice then. HPB herself followed a vegetarian diet at various times, but the difficulty of maintaining that diet in many parts of the world in the late nineteenth century was so great and her health was such that she did not do so consistently. She treats the subject in *The Key to Theosophy*, section 13 "On the Misconceptions about the Theosophical Society."

DATE: The date, which is conjectured, places this letter next to the following, as both treat similar subjects, albeit in quite different tones.

SOURCE: Russian original unavailable. Copied from a translation in *Path* (NY) 9 (Dec. 1894): 268–9. Another translation in *Path* (London) 3 (Nov. 1912): 169–70.

Letter 85

To A. N. Aksakoff   *June 15, 1877*

Our Theosophists (the local ones) are expected not only not to take a drop of drink, but to fast frequently as well.[1] I am teaching them not to eat anything; if they do not die, they will learn, but if they cannot hold out, so much the better for them. They will set off straight for Nirvana, and we shall cremate them solemnly with a pagan ceremony. There is Judge, who is simply becoming a holy Arhat. He sees visions and flies about; and he asserts that every night he oozes out of his body and roams in infinite space. I ring a bell on 47th St. (in my room), and he hears it in Brooklyn, eight miles away, and starts off at once, and in two hours he turns up at my call.

NOTE:

1. Letter 84, to her relatives, treats the same subject but in a serious vein rather than in the bantering tone of this letter.

SOURCE: Russian original unavailable. Translated by Boris de Zirkoff from Solovyov's *Sovremennaya* 286–7. Another English translation by Walter Leaf in *Modern Priestess* 276.

Letter 86

To V. de Zhelihovsky   *[ca. June 1877]*

Imagine my pleasant surprise! For my latest article[1] sent to the *Tribune*, on esotericism and Nirvana in the Buddhist religion, I expected to receive from $100 to $150; instead, they sent me $400! . . . It means that I have become fashionable. There is no end to requests. For a trifling article written by me at one stroke, just to get rid of some tiresome requests, they give me from $60 to $70. Previously, I used to be happy if they paid me $20 for a much more serious contribution carefully worked over by me. Actually, do they pay me for the merit of the article itself? . . . They pay me for my name. Even before, I didn't write so badly, and perhaps even worked over my articles much more carefully—but they didn't know my name. . . . Now, however, it has become known, and so the editors do not leave me in peace; they all want it and compete with each other as to payments! . . . It is a good thing they didn't find me a vain person; the daughter of my father is rather humble and hasn't big ideas about herself![2]

NOTES:

1. This article has not been identified.

2. The version of this letter in *Incidents* is as follows:

> Fancy my surprise . . . I am—heaven help us!—becoming fashionable, as it seems. I am writing articles on Esotericism and Nirvana, and paid for them more than I could have ever expected, though I have hardly any time for writing for money. . . . Believe me, and you will, for *you* know me, I cannot make myself realise that I have ever been able to write decently. . . . If I were unknown, no publisher or editor would have ever paid any attention to me. . . . It's all vanity and fashion. . . . Luckily for the publishers I have never been *vain*.

DATE: This letter talks about what is apparently the same article as that mentioned in letter 82, dated June 8, 1877. In that letter HPB says an editor is pleased with the article. In this letter, she mentions payment for the article. Therefore this letter dates from approximately the same time as that, or perhaps slightly later than it.

SOURCE: Russian original unavailable. Translated by Boris de Zirkoff from *Rebus* 2 (Dec. 4, 1883): 429. Partial English translation with variations in *Incidents* 205 and in "Mystical History" 62.

Letter 87

To V. de Zhelihovsky   [ca. June 1877]

It is lucky for me that I am not vain. As a matter of fact, I have hardly any time to write much for other publications and for money. . . . Our work is growing. I must work, write and write; I hope there will be publishers for what I write.

DATE: As this fragment is very similar to the end of letter 86 and may even be another partial version of that letter, it is assigned the same date.

SOURCE: Russian original unavailable. Translated by Boris de Zirkoff from *Russkoye Obozreniye* 2 (Nov. 1891): 269. Another English translation in *Path* (NY) 9 (Jan. 1895): 301, where it is combined with letter 80.

⌒

Letter 88

To N. de Fadeyev   *July 19 [1877]*
                                                          New York

Nadyezhinka, friend of my soul,

Do not be astonished that I am not writing you on regular *letter-paper*. I do so because I feel the need of talking to you very seriously. From the very day I received your letter—and may the Heavenly Powers grant you happiness for writing it—I have been thinking and thinking, and finally have decided to write to you the whole truth, such as it is. I shall lay before your eyes all my "innards," my soul, my heart, and my brain and then—come what may! If you understand me—thanks be to God, fate will have favored me; if you do not, and get angry—unhappiness and grief will be mine. In the next world, in our future life, *where we shall certainly meet*, everything will become clear; we will know who is right and who is wrong; but meanwhile, as we are both sincere and obey our consciences, and do not deceive anyone through cowardice or vile complaisance, however much we may be mistaken in our deductions, our hopes, and our beliefs, we nevertheless remain honest people. If you were Madame von Hahn or that turkey-hen Romanova, I would not have written about such things. But you know yourself that you are a person of unusual intelligence and actually a thousand times more learned than I, for your learning is the sturdy progeny of your own brain and understanding, while mine is derived from my Superior. I am nothing but a *reflector* of someone else's bright light. However it may be, this light has little by little entered into me, has been filtered into me, has permeated me, as it were; thus I cannot help it; all these ideas have entered into my brain, into my very soul, and so I am sincere, although perhaps I am wrong.

The mere fact that you and uncle, owing to goodness of heart and family feeling, wish to have two copies of my book does not justify this long preface. The first volume, "Against Exact Science," will no doubt interest you very much. But I am anxious about the second volume, "*Against Theology and for Religion.*" I know what a devoutly religious person you are; how clear and pure your faith is; and my only hope is that you will understand that my books are not aimed *against religion*, against the Christ, but against the heinous hypocrisy of those who murder, burn, and kill in the name of the Almighty Son of God, ever since the moment of his death on the Cross for the sake of *all* humanity, and especially the sinful, fallen men, the heathen, the fallen women, and those who have gone astray. Where is truth? Where to find it? Three enormous, so-called Christian Religions. In England, Germany, and other Protestant countries there are 232 sects, and in America, 176. Each one of them demands respect and wants its doctrines and dogmas to be acknowledged true and those of its neighbors a bunch of lies. "Where is truth—what is it?" asked Pilate of Christ 1877 years ago. Where is it? I myself, poor sinner, am asking, and nowhere do I find it; everywhere deceit, falsehood, ferocity, and—the sad results of the Jewish Bible which burdens the Christians, and by means of which half of the Christian world has stifled the actual teachings of Christ!

Understand me; our own Orthodox Faith stands by itself. The book does not mention it. I have *refused point blank* to analyze it, as I wish to preserve at least one small corner of my heart where suspicion could not crawl in, a feeling I put down with all my strength. The Orthodox people are *sincere*; their faith may be blind, unreasoned, but it leads them to the good; and though our priests are drunkards and thieves, and often fools also, the faith of the people is pure and can lead only to the good. The Master himself admits this and says that the only people in the world whose faith *is not a speculation*, are the Orthodox people. As to our privileged classes—let them go to the devil. They are the same hypocrites as elsewhere; they do not believe in either God or Devil, and being full of nihilistic ideas, they materialize all that exists. I am not talking about them, but about universal religions.

What is the essence of all religion? "Love your neighbor as yourself and God above all."[1] Are these not the words of Jesus? Has he left behind even one single dogma, has he taught a single one of the thousand articles of faith that the Church Fathers have afterwards invented? Not one. On the Cross, he prayed for his enemies, and in his name, as much as in the name of Moloch, 50 to 65 million people have been thrown into the fire and burned. He spoke against the Jewish Sabbath and purposely belittled it, and yet here, in free America, *fines* and *imprisonment* are imposed for the violation of the Sabbath, called just that, *Sabbath day*, although they have altered it to Sunday. What then have they done? Saturn has been changed into Sol, *Dies Solis*, i.e., that day of the Sun and of Jupiter. With us Russians, at least, Sunday reminds us of the day of *Resurrection*.[2] But with these heathen Protestants and Catholics, it is simply the day of the Sun—*Sunday*. St. Paul clearly says that anyone can have it his own way: one man likes one day, and the other likes another. St. Justin Martyr is definitely opposed to the observing of Sunday because the heathen on that day observe the day of Jupiter; and here people are put in jail for it. If we are to believe in the New Testament, then we cannot believe in the Old. Jesus goes directly against the Old Testament and the Law. His Sermon on the Mount (see Matthew [5–7]) is a teaching diametrically opposed to the Ten Commandments of Sinai. "On Sinai, in the Books of Moses, it is said so-and-so—*a tooth for a tooth*, etc.; *but I say unto you*, etc." What is it if not a rebellion against the old institution of the Synagogue? Let all the Churches rise against me, let *people* curse me, God, the Great Invisible God, sees *why I rebel against the teaching of the Church*. I shall never believe that the purest Divine Person of Christ was the son of the Jewish Jehovah! Of that wicked, crafty Jehovah, who purposely hardens the heart of the Pharaoh and then chastises him for it; who *tempts*—personally tempts—the people and then throws stones at them from behind the clouds like Spanish guerillas; who materializes himself in the cleft of a rock and shows his behind to Moses!! Lord, what a blasphemy, that Bible! See Exodus 33.18–23. If Christ had believed in Jehovah, he would not have been crucified. Has he ever, even once, mentioned his name? Jehovah is a purely *national* deity of the Jews. And they would not have permitted him to be the god of anyone else but the people chosen by him. What a chosen people! Jehovah is simply Bacchus and this can be proved just as two and two make four. One of the names of Bacchus was Sabazios, and El and Iacchus. Bacchus was Dionysos, DIO-NYSOS, the God of Nysa; also Osiris, born on Mount Nysa—Sinai; and the Egyptians called Sinai "Niza."[3] And what do we find in the Bible? "And Moses built an altar, and called the name of it Jehovah-Nissi." (See Exodus 17.15.) We find that all the names of Jehovah belong to heathen gods, *all of them*. Solomon has no idea of Jehovah, and David borrowed that name from the Phoenicians. *Yago* was one of the four Kabeiri Gods— secret gods that were part of all the mysteries. Jewish "nationality" is but a lie. There was no Jewish nation until the second century BC; all their books are spurious. Where are the historic documents to prove that their Scriptures

are authentic? Which is the first Jewish Scripture mentioned? The Septuagint—a translation made by seventy
men, on order of Ptolemy. Who mentions it? Josephus
alone, a writer who upholds the Jews with all his might and
lies for all he is worth. Why is this story of the seventy
translators never confirmed in any work of Greek writers,
or in any archive or chronicle? Who knew better the deeds
of Ptolemy than the Greeks and Romans? If all the learned
theologians of the world united, they would never find *in
any history or in any writing* a single word on the Jews as a
nation. Who ever heard of it? Herodotus, the most accurate
writer, a traveler and historian, whose every word and observation is daily confirmed by archeology, paleology, philology, and other sciences, was born in 484 BC and died in
424 BC He traveled in Assyria and the Babylonia of Cyrus.
Hardly half a century had elapsed since Nebuchadrezzar
was turned into a bull by the prophet Daniel; seven years
did that King bellow like a bull—42,000 Jews, under the
guidance of Zerubbabel, returned to Jerusalem (538 BC)
after their exile, to build a temple; and yet Herodotus, who
resided there several years, who described so accurately and
often with tedious minuteness (see book 6.98) the reign of
Nebuchadrezzar (584 BC) and how he took Jerusalem, and
who wrote of Cyrus, Darius, and Artaxerxes, does not say a
single word either about the above mentioned metamorphosis, or the Jews, or the prophets, or about any single
Jew whatsoever. Except for a few lines, where he casually
mentions that the Syrians inhabiting Palestine learned
the practice of circumcision from the Egyptians—there is
nothing else. Is this possible? An event like the metamorphosis of the King into a bull by the Head and Chief of the
Magi (Daniel), would it not have been described by other
historians, at least as a legend? Then again, if the chronology of the Scriptures established by our learned theologians is correct, how is it that the prophet Ezekiel, who

wrote in 605 BC, speaks twice of Daniel as of an ancient sage, while Daniel had not yet been born?[4] If Judea was a nation with Solomon, David, Saul, and *tutti quanti* [*It.* all the rest], why is there nowhere in the world a single ancient coin with a Hebrew inscription, i.e., a Jewish coin, while there are any number of Samaritan coins? Would the Jews, who hated the Samaritans, have consented to use the coins of their enemies without coining their own money? Coins thousands of years older are found; tombs of people who lived before Moses are uncovered, even though these are but a flimsy proof of their existence. But of the Jewish nation—not a trace. Neither tombs nor coins—nothing at all. As if all had evaporated and disappeared by magic. Only the Sacred Scriptures remain, which people (whose God was killed by the Jews) must believe blindly. Can such events as the Exodus out of Egypt of nearly three million people (from the seventy brought by Jacob hardly 150 years earlier?—that would mean they had multiplied quicker than red herrings—figure this out according to statistical law!), can such events leave no trace on monuments, tombs, or in some ancient chronicles? Yet there is nothing but dead silence! No answer anywhere, nowhere the slightest confirmation! Just think! And as to the Scriptures themselves, where is the historical confirmation of their existence earlier than 200 or even 150 BC?

The Hebrew language, i.e., the extinct language called ancient Hebrew, never existed: it is a language without a single original root; it is a composite language formed of bits of Greek, Arabic, and Chaldean. I have proved this to Professor Rawson (Yale College). Take any Hebrew word whatsoever, and I shall prove to you that its root is either Arabic, Greek, or Chaldean. It is like a harlequin's coat. All the Biblical names are composed of foreign words and suggest *why* they have been thus composed. It is an Arabic-Ethiopian dialect with an admixture of Chaldean; and the

Chaldean itself comes from Sanskrit. It has now been proved that Babylon was at one time a seat of Brahmanas and had a School of Sanskrit. The Akkadians invented by our Assyriologists, and who (according to Rawlinson) are supposed to have come from Armenia and to have taught the Magi an alleged sacerdotal or sacred language, are simply Aryans, from whom our own Slavonic language came also. Here is an example (pardon the digression) from the Rig Veda:

> Dyaur hi vah pita, prithivi mata,
> somah bhrata, aditih svasa.
> Hymn to the Maruts, Mandala 1.191.6.

which translated runs:

"The Sky (*Dyaur*) or Day is your Father (*pita, pater*); the Earth, your mother (*mata*); Soma, your brother (*bhrata*); Adita, your sister (*svasa*)."

Therefore, to demand the recognition of the Hebrew manuscripts as ancient revelations or the word of God is simply a farce. God would never have written or dictated anything that would give occasion at the same time for the earth created by Him, mankind, science, and the rest of it, to expose Him as a liar. To believe *implicitly* in the Jewish Scriptures, and at the same time in the Heavenly Father of Jesus, is absurd; worse than that—it is blasphemy. If our Father of Heaven and Earth, the Father of the whole limitless Universe, had to write, He would not have allowed mankind to be obliged to accuse Him of senseless contradictions and such like. 64,000 mistakes have now been found in the Bible by the revision Society, and no sooner were these mistakes corrected, than as many contradictions were also found. This was all due to the Jewish Masorah. Even the most learned Rabbis have lost the key to their books and do not know how to correct them. It is a well-known fact that the Rabbis of Tiberia constantly amended their Bible, altering words and numbers, and borrowing from the Christian Church Fathers the bad habit of distorting both texts and chronology whenever a controversy arose, in order to defeat their opponents. And that is how they made a mess of it. We have no manuscript of the Old Testament earlier than the tenth century. The Bodleian Codex is considered to be the oldest. But who can vouch for its authenticity? Tischendorf is the authority for it and has convinced the whole of Europe that he had discovered on Mount Sinai the so-called Codex Sinaiticus. And now two other scholars (one of them a Theosophist of ours), who have spent several years in Palestine and have been on Mount Sinai, are about to prove that such a Codex never existed in the Library. They have conducted investigations for two years and have searched all the hidden places, with the help of a monk who has lived there for the last sixty years and who knew Tischendorf personally. And this monk stated under oath that he had known for years every manuscript and every book, but had never heard of the one spoken of. The monk, of course, will be tucked away; and as to Tischendorf, he simply deceived the Russian Government by a counterfeit. Out of 620 manuscripts of the Old and New Testament, in Hebrew, Greek, and other languages, there are no two that read alike. And is this to be wondered at? The Books of Moses had been lost for several centuries. Suddenly, in 600 BC, Hilkiah finds them. Solomon's Temple is destroyed, the Sodomites are driven out, etc., etc. (2 Kings 23), and the books disappear again, to the last one. In 425 BC, Ezra writes them down from memory (40 books!) in forty days. Then they are lost again. Antiochus Epiphanes is supposed to have burned them all in 180 BC. Miraculously, they are found once more. All this, however, is mere tradition; there is not a single historical fact. And now comes the famous Masorah. Jehovah is changed into Adonai and Adonai himself might as easily be transformed, with the help of the Masoretes and their clever points, into an Ivan Petrovich. Yet their Kabbalah and also Onkelos, the most famous Rabbi of Babylonia, teach that Jehovah is not God by any means, but Memro—which means Logos. Analyse the word Yod-he-vau,[5] and you will have Adam and Eve; Jehovah is, therefore, the first Adam—not of the second chapter of the creation of the world, not the earthly Adam, but of the first; "male and female created (*bara*) Elohim man,"[6]—i.e., Adam Kadmon, fantastic, bisexual, whose name is composed of the letter Yod and the three letters of Eve, הוח = י 8[7] namely, Jehovah, the personification of sinful humanity. But enough of these Jewish fables.

So then, my dear, I fear that you will reject me because of this. Lord forbid, but I cannot alter facts. I believe, but in my own way; I firmly believe, and believe that since the creation of the world (not creation, but progressive emanation or evolution of the world out of its spiritual prototype) the *incarnation* of God in a man is repeated every few thousand or hundred years. A chosen man becomes the temple of God; the pure and holy Spirit manifests in him, uniting itself with the soul and body, and thus a Trinity appears on earth. The Brahmanas have also their Christna or Krishna, which is also a Trinity, the *Trimurti*. If the early Christians did not believe in these periodic incarnations, they would not have sought safety for themselves through their belief in the Antichrist and the Second Advent of Christ, in case of such an incarnation. I believe in an invisible and Universal God, in the abstract Spirit of God, not in an anthropomorphic Deity. I believe in the immortality of the Divine Spirit in every man, but *I do not believe in the immortality of every man*, for I strongly believe in the justice of God. Everyone must take the Kingdom of God *by force*, i.e., by good works and a pure life; but to believe that every scamp, every godless man, every murderer, by the mere fact of having in the last moment of life kicked his legs and exclaimed in fear: "I believe! I believe that the Son of God shed his blood for me," will be next to the good and righteous man—that I cannot believe. This dogma, as it is now taught by the Christian Church, is a fatal dogma for humanity. This blasphemous idea that we can pile all sorts of mean acts, murders, and injury to our fellowmen upon the long-suffering shoulders of Jesus Christ, results in the fact that every week people are hung here for the most curious crimes; and Protestants as well as Catholic priests assure the people in front of the gallows that *thus and so* the murderer has *made his peace* with God before his death and has no need to fear any longer. So then, go right to it! He who does not fear death—and there are many such—can steal and murder to his heart's content. It may even encourage him; if he had not killed, he would not have made his peace with God so solemnly and might have missed Paradise. But what about his victims? Is this *God's justice?* If, at the very moment when the criminal was reconciled with God, the forgiveness of his sins was confirmed by the return to life of his victim or by the restitution of the possessions of the one dispossessed or his orphans; in other words, the complete restoration of the disturbed equilibrium of good and evil, then one could have believed. There would be some reason, some logic. But otherwise, what do we have?

Picture to yourself a lake or a limitless sea, with a surface as smooth as a mirror, and underneath, perhaps, hidden reefs and shoals, whirlpools, and other such things; everything goes on in its appointed way, everything seems to be in its own place and in order. Thus is humanity: it is born, it lives and dies. The life of every drop (man) of that sea depends greatly on outward circumstances, but above all on itself (for the sake of the metaphor, imagination must admit free choice and individuality in every drop). I approach the shore of the lake, take a stone, and throw it into the water! That stone produces a disturbance in proportion to its size; one wave pushes another, the other pushes the next; circle after circle spreads out, and the motion of the water is transmitted to the lower layers of the atmosphere. From below and from above, visibly and invisibly, dormant forces arise, and this motion is imparted from one atom to another, spreads further and further from one stratum to another, from one layer to another, and disappears in infinite and immeasurable space. An impulse has been given to matter, and such an impulse, as even physicists know, *is eternal in its effects*.

There you have the picture of any crime, of any evil deed, as well as of a good one. Would Divinity, which created once and for all the eternal, immutable laws of Nature, in the physical as well as the moral worlds, wish, even if it could do so, to arrest the course of these laws, making *nonexistent* that which once had taken place? Can the stone, once thrown, come back to the hand of him who threw it into the depths of the water? Can the motion of water and the natural progress of spirit as well as matter be arrested? The criminal may be forgiven by God—but what about the victim? The victim of the moment is but a small thing as compared with the aftereffects—the countless victims of that *which comes about as the result of the victim*. A man is killed, and the work that had been allotted to him is forcibly interrupted. Every man, however insignificant he may be, in his own sphere is a link holding on to another link in its appointed orbit; if it breaks, all goes haywire, other links are caught, and so forth.

No, Ma'am! Forgiveness of sins without erasing the consequences of the offence is no supreme justice, as we, Theosophists, understand it. God is something so great, so unthinkable to us, worms of earth, that we need waste no time in speculating on the Divine Essence. A manifestation, an appearance of God in flesh takes place—"Ecce Homo" [*Ln.* Behold the Man]; follow Him, walk in His footsteps! As long as He lives, ask His help; in this I fully believe—not in the help of the Highest God—for what are you in His eyes?—but of *His Son*, who represents humanity, which is every moment crucified by evil. He has shown us the way, not in synagogues or temples, as the Pharisees did, but in His own Divine Temple, in the depth of everyone's heart. "Know ye not that ye are the Temple of God" (1 Cor. 3.16), asked St. Paul of *every* man. Try to erase your sin by means of good, not through vain penitence, but by deeds, and the *law of retribution* will lose its hold on you. Try during your frail life to unite yourself as firmly as possible with *your own personal God*, with your own Divine Spirit; then your soul will become immortal. But if you break the bond with it and turn away from the messenger of God, the CHRIST, then He too will turn away from you. Your soul will perish, not in a hell with its bonfires of oak and pine, and its "horned and tailed" stokers, but in that *eternal Gehenna, where there is weeping and gnashing of teeth.* This means that your soul, the astral spirit, your second ethereal *ego*, or that which St. Paul calls the Spiritual Body (1 Cor. 15.46), which is only semi-immortal, if not firmly united with the Spirit, must *disintegrate* after the death of the body into the elements, from the constituent particles of which—fire, air, earth and water—all the Universe, including the human soul, is composed. The *subjective* alone is eternal; all that is objective comes to an end, and as the spiritual sheath of man, however ethereal it may be, is nevertheless endowed with form and color, it cannot therefore be eternal. There is your *Hell!* Hell consists in anguish of conscience, in wanderings upon the earth, in places where we have directly or indirectly committed evil, and, at the end, in complete disappearance of our personality.

As far as the *white* and *black* forces are concerned, you are right. It could not be otherwise. The world is upheld by centrifugal and centripetal forces; right and left, interior and exterior, and so forth. Were there no night, we should not know day; were there no evil, there would be no good. As to actual devils, devils by origin and nature, there cannot be any such, for that would mean giving rivals to God in creating. The Devil, or rather the idea of an opposing power, is the lever of Archimedes on which the world turns. It is a field where grows the good, for wherever the manure is the richest, the grain grows best. Had I not been *the devil knows what*, to my shame and sorrow (one cannot relive one's past, one can only try to erase it according to one's strength), if I had not been foolish in my younger days, I would not have been able, as I have done, to place seven people on the true path. First Olcott, who did not believe in God or Devil three years ago; he was a reveler, drank in clubs, kept mistresses; and now he has become pure and clean, and fears my glance; he believes that I would know at once his smallest thought; he is worse than a three-year-old child. It is the same with Judge, and Cobb, and Harley, and Marble, and Webster; and in London, Professor Stainton Moses, whose shadow or double has appeared before us twice, out of five experiments, he had failed three times. I shall try to appear before you, but we must figure out when you are alone in your study, or are sitting down with aunt, for if the children were to raise a howl, they might kill my physical body, into which I would not have time to return quickly enough.

You have guessed right. I am writing about Storozhenko and am proving the *possibility* of the existence of vampires. The whole book is full of such stories, and I show the how and the why. I am uneasy only about two or three chapters in volume 2, because I inveigh against the Catholics and the Protestants and their Saints, living or dead, and defend the philosophy of ancient Brahmanas and Buddhists. As to the Russian Church—there is *not a word* about it. Still, will they let the book through? How should I send it to you? As to the money, and the sending of it, that's a mere trifle, if only they do not confiscate it. Perhaps you will no longer want it! I am terribly afraid, Nadyezhda Andreyevna, of upsetting you, for I love you so much, and all of you too; still I write but the truth. Well, forgive me my long chatting.

May the Most High safeguard you all.

Helena

NOTES:

1. Luke 10.27, based on Leviticus 19.18 and Deuteronomy 6.5.

2. The Russian word for "Sunday," *voskresenye*, is based on a root meaning "resurrection."

3. Cf. *Isis Unveiled* 2:165.

4. The dates HPB cites, based on a chronology "established by our learned theologians," are in error (cf. Glossary, "Ezekiel").

5. Hebrew does not normally write vowels, but only consonants. These three letters, Y H V, are those needed to spell the name "Yahweh," transcribed in Christian tradition as "Jehovah," although the letter H has to be used twice to do so: YHVH. The Hebrew letter represented by V can be transliterated as either *v* or *w;* similarly Y can be transliterated as either *y* or *j.*

6. That is, "Elohim (the term for God in the first chapter of Genesis) created (Heb. *bara*) man (Adam Kadmon, Primordial Man) as male and female (hermaphroditic)."

7. The interpretation of this passage is not wholly clear, and the last character, here transcribed as "8," is of uncertain reading in the manuscript. The "three letters of Eve" are the Hebrew letters ה ו ח, Ch V H, or chet, vau, he, which are the consonants that spell the name "Chavah" or "Havah" (that is, "Eve"). It is not quite correct that the name י ה ו ה, YHVH, or yod he vau he, "Yahweh" (that is, "Jehovah") "is composed of the letter Yod and the three letters of Eve," but the Hebrew letters chet and he are written much alike and are often both transliterated by the Roman letter "h." With the substitution of he for the initial chet of "Chavah," HPB's statement

327

holds true. Each letter of the Hebrew alphabet corresponds to a number; the number of chet, the first letter of Chavah, is 8, which might represent the whole name "Chavah" in the formula ח ו ה = י 8 , which would then be saying that ChVH, "Chavah," or "Eve" equals YHVH, "Yahweh" or "Jehovah"; that is, the archetypal feminine is the same as the archetypal masculine. But this is mere speculation.

DATE: HPB's reference to "Christ 1877 years ago" fixes the year of this letter, otherwise dated only July 19.

SOURCE: Translated by Boris de Zirkoff from the Russian original in the Archives of the Theosophical Society, Adyar. Other English translations in *Theosophical Quarterly* 5 (Oct. 1907): 126–35; *Theosophist* 53 (Oct. 1931): 32–40 and (Nov. 1931): 161–6; and *HPB Speaks* 1:165–88.

⌁

Introduction to Letter 89

Shortly after HPB moved to Annie Besant's house in St. John's Wood, London, in 1890, the *New York World* published an account of the doings of the London Theosophists. The article was illustrated with a portrait of HPB copied from an older photograph, which must originally have been one of those that HPB exchanged freely with her friends and associates. A note on its reverse side was written during HPB's New York days. References to the exchange of such pictures occur in a number of the letters from this period.

The text on the back of the photograph is notable for its abundance of Masonic allusions. The second and third paragraphs refer to the preparation of a candidate for initiation into Freemasonry and his admission into the Masonic Temple.

The article in the *World* commented:

On the back of the photograph is this specimen of aesoteric composition, inscribed in as fine a hand as copper-plate:

Letter 89

To E. Hardinge Britten   *[ca. July 1877]*

To Mrs. H. B—, with the kindest regards and sincere friendly love of a poor Buddhist pilgrim, daily stoned in the free State of New York.   M. [sic] P. Blavatsky.

"Neither naked nor clothed, barefoot nor shod," I knock thrice for admission at the "inner door" of the temple. Let your heart be Jachin and Boaz, the main pillars of Solomon's Temple, and allow a poor candidate with the left breast, knee and foot naked pass through, that the unity added to the Binary might produce the sacred Friend or Trinity but shut tight your heart against the rest of the cunning craft. Amen.

Remember, O, my sister fellow of the Theosophical Society, that the cable toe [tow] encircling the Mason's waist is twin brother of the sacred Brahminic cord. And to the modern Mason who may doubt, chant the following Hindoo hymn and ask him what it means:

Thou, O wise god Varuna, Lord of all, of heaven and earth, listen on thy way:

That I may live, take from me the upper rope, loose the middle rope and remove the lowest rope.

                    —*Hymn to Varuna, R. V.* 1:25[1]

NOTE:

1. The final two verses of hymn 25 in book 1 of the Rig Veda.

DATE: The note could have been written anytime between the founding of the Theosophical Society (as HPB refers to Emma Hardinge Britten as her "sister fellow of the Theosophical Society") and HPB's departure from New York for India, that is, between late 1875 and late 1878. Because of the quotation from the Rig Veda in the note and another quotation from that same scripture in HPB's letter (88) to Nadyezhda de Fadeyev of July 19, 1877, the two letters have been grouped together, and this one dated the month of the other.

SOURCE: Original unavailable. Copied from the *New York World* (Sept. 21, 1890), 7.

⤿⤾

BACKGROUND ESSAY K

The Writing and Publication of *Isis Unveiled*

Isis Unveiled was HPB's first book. In December 1874, in a letter (12) to A. N. Aksakoff, she wrote:

> The most eminent Spiritualists, such as Robert Dale Owen, Dr. Child, and others have written me letters, and the editors of the largest publishing company in America, here at Hartford, have written me asking me to get together a volume of letters concerning different phases of Spiritualism and of the *physical* manifestations of the spirits that I had seen in India, in Africa, and elsewhere. They are desirous of buying such a work.

Nothing came of the idea at that time, but HPB kept the thought of writing a book in mind. The actual origins of *Isis Unveiled* were, according to H. S. Olcott, "commonplace and unostentatious," and he continues (*ODL* 1:202–3):

> One day in the Summer of 1875, H. P. B. showed me some sheets of manuscript which she had written, and said: "I wrote this last night 'by order,' but what the deuce it is to be I don't know. Perhaps it is for a newspaper article, perhaps for a book, perhaps for nothing: anyhow, I did as I was ordered." And she put it away in a drawer, and nothing was said about it for some time.

HPB's own account of the origin of the book agrees with Olcott's recollections. In an essay on "My Books" (*CW* 13:197–8), she remembers:

When I started to write that which developed later into *Isis Unveiled*, I had no more idea than the man in the moon what would come of it. I had no plan; did not know whether it would be an essay, a pamphlet, a book, or an article. I knew that *I had to write it, that* was all.

Olcott's book *People from the Other World* had been published on March 11, 1875; it may have suggested to HPB the idea of producing a more extensive work herself to deal with the philosophical implications of the Eddy phenomena that Olcott treated in his book. On July 15 and 22, the *Spiritual Scientist* published her article "A Few Questions to 'Hiraf'" (*CW* 1:101–19), which she called "My first *Occult* Shot" and which served as a prelude to her work on *Isis*, even in its imagery, including its final words (*CW* 1:115, 118):

> The only cause for the horror and dread we feel in the presence of death, lies in its unsolved mystery. A Christian will always fear it, more or less; an initiate of the secret science, or a *true* Spiritualist, never; for both of the latter have lifted the veil of Isis, and the great problem is solved by both, in theory and in practice. . . .
>
> I will close by startling, perhaps, even Orthodox Spiritualists by reaffirming that all who have ever witnessed our modern materializations of genuine spirit-forms, have, unwittingly, become the initiated neophytes of the Ancient Mystery; for each and all of them have solved the problem of Death, have "lifted the veil of Isis."

In mid September 1875, HPB went to spend several weeks with Cornell University Professor Hiram Corson and his wife in Ithaca, New York. While there, she spent most of her time working on the manuscript of the future *Isis*, which she says in a letter (55) to A. N. Aksakoff was then to be called, on the advice of "John King," *Skeleton Key to Mysterious Gates*. Olcott recalls her description of the work, which she sent to him from Ithaca (*ODL* 1:203):

> She wrote me that it was to be a book on the history and philosophy of the Eastern Schools and their relations with those of our own times. She said she was writing about things she had never studied and making quotations from books she

had never read in all her life: that, to test her accuracy, Prof. Corson had compared her quotations with classical works in the University Library, and had found her to be right.

After HPB returned to New York City from Ithaca in October, she became involved in other activities and did little more on the book for about six weeks. Then at the end of November, she and Olcott both rented rooms on adjacent floors at 433 West 34 Street, and work on the book resumed. Eventually the "John King" title was dropped; in letter 64 (January 8, 1876), HPB says she has given "John" up. Shortly before then and for some while after, HPB referred to the work simply as "my book" or "the book" (for example, letters 59 of November 1875, 64 of January 1876, 71 of August 1876, 74 of November 1876, in which she alluded to "the veiled Mother Isis," and 75 of December 1876). In letter 43 (probably summer 1875), HPB had spoken of peeping out from "under the veil of Isis," showing the persistence of the image in her mind. In an undated letter (62), probably written sometime in 1876, she finally refers to the book as *Isis*. And a newspaper interview with HPB published on January 23, 1877, identifies the title as *The Veil of Isis*, echoing the use of that phrase in "A Few Questions to 'Hiraf'" eighteen months earlier. The final title, *Isis Unveiled*, was adopted after the book was already in production, as HPB explained in letter 95: "The book was to have been called 'The Veil of Isis', and the first volume was stereotyped before I learned that Mr. Winwood Reade had anticipated me, and I had to do my best to alter the title of my work."

HPB had help from a variety of sources in writing the book. Olcott describes working with her after the evening meal until 2:00 AM many days and characterizes his role as that of amanuensis, proofreader, and collaborator. In writing her long books, HPB seems to have used others as sounding boards and stimuli. Olcott's description of their working arrangements on *Isis* (*ODL* 1:205) is not unlike her later procedure with others on *The Secret Doctrine*:

> As a part of my educational training she would ask me to write something about some special subject, perhaps suggesting the salient points that should be brought in, perhaps just leaving me to do the best I could with my own intuitions. When I had finished, if it did not suit her, she would

usually resort to strong language and call me some of the pet names that are apt to provoke the homicidal impulse; but if I prepared to tear up my unlucky composition, she would snatch it from me and lay it by for subsequent use elsewhere, after a bit of trimming, and I would try again. Her own manuscript was often a sight to behold; cut and patched, re-cut and re-pasted, until if one held a page of it to the light, it would be seen to consist of, perhaps, six, or eight, or ten slips cut from other pages, pasted together, and the text joined by interlined words or sentences.

As a specific example of his contributions to *Isis*, Olcott (*ODL* 1:240) offers the following: "That evening I wrote the paragraphs about him [Paracelsus] that now stand on p. 500 of Vol. II of *Isis*." He likewise comments on the contributions of others (*ODL* 1:205-6):

> From the date of her first appearance in the *Daily Graphic*, in 1874, throughout her American career, she was besieged by visitors, and if among them there chanced to be any who had some special knowledge of any particular thing cognate to her field of work, she invariably drew him out, and, if possible, got him to write down his views or reminiscences for insertion in her book. Among examples of this sort are Mr. O'Sullivan's account of a magical séance in Paris [*Isis* 1:608–11], Mr. Rawson's interesting sketch of secret initiations of the Lebanon Druses [*Isis* 2:313–5], Dr. Alexander Wilder's numerous notes and text paragraphs in the Introduction and throughout both volumes, and others which add so much to the value and interest of the work.

Concerning Wilder's contributions to the work, HPB says in the article "My Books" (*CW* 13:198):

> When the work was ready, we submitted it to Professor Alexander Wilder, the well known scholar and Platonist of New York, who after reading the matter, recommended it to Mr. Bouton for publication. Next to Olcott, it is Professor Wilder who did the most for me. It is he who made the excellent *Index*, who corrected the Greek, Latin and Hebrew

words, suggested quotations and wrote the greater part of the *Introduction* "Before the Veil."

Wilder seems to have read at least a portion of the work in progress by August 1876, for he and HPB then had an exchange of correspondence (letter 71) about points in the book. He much later recollected his role in the production of the book in a 1908 article, "How 'Isis Unveiled' Was Written." He was serving as a manuscript reviewer for the publisher J. W. Bouton, and in that capacity received all or part of the *Isis* manuscript from Olcott. Wilder recommended favorably on the content, but told the publisher it was too long to be a profitable book. Bouton nevertheless entered into a contract with HPB, in which he acquired the copyright and engaged Wilder to shorten the book as much as possible. Wilder proceeded to do so:

> I had aimed only to shorten without marring the work. It should be stated, however, as a fact in the publication of this work, that Madame Blavatsky continued to add matter, after Mr. Bouton began the undertaking, and I think that much of the second volume was then written. I have no recollection of much of it except in proof sheets at a later period. ["How 'Isis Unveiled' Was Written" 82]

The fact that HPB used people she knew as sources, much as every author uses reference works, does not deny her own remarkable knowledge of the subjects on which she wrote. Olcott continues his account (*ODL* 1:206–7):

> I have known a Jewish Rabbi pass hours and whole evenings in her company, discussing the Kabballa, and have heard him say to her that, although he had studied the secret science of his religion for thirty years, she had taught him things he had not even dreamed of, and thrown a clear light upon passages which not even his best teachers had understood . . . and in her better moments of inspiration— if the term be admissible—she astonished the most erudite by her learning quite as much as she dazzled all present by her eloquence and delighted them by her wit and humorous raillery.

Olcott and others have also observed that the sources available to HPB do not account for the range of information covered in the book (*ODL* 1:208):

> Then, whence did H.P.B. draw the materials which compose *Isis*, and which cannot be traced to accessible literary sources of quotation? *From the Astral Light*, and, by her soul-senses, from her Teachers—the "Brothers," "Adepts," "Sages," "Masters," as they have been variously called.

Olcott gives many examples of HPB's mental contact with those Teachers. After considering a range of possible alternative explanations of who or what they were (*ODL* 1:220–54), he summarizes the question of authorship as follows (*ODL* 1:255):

> *Isis Unveiled* . . . is unquestionably a collaborated work, the production of several distinct writers and not that of H.P.B. alone. . . . [But he also adds:] The personality of H.P.B. was the mould in which all the matter was cast, and which, therefore, controlled its form, colouring, and expression, so to say, by its own idiosyncrasies, mental as well as physical.

HPB herself, especially in her correspondence with her relatives, describes writing the book in what might be called an ecstatic state. So she writes her sister (letter 62):

> I am writing *Isis*; not writing, rather copying out and drawing that which she personally *is showing* me. . . . I am sitting with my eyes open and, to all appearances, see and hear everything real and actual around me; and yet at the same time I see and hear *that which I write*. I feel short of breath; I am afraid to make the slightest movement, for fear the spell might be broken. Slowly century after century, image after image, float out of nowhere and pass before me as if in a magic panorama . . . . It stands to reason, it is not I who do it all, but my *Ego*, the highest principles which live in me; and even then with the help of my *Guru*, my teacher, who helps me in everything.

HPB similarly writes to her aunt (letter 79):

Now then, tell me: how could it have happened that I, a perfect ignoramus up to my mature years, as you know, have suddenly become a phenomenon of learning in the eyes of people who are really learned? . . . This is an impenetrable mystery! I—a psychological enigma, a puzzle for future generations, a Sphinx! . . . Where does it all come from? Am I a changeling?

Concerning the progress of work on the book and its completion, the evidence is unclear. About three months after returning from Ithaca, HPB wrote Corson (letter 64): "My book is finished . . . It is no more what it was, when I was writing it in your place than one chapter of twenty or thirty such." This may refer to an early draft that was much rewritten later, or it may be an example of the optimistic projection of completion that authors are prone to. In fact, when she wrote that letter in January 1876, the book still had well over a year of serious writing for its completion. About August of 1876, HPB and Olcott moved to the "Lamasery," on the corner of 47th Street and 8th Avenue, where most of *Isis* was written.

Another curious statement concerning the timing of the book is in a letter to A. P. Sinnett, in which KH says that "she was ordered to write Isis—just a year after the Society had been founded" (*ML* 81/52). A possible solution to the inconsistency of HPB's premature statement of completion in January 1876 and KH's statement that she was instructed to write the book in September 1876 is that the manuscript changed in some significant way between those times. That possibility has some support from a report by Olcott (*ODL* 1:217–8):

We had laboured at the book for several months and had turned out 870-odd pages of manuscript when, one evening, she put me the question whether, to oblige—(our *"Parama-guru"*), I would consent to begin all over again! I well remember the shock it gave me to think that all those weeks of hard labour, of psychical thunder-storms and head-splitting archæological conundrums, were to count—as I, in my blind-puppy ignorance, imagined—for nothing. However, as my love and reverence and gratitude to this Master, and all the Masters, for giving me the privilege of sharing in their work was without limits, I consented, and at it we went again.

In any case, the manuscript, or at least a substantial part of it, must have been delivered to the publisher, J. W. Bouton, by early 1877, for on February 8, Olcott wrote to General Lippitt (in a letter preserved in the Archives of the Theosophical Society, Adyar):

> Dear General Lippitt .
>
> I enclose Adams Ex [*i.e.,* Express] receipt for your John King picture. This is the last you or any one will get from him, as the genuine spirit of that appellation has passed into another sphere & lost all attraction for the Earth.
>
> Mme B's publisher (J. W. Bouton) will soon rush in the proof sheets upon us at the rate of 30 pp per day. The book will be a monumental one—full of the profoundest learning and of interest.
>
> For a year and a half she has worked about 17 hours a day upon it.[1] Her constitution must be made of adamant. This has been a precious opportunity for me to learn Occult philosophy & I have availed of it to the Extreme.
>
> Wishing you every good-fortune
> > I remain,
>
> > > > Yours truly
> > > > H. S. Olcott
>
> PS. On Monday evening Hon J. L. O'Sullivan spent several hours with Mme B & was delighted with her conversation, he tells me.

NOTE:

1. HPB's concentrated writing on the book is first recorded during her visit to the Corsons in September-October 1875, just a year and a half before this letter.

In mid May Bouton wrote Olcott, complaining of the changes that HPB was making in the proofs. Those changes were so many that he feared the book would cost more to produce than it could be sold for. She made alterations at every stage of production: galley proofs, page proofs, and final plate proofs. In July, Olcott prepared the table of contents for volume 1, and Emily Kislingbury, who was visiting from England, did the same for volume 2. In view of the chaotic state of the text, both found the task a challenge. In September Alexander Wilder made the index for the book and by the end of that same month *Isis Unveiled* was published in a first printing of 1000 copies that sold out in ten days.

The continuing addition of new material, which both Olcott and Wilder mention, resulted in a surplus of unused copy because Bouton finally put his foot down on changes (*ODL* 1:217):

> Then, again, when the publisher peremptorily refused to put any more capital into the venture, we had prepared almost enough additional MS. to make a third volume, and this was ruthlessly destroyed before we left America.

Olcott's characterization of HPB's work process presages the nature of the final product (*ODL* 1:204):

> She worked on no fixed plan, but ideas came streaming through her mind like a perennial spring which is ever overflowing its brim. Now she would be writing upon Brahma, anon upon Babinet's electrical "meteor-cat"; one moment she would be reverentially quoting from Porphyrios, the next from a daily newspaper or some modern pamphlet that I had just brought home; she would be adoring the perfections of the ideal Adept, but diverge for an instant to thwack Professor Tyndall or some other pet aversion of hers, with her critical cudgel. Higgledy-piggledy it came, in a ceaseless rivulet, each paragraph complete in itself and capable of being excised without harm to its predecessor or successor. Even as it stands now, and after all its numerous re-castings, an examination of the wondrous book will show this to be the case.

HPB's own judgment (*CW* 13:191–2) of the coherence of the book is the same as Olcott's and, indeed, paraphrases his:

> Of all the books I have put my name to, this particular one is, in literary arrangement, the worst and most confused. . . . And I might have added with as much truth that, carefully analysed from a strictly literary and critical standpoint, *Isis*

was full of misprints and misquotations; that it contained useless repetitions, most irritating digressions, and to the casual reader unfamiliar with the various aspects of metaphysical ideas and symbols, as many apparent contradictions; that much of the matter in it ought not to be there at all and also that it had some very gross mistakes due to the many alterations in proof-reading in general, and word corrections in particular. Finally, that the work . . . has no system in it; and that it looks in truth, as remarked by a friend, as if a mass of independent paragraphs having no connection with each other, had been well shaken up in a waste-basket, and then taken out at random and—published.

And yet this disorganized and flawed book has continued in print ever since. The initial notices were mixed, as is to be expected. Olcott (*ODL* 1:295–7) cites examples of both types, including: "one of the most remarkable works for originality of thought, thoroughness of research, depth of philosophic exposition, and variety and extent of learning that has appeared for very many years" (*Philadelphia Press*), "a most valuable contribution to philosophical literature . . . one of the remarkable productions of the century" (*New York Herald*), "a large dish of hash" (*Springfield Republican*), "discarded rubbish" (*New York Sun*). He concludes: "The truest thing ever said about *Isis* was the expression of an American author that it is 'a book with a revolution in it.' "

The revolution that *Isis Unveiled* evoked had repercussions long after its first appearance. For example, nearly twenty years following the book's publication, Gordon Rowe wrote an imaginative spiritual biography of "George Holly of Sevenoaks Lodge, Crickhowel," Wales, for the short-lived magazine *Theosophic Isis* (Nov. 1896, 328–32). There is no historical record of such a George Holly, and he and his biography are almost certainly fictions. The biographical sketch has Holly contacting Theosophy in 1877 as the result of a letter from America mentioning the publication of *Isis Unveiled*. Holly impulsively writes to HPB and, having no better address for her, sends his letter to "Mme. Blavatsky, New York." The next day he receives a telegram concerning a business matter that summons him from Wales to London. Arriving there the next morning, he looks again at the telegram and then sees on the back of it a precipitated letter to him from HPB:

> Theosophy *is* true. Your opportunity is great. Study. Propagate our ideas, for the time is short. Who teaches the wisdom of the GODS, to them the GODS (incorporeal minds) reveal themselves. Yours, dear lad, as in past lives.—H. P. BLAVATSKY.

This letter, which has sometimes been mistaken for a genuine one, is a literary device, "merely corroborative detail, intended to give artistic verisimilitude" to the narrative, a piece of late Victorian fiction drawing a moral about the importance of responding positively to one's inner promptings. It also, however, demonstrates the continuing reputation of *Isis Unveiled*—even after the publication of *The Secret Doctrine*—as a revolutionary book that has changed lives.

Introduction to Letter 90

A report of the publication of *Isis Unveiled* in HPB's surviving correspondence appears first in the following letter:

Letter 90

To A. N. Aksakoff   *October 2, 1877*

Well, my book has appeared at last. The darling was born last Saturday, September 29th, but a week earlier my publisher sent advance copies to the editors of all the papers; I enclose herewith the review of the *New York Herald*. When I read it I almost fainted. I was prepared for all sorts of abuse, and lo, here is such praise, and that from one of the most conservative and Catholic of papers. Look at the last paragraph, where it says that *Isis Unveiled* is "one of the remarkable productions of the century." Perhaps they will abuse me yet, but all the same the entire first edition (1,000 copies) has been sold out in two days, so that even the subscribers are obliged to wait another week, until the second edition is out. . . . The book is handsomely got up, two huge volumes in red binding and with a gilt back, on which Isis Unveiled sits astride. I am quite proud of the index. It was made for me by Professor Wilder, our Vice President and a famous American archeologist. . . . We have now numerous corresponding fellows in India, and we are thinking of going to Ceylon next year in order to settle there, as the Headquarters of our Society.[1] I have received the degree of "Arch-Auditor" from the principal Masonic Lodge in India.[2] It is the most ancient of the Masonic Lodges, and is said to have been in existence BC.

NOTES:

1. This is the first mention in the correspondence of HPB and Olcott's plans to move the Society headquarters to India or Ceylon.

2. HPB's Masonic credentials were due to John Yarker, an Englishman who specialized in alternative or "fringe" Masonic rites. Charles Sotheran, a mutual friend, introduced HPB to one of Yarker's books, *Notes on the Scientific and Religious Mysteries of Antiquity; the Gnosis and Secret Schools of the Middle Ages; Modern Rosicrucianism; and the Various Rites and Degrees of Free and Accepted Masonry*, which HPB cited favorably in the manuscript of *Isis Unveiled*. In August 1877, Yarker was made an honorary member of the Theosophical Society. In September, *Isis* was published with the citations to Yarker (2:316-7, 374n, 376-7, 394). Sotheran had suggested to Yarker that HPB be given Masonic recognition, so Yarker first sent her "the certificate of the female branch of the Sat Bhai (Seven Brothers, or seven birds of a species, which always fly by sevens); it was a system organized at Benares in India by the Pundit of the 43rd Rifles, and brought to England by Major J. H. Lawrence-Archer, 32°-94°." HPB alludes to the degree in this letter. In November 1877, Yarker sent her a certificate of the highest degree (Crowned Princess 12°) of the Rite of Adoption (a form of female Masonry), which had developed in France, to which HPB alludes in letter 106. (HPB's connections with Freemasonry are dealt with in Algeo, *Blavatsky, Freemasonry, and the Western Mystery Tradition*.)

SOURCE: Russian original unavailable. Translated by Boris de Zirkoff from Solovyov's *Sovremennaya* 287. Another English translation by Walter Leaf in *Modern Priestess* 276-7.

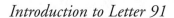

Introduction to Letter 91

After the publication of *Isis Unveiled*, HPB corresponded in late 1877 with William H. Burr, a skeptic about Spiritualism who was interested in Gnosticism. Several letters of his, dated October and November 1877, are in the Archives of the Theosophical Society, Adyar. None of her letters to him are known to survive, except the following two published fragments, which Burr himself quoted. Although Burr does not link the two fragments, it is likely that they are from the same letter.

Letter 91

To W. H. Burr   *October 10, 1877*

My only curse is, that I know English so imperfectly. I am going to study it now that I have nothing better to do.
. . . . .

I do not believe in Spiritualism, but I believe in the phenomena, which, as it takes place, must proceed from some natural causes as yet undiscovered by science.

DATE: Burr implies that the first fragment is from a letter HPB wrote him after *Isis Unveiled* had been published (on September 29). A letter from him to HPB dated October 14, 1877 (Archives of the Theosophical Society, Adyar), replies to one she wrote him in response to an article he had written about a review of *Isis*. As the second fragment is dated October 10, 1877, both are probably from HPB's first letter to Burr.

SOURCE: Original unavailable. Copied from Burr's *Madame Blavatsky*, 1, 4.

Letter 92

To N. de Fadeyev   *October 28–29 [1877]*

Well, my dear friend, try to be patient and do not grumble. I received two of your letters and found in them eighty-nine questions, which I now propose to answer as far as my strength and capability go. It is a pity you do not read English; otherwise you would find all the answers in *Isis*. Have you received the two copies of it sent to you? Please let me know as soon as you receive them. Of course you will not find one word therein against the Orthodox Church. Why? Your Church is the purest and the truest, and all the ugly human things, as well as all the little "enemies" of Father Kiriak will not suffice to desecrate it. In the Russian Orthodox Church alone is *Divine Truth* established, firmly established. But it is buried in the foundations; it cannot be found on the surface, unless it be in such pure, angelic hearts as Father Kiriak, or in such deeply philosophical intellects as the Most Reverend Nil. Please find out whether it is possible to obtain that book, *On Buddhism*,[1] by Bishop Nil, which you wrote about. Can it be had apart from his other writings, for I am interested only in his opinions on Buddhism. Thank you for the book *On the Edge of the World*. It may well be a novel belonging to "Flying Sketches," but it will not fly away from my head. It is such a deep and true story that if all the Christian Bishops, priests, and monks were such as these, there would be no outlandish sects, no warring religions, and all the world would be—I will not say *Christian*, but *Christ-like*.

You are right, my bright soul; the *Master* likes the former so much that he almost called me stupid when I humbly confessed that I had never heard about Nil. And he, you see, must have known him. Now I shall start translating it into English, somewhat abridged of course, and the Master will try to get it translated into three or four dialects of Hindostan, to make it known among the Buddhists, and to strengthen the friendship between them and the Russians. I shall finish it in three days and will send the translation to Ceylon, to Colombo, to the Buddhist College and to the High Priest and President of the College, Mohottiwatte

Gunananda, as he is called. He has already ordered fifty copies of my book, in order to translate some portions of it. He has also translated the writings of Bishop Colenso and *Matter and Force* of Büchner, with notes and arguments, and has smashed the German into smithereens. Last month, at a public debate, he defeated the greatest Methodist orator, Bishop Gringood, so much so that the latter broke his eyeglasses; and he proved the superiority of *practical* Buddhism over theoretical Christianity.

You are wrong in expressing the opinion, my friend, that I only "cast a glance" towards Christ, but in reality yearn for the Buddha. I look straight into the eyes of Christ, as well as of Gautama the Buddha. That one of them lived twenty-five centuries ago and the other nineteen does not make the slightest difference to me. I see in both of them the *identical* Divine Spirit, invisible but clearly felt by me. Heaven help me from ever imposing my ideas on anyone, and still less on *you*, but if, out of kindness and generosity, you allow me (contrary to the dogmatists) to lay open my soul to you, then I will do so as completely as I would be compelled to do before Christ and the Buddha themselves, when I will have become worthy by growth and achievement (by means of *deeds* and not words) to meet them in a better world. In words and deeds, as well as in the practical life of both of them, I feel with all my spiritual being the same *substratum* of Divine Truth. For me neither the dogmas of Christianity nor those of Buddhism and Brahmanism exist. Neither Christ nor Gautama the Buddha nor the Hindu Krishna have ever preached any dogmas. *Not a single article of faith*, except these greatest truths: "Love thy 'God' more than thyself, and thy brother as thyself." (Excuse my altering the text.) Among the points with which you do not agree in the story of Nil (by Leskov), one is probably the satire concerning the "remittance of sins by the priest"; and it is just these last pages which constitute for me the whole delight and philosophy of the story. The baptized Yakut ate up the sacraments and abandoned poor Father Kiriak. He committed a most heinous crime. Why? Because his catechism taught him there is no crime which is not redeemed by the blood of Christ; that the priest of Christ can do everything, that he has the power to remit any sin, for this power is given to him by the dear Christ himself. Why then not do something even worse? Three days ago a Negro Methodist was hanged here. He cut his wife to pieces and burned his five-year old daughter bit by bit in the open fireplace, beginning with the feet and ending with the head, torturing her for *one hour!!* When the noose was put on his head the Negro began to shout in a sort of ecstasy: "Oh, I see my Savior; I see, I see the bright face of my Christ the Lord, He smiles at me. . . . He opens his arms to me!!" etc. Lots of people purchased bits of the garment of the hanged man and, cutting them to pieces, kept them as a kind of relic. All his life this Negro had been a thief and a drunkard and finally became a bestial criminal, but ONE HOUR BEFORE being hanged he seemingly repented and received communion, and now, according to the words of the pastor, "he has been united forever with Christ and lives the eternal life on His bosom"!!! Oh Lord, what a sacrilege! These are the results of Christianity. No, Nadyezhenka, I am not against Christ or in favor of the Buddha, but against man-made dogmas. Buddhism teaches that one merits the Kingdom of Heaven—*Nirvana*, by means of deeds and not empty words. It teaches there is no mediator at the Great Judgment of the Future and of the Unknown God but our own deeds. For us, Christ, and for the Buddhists, Buddha. Both taught the blind people how to see truth, but the apostles of both distorted a great deal, some out of spiritual and bodily weakness, some out of ill will and selfish ambition like that of the Papacy. You are unable to believe in the periodical embodiments of the Unknown

Deity, which means the Holy Ghost, according to Christianity, and, according to Buddhism, the Holy Wisdom, Adi-Buddha, which is the same thing; and I, sinful creature, believe it so; for it seems to me *impossible* and incomprehensible that, if there is an individual, an intellectual Personality called the Most High Creator, it could wait for so many hundreds of thousands of years from the time of the objective manifestation of our earthly globe in the midst of the universe, to finally appear 1877 years ago. Were human beings worse in ancient times, say twenty thousand years ago, than we are now? Or were they such pure angels that there was no need for Divinity to manifest itself at all? It is unthinkable. I am not a Buddhist, but I am afraid I am not a Christian either, in the ordinary Church sense. I believe blindly in those words of Christ that I clearly understand and still more in those that were expressed by Him in the Sermon on the Mount, for I find them literally repeated in the Buddhist sermons of Gautama, in the Dhammapada and in the Sastras of Siddhartha Buddha, as well as in the Egyptian Book of the Dead. If Divine Truth was and is one, then, in all ages, men of righteousness and purity of spirit should have seen it as white, and not black or green. In practice, the Buddhists are a thousandfold more Christlike than Christians. I remember and see an example of it in myself. It seems to me that from the day I was born I never was a Christian, yet there were moments when in a sort of fit I believed deeply that *sins could be* remitted by the *Church*, and that the blood of Christ has redeemed me, together with the whole race of Adam. And what? . . . No! It is bitter and painful to remember the past. You know what I am hinting at. I'll tell you one thing, Nadya: *If I had been born a Buddhist and not a Christian, I would not have shamed the heads of those whom I loved more than all else in the world*, grandmother and aunt and yourself and the whole family. I remember how at Tiflis two days before confession and communion, being convinced that all my sins would be forgiven in any case *wholesale*, however few or many, it did not matter, I continued to stain my damned soul. And of such as myself, weak in spirit and flesh, there are millions, and thousands of crimes are committed every day, simply because people believe in the remittance of sin, not through repentance and good deeds, but merely through the power of the priest. That is why I believe, and am unable not to believe, that such periodic embodiments have a sense and are indispensable. Buddha does not stand in the way of Christ or the other way about. The word Χριστός, *Christos*, was derived by the Greeks from χριω⸱, "to be anointed." And the word Chrestos existed—as has now been clearly shown by ancient *pre*-Christian inscriptions, several thousand years BC. Jacolliot may be foolish and a humbug in many ways—he is a Frenchman—but in his etymology of the word *Jezeus-Christna* he is right. This word means *pure essence*, in other words Divine Spirit; and if the word *Krishna* means "black" in Sanskrit, the word хрисс [? *cf. Russian* Христос "Christ"] means something springing forth from the Divine, or Divine Essence, just as he tries to prove. However, I have not read much of him and do not like him, for he lies too much and slanders the highly ethical priesthood of Buddhism, identifying it in his hate of all Churchianity with the Catholic clergy. However, I am drawing my proofs not from the humbug Jacolliot but from the most ancient manuscripts of Ceylon and central India, from the Book of the Dead and the Egyptian inscriptions of the fourth and seventh dynasties of pharaohs. "Chrestos" is a word identical with *Onnofre* (one of the names of Osiris)—Divine Essence or Mercy again. All the most ancient philosophies prove that this "essence" meant the immortal spirit—the spark of the infinite and beginningless ocean, called God, a spark with which every human being is endowed from birth by the Divine, that it may overshadow him during all his earthly life; and after the death of the body either to blend with the soul (périsprit) to make him immortal, or—if the man was a beast during his life—break the spiritual thread uniting the animal soul, the individual intellectuality, to the immortal spirit, leaving the animal entity at the mercy of the elements constituting its subjective being; after that, following the law of *perpetuum mobile* [*Ln*. perpetual motion, constant change], the soul or *ego* of the former man has unavoidably to dissolve in time, to be *annihilated*. It is this immortal spirit of ours that is and always was called Chrestos or Christos. Do we really have to believe with Doctor Müller[2]—the Bishop-orator here—that during Christ's (Jesus') stay on earth there was no God either in Heaven or the rest of the universe? The invisible world was empty and left without a ruler, like France during its periods of anarchy? This is a question of simple logic: Hamlet's to be or not to be. Either the *whole* essence of Divinity was centered in Christ—then Müller is right and there was nowhere another God—or only a part of the Universal Great Spirit descended into Jesus; then we Theosophists (our own party!) are right. The Holy Spirit was embodied in Christ, but it was neither the first nor the last time since the beginning of the world; for this spirit was of the same essence with the immortal spirit of every man, with this difference only, that all other men were more or less sinful, while Jesus was chosen by the Divine Spirit, which descended into him instead of overshadowing him from a greater or lesser distance; and for the purpose of redeeming the human race, or rather to redeem forthcoming generations of men who had forgotten other Saviors, who had appeared in other times and countries. I fully realize that all this will appear to you as pure *heresy*. But Nil also regarded as heresy what Father Kiriak told him. My Master has the same reverence for Jesus of Nazareth as for Gautama of Kapilavastu, but he does not look on either of them as gods; he regards them both as simply mortals and worships the spirit of Christ and the spirit of Buddha in the same way, realizing that both are identical, both are particles of the One Great Divinity. All the rest—dogmas and rules—are purely human. If we behaved as Christ and the Buddha behaved, when embodied as two mortal men, we and any one of us would become like Christ and Buddha, namely united and blended with the Christ-Buddha principle in us, with our immortal spirit; but of course only after the death of our sinful flesh, because how could we, with our beastly snout, climb into paradise in this life? Be charitable, do not accuse me of sacrilege. Perhaps I am heretical in regard to the Church and human religion, but, as far as my feeble understanding goes, I am not sinning against the Holy Divine Truth. I repeat that I am using the word "Buddha" in its *abstract* sense, which means the Divine or God-like *Wisdom*, not taking into account either the man Jesus or the man Gautama, Prince of Kapilavastu.

About the "peisahs"[3] of the Bible I will speak no more. It is these "peisahs" who have caused so much trouble. It may be that the learned chronologists and theologians will not accept the teaching at once, but future discoveries in the world of scholarship will soon prove that the monotheism of the Jews is but slightly older than our Christian era. As to *Jehovah*, he was born at the same time as the bluff of the Masoretes, and was not firmly established any earlier than the fourth century. You will have to agree that out of the four consonants JHVH, which can be found in all the manuscripts *prior* to those of the Masorah, it was possible for the Jewish Masoretes to make *Johivy* and *Jehavhu* and what not, according to their tastes and needs. The vowels of the Masorah were invented only in the last century BC. Of course the Jews and their forefathers existed even before Ezra, the fabricator of the Old Testament, but as a nation they were unknown to any of the educated philosophers and writers. They may have been the Hyksos—the Shepherd-Kings or Pharaohs, and may have been called Phoenicians or Syrians; but they were called neither Judeans nor Hebrews nor Jews until 150 BC, nor were they ever in Babylonian captivity. In Cochin, just a stone's throw from Madras, there is a colony of Jews who settled there before the Christian era; they have all their papers and documents, and they have the Bible of Moses, but this Bible is in no respect like the real Bible, but rather like a Samaritan one. They also have their idols and even bow before the Brazen Serpent of Moses—the *Nehushtan* [2 Kings 18.4]. And not one learned man knows anything about this colony; only some of *our* people belonging to the Sat-Bhai Society fraternize with some of their Kabbalists. Their papers and charters granted to them by the Kings of Travancore 400 years after the death of Gautama the Buddha, i.e., 200 years BC, prove their origin, and they call, or rather used to call themselves, Phoenicians. They *prove* that they have kept the faith of their fathers and of Moses in the purest spirit. They intermarry among themselves and never mix with the "heathens."

October 29

Now let us talk about the individual God, the personal or anthropomorphic God. You say and reproach me for the fact that I do not believe that the "Great Essence" could be interested in me. Let us talk it over. If we are to discuss it, let's do so thoroughly. I shall play it clean.

Who is teaching us, or has taught us about the *anthropomorphic* existence of God, namely a God or Gods endowed with purely human attributes and qualities, a God that is good, just, omniscient, and all-forgiving? The RELIGIONS of all times and of all peoples? From its very creation, the world has always been full of a number of religions—fruits of human and purely physiological imagination. Everywhere, on the mountains and in the valleys, incense was burned to God and gods; at all times and from everywhere earnest prayers went upward, silently and otherwise. Religions are spread in all the corners of the earthly globe. If religion—as it is preached to us by the clergy—is the mother of virtue and happiness, these should reign everywhere where there is religion, especially the *Christian* one. But is it so? Look around you; cast a glance at the Danube and Asia, where the Cross is struggling with the Crescent; *Truth*, we are told, with idolatry and error. Is it likely the *God* of Truth would help more or pay more attention to the Christians than the Turks? Compare the statistics of crimes and sexual laxity, of sin and abomination in Christian countries with those in heathen countries. For every 100 crimes in Christian cities you will not find even one among heathen nations. A Buddhist, Brahmanist, Lamaist, and Mohammedan does not imbibe alcohol, does not steal, does not lie, as long as he holds fast to his own heathen religion. But as soon as the Christian missionaries appear, as soon as they *enlighten* the heathen by means of faith in Christ, the *heathen* becomes a drunkard, a thief, a liar, and a hypocrite! While they are heathen, every one of them knows that every sin of his will return to him, according to the law of retribution and justice. A Christian ceases to rely on himself and loses self-respect. "I shall meet a priest, he will forgive me," as answered a newly "enlightened" one to Father Kiriak. Something similar exists, although on a far smaller scale, in vulgar, *popular* Brahmanism. No, the world is full of religions, and fuller yet of suffering and injustice, and especially so where present-day refined Christianity, adjusted to the laws of the nineteenth century, reigns.

I assuredly cannot write you several volumes, but I will send you a little article translated from an ancient, very ancient Singhalese manuscript. If you or any other—the most learned theologian—could give us an answer to it, it would mean a victory for you. Now I will answer your direct questions. The idea that people are repentant devils is the idea of Yevgeniy Ivanovich, in Saratov days, but that is something I will reply to some other time.

It seems strange to you that a Hindu, the Sahib,[4] intrudes like a "host" into my house? Once admit that the human soul, its *périsprit*, is a completely separate part of man, that it is not pasted down with some sort of glue to the physical "giblets," and that it is just this very *périsprit*— which exists also in every animal, from the elephant to the infusoria—that differs from the animal *double* by being more or less overshadowed by the immortal spirit, and capable of acting independently—in the *noninitiated* man during his sleep and in the *initiated* Adept at all times—and everything will become clear to you. This fact has been known and believed in from immemorial antiquity. Hierophants and Adepts of the "heathen" Mysteries were initiated into these secrets; and St. Paul, who alone among the Apostles was an Adept of the Greek Mysteries, hints at this rather openly when he tells about a certain young man who "whether in the body . . . or out of the body, I cannot tell; God knoweth," was caught up to the third heaven. And Rhoda, was she not told, "It is not Peter, but his *angel*" [Acts 12.13-5], i.e., his double, his spirit. Remember about Philip, of whom it is said that the Spirit of God caught him up and carried him to Azotus [Acts 8.39-40]. Surely it was not his physical body that was caught up, but his *périsprit*. Read Apuleius, Plutarch, Iamblichus, and other philosophers; all of them hint (the pledge they took at initiation did not allow them to speak openly) at this phenomenon. What the mediums are doing *unconsciously* under the influence and with the help of the spirits of the dead and of the elementals, the Adepts do consciously and in full awareness. Sahib has been known to me more than twenty-five years; he came to London with the Premier of Nepal and the Queen of Oudh. Since then I have not seen him, until I received a letter from him through a certain Hindu, who had come here three years ago to lecture on Buddhism. In this letter he reminded me of several things that he had foretold in London, when he looked at me with the greatest of disdain (deserved) and asked me if I was ready now to renounce the unavoidable *annihilation* after death and to believe him. Look at his portrait; as he was then, so is he now. He who could be on the throne, according to his birthright, renounced all to live quite unknown and gave all his enormous income to the poor. He is a Buddhist, but not of the dogmatic Church, but belongs to the Svabhavik-as, the so-called Nepal *Atheists* (?!!). He lives in Ceylon, but what he is actually doing there—I do not know. I cannot, *I have no right to tell you all*, but it ended by my leaving New York and staying seven weeks in the wilderness, in a forest—in Saugus, where I saw him every day; at first in the presence of a Hindu lecturer on Buddhism, and later alone, and I almost passed out from fear every time. This Hindu was not a double but in his physical body—and was the first one to organize the Theosophical Society. He also chose almost all the members and foretold about Baron de Palm's death the following May, ordering him to arrange for the cremation of his body. All was done accordingly. The Hindu left after giving us several dozens of names of Hindus in India, all Kabbalists and Masons, but not of the stupid European and American Lodges, but of the Grand Eastern Lodge into which Englishmen are not admitted. The fakir Kovindasami[5] about whom Jacolliot writes (you probably read in the *Revue Spirite*), belonged to the subalterns of this Lodge. (If you have not read, you had better read Jacolliot's *Le spiritisme dans le monde*.) All these people are such thaumaturgists that the best of mediums are mere asses compared to them, with all their *shishimori*-spirits. When this

Hindu was here, he purposely went to the powerful mediums, and his presence alone paralyzed all the manifestations. Nothing happened! They despise all mediums, call them innocent and unconscious blasphemers, and regard the spirits as stupid *kikimoris*, earthly, elementary demons; they do not recognize anything higher either on earth or in heaven than the human, immortal, all-powerful spirit. Higher than this individual spirit, there is only the Unknown Great Divinity—or rather the Essence of the Highest Divinity, as they all deny a personal God, as you know. An enormous bronze statue of Jesus, forgiving Mary Magdalen, stands in one of the underground temples. Next to it is a statue of Gautama giving water to a beggar from his palm, and of Ananda, his pupil and brother [word illegible]; also one of Buddha, who drinks at a well out of a cup extended to him by a pariah prostitute. *This I know*. But what is the secret meaning of these three statues, they, the "initiated" adepts, know better than I. I know only that my "host" is more Christ-loving and Christ-like than the best of present-day Christians and certainly reveres the Christ more than does the Pope of Rome, or Luther, or Calvin.

When his double, or the real Sahib, leaves temporarily his outer sheath, the bodily envelope is left in a state similar to that observed in a calm but mindless person. He either orders it to sleep, or it is guarded by his men. At first it seemed to me he would squeeze me out of my body, but soon I became accustomed to it and now, during the period of his presence in me, it merely seems as if I were living a *double* life. When they wanted to operate on my leg, and gangrene was developing, the "host" healed me; he was standing next to the old Negro and placed a little white dog on my leg. Do you remember I wrote you about it? Now he will soon take me and Olcott and several others to India for good, only we must first organize the Society in

London. Whether he dwells in some other corporeal vehicle than mine, I do not know. But I know that when he is not here—sometimes for many days—I often hear his voice and answer him "across the sea"; Olcott and others often see and hear his shadow; sometimes it is solid like a living form, often it is like smoke; still more often it is invisible but is *felt*. I am only now learning how to leave my body; I am afraid to do it alone, but with him I am afraid of nothing. I shall try it with you; but kindly do not resist and do not scream, otherwise you will ruin

Your devoted,
Lulushenka

NOTES:

1. *Buddhism, Examined in Relation to Its Followers Who Were Living in Siberia*, by Nil, Archbishop of Yaroslavl (St. Petersburg: At the Printing Press of Grigoriĭ Trusov, 1858).

2. The identity of this "Dr. Müller" is unclear.

3. The context suggests that "peisahs" refers to those persons who produce *peshat*, "a literal interpretation of Biblical texts."

4. "One of the names that my sister gave (at first) to her 'Teacher' or 'Host' " (footnote added by Vera de Zhelihovsky, HPB's sister).

5. Perhaps Govinda Swami.

DATE: The reference to the incarnation of Christ "1877 years ago" fixes the year of this letter, which was apparently written over a two-day period: October 28 and 29. In addition, *Path* (NY) 9:298, quoting HPB's sister Vera, introduces its fragment of the letter thus: "Directly Isis Unveiled was published, H.P.B. wrote to Madame Jelihovsky," indicating the year 1877, and HPB refers in the first paragraph above to having sent Nadyezhda two copies of *Isis*.

SOURCE: Translated by Boris de Zirkoff from the Russian original in the Archives of the Theosophical Society, Adyar. Another English translation in *Theosophist* 71 (May, Aug., Sept. 1950): 79–85, 293–7, 365–9, and in *HPB Speaks* 1:203–25.

This letter has a curious history, described in part by C. Jinarajadasa in his introduction to the translation he published (*Theosophist*
71:79 and *HPB Speaks* 1:189):

> There are three remarkable letters of H. P. Blavatsky which
> came to Adyar in 1947, presented by the Society in England.
> The story is interesting. Somebody sent Mrs. Doris Groves,
> General Secretary, a newspaper cutting announcing the sale
> of some manuscripts, among them some letters of H.P.B.,
> from the library of the late Earl of Crawford and Balcarres.
> Evidently in 1881 this gentleman was interested in the
> teachings of the Mahātmas and had come into touch with
> A. P. Sinnett. There is a reference to him in *Mahatma Letter
> No. VIII.* How three letters of H.P.B., sent evidently to her
> aunt, came into his possession is a mystery. Mrs. Groves sent
> one of her staff to be present at the auction, where there
> were two others bidding for the letters, but finally Mrs.
> Groves' messenger outbid them and purchased the collec-
> tion, which Mrs. Groves brought to Adyar. Among the mate-
> rial are three letters of H.P.B., the remainder being evidently
> a transcription in Russian of parts of H.P.B.'s book, *Caves
> and Jungles,* not in her handwriting but presumably in that of
> her niece. As the first of these letters dates back to 1877, they
> are of particular interest.

Even more curious is the fact that a portion of the latter part of
this letter starting with the paragraph beginning "It seems strange
to you that a Hindu, the Sahib, intrudes like a 'host' into my
house?" was printed in two quite divergent translations both in
January 1895. Each of these early translations also adds material to
the text of this letter. The provenience of the Russian version(s)
from which these early translations were made is unclear. One
translation was made by HPB's niece, Vera Zhelihovsky Johnston:

1895 *Path* Version

It seems strange to you that some Hindu Sahib is so free and
easy in his dealings with me. I can quite understand you: a person
not used to that kind of phenomenon—which, though not quite

unprecedented, is yet perfectly ignored—is sure to be incredulous. For the very simple reason that such a person is not in the habit of going deeply into such matters. For instance, you ask whether he is likely to indulge in wanderings inside other people as well as me. I am sure I don't know; but here is something about which I am perfectly certain: Admit that man's soul—his real living soul—is a thing perfectly separate from the rest of the organism; that this perisprit is not stuck with paste to the physical 'innerds'; and that this soul which exists in everything living, beginning with an infusoria and ending with an elephant, is different from its physical double only inasmuch as being more or less overshadowed by the immortal spirit it is capable of acting freely and independently. In the case of the uninitiated profane, it acts during their sleep: in the case of an initiated adept, it acts at any moment he chooses according to his will. Just try and assimilate this, and then many things will become clear to you. This fact was believed in and known in far distant epochs. St. Paul, who alone among all the apostles was an initiated Adept in the Greek Mysteries, clearly alludes to it when narrating how he was 'caught up to the third heaven, whether in the body or out of the body I cannot tell: God knoweth'. Also Rhoda says about Peter, 'It is not Peter but his angel'—that is to say, his double or his soul. And in the *Acts of the Apostles,* ch. viii, v. 39, when the spirit of God lifted up Philip and transported him, it was not his body that was transported, not his coarse flesh, but his Ego, his spirit and his soul. Read Apuleius, Plutarch, Jamblichus, and other learned men— they all allude to this kind of phenomenon, though the oaths they had to take at the time of their initiation did not allow them to speak openly. What mediums accomplish unconsciously, under the influence of outside powers which take possession of them, can be accomplished by Adepts consciously at their own volition. That's all. . . . As to the Sahib, I have known him a long time. Twenty-five years ago he came to London with the Prince of Nepaul; three years ago he sent me a letter by an Indian who came here to lecture about Buddhism. In this letter he reminded me of many things, foretold by him at the time, and asked me whether I believed him now and whether I would consent to obey him, to avoid complete destruction. After this he appeared repeatedly, not only to me but also to other people, and to Olcott whom he ordered to be President of the

Society, teaching him how to start it. I always recognize and know the Master, and often talk to him without seeing him. How is it that he hears me from everywhere, and that I also hear his voice across seas and oceans twenty times a day? I do not know, but it is so. Whether it is he personally that enters me I really cannot say with confidence: if it is not he, it is his power, his influence. Through him alone I am strong; without him I am a mere nothing.

SOURCE: *Path* (NY) 9 (Jan. 1895): 298-9. Another English translation of most of this version in *Path* (London) 3 (Dec. 1912): 211-2.

The other early printed version is even more divergent. It is, however, an English translation of a French translation, perhaps of the original Russian or perhaps of an inaccurate copy of the original Russian. It has no authority but is included here as a demonstration of the complex textual history of these letters:

1895 *LUCIFER* VERSION

It is evident that it is difficult for you to comprehend this psychic phenomenon, notwithstanding that there are precedents of which history speaks. If you will allow that the human soul, the vital soul, the pure spirit, is composed of a substance which is independent of the organism and that it is not inseparably linked with our interior organs; that this soul, which belongs to all that lives, to the infusoria as well as to the elephant and to each one of us, is not to be distinguished (from our shadow, which forms the almost always invisible base of its fleshly envelope) except in so far as it is more or less illumined by the divine essence of our Immortal Spirit, you will then admit that it is capable of acting independently of our body. Try and realize that—and many things hitherto incomprehensible will become clear. As a matter of fact, this was well recognized in antiquity. The human soul, the fifth principle of the being, recovers some portion of its independence in the body of one profane during the period of sleep; in the case of an initiated Adept it enjoys that state constantly. St. Paul, the only one of the Apostles initiated into the esoteric mysteries of Greece—does he not say in speaking of his ascension to the third heaven 'in the body or out of the body' [2 Cor. 12.3] he cannot tell; 'God knoweth.' In the same sense the servant Rhoda says when she sees St. Peter, 'It is not him, it is his "angel," ' that is to say, his double, his shade [Acts 12.13–5]. Again in the *Acts of the Apostles* (viii. 39), when the Spirit—the divine force—seizes and carries off St. Philip, is it in truth he himself, bodily and living, that is transported to a distance? It was his soul and his double—his true 'ego.' Read Plutarch, Apuleius, Jamblichus. You will find in them many allusions to these facts if not assertions which the initiated have not the right to make. . . . That which mediums produce unconsciously under the influence of outside forces evoked during their sleep, the Adepts do consciously, working by understood methods . . . *Voilà tout!* [*Fr.* That's all!]

SOURCE: *Lucifer* 15 (Jan. 1895): 361–2.

Letter 93

To N. de Zhelihovsky[1]   *November 6, 1887 [1877]*
                                            New York

My most kind—and, so far the *only one* of my nieces deserving esteem, Nadya, write to me—has your unconscientious Mamma received the books that I sent her a long time ago—some two or three months back? Together with the latest *Isis*—namely the one produced by your aunt (which was not written about you), there were altogether *eight* books. Your hard-hearted and taciturn parent has not written a single word about it. Tell her also that I have not been receiving any *barrack memories*. I have received one of her articles for translating and publishing in *World*, which will probably be included shortly. Is that what she calls "the attitudes of our soldiers to the Turks"? I have not received any others.

Fedya, Rostya, Verochka, you, Valka and Lenochka (pshaw! my godfathers, what a phalanx there is of you!) I firmly kiss and ask you all not to forget your aged aunt, who is somehow starting to love you all too much, which is not at all compatible with the stern ancient philosophy.

May the Lord God keep you.
I kiss you, firmly my dear, precious girl.

Your aunt—Elena Blavatskaya

NOTE:

1. HPB's niece, the daughter of her sister, Vera de Zhelihovsky. The girl was in her early to mid teens at the time of this correspondence.

DATE: The dating 1887 is an error for 1877. Russia and Turkey engaged in a series of conflicts from the seventeenth to the nineteenth centuries, the last of them in 1877–8, which must be the one alluded to here. HPB published an article on "Turkish Barbarities" (*CW* 1:255–60) in the *World*, August 13, 1877. HPB's mention of having sent Vera eight books, including *Isis Unveiled*, "some two or three months back" agrees approximately with her statement of October 28 (letter 92) of having already sent two copies of her book to her aunt after its publication on September 29.

SOURCE: Russian original unavailable. Translated by Anatol Kagan from *Questions of Theosophy*, 2nd ed. (St. Petersburg, 1910), 93.

Introduction to Letter 94

In the early 1870s (letters 5 and 10 endnote), HPB's references to the internationally known physical medium D. D. Home were neutral, but from 1876 onward they become increasingly bitter. The antagonism perhaps stems ultimately from HPB's insistence that the physical effects of mediumship were not produced by the spirits of the departed, as mediums like Home maintained, but by elementals (semiconscious forces of nature) and elementaries (the cast-off psychic shells of dead human beings, left behind after the spirit has departed from them).

More immediately the quarrel seems to have begun with an objection by Home to Olcott's characterization of HPB as "one of the most remarkable mediums in the world [whose] mediumship is totally different from that of any other person I ever met; for, instead of being controlled by spirits to do their will, it is she who seems to control them to do her bidding" (*People from the Other World* 453). HPB did not claim to be a medium, "except perhaps, in her earliest youth" (*CW* 1:203), but Olcott's characterization focused on the difference between her phenomena and that of mediums like Home, to the latter's disadvantage. Then, in an article published in March 1876 (*CW* 1:194–203), HPB took Home to task for his failure to support the imprisoned Leymarie (French editor of the *Revue Spirite*), for his conversion to Roman Catholicism (one of her bêtes noires), and for his attacks on various Spiritualists and mediums, which Olcott also commented on (*ODL* 1:74–5n).

In 1877, Home published simultaneously in London and New York a history and critique of Spiritualism and persons associated with it: *Lights and Shadows of Spiritualism*, whose thesis has been characterized as a statement that, although his own mediumship was genuine, all other practitioners of the art were frauds. In it, he made a number of critical comments without identifying the object of his criticism, who was, however, clearly HPB (244, "America's chief Occultist"), but he was also highly critical of the Theosophical Society and Olcott, focusing especially on elementals and elementaries (245–8) and on Olcott's book *People from the Other World* (252–75). Home's book greatly exacerbated the quarrel between him and the Theosophists.

Letter 94

To A. N. Aksakoff   *November 6, 1877*

That is why I am going *to India for good*, and because of my shame and sorrow, I am going where no one knows me . . . Home's malignity has ruined me forever in Europe. He must have written some nice things, when his wife was obliged to write to Mr. Martheze in London, not to pay any attention to her husband's letters as he (Home) was crazy!! As for Home's book,[1] neither Olcott nor I have read it, we have never so much as set eyes on it. Before it appeared, Olcott vowed never to open it, and has kept his vow. He has had several offers to answer it, and one of the publishers of the London *Athenaeum* has written to him suggesting that he should reply to it point by point in his review. But Olcott refused.

NOTE:

1. D. D. Home, *Lights and Shadows of Spiritualism* (New York: G. W. Carleton, 1877).

SOURCE: Russian original unavailable. Translated by Boris de Zirkoff from Solovyov's *Sovremennaya* 287. Another English translation by Walter Leaf in *Modern Priestess* 278.

$\backsim$

Letter 95

To A. R. Wallace   *November 7, 1877*
                    302 W. 47th St., New York

Alfred R. Wallace Esq[re]
Dear Sir,

I hope that in venturing to ask your acceptance of the first work I have ever written—"Isis Unveiled" you will not think me too presumptuous. Better than anyone else I know its faults and deficiencies. But, while I can expect no indulgence from the ordinary critic on the score of being a foreigner and quite unaccustomed to literary work, I yet hope that a few of the facts of my personal experiences may interest you, who have given so much attention to Spiritual and psychological phenomena and are so exceptionally competent to appreciate the weird and endless mysteries of the invisible world of Spirit.

My title is really a misnomer for *I do not* reveal the arcane secrets of the dread goddess—Isis. Needless to tell you who has lived in the East, that the *final* mysteries and secrets of initiation are never given to the general public. The book was to have been called "The Veil of Isis", and the first volume was stereotyped before I learned that M[r] Winwood Reade had anticipated me, and I had to do my best to alter the title of my work. There are, however, facts in my book that should be known alike to those who advocate and those who oppose the study of Spiritualism. If the latter does not soon develop into a philosophy and a Science its fanatical votaries will drag it down, and it will fail to satisfy the reasonable expectations of a public which is outgrowing the tyranny of Theology and materialistic Science.

If I do not uncover altogether the Saitic[1] goddess, I hope to have at least sufficiently indicated where the Veil of her shrine can be raised by those who are ready to conform to the four cardinal rules of so called "Magic" or occult Psychology—to Know, Will, Dare, and Keep Silent. Behind the veil lies the Key to modern Spiritualistic phenomena, and there alone can be discovered the Secret of Secrets: what is man, his origin, his powers and destiny.

With assurances of my profound regard
Believe me, Dear Sir,
faithfully yours
H. P. Blavatsky
Corresponding Secretary of the
Theosophical Society of New York

NOTE:

1. Related to Saïs, an ancient Egyptian city in the Nile delta.

SOURCE: Transcribed from the original in the British Library, Department of Manuscripts, Wallace Papers (ADD 46439, fol. 72 recto and verso); reproduced photographically and transcribed with minor differences in the *Eclectic Theosophist* No. 73 (Jan.-Feb. 1983): 6–7.

Letter 96

To M. D. Evans   *November 16, 1877*
New York

Dear Mr Evans,

It will give me much pleasure to see Mr Pusey and yourself upon the evening you name. If you want to enjoy a good laugh read the article in this morning's New York "World" upon "Theosophs at the Circus."[1] The writer is a wag of a fellow who never loses an opportunity to poke fun at us in a good natured way. His present story is based upon the slender foundation that Col. Olcott and I did go to the circus with him, did feed the elephants, and did have an interview with the putative "Egyptian Jugglers" a couple of French humbugs who are no magicians at all but only passable as *prestigitateurs* [*Fr. prestidigitateurs* prestidigitators, slight-of-hand artists].

Thanks to Brahma and all the holy family of gods dwelling in the Moksha the second edition of "Isis" is selling as rapidly as the first. This one has "a table of contents in it"—a great improvement. The London publisher Quarritch[2] has sent for a fourth supply, and to morrow's steamer takes the first shipment to the corresponding Fellows of the Theosophical Society in India.

With remembrance and my kindest regards to M[rs] Evans, M[rs] Ames and other friends,

yours sincerely
H P. Blavatsky

NOTES:

1. The article is reproduced below.

2. Bernard Quaritch, a London publisher and rare book dealer.

SOURCE: Transcribed from a photocopy of the original in the Dreer Collection, by courtesy of the Historical Society of Pennsylvania. Published in a slightly different form in *Canadian Theosophist* 71 (Sept.-Oct. 1990): 78–9.

The article mentioned by HPB is reproduced below. It is an imaginative jeu d'esprit, not a factual report, but it shows the popular interest that the early Theosophists evoked and HPB, who appreciated parodies of herself, clearly enjoyed it.

THEOSOPHS AT THE CIRCUS.

A VERACIOUS CHRONICLE WHICH NOBODY
WILL PRESUME TO DENY.
THE MARVELOUS THINGS WHICH HAPPENED BETWEEN
MME. BLAVATSKY AND THE JUGGLERS.

"Colonel, we will go to the circus to-night. Bis mallah!" said Mme. Blavatsky suddenly, while seated at the well-appointed dinner-table in the lamasery, at the corner of Eighth avenue and Forty-seventh street, last evening. "This WORLD it says well that the Egyptian jugglers present a promising subject for inquiry by the Theosophical Society."

"To hear is to obey," said Hierophant Olcott, stroking his ample beard thoughtfully and relapsing into silence as he bent the gaze of his astral man upon the quaint little image of Buddha in an adjoining room. The WORLD reporter, who was present, once asked the Hierophant why Buddha gazed forever at his umbilical, thinking to hear words of wisdom in reply. "He tries to think what it is for," said the Colonel thoughtfully, and after a pause: "Perhaps you can tell me why the Etruscan serpent swallows his tail?" The reporter gave it up.

"And you, too, will go with us," said Mme. Blavatsky in a tone of courteous command to an acolyte of the lamasery who was neglecting his soup to listen to the tinkling music of Pou Dhi, Mme. Blavatsky's favorite elementary spirit.

"I will go," said the acolyte, absently. He is a very solemn looking man, with a very black beard and very large spectacles, who is very devoted to the high-priestess and very much in earnest in his studies. He looked, however, very much as though he thought it a very trifling way of passing the time.

"Will Fiske go with us?" asked the WORLD man after he had accepted an invitation to join the party. Fiske is the stuffed ape in the corner of the drawing-room, and is the abode of various speaking spirits. His deep base voice is sometimes startling to the casual visitor, but to those who are familiar with him he appears harmless.

"Ah, do not talk flap-doodle, my friend," said Mme. Blavatsky.

Mme. Blavatsky is writing a second book, intended to supplement "Isis Unveiled." That work treats more of the theories of mysticism, and the second book, "White and Black Magic," relates to the phenomena of magic. It was plain that the Egyptian jugglers were to pass the crucial test of an interview with the learned author.

As the party approached Gilmore's Garden, Mme. Blavatsky sniffed delightedly: "It is like India, this circus," she said. "There is the beautiful smell of the wild beasts." Inside she was greatly interested in the trained elephants, but not much in the rest of the show till the jugglers appeared. The Hierophant, on the other hand, seemed most interested in the young women who performed on the trapeze. "How much do they earn?" he asked of the WORLD reporter, who did not know. "They would make nice Nautch girls for the temple we are going to build," he said absently.

"I wonder if they are Buddhists," he continued, but the reporter did not know that either. The acolyte was interested in everything. "Do they have many elephants as large as that in India?" he asked, modestly.

"As large as——By the point of Cleopatra's Needle, but these are not large," cried Mme. Blavatsky. "They are the largest I have seen in this country, but in India they are much larger. But these are wonderfully intelligent," she continued, patronizingly.

"And is that magic?" asked the acolyte, when the jugglers appeared and began their performance.

Mme. Blavatsky looked for a moment and said—a little sadly, the reporter thought, "No, it is not true magic. It is clever juggling, but not magic. The true white magician does not perform his wonders for money. But we will see these men after the performance, and learn more of them."

Accordingly, the party thridded its way through the crowd in the menagerie, Mme. Blavatsky stopping to fondle the elephants, and feeding them with apples when they responded with ponderous winks and jovial flappings of their great ears to a phrase of some prehistoric language that she whispered to them. One of them extended his trunk—the reporter swears it stretched a yard beyond its normal length, and, first touching the lower edge of the ermine pelisse in which the lady was wrapped, made as if to whisper in her ear. The acolyte misinterpreted the motion and stretched out his hand to interfere, thinking to save the bonnet of the priestess.

"Ouch!" he yelled, as his arm dropped suddenly.

"Is it a cramp!" asked the reporter.

"No," whispered the hierophant. "His arm is withered. But I have some magic oil at home. Perchance I may restore it."

"This elephant, I will speak with him," said Mme. Blavatsky suddenly. "It is a magician imprisoned. Colonel, give to me the umbrella with the mystic point."

Grasping the weapon, she began drawing the ring of Arbaces, and getting on the further side of the elephant as she completed the mystic circle, vanished entirely.

The party waited awhile in silence, and the audience, not having noticed the incantation, manifested the greatest surprise at the white solemnity in their faces. Presently Mme. Blavatsky appeared around a far corner of the elephant, and rejoined her friends, a serene smile on her face and a little of the straw of the elephant's litter clinging to her right ear.

"What did he—" began the acolyte, but the high-priestess stopped him with a gesture.

"Would you penetrate the arcane, you, with your withered arm not healed?" she said, and the acolyte prostrated himself in humiliation. Suddenly the two jugglers appeared in a mysterious way from a side door, and the entire party adjourned to a small room hard by.

Not knowing many languages the reporter is unable to give the whole of the conversation. His eyes were busy, however, and while he gathered a few scraps of the story the jugglers told, he witnessed what made his brain whirl. There were only two chairs in the room as they entered, yet in a moment all six of the party were seated, and the reporter saw that each had a chair. Cigarettes of fragrant Latakia appeared suddenly, floated in the air and were mysteriously placed in the mouths of all the persons present. As they smoked they talked. The jugglers, it appears, were born in Egypt, near Cairo, of a French father and an Egyptian mother. Embracing the religion of their mother they fled from home after her death and took refuge in a temple of Isis, where they devoted themselves to a religious life and drank deep at the fountain of wisdom-religion to which they were led. Straying too far from the sanctuary, they were one day captured by emissaries of their Christian father, and being over-powered they were bound and carried to France. Making their escape after two years of captivity, they resolved to see the world before returning to Egypt.

"We support ourselves by juggling," said the elder brother to Mme. Blavatsky when she asked why holy men juggled for hire, "but we do not practise magic. Of course you have seen that," he added, with an obsequious salaam, after Madame had made a mystic sign and whispered a holy word in his ear.

"Do you carry serpents in your pockets?" asked the acolyte, curiously.

"Certainly, and much larger than those in your pockets," said the elder brother, smiling.

"But I have no—" and the acolyte stopped. Two hissing heads had suddenly thrust themselves in his face as two boa constrictors wiggled their way out of his coat-tail pockets.

"Great Allah! I've got 'em again," he said as he dropped in a faint. The serpents laughed diabolically, and at a signal from the two magicians, who opened their mouths wide, they slid rapidly down the two gaping throats. Mme. Blavatsky grabbed a vial of strange perfume that floated casually through the air and sprinkled nine drops on the acolyte's left temple and he sat up bewildered.

The reporter suggested that it was a favorable time to produce some manifestations that, being duly chronicled in THE WORLD, would remove the slight doubts that had perplexed many citizens who were unable to accept the Buddhist faith unreservedly. Mr. Olcott was divided in his mind. As Colonel he wanted to second the suggestion, as President of the Theosophical Society he maintained that the annuals of that society were the proper place in which to record all marvels, and as Hierophant and Buddhist priest he strongly opposed the notion. But Mme. Blavatsky was decided at once.

"You are my friend," she said to the reporter, who bowed low, "and you shall see what the holy men of the East can do, and I myself will show them what I can do," and she waved her hand, whereat a huge crocodile trotted into the room and bending his tail gracefully presented each of the jugglers with a slip of paper, at which they clanked and turned pale. The reporter gazed at one of these afterwards and saw that it was a bill for six weeks' board.

"Great lady, we bow to thee," said they together and salaamed continuously for some minutes.

"But these people in New York who scoff at me I will give them no signs—the Thomases," continued the lady, wrathfully. She did not bind the reporter, however, by any promise, and though the notebook he had in his pocket was not visible during the séance, it was yet filled with notes when he drew it out in the horse-car afterwards, which magical occurrence, he considers, frees him from any obligation of secrecy.

"I would like to see a man vanish," said the acolyte modestly, and instantly the younger juggler, who sat near the door, was no longer seen. Every one gazed agape for over a minute at the chair in which he had been sitting, when suddenly the window opened and he leaped lightly in.

"That is only the astral man that is now visible," whispered Colonel Olcott to the reporter. "Presently, when you are not looking, he will get into his physical body, and that will be visible again."

"It is getting very hot," said the reporter, and the words were hardly out of his mouth when a little bell that was on the table was lifted high and swung tinkling through the air, and presently an Ethiopian dwarf entered with a tray of sherbert. It was aromatic and refreshing and though it seemed a mild drink as it was swallowed, it produced strange effects. The acolyte flourishing his empty goblet in the air chanted loudly a song in some strange tongue, of which the reporter was only able to catch the refrain. It ran:

> "Wew ontg oho metillm orni
> Ngti Ilda ylig htde thapp earrrr."

Of the mad revel of *diablerie* that followed nothing could be told without exciting the reader's doubt. The reporter vainly strove to persuade the Hierophant to join him in a cocktail as they stepped out in the night, some two hours later, but the acolyte looked after the reporter longingly as he tottered away, his nerves shattered and his brain reeling.

SOURCE: *New York World,* November 16, 1877, 8.

Letter 97

To W. H. Burr   *November 19, 1877*

Let us settle, once for all if you please, as to the word "Spiritualist." I am not one—not at least in the modern and American sense of the word. I am a Shwabhavika, a Buddhist Pantheist, if anything at all. I do not believe in a *personal* God, in a direct Creator, or a "Supreme" [Being (Burr's addition)]; neither do I confess to a *First* cause, which implies the possibility of a *Last* one—and if so, then what comes next? I believe in but one eternal, indestructable substance, the Shwabhavat, or invisible, all pervading matter, whether you call it God, or many Gods in partnership. But this is not the First cause, but only the eternal emanation of the universal, *incomprehensible* something, which is neither first nor last, but had neither beginning, neither will it have an end. The epithet "Atheist" in my book [Isis Unveiled (Burr's addition)] does not apply to those who disbelieve in a personal God, but to them who equally reject the God of the Christians and the "Anima mundi" [*Ln.* world soul] of the ancients; who attribute the whole of the visible and invisible world to blind *chance*—which is a word void of sense in relation to the economy of nature as a whole and can, at best, be applied to individuals, the results of the everlasting work of this *whole*. If you did not know of any Atheist who had nightmares I did. And my own brother to begin with, one of the brightest intellects of the Moscow University. Unable to solve the problem, What is God? (the God of the Christians,) whence he proceeded and who created him, the young fellow had brain fever and went mad. He was cured with great difficulty in a lunatic asylum in Germany, where he remained from 24 to 31 years of age. Then again Schleiermacher, the German Professor of Theology and several others.

You are right in saying that you see no inconsistency in
being an Atheist and at the same time a Spiritualist. I am
an Atheist in the Christian sense of the word and yet I
believe in the survival of the *real inner* man after the disso-
lution of his physical body or his outer terrestrial garment,
and I believe in the immortal or third principle in man. But
I do not believe the following:

1. I deny that immortality is achieved by every man,
woman or child. Immortality must be won, or as John says,
"The kingdom of heaven must be taken by violence."
["From the days of John the Baptist until now the kingdom of heaven suffereth violence." Math. xi:12 (Burr's
addition)] But a very small percentage of the human race
becomes immortal, i. e. very few individuals become *gods*.
"Know ye not ye are gods?" ["Is it not written in your law,
I said Ye are gods?" John x:34 (Burr's addition)] The rest
are sooner or later *annihilated*, and their bodies and souls
are disintegrated, and while the atoms of one return to the
elements of physical nature, the more sublimated atoms of
the other, when no longer cemented by the presence of their
individual "spirits"—which are alone immortal, as everything real becomes subjective—are violently torn loose from
each other and return to the more sublimated elements of
spiritual nature.

2. I emphatically deny that the spirits of the dead can
show or manifest themselves objectively in any way or
manner. But I do believe and know that these spirits have
the power (if their finer astral entity survives) to impress
mortals on earth, to inspire and teach them, etc.

3. I do not believe in the so-called materializations of
our dead ones. But I believe that the astral souls (erroneously called spirits) within a living body have the same
powers or faculties as those who have forced themselves
from their earthly presence. Therefore I believe in some of
the manifestations produced by mediums, but hold that

pretty nearly all such phenomena are the result of the freaks of the spirits of the mediums themselves, unconscious to themselves, and are often helped by the "elementary," or those disembodied men and women who, having parted forever from their immortal spirits, vegitate [sic] within the atmosphere of the earth, which alone attracts them, and use the organs of weak mediums to lead through them a fictitious life, and cheat *annihilation* for a short time yet. If the *inner man* of a sleepwalker, who is ignorant sometimes even of reading and writing in his normal state, can write very often beautiful poetry, play the violin and do that which his body would never do when awake, why not believe that their spirits or *inner selves*, when disembodied, can do the same? Why wonder and attribute the phenomena to the agency of disembodied spirits when they are simply due to the invisible and real self of the medium?

Thus, as I do not believe what your Spiritualists teach, I am *not* a Spiritualist. But as I believe in the survival of the astral soul, and the immortality of the "spirit," I am not a nihilist, either. I confess that the term "Atheist" is improperly used; but this is the fault of the English language, not mine. What other term would you use? Even the modern Hindostanee—let alone the mother tongue of all, the Sanskrit—has expressions which are utterly untranslatable into your European poor tongues. I am not an Atheist— quite the reverse; and yet I completely reject the idea of a Creator or a Supreme God, who is in the least concerned in the government of this world. How would you call me then? Neither am I a Pantheist, pure and simple, for beyond visible nature, and within its immutable, eternal laws, I place a spiritual, purely subjective intellect, the unconscious *Deus ex Machina* of all, though neither its guide nor Ruler. Buddhist philosophy and metaphysics, even in their exoteric literature, are beyond the comprehension of the average civilized Christian; as to the esoteric Eastern teachings they are simply inaccessible to the greatest metaphysical European mind—unless he is *shown* that which he cannot comprehend by simple argumentation, and all his five senses are brought together to testify to his reason that which he is allowed to learn practically as well as theoretically within certain sanctuaries and through imitation.[1]

Excuse my long and not very clear arguments. I would if I could express myself more clearly. But besides being a foreigner, with a very limited knowledge of English, I am placed face to face with a public, which, however, intelligent and scientifically trained, is yet unable to grasp even theoretically that which is demonstrated practically in certain pagodas, and therefore perfectly plain to me.

* * * * *

P.S. I have read over the present scribble, and I know that your verdict upon reading it will be that I am a d—— fool. So be it, nor do I blame you for sharing the ideas of every respectable and civilized citizen of America in regard to my religio-metaphysical views and unconventional habits.

NOTE:

1. The reprint in the *Canadian Theosophist* reads "initiation" rather than "imitation." The amendment fits the context well, but the word in the pamphlet is also possible and is retained because it is the reading in the oldest surviving text of the letter.

SOURCE: Original unavailable. Copied from Burr's *Madame Blavatsky* 4–7. Reprinted in *Canadian Theosophist* 71 (Sept.-Oct. 1990): 79–81.

Letter 98

To her relatives   [late 1877]

Upon my word, I can hardly understand why you and people generally should make such a fuss over my writings—whether Russian or English! True, during the long years of my absence from home, I have constantly studied and have learned certain things. But when I wrote *Isis*, I wrote it so easily, that it was certainly no labor, but a real pleasure. Why should I be praised for it? Whenever I am *told* to write, I sit down and obey, and then I can write easily upon almost anything: metaphysics, psychology, philosophy, ancient religions, zoology, natural sciences—or what not. I never put myself the question: "*can* I write on this subject? . . ." or—"am I equal to the task?"—but I simply sit down and *write*. Why? Because *He who knows all* simply dictates to me. . . . My MASTER, and occasionally others whom I knew years ago in my travels. . . . Please do not imagine that I have lost my senses. I have hinted to you before now about Them . . . and I tell you candidly that whenever I write upon a subject I know little or nothing of, I address myself to *Them*, and one of Them *inspires* me, *i.e.*, he allows me to simply copy what I write from manuscripts, and even printed matter that pass before my eyes, in the air[1] . . . It is that knowledge of His protection, and faith in *His* power that have enabled me to become mentally and spiritually so strong . . . and even He (the Master) is not always required; for, during his absence on some other occupation, he awakens in me his substitute in knowledge. . . . At such times, it is no more *I* who writes, but my *inner ego*, my "luminous Self," who thinks and writes for me. Only see.[2] Is it possible that in a few years I should have become so very learned as to write without hesitation page after page of *Isis*, with all its *verbatim* quotations from, and innumerable references to, books that I had never seen, nor could I ever see them? Then all this running after me of reporters and journalists, and of Russian editors after my articles. . . . What is it caused by? . . . Whence all this knowledge?

NOTES:

1. *Incidents* has at this point: "during which process I have never been *unconscious* one single instant."

2. *Incidents* has as the rest of this sentence: ". . . you who know me."

DATE: The reference early in the letter to having written *Isis* and being praised for it suggests a date shortly after the publication of that book.

SOURCE: Original unavailable. Copied by Boris de Zirkoff ("Introductory," *Isis Unveiled* 1:[23–4]) from HPB's English translation of her Russian letter, a slightly shorter version of which is in "Mystical History" 63 and a slightly variant one in *Incidents* 205–6 (2nd ed. 156–7). Portions of this letter are in *Rebus* 2 (Dec. 4, 1883): 429–30.

⌒

Introduction to Letter 99

The following letter came to light some fifty-two years after it was written. In 1929, the Madras *Hindu* newspaper published the letter under the following headings and introduction:

CHRISTIAN THEOLOGY AND EASTERN FAITHS

M. BLAVATSKY ON HER BOOK

The following copy of a letter dated 20th November 1877 written by the late Madam H. P. Blavatsky, founder of the Theosophical Society, from New York, to the late Sir T. Madhava Rao, will be read with interest:

Letter 99

To T. Madhava Rao   *November 20, 1877*

Permit a woman—whose only claim on your attention is the sincere devotion she bears to your country and her love for its great Hindu race—to present you with her work—the fruit of many years' study. Though born in Russia and under the spiritual jurisdiction of the Greek Church, I have from an early age felt myself drawn towards India as though it were my own country, and to its time-sanctified religion and philosophy as the only teachings that would satisfy the longing of my spirit. Three times I have visited your fairy land, each time I quitted it with regret—with heart-felt distress; the more I studied its philosophies hoary with age and replete with wisdom, the more I saw of its peoples and learned to understand the secret meaning of its exoteric worship, the more I felt convinced how utterly both the people and their religion were misunderstood, hence—misinterpreted and shamefully disfigured even by those who should have known them better,—from Sir William Jones down to the Sanskrit scholar Max Muller. As to ways and policy on these questions adopted by the so-called "Christian Missionaries" they are beneath contempt. It is against their lies, their shameful behaviour and diabolical hypocrisy in foreign, "heathen" (?) lands as well as to their homes that the greatest portion of my work "Isis Unveiled" is chiefly directed. Christian theological dogmas I have ever abhorred, not alone for its unacknowledged robberies of the oldest sacred writings, but also for their debasement of priest and people by the abominable doctrine of the "vicarious atonement." The only "Old Testament" I have revered is the "Vedas"; my only "New Testament" is the Mahabharata, Manu and your Vedanta.

I have waited for many years for some man to do justice to India and by quotations from her sacred literature brand this Western theology with the stamp of shame. I have waited in vain to find one who had both the knowledge and the courage to say what Truth demanded. Jacobhot,[1] a Frenchman, ex-Judge at Pondicherry, moved by a sincere admiration for India, tried in over twenty volumes to do her religions and people justice. But in his fanatical hatred of all priesthoods, he included the Hindu Brahmans of the temples in the same sweeping denunciation as he gave to the Jesuits. No priest, in his eyes, could be pure and holy; As to other authors—if materialists, they have some official position at stake, perhaps; they know the whole truth about India, they have read but they conceal; those who are ignorant—defame and denounce the more unscrupulously to hide that ignorance; as to the Christians, the believers in and followers of their meek Jewish God Jesus, they are to-day led from their tender infancy to believe all the non-Christian people vowed to "eternal damnation" after their death; hence—they damn them during life, and for them to tell the most bare-faced lies about the "heathen" is a meritorious and sacred duty.

[WHY "ISIS UNVEILED" WAS WRITTEN]

Finally, tired of fighting Christians in words, I determined that I myself, albeit a woman, a foreigner, and with no pretensions to scholarship would do the work that others neglected. I came to America, the only country where a woman is entirely free to say as well as man what she likes upon religious matters, and I have written a work of which a copy is now respectfully offered to Your Excellency for acceptance. It is in two large volumes, one devoted to a comparison of modern science with ancient, the other to a demonstration that this pretended divinely-given Christianity is but a mongrel mixture of various older Eastern faiths. I call the book "Isis Unveiled" because Western people are familiar with the Egyptian goddess who represents nature and its sacred mysteries.

That such a work was needed is proved by the public reception mine has met with. Within a week it had reached its second edition.[2] That it tells the public and the Christian theology very disagreeable truths is shown by its abuse by the clergy and the church-going hypocrites. The Russian Government has already decreed that it shall not be allowed to cross the frontiers of my native land and its sale is prohibited. I was just informed that the sacred college at Rome has placed it upon the "Index Expurgatorus"[3] Let these signs indicate to Your Excellency and other sons of India whether I have done my duty in defending them and the religion of their forefathers, as conscience and sincere and affectionate admiration would prescribe.

Christianity is so unspiritual, so rotten at the core, that it is splitting into two great parties of materialists and Christian dogmatists of every colour—one representing blind reason, and the other blind faith. To attempt to save the middle party from the inevitable despair which attends the existence of man's knowledge of the world of spirit, I have contrasted the psychological achievements of your gurus, sanyasis and fakirs with the childish miracle (!) of Christian saints, and the revolting and absurd phenomena of modern spiritualism and its so-called "medium."

In asking your Excellency to accept a copy of my book which will be forwarded to you by Mooljee Thackersey of Bombay, North Brook Gardens—I offer the only tribute I can pay to a statesman whose character for justice and great ability is known to every lover of India at this side of the oceans, and at home. This reputation has—as Manu expresses it— "made the people run to him as the rivers to the ocean."

Praying that you may be long spared to promote by your public services and private example the interests and welfare of your too long oppressed Mother-land, which at the present juncture so much needs the help of her ablest patriotic sons.

NOTES:

1. Louis Jacolliot.

2. That is, second printing.

3. The Index Expurgatorius is a list of books that Roman Catholics were forbidden to read.

SOURCE: Original unavailable. Copied from the Madras *Hindu* 53 (Dec. 18, 1929): 16.

Letter 100

To N. de Fadeyev

December 11, 1877
New York

From your letters I see that you did not receive some of mine, and that I also did not get all of yours. It is most unpleasant. For instance you write that one of these days you told all about Sasha's[1] wound—I never got that. And now you say that you do not know whether I received *Laughter and Sorrow*, when I wrote to you long ago that not only did I receive the book, but that I also read it in Odessa, soon after the corporal punishments on the public square. Don't you remember that even I thought of translating it, but auntie objected out of patriotism.

You are right, let us drop theology, as neither of us is likely to convince the other, and we shall probably lose time for nothing. But one thing you must give me leave to reply. In spite of the fact that India is really no *terra incognita*—though very *incognita* in some respects—Russian missionaries know hardly anything about it, and the Protestant and the Roman Catholic missionaries tell lies to their hearts' content. Read any work on India of any learned and dispassionate person, of any of the officers who have spent years in that country, even the statements of the enemies of India, and you will find everywhere that a Hindu never takes either liquor or wine, that he eats no flesh, and that it is difficult to find anyone more honest, more truthful and more gentle. I am speaking about the real Hindu[s], followers of Brahminism, not the cowards who become Musulmans, or drop all religion, becoming thugs and brigands. Please do read what the missionary Dubois says about it. Also read St. Francois Xavier, who spent years in Japan and says that the scrupulous honesty of the Japanese could give lessons to the Christians.

Buddhism (not the idol worship, of course) is the purest and the highest of Asiatic religions. In Ceylon, Burmah, and Siam, monogamy is the rule, having two wives is considered very immoral and is punished severely. It is possible that the Samoyeds, Tunguzes and Buriats and other nomads have learned to drink *vodka*, but believe me that nowhere in Southern India or Ceylon could you find a member of the priesthood who either drinks or is immoral.

Do not be guilty of injustice, Nadejinka, but remember the great rule of the Buddhist religion, a rule which, in spite of the embodiment of gentleness, charity and justice in Christ, and in spite of his precept, has never as yet become a rule amongst the Christians or their clergy. Here are the words Gautama Buddha spoke, before his last words: "Hold fast to your faith, honor it above everything else, but also respect the faiths of other people." And his last words were: "All form (*composé* [*Fr. composée* compound substance]) is finite, and doomed to destruction. The spirit of man alone is immortal, without beginning, as without end. I am going to Nirvana."

Now I shall answer all your questions, and will try to explain what you do not understand.

NIRVANA is a word which none of our Orientalists have as yet rendered with any degree of accuracy. Barthélêmy Saint-Hilaire, Burnouf, and Max Müller (the latter twenty years ago, for of late he has changed his opinion for another, which is just as inaccurate) have discussed the question, and tried to prove that Nirvana means the ultimate, the complete destruction of the human individual. Other Sanskrit scholars maintained that Nirvana meant something quite different. Think of the absurdity of the idea that over 400,000,000 people, for the Brahmanists also believe in Nirvana, calling it Moksha, pray all their lives, mortifying themselves with fasting, self-abnegation and renunciation of all physical and moral comforts, all in the hope of obtaining Nirvana or "annihilation," when this annihilation is to overtake them, in any case, upon the death of their bodies, so long as they do not believe in the immortality of the soul. Yet the absurdity of this did not prevent the Orientalists from preaching their theories.

Their argument was founded on the etymology of the technical term. In Sanskrit, Nirvana means the "blowing out" of fire or flame, the destruction of the spark, and is composed of two words: "Nir" and "Vana," that is, "extinguish" and "light."[2] "Moksha" also means "liberation," in Sanskrit "Nirvritti,"[3] "end to everything," or the "ultimate cessation." They found the explanation of the word in the Mahabharata, which claims that Nirvritti means "the extinguishing of life in the fire, as well as in the wise man." But as I proved to the Philological Society of New York, in the Amara Kosha, a philosopher of antiquity interprets the term "Nirvana," "flameless," in "Nirvana," as the perfect stillness, a state of windlessness, in which the spirit of man (the symbol of which, with the Christians, is a fiery tongue), as a spark of the eternal, invisible hearth (foyer), of the Great Spirit, or Anima Mundi, is for ever freed from all accidents. The question is, to understand correctly the metaphysical concepts of the early Aryan races, the Vedas, and also the "Four Truths"[4] of Gautama Buddha, Siddhartha. Their philosophy does not admit the idea that the Matter in anything composite or concrete can count for anything. Matter, even sublimated, that is, invisible, as even all our moral functions, thought, the affection of one person for another, as desire, in fact, all the attributes of the living, thinking man, which *are* Matter, as is now proven by Tyndall, who stole his idea from Schopenhauer and Van Helmont, who borrowed it from the Neo-Platonists, who inherited it from the Hindu Kapila, the greatest philosopher of prehistoric times. In fact, everything that has shape or color, or can be formulated by the tongue of man, or perceived by the thought, does not exist (in eternity), but is merely a meteor which, lightning-like, flashes out and is lost at the moment of its birth and being. All this is Maya, an illusion of the objective perception, *ergo* it is finite, having a beginning and an end, the interval between which is not worth noticing, as even many thousand years are but an instant in eternity. Time, and the distribution thereof, are the creations of human fancy, and as the beginningless and the endless cannot be created by the finite and the short-lived, such as is man, time itself is but an illusion of our senses, which also are an illusion, like everything else. Only that actually exists in eternity which is subjective, in the spiritual world, the Subjective of the very highest grade, in which there is no more any trace of human thinking, but everything is divine and pure: it is without beginning, as without end, it always was. This is Nirvana, the spiritual plane, the reflections of which light up all the worlds of the boundless universe, and as soon as these reflections reach the bounds of the subjective, they immediately become "breaths," "spirits," and "sparks," or the souls of Humanity. Which means that Nirvana is God. Not the anthropomorphic God capable of taking definite shape in the mind of man, but the All-containing, the Omnipresent, the Life-giving Spirit of God. After every Pralaya, or temporary disappearance of the Universe from the region of the Objective, this Spirit of God broods over the watery abyss, that is, Chaos, once more imparting life to every atom of this Abyss, which sweeps the atoms towards the whirlpools (so to speak), of self-creation, and a new appearance in the region of the objective but not real.

Next. Now I shall explain what Pralaya is. The atoms of which Matter is composed, are in themselves eternal and indestructible, which is proved, or rather half-proved, by modern Science; because it is not Matter itself, but only its essence, the atoms, that are indestructible and eternal. And this is why the Svabhavikas, a school of the highest Buddhistic philosophy in Nepal, claim that nothing exists in Nature but Nature itself, or the Substance, and that this substance (to use the right Russian word) has its existence in itself, is *Svabhavat*, without any Creator or Ruler; for which the Svabhavikas are called, very unjustly, Pantheists, and even Atheists. This injustice I also proved in my article.

This self-existing Matter (perhaps better, Substance) or Svabhavat, they teach, exists in eternity, and from all eternity, in two forms: in the state of Pravritti, or activity, and in the state of Nirvritti (Nirvana), or passivity. When it is in the state of activity, it is the ever-busy, ever-transforming Nature, or the Spirit of God itself, which animates every atom, and is crystallized in it. And so, though at first sight it may seem absurd, or even blasphemous, in my understanding it is the highest conception of the reflection of the Godhead, which is everpresent everywhere.

And when this Svabhavat is in its passive state (N.B. in the human sense of the term), or in Nirvritti, it does not exist for man, because the latter will never be able to define, or to understand, what God is.

The Buddhists of all schools believe in Nirvana; they believe in God; but they will never consent to belittle this Something unimaginable by lowering it to the level of human ideas. That is all.

This is proved by the profound remark of Gautama, which was translated only recently, and is preserved in the original, in the Bodleian Library: "Sadasad vikaram na sahate," which means that "ideas of Being and non-Being do not admit of discussion." And so our learned sillies promoted Buddha to the rank of an atheist.

Human beings who, in the physical sense, also self-create themselves like the rest, under the law of Nature, ought to do all they can to assimilate in this life the state of Nirvana as much as possible, that is to say, they ought to keep in mind that everything earthly whether physical or moral, is but an illusion, a vanity of vanities, and to aspire with all their moral and spiritual being to life eternal, or that state which for the present is but subjective for us, yet nevertheless is the only objective state in reality. In other words, we must love our neighbor, and honor our father and our mother, and feel joy and sorrow, and give ourselves to every emotion, only in so far as we have failed to conquer that emotion, even to destroy it in ourselves, but not any more. We must do good, yet not for our own sakes, but for the sake of our duty to Humanity. We must love and respect our parents, our children, our husbands and wives, but only with the object of making them happy. And as to ourselves, our physical selves, our husks, we must disregard them, aspiring with all our hearts to Nirvana, to that state after death in which the flame of our spiritual individuality is liberated from all the functions and attributes even of our spiritual man, whilst he is in the body, in which the flame is extinguished, as a separate thinking, and therefore imperfect personality, and is merged (though not lost) in the divine essence of Nirvana, or, speaking more clearly, it lives in God, and God lives in it.

Here is Buddhistic "atheism" in a nutshell.

Christian theologians, and especially missionaries, turn up their noses at Nirvana, abusing it, and getting perfectly shocked by this doctrine, and say: "Buddha teaches us to despise Humanity and ourselves. He teaches egotism, maintaining that filial and parental affection, these most sacred things in all creation, are nothing but vanity, that man must aspire to Nirvana alone, to complete annihilation." And all this is nonsense, sometimes even intentional nonsense, with full knowledge of the opposite side. Does not Christ teach just the same? Did He not go on the path of self-denial and renunciation of everything earthly, even farther than Buddha? "He that does not leave father and mother, and follow me, is not worthy of me." And has not Saint Jerome made of this highly philosophical attitude toward life a monstrous fanatical doctrine, when he taught: "if thy father prevents thee from becoming one with the Church, go kill thy father; if thy mother prostrates herself across the threshold to hold thee, trample with thy feet the breast that suckled thee, and run; unite thyself to God and to his Church which is calling thee." Here is a proof that scholars and theologians, since the very first centuries, have not understood either Buddha or Christ, did not understand them at any time, and still do not understand them.

That which seems to us non-existent is alone, in the eyes of the Buddhists, worth the effort; the complete annihilation of everything objective, which exists in this temporary world, and therefore is temporary itself, is the beginning of life eternal, which is subjective for us, and therefore is called unreal, *nihil*.

I know that uncle will understand the idea, though for me it is awfully difficult to explain it in Russian, without any knowledge of the accepted philosophical and metaphysical terms.

Next. Why does the Hindu (do you mean my Master?) have little love for the "spirits" (of the mediums)? Well, exactly because of that same Nirvana, and Metempsychosis. I do not mean human souls entering dogs, pigs and vultures, because all this is nothing but a religious metaphor. I mean the transmigration of the second principle of man, according to its deserts, and not of his highest immortal spirit, into wicked pig-like creatures into "spooks," which bark like chained dogs. Good, pure spirits will not, I can assure you, throw about tambourines in dark *seances*; they will not talk nonsense and entice people to sin, just like devils.

"Spirits" of this kind disjointed from their bodies after death, if they were exceptionally material, drunkards and immoral, are so strongly attracted by everything earthly, that they will not go far from the atmosphere of the earth. They may roam about the wide world, trying to take possession of mediumistic people, living once more a factitious life through their organs, a temporal life, instead of attempting by repentance to reach Nirvana, and the final purification of everything fleshy. Or else, if they are altogether done for, these "spirits" or rather "*perisprits*," may disappear altogether, and their immortal souls, their guardian angels, will return to Nirvana.

The Ego within us is also Matter, sublimated and invisible to the eye as it is. If a pure spirit, once having broken through the prison of the living body, is still willing to come into contact with objective Matter, it proves that it can stand such a pollution, and if so, it shows that it is not altogether pure itself.

"The Hindu" does not despise the spirits which inspire the medium spiritually, nor those who influence people to speak, write or act under inspiration, nor those who are seen by clairvoyants, but only those who crowd into materialization, who clothe themselves with the effluvia of the medium and those present, with their magnetic sweat and other fluids, who lower the dignity of the immortal by giving themselves out to be immortal, and even by manufacturing out of the sweat and effluvia visible bodies which resemble the departed relations of the spiritualists. Of course these are also human souls, but as one soul is different from another, some, as I said, progress, and reach Nirvana; others disappear. The latter are no better than devils, save for the horns and tails, perhaps.

Through long habit, you mix up the human spirit with the human soul. They are two entirely different things. The one is identical with Deity, the other is merely the etherial man; for the most part invisible but in some cases capable of assuming a visible form.

As to how the body becomes a harmless idiot, when the soul (peresprit) gets out, it is easy to explain. The functions of life, or vital principles, have nothing to do, with the true soul, or the Ego of man. Consider insanity. People become insane, just because, whilst the fit lasts, the soul is away from the body, of which the insane is entirely unconscious. And in cases of incurable insanity, the soul has left the body altogether, promenading somewhere else, and pretending it does not know its body, though so long as the body lives, it is tied to it by a thin thread. And in cases where the body has become vacant, either through illness, or because the man has been convulsed by sudden despair, or because he has been intensely thinking of some person or some object, which magnetically drew his soul, together with his thought, out of his body, and toward that person or that object,—in all such cases, it sometimes happens that the vacant body is taken possession of by another soul, a "spook," whose kind are forever roaming about the earth, and who establish themselves very comfortably in the deserted body, controlling the functions of its physical brain, and impressing it to think that "I am, let us say, Caesar, or Alexander the Great, or even Christ himself." Such things do happen. The demoniacs of the New Testament tell you clearly that it is so.

The evil spirit is not the devil of popular fancy; it is the malicious, wicked soul of any sinner who has died without repentance, and who will go on existing until it is dissipated into the dust of the elements. This is why they are called Elementaries by Paracelsus, and all the other mystics who have studied Cabalistic sciences. There are also elementary spirits, but these are not the souls of men, but merely forces of nature, like Salamanders, Undines, Sylphs and Gnomes, of which there are hundreds of subdivisions.

Next. If I go to India, it will be because all our Society goes, I shall not go alone, and the mail goes to India, as to anywhere else.

Then how can you think that the Society will be destroyed? We simply transfer the Society to Madras, or to Ceylon, to be nearer to the Yogis, and thaumaturgists, the wonder-workers of India.

Next. When the soul gets out of the body, and is seized or suddenly frightened (I mean people who have but little experience, like myself), the peresprit may bound into space from fright, instantaneously breaking the thread which joins it to the body; then the body will die.

Well, I suppose I have tired you out. Good-bye! May the Superior Authorities take care of you all. I kiss everybody. Have you received my MS. for *"Pravda"* and my letter to the Editor? Please let me know.

HELENA.

P. S. I thought I had done, when look what happened in London: Three learned gentlemen were investigating Monck, the medium; they held him, in a lighted room, by his hands and feet, he being in a dead trance. And lo and behold, a light, white cloud-like vapor began to pierce through his coat and waistcoat, from the region of his heart. It began to rotate. It grew. It increased, and formed into the white shape of a woman, which moved away from the medium, and walked about the room, still remaining tied to him by a thread which was also vapory. Then she dwindled, grew vague, until, losing all outline, she became a cloud again, which was, so to speak, sucked back into the medium through his heart. Then it came out again, but as a tall man this time, evidently belonging to a different race. Same process. When the cloud came out for the third time, they all recognized the double of the medium. All three figures walked as if on springs, automatically, as if moved by some *outside power*. This outside power is nothing but some "spook," controlling the medium and his peresprit, endowing it, like a sculptor with Protean shapes.

So you see that what I have written to you about is beginning to take place in the sight of men, and learned skeptics at that. Unless the medium is a man of perfect moral purity, he will be controlled by "spooks." As to the Adepts, like my "Master," they will not let the spooks come near them, getting out of their own shells at will, moving perfectly freely, and working various wonders. And this is because their life is the life of virtue, of holiness, of self-abnegation and purity.

Devils have controlled me quite long enough, until my old age! Now I am rid of them, for Master is on my side!

Good-bye. Perhaps we shall see each other. In spring, I may have to go to London. Won't you come too?

I have read about Sasha (Major Witte); he is a fine fellow. God keep him!

All London is bubbling and chattering over this wonderful (?) occurrence; yet it is quite ordinary. Send me, oh my friend and my soul, a dictionary, and also see that, if I am to write for *"Pravda"*, I should be legally made their correspondent, with all due forms.

NOTES:

1. The pet name for Alexander Yulyevich de Witte, who was about 31 and a Major in the Russian army.

2. *Nir-* is a prefix meaning "out," and *vana* is from the verb *vāti* "it blows" (cognate with the English word *wind*), the combination meaning "blowing out, cooling, extinguishing." David and Nancy Reigle (private communication) note, however, that "the lexicon Amara-kosa by Amara-simha does indeed interpret nirvana as she says [in the third following sentence] (3.1.96)."

3. David and Nancy Reigle (private communication) observe that HPB's comments about *"pravritti* and *nirvritti* are taken from Brian Hodgson, who first made known the Svabhavika school of Buddhism (later found to be nonexistent). Although even Buddhist writers confuse these words, *nirvritti* is not really the correct spelling. That is what Hodgson has, but it should be *nivritti* or possibly *nirvriti.*" They add, "*Pravritti* is a common word in both Hindu and

Buddhist texts for activity, or functioning, in regard to anything
. . . . *Nivritti* is its opposite, meaning cessation. (*Nirvriti* is a synonym
of *Nirvana*.) In the Bhagavad-gita, *pravritti* is the outgoing path of
worldly activity, while *nivritti* is the path of renunciation leading
to liberation." *Nivritti* is from *ni* "back" and the verbal root *vrit* "to
turn." The Reigles quote Hodgson's *Essays on the Languages, Literature, and Religion of Nepal and Tibet* (23): "The Swabhavikas deny the
existence of immateriality; they assert that matter is the sole substance, and they give it two modes, called Pravritti, and Nirvritti, or
action and rest, concretion and abstraction. Matter itself, they say,
is eternal, (however infinitesimally attenuated in Nirvritti); and so
are the powers of matter which powers possess not only activity, but
intelligence." They observe, however, that Hodgson's "matter" is an
inaccurate translation of "dharma," and they add, "In brief, all of
Hodgson's statements about matter in Buddhism are fundamen-
tally in error" and "The matter and atoms and substance teachings
in relation to svabhava are apparently from her teachers, as they are
not in Hodgson."

4. Life involves suffering; there is a cause for suffering; there is an end
   to suffering; there is a way to that end: the Noble Eightfold Path.

SOURCE: Russian original unavailable. Copied from a translation in
Theosophical Quarterly 5 (Jan. 1908): 239–46.

Letter 101

To P. C. Mittra   *December 12, 1877*
                              The Theosophical Society
                        302 W. 47th Street, New York

Peary Chand Mittra, Esqre

Dear Sir,

I am instructed by the "Society" to inform you of the fact
that a dispute has arisen for the settlement of which your
aid as a Corresponding Member of the Theosophical Society
is desired. It involves the correctness of certain statements
made [by] some of our unprejudiced scholars respecting
the Brahmanical calculations by the Zodiac. They seek to

demonstrate that India is not alone the cradle of the human race, but also the source of civilization and Science.

Some orthodox Christian writers aver that of the great astronomical cycle—the precession of the equinoxes which is completed in 25,868 years—less than one fourth has passed since the world was created and man appeared upon earth. In short, that not even the first cycle has yet accomplished its revolution. This is the old ridiculous and exploded notion based upon the pretended Biblical chronology.

To this, we Theosophists answer that not only one but many cycles have been passed through—so many that no man can calculate the number, expect [*i.e.*, except] perhaps in India. For proof we point to the Zodiacs of the Brahmanic pagodas, which we claim to be the nearest infallibility as to correctness; all Christian scorn and abuse to the contrary, not withstanding. You are in a position to verify our assertions by being upon the spot; and since you have expressed a willingness to labor with us in our researches, the Society will be pleased to hear from you at your early convenience.

We wish to know, which pagoda contains the most ancient calculations, and at what age its historical records begin. If the records of different pagodas vary in antiquity, we would know how far back the learned Brahmans respectively place the beginnings of their infallible astronomical chronology. We do not ask what age they ascribe to the earth, for of course, that may be known by the four yugs, and the respective number of years of the four summed up very easily. But when does your *historical* period begin? In what pagodas are the records preserved? Where are these temples situated and what are their names, and how old is each known to be?

The western world depends for its facts about the orient upon missionaries, and civilians of various grades interested in supporting Christianity—the gigantic fraud of so-called "civilized" nations. In other words, garbled facts are presented to a prejudiced court, by interested witnesses. Our work is to show the truth, and to do it we count upon the help of our affiliated correspondents and the other native scholars whom they can enlist in the good cause.

Hoping for a favorable answer.

I am, Dear Sir, with respect and esteem for yourself (and devoted love for your country)

your's very truly

H P Blavatsky,

Corresponding Secretary of the Theosophical Society

SOURCE: Transcribed from the original in the Archives of the Theosophical Society, Adyar. Published in *Calcutta Review*, 3rd series, 45 (Nov.-Dec. 1932): 285-7; and with slight variations in *Canadian Theosophist* 71 (Nov.–Dec. 1990): 101-2.

Mittra replied to this letter on February 6, 1878, as follows (transcribed from the original in the Archives of the Theosophical Society, Adyar):

Madame H P. Blavatsky
302 W. 47 Street
New York

Dear Madam

Your esteemed favor of the 12 Decr last has come to hand for which I feel flattered and honored. Your learned work has not yet reached our city and I long to read it as soon as it is available here. In compliance with the wishes of our mutual friend I am getting it noticed in the native papers. I find on enquiry that there is no temple in India which contains ancient records of astronomical calculations. The records of the temples in different parts of India are historical. If you will refer to Wilson's Edn of Mills' British India, you will find some information in the points mooted in your letter. Wilson makes mention of several works which might throw light on some of the enquiries.

Wilson has also treated of our chronology and history. I regret that it is not in my power at present to give you any further information—I hope to be able to send you a copy of my paper "Commerce in Ancient India" as soon as it is received from the Pub. I suppose my articles in the English spiritualist and my paper on the "Developement of the Female Mind in India" sent to our mutual friend Colonel Olcott have met with your approval.

With my admiration for your devotion to the cause of truth and most sincere respect for your good self

I remain
with great esteem
yours most respectfully
Pearychand Mittra

P.S. I have posted by this mail a copy of my Life of David Hare for your kind acceptance. PM

Introduction to Letter 102

The introduction to the following letter in the *Path* explains the background of the letter:

> H.P.B. wrote to Madame Jelihovsky (date unknown) that she was learning to get out of her body, and offering to pay her a visit in Tiflis "in the flash of an eye." This both frightened and amused Madame Jelihovsky, who replied that she would not trouble her so unnecessarily. H.P.B. answered:

Letter 102

To V. de Zhelihovsky [1877]

What is there to be afraid of? As if you had never heard about apparitions of doubles. I, that is to say, my body, will be quietly asleep in my bed, and it would not even matter if it were to await my return in waking condition—it would be in the state of a harmless idiot. And no wonder: God's light would be absent from it, flying to you; and then it would fly back and once more the temple would get illuminated by the presence of the Deity. But this, needless to say, only in case the thread between the two were not broken. If you shriek like mad it may get torn; then Amen to my existence: I should die instantly. . . . I have written to you that one day we had a visit from the double of Professor Moses.[1] Seven people saw him. As to the Master, he is quite commonly seen by perfect strangers. Sometimes he looks just as if he were a living man, as merry as possible. He is continually chaffing me, and I am perfectly used to him now. He will soon take us all to India, and there we shall see him in his body just like an ordinary person.

NOTE:

1. No other information about this visit is known.

DATE: By Boris de Zirkoff, "sometime in 1877."

SOURCE: Russian original unavailable. Copied from a translation in *Path* (NY) 9 (Jan. 1895): 299–300. Another English translation of the first part of this letter in *Path* (London) 3 (Dec. 1912): 212–3.

Letter 103

To V. de Zhelihovsky   *[late 1877]*

You simply do not believe that I am writing you the truth concerning my *teachers*. You think they are myths. . . . But isn't it obvious to you that I, myself, *without help*, could not have written "about Byron and grave matters," as Uncle Rostya[1] puts it. What do we know, you and I, about metaphysics, ancient philosophies and religions, about psychology and other wise things? . . . Have we not been studying together, except that you did very much better than I. . . . And now, look at what I am writing, and people too, professors and scholars, read and praise. Open *Isis* wherever you please, and decide for yourself. I am telling you the truth: it is the *Master* who is explaining and showing all this to me. . . . Pictures, ancient manuscripts, and dates pass before me; I am merely copying them and write with such ease that instead of its being an effort, it is the greatest pleasure.

NOTE:

1. Rostislav Andreyevich de Fadeyev, HPB and Vera's maternal uncle (*CW* 1:lxix).

DATE: The reference to *Isis*, copies of which HPB had sent to her relatives shortly after its publication (letters 92, 93), suggests an approximate date for this letter.

SOURCE: Russian original unavailable. Translated by Boris de Zirkoff from *Russkoye Obozreniye* 2 (Nov. 1891): 269. Russian text also in *Rebus* 2 (Dec. 4, 1883): 429–30. Another English translation in *Path* (NY) 9 (Jan. 1895): 301.

Letter 104

To her relatives   [late 1877]

Do not believe that Theosophy contradicts or, much less, destroys Christianity. It only destroys the tares, but not the seed of truth: prejudice, blasphemous superstitions, Jesuitical bigotry. . . . We respect men's freedom of conscience and their spiritual yearnings far too much to touch religious principles with our propaganda. Every human being who respects himself and thinks has a holy of holies of his own, for which we Theosophists ask respect. Our business concerns philosophy, morals, and science alone. We ask for truth in everything; our object is the realization of the spiritual perfectibility possible to man: the broadening of his knowledge, the exercising of the powers of his soul, of all the psychical sides of his being. Our theosophical brotherhood must strive after the ideal of general brotherhood throughout all humanity; after the establishment of universal peace and the strengthening of charity and disinterestedness; after the destruction of materialism, of that coarse unbelief and egotism which saps the vitality of our country.

DATE: The subject of the letter is similar to that of others HPB wrote her relatives after the publication of *Isis Unveiled*.

SOURCE: Russian original unavailable. Copied here from *Path* (NY) 9 (Jan. 1895): 302. Russian text in *Russkoye Obozreniye* 2 (Nov. 1891): 270.

Letter 105

To her relatives   *[late 1877 or early 1878]*

What kind of Spiritist can you see in or make of me, pray? If I have worked to join the Theosophical Society in alliance offensive and defensive with the Arya Samaj of India (of which we are now forming a branch within the Parent Theosophical Society), it is because in India all the Brahmins whether orthodox or otherwise are terribly against the *bhoots*, the mediums, or any necromantic evocations or dealings with the dead in any way or shape. That we have established our Societies (Arya Samaj and Theosophy) simultaneously in order to combat under the banner of Truth and Science every kind of superstitious and preconceived hobbies. That we mean to fight the prejudices of the sceptics as well as the abuse of power of the false prophets, ancient and modern; to put down the high-priests Calchases[1] with their false Jupiterean thunders, and to show the fallacy of the Spiritists. If we are anything, we are *Spiritualists*, only not on the modern American fashion but on that of ancient Alexandria with its Theodadiktoses,[2] Hypatias and Porphyries.

NOTES:

1. Persons like Calchas, the Greek soothsayer.

2. Theodidaktos(es), "God-taught."

DATE: The letter is dated 1877 in "Mystical History." The reference to the Arya Samaj "(of which we are now forming a branch within the Parent Theosophical Society)" suggests a date of late 1877 or early 1878. Correspondence with Dayanand Saraswati began about September 1877 (CW 1:lxi). The decision to ally the Theosophical Society with the Arya Samaj was made in February 1878 (CW 1:lxii), and the title "The Theosophical Society of the Arya Samaj of India" was adopted in May 1878 (CW 1:lxiii).

SOURCE: Original unavailable. Copied from a translation in "Mystical History" 31. A slightly variant version in *Incidents* 179–80 (omitted from the 2nd ed.) and a different, abridged version in *Lucifer* 15 (December 1894): 275. Russian text in *Blue Hills* xi.

Letter 106

To her relatives   *[late January 1878]*

Listen, Brethren! I am sending you something curious: the English Freemasons, whose head is the Prince of Wales, sent me a diploma, for my *Isis*.[1] . . . That means I am now a "Mysterious Mason"! . . . I am expecting to be installed as the Pope of Rome for all my virtues. . . . I am sending you a clipping from a Masonic journal.[2] As to the decoration, it is very beautiful—a ruby cross and a rose.

NOTES:

1. The reference is actually to the certificate or diploma of the highest degree in a Rite of Adoptive Masonry sent to HPB by John Yarker (letter 90, note 2). The diploma is reproduced in *HPB Speaks*, frontispiece, and in *CW* 1, opposite p. 305.

2. *CW* 1:307–12 contains what has survived concerning HPB's Masonic diploma in this journal.

DATE: John Yarker says he sent the certificate on November 24, 1877 (*CW* 1:31–2), and the report of it was published in the *Franklin Register and Norfolk County Journal* on January 18, 1878 (*CW* 1:307); so this letter was probably written shortly thereafter.

SOURCE: Original unavailable. Translated by Boris de Zirkoff from *Blue Hills*, xvi. Another English translation in *Path* (NY) 9 (Feb. 1895): 382–3.

⌒

Letter 107

To J. C. Bundy   *January 26, 1878*

I am a *true, firm*, and if anything *too exalted Spiritualist*. Desiring, as I do, to leave no stone unturned to force Spiritualism and its higher and nobler truths upon the world of scientists in general and skeptics especially, I try to show the readers that I am neither credulous nor blind to the imperfections and shortcomings of Spiritualism as it is now. I work in my own way and try to do my best. Why believe me a deceiver and a schemer? . . . I feel pained to see that I have no greater enemies in the world than Spiritualists themselves, whose faith or rather philosophy I would see spread throughout the whole world and become the *only* and universal belief on earth. Please pitch into myself, cigarettes, entourage, fatness, Calmuck nose, etc., etc., as much as you like, and I will be the first to laugh, but *do not* represent me as an enemy of true Spiritualism. Olcott is as sincere as myself in that. If he has several times protested against being called a Spiritualist, I have as many times pitched into him for that. He may be a flapdoodle in his loose expressions, but he has always been a true Spiritualist.

SOURCE: Original unavailable. Copied from *Carrier Dove* 8.11 (Nov. 1891): 298. Published with variant transcriptions in *Canadian Theosophist* 71 (Nov.–Dec. 1990): 102.

The Arya Samaj
and Hurrychund Chintamon

The Arya Samaj and the Theosophical Society made an odd couple during their short-lived association, yet they had some things in common.

The Arya Samaj was founded by Dayanand Saraswati in 1875, the same year as the Theosophical Society, and was also a reform movement that looked to the past for its innovations in present-day beliefs and practices. It rejected idol worship and modern cultic practices, but promoted traditional practices like the honoring of cows and Vedic rituals such as the fire sacrifice. It rejected caste differences, child marriage, temple offerings and priestcraft, polygamy, doweries, and suttee. It promoted social reforms such as the education of women, intercaste marriage, the right of widows to remarry, divorce, orphanages, homes for widows, medical services, and famine relief. It was monotheistic, viewing the Vedic gods as different names for the same divine reality.

In some ways, however, the Arya Samaj was quite different from the Theosophical Society. It based itself on its founder's interpretation of the Vedas, regarded as infallible revealed truth and the source of both spiritual and practical knowledge. Its philosophy was dualistic and its theology theistic. It actively proselytized both Hindus who had been converted to Islam or Christianity and non-Hindus. It was nationalistic, dogmatic, and militant.

The Theosophists' future association with the Arya Samaj began as early as 1870, when Olcott, returning to America from England, met an Indian, Mulji Thackersey, aboard ship. Seven years latter, both the Theosophical Society and the Arya Samaj having been founded in the meanwhile, Olcott learned of Thackersey's address from a visitor who had recently returned from India, where he happened to have met Thackersey in Bombay. Being at that point interested in making Indian contacts, Olcott wrote to Thackersey about the new Theosophical Society. Thackersey replied, joining the Society and telling Olcott about Dayanand Saraswati and his new Arya Samaj, as well as putting Olcott in touch with Hurrychund Chintamon, President of the Arya Samaj in Bombay. Olcott wrote to Chintamon and through him contacted Dayanand Saraswati about September 1877.

After various correspondence, in February 1878 Hurrychund Chintamon proposed an amalgamation of the two groups on the basis of their similar views and goals, and the Theosophical Society began moving toward an alliance with the Arya Samaj. There were early warning signs, such as an Arya Samaj leaflet on theism received about April, which caused some concern as presenting an anthropomorphic view of God, but plans leading toward a merger went ahead. In May, the Society renamed itself "The Theosophical Society of the Arya Samaj of India," recognized Dayanand as its Chief, and began sending initiation fees to the Arya Samaj through Chintamon. HPB, who had earlier advised Olcott that a Himalayan Adept was occupying Dayanand's body, wrote to Chintamon, "I am *officially* and *personally* subject to his [Dayanand's] orders" (letter 120) and wrote an article for Charles Sotheran's short-lived publication, the *Echo*: "The Arya Samaj: Alliance of Theosophy with a Vedic Society in the Far Orient" (*CW* 1:379–84).

By late summer, the rules of the Arya Samaj arrived in America and made it clear that Dayanand's group was no Indian equivalent of the Theosophical Society, but a sect of Hinduism. The Theosophical organizational structure was quickly rethought, the result being the establishment of two groups: the original Theosophical Society continuing along its own lines and a link organization, the Theosophical Society of the Arya Samaj of Aryavart, recognizing Dayanand as its guru. These parallel Theosophical Societies continued in theory for about two years, after which the second faded into oblivion.

We have six early letters between HPB and Chintamon, or rather records of parts of six letters—and that difference is important, as is the background of the survival of those records. In 1878, HPB corresponded with Hurrychund Chintamon in preparation for the Founders' trip to India and in connection with the short-lived alliance of the Theosophical Society with the Arya Samaj. After HPB's death, copies of some of her letters to Chintamon were added to the files of the Society for Psychical Research in the following way.

On November 4, 1891, Henry Sidgwick wrote to Chintamon, then resident in London, asking for copies of HPB's letters to him. Chintamon replied on November 6, sending two letters. On November 14, he wrote to Sidgwick again, sending three more letters, and commenting—apparently in reply to a question from Sidgwick—about HPB's request in letter 108 for a photograph of a fakir suspended in the air. Copies of the three letters between Sidgwick and Chintamon about the latter's correspondence with HPB are in the Archives of the Society for Psychical Research (SPR) in Cambridge University Library, but there clearly was other correspondence between Sidgwick and Chintamon that seems not to have been preserved.

Copies of parts of six letters from HPB to Chintamon are also in the SPR Archives (letters 108, 115, 116, 117A, 118, and 125)—the originals presumably having been returned to him. The copies were probably made by Eleanor Sidgwick, who freely abbreviated and paraphrased the material and interjected personal opinions about it. She rephrased passages and described what she saw in the letters, often writing about HPB, rather than recording HPB's actual words. Her general skepticism about paranormal matters, amounting to a prejudice that distorted her perception and judgment, has been noted by Brian Inglis (360-1). In her transcriptions, it is not always clear what is quotation from the letters and what is paraphrase or comment. The material in quotation marks was presumably quoted directly from the letters, but quotation marks are not used consistently. Some of the parenthetical commentary and summary is in square brackets, but most is not. When the square brackets in the following transcriptions of these letters are from the SPR copies, that fact is noted; otherwise, such bracketed material has been added here.

These copies, gathered after the fact and apparently in support of the SPR's earlier negative Hodgson Report as part of a "case for the prosecution," omit parts of the original letters considered not relevant to the purposes of the SPR case, and so they are not full, accurate, and reliable records. In particular, the copies do not represent HPB's style of writing and, because of the omissions and paraphrases, do not accurately represent the content of the original letters either. Although they must be used with discretion because they are very imperfect representations of the originals, they are included here as the only available, albeit flawed, copies of what are doubtless genuine letters from HPB. Vernon Harrison has made a detailed analysis of evidence used for the Hodgson Report to the SPR: *H. P. Blavatsky and the SPR: An Examination of the Hodgson Report of 1885*. The SPR and the investigation that led to the Hodgson Report are further considered in volume 2 of these letters.

Letter 108

To H. Chintamon   *February 9, 1878*

Mad B. sends her *Isis*—Flattery about his book—Artist in Paris mentioned known & c. His Photograph about her Secret society work hinted at.

Indian 'psychological marvels' not miraculous but true. Yet European science scorns & calls Jacolliot an 'unmitigated humbug'. Science to have a slap in the face. Will Hindoo brother give the means—For instance by sending "a good photograph of either a Fakir, or Sannyâsi, sitting self-supported, in the air," which will be engraved in Harper's Weekly circulation of 100000 in America and Europe. "Science might turn up its aristocratic nose but it will have to explain this phenomenon, and confess that if it will know the occult forces in Nature, it must go to India to learn the alphabet at the feet of some Brahmans." Abuse of Spiritualism & Clergy—both said to have attacked Theosophy 'fierce wrath upon our heads' . . . "Learned Brahmans believe no more than you or us, that devils or angels have to do with the marvellous phenomena exhibited by their fellows. But how are they produced? *I know*; perhaps you do also, and if so, you know that it is no 'jugglery'. There is a psycho-physiological power in man, which, whatever Greek or Latin name may be given it, is a force which survives our physical death whether as an [?] *immortal* in the full sense of the word or not. We are trying to instruct these people about that. Unhappily their unintuitive minds require ocular proof before they can admit the basic ideas of philosophy.

Remember, the whole superstructure of Xn [*i.e.,* Christian] theology rests upon the absurd dogma of *miracle*. Until we can prove their 'miracles' as no transgressions of natural law but phenomena producible by the poor 'heathen' to a perfection never attained by pretended Xn saint or divinity—certainly not now by a single priest,—we cannot hope to crush Xnity.

See therefore the vast importance of the commission we give you, our esteemed Brother. Sketches may be made & deceive, verbal descriptions may be totally false, but a photograph from nature tells the truth so faithfully that denial becomes impossible. I know you hate superstition. So do we. But right between superstition and utter skeptical materialism, is the domain of fact, and if we, as philosophers will give a priest-ridden public . . . [indecipherable word] we must approach them with an array of invincible FACTS." Dr Peebles & his ascription of spiritualism & mediumistic power to Hindus [long space] "Yet the so called 'materialisation' phenomenon does occur, and has convinced even such great scientists as Wallace, Crookes, Wyld and others as well known, that 'Spirits' can return & take bodily shape. Ours is the duty as Theosophists to explain the occult laws of nature to which these facts must be ascribed. We give you the general commission to send us photographs (the cost of which, we are quite willing to defray) of fakirs and even jugglers in the act of performing feats inexplicable by Western Scientists."

Exchange of Theosophical publications prepared from clips from Indian papers showing irregularities of missionaries—and from pamphlets etc about the religious philosophies of India, whether Brahminical, Buddhistic or Parsee. "Also if you happen to find printed accounts of feats of jugglery, 'miracles' and so forth in the presence of trustworthy witnesses—" An opening said to be in America for Brahman lecturers—Great command of American press by Theosophical Society—"Whatever you choose to write, whether anonymously or otherwise we can give an enormous circulation. Things that British papers would not admit or will get a wide currency for. Please spread this information among your friends, and tell me [?] and to count upon the Theosophical Society as a devoted ally. You know, of course, that we are all sworn *to secrecy* and that whatever is given to us by 'Fellows' in confidence is kept inviolate."

Mad B's masonic diploma etc etc—

SOURCE: Original unavailable. Transcribed from a copy now in the Archives of the Society for Psychical Research in Cambridge University Library. The copy, of poor legibility, was made presumably by Eleanor Sidgwick, who freely abbreviated and paraphrased the material she copied (see background essay L).

Introduction to Letter 109

Early in 1878, HPB was examined by a phrenologist, perhaps Joseph R. Buchanan, author of the *Manual of Psychometry*, and in March of that year an article on her was published in the *Phrenological Journal and Life Illustrated* 66:134-7. It consisted of a phrenological analysis and a biographical sketch, which ends: "our acknowledgments are due to Prof. J. R. Buchanan, M.D., for contributions to our phrenological notes." Whatever the basis for the following phrenological analysis (134-6), its character sketch of HPB is of some interest as a contemporary impression of her:

The head of Madame Blavatsky is one of remarkable strength in many elements of character. With her fine physical constitution and temperamental balance her brain is capable not only of prolonged labor, but of extraordinary exertion under excitement. She is not of that quiet, scholastic mould which is so often found in literary pursuits, but possesses an intensely emotional and energetic nature, adapting her to fields of robust action.

With a large head, whose intellectual development is very marked, particularly in the perceptive region, she exhibits a strong leaning to observation and the study of facts and things as they exist. We do not find much evidence of the disposition to trust to mere impressions, or to be won over by probable or plausible showings; she is rather skeptical, more inclined to be iconoclastic in her attitude toward philosophy, religion, and literature, than to build up a system by negative reasoning, or by speculation. The type of her intellect renders her critical, and that, assisted by her cautious skepticism and strong individualism, makes her a stubborn and fearless partisan of her own convictions. She has a great deal of firmness, and the sense of justice, duty, and of honor is nearly equal to her firmness; hence, whatever cause she may espouse she will maintain with enthusiasm. When she has confidence in persons, or in the sources of her information, she accepts and acts upon them to the fullest extent.

Her social nature is influential, but on account of her moderate Spirituality and Intuition, her full Secretiveness and critical intellect, she may be said to watch mankind closely, and is thoroughly distrustful where she perceives cause for distrust. So in society she combines a vigilant observation of persons with a great deal of earnest friendship. Her highly sanguine temperament and energetic nature lead her to adhere to friends through good and evil report. Being as earnest to conquer opposition in social as in intellectual relations, she is highly capable of love and friendship which are real and practical, but disposed to laugh at what people generally term sentiment in literature and character, relegating it mainly to effeminacy and weakness.

She has a great love of freedom, and aversion to almost any kind of restraint which prevents her from taking an independent course, and acting out her own convictions. In emergencies she would generally show great coolness and boldness. She has a great deal of hope and enthusiasm for the elevation of humanity according to her own peculiar views; and her views in most cases are likely to appear peculiar and extreme to others, notwithstanding her caution and self-control. She is patriotic, and would be brave in the defense of country, home, family, and faith. Her attachments would tend ever to carry her back to the country and home of her love, especially if it were among a people whom she could impress by her mental force. She would never feel at home among people of a gloomy and cynical temperament.

Her development of Self-esteem is not large, so that she does not believe so much in herself as in her knowledge, experience, duty, and purposes. Her temperament ministers great activity to an energetic, thorough-going nature; so her force and ambition lead her into a bold career, but in such a career she does not make her accomplishments redound so much to her own honor and elevation, as a woman of greater self-esteem would.

The reader must have been struck at first sight by the unusual development of Language which renders her a natural linguist, and gives remarkable ability in the expression of her thought. Madame Blavatsky has a masculine order of intellect, and a masculine energy with a woman's temperamental susceptibility and social feeling. Hence we should not expect her to follow the conventional routine of the society lady, nor yet to adopt the passive round of most society men, but we should expect her to display unusual qualities and pursue a career unique, individual, and exceptional in achievement, as she is exceptionally endowed.

It is rare for us to meet a person, man or woman, so advanced in life with so much physical freshness and youthful ardor and capability. She would pass easily for a lady of but fifty[1] or so, while she differs from most people of fifty, in being still an earnest student of life and literature, taking up and pursuing new subjects with vigor and success.

NOTE:

1. The biographical sketch in the *Phrenological Journal* refers to "Mme. Blavatsky's long life—for she is upward of eighty years old, yet wonderfully young in body and fresh in mind." At the time of the article's publication, HPB was 46 years old. Olcott (*ODL* 1:265) comments:

> So as to her age, she told all sorts of stories, making herself twenty, forty, even sixty and seventy years older than she really was. We have in our scrap-books certain of these tales, reported by successive interviewers and correspondents to their journals, after personal interviews with her, and on sundry occasions when I was present myself. She said to me in excuse that the Somebodies inside her body at these various times were of these various ages, and hence no real falsehood was told, although the auditor saw only the H.P.B. shell and thought what was said referred only to that!

Letter 109

To V. de Zhelihovsky   [*ca. March 1878*]

And so this poor victim (victim in view of his awful task) was sent to me—a phrenological occultist, who came in the company of a huge bouquet (as if I were a prima donna!) and with three trunk-loads of compliments. He fingered my head and fingered it again; he turned it on one side and then on the other. He snorted over me—snorted like a steam-engine, until we both began to sweat. And at last he spat in disgust. "Do you call this a head?", he says; "It's no head at all, but a ball of contradictions." "On this head", he says, "there is an endless war of most conflicting bumps; all Turks and Montenegrins.[1] I can't make anything of this chaos of impossibilities and confusion of Babel. Here, for instance", he says, poking my skull with his finger, "is a bump of the most ardent faith and power of belief, and here, side by side with it, the bump of scepticism, pessimism, and incredulity, proudly swelling itself. And now, if you please, here is the bump of sincerity for you, walking hand in hand with the bump of hypro-crisy [sic] and cunning. The bump of domesticity and love for your country boxes the ears of the bump of wandering and love of change. And do you mean to say you take this to be a respectable head?" he asked. He seized himself by the hair, and in his despair pulled a considerable lock from his own respectable head, answering to the highest stan-dards of phrenology. . . . But all the same he described, drew, and published my poor head for the amusement of the hundred thousand subscribers to the *Phrenological Journal*. Alas, alas, "heavy is the crown of Monomach!"[2] The aureola of my own greatness, acquired so undeservedly, is simply crushing me. Here, I send you a copy of my poor head, which you are requested to swallow without any sauce. A hundred thousand Yankees are going to feast upon it, and so I am certainly going to save a bit for my own blood!

NOTES:

1. Inhabitants of Montenegro in the Balkans, closely related to the Serbs and like them Eastern Orthodox in religion, having a long history of conflict with the Turks after the Turkish defeated the Serbians at Kosovo in 1389.

2. A reference to an imperial Russian crown, a gold skullcap of eight panels decorated with filigree, jewels, fur, and a finial ornament at the top. According to legend, it was given to Prince Vladimir Mono-makh of Kiev by the Byzantine emperor Constantine Monomachus in the 12th century; also perhaps an allusion to the etymological sense of *monomach*, "one who fights alone."

DATE: Estimated from the March date of the article referred to in the letter.

SOURCE: Russian original unavailable. Copied from a translation in *Path* (NY) 9 (Feb. 1895): 382.

⌒

Letter 110

To P. C. Mittra   *April 10, 1878*
                                         New York

Peary Chand Mittra Esqre

My dear Sir,

I cannot thank you enough for the various publications you have been kind enough to send me. They have all been attentively read and appreciated. Of them all, the one which treats upon the condition of women in India, has perhaps, pleased me most, though the biography of David Hare has nearly reconciled me with European races, which I most cordially hate, By showing me that they are not altogether contemptible and that there are truly good, *godly* people among my Western countrymen. The disabilities under which the female sex labors among Western peoples spring mainly from the [fact] that men regard them for the most part as instruments of lust than as equals and companions. Despising them when gratified in this direction, they of course cannot respect them. And women in their turn accept their degrading position, and busy themselves principally in making their physical charms more alluring. Speak of the Ceylonese and Travancore women going naked, with but a short skirt! An English woman would turn in disgust from her, but at the same time attend the Queen's "drawing room" in a costume so provokingly immodest—wearing but a *sash* instead of a bodice—as to make men themselves blush to their ears for shame! Even the London Court papers have recently protested against such a *naked* exhibition,—the new fashion. In my eyes, your poorest woman, who goes about as God created her, is thousand times more respectable than these European prostitutes of the Courts—the aristocracy of the various Kingdoms. The more I see of Christianity and Christendom, the more disgusted am I with both, and the warmer grows my love and respect for the dark-skin[n]ed races. I was myself brought up with the Buddhist Kalmucks. in the steppes of Astrachan (Caspian Sea) till the age of ten.

I am sorry that you have not given me the information I wanted about the Brahmanical calculations of the Zodiac. I hope you do not place too great a value upon European Sciences: in my opinion, the greatest of the Tyndalls is but a puling babe beside some of your Brahmans, who, scorn to disabuse Europeans who take them for ignoramuses. What I want is their legends, what they maintain in *their* teachings about the age of the world and *man*. From European Science, the public gets nothing but misrepresentations and crude guesses. Generally slaves of public opinion, they care but for their official positions and wages, and so, stick to the old exploded notions of the Jewish Bible with its 6,000 [years] of the world.

Do please tell me, *theosophically* and "on the square," as Masons say, whether you believe with Peebles and other Spiritualists, in the so called "materialization" of Spirits, of pure disembodied man. I infer from your writings that *you do not*. But Peebles would have us all understand, that not only you but all other Hindu gentlemen who justly believe in the Soul's immortality and a *subjective* communication between the two worlds are *Spiritualists* like himself. I presume you have seen the controversy between us (theosophists) and the orthodox Spiritualists that has been going on for some months past in the London Sp^t papers. Some of the best men have come around to our side, and we are constantly growing stronger. While the *Spiritualist* and the Banner of Light in days past have classed me as a *non* Spiritualist, the "Indian Daily News" of Calcutta and various secular papers in other countries abuse me and my book for its author being a "Spiritualist"!! This is comical

410

and perplexing. *I am a Spiritualist*, but of another sort, and I flatter myself of a little more philosophical sort. I will never believe that a *pure* spirit can reclothe itself in gross matter (which smells at seances like a *corpse*), nor that all mediumistic communications are of necessity from a "Spirit" source or individuality. And on this question, some of your Brahmans are more than other men competent to discriminate. Will you kindly tell us whether we err or not? Will you help us to be enlightened? People (foolish Spiritualists) call and believe me an "*adept.*" They verily [believe] that *I was initiated in the pagodas!* I, a woman, and a European!! The absurdity of such a notion is really [illegible] calculated to make one stare in amazement! *I*, at least never pretended such a flagrant lie. I know too much of India and its customs not to be well aware that no European man—let alone *a woman*, could ever penetrate into the inner recesses of the pagodas. But I have had many friends among Buddhists and knew well two Brahmins at Travancore and learned a good deal from them. I belong to the secret sect of the Druzes of the Mount Lebanon and passed a long life among dervishes, Persian mullahs, and mystics of all sort. Therefore, I am well acquainted with the phenomena—loosely called Spiritual in every case,—and came to the conviction that most of the phenomena can be produced without there being either jugglery and fraud or *Spiritual* manifestations. I have in short, too great a veneration for the Spirit of disembodied man, to believe that he who was a good and pure man on earth instead of pursuing as in his progress toward "Nirvana" or "Moksha" will degrade his Spirit by returning on earth to throw guitars and bells at the people's heads, for 50 cents the seance! But in *subjective* communication I believe thoroughly, for I *know* it to be true. I believe in the *possession* and *obsession* by Spirits, etc.

Hoping you will excuse this uncalled for "profession of faith," which I wanted you to know in case you should read my book, I will now close. I am very sorry to have to deny myself the pleasure of sending you a copy of "Isis Unveiled" for the present, but the fact is, that *not a single copy* of the 3ᵈ edition[1] remains in the publisher's hands; and of a Bombay order for 100 copies he could send but 34, until he gets out the fourth edition.

Hoping for a reply at your early convenience, I remain,
Dear Sir, very gratefully and sincerely yours.
H. P. Blavatsky

Please excuse the horrid writing.

NOTE:

1. Today this would be called a third impression or printing, the term "edition" being reserved for reissues with major changes of content.

SOURCE: Transcribed from the original in the Archives of the Theosophical Society, Adyar. Published in *Theosophist* 52 (Aug. 1931): 626-9 and *Calcutta Review*, 3rd series, 45 (Nov.-Dec. 1932): 287-90.

Letter 111

To N. de Zhelihovsky[1]
April 25, 1878
New York

My much beloved Niece and dear Sheep of the "Golden Fleece," in spite of your progress in algebra, it is evident, my brother, you are far from having studied mathematics and geometry sufficiently, as you do not know that "the whole is equal to the sum of all the parts taken together," or that "the lesser can not contain the greater." In the language of the mere unlearned mortals, all this means that it is impossible for your aunt—though she does enjoy the reputation of an Eastern Magus—to write more letters a day than she now succeeds in writing, often depriving herself of sleep.

However, I do not want to give you the impression, that I intend to deprive myself of a correspondence with such a learned latinist and algebraist, as you show yourself to be. My next work we shall write together, I hope, and we shall call it *"The fifth dimension of space, as it exists between the Cities of New York and Tiflis, from the point of view of an American aunt and a Tiflis niece, etc., etc.: in nine (9) volumes and three and a half (3½) chapters."*

Well, the news is that I have bought a doll for Lena,[2] and a toy telephone. The latter is not particularly good. One of these days I was given a most wonderful object, which I am thinking of despatching to you. But my wish is that it should remain in Mama's keeping, until you are old enough. This object is a golden cage (*golden* to the eye only, it goes without saying, all is not gold that glitters). Well, you will say, there is nothing wonderful in a cage. True enough, but there is a bird in this cage. Why, you will say, how can anybody wonder at a bird, it is a creature well known to everybody of old, ever since the world was started. But my bird sings! And again, I know, you will object, that all birds sing, when they do not simply twitter. Yes, but dont you see that my bird can be made to sing for two hours consecutively or it can be silenced the moment you are tired of song. The thing is a very curious mechanism, and here it costs, in all probability, at least $150, and in Tiflis you won't buy it for $1,000. But when it arrives, mind you do not touch it before you have read the instruction. You may damage the thing, and nobody will be able to mend it. The members of the Society, which I serve as secretary, have presented me with the bird on a pretended birthday of mine. I do not care in the least how much I startle them: I simply have a birthday any time I like. Here in New York I always have several, and well, it comes off excellently every time. It will soon become a universal fashion here for one and the same person to have the right to have been born in several different places, and at different times too. When you have learned algebra well and know something about the *unknown quantity* (I don't know what you call it in Russian), then you will understand. In the meantime, little brother, take it on my word. Also don't write *you* to me, I don't like it.[3] To begin with I am a democrat, and then I do not care for this old-fashioned manner to say *you* to relatives, if you love them. Don't we say *thou* and not *you* to God?

Also you must not forget that the day I left Tiflis you howled so that all the block heard you and, having crawled under a bed, you cried: "Auntie, you are a fool, you are." This is my last impression of my affectionate niece.

Well, I really don't know how to have this bird sent to you. They won't take it at the post office. I shall have to find out some Parcel Company. However, this need not concern you.

To-morrow I am to start for California, where I shall stay about a month, doing some work.[4] I may write from there, but possibly I shall have no time. I am sent there by the Society, which I serve, to investigate the treatment of illness by mesmerism in vogue amongst the Red Indians. I don't know what B.[5] will think of this subject for an article, otherwise I would describe it for your newspaper.

By the way, my dear sir, I tell you what you will have to do: you will have to take the trouble to carefully write down for me B.'s full name, as your progenitress forgot to do so, with her usual light-headedness; so that when I tried to write to him, I felt as stranded as a cray fish on a sand bank.

From your last photographs I see that you and Rostia[6] bear much resemblance to the Imperial family, in your noses and lips, and, as I think, it is the Romanoffs and not you who are the gainers. Thank you for Rostia's portrait. He is a great fellow, and, with God's help, he shall soon be promoted to an officer's rank. But for all this, I wish he would stay home, instead of fighting the Turks. Do write to me about every single one of you: about Sasha, Fedia,

Valia, Lena, Masha.[7] Especially about Masha, I hope she is still with you?

I want you to do me a great favour. If my letters are published in the Herald,[8] get clippings of my articles every time and send them to me. I need two copies every time, you understand, to paste them into my scrap book, that is a kind of an album in which I keep all my newspaper articles.

I do hope that B. will send the newspaper regularly. This year I have never had a single copy as yet. But I expect the paper will be sent to me beginning with the day when my article appears. Do try to get No. 15 for this year for me; even two copies of it if the notice of my "Isis" was printed on both sides of the page. You understand, don't you? If you do as I ask, I shall send you ten or even fifteen dollars, as soon as I get them changed for Russian roubles here. I have already ordered them.

So, dear soul, please don't be neglectful, and see that it is done. Your mama is not to be trusted.

And how is papa? Kiss the tip of his nose for me.

I do not share your passion for the theatre. I have free tickets for most theatres, because I write about them for the newspapers.[9] But I must confess that the moment I am comfortably in my seat, I go to sleep. I am very tired of most things. Both the Paris "Figaro" and the "Revue Spirite" ask me to write. But as it is, I have no time to breathe. It is half past three, and I still sit and write, because until midnight I had visitors. No holy incense can smoke them out.

Well, good bye to you. I am really altogether done up. I embrace you all with all my heart.

But you really must stop counting letters with me. If I do not write, it means that I have not a minute.

You were my pet, when you were a baby. Now I hope I shall have a chance to make pets of you all.

Your loving American "uncle" of female sex,
H. Blavatsky.

NOTES:

1. HPB's niece, Nadyezhda Vladimirovna, the daughter of her sister, Vera de Zhelihovsky. The girl was in her mid teens at the time of this correspondence.

2. A pet name for "Helena," here Helena Vladimirovna de Zhelihovsky, a younger sister of Nadyezhda's, about the age of four or five at the time of this correspondence.

3. Russian (like French, German, Spanish, and English of an earlier time) has two forms of the second-person personal pronoun. The formal or respectful one (historically in English, "you") is *vy*, used between equals on formal terms and by inferiors to superiors (servants to bosses, children to adults). The informal or intimate one (historically in English, "thou") is *ty*, used between equals on close terms, by superiors to inferiors, and in addressing God. In English the informal pronoun was generally replaced by the formal one in the late Renaissance or early Modern period. In most other languages the difference was maintained longer, but is in the process of erosion. HPB urges her young niece to address her with the informal and "democratic" familiar pronoun.

4. This prospective trip seems not to have been taken. Evidence for it is lacking, and HPB's correspondence, apparently from New York, continues through the period anticipated for it. In letter 121 of July 3 to her aunt, HPB reports just having returned from a trip "almost as far as California," which the evidence also suggests did not occur.

5. The identity of "B." is uncertain. It is possibly A. A. Brussilov, who was at this time in his mid twenties and whom HPB's niece Nadyezhda later married. Perhaps an engagement had already been made.

6. Rostislav Nikolayevich de Yahontov, HBP's nephew and Nadyezhda's younger half brother by her mother's first husband, Nikolay Nikolayevich de Yahontov, who died the year of his son Rostislav's birth. The son was about 20 years of age at the time of this letter.

7. The pet names are as follows: Sasha may be Alexander de Witte (age 32), HPB's nephew and Nadyezhda's cousin. Fedia is Feodor Nikolayevich de Yahontov (age 24), HPB's nephew and Nadyezhda's older half brother by her mother's first husband, Nikolay Nikolayevich de Yahontov. Valia is Valerian Vladimirovich de Zhelihovsky (older teenager), HPB's nephew and Nadyezhda's older brother. Lena is Helena Vladimirovna de Zhelihovsky (age 4 or 5),

HPB's niece and Nadyezhda's younger sister. Masha is a pet name for Marya (or Mary), an unidentified person.

8. A newspaper whose Russian name is unidentified, but perhaps the *Herald of Odessa*.

9. No theater reviews by HPB have been identified.

SOURCE: Russian original unavailable. Copied from *Theosophical Forum* (NY) 9 (Dec. 1903): 144-7.

Letter 112

To H. Chintamon?   *[April 1878]*

Is our friend a Sikh?[1] If so, the fact that he should be, as you say, "very much pleased to learn the object of our Society" is not at all strange. For his ancestors have for centuries been—until their efforts were paralysed by British domination, that curse of every land it fastens itself upon—battling for the divine truths against external theologies. My question may appear a foolish one—yet I have more than one reason for asking it. You call him a Sirdar—therefore he must be a descendant of one of the Sirdars of the twelve mizals,[2] which were abolished by the English to suit their convenience—since he is of Amritsir in the Punjâb? Are you personally acquainted with any descendant of Runjeet Singh, who died in 1839, or do you know of any who are? You will understand, without any explanation from me, how important it is for us, to establish relations with some Sikhs, whose ancestors before them have been for centuries teaching the great "Brotherhood of Humanity"—precisely the doctrine we teach. . . .

As for the future "Fellows" of our Indian Branch, have your eyes upon the chance of fishing out of the great ocean of Hindu hatred for Christian missionaries some of those big fish you call Rajahs, and whales known as Maharajahs. Could you not hook out for your Bombay Branch either Gwalior (Scindia[3]) or the Holkar of Indore—those most faithful and loyal friends of the British (?). The young Gwikovar is unfortunately scarcely weaned as yet, and therefore not elligible for fellowship.

NOTES:

1. The person referred to is unidentified.

2. Cf. "Mahan Singh, the father of Ranjit, had set off the Sikhs into twelve misls or divisions, each having its own chief (Sirdar), whose secret Council of State consisted of learned Gurus" (*CW* 1:373).

3. Sindhia, the family name of the rulers of Gwalior.

DATE: The addressee of this undated letter is not identified in the source, but the letter appears to be one of those to Hurrychund Chintamon, which otherwise span the period of February 9 to August 21, 1878. In addition, certain of the subjects of this letter, namely the Sikhs, the Sirdars of the twelve misls ("mizals"), Ranjit ("Runjeet") Singh, and the "Brotherhood of Humanity" or "Brotherhood of Man" are all topics dealt with in the second half of an article HPB probably wrote in April 1878 (*CW* 1:369–75, specifically 372–4). So that date is postulated for this letter as well.

SOURCE: Original unavailable. Copied from *Hodgson Report* 316. Published in *Canadian Theosophist* 71 (Nov.-Dec. 1990): 103.

BACKGROUND ESSAY M

Thomas Alva Edison

Thomas Edison was a member of the Theosophical Society, although not an active one. HPB referred to him in print several times, as the index to the *Collected Writings* shows, for he was a distinguished member and certain of his views were consonant with Theosophical thought. He had an abiding interest in unexplained laws of nature and latent human powers, as well as a conviction about the existence of a pervasive intelligence in the universe, from which human intelligence is derived:

On the second tier of Edison's twelve-thousand-volume, gymnasium-sized library building in his West Orange laboratory complex there are several shelves devoted to books about psychic power and reincarnation, including an inscribed copy of Mme. Blavatsky's *The Key to Theosophy* (1889) alongside Emanuel Swedenborg's *Heaven and Hell*. In keeping with his expansive and recurrent style of thinking, Edison took as his province not only the whole knowable world, but, by extension, as much of the spiritual world as anyone could humanly assimilate. And despite the fact that this persistent inclination to explore the unquantifiable aspects of reality undercut his scholarly credibility, Edison visited and revisited these mystical spheres periodically throughout his life, up until the utter end. [Baldwin 95-6]

"People say I have created things," the mystical Edison said in an obscure 1911 essay published in the Gary, Indiana, *Gazette*. "I have never created anything. I get impressions from the Universe at large and work them out, but I am only a plate or a record or a receiving apparatus—what you will. Thoughts are really impressions that we get from outside." Several days later, Edison elaborated in similarly transcendental fashion in *The Columbian Magazine*. While he did not believe in a "Supreme Being," calling such an image of "creedism . . . abhorrent and fallacious," he did on the other hand fervently espouse the existence of a Supreme *Intelligence* ("I do not personify it"), which acted as a kind of "Master Mind" informing all singular intellects on the planet. [Baldwin 376]

Edison had spoken on occasion publicly of metaphysical concerns, his belief that within every atom, every subdivision of nature, there could be found "a certain amount of primitive intelligence. . . . Look at the thousand ways in which atoms of hydrogen combine with those of other elements, forming the most diverse substances. Do you mean to say that they do this without intelligence? When they get together in certain forms they make animals of the lower orders.

Finally they combine in man, who represents the total intelligence of all the atoms."

"But where does this intelligence come from originally?"
he was asked.

"From some greater power than ourselves," was the reply.
[Baldwin 172]

Edison's initial contact with the Theosophical Society was the
result of a visit from H. S. Olcott, who wanted to solicit Edison's
participation in an industrial exhibition to be held in Paris. Olcott
was honorary secretary of the Citizen's National Committee, whose
aim was to further American involvement in that exhibition. Olcott
therefore went to see Edison on March 11, 1878, announcing his
impending arrival with a telegram:

Came here to see you on important business. Return by next
train. Will go straight to Church St answer. H. S. Olcott

Olcott (*ODL* 1:467) describes how the resulting visit led to a discussion of other subjects:

Edison and I got to talking about occult forces, and he interested me greatly by the remark that he had done some ex-
perimenting in that direction. His aim was to try whether a
pendulum, suspended on the wall of his private laboratory,
could be made to move by will-force.

On his return to New York that same day (a Monday), Olcott
told HPB about his conversations with Edison and immediately
sent Edison an invitation from HPB for dinner and conversation
about those occult forces:

302 West 47th St
N.Y. M[ar]ch 11, 1878

Thos A. Edison Esq

Dear Sir

Mme Blavatsky hopes you will be able to dine with her
on Thursday at 6 p m and will be pleased to explain to you
something about the occult forces that you desire to know.

If, however, you should be unavoidably prevented from coming in town on that day, & will telegraph her on Wednesday Evening so that she can make necessary arrangements, she will come out, agreeably to your polite invitation, with me on Friday by the 11 a m train & return at 3 o'clock.

Yours truly
H. S. Olcott

Edison did not reply, and so on the following Friday Olcott wrote him again:

71 Broadway
N.Y. March 15, '78

Dear Sir

As the visit of Mme Blavatsky and myself, today, was made conditional upon receiving a telegram from you on Wednesday Evening, and no word was received from you, we, of course, have remained in the city.

The copy of "Isis Unveiled" awaits your coming to Mme B's house—302 W 47th St—which she trusts may not be long deferred. If you should find it only possible to call in the morning, or before her dinner hour—6 pm—you will do well to let her know a day ahead, as she has Engagements at present that take her out frequently, and she would not like to miss the pleasure of seeing so thoroughbred a Heathen—as you say you are. Good people of our kind are scarce in this pretended Christian country!

Yours
H. S. Olcott

(Olcott's communications to Edison are transcribed from photographic copies of the originals provided by courtesy of the Edison National Historic Site, National Park Service, US Department of the Interior, West Orange, NJ, and its archivist, Leonard DeGraal. They have also been published in *Theosophical History* 7 [1996]: 54–5; the article by Deveney, Godwin, and Gomes in the same issue provides a good overview of the Edison-Olcott-Blavatsky correspondence.)

The proposed visit of Edison to HPB never occurred, so a copy of *Isis Unveiled* was sent to Edison, and also an application for joining the Theosophical Society with the form for promising the secrecy that was required of all members at that time. Edison signed the forms and returned them to Olcott on April 4, with an acknowledgment of HPB's book:

> Dear Sir,
>
> I herewith return signed, the forms of the Theosophical Society, and thank you for the same. Please say to Madame Blavatsky that I have received her very curious work and thank her for the same. I SHALL READ BETWEEN THE LINES!
>
> Yours truly,
Thomas A. Edison

A copy of Edison's note was made by Walter R. Old, General Secretary of the British Section in 1889 (provided by courtesy of the Edison National Historic Site, National Park Service, US Department of the Interior, West Orange, NJ, and its archivist, Leonard DeGraal). A photograph of Edison's signed pledge, dated April 4, 1878, is in Jinarajadasa's *Golden Book* (29) and the *Theosophist* 53 (November 1931): 129.

Olcott's contact with Edison led to the following letter from HPB, concerning his recent (1877) invention, the phonograph. Other references to Edison's phonograph are in letters 115 and 133.

Letter 113

To T. A. Edison

April 30, 1878
The Theosophical Society
302 W. 47th St.

Thomas A. Edison Esqre

Dear Sir,

I have just finished translating into the Russian language, your paper on the phonograph in the *North American Review*,[1] for two newspapers—at Odessa and St Petersburg, of which, I am Correspondent. This publication will, I know, excite a profound interest, the more so, as what has appeared in the Russian papers until now, has been a mass of absurdities.

I know that, I will undoubtedly be applied to for information, as to the terms upon which the instrument can be bought. So, the object of my present note is, to ask you, to kindly inform me, what are the wholesale and retail prices of the instruments and *where* they can be procured. I will send this information along with my MS., so that the public may be informed from the start. Please, do not for a moment think, that I have any personal interest to serve, or that my inquiry is suggested by any commercial consideration. Now, that you are a "Fellow" of our Society,—*which is more than proud of its New Son*—it is alike the duty and pleasure of every "Fellow" to look after your interests and reputation in every practicable way. I for one, have been trumpeting you from the White Sea to Persia.

believe me your's fraternally
H P Blavatsky.
Corresponding Secret^y of the Th. Society

NOTE:

1. "The Phonograph and Its Future," *North American Review* 126, issue 262 (May 1878): 527-37. The article is a promotional piece describing the phonograph and predicting its possible uses for letter writing, dictation, talking books for the blind and infirm, education, music, family records, talking books for the general reader, music boxes, toys such as talking dolls, clocks, advertising, oral history, and communication.

SOURCE: Transcribed from a photographic copy of the original provided by courtesy of the Edison National Historic Site, National Park Service, US Department of the Interior, West Orange, NJ, and its archivist, Leonard DeGraal. Published in *Theosophical History* 7 (1996): 55.

In the fall, Olcott sent Edison his diploma or membership certificate, which he acknowledged on October 7, 1878 (in the Archives of the Theosophical Society, Adyar, and published in the *Theosophist* 53 [November 1931]: 128):

My Dear Olcott,

Your favour of the 1st was duly received. Thanks for the Diploma. I have placed it in my honor box, that is a receptacle where I place "rewards of merit". I should like very much to make an appointment with you, but I am pulled, driven, and banged about to such an extent that I cannot call any time my own. I am working 18 hours out of the 24 and have crowds of scientists, curiosity seekers, etc., calling on me, so that the "leisure" you refer to, is to me a thing of the past, and a faint possibility of knowing something of it again in the future. However I will try and call on you but cannot undertake to appoint a time. I should be pleased to meet Mme. B. before her departure but fear that I will be unable to do so.

Very truly
T. A. Edison

The story of Edison, his phonograph, and the Theosophists is continued in letter 133.

Letter 114

To V. de Zhelihovsky [ca. May 1878]

I have not written to you for a month, my well-beloved friend, and could you guess the cause of it? One beautiful Tuesday morning in April I got up as usual, and as usual sat down at my writing table to write to my Californian correspondents. Suddenly, hardly a second later, as it seemed to me, I realized that for some mysterious reason I was in my bed-room and lying on my bed; it being evening and not morning any more. Around me I saw some of our Theosophists and Doctors looking at me with the most puzzled faces, and Olcott and his sister Mrs. Mitchell—the best friend I have here, both of them pale, sour, wrinkled, as if they had just been boiled in a sauce-pan. "What's the matter? What's gone and happened?", I asked them. Instead of answering, they heaped questions upon me: what was the matter with me? And how could I tell—nothing was the matter with me. I did not remember anything, but it certainly was strange that only the other moment it was Tuesday morning, and now they said it was Saturday evening; and as to me, these four days of unconsciousness seemed only the twinkling of an eye. There's a pretty pair of shoes! Just fancy, they all thought I was dead and were about to burn this dismantled temple of mine. But at this, Master telegraphed from Bombay to Olcott: "Don't be afraid. She is not ill but resting. She has overworked herself. Her body wanted rest, but now she will be well." Master was right. He knows everything, and in fact I was perfectly healthy. The only thing was I did not remember anything. I got up, stretched myself, sent them all out of the room, and sat down to write the same evening. But it is simply awful to think about the work that has accumulated. I could not give a thought to letters.[1]

NOTE:

1. The episode of unconsciousness that is the subject of this letter is otherwise undocumented. Olcott's diary for the period March-June 1878 has many references to HPB, but none to this episode, nor is there a reference in *Old Diary Leaves*.

DATE: Vera de Zhelihovsky dates the episode of HPB's unconsciousness as spring 1878 (*Lucifer* 15:364). Boris de Zirkoff dates it as most likely April 2–6 or April 9–13 (*CW* 1:lxiii). The letter was written after that event and at least a month after her last letter to Vera, according to HPB. The last previous letter to Vera that we have evidence for was probably written in March, so sometime in May is a likely date for this letter. On the other hand, Vera's date for the letter, which is the only evidence we have for its time of writing, may be wrong; her dates are sometimes inaccurate. During approximately April and May of 1876, Olcott's sister, Mrs. Mitchell, was living in the same apartment house with the Founders, but she was a visitor at other times as well, so her presence during the episode requires no special explanation. The telegram from Bombay mentioned in the letter suggests a date after September 1877, when the correspondence with Dayanand Saraswati began, or even after May 16,

1878, when the Founders were directed to prepare to go to India (Ransom 106). So on the whole, Vera's date is reasonable.

SOURCE: Russian original unavailable. Copied from a translation in *Path* (NY) 9 (Mar. 1895): 411-2.

Letter 115

To H. Chintamon   *May 4, 1878*

Compliments . . . . "The woes of India affect me far more" . . . etc "What you say of the 'deplorable conditions' of the native princes under your bastard Empire gives me great pain. Had I the secret guidance of things I think I should contrive to have the Russians drive the English into the sea, and then the Hindus to unite to a man to kick the Russians over the crest of the Himalayas in their turn, with the Mussulmans in their company etc—And yet—much as I hate the English . . . I would far rather see them in India than my sweet Greek-orthodox countrymen." etc "Ye gods! What a lunatic fuss, when we come to think of it, the indecently public and *osmosic*[1] amours of a Holy Ghost with his Jewish *belle*."[2]

"Mr W. Paris[3] has been spending the evening here" etc "Poor Paris is dead in love and on the edge of committing moral suicide by marrying" etc—offensive description of the girl . . . "I have tried hard to make him a theosophist of the *inner* ring—an English Swamee, but—failed most signally"

Sending her photograph— . . . The unfortunate matter of *Isis*—a book upon which I now look with horror, as it does not say half of what it ought to say, and much of that which never ought to have been published at all. It looks as if I had the *delirium tremens* when I wrote it" . . .

"I also hope that you will be able to send to me these photographs of holy men sitting self-supported in the air. It is so important for our Society, because both spiritualists and Xns[4] are such a set of asses here. You know best yourself what we need to convince the fools we have to deal with. They cannot understand that there may be a middle ground between *fraud* and *miracle*, and that mother nature has more than one secret force hidden in the store rooms of her laboratory of which our greatest European scientists are wholly ignorant. In Vol I of Isis p. xxiii seq I discuss this subject of the scientific possibility of admitting levitation without at all violating the laws of nature—on the theory of polarity. Please give me your views—tell me what you have seen yourself in the way of *seeming* miracles produced by some of your ascetics and holy men, and how you explain it. As I said to you I do not believe in miracles, supernaturalism or 'spirit agency' but I *do* believe in the occult and as yet unknown (in the West NB[5]) forces of nature, as I *do know* that the East especially India—has inherited all the wisdom and knowledge of occult sciences of old. That some of your Fellows & Swamees—produce the most extraordinary phenomena, apparently in utter contradiction with the known laws of nature, that I believe, for having repeatedly seen such things I know them to be a fact— When a child . . . Kalmuck Buddhists . . ." Then comes account of associating with Fire-worshippers—of running away from aunt when 16 because as she would not kiss hand of the Metropolite[6] they meant to shut her up in a convent for a year & then marry her "to a man of 73. For years I have roamed about and travelled and spent several fortunes with the Shamans of Siberia, and Buddhistic Lamaists who live in Russian possessions. I have learnt too well with them the secrets of animal magnetism and electricity to be either astonished or appalled at any amount of phenomena. Of course, I spoke to you about all this "on the square" and because I know you better—far better than you will ever know me. If only I had the right to speak— which I have not—of my life in India, nothing or very little would astonish *you*, who are well versed in many of the mysteries of your country." But—never mind. Some day you will see me personally, and—either become my fast friend or—turn away in disgust from me . . . ."

Then—paragraphs about native princes & abuses of Prince of Wales—about tyrannical measure as regards the Calcutta press— . . . Edison a Theosophist—description of phonograph—(graphic and clear)— . . . phonographs might as easily as not be placed in the statues of the caves of Ellora and Elephanta and the *gods* made to speak to the multitudes for hours—truth and to convert them to pure atheism by the thousands. The best *phonograph* costs less than a 100 dollars and very soon will be had for half the price. Edison promised me one. Don't you think in consideration of the Oriental lazziness (sic)[7] of our Esteemed Brother Mooljee Thackersey I better send him one?" [Then chaff about Mooljee & how he might speak into phonograph though he would not write][8]

"I have a question to ask you, my dear Sir & Brother, hoping that you will forgive me the indiscretion if it is one. I read every word of your writings that were sent to me, and studied particularly the *Introduction of the Science of Universal Theism*. In the latter you call God an "immaterial Being" Do you then believe in a *personal* god?" etc [a page and a half about pantheism etc][9]

Zollner & a fourth dimension . . . Slade selected by Mad B & Col. Olcott for a Russian committee. His adventure in London "The outcome of this now was that Slade on his way to Russia stopped at Leipzig and that Professor Zollner—a great academician discovered the *fourth* dimension. A report of it translated by me into English from a Russian paper, I now send you.—Whilst it is very plain from your words and letter to me, that no more than ourselves you personally believe in miracles and devils, yet it is not plain from your letter to what extent you admit the reality of phenomena indicating the action of psychical powers. India is the land and home of such phenomena. You promise to send me the photograph of a fakir 'self supported in the air'—then, the same as ourselves,—you admit the fact of levitation? You say, that all such beliefs in 'Spirit agency' etc were considered by the ancient Aryans, as offsprings offsprings [sic] of ignorance and superstition! The *alleged cause* of such effects, you mean? —not the effects themselves proceeding entirely from some unknown psycho-physiological cause—though not from 'Spirits'? Would you mind—as a 'Fellow' of our Th. Soc. to give serious attention to such phenomena in India, while Crookes, Wallace, Prof. Hare, Thury, the astronomer Flammarion and many other scientists ending with Zöllner of Leipzig give theirs to the Sp[iritualist] mediumistic phenomena in Europe & America?

Then more philosophical discussion to show that learned Brahmans had always known a fourth principle answering to Zollner's fourth dimension . . . "Read attentively the article on the fourth dimension, I sent you and tell me, whether your Aryan philosophers and even your modern learned Brahmans—those who train fakirs from their childhood to produce phenomena—did not know of this *fourth* dimension and called and yet call it—*Akasa* in its generic name?" . . . etc. etc. "It is eternal *motion*—the Narayana, or spirit of Brahma moving on the waters of chaos, darkness or matter. It is *not* a dimension, but a quality, the direct effect of Spiritual force upon matter, and—it does exist. And *if once science proves it to exist*, then the 'permeability of matter' (hitherto denied) or 'passage of matter through matter' must also be accepted." etc etc—etc—

"It may so happen that you will see all this in quite a different light; and that the only thing I will have succeeded in demonstrating to you clearly will be—my idiocy." Then various statements about her ignorance of Indian languages etc calculated to suggest that he had considerable knowledge of them—etc etc

[The whole tone of the letter is confidential and deferential while suggesting great learning and intimacy with Indian affairs, feelings, and philosophy and critical of European beliefs and customs a flattering kind of letter.][10]

NOTES:

1. Presumably *osmotic*, "pertaining to osmosis," alluding to Mary's virgin conception of Jesus.

2. This sentence is in a different hand, added at the foot of the page, with an insertion mark at this point in the copy of the letter.

3. W. Paris is otherwise unidentified.

4. Christians.

5. Nota bene, Latin for "mark well," used to call attention to something important or unusual.

6. Metropolitan bishop, especially in the Orthodox Church.

7. Parenthesis in the manuscript copy.

8. Brackets in the manuscript copy.

9. Brackets in the manuscript copy.

10. Brackets in the manuscript copy.

SOURCE: Original unavailable. Transcribed from a copy now in the Archives of the Society for Psychical Research in Cambridge University Library. The copy, of poor legibility, was made presumably by Eleanor Sidgwick, who freely abbreviated and paraphrased the material she copied (see background essay L).

Letter 116

To H. Chintamon   *May 9, 1878*

Encloses a newspaper cutting about conversion to Xtianity and asks if it is true—Abuses of Xtianity.—"Let the Brahmans worship such a deity if they will—we *Theosophists* trample the idea under foot. The Brahma Somaj seems to us but a caricature, a pale reflection of Judaic Protestantism, without even the excuse that those white people have that they have been brought up in ignorance of Vedic philosophy. If the Jewish Jehovah were a candidate for election to Fellowship in the T.S. he would not get a high vote in our council, nor ever be complimented by taking a ballot! If I had a *hundred* lives I would give them all to the last drop of my blood to save India from this thrice accursed Christian system, and our President agrees with me fully. Don't be surprised at this language, my respected Brother, for one day you may discover that it is no exaggeration. You cannot imagine how I hate a theology which has bathed the world in tears and blood to propagate a system of the most blasphemous lies! Since last night, when I read that vernacular Press act, I have been boiling over with resentment; I could not close my eyes for the whole night."

"The President has already secured the republication in the New York *Herald* and written an editorial commenting upon the subject. Copies will be sent you *enclosed in envelopes of course*. Bravo, for England!" etc

"We are very much disappointed that you should have sent in the rules of the *Arya Somaj* without an English translation, as not one of our members reads or understands Sanskrit" etc— . . . "Having devoted a whole day to decipher your *Rules*, I think I understand well enough to make myself a correct idea of them, and yet, notwithstanding

Col. Olcotts desire I *cannot* take upon myself the responsibility of giving forth your ideas, which after all I may have misunderstood more than once." etc . . . We are all very anxious to study these rules as correctly as possible, for every member of the council is heart and soul for joining or rather blending members to your Arya Somaj. The President will write to you himself about that, and I, for one, if you will only kindly condescend to give me your order to do anything I can for the Arya S. am ready to pledge myself to it's work for the rest of my life." She is going to study Hindostani again— . . .

"Please then, to let me know, what I ought to do, to become in any degree useful to the Arya Somaj of my mind and strength and even—of MY VERY LIFE: I have nothing in this world to attach me to it; no ties of country or kindred paramount to the claims of India. Very likely—you may despise the offer." etc. —explains her strength & power and how she fought with Garibaldi in 1867. . . . "There is plenty of me left, for more bullets and more scars, if need be, when the hour again strikes to summon to-gether the friends of human progress and welfare—only (some oriental language)—and I will be at my post—however much (like an old idiot that I am) I have forgotten Hindostani"

SOURCE: Original unavailable. Transcribed from a copy now in the Archives of the Society for Psychical Research in Cambridge University Library. The copy, of poor legibility, was made presumably by Eleanor Sidgwick, who freely abbreviated and paraphrased the material she copied (see background essay L).

Introduction to Letter 117

The following letter has survived in two different versions: one as abridged by Eleanor Sidgwick for the files of the Society for Psychical Research and another as abridged in Sarda's *Life of Dayanand Saraswati*. A comparison of the two versions raises the question of how much has been omitted from other letters of which we have only a single version abridged (with or without acknowledgment) by the recorder.

Letter 117

To H. Chintamon   *May 21, 1878*

117A. SIDGWICK VERSION

She sends out her books some 250 volumes to India—to be used till she comes and to belong to any Somaj he likes if she dies. Some are good—some "I call 'flapdoodle' character."—but worst specimens thrown away. . . .

Different ages ascribed to her by newspaper interviewers—25 to 90. . . . [long space] "As you will see by my signature on the slip enclosed I sign myself a 'Buddhist', i.e., a HEATHEN, for I am no more a Buddhist than I am a Christian; but, as these Christian folk generally call me a 'Buddhist' as they would call me a 'murderess' by way of abuse, so I take pleasure in signing myself with all the *anti Christian* names I can think of."

Excuses for writing so often etc

SOURCE: Original unavailable. Transcribed from a copy now in the Archives of the Society for Psychical Research in Cambridge University Library. The copy, of poor legibility, was made presumably by Eleanor Sidgwick, who freely abbreviated and paraphrased the material she copied (see background essay L).

117B. SARDA VERSION

My dear Sir and Brother,

As I am about to leave the city of New York to take a needed rest at the sea-shore, with no probability of my returning before I sail for Europe and India (whether I will stop in London one month or one year, fate alone knows), I have decided to send a portion of my books direct to Bombay to await my coming (some 250 volumes and as many unbound books). The President adds some of his. If any accident should prevent my coming there in person, you will please present them to any library of Arya Samaj. By *accident* I mean Death: for nothing except death will prevent our coming to India in due season. I have decided, as soon as I am in the Motherland to present the greater part of the volumes to such Samaj as you may designate: and I hope to bring a load more from England (and Olcott also). I hope you will not feel annoyed at my writing and bothering you so often, but I assure you I never breathe so easily as when I either write to, or receive letters from India. It seems to me as if I was sending a portion of my heart and soul to the blessed Motherland every time.

H. P. Blavatsky

To the above letter, Olcott added the following:

Dear Brother,

I will add a few lines to our sister's letter to say that I have read its contents, and its several propositions have my unqualified approval. In suggesting that our society should make itself known as a branch of Arya Samaj subject to P. Dayanand's control and myself, *I am proud to acknowledge fialty to such an instructor and guide* as that wise and holy man. There is much work to be done by us before we can expect very great results. As you say, let us work together in hearty co-operation and we will be able to effect wonders.

H. S. Olcott

SOURCE: Original unavailable. Copied from Sarda, *Life of Dayanand Saraswati* 527. Reprinted in *Canadian Theosophist* 71 (Nov.–Dec. 1990): 102–3.

Letter 118

To H. Chintamon   *May 22, 1878*

Personal and Confidential

Acknowledges letter of April 22 announcing adherance of 7 Hindus. About changing name of T.S. to "Theosophical Society of the Arya Somaj" & complete subordination to Arya Somaj & asking for directions or orders from Dayanand—some American members want [?] to abandon all and go to India. "We have others in London, who only require a little persuasion to do likewise, but they will be more useful in England than in India. Among them are persons of great ability learning & talent, and persons of rank and great wealth. One of these Theosophists—the editor of the late Anthropological Review offers to take the management of the Theo. Review[1] & will start it. Another, and the most devoted perhaps in England, is Charles Carleton Massey (Athenaeum Club) son of an M.P. who was formerly Minister of Indian Finance. C.C.M. is what you may call a *congenital mystic* and I feel perfectly sure, that if Pundit Dyânând will write to him any request he will joyfully comply. English Spiritual[sm] is the great opposing force to Theosophy as you may have noticed in the papers sent you (*Spiritualist*) C. C. Massey has for three years bravely defended theosophy, our Society and selves. But what can we do? He hungers after truth, and the sight of a *fakirs* phenomenon (however fanatical and idolatrous) would make him do anything in the world. Another brave loyal heart is Miss Emily Kislingbury, secretary, guiding spirit and in fact soul of the B.N.A. of Sp[ts][2] She has courage enough to make herself a heroine, and her motives and character are as pure as gold. But, like most women her emotional nature calls for a proof to lean upon; and for lack of that (since we all repudiate mediumship) she feels as though she would turn to the Xn church for support. . . . Here is a prize—or rather two—worth the having. This little woman gathers about her some of the first writers in England, and is a *power* for good under wise direction. We want you to secure her from her weaker self. Write to her in the name of the Arya Somaj and to C. C. Massey (I send you both addresses) and in the name of TRUTH save them both! A direct letter from India would fire the zeal of both, for it is what they have been waiting and hoping for for three years. They regard India as the land of mystery, wisdom and *Spiritual Power*. My devotion, love and enthusiasm for India has fired them both (for last year they have come both—C. C. Massey and Emily Kislingbury—accross the ocean to see me and lived with me) but unfortunately I am but a white-faced IDIOT not a Hindu, what *can I* do more! In the name of truth then and the great Unseen, Power, help me to rescue both these enthusiasts either from Christianity—worse than that—Catholicism, into which both are diving rapidly and give them work to do—*real hard* work, for both are of the stuff that helps making MARYTRS. Show this letter to our revered pundit—perhaps, he will consent to help and advise me. The *more mystery* you can throw about the communication the better and deeper impression it will make. If it would not be deemed impertinent in me to suggest a form of a letter I would propose the following:

'Charles Carleton Massey Esq
Atheneaum Club—London
Dear Brother

The 'Brothers' in India look to you to take the Presidency of the British Theosophical Society of the Arya Somaj. Great consequences may follow. After three years of expectation the WORD comes. Are you ready? If so—act.'

(Here let the Pundit write his name in *Sanskrit characters* and date it from wherever he likes.)

The letter to Miss Kislingbury should be worded:—

'Emily Kislingbury, 38 Great Russell Street London
Dear Sister

Only the weak need a crutch. There is no primal truth in Earthly writings outside the Vedas: all else is derivation If you seek consolation seek it there; if support it is there to be found (or something to that effect—you know better what to say.) *The reality of the Word made Flesh is to be found in Humanity*—The highest avatar of the Son. Have patience & work for your fellow creatures and you will see Light in the East. A true Theosophist of the Arya Somaj will not wait in vain.'

(Follow again the pundits or any other signature in Sanskrit)

We know the mind to be worked upon and will guarantee results if the Pundit kindly permits the letters to be written. Deeply as C C Massey and Emily Kislingbury love us, good theosophists as they are, nothing that we could do will *have such an effect* as these letters from India. For the present, it will be far better that these two should not know *who* addresses them. Later when the London branch is actively working, we will put you in full communion. Do not think we are resorting to childish method. Believe me, we know what is best for these EX-Spiritualists—these half-born theosophists. There are others, in different parts of Europe to whom after a little we will ask you to address ourselves. And now dear Brother, can we reciprocate? Is there any one in India to whom you would have us write? If so *command us.*"

Then other remarks about portraits

NOTES:

1. No periodical of this name has been identified. It may have been a projected publication that was never realized.

2. British National Association of Spiritualists.

SOURCE: Original unavailable. Transcribed from a copy now in the Archives of the Society for Psychical Research in Cambridge University Library. The copy, of poor legibility, was made presumably by Eleanor Sidgwick, who freely abbreviated and paraphrased the material she copied (see background essay L).

⌒

Introduction to Letter 119

Part of the Theosophists' correspondence with Dayanand Saraswati was carried on with the assistance of a young Indian named Shyamaji Krishnavarma, who served as a translator. The following extracts may be from the same letter or from two letters written on the same day. The fragments in the first extract relate to Krishnavarma's services as translator and appear to be partly quotation and partly paraphrase. The second extract alludes to Krishnavarma's ambition to go to England to study with and work for the Oxford Professor of Sanskrit, Monier-Williams, for whom HPB had little regard. Her unsuccessful efforts to dissuade Krishnavarma from that course are more explicit in letters 120 and 124.

Letter 119

To Shyamaji Krishnavarma   *May 30, 1878*

... the thanks of the President and the Council of the Theosophical Society for the translation you kindly made of the letter of our revered Pandit Dayananda Saraswati Swami to ourselves. . . . the Council of New York had adopted an unanimous resolution to ask you to accept the Diploma of a "Corresponding Fellow" of the Theosophical Society.

While I have no right to obtrude opinions unasked, yet being

European myself and knowing the white race—the English scientific world—I feel like quoting to you one of the very few passages in the Christian Bible which I can thoroughly endorse, viz. "Cast not your pearls before swine, nor give that which is holy unto the dogs, for they will turn and rend you." I have a poor enough opinion even of the Oxford Professors to believe that they form no exception to the rule.

SOURCE: Original unavailable. Copied from Yajnik, *Shyamaji Krishnavarma* 30–1.

Letter 120

To H. Chintamon   *May 30, 1878*
                                                              New York

private—except to the Swamee Dyanand

Dear Brother,

I had hardly mailed my last letter to you in which I ask the assistance of our revered Master Dyanand Saraswati Swamee and your's—in the cases of C. C. Massey and Emily Kislingbury—when I received another letter from our London theosophist—(Charles Carleton Massey). I inclose and send it to you. Please read it carefully and let it be a proof to you, of the worthiness of this young man whom we would save from himself. A truer and more faithful heart never beat in an English bosom. He is possessed of the qualifications of a leader in reform, but he requires instruction, support and guidance as well. I have underscored passages which will show you the man's inner nature. We look to him as the future leader of an Arya Somaj in England—if you help us. You see, he want's *to be tried*, he desires to receive *orders*; and I, without your help can do nothing for him. It is *impossible* that he should without much more preliminary training and a disruption of certain present, social relations, be accepted in certain orders in the East—of which perhaps you have knowledge—but he is as well calculated as any one I know in England to head an Arya Somaj movement. I am loath to answer his questions about his "spirits" and their physical manifestations, proofs of identity etc. I have an expression of the Swamee Dyanand's wishes, (for since the receipt of his letter of April 21, I am *officially* and *personally* subject to his orders. You know that Europe and America are deluged with these nether-world phenomena. I have learned from the adepts of the East (Druzes and Lamas) that they are *not* phenomena produced by "spirits" but by forces with which it is neither profitable nor safe to dabble;—though I believe in neither Christian "devil" nor supernatural agencies—yet "a man cannot touch pitch without being defiled." But, there are millions of well meaning persons, who fancy they get in these physical phenomena the comforting assurance of man's immortality. Our brother Massey is one of these, though with philosophic instinct, he reaches above them to a communion with our Eastern adepts. People call *me* an adept; now, that's *perfectly ridiculous*! I have tried hard for nearly 30 years to learn and study, and I have known "adepts" and philosophers who taught me a little of everything—but that's all. I know enough anyhow to say that these phenomena are not produced by "spirits." While the concurrent testimony of many scientific men proves the occurrence of *the phenomena*. For saying this much, the Western papers have covered me with abuse; but nevertheless, to this day they have not been able to shake my position. The time is ripe for the preaching of an Aryan crusade throughout Europe and America. Thousands of intelligent persons falling away from the Churches yearn for a better religious system, and doubtless, they would welcome Aryanism with open arms. The first recruits I believe will come from the intelligent Spiritualists who are already enfranchised from priestly rule. But we must educate them first as to the nature of their mediumistic phenomena and second as to their own powers, duties and responsibilities; and the Theos. Society is a bridge on which they may cross the chasm from their absurd exoteric-notions (whether about Christianity or Spiritualism) to the sublime truths taught by the *Vedic* Arya Somaj. Ignorant ourselves as to the best method of bringing the C. C *Masseys* of this great body of inquirers hungering after truth—from the *materialism* of their *Spiritualism* to the pure philosophy and ethics of Aryanism, we wait the orders and implore the counsel of the revered Swamee. If he would graciously comply with our request to send the few lines I suggested in my previous letter to you, to Brother Massey, the latter would unquestionably organize the "British Theosoph. Society of the Arya Somaj" at once, and so President Olcott and I, on reaching England— which we hope to do in a couple of months—would find our mission in that country thoroughly well begun.

I beseech you, then, to read attentively the enclosed letter. To lose Massey, would be to lose our strongest prop in England. You see he says that he has "sacrificed" already "the practical ends and prospects of life to devotion to psychological phenomena" and adds—*"If I fail in these I fail in all."* We must not let him lose all, but he would, if we should drag him away, from his *Spiritual* phenomena, without showing him what they really are, and what is their true value. And who can teach us, so well what we ought to do and say as the Swamee Dyanand to whom few philosophical secrets are unknown—as he is a *Swamee*?

I have shown your letter to Brother Olcott, and he has answered your inquiries about Shyamaji Krishnawarma. Does Monier Williams think that he knows the Sanskrit better than the Swamee? And does he imagine that the Arya Somaj would take the insult of making its *chief's* pupil a lackey to carry his Oxford books after him? This is how we *theosophists* look upon this proposition: may be, that we are mistaken and that some Hindus *do* believe that there is more Science in the West than the East, and that English know better Sanskrit that [*i.e.*, than] the descendants of the Aryas who first spoke it? If he does desire to go to England, then, when the branch of the Theos. Soc. of the Arya Somaj is established there and in working order then it would be *their duty* and pleasure to raise the money to [defray][1] the expenses of his mission. He is so young as yet, that [*word missing*] a little delay would be of no consequence. A recent review of a new book by Monier Williams credits him with saying that there is more wisdom in one volume of modern Scientific literature than in all the pretended treasures of Eastern religious books—Sanskrit and Arabic. Should our young missionary be entrusted to the government and teaching of such a conceited ass? They are all alike these Western Scientists, for from Max Müller down they think that our Eastern people are indebted to Western philologists for the little glimmering of light they—poor imbeciles—have of the meaning of their ancestral literature! It makes my blood fairly boil to read these exhibitions of their insufferable vanity. And as my blood is in that condition at this moment from the recollection of what I have read, [it] will be best for me to bring this letter to an abrupt [close.]

Waiting for you to kindly answer these several questions you have *promised me to answer*, and with best wishes for the health and happiness of all our Brothers,

I am yours fraternally
H P Blavatsky.

Hurrychund Chintamon Esq—

[*word missing*] you seem to laugh at me in the "Indian Spectator" of April 28th about what I say of the *Fakir* and the *Ju[ggler.]* But a *fact* IS *a fact*; and I have seen it with my own eyes in the presence of two other Russians whom I do not name in my book. How do *you*, account for it?

NOTE:

1. The letter is torn at this point and several subsequent places, the word missing here being supplied from the text in Yajnik, *Shyamaji Krishnavarma* 30.

SOURCE: Transcribed from the original in the Archives of the Theosophical Society, Adyar.

Letter 121

To N. de Fadeyev   *July 3 [1878]*
                              Scorching heat like inside an oven.

Well, Nadyezhenka, my dear, I have received your letter which, as soon as it had been read, was carried off by Krishnavarma who came two weeks ago from Multan (Panjab) in a [word indecipherable] and is now staying with us. The Devil knows how, but he translated into English for me the entire paragraph written by you in Russian about your *doubts* and fears concerning my alleged denial of Christ, and he asked insistently for the letter. He said to Olcott: "If we could find only one dozen European members with such character, such unshakable faith and principles, the world would be saved." You don't believe it? As you like, but he said just those words and sent your letter to Swami Dayananda. Don't be angry with me, friend. He respects you for your principles and I could not refuse him. But remember the following:

The Arya-Samaj has *no religious dogmas or rules*. The only article of compulsory faith, as I once wrote, is the oneness of God; whether in three persons (as you believe) or in trillions of quintillions, namely, in every bit of dust, in each

atom separately, and in the ONE WHOLE (as we believe)—
does not really matter. Everyone is free to believe in his
own way. One fact remains: there is the One, All-powerful,
Uncreated and Eternal Divinity that is manifesting itself
every second in all its creation, from dust to man. Neither
your belief nor ours can change this fact one iota. As He is
so He was, and will be for all ages; and the fact that John
sees Him as an old man and Peter as a youth, you as a
Trinity and I in innumerable beings, is no sin against Him,
provided we believe in His existence; *ergo*, the Materialists
are kept out of the Society—this is *mandatory*. As in Nature
there are no two leaves identical one to the other, nor a
man, even among identical twins, absolutely like another,
so there cannot be two people believing *literally* the same.
Faith and the picture it evokes depend upon the physiological and psychological construction of the brain. Aunt
is probably as good a Christian as you, yet if you tried to
dig deeper into her brain, you would find there is an enormous difference in the intimate details of your respective
faiths. People's faith does not depend upon themselves but
upon their constitution. Hence let us be just to everyone.
Every man believes in his own way, just as with taste, one
may like tomatoes, while they make another sick; one loves
the color red, while it gives eye-ache to another. It is the differences in religious dogmas, invented not by saints but
by all-sinful mortals, and the great number of varied and
diverse beliefs, that divide humanity into inimical nations
and races. Were there no dogmas, were there no Protestants, Catholics, Buddhists, Brahmanists, etc., all would
believe in One God, one Life-giving Lord; all would regard
themselves as brothers, and, as children of one Father,
would be ashamed to let their brothers see how they kill
and cut each other to pieces in wars, rend each other like
wolves, and condemn each other to HELL. I shall never forget one memorable day, or rather night, at Odessa, in your

house at supper. Aunt was debating with me about religion and was insisting that no Jew or idol-worshipper could ever enter the Kingdom of Heaven and will never be found therein. From that very moment I began to brood on these words. "If even Aunt," I thought, "such a good, noble and just woman, is so blinded by Christian faith that she can believe in such a strange and terrible injustice of God, then what must other Christians be like, many of whom are not worth her little finger?" Till then I still believed from time to time in Christianity. A few months after that I became a Theist, if not a complete Atheist. Then came my journey to America, to the woods of *Saugus*, near Boston. But I am digressing. That's enough about me!

Having no dogmas and forcing neither this nor that belief upon our members, we accept and respect, equally with the Hindus, all Christians, with the exception of Catholics—and this is another basic rule. Not because there are not among Catholics people just as good as in any other religion, but because their priesthood is so mean and Jesuitical, and forces everything out in confession, even that which has no bearing upon religion. In short, it is strictly forbidden; and also because the Catholic Madonna in a crinoline and with an umbrella is a worse idol than Kali, the consort of Siva, and we are going dead against any idol-worship. In the beginning of Brahmanism they actually had but one God—Vishnu; but instead of *three aspects*, the people began to represent it in a thousand images, and these images, from having been at first merely emblems of its innumerable qualities, little by little dissociated themselves from each other, and, from having been abstractions at first, became something concrete and were transformed into personalities—gods. This is the ABC of the *Veda*. Every philologist and Indologist who can read Sanskrit knows it. Brahmanical priests took advantage of this in order to enslave and subjugate stupid, superstitious masses, just as

Catholics and others have done. In regard to the precepts and parables of Christ, how can we believe in them when we find them *word for word* in the "Moral Precepts" of Krishna, Gautama the Buddha and others many years B.C. The whole of Buddhism is contained in the *Vedas* of the Aryans. The priesthood has distorted the *Vedas* and Gautama the Buddha undertook to explain to the people the essence, the secret meaning of the distorted dead letter. Later the Buddhist clergy also began to distort it and perverted the truth because of unreasonable devotion. Thus I believe in the truth of the *Vedas* which radiates forth the One God and the Eternal spirit. With the exception of dogmas established later by sinful men, and with the help of such a monster as St.(?!) Constantine, we believe in the same thing as you do. "Do not do unto others what you do not wish them to do unto you," says Confucious, Buddha, and Krishna. "Love thy neighbor as thyself and God above all," they tell us also. "*If the blind lead the blind, both will fall into the pit,*" is written in the *Prakhya* from the *Aitareya-Brahmana* of the *Rig-Veda*, the existence of which books has been established without a doubt, if not twenty thousand years ago as the Bramanas assure us, then at least two thousand years B.C., according to Max Müller and Dr. Haug, the latter having been the best Sanskrit scholar of our era. There is no saying of Christ which could not be found in the *Vedas* and the *Mahabharata* of Krishna. You believe in the Trinity, while we believe in the *Trimurti* (literally, *three faces*, in Sanskrit); but you believe in the Church dogma of the Trinity—God the Father, God the Son, and God the Holy Ghost, in the anthropomorphic sense, *i.e.*, making of them three separate persons in One. In the same way the Brahmanas believe in the Trimurti composed of Brahma, Vishnu, and Siva—the Creator, the Sustainer, and the Destroyer. But we, followers of the pure and monotheistic religion and philosophy of the ancient Aryans, believe in the Trinity in its scientific, philosophic and Divine sense. We believe and understand thus: God the Father—the Universal Soul, the Creative Power which has brought forth and is creating every minute everything that exists in the Universe. God the Son—the Universe that is, the whole world order, *i.e.*, *Spirit in the flesh*, the clear and visible manifestation of the invisible creative Power. . . .

[Page of the original letter missing.]

. . . like yourself. As the Gospel says, in the House of our Father there are many mansions—there is work for everyone. Christians can rail against materialism and atheism, and *non*-Christians against Catholicism and Protestantism. Certainly hypocrites [text illegible], but as people who recognize that God, by whatever name he may be called, is still the Unchanging One God, and that all men are brothers. It is only the foolish Wittgenstein (a portion of whose letter I am enclosing) who felt offended that the poor Leymarie (*Revue Spirite*) wrote him "Mon cher frère en croyance" [*Fr.* My dear brother in belief], and adds—"l'animal! un peu plus et il me tutoyerait" [*Fr.* the brute! a little more, and he'd be addressing me in familiar terms]!!! And that is a Theosophist!! He is also a Christian, namely, he believes in Christ, but is vehement against the priesthood of whatever color.

No, my darling, we will not let you leave our Society; you are an "Honorary Fellow," and don't you yourself want to fight all idol-worship? It stands to reason that we have too much respect for our Fellows to allow ourselves to ask them to act against their convictions. Hence have no suspicions. You are a Theosophist (Christian) for good. Böhme the mystic was also a Christian and all the mediaeval Kabalists were Theosophists, as was Swedenborg.

The Dictionary has been probably received by now. I have received notification about a book from Europe through

Hull, as is stated in your note, but it is so hot there is no strength to go out. I just returned three days ago; I was almost as far as California with Krishnavarma and Olcott.[1] One of our Fellows is the editor of a journal in Sacramento and we had to talk over some business matters with him. He came half way to meet us. At Milwaukee and in Nevada all the ladies walked in procession by the windows of our hotel and the terrace where we were sitting, in order to stare at Krishnavarma. He is remarkably handsome even though swarthy like the color of coffee. In his long, white, muslin garment and a white, narrow turban on his head, with diamonds on his neck and barefooted, he is really a curious sight among the Americans in black coats and white ties. Photographers came to ask me to allow them to take his picture, but he refused all of them, and everyone wondered at his good and pure English. The Lord knows how old he is. When one sees him for the first time he seems not more than 25, but there are moments when he looks like an old man of 100 years. You ask why the Hindus are not paying for my work. Is it possible to ask money for religious convictions and for what one does in the name of God? They will not allow me to starve, this has already been proved to me; but I will not ask for money. Krishna-varma who is leaving tomorrow for South America brought 40 thousand Rupees (20 thousand dollars in gold) for the Society and has given me 200 English gold pieces for two weeks of his stay with me, yet except for tea which he prepared himself, he hasn't eaten any of our supplies. Every morning his old man—maybe his servant, I do not know—went to town to buy fruit for him, and himself cooked the rice in his own silver vessels. This old man seems to me to be a thousand years old. He is so old his face is like parchment, but what strength! A few days ago, some boys and a few grown people annoyed him a lot by running after him and calling him "heathen." He seized one of them by the neck and threw him on the other side of the street into a ditch full of filthy water, and sent another tumbling some 50 steps. The crowd got angry, but Krishnavarma threw a handful of gold coins into their midst and they jumped on the money like wild beasts and shouted Hurrah for both of them until they entered our house. To avoid scandal, Olcott is accompanying the old man now when he is shopping. The *other* Krishnavarma Shyamji, the chief Apostle and pupil of our Swami, will come here next winter to preach. He intends to show by facts and statistics that the few Hindus who were converted to Christianity invariably became drunkards, liars and thieves after conversion; that no Christian European family would ever hire a Hindu Christian as a servant, but prefer a heathen who never lies and has preserved some of the good qualities of his ancestors.

I enclose herewith a card of Colonel Chaille Long of the Egyptian Army for Uncle; he wrote to him a few words. Chaille Long is my great friend and comes often to see me. He knew Uncle in Egypt, at Alexandria and Cairo, in the Abbot Hotel. I did not know that Uncle was in Egypt after I was. Chaille Long praises him a great deal, saying that he is the cleverest man in the world and an excellent diplomat. Send this card to Uncle. Has he sent *Isis* to the Moscow Professor or not? Good Lord, how the English *Pall Mall* praises it!

You write that you will find some way to publish my articles which were rejected by *Pravda*. Could you find a magazine in Russia where I could send my articles from America, England and India? In India there are no Russian correspondents. You would greatly oblige me. I could also find out some things about politics and describe the country in an interesting way, even in archaelogical or geographical magazines. Do try, my dear soul. I have sent to Dobrovolsky seven articles in all at two different times. He sent three of them back, published two, and rejected the last two. It means that I have lost more than 200 Roubles on these five articles, as he asked for two articles each month at 50 Roubles per month. Even for the two which he published he has not paid. What a pig! Of course I shall not write for him any more. Poor Vera[2] begs in the name of Christ to write for her sake at least two articles per month. For the last two she received 80 Roubles, and it is a great help to her. Do you really like my articles? I really thought they were foolish. Well, I am glad.

So Natashka[3] got married? God give her happiness. And what about Katherine?[4] Is she still cursing the bones of her dead parents or has she stopped drinking and cursing? On the whole she is a good and devoted woman. Such are rare.

Of course Edison has kept all the promises and will keep them. Foolish Dobrovolsky has omitted a good deal from my article, and the most interesting part of it, to be sure. He accomplishes real miracles. You know that he is your *"brother."* He is a Fellow of our Society, and Krishna-varma has taught him two more things, so that with a small, almost invisible mechanical contrivance on their neck the deaf will hear quite well.

Well, good-bye. I have written a lot; have to write yet to Vera; I kiss everybody warmly. And here is Val'ka[5] who is writing a letter, and Vera, and Verochka[6] also: they are all asking me to come to them for a visit from London. Am I free to do so? And where is the money for it?

Sal'ka[7] is an awful dunce. Never writes a single word, and Olya[8] and Sasha[9] likewise; and Sonya[10] has cheated me with her portrait. Write my friend, more often,

Helena.

NOTES:

1. A trip of the sort implied by these remarks does not seem possible. HPB says she returned from the trip with Olcott and Krishnavarma

"three days ago," which would have been June 30; she wrote Hurrychund Chitamon from New York on May 30, so the trip would have been taken during the month of June, but Boris de Zirkoff's chronology (*CW* 1:lxiv) shows that on June 4, HPB was in Hoboken, New Jersey, with Belle Mitchell and Edward Wimbridge; on June 16, Olcott was in Albany, New York, and HPB was visiting Belle Mitchell again and did not return until June 22; on June 26, HPB and Olcott took a night boat down the Hudson River; and on June 28, HPB was interviewed by the *New York Star*. In addition, the identity of "Krishnavarma" is unknown; he is, HPB says, not Shyamaji Krishnavarma of the Arya Samaj. The episode has a fictional air about it. It is not improbable that HPB, who was known for the stories she told her relatives and companions in their childhood, is still making up a good yarn for them.

2. Vera Petrovna de Zhelihovsky, HPB's younger sister.

3. A pet name for Anastasia. The person referred to is unidentified.

4. The person referred to is unidentified.

5. A pet name for Valerian, here probably Valerian Vladimirovich de Zhelihovsky, HPB's nephew, her sister Vera's son.

6. A pet name for Vera, here probably Vera Vladimirovna de Zhelihovsky, HPB's niece, her sister Vera's second daughter.

7. A pet name. The person referred to is unidentified.

8. A pet name for Olga. The person referred to is unidentified.

9. A pet name for Alexander or Alexandra. The person referred to is unidentified.

10. A pet name for Sofya (Sophia). The person referred to is unidentified.

DATE: The reference to *Isis* shows that the letter was written after the publication of that book in September 1877. July 3, 1878, seems probable also because of the reference to Krishnavarma of the Arya Samaj, with whom HPB was corresponding in this year.

SOURCE: Translated by Boris de Zirkoff from the Russian original in the Archives of the Theosophical Society, Adyar. Another English translation published in *HPB Speaks* 1:190–203.

◡⟶

Letter 122

To N. de Fadeyev   *July 8, 1878*

My dearest, I write to you because otherwise I would burst with a strange feeling which is positively suffocating me. It is the 8th of July to-day, an ominous day for me, but God only knows whether the omen is good or bad. To-day it is exactly five years and one day since I came to America, and this moment I have just returned from the Supreme Court, where I gave my oath of allegiance to the American Republic and Constitution. Now for a whole hour I have been a citizen with equal right to the President himself. So far so good: the workings of my original destiny have forced me into this naturalization, but to my utter astonishment and disgust I was compelled to repeat publicly after the judge, like a mere parrot, the following tirade: that I "would renounce for ever and even to my death every kind of submission and obedience to the emperor of Russia; that I would renounce all obedience to the powers established by him and the government of Russia, and that I would accept the duty to defend, love, and serve the Constitution of the United States alone. So help me God in whom I believe!" I was awfully scared when pronouncing this blackguardly recantation of Russia and the emperor. And so I am not only an apostate to our beloved Russian Church, but a political renegade. A nice scrape to get into, but how am I to manage to no longer love Russia or respect the emperor? It is easier to say a thing than to act accordingly.

SOURCE: Original unavailable. Copied from an English translation in *Path* 9 (February 1895): 385. A partial Russian text is in *Blue Hills* xvi.

Letter 123

To C. H. van der Linden?[1]

July 30, 1878
302 W. 47th St.
New York

Dear Sir:

The printed circular enclosed will indicate to you the conditions of membership in the Theosophical Society. I may add, however, that since it was issued we have affiliated with the great Indian Brotherhood of the Arya-Somaj, and, by vote of Council have changed our title correspondingly. Henceforth our Society will be known as "The Theosophical Society of The Arya-Somaj of India." Thus, instead of exacting fees from the applicants for the benefit of our Society—now, that we are allied to an Oriental Body engaged in a just and worthy work, we have voted and passed a resolution that the fee of five dollars should be remitted in each case to Bombay, for the benefit of the Arya-Somaj.

Herewith, you will also find blank applications and obligations for yourself and son to sign, provided that after reading our Circular you still desire to unite with us. In such case, you will please procure and send me a postal order for £2, sterling, payable to Mr. Hurrychund Chintamon, 6 Meadow Street, Fort, Bombay, India. He is the representative of our Society near the Arya-Somaj and will remit you a receipt in due course of mail and—instructions.

That you are Hollanders by birth strongly commends you to our regard, for we all have a lively appreciation of the sterling qualities of your national character, and believe that you yourself can materially aid in forwarding the reformatory work of our Society. As it is proper, that in joining us you should know what is the Arya-Somaj, permit me to give you an idea of it, as of the Chiefs to whom we have unanimously voted our allegiance.

It is a Society (Somaj) organized by the orders and under the supervision of that mysterious body (mysteries—to the *non*-initiated, of course) of adepts and philosophers, whose existence in India I have hinted at in my book. The founder and responsible chief of it is a very noted Swamee (a holy man) named—Dya Nand Saraswati—at once the purest and most erudite man of the Hindu pandits. Branches have been established in all parts of India, and one has just been organized in London. The object is to restore the primitive Vedic philosophy and teach with its help the now nearly lost to the outward world—psychological sciences, the knowledge of which gives to man the material and mathematical certainty of our Spirit's immortality and develops in man god-like powers. Of course, once that we accept the Aryan philosophy, seek to make the world converted to its great truths, we are bound to break down the superstitious observances and dogmas of every *exoteric, human* religion—especially that of Christianity. What our philosophy is until you are furnished with certain documents of the Arya-Somaj you can abundantly learn from "Isis," which was written under orders.

All who enter our Society pass through different degrees and sections (as in Masonry) from lowest to highest. Promotion depends upon *personal merit* and devotion to the cause. A Ritual, Ceremonial, will be provided from India, and later we will communicate with you in regard to the work you are expected to do for the common cause. If you desire so, you can become yourself the president of a Branch Theosophic Society of the Arya-Somaj in your place. I can write to the chiefs in India, and provide you with a charter. It is their desire that as many Somajses (Societies) as possible should be started in various countries in Christendom, for nowhere else is there so loud a call for reformatory work in ridding the people from bigotry and superstition as in these countries. We aim to establish a *Universal* Brotherhood of Humanity, and—with the help of the "Supreme *Unknown*"—we will succeed. If, according to a French saying: "A brebis tondue, Dieu modere le vent" [*Fr.* God tempers (*modère*) the wind to the shorn lamb]—we, who have two millions of "Brothers" behind our backs in India must certainly succeed.

Awaiting your reply and, on behalf of the Society, accepting the hands which you and your son extend to it,

I remain, Sir, yours faithfully,

H. P. Blavatsky.

NOTE:

1. The copy of this letter published in the *American Theosophist and the Theosophic Messenger* is illustrated with a reproduction of the membership certificate of Peter van der Linden, dated September 1878. Peter and his father, C. H. van der Linden, were both members of the Society. Because the letter refers to "yourself and son," the addressee was presumably the father.

SOURCE: Original unavailable. Copied from *American Theosophist and the Theosophic Messenger* 14 (May 1913): 623–5. Published in *Canadian Theosophist* 71 (Nov.–Dec. 1990): 104–5, with slight differences.

~~~

Letter 124

To Shyamaji Krishnavarma
August 7, 1878
New York

Mʳ Shyamaji Chrishnavarma

Dear Brother,

Your's of July 5ᵗʰ just received and I feel more than flattered by your confidence in me—I feel profoundly *touched*, and certainly will do all that lies in my power to prove to you that such a confidence on your part is not misplaced. As you come out so freely and sincerely and ask my advice and opinion, do not take it amiss if I answer you just as sincerely. You may either follow this advice or let it alone; only when I will have stated all—I do not believe that either our respected Brother Hurrychund Chintamon or yourself will find reasons to object to it.

In the first place you are a member of the Arya Somaja—ain't you? You are the pupil and disciple of the most venerated Pandita Dyanand S. Swamee? And in these two capacities is it not your right duty regardless of every selfish end or object to *"exert yourself for the prosperity of the Society with more zeal than what you would apply for the rise of your own family"* (Art. 9. of the Rules)—and— *"do your utmost to defend the rights and elevate the position of the Arya Somaja . . . . even at the expense of your own pocket & life"* (art. 25.)

Either the "Rules" of the Somaja mean what they say and have to be enforced, or they are simply a moonshine.

Now, let us see the position in which you place the Arya Somaja,—you one of its prominent and most promising members on account of your relations to the revered Swamee—if you accept this most *infamous* and most *impudent* proposal of Monier Williams.

To begin with, and from the simple stand-point of logic and legality, Monier Williams' written document is not worth a rotten penny in the eyes of the law. Everything thing [sic] therein concerning your pay and his (the Professor's) obligations of payment is conditional. You have to sacrifice to him three years of your young life—the best years, "help him in preparing for him his books for publication"—in other words to *edit* them for him—and "in teaching," and not only has he the impudence to offer you a salary, which for its paltriness I would blush to offer to my servant or cook, but he reserves himself every right before the law to either pay you *or not* as he chooses!! For what can the man mean by the following words: "No money can be given *unless Mr Shyamajee is punctual, diligent and efficient in his duties*"—if not that he reserves himself

456

every legal right at his own option to either pay you like a menial or kick you out without pay after three years labor and loss of time!

This is positively *infamous* on his part, he is no gentleman but an arrogant, conceited ass, stewed up in his own vanity, and soaking through all his pores—British arrogance. I know England, and I know Oxford; my nephew was there for two years and I know that no young man can live there, have a room, board, pay for his washing etc for £1.-5s. a week, unless he lives in a garret and eats salt herrings with Irish potatoes. And what would become of the respect due to our Somaja if people in England knew that the favourite pupil of the revered founder of the Arya Somaja, was serving in that capacity a professor, who does not even belong to the first class scientists? I have read his latest work—it is a scientific trash calculated only to mislead the reader as to the religions of India. It was torn to pieces here by Professor Whitney, the first Sanskrit scholar in America and holding a high position at the Yale University.

Objection Nᵘ 2.—Mon. Williams though not on the best terms with Max Müller and other Orientalists of the same school, yet belongs to it—i.e. he takes the same views of the Vedas as given by that school which has shaped them entirely on the Commentaries of Sayana Mahidhar which our Swamee finds spurious. Very soon, when Veda Bashya[1] will be read and criticized by English Orientalists such as Max Müller, a storm will be raised in England and Europe generally against Pandita Dyananda Saraswati, which will prove a little more dangerous than the childish criticisms of the Pandits of High Schools and Oriental Colleges in India. The native Pandits object to the Swamee's interpretations of the Vedas only in fear for their bread and butter; they are soap-bubbles and must burst through their own emptiness. But the war declared to Veda Bashya by the European scholars—so called—involves something more serious. It involves their authority as Scientists and threatens to turn the tables of ridicule on these conceited donkeys who pasture on fields of fiction. I tell you there will be a general crusade against the Bashya, for Scientists are no less intolerant and dogmatic than their lying clergy, and will maintain a lie if it involves their interest to their last breath. There never was yet either a religious reformer or a Scientific discoverer of some new truth which upset an earlier doctrine, but that had to become a martyr. And will you, the pupil of your venerated master stand by and endorse views of the Vedas totally opposite to those which were taught to you by our Swamee, or—which is worse yet—silently stand by and hear him criticized and abused? And *you will have to do* it, unless you risk to give M: Williams a good opportunity for cheating you out of your money, and to his pupils another one for turning their backs on you and becoming your enemies. I do not and *cannot* believe it, for if it were so, you would be worthy neither of the Arya Somaja nor of our Swamee's affection. Believe me, my dear young Brother, believe the words of an old woman who knows the world in general and Scientists in particular, and whose whole life was one constant battle against LIE in every form and shape. I do take an interest in your welfare; *first*, because you have lived and studied with one who has my utmost respect and veneration; *secondly* because you belong to the Arya-Somaja; and *thirdly* because you are not only a Hindu by birth but one of the most promising intellects of your country, one, in short, who can become in time one of the Saviours and defenders of his country which needs all her best children to defend her rights crushed and paraly[s]ed by a selfish, heartless nation. Do not think, that I preach revolution and rebellion. Far from it, for no one is more against physical strife in this case than I am. It is by intellectual and mental *Force* that the children of India have to assert their hereditary rights. It is by showing to the world at large and to their enslavers in particular that intellectually they are their equals and in many cases their superiors. And is it by serving a Monier Williams, an arrogant, conceited donkey and by yielding to his views that you will serve the Cause of Truth and your Holy Country? You say yourself that even in India where mental as well as physical labor are so cheap you got £4. a month by teaching. And would you accept for £1 or more such a physical and mental slavery beyond the seas, in a country where people will look at you as if you were a being inferior to them—a slave? Where Christian hypocrites and lying missionaries will be buzzing around you, calling you a "heathen" to your face, belittling the religion of your fathers and insulting you by seeking to make of you a renegade to your country, a convert to Christianity? No, no! Whatever you do, do not place yourself in such a *dependent* position. If you believe that you cannot improve your prospects otherwise than by going either to Europe or America (though my ideas are perfectly opposite to your's in this direction) then go to one of these countries as an *independent* man, your own master. Have patience. A branch of the Theos. Society has just been established in London, and its *President* is Mr C. Carleton Massey, a distinguished barrister at law, a man of means and the son of a member of Parliament, an ex-Financial Minister of India. He is an honest good man, and a *gentleman* to the tip of his fingers; he is my greatest personal friend moreover,—Brother Hurrychund will tell it to you for he knows it. I will write to him and see what he can do for you. He desires to belong to the Arya Somaja and his whole aspirations are to get in communication with the ascetics and holy men of India. He is a Spiritualist—for hitherto he had no better explanation of the phenomena produced through "mediums" than the one given by those invisible intelligences, to viz: that they were the Sp[irits][2] of disembodied men

and women. He needs t[he] advice on the subject of some
learned holy man like our Swamee. I, n[ow] am bound by
my vows and cannot teach him that whic[h] I have learned
in India and elsewhere; but I know that Pandit Dyn. Saraswati *could* if he only had a mind [to.] A "strange coincidence, you say? You find it "remarkable" t[hat] our T. S.
was founded in New York in the same year as your Bombay
Arya Somaja? I—do not. For, I have received a letter from
India in July 1875 with ORDERS to found our Socie[ty.] I
chose Col. Olcott—according to the same orders and he
established the Society. That's all what *he* knows about
that; and I have no right to say more. Ask our Swamee
about that; may be that he can tell you something more,
though it is but a guess of mine. Do you think Our venerated Master, will tell you or any one else *all* that he knows?
I *guess* not—as the Yankees say. I do not believe in blind
chance nor in "coincidences" either. I believe in an *intelligent* Fate, in the Law of Compensation & Retribution,
though, as I said before to our Brother Hurrychund I do
not believe in the Christian "special Providence" as I reject
their Jewish Jehovah—a fickle, [cr]uel, unjust and half-
crazy demon, good only for such pariahs [as] the Jews, [the]
ancient *Chandalas* & brick-makers of old Ary[an] India.

I will also write about you to Professor Whitney of the
Harvard [U]niversity. America is another kind of place than
Engla[nd.] [I]n America every one—even a beggar—is on the
same [lev]el with the President of the U.S. and if the latter
offends the [for]mer, he has the right to either thrash him
or drag him before [*several words missing*]. May be Whitney
will want your services to help him teaching the Sanskrit.
In a fortnight or a month—at the latest I will be able to give
you some news. Only have patience. Why, we are coming to
Bombay and we will be at least five of us if not more. And
between us all I do hope that we will be able to do some-

thing for you either in Bombay or England.

Excuse my free talking—but I am accustomed to always say to people what I think. I hope I will hear from you. Please give my most humble and sincere respect and the expression of my greatest devotion to our revered Swamee. Tell him that I am his slave to the end of my life, and that he can dispose of me as he likes, for the promotion of our Holy Cause.

believe me, meanwhile

Your's sincerely and fraternally

H P Blavatsky

NOTES:

1. The *Veda Bhāshya* is Dayanand Saraswati's commentary on the Vedas, for which he tried unsuccessfully to secure both government subsidy for publication and adoption as a text in Indian schools.

2. The paper on which the letter is written has suffered several tears, notably on the upper right side and the lower left corner. When the missing text can be reasonably inferred, it is put in square brackets; otherwise the fact of the missing text is similarly noted.

SOURCE: Transcribed from the original in the Archives of the Theosophical Society, Adyar.

Letter 125

To H. Chintamon   *August 21, 1878*

"Will you permit me, this [?] to the most *devoted* friend you have in this hemisphere to speak with you openly? I want you to keep this letter secret from every one. . . . I do feel as if I were morally obliged to tell you what *I know* to be the best course for us to persue [(sic)]¹ Well, I believe you will take an imprudent step if you write to Massey what you have written to me, namely: that though you admitted the phenomena produced by the Hindoo Sanayâsi & fakirs to be a fact, yet—how they were produced was "a mystery" to you. Brother Massey is an uncompromising, devoted *Spiritualist*. He imagines that every one must believe in *bhoots* [ghosts] as he does, otherwise, he takes the skeptics for materialists and—drops them. We will never reach our object with him to viz: to make him join the Arya Somáj and make others join it unless he believes that the Aryan philosophy can teach him more than his Spiritual phenomena about the powers hidden in the *inner* man. Mind you, I do not ask you to go and speak to him of what you do not know, or assume a false appearance with him. But there is a way to avoid his questions—which he is sure to offer you—by answering him that you do not feel ready yet to answer them, and that he must first become a member of your society before he has a right to receive instructions'. . . . (2/3 of page omitted here) I believe that a bit of cautious diplomacy is no sin nor lie either. If you tell him at once that you are neither a spiritualist nor do you know anything of *bhoots* he will take you to be a materialistic sceptic. And if, without precising to him what you do, or do not believe and know, you left him *in the dark* as to your knowledge then we may hope—in good time to draw to our Arya Somaj several thousands of Spiritualists why . . .

I do not know what you have written to him but he writes to ask me particulars about you; who you are besides being Pres^t of the Arya Somaj of Bombay; whether you are an "*adept* in occult lore", whether you can produce phenomena etc. etc. I answer him that I do not know whether you are an *adept*, nor do I know whether you can or cannot perform miracles, *à la* fakeer. But that . . . being the President of the Arya Somaj you must be certainly in communication with those ascetics who could teach him (Massey) certain religious philosophy and etc In short, I tell him that it is not the Arya Somaj—if he becomes its member—that can lead him to the *truth* he is searching for;

that the A.S. is the first step toward true knowledge and that his only chances of becoming in his old age an ascetic with psychological powers is to begin to study the Vedas etc—[Then she goes on to hint at the Mahatmas etc for Chintamon's benefit][2] . . . But as you seem to know little yourself of this *occult* philosophy of your country, then, if Massey puts to you direct questions, as to what is the Arya Somaj, answer him that exoterically it is but what its 'Rules' show it to be, and that you have no right to speak of other matters with outsiders. To learn more, let him join the A.S. put himself in direct communication with our Swamee, etc or with those holy men of India etc . . . who can produce at will . . . phenomena. . . . Say what you like, only do not confess to him your ignorance of how such phenomena take place. . . .

And now, another thing. Do, make them feel that the Arya Somaj is no easy thing to reach. They must not hold it so cheap as that. They must respect and run after you, not you after them. Please do not put yourself in your great kindness on *a level* with them. Otherwise the best of them would immediately begin to *patronize* you. I know this arrogant, haughty set called the English better than you do perhaps. We must force them to respect the Arya S. whether they join it or not, and you the President of the Bombay A.S. In my letters to you I have been placing you on an immeasurable distance above them—so do not contradict me and destroy what I have done by writing to them *friendly* letters. If you do, then you will be working against myself as much as against the Arya Somaj which I seek to glorify by every available means (soon will appear in the French press at Paris an article of mine on the Arya Somaj) I want to place our Somaj and its venerated founder on an eminance that would force the Europeans to crawl on their knees to get at one of them. Will you help me? Will you work with me not against me? I may be—and no doubt

I am—capricious, passionate and self-willed, it is the evil effect of the education I have received from the proudest and haughtiest of parents—but all these vices appear but in private life. Believe me, they all disappear whenever serious work is to be done. . . . Thus I have the power in me to *psychologize* whole crowds, and make them do as I wish, the Theosophical Society is a good proof. I do not boast when I say that I never found *my master* yet, among the Europeans or Americans, and I have never failed in what I have once seriously undertaken. Only I repeat it, *you must help* me.

NOTES:

1. Brackets in the manuscript copy.

2. Brackets in the manuscript copy.

SOURCE: Original unavailable. Transcribed from a copy now in the Archives of the Society for Psychical Research in Cambridge University Library. The copy, of poor legibility, was made presumably by Eleanor Sidgwick, who freely abbreviated and paraphrased the material she copied (see background essay L).

⟡

Letter 126

To C. R. Corson

August 28, 1878
302 West 47th Street
New York

Dear Madame Corson,

You were right in following your good inspiration to take up your pen and write me. Having always had more enemies than friends, your silence, sudden and without any apparent reason, did not surprise me although—it really grieved me. But, let us say no more about that; you had your reasons, and that is enough for me. On the other hand, I am delighted to learn the cause for the break which I so little expected; I had attributed it to an entirely different reason, and like a cat that always feels guilty after having stolen a piece of meat, I had thought that through someone in Philadelphia you had learned the truth concerning the mystification which we had amused ourselves with for three months: I am referring to the marriage advised by the "spirits" between myself and that imbecile who was twenty years younger than me. To make fun of the Spiritualists, of the spirits and especially of my *ex*-friend, Mrs Louisa Andrews—who as soon as I informed her of my *alleged intention*, started writing me letters full of jealousy,— I communicated that news *as a secret* to several of my friends, making them believe that all was *consumatum*[1] and that I was *married*. It was stupid of me, and I have repented of it quite often; for it gave rise to evil talk, especially as this gentleman, no sooner had I left you at Ithaca, publicly married a Miss Allan.[2] I hope that I did not lie to you too much, during my stay with you? I remember, that immediately on returning to New York, I intended to write you that it was only a bad joke. But—you did not give me any time to do so. I pray you, dear Madame Corson, don't talk about it to anybody any more; everybody has forgotten it, and I am positively *ashamed* to have lent myself to that comedy, which, according to the laws of N. Y. and of Philadelphia could have resulted in unfavorable consequences for me, because there were many people who took it seriously.

I am sending you the letter that you asked of me for Mr Aksakof; and, I am going to write him another from here. I will do everything in my power, but, I do fear that [because of] the state of Russian finances at the moment, after this war and the pockets that have been forcibly emptied, the moment may be ill chosen. But—who knows? Maybe you will have luck after all. Write to Mr Aksakof everything you have written to me; he knows everybody and it may be that he can find you a good place. I am purposely writing to him on *theosophical* letterhead, for, as a member of the T.S.

he will feel himself *obliged* to do everything he can. It is one of the rules of our Society to help each other mutually and always work for one another. Our Society has grown, dear Madame, and from a child malformed and hooted at by everybody, it has developed into a giant that counts its members by the thousands, and has recently *affiliated* itself with the greatest Esoteric Fraternity of India—the Arya-Samaj. We have Hindu members, now, by the thousands; and our supreme chief, Swâmi (Saint, he who performs "miracles") Dayanand Sarasvati, the greatest *scholar* of India, the most distinguished orator who captivates all those who hear him preach—orders us to come to India. There are already two million Arya-Samajees in India, and new members are recuited every day. Apart from psychological science and the study of occult sciences our Society, whose object is to establish a "Fraternity of Humanity," is also a reformist society. We go dead against *idolatry* in every shape & color, whether in the heathen or Christian religion; for, let's see dear friend, you will admit that the male and female Saints of the Greek and Latin churches are just as much idols as those of the Hindu Pantheon? Our Arya Samaj is a reformist society, and the newspapers call our Chief the "Luther of India." And, I bet that "my wife's sister's niece's child"[3] would give a lot to witness the marvelous phenomena that our Hindu "brothers" produce at will, without laying them either on the back of the "Spirits" or on that of the Good Lord, for our philosophy rejects any "miracle" and does not believe in anything *supernatural*. Have you read or seen my book? I wanted to send you a copy when the first edition came out last October, but I was afraid you might send it back to me. The first edition[4] (1000 copies) was sold in *nine* days, and the two others were exhausted long ago. My publisher—Bouton, is having a fourth edition printed in October. The English newspapers have lauded it even more than the American critics, and there has been only the "Sun" alone that has torn my work to pieces before even reading it, that has knocked it. The "Herald" gave the most flattering notice. Well—I don't give a damn! I'm off to India and—three cheers for the "Heathen Hindoos!!"

It is likely that we will not see each other ever again, but, believe that the affectionate friendship I have always had for you, and my esteem for Mad. C. R. Corson will never weaken. If your "Wife's sister's niece's child" has nothing against me any more (??) tell him that I embrace him. If not, and if he still has something against me tell him I do not embrace him, but that I will always love him.

It is a pity that I didn't know your son was in Vienna. Two of my aunts,—Madame Witte and Fadeyev, my sister, Mme Bieloy[5] and two of my cousins have been there since spring. Now they have all gone to Karlsbad.

Your son would have found them to be agreeable company. They all speak English and French.

And now goodbye, dear Madame Corson; believe me, my most sincere wish is to see you happy and content, for you have well deserved it.

Yours with all my heart,
H. P. Blavatsky.

NOTES:

1. Consummatum "completed." The term is most familiar from Jesus' last words on the cross (John 19.30), "Consummatum est" (It is finished). The allusion to HPB's short-lived marriage is ironic.

2. An unidentified person. If the "imbecile who was twenty years younger than me" was Betanelly, he married HPB on April 3, 1875, and they were divorced on May 25, 1878. HPB visited the Corsons between approximately September 17 and October 12, 1875. The surviving correspondence between HPB and Mrs. Corson before this letter was that of March 12, 1876, nearly two and a half years earlier.

3. This catchphrase, first introduced in letter 57, is explained in note 1 to that letter. Here it is used as a byname for Hiram Corson.

4. That is, "printing," and so subsequently. A new edition is properly a reprinting with significant changes.

5. Presumably Elizabeth Petrovna Beliy, HPB's half sister.

SOURCE: Translated partly from a photocopy of the French original in the HPB Library and partly from the text in *Unpublished Letters*. Published in Corson, *Unpublished Letters* 195–8 (French original) and 199–202 (English translation).

Letter 127

To A. N. Aksakoff   *August 28, 1878*

M. Alexander N. Aksakof,
6, Nevsky Prospect,
Saint Petersburg.

Highly Respected Alexander Nikolayevich,

Permit me to introduce to you Madame C. Corson—wife of Mr Hiram Corson, Professor at Cornell University in Ithaca, N.Y. (U.S. of America)—in Heidelberg, both, at the moment; and to whom, according to her wish, I am sending this letter—to do with as she pleases.

Apart from the honor that she does me in calling me one of her friends, Madame C. R. Corson—according to the unanimous opinion of all those who know her—is a lady whose sound and brilliant education, her goodness of heart and her irreproachable character make her loved and respected by all who come in contact with her. You will remember, perhaps, that some three or more years ago I wrote you several letters from Ithaca and, from the very house of Madame and Mr Corson. Both of them and for several weeks, extended to me one of those open, cordial, and most kindly welcomes, which I do not easily forget; all the more so, since my *inextinguishable* cigarette, and my manners of a Prussian grenadier on furlough leave me generally, very little hope of often receiving anything like it.

Madame Corson, will herself explain to you—and better than I, what she wishes. For my part, my role must be limited to recommending her to you as warmly as possible. I am happy to seize this opportunity of rendering her a small service, if only to prove once more, that ingratitude has never been among the vices with which public and such very Christian charitableness adorns me so abundantly and with a generosity of the rarest kind.

On that note, dear Mr. Aksakof,

Please believe in this expression of the most sincere and affectionate esteem of your correspondent

H P Blavatsky

(who begs you to remember that it will soon be four months, since she has received a word from you)

SOURCE: Translated from a photocopy of the French original in the HPB Library. Published in Corson, *Unpublished Letters* 203–4 (French original) and 204–5 (English translation).

⌒

Introduction to Letter 128

On October 13, 1878, the *New York Sun* printed two articles that elicited a letter from HPB. The first article (on page 4), which was also the primary motive for her reply, editorialized about Christian missionaries in the East and superciliously about the prospective trip of HPB and Olcott to India, treating the latter as a reverse mission to reinforce the "heathen" and propagate Brahmanism in the West:

A Mission Against Christianity.

For hundreds of years the Occidental World has been unceasing in its efforts to convert the heathens of the East to the Christian faith. Millions of treasures and thousands of lives have been expended in this propagandism, and in

spite of much that is discouraging in the past and comparatively little that is hopeful in the present, all the different
branches and sects of the Christian Church, with insignificant exceptions, are to-day as zealous as ever in the work of
heathen conversion.

No religious contributions are more regular and very few
are larger than those collected to pay the cost of carrying the
Gospel to heathen lands. Christian missionaries are scattered
throughout the East, the Bible has been translated into nearly all the tongues of the world, the prayers of myriads of the
faithful ascend to heaven for the success of the efforts at heathen evangelization, and the theological seminaries have constantly in training recruits for the foreign missionary field.

Doubtless progress has been made in the work since the
Church first undertook the tremendous task of converting
the heathens. The reports of the foreign missionary societies
present encouraging facts and stimulate the religious to further self-sacrifices, to the end that the ancient faiths of the
East may be broken down and the purer truths of Christianity substituted for them. But it cannot be denied that so far
not even the outworks of heathendom have been taken by
the army of Christian missionaries which has steadily assailed
them from the early days of the Church up to the present
moment. In the Indies Brahmanism still has more followers
than Christianity, and the Oriental mind turns away from
the religious teachings of the West.

Our missionaries to India, China, and Japan do not go to
rude and unlettered peoples, like the Fiji Islanders, or the
African savages, or the Sandwich Islanders, as they were a
hundred years ago, but to races who have a developed creed
and who can give a reason for it, a creed which has many
learned expounders and deft logicians to defend it. They are,
therefore, unless they are very clever men, sometimes actually beaten in the argument with the heathens they set out to
convert, and are driven to their wits' ends to save themselves
from appearing to need conversion to Brahmanism, instead
of having a superior religion of their own to offer. It is very
great folly to send a dull and stupid man, a minister who is

not bright enough to get on at home, to convert the Oriental heathens. They are pretty sure to be too sharp for him.

Our missionaries, no matter how learned and how devoted, suffer under many disadvantages in trying to propagate Christianity in the East. It is up-hill work with them from the start and all through. They must be content with accomplishing comparatively little, and yet keep alive the zeal of the faithful, who send them out in ignorance of the difficulties of the task of supplanting a faith so old, and so deeply rooted as that of Brahmanism.

But hard as the work now is, and expensive as it has always been, it seems it is hereafter to be made more arduous and more costly. The heathens are about to gain recruits from the West, who, instead of conducting a defensive warfare, will at once throw their columns against the walls of Christianity itself! We are informed that Hierophant OLCOTT and Mme. BLAVATSKY, the Theosophists, are now packing their trunks preparatory to a pilgrimage to India, there to challenge the Christian missionaries to debate the respective merits of Brahmanism and Christianity!

The intelligence is the more startling because the Hierophant has lately been received into the Brahmanical sect, and is now Pandit of New York, and Madame BLAVATSKY, who has long been known as an out-and-out Brahmanist, with a contemptuous opinion of Christianity, has set her heart on overthrowing the Bible and substituting the Vedas in the United States. The Pandit OLCOTT has all the fire and zeal of a new convert, and Mme. BLAVATSKY's mind is an arsenal of arguments which can be used against our religion. Their plan of operations is a bold one. Their intention, evidently, is first to meet and conquer the missionaries in the home of the ancient faith to which they have been converted, and then, flushed with victory, to plant the standard of Brahmanism in America, and go forth exhorting the people to return to the old Aryan religion, with its mystical doctrines of metempsychosis and the rest and peace of annihilation.

This is a plan of assault not contemplated by our foreign missionary societies. They have been wont to regard the

Brahmanical as a quiescent faith, against which they could bring to bear the forces of Christianity—a faith on the defensive merely. But now, inspired by the zeal of Hierophant OLCOTT, the Pandit, and Mme. BLAVATSKY, the seeress, the Brahmans are about to begin an aggressive warfare against Christianity, and establish a propaganda of their own in the West to offset that which has been so long carried on by Christians in the East.

We are not informed as to the exact plan of campaign of the Pandit, nor do we know the means he intends to use to get the missionaries into a defensive position; but both he and Mme. BLAVATSKY are full of resources, and we doubt not they have carefully considered their strategy. Nor do we hear from India that there is yet any great excitement among the Brahmans over the prospect of their arrival. They ought to be received with great pomp, however, for they are the first allies the United States have sent out to the heathens, and Hierophant OLCOTT is the first and only American Pandit. It would be a pity if both he and Mme. BLAVATSKY should land in India to be received without honor, and nothing would give them such a start as a rousing ovation at Calcutta and throughout Hindostan. The Pandit will probably early make a trip to the furthest fastnesses of the Himalayas, where, he says, the only true and ancient doctrines are kept locked up, and perhaps spend a year or two in mastering them ere he sets out on his campaign against the missionaries. We certainly advise him to do that, for the work he has taken in hand is great, and no man can find out all about the ancient Aryan faith in a day.

As to the Christian missionaries, we advise them to let the Pandit alone and to avoid all argument with Mme. BLAVATSKY. Hierophant OLCOTT is one of those men who enjoy an argument, but let the missionaries leave him to debate with the Brahmans, who know very well how to chop logic, and who can teach him many things about his new religion of which he is now as ignorant as of the history of the Aryan race. And as for Mme. BLAVATSKY, why never dispute with a lady.

We trust the Pandit will keep us advised as to the progress of his warfare against the missionaries, and let us know in due time when he proposes to begin operations at home, so that we shall be prepared to report his discourses with the necessary learning and eloquence.

The second article (on page 6) dealt with a prospective conference on the second coming of Christ, followed by what is sometimes called the "Rapture," the "Great Tribulation," and eventually the Final Judgment. The article included an extensive interview with one of the organizers of the conference, the Rev. Dr. Stephen H. Tyng, Jr., an Episcopalian clergyman of New York City. HPB cites this second article to show that the views of "heathen" Buddhists and Brahmins are no stranger than those of some mainline Christians who interpret their scriptures literally and probably to call attention to the fact that the *Sun* reported the literalist views without the superciliousness of tone used in commenting upon the Theosophists.

HPB's letter to the editor is headlined:

MME. BLAVATSKY'S INTENTIONS.

She is Not Packing her Trunk to Quit these Shores, but Wishes that she Was.

Letter 128

To the editor of the New York Sun

October 13, 1878
New York

TO THE EDITOR OF THE SUN—*Sir:* You really do me too much honor. The idea that my humble and tongue-splitting name is just now being laboriously spelt out by the 800,000 readers of THE SUN at the risk of their getting the lockjaw, is alone overwhelming. Your editorial of Sunday, Oct. 13, using up a whole column to tell the public what we may perhaps do (though we have no idea of doing it), and the interesting interview of THE SUN's reporter with Dr. Tyng were respectfully read. Both, viewed together, suggest a train of thought which I crave permission to lay before you, hoping that a few rays of THE SUN may perchance penetrate my beclouded intellect. We all know that its fiery darts sometimes scorch, and yet, since it opens its columns to every bereaved one, whether in love or politics, who seeks advice from its wisdom, it will surely not refuse to enlighten a foreigner, however benighted, who only seeks for truth. I, for one, notwithstanding the SUN-strokes I have often received, still place the fullest confidence in its ability to satisfactorily settle all questions of a delicate character. And if, adding kindness to generosity, THE SUN will permit me, previously to propounding my main question, to correct a few errors in its editorial, it will have earned my eternal gratitude.

I read that "Mme. Blavatsky has long been known as an out-and-out Brahmanist." I thought THE SUN had repeatedly stated last year that I was an out-and-out Buddhist. Moreover, at a discreet, yet not a very great distance from the editorial which gives the world this new version, I find Col. Olcott's modest card,[1] which states explicitly that, together with the Arya-Samaj in India, we are "engaged in a warfare against idolatrous Brahmanism." This would appear to conflict somewhat with the above statement.

We hear that we are "packing up our trunks." I wish sincerely we were; but we are not. America, my adopted country, will have to bear with me a little longer. And, intense as may be Col. Olcott's aversion to idolatry, whether monotheistic or polytheistic, yet I doubt whether he is fully prepared to pass the rest of his natural life in the unprofitable occupation of sitting perched upon a pillar, and—fakir or Simon Stylites like, with his gaze concentrated upon the tip of his nose—ponder on the eternal unfitness of things. The Colonel is out of town, therefore I speak but for myself, and must strongly protest against the chronic habit the papers have of constantly hitching our two names together, like a runaway team bound on a race of destruction.

I have already declared that I am neither Brahmanist nor Buddhist in the accepted or orthodox sense. But supposing I were? Surely, I might claim the same right to expect the personal advent of either Maitree-Buddha, or that of Vishnu, the Hindoo Saviour, who, at the Kalki-Avator, descending from his eternal abode in Swarga, will come again to judge the wicked, and, catching the righteous, take them bodily with him to heaven, as Dr. Tyng has to expect the "Second Coming of Christ?" Difference of opinion with regard to names or minor details does not necessarily make of one a glorified saint and of the other a doomed demon. If your most scholarly and fashionable clergymen are allowed to believe, unmolested and secure from criticism, in the second advent of Christ in body and as he was when in life, why should not Brahmanists and Buddhists be entitled to the same privilege of belief in their respective Saviours in this free country—if this be a free country? If the antiquity of this doctrine, "as old as the Church," is quoted as any proof of its authenticity, how much stronger must be the inherent truth of the same doctrine as held by Buddhists and Brahminists, the former alone numbering over 400,000,000, and which belief, as we all know, antedates Christianity by many centuries. The sincerity of their faith is shown in the remark made in the editorial in question, when it says that it was "an up-hill work" with the missionaries to convert the heathen, "from the start and all through." I sincerely hope that it will prove the more so hereafter. Better leave the "heathen," with their horror of shedding the blood even of an insect, than to convert them to a faith which does not prevent Christian Americans from cutting daily the throats of their neighbors—including their own fathers, mothers, and wives—and employ the millions thrown on the profitless missionary work in converting the pagans of this republic to a more worthy life.

Dr. Tyng asserts "that the Lord will come visibly;" that "he may not come on earth, but he will be visible to his people." In these days of improved telescopes, we would not wonder if he were. Disagreeing with most of the ideas enunciated by the reverend gentleman during his interview with THE SUN's reporter, I yet welcome some of his thoughts most enthusiastically. I was especially delighted to learn that after the resurrection of the dead "those of the children of Christ who are alive will be caught up into the clouds . . . their bodies will change, and they will dwell in heavenly places." It was very reassuring, also, to find that "their disappearance will not affect society;" and, though surprised, we heartily agree with the reverend Doctor when he expressed a hope that "there won't be many preachers left in the pulpit." Amen! Godspeed to him and all others.

Perhaps it would be asking too much were I to desire THE SUN to shed a little light upon the following question: Can it show us in what respect the expected advents of Maitree-Buddha and Vishnu may differ in scientific and philosophical points from those of the second coming of Christ? Or, would THE SUN prefer to leave the solution of this question to spiritualistic papers?

H. P. Blavatsky

NOTE:

1. In America the term *card* developed an extended meaning as early as 1769: "a short advertisement of one's business, or a personal statement of any kind, in a newspaper or other periodical" (*Century Dictionary, Dictionary of Americanisms*). That is the sense here.

SOURCE: Copied from the *New York Sun*, Oct. 18, 1878, 2. Published in *Canadian Theosophist* 71 (Jan.-Feb. 1991): 135–7.

⌒

Introduction to Letter 129

The *New York Sun*, continuing its commentary on HPB and Olcott and their Eastern associations, on October 25, 1878, printed an editorial (on page 2), quoting a critical comment about the Arya Samaj from the London *Pall Mall Gazette*:

The *Pall Mall Gazette*, speaking of the various religious sects among the Hindoo population of India, says:

"Now JUGGERNAUT is at a discount. We have a new religion which has just been evolved from the consciousness of some dwellers in Bombay and at Amritsir. This is termed the Arya Somaj. Few Hindoos as yet appear to have joined the standard of the Arya Somaj."

It has recently been announced by Col. OLCOTT, the deeply initiated Hierophant of the Theosophical Society, that an American branch of the Arya Samaja has been established in this city, he himself being its chief. Col. OLCOTT is a very earnest man. We have no doubt that he is sincere in his belief that this new religiosophic organization, which, judging from the *Pall Mall Gazette's* account, is making less headway in Bombay than in the Eighth avenue, aims at the restoration of the pure theism of the primitive Aryans and the abolition of corrupt practices introduced by a sensual priesthood. Is it possible that Col. OLCOTT has been imposed on? The *Pall Mall Gazette*, which is usually well informed upon Oriental matters, goes on to say of the Arya Somaj:

"Its tenets comprise a revival of most of the 'fair humanities of old religion' which are associated with some of the mysterious rites of which the trustees of the British Museum prudently keep the memorials in a cellar."

This hints strongly at something in the practices of the Bombay brethren of Hierophant OLCOTT's new sect, not exactly suitable for family reading. What does it all mean? Hierophant OLCOTT's charter comes from the Swamee DYA NAUD, chief of the Bombay society. Hierophant OLCOTT says that the Swamee DYA NAUD is "one of the profoundest scholars and saintliest characters of our epoch." Can it be that the Swamee is not really a saintly character but is a bad and crafty Hindoo, who has deluded the Hierophant into rendering allegiance to an organization which all respectable citizens ought to keep clear of? Or are there two societies of the same name in Bombay, one saintly and pure in its aims and the other just the reverse?

The *Sun* editorial elicited the following letter from HPB to the newspaper's editor, whom she had already met through his connection with H. S. Olcott and his interest in investigating the paranormal:

Letter 129

To E. P. Mitchell   *October 25, 1878*
                                                    302 West 47th Street

My dear Sir:

I hope that *The Sun* will prove just and fair in every case and will give even the Devil his due. Once that you have quoted from and commented upon the disgusting, infamously lying paragraph published against the Arya Somaj in the *Pall Mall Gazette* of October 9 I would humbly advise you to turn to the number of the same paper of the 11th instant and find therein an answer to the sensation or rather to the cowardly insinuation.[1] This answer was sent in by one of our English Theosophists who, as you will see, proclaims his allegiance to the Arya Somaj publicly. . . . The writer of the first paragraph (October 8th) is an old member of the Society of Jesus who got into our brotherhood by cunning and craft and now turns a traitor as every Jesuit is bound to be, and he who answers is a well known barrister in London, the son of a member of Parliament and highly respected in the best circles of English society.

If you want a *sensation*, better ask Olcott to come and see you. There's a grand conspiracy against us. . . . You will find Jesuits trying to pull down Arya Somaj, theosophy and all, and getting knocked on their heads for the trouble. An ex-Jesuit, pretending to have been excommunicated, gets inside our fold, betrays us, is ignominiously turned out by our Council and now swears *revenge*. I have his letter. But he will lose his time for nothing. The Arya Somaj *is not a secret body*. You may read what it is in the *Nineteenth Century*[2] of September last—an article by Professor Monier-Williams, who knows our Swamee Dya Saraswati *personally* and can tell the world—bigoted Christian as he is—whether the Arya Somaj is not the noblest Society in the world.

At all events, remember, dear Sir, that the Theos. Soc. has spread itself over the whole globe; that we have thousands of members in America and Europe, and over one million in India who belong both to the A.S. and the Theos. Soc.; that it includes the highest personages among its members—aye, some of them closely connected with Royal and Imperial families; that it is a purely religious and reformatory society having nothing to do with the politics whatever; and as such having naught to fear from the Indian Govt. or the whole Scotland Yard. And above all know, my dear Mr. Mitchell, and bear in mind that however ridiculed, tabooed, slandered and persecuted—every true theosophist is ready to lay down his very life for the Arya Somaj and its chiefs and die a thousand deaths in its defence.

Yours respectfully and truly,
H. P. Blavatsky

NOTES:

1. Michael Gomes points out (*Canadian Theosophist* 71 [Jan.-Feb. 1991]: 138) that in HPB's Scrapbook 8:49, the author of the October 9 *Pall Mall Gazette* article is identified as C. Carter Blake and the author of the October 11 response as C. C. Massey. On the upper right corner of that page of the scrapbook there is a picture of a demonic face labeled "('C. C. Blake's controlling 'guide')," graphically expressing HPB's attitude toward Blake at that time.

2. Michael Gomes reports that this article on the Arya Samaj was published in the September 1878 *Contemporary Review* rather than the *Nineteenth Century*.

SOURCE: Original unavailable. Copied from Mitchell, *Memoirs* 191-2. Published in *Canadian Theosophist* 71 (Jan.-Feb. 1991): 137-8.

~~~~

Letter 130

To Mrs. C. Daniels   *November 28 [1878]*
                                                    New York
                        "Thanksgiving day"—probably to
            the devil? & thanking him for all the evils
            bestowed by him so generously upon America?

My dear "Wide awake",[1]

Allow me to offer you my thanks for various favours received, & also those in prospect. You seem to be determined to take my aged heart by storm. Well—go on.

Mr Hayden will always be welcome. I wish he would come. But I do hope that he will not do as a Mr Evans,[2] of Washington, a newly baked "brother" did last week. Fancy, a man showing after two years of correspondence an intense desire to join the T.S.—Duly elected & *diplomed*. Writes craving permission to come to N.Y & be initiated in the Lamasery. Receives graceful permission thereupon—also warm invitation. Telegraphs that he is coming Monday.— *Re*telegraphs that he is *not* coming Monday but Wednesday. Telegraphs Wed:—"I'm a'coming."—and—does not come. —Writes he is sure to come on Saturday & pass Sunday with us. Friday morning sends a cable despatch. "Cannot come to morrow, will come to night—Friday, by the last train—10 1/2/ Great preparations and a sumptuous banquet spread for the benefit of his hungry guts. 11, 12 o'clock —no Evans. No more of him Saturday morning. Finally a letter from him on Tuesday, in which he pours out a whail of despair! Took train, came in good time to N.Y. went to my house, rung bell for half an hour, got chilly, despairing, rung for the last time, and as the door did not open, went back, i.e., crossed over to New Jersey, slept in an hotel, and taking the noon train went back to Washington without seeing us!!!!!!!

I have met with flapdoodles in my life; never—with one, of such 50 horse power of flapdoodle!

Shin is *not* a Theos: but Shin came here last night, & warmed his shins at the cold stove, & his heart in the depth of my beauteous classical features. Says his article does not interfere with yours. He means to write up a *"cameo"*— (whatever it may mean—) of H. P B. and you crave for a *biography* I understand? Well, & who the devil prevents you writing one? Say, I am born in three different places, at two distinct periods of the last four centuries, from seven mothers and a half of one father. Tell 'em, I am between 273 and 19 years of age, my nose being the most classical feature of my *phrenology;* you may add that the above named *proboscis* having something else to do at the time of my birth, (or rather, "last birth") could not present itself in *propria persona*, but left instead its "visiting card" upon my classical countenance. That, I was reared by the Astrakhan Kalmucks, and benevolently brought up and nursed by camels and the mares of the Prince of these Kalmucks, the Prince Tzereta-Korchay-Tungu Tchichmak-Zuru. That— surprisingly enough, I was born with a cigarette of Turkish tobacco in my mouth, and an emerald ring on my left big toe, a small gooseberry bush, moreover, growing out of my navel. That I was called *Heliona* (not Helen as people call me) a Greek name, derived from that of the Sun—*Helios*— because (1st) there was an eclipse of the luminary on that day, who knew prophetically, we must infer, that it would be eclipsed for long years by the newly born babe, and also (2nd) because of the possibility it gave the clergy

& missionaries of the 19th century to spell it with a double L— (thus—*Hell*iona) and assure the more readily their congregation that I was an imp of Hell.

Now, isn't there facts enough to make Mark Twain himself die of a fit of *cholera morbus* brought on by envy & rage?

Permit me now, lovely "Lucreta" to say to you a few words seriously. Please, let Miss Burr (the Editor's sister)[3] know them.

While our Society received $5 initiation fees & $6 for the yearly pay, we had regular meetings, every month, had a Hall (Mott's Memorial Hall) a library & all the paraphernalia required. But while the "Fellows" residing all over the States, were regularly notified of every meeting, they never attended them and even very few of those who reside in New York. Yet these notifications, stamped letters, stationary etc. cost the T.S. more than the fees could cover. There was a general meeting of the Council a year ago; and it was resolved to suspend general meetings, and for the Council alone to meet, once a week. Three months after that we joined *publicly* our mother Society the Arya Samaj of India & it was resolved that all the initiation fees would go to the A.S. of Bombay as you know. Thus, our Society has no means of its own & depends on the liberality of its Council. For the last year Olcott pays for the stationary himself, and I pay for the postage stamps. And it is a drag on my pocket— I assure you. That's all the secret. Two days before the last ceremony described in the *Sun*[4] (the throwing into the Sea of the Baron's de Palm ashes) one of our Hindoo brothers came over from England, summoned the Council together plan[n]ed the ceremony and performed it on the following night. There were but 21 persons present, mostly those of the Council & the chief officers, not a single *theosophist* was present (of the general crowd of theosophists I mean).

Now, as I am going away in about three weeks (before Christmas surely) and even if Col. Olcott starts but in spring and does not go with me, we are going to have a meeting called before my departure, for we have to elect a new acting President & a Corresp. Secretary. General Abner Doubleday, (of Fort Sumner)⁵ is to be elected. Vice Presᵗˢ are Dʳ Alex. Wilder 565 Orange St. Newark—a great philologist and an archeologist here, & Dʳ J. Weisse, a well known philologist here. (Oh, Paris has applied for membership!!)

We have over a 1000 theosophists scattered in this republic. Don't you know the signs and pass word & grip. Why don't you try it on those you meet, and so find out whether they are "brothers"? I cannot name them all to you.

By the bye Mʳ Hayden has *not* sent his photog. card to us. He must send his portrait. I am going to write to him for it. Olcott is gone to Providence again Maybe he will see him. Remember Mʳ Judge's address. He is the Recording Secretary of the Society & you can learn everything from him. address 71. Broadway. Wᵐ Q. Judge Counselor at Law. I suppose that under the Presidency of General Doubleday there will be meetings held. Anyhow, we have two new branches of our Society established: one in Corfu (Greece) and the other in Constantinople. (Turkey as you have been, doubtless, taught at school) The President of the London Branch is C. *Carleton Massey;*—that of Constantinople, the richest Editor of the country one who has a dozen of papers at least, *Angelo—Nikolaides;* and—that of Corfu is— *Paschale Menelao.* Another branch is now started in Paris. Whom they will elect for Presᵗ I dont know, but Mʳ P. G. Leymarie, Editor of the *Revue Spirite* 5, *Rue des Petits Champs* will always know. So you see, any *Fellow* going abroad, and in whatever direction, will always find "brothers"—*who have to lay down their lives* in case of necessity, for any other *brother,* of whatever race, color, or creed.

Please let this be known to Miss Ellen Burr. I will write to you from India and so give you a chance for more than one startling article.—Mr Hayden too But I *want his portrait* —otherwise he be *"anathama marathon"*!⁶

Miss Bates is gone to London, preceding me like a theosophical *Precursor*, and my four trunks are gone to Liverpool to await for me. So you see, I am ready. If you really want any points for my biography name them plainly. Good bye. your's ever truly

H P Blavatsky

NOTES:

1. Wide Awake, also called "Lucreta" (*i.e.,* Lucretia) later in the letter, is identified by C. Jinarajadasa (*HPB Speaks* 1:109) as Mrs. C. Daniels.

2. Identified by C. Jinarajadasa as presumably Mordecai D. Evans.

3. The editor is Frank L. Burr, editor of the *New York Times*. His sister is F. Ellen Burr.

4. *New York Sun*, November 21, 1878.

5. Fort Sumter.

6. *Anathema maranatha*, "cursed or excommunicated" (1 Cor. 16.22).

DATE: The reference to "going away in about three weeks" and the promise, "I will write to you from India" identifies the year as 1878, when HPB and Olcott boarded a ship in New York harbor to travel to India on December 17, just less than three weeks after the date on this letter. Also, in 1878, November 28 was the last Thursday of the month, Thanksgiving Day.

SOURCE: Transcribed from a xerox of the original in the Manuscript Room of the Archives Department of the Library of Congress, Washington, DC, supplied by the Archives of the Theosophical Society, Pasadena. Published with variations of transcription in *O.E. Library Critic* 27 (July-Aug. 1940): 4–5; *Theosophical Nuggets* 1.6 (Aug. 17, 1940): 1–5; *HPB Speaks* 1:102–9; and *Eclectic Theosophist* No. 78 (Nov.-Dec. 1983): 6–8, with a photostat of the first page of the letter.

Letter 131

To J. D. Buck

November 29, 1878
The Theosophical Society
Mott Memorial Hall
64 Madison Avenue
302 W. 47th St.
New York

J. D. Buck, M. D.

My dear Sir,—your kind favour of Nov. 26th received this morning & I will endeavor to answer your questions at once.

You will find the aims & purposes of the T. S. in the two enclosed circulars. It is a Brotherhood of Humanity, established to make away with all and every dogmatic religion founded on *dead letter* interpretation, and to teach people & every member to believe but in one *Impersonal* god; to rely upon his own (man's) powers; to consider himself his only Saviour; to learn the infinitude of the occult psychological powers hidden within his own *physical* man; to develope these powers, & to give him the assurance of the immortality of his divine Spirit and the survival of his Soul; to make him regard every man, of whatever race, colour or creed (except, if he is a bigoted sectarian) and to prove him that the only truths revealed to man by *superior men* (not a god) are contained in the *Vedas* of the ancient Aryas of India. Finally, to demonstrate to him that there never was, will be, or are any *miracles;* that there can be *nothing* "supernatural" in this universe, and that on earth at least the only god is man himself. It lies within his power to become and continue a god after the death of his physical body. Our Society receives nothing, the possibility of which it cannot demonstrate *at will.* We believe in the phenomena, but we disbelieve in the constant intervention of "Spirits" to produce such phenomena. We maintain that the *embodied* Spirit, has more powers to produce them than a *disembodied* one. We believe in the existence of "Spirits" but of many classes, the human Spirits being but one class of the many, etc.

The Society requires of its members but the time they can give it without encroaching upon that due to their private affairs. There are 3 degrees of membership. It is but in the highest or *third* that members have to devote themselves *quasi* entirely to the work of the T. S. which has joined now the *Arya Samaj* of India, a Society full of adepts.

Every one is eligible, provided he is an honest, pure man or woman, no free-lover and especially—no bigoted Christian. We have over 2,000 members scattered about in the U. S.; and also branch Societies in London, Paris, Berlin, Constantinople, Corfu and Hungary. In India we have over one million of members, as the *Arya Samaj* is our mother Society.

The membership in our Society gives the *Fellow* the right (in the 1st and 2d degrees) to correspond with Hindu adepts of the A.S.; the right to the protection of & help of every brother he may chance to meet, and which he recognizes by certain pass-words, grip & signs. It is as in Free masonry.

We go dead against *idolatry* and as much against materialism. The Xtian clergy are our enemies; therefore, I prefer taking your simple word for your own recommendation than to have anything to do with a *Reverend*.

I am leaving the country before Christmas, for India, where I am called by my chiefs. Should you desire to become a member you have to sign the enclosed application with your name at both places where you find them marked with a cross. If you desire to be initiated by the President, you better come to New York, for a few hours once you receive your diploma. Otherwise, you will have to wait till you do come, & be initiated by W. Q. Judge, 71 Broadway, our Recording Secretary and Counselor of the T. S. If you do not want to join us, then you can send me back the application.

There are no fees to pay, but once; and that is not for our Society, but has to be forwarded after every initiation ($5) to Bombay, India to the Pres^t of the Arya Samaj. The *rules* you will find on the double circular apply only to those theosophists who have joined the Arya Samaj, not to theosophical *Fellows* proper.

I think I have answered every question. If there are any more I am, dear Sir, at your service.

Please excuse this writing. I have badly cut my finger this morning and can hardly hold the pen.

With sincere regard
your's truly,
H. P. Blavatsky

If you want to know more about the *Arya Samaj* of India, get Frank Leslie's *Sunday Magazine* of Dec. 1, 1878, and read article on "The Martin Luther of India" by D. A. Curtis. The picture of the Hindu there is that of our chief Dyanand Saresvata.

SOURCE: Transcribed from the original in the Archives of the Theosophical Society in America, Wheaton, Illinois. Published in *American Theosophist* 44 (Nov. 1956): 214, 229, somewhat abridged.

Letter 132

To F. E. Burr   *December 10, 1878*
302 West 47th Street, New York

My Dear Miss Burr,—friend and "Brother":

Your disappointing letter with no portrait in it, but with a vile dollar, received. Well! this is an idea to send me money for my portrait! The latter you will have as soon as ready. I had one taken yesterday. But your dollar I changed into a silver one and dropped it into the pyramid of the Arya Samaj fund, spoken about in the *Star* article I send you.

Excuse my vile writing. It is always infamous, but to-day particularly so, as everything was sold yesterday at auction, and I am obliged to write my letters on a barrel, sitting on a spittoon, which may be a novel and eccentric way of answering correspondents, but by no means a comfortable one.

'Pon my word, it's a shame that you deprive us of your portrait! Do have one taken; you can do so instantly by having it done in tin-type and sending it to us on the same day. Please do so. Why should you come out bad on them? I will do *anything* for you if you only send it. It's a theosophical duty, you know.

Lo! how the reporters begin pursuing me again now that I am going away! Did you read the article in to-day's *Herald*? What a cut I did receive at the conclusion of it, to be sure! I am not sure that I will be able to survive it.

I have twenty letters to write, and so excuse the briefness of this one. You will receive my mug by Saturday.

Yours fraternally,
H. P. Blavatsky

SOURCE: Original unavailable. Copied by Boris de Zirkoff from an unknown source. HPB mentions her correspondence with Ellen Burr in her diaries (*CW* 1:429).

Introduction to Letter 133

When HPB and Olcott prepared to leave for India, they decided to take with them one of Edison's phonographs with recordings of the voices of American members of the Society for prospective Indian members to hear. Olcott accordingly telegraphed Edison on December 14, 1878, in an effort to bring down the cost of the machine:

If you will waive Royalty Phonograph Company will give at cost an instrument for Bombay Society tomorrow evening at Blavatsky's, Johnson[1] will meet the Theosophists to take voices Send to India. Can he speak for your voice please answer care Bergmann[2] Immediately

H. S. Olcott

[Endorsed by Edison:] Dec 14 78 / Telegram from R S Olcott / Replied "Yes"

NOTES:

1. Edward H. Johnson, a colleague of Edison's whom he sent to represent him at the "voice-receiver" party when the recordings were made (Baldwin 80, 94).

2. Sigmund Bergmann, a colleague of Edison's who leased phonographs in Manhattan (Baldwin 91).

SOURCE: Transcribed from a photographic copy of the original provided by courtesy of the Edison National Historic Site, National Park Service, US Department of the Interior, West Orange, NJ, and its archivist, Leonard DeGraal. Published in *Theosophical History* 7 (1996): 56.

The machine, according to HPB (*CW* 1:430) weighed 100 pounds. She wrote Edison to bid him goodby and to thank him for letting them have the machine at a discounted price:

Letter 133

To T. A. Edison   *December 14, 1878*
                                              New York

Thomas A. Edison, Esq F.T.S.

Dear Sir,

I deeply regret that I shall have to leave America for good, without having seen you. In Hindoo psychology and natural philosophy the laws of force correlation are all explained and I would have been glad to have given you some little glimpse of what lies beyond the threshold of physical science. I have not the slightest doubt, however, but that you will do very well without any body's help. I mention it only, because, you are one of the few scientific experimenters whom we would care to have on our master-roll. We have sent your portrait to our branches at London, Paris, Perth, Constantinople, Corfu, Bombay, etc. as the greatest of American, or rather—world—inventors of the present day.

The Council thanks you for waiving your royalty on the phonograph purchased for the Bombay Branch of the Theosophical Society. Doubtless, this one machine will lead to many orders for duplicates, in which case Col. Olcott will communicate with you from India. Our greatest regret is, that you could not be present at the meeting of to morrow (Sunday) evening to give your voice *personally* to send to India.

By direction of Col. Olcott I enclose blank application, and obligation of secrecy for Mr Griffin,[1] your assistant to sign, if he desires to join us. When signed they may be returned to Mr William Q. Judge 71 Broadway, N.Y. our Recording Secretary who has orders to *initiate* you & Mr Griffin, whenever you can make it convenient. Major General Abner Doubleday U S.A. will be acting President in Col. Olcott's absence from the country and Professor Alex. Wilder M.D. and John A. Weisse M.D. are our Vice-Presidents.

Wishing you prosperity in all your brilliant endeavors.

I am with sincere regard
fraternally your's
H P. Blavatsky.
Corresponding Secretary of
the T. S. of the A. S.

[Edison endorsed the letter]: NY Dec 14 '78 / Madame Blavatsky / No reply

NOTE:

1. Stockton L. Griffin was Edison's secretary (Baldwin 129).

SOURCE: Transcribed from a photographic copy of the original provided by courtesy of the Edison National Historic Site, National Park Service, US Department of the Interior, West Orange, NJ, and its archivist, Leonard DeGraal. Published in *Theosophical History* 7 (1996): 56–7.

On the evening of December 15, the voice recordings were duly made. According to Olcott (*ODL* 1:480-1) and HPB (*CW* 1:430), some two dozen persons were recorded, including themselves, W. Q. Judge, and Alexander Wilder. The phonograph, however, was irretrievably damaged in being shipped to England, where it was replaced by another, presumably smaller and cheaper one. The financial reports of the Society (*Theosophist*, Supplement May 1881, 2:2) record the expenses:

Large phonograph for Society (damaged on voyage and left
    in London); album for Samaj (given to President,
    Bombay Samaj); books, pamphlets, &c. (from Dec.)
    ... Rs. 864
Second phonograph bought in London (15 guineas)
    (January 15, 1879) ... Rs. 188 a. 12
Examination of the first phonograph (January 13, 1879)
    ... Rs. 6

The recordings themselves fared no better. Olcott (*ODL* 1:480) recounts their fate:

... in May, 1895—I sent these tinfoil records to Edison's London office, to see if they might not be received on one of the modern wax cylinders and so saved for posterity. Unfortunately, nothing could be done with them, the indentations made by the voices having become almost flattened out.

⌒

Letter 134

To F. E. Burr   *December 16, 1878*
                                                              New York

My very Dear Friend:

I do hope we will remain friends in correspondence, at least. According to promise, I send you the exact copy of my mug. Please accept this likeness of a Hindoo Cossack from the Caspian shores, and accept the assurance of my real, sincere, genuine regret for having known you at so late a date.

Yours fraternally,
H. P. Blavatsky.

In the envelope enclosing her picture, was another envelope with her Bombay address "Care of Hurry Chund, Chintamon, Esq. President of the Arya Samaj, 6 Meadow St. Fort Bombay, India," on which H.P.B. wrote:

Did I send you the circulars? Ye Gods of the Swarga! I lose my head and the remains of my brains in the work of preparation to sail.

I mean the circulars of the T.S. and the Arya Samaj?
H.P.B.

SOURCE: Original unavailable. Copied by Boris de Zirkoff from an unknown source.

⌁

$\mathcal{L}$etter 135

To A. Sturge   *January 1, 1879*

To the Revd A. Sturge.—
—with the warmest regards of one, who, though the friend
of the "Heathen" and "Champion Heathen" herself—yet
respects the sincere of all faiths—even Christians.

respectfully
H. P. Blavatsky
Cor. Sec. of the Theosophical Society of India
Jan 1. 1879
Steamship Canada
British Channel

SOURCE: Transcribed from the original in the Archives of the Theosophical Society, Pasadena, written on the back of an 1878 photograph
of HPB wearing a black fur Russian-style hat and a white fur stole
across her breast from her left shoulder. The photograph is signed
"H. P. Blavatsky."

⌁

BACKGROUND ESSAY N

English Reactions to HPB

Shortly after Blavatsky and Olcott left England, notices of their
visit appeared in the press. The *Spiritualist Newspaper* of January 24,
1879 (14:41–2), included two letters about their stay. The first, by C.
C. Massey, focuses on the ideas that HPB was attempting to propagate rather than the phenomena she produced. Massey mentions
the phenomena but emphasizes the social, moral, and spiritual
aims of Theosophy. The second letter, by George Wyld, is primarily
a character sketch of HPB, depicting both her strengths and her

foibles. Together, these two letters show how HPB and the Society were viewed by English Theosophists at the beginning of Theosophical activity in Britain.

MADAME BLAVATSKY AND COL. OLCOTT IN ENGLAND.

SIR,—It may interest some of your readers to learn that Madame H. P. Blavatsky and Col. Olcott have been paying a brief visit to this country on their way from the United States to India. They arrived on the 3rd instant, and were the guests of Dr. and Mrs. Billing, at Norwood, until Friday last, the 17th, when they left for India, direct from Liverpool. Their stay was prolonged beyond their original intention at the desire of the recently formed British branch of the Theosophical Society of the Arya Samáj; and I think all the members who had the privilege of meeting them will acknowledge the advantage that has been derived from their presence and instructions. In New York Madame Blavatsky had become a celebrated character. In concert with Colonel Olcott she had brought together a large number of earnest students of psychology and spiritual science, including some highly gifted and famous persons. The Theosophical Society there is established on a firm and permanent footing. Its founders, especially the Russian stranger, had in its early days to encounter the ridicule of the public press, the obloquy of Spiritualists, and the slanders of certain mediums whose "divine powers" she laughed at, and whose frequent rogueries she mercilessly exposed. Indeed, it seemed likely at one time that the mediumistic fraternity, with its enthusiastic following, would make common cause against the most formidable critic whom its pretensions had ever encountered. But Madame Blavatsky's practical acquaintance with the phenomena of Spiritualism made her the friend of honest and genuine mediums; and as agent of the Committee of the St. Petersburg University, she was instrumental in sending to Europe Dr. Slade, whose career there, notwithstanding the abominable treatment he sustained in this country, has done so much to promote public and scientific investigation. And

Madame Blavatsky has no warmer friends and admirers than some of the well-known private mediums. Among them I may mention her late hostess, Mrs. Billing (formerly Mrs. Hollis), whom she regards as one of the greatest depositaries [sic] of these powers that America has produced—an opinion thoroughly justified by what, in common with other guests, I have been privileged to witness at the interesting *séances* which sometimes concluded our Norwood evenings. The publication of *Isis Unveiled* attracted to the Theosophical Society a host of inquirers, and was the occasion of making the authoress favourably known to a large section of American society. And when she and Col. Olcott left New York last month, they were the theme of a number of respectful and complimentary notices in the newspapers, and were accompanied by the regrets of a multitude of private friends. That Madame Blavatsky is a person of extraordinary powers, no one who has been frequently in her society can doubt. But she is intent on higher objects than display, which she contemptuously designates "psychological tricks." With some of these, however, she occasionally indulged the guests at Dr. Billing's hospitable house, where all of us were made welcome by day and night. I will not expiate on wonders which, by Spiritualists who do not believe in the mighty powers attainable by the cultivation of the will, would certainly be attributed to mediumistic gifts that Madame Blavatsky utterly disclaims, or rather repudiates. I will only mention the voluntary production of the "spirit rap" in bright light, and with a profane disregard of all the "conditions" of the circle. She amused herself and us by producing this in any number desired—on a chair, a table, or on our heads—ascribing it entirely to electricity directed by her own will. With the medium the will is unconscious; it is not distinct volition—and that is all the difference. But, on the whole, she discouraged our appetite for phenomena, exhorting us rather to a study of the principles upon which these apparent marvels are shown to be in entire accordance with natural laws. And even this pursuit seemed subordinate in her mind to the great social, moral, and spiritual objects of the Arya Samáj, to which she is entirely devoted. "The Brotherhood of Humanity" is with her and Colonel Olcott no mere sentimental phrase or visionary aspiration. To break down all the barriers of race and religion between man and man by the eradication of prejudice, and to emancipate the mind alike from its theological and materialistic trammels, are the main objects of the great Indian society, of which she has been so active and efficient an agent in the West. No greater undertaking, and none with more hard fighting before it, has ever been attempted. In every age and country exemption from superstition and from popular misconceptions of religion has been the privilege of a cultured and reticent few. And in all but the higher class of minds the emancipation from theology has simply meant the loss of faith in the unseen. The masses of the people, alike in East and West, are brought up as passive recipients of the degenerate beliefs by which the world is bitterly divided. It is believed that all the popular religions are corrupt offshoots of a primitive truth, and that this truth is to be found in a right interpretation and comprehension of the Vedic writings. The work of the Arya Samáj, as a public exoteric body, is educational and missionary. It has already established schools over a great part of India, in which are taught the purest devotion and morality, and which are proving the more efficacious against the wretched idolatry of the people than all the attempts of Western zeal to substitute conceptions of religion which are fast losing their hold over ourselves. The answer of the Arya Samáj (which must not be confounded with the Brahmó Samáj) to these attempts is to be seen in the foundation of its Western branches, as theosophical societies, already established in several countries. The members of these, for their own edification, will devote themselves to the study of religion and of the laws of nature, and by so doing will second the tendencies of modern science, research, and speculation, to uproot the fallacies that are conserved by Church organisations. Convinced that religious truth is the surest and soundest basis of all human development, the Arya Samáj has no

political sympathies or designs, as has been absurdly suggested by an English opponent. Its founder and chief in
India is a profound scholar and eloquent expositor of doctrines, which even to the most accomplished Orientalists of
the West are enveloped in much doubt and obscurity. It is
not, of course, to be supposed that the Theosophical societies are composed of persons equally competent in this
respect, or, on the other hand, who have blindly embraced
what would be to most of them an unknown religion. But
we believe, as we are taught, that knowledge is not a mere
result of research or speculation, but is inseparably connected with action. There are in our societies sections and
degrees in which the obligations and attainments differ
greatly. We have evidence that the highest development of
spiritual life in the most secret and esoteric lodges of the
parent fraternity is marked by the recovery of that knowledge of and power over the forces of nature—blind and intelligent—which Cabalists and Gnostics tell us are the original
prerogatives of man. Few of us, probably, will reach these
heights. But all who do not dishonour the profession of
theosophy by negligence or self-indulgence may hope to
attain some knowledge of the Divine-human spirit, its
nature, and powers. The doors of our Society are open to all
who are in sympathy with the public objects of the Arya
Samáj, and who wish in all sincerity and earnestness to avail
themselves of the instructions and help in occult researches
which we expect to receive. But we have no phenomenal
wonders to promise, and with the exception of such mediums as we have among us, are not at all distinguished from
the most commonplace people by the possession of occult
powers. Nevertheless, as I have had many questions addressed to me from time to time on the subject, it is possible
that this short and necessarily imperfect account of our
objects, so far as they are at present developed, may be
acceptable. And it seemed appropriate to introduce it into a
notice of the short visit which we have had from our friends
Madame Blavatsky and Colonel Olcott. I should add that
they both felt much regret that the time at their disposal did

not permit them to make any visits of compliment, or to seek any acquaintances outside the circle of the Theosophical Society. One of Madame Blavatsky's objects in visiting London was to consult certain books and manuscripts at the British Museum, where most of the time she could spare from Norwood was passed. Two other members of the New York Society accompany them to India, with the intention of permanently residing there. Colonel Olcott goes as a Commissioner from the Government of the United States to report upon the state of commerce and the means of promoting intercourse for trade purposes between the two countries. Madame Blavatsky will be the Indian correspondent of one of the leading Russian journals.

C. C. MASSEY

Jan. 19.

SIR,—The readers of *The Spiritualist* will be surprised and interested in knowing that Colonel Olcott and Madame Blavatsky have been living for the last ten days with Dr. and Mrs. Billing at Norwood, and have just sailed for Bombay.

The mysterious authoress of *Isis Unveiled* desired that her presence here should remain a secret, as her time was so short, and she feared being disturbed by a number of curious inspectors. She, therefore, saw only the few members of the Theosophical Society now in London.

Colonel Olcott is a man at once easily understood. A man of robust health and strength, of great vigour, soundness, affection, and truthfulness of mind, and of indomitable perseverance; and one of whom you feel that once to be his friend is to be his friend for ever.

Madame Blavatsky, or H.P.B., as she prefers to be called by her intimates, is not so easily understood, for she is *sui generis* and unique, a mystery and an enigma.

Swarthy, and of Tartar aspect, she is tall, strong, vigorous, and in perfect bodily health. She resembles a very powerful woman, about fifty-five years of age, but she asserts that she is eighty-two years of age. Her jaws are large, and furnished with perfectly regular and strong teeth; and her eyes, though almost without colour, yet can read without glasses the smallest print, and can look you through and through, and can read your character and thoughts at will. She is highly accomplished in languages and music, but is totally indifferent to the exhibition of these accomplishments, and to personal appearances, although she is possessed of a form and bearing of queenly dignity, if she only condescended to assume the garments and the mien. With irresistible powers of fascination, she seems only to despise the use of these powers. Enjoying enormous fits of laughter, she is yet for ever restless and sad. She possesses that powerful dramatic force which proceeds from the intense convictions of a powerfully emotional nature. She declaims on all subjects, rapidly passing from one to another, yet ever returning to her central idea; the spiritual wisdom and power of the East, from which must appear the coming man to rule the spiritual world.

Of truly a great nature, but with, to my mind, one extravagant defect, shown in her book and in her talk, an unreasoning and intolerant hatred of the doctrines and works of all Christian teachers.

If you explain to her that your form of Christianity is spiritual and esoteric, and show that the essence of esoteric Brahmanism, Buddhism, and Christianity are one and identical, namely, to find your hidden spiritual light, and unite this with the fountain and centre of all light, she at once accepts you as a spiritual brother; but she cannot rest in this, but noisily and for ever persists in confusing the essence with the external garments of Christianity.

This habit of mind arises from her vehement reverence for her Eastern lords and masters, who are for ever being reviled by Christian missionaries. You may criticise herself freely as you like, but if you whisper a word of treachery against her revered chiefs, you convert her into an implacable enemy, and from this characteristic it will be seen that she is very far from having reached that dignified and calm repose and sublime toleration which all who attain to the wisdom of the soul possess.

Beyond all doubt she is a magician controlling the movements of matter and counteracting the action of *poisons*, as I experienced in my own person.

She is wonderful and unique, and to have known her as I have, is always to remember her with affection, admiration, and respect.

GEORGE WYLD, M.D.

Letter 136

To V. de Zhelihovsky   *January 14, 1879*
London

I start for India. Providence alone knows what the future has in store for us. Possibly these portraits shall be the last. Do not forget your *orphan*-sister, now so in the full meaning of the word.

Good-bye. We start from Liverpool on the 18th. May the invisible powers protect you all!

I shall write from Bombay *if I ever reach it.*

Elena

SOURCE: Russian original unavailable. Copied from *ODL*, 2:1–2.

Bibliography

Algeo, John. *Blavatsky, Freemasonry, and the Western Mystery Tradition.* Blavatsky Lecture. London: Theosophical Society in England, 1996.

American National Biography. Ed. John A. Garraty and Mark C. Carnes. 24 vols. New York: Oxford University Press, 1999.

Baldwin, Neil. *Edison: Inventing the Century.* New York: Hyperion, 1995.

Blavatsky, Helena Petrovna. *Collected Writings.* 15 vols. Comp. Boris de Zirkoff. Wheaton, IL : Theosophical Publishing House, 1950-91. Vols. 1-4 were first published as *The Complete Works of H. P. Blavatsky* (London: Rider, 1933-6). Vol. 15, Cumulative Index, ed. Dara Eklund.

——. *From the Caves and Jungles of Hindostan.* Wheaton, IL: Theosophical Publishing House, 1975. Originally published in Russian, 1883-6.

——. *H.P.B. Speaks.* 2 vols. Ed. C. Jinarajadasa. Adyar, Madras: Theosophical Publishing House, 1950-1.

——. *Isis Unveiled: A Master-Key to the Mysteries of Ancient and Modern Science and Theology.* Ed. Boris de Zirkoff. Wheaton, IL: Theosophical Publishing House, 1972. Originally published 1877.

——. *The Key to Theosophy: Being a Clear Exposition, in the Form of Question and Answer, of the Ethics, Science, and Philosophy for the Study of Which the Theosophical Society Has Been Founded.* London: Theosophical Publishing Co., 1889.

——. *The Letters of H. P. Blavatsky to A. P. Sinnett and Other Miscellaneous Letters.* Ed. A. T. Barker. Facsimile ed. Pasadena, CA: Theosophical University Press, 1973. First published 1925.

——. *The Magicians of the Blue Hills.* [Russian.] Gomes, *Theosophy in the Nineteenth Century* (196), says: "Originally printed in *Russkiy Vestnik*, Moscow, Dec. 1884-Apr. 1885, and published in book form with 'The Durbar at Lahore,' St. Petersburg, 1898."

——. *The Secret Doctrine: The Synthesis of Science, Religion, and Philosophy.* 2 vols. London: Theosophical Publishing Co., 1888.

——. *Some Unpublished Letters of Helena Petrovna Blavatsky.* Ed. Eugene Rollin Corson. London: Rider, 1929.

——. *The Theosophical Glossary.* London: Theosophical Publishing Society, 1892.

Blue Hills = Blavatsky. *The Magicians of the Blue Hills.*

Bowen, P. G. B. "The Secret Doctrine and Its Study." Reprint in *Foundations of Esoteric Philosophy from the Writings of H. P. Blavatsky*, ed. Ianthe H. Hoskins. 2nd ed. London: Theosophical Publishing House, 1990.

Britten, Emma Hardinge. *Modern American Spiritualism: A Twenty Years' [1848 -1868] Record of the Communion between Earth and the World of Spirits.* 3rd ed. New York: The Author, 1870.

Burr, William Henry. *Madame Blavatsky.* N.p.: n.p., n.d.

Caldwell, Daniel H., comp. *The Esoteric World of Madame Blavatsky.* Wheaton, IL: Theosophical Publishing House, Quest Books, 2000.

Caracostea, Daniel. "Louis-François Jacolliot (1837–1890): A Biographical Essay." *Theosophical History* 9.1 (January 2003): 12–39.

Carlson, Maria. *"No Religion Higher Than Truth": A History of the Theosophical Movement in Russia, 1875–1922.* Princeton, NJ: Princeton University Press, 1993.

Cranston, Sylvia, and Carey Williams, research assistant. *HPB: The Extraordinary Life and Influence of Helena Blavatsky, Founder of the Modern Theosophical Movement.* 3rd rev. ed. Santa Barbara, CA: Path Publishing House, c. 1993 [1999].

CW = Blavatsky. *Collected Writings.*

DAB = *Dictionary of American Biography.*

Dayanand Saraswati. *Autobiography of Dayanand Saraswati.* 2nd ed. Ed. K. C. Yadav. New Delhi: Manohar, 1978.

Deveney, John Patrick, Joscelyn Godwin, and Michael Gomes. "Correspondence of H. P. Blavatsky and Colonel Olcott with Thomas A. Edison." *Theosophical History* 7 (1996): 50-7.

Dictionary of American Biography. 20 vols. New York: Scribner, 1928-36.

Dictionary of National Biography. 22 vols. London: Oxford University Press, 1963-5.

Dictionary of Scientific Biography. 16 vols. Ed. Charles Coulston Gillispie. New York: Scribner, 1970–80.

DNB = Dictionary of National Biography.

DSB = Dictionary of Scientific Biography.

Encyclopædia Britannica. Compact disk ed. 1999.

Encyclopedia of Occultism and Parapsychology. 4th ed. 2 vols. Ed. J. Gordon Melton. Detroit: Gale, 1996.

Ennemoser, Joseph. *The History of Magic.* 2 vols. Trans. William Howitt. London: Bohn, 1854. Original German 1844. Reprint. New Hyde Park, NY: University Books, 1970.

EOP = Encyclopedia of Occultism and Parapsychology.

Flint, Charles Ranlett. *Memories of an Active Life: Men, and Ships, and Sealing Wax.* New York: Putnam's, 1923.

Fuller, Jean Overton. *Blavatsky and Her Teachers: An Investigative Biography.* London: East-West, 1988.

———. *The Comte Saint Germain, Last Scion of the House of Rákóczy.* London: East-West, 1988.

Godwin, Joscelyn. *Robert Fludd: Hermetic Philosopher and Surveyor of Two Worlds.* London: Thames and Hudson, 1979.

Golden Book = Jinarajadasa. *The Golden Book of the Theosophical Society.*

Gomes, Michael. *The Dawning of the Theosophical Movement.* Wheaton, IL: Theosophical Publishing House, Quest Books, 1987.

———. *Theosophy in the Nineteenth Century: An Annotated Bibliography.* New York: Garland, 1994.

Grand Larousse de la langue française, 7 vols. Paris: Librairie Larousse, 1976.

Grimes, John. *A Concise Dictionary of Indian Philosophy: Sanskrit Terms Defined in English.* Rev. ed. Albany, NY: State University of New York Press, 1996.

Hall, Trevor H. *The Enigma of Daniel Home: Medium or Fraud?* Buffalo, NY: Prometheus Books, 1984.

———. *The Spiritualists: The Story of Florence Cook and William Crookes.* New York: Helix, 1963.

HarperCollins Dictionary of Religion. Ed. Jonathan Z. Smith. New York: HarperCollins, HarperSanFrancisco, 1995.

Harper's Bible Dictionary. Ed. Paul J. Achtemeier. New York: HarperCollins, HarperSanFrancisco, 1985.

Harrison, Vernon. *H. P. Blavatsky and the SPR: An Examination of the Hodgson Report of 1885*. Pasadena, CA: Theosophical University Press, 1997.

Hawkins, R. E. *Common Indian Words in English*. Delhi: Oxford University Press, 1984.

Haynes, Renée. *The Society for Psychical Research, 1882–1982: A History*. London: Macdonald, 1982.

Higgins, Godfrey. *Anacalypsis: An Attempt to Draw Aside the Veil of the Saitic Isis; or, An Inquiry into the Origin of Languages, Nations and Religions*. 2 vols. London, 1833, 1836. Reprint New Hyde Park, NY: University Books, 1965.

Hodgson, Brian Houghton. *Essays on the Languages, Literature, and Religion of Nepál and Tibet: Together with Further Papers on the Geography, Ethnology, and Commerce of Those Countries*. London: Trübner, 1874.

Home, Daniel Dunglas. *Lights and Shadows of Spiritualism*. New York: G. W. Carleton, 1877; London: Virtue, 1877 (differently paged editions; references in this volume are to the London edition).

HPB Speaks = Blavatsky. *H.P.B. Speaks*.

Hutchinson Guide to the World. 3rd ed. Phoenix, AZ: Oryx, 1998.

Incidents = Sinnett. *Incidents in the Life of H. P. Blavatsky*.

Inglis, Brian. *Natural and Supernatural: A History of the Paranormal from Earliest Times to 1914*. Rev. ed. Bridgport, Dorset: Prism Press, 1992.

Isis (Unveiled) = Blavatsky. *Isis Unveiled*.

Jinarajadasa, Curuppumullage, ed. *The Golden Book of the Theosophical Society: A Brief History of the Society's Growth from 1875–1925*. Adyar: Theosophical Publishing House, 1925.

——, ed. *Letters from the Masters of the Wisdom, 1870–1900*. First Series. 5th ed. Adyar, Madras: Theosophical Publishing House, 1964. 1st ed. 1919.

——, ed. *Letters from the Masters of the Wisdom*. Second Series. 2nd ed. Adyar, Madras: Theosophical Publishing House, 1973. 1st ed. 1925.

Judge, William Quan. *Echoes of the Orient: The Writings of William Quan Judge*. 4 vols. Comp. Dara Eklund. San Diego, CA: Point Loma Publications, 1975–93.

Lippitt, Francis J. *Reminiscences of Francis J. Lippitt, Written for His Family, His Near Relatives and Intimate Friends*. Providence, RI: Preston and Rounds, 1902.

Kingsland, William. *The Real H. P. Blavatsky: A Study in Theosophy and a Memoir of a Great Soul*. London: Watkins, 1928.

LBS = Blavatsky. *The Letters of H. P. Blavatsky to A. P. Sinnett*.

Leaf, Walter. *A Modern Priestess of Isis*. = Solovyov. *Sovremennaya zhritza Isidi*.

LMW1 = Jinarajadasa. *Letters from the Masters of the Wisdom*. First Series.

LMW2 = Jinarajadasa. *Letters from the Masters of the Wisdom*. Second Series.

Mahatma Letters to A. P. Sinnett from the Mahatmas M. & K. H. Comp. A. T. Barker. 3rd ed. Ed. Christmas Humphreys and Elsie Benjamin. Adyar, Madras: Theosophical Publishing House, 1962.

———. In Chronological Sequence. Comp. A. T. Barker. Ed. Vicente Hao Chin, Jr. Quezon City, Manila, Philippines: Theosophical Publishing House, 1993.

Malin, James C. "Kansas Philosophers, 1871—T. B. Taylor, Joel Moody, and Edward Schiller." *Kansas Historical Quarterly* 24 (1958): 168–97.

Medhurst, R. G., ed. *Crookes and the Spirit World*. London: Souvenir Press, 1972.

Merriam-Webster's Collegiate Dictionary. 10th ed. Springfield, MA: Merriam-Webster, 1993.

Merriam-Webster's Encyclopedia of World Religions. Ed. Wendy Doniger. Springfield, MA: Merriam-Webster, 1999.

Mitchell, Edward P. *Memoirs of an Editor: Fifty Years of American Journalism*. New York: Scribner's, 1924.

ML = *Mahatma Letters to A. P. Sinnett*. Chronological Sequence.

Murphet, Howard. *Yankee Beacon of Buddhist Light: Life of Col. Henry S. Olcott*. Wheaton, IL: Theosophical Publishing House, 1988. First published as *Hammer on the Mountain: Life of Henry Steel Olcott*, 1972.

"Mystical History" = Zhelihovsky. "Fragments from HPB's 'Mystical History.'"

Neff, Mary K., comp. *Personal Memoirs of H. P. Blavatsky*. New York: Dutton, 1937.

New Columbia Encyclopedia. New York: Columbia University Press, 1975.

ODL = Olcott. *Old Diary Leaves*.

OED = *Oxford English Dictionary*.

Olcott, Henry Steel. "Inaugural Address of the President of the Theosophical Society, Delivered at Mott Memorial Hall in the City of New-York, at the First Regular Meeting of the Society, November 17th, 1875." New York: The Society, 1875. Reprint *Theosophist* 53.11 (August 1932): 502–16.

———. *Old Diary Leaves*. 6 vols. Adyar, Madras: Theosophical Publishing House, 1895–1935.

———. *Old Diary Leaves: The Only Authentic History of the Theosophical Society*. Second Series, 1878–83. London: Theosophical Publishing Society, 1900.

———. *Old Diary Leaves: The True Story of the Theosophical Society*. Vol. 1. New York and London: Putnam's, 1895.

———. *People from the Other World*. Hartford, CT: American Publishing Co., 1875.

Old Diary Leaves = Olcott. *Old Diary Leaves*.

Owen, Robert Dale. *The Debatable Land between This World and the Next: With Illustrative Narrations*. New York: G. W. Carleton; London: Trübner, 1872, 1873.

Oxford Companion to the Bible. Ed. Bruce M. Metzger and Michael D. Coogan. New York: Oxford University Press, 1993.

Oxford Dictionary of World Religions. Ed. John Bowker. Oxford: Oxford University Press, 1997.

Oxford English Dictionary, 2nd ed. on Compact Disc, 1992.

People = Olcott. *People from the Other World*.

Personal Memoirs = Neff. *Personal Memoirs of H. P. Blavatsky*.

Podmore, Frank. *Modern Spiritualism*. 2 vols. London, 1902. Reprint as *Mediums of the Nineteenth Century*. New Hyde Park, NY: University Books, 1963.

Prothero, Stephen. *The White Buddhist: The Asian Odyssey of Henry Steel Olcott*. Bloomington: Indiana University Press, 1996.

Ransom, Josephine, comp. *A Short History of the Theosophical Society*. Adyar, Madras: Theosophical Publishing House, 1938.

Reigle, David. *The Doctrine of Svabhāva or Svabhāvatā and the Questions of Anātman and Śūnyatā.* Book of Dzyan Research Report. Cotopaxi, CO: Eastern School Press, 1997.

Rosicrucian Miscellanea. The manuscript commonplace book of Francis G. Irwin and Herbert Irwin, now in the United Grand Lodge of England Library, Freemasons Hall, London.

Sarda, Har Bilas. *Life of Dayanand Saraswati, World Teacher.* 2nd ed. Ajmer: Paropkarini Sabha, 1968.

Short History = Ransom. *A Short History of the Theosophical Society.*

Sinnett, Alfred Percy, ed. *Incidents in the Life of Madame Blavatsky Compiled from Information Supplied by Her Relatives and Friends.* London: Redway, 1886. 2nd ed. London: Theosophical Publishing Society, 1913.

Smith, Richard Penn. *Caius Marius: A Tragedy.* Ed. Neda McFadden Westlake. Philadelphia: University of Pennsylvania Press, 1968.

Solovyov, Vsevolod Sergeyevich. *Sovremennaya zhritza Isidi.* St. Petersburg, 1893. The Russian original of *A Modern Priestess of Isis,* abridged and trans. on behalf of the Society for Psychical Research from the Russian by Walter Leaf. London: Longmans, Green, 1895. Reprint. New York: Arno Press, 1976.

Stutley, Margaret, and James Stutley. *Harper's Dictionary of Hinduism: Its Mythology, Folklore, Philosophy, Literature, and History.* New York: Harper & Row, 1977.

Tripp, Edward. *Crowell's Handbook of Classical Mythology.* New York: Crowell, 1970.

Unpublished Letters = Blavatsky. *Some Unpublished Letters of Helena Petrovna Blavatsky.*

Vania, K. F. *Madame H. P. Blavatsky: Her Occult Phenomena and the Society for Psychical Research.* Bombay: Sat Publishing Co., 1951.

Waterman, Adlai. *Obituary: The "Hodgson Report" on Madame Blavatsky.* Adyar: Theosophical Publishing House, 1963.

Webster's Third New International Dictionary of the English Language. Unabridged. Ed. Philip Babcock Gove. Springfield, MA: G. & C. Merriam, 1971.

Wedderburn, William, Sir. *Allan Octavian Hume, "Father of the Indian National Congress," 1829–1912: A Biography.* London: Unwin, 1913. 2nd ed. Ed. Edward C. Moulton. New Delhi: Oxford University Press, 2002.

Who's Who in America. Chicago: Marquis, 1899–.

Who Was Who in America. Chicago: Marquis, 1942–; H = *Historical Volume 1607–1896,* 1963.

Wilder, Alexander. "How 'Isis Unveiled' Was Written." *Word* 7.2 (May 1908): 77–87.

WWA = *Who's Who in America.*

WWWA = *Who Was Who in America.*

Yajnik, Indulal Kanaiyalal. *Shyamaji Krishnavarma: Life and Times of an Indian Revolutionary.* Bombay: Lakshmi Publications, 1950.

Zhelihovsky, Vera Petrovna. "Fragments from HPB's 'Mystical History'." Ed. Michael Gomes. *Theosophist* 112–3 (May–Nov. 1991): 288–97, 437–43, 475–82, 520–8, 552–60, 28–33, 61–7. An English translation, perhaps by HPB, of "Pravda o Yelene Petrovne Blavatskoy" [The Truth about Helena Petrovna Blavatsky], by Vera Zhelihovsky, in the Russian periodical *Rebus,* 1883.

——. "Helena Petrovna Blavatsky." *Lucifer* 15–16 (Nov. 1894–Apr. 1895). This article is translated from the French of the *Nouvelle Revue,* and therefore its versions of HPB's letters to her family are at least two languages removed from their original Russian.

Zirkoff, "Introductory" (essay to his ed. of *Isis Unveiled*) = Blavatsky. *Isis Unveiled.*

Glossary-Index

This index includes glosses on many terms to help identify them and to provide the reader with information that may be useful; they are not general definitions, but identifications. Boldfaced forms are those that appear in the letters or commentary; lightfaced forms in the entries are additional spellings common elsewhere. For sources and their abbreviations, see the bibliography, which lists the abbreviations in their alphabetical sequence as well as a complete bibliographical entry for the source.

Other abbreviations are the following:

b.	born	It.	Italian
c.	century	Josh.	Joshua
ca.	circa	Lat.	Latin
cf.	compare	lit.	literally
Chron.	Chronicles	Matt.	Matthew
d.	died	myth.	mythology
Dan.	Daniel	n.	note
et al.	and other	Num.	Numbers
Exod.	Exodus	orig.	originally
fl.	flourished	Russ.	Russian
fn.	footnote	s.v.	under the term
fr.	from	Sam.	Samuel
Fr.	French	Skt.	Sanskrit
Gen.	Genesis	Thess.	Thessalonians
Gk.	Greek	Turk.	Turkish
Heb.	Hebrew		

A. The Protestant clergyman and Biblical commentator, otherwise unidentified, who sought the aid of two rabbis (Adler and Goldstein) to prove HPB wrong about "the Chaldean Bible of Onkelos." 298

Abbot Hotel. A hotel in Alexandria or Cairo, Egypt, where an uncle of HPB's once stayed. 449

Abdin, Rue d'. A street in Cairo where HPB tried to organize her Société Spirite. 18, 19

Abet, Raphael. A person in Egypt whose estate, HPB says, was exploited by Russian officials. 25

Abich, Otto Hermann Wilhelm von (1806–86). A German geologist who was an authority on the Caucasus, where he lived for a number of years, and who corresponded with HPB's maternal grandmother, an accomplished amateur scientist. (Biographical data: *CW* 2:521.) 267, 269

Abieh. *See* Abich.

"About Spiritualism." HPB's second published article (*CW* 1:36–44). 37, 52, 173

Abraham. A Hebrew patriarch whom HPB compares with Enoch, Hermes Trismegistus, Thoth, and Brahma. 176, 204, 205, 213

Acts of the Apostles. The fifth book of the New Testament, dealing with the history of the early Christians. 306, 357, 359

Adam. The first human being, the earthly man of Gen. 2. 49, 306, 322, 346

Adam Kadmon. *Heb*. A Kabbalistic image of the most perfect divine manifestation that the human mind can conceive; the heavenly or real man; the primordial or archetypal and hermaphroditic human of Gen. 1. 302, 322, 327

Adams, Charles Frederick. A New York lawyer with whom "John King" corresponded and one of the five men who participated in discussions that led to the publication, under the pen name HIRAF, of the article on "Rosicrucianism," to which HPB replied with her "first *Occult* Shot." 179

Adams Express Company. A shipping firm used to send the painting by "John King" to Gen. Lippitt. 137, 337

Adi-Buddha. *Skt*. The primordial, supreme Buddha, the Unknown Deity or Holy Wisdom. HPB calls it "the Wisdom-Principle, which is Absolute and therefore out of space and time" (*CW* 14:391). 346

Adler. A Rabbi and Talmudist, otherwise unidentified, with whom HPB entered into private controversy at the instigation of a Protestant clergyman. 298

Adonai. *Heb.* "my Lord." A term substituted in pronunciation for the scriptural name of God, YHVH, and associated by HPB with Adonis. 205, 207, 265, 322

Adonis. *Gk. myth.* A handsome young man, beloved of Aphrodite, slain in his youth by a boar; associated by HPB with Adonai, Baal, Bacchus, Bal, and Osiris. 265, 266

Adoptive Masonry. Any Masonic-like rite for women. 397

Adversus Haereses. *Lat.* "Against Heresies." The most important work of St. Irenaeus, a defense of orthodox Christianity against Gnosticism. 308

Adyar. The headquarters and international center of the Theosophical Society. 356

aether. *See* ether.

Africa. 43, 49, 50, 127, 141, 240, 278, 330

African peoples. 269, 470

"After the Storm Comes the Sunshine." An article by Henry Child responding to HPB's attack on him in her article "The Philadelphia 'Fiasco,' or Who Is Who?" 64, 94, 95, 96, 114, 116, 120

Agrippa von Nettesheim, Heinrich Cornelius (1486–1535). A German public servant, teacher, theologian, philosopher, and mage, whose book *De occulta philosophia* became a standard Renaissance study of magic. It expounded a form of Christian Kabbalism and Pythagorean numerology, proposing magic as the best way of coming to knowledge of God and the world. During his life Agrippa served as court secretary to Charles V of France and as physician to Louise of Savoy. He taught at the universities of Dôle and Pavia and was orator and public advocate at Metz. He was frequently in legal difficulties himself for defending a woman accused of witchcraft in his office as public advocate, for opposing the inquisitor of Cologne, for criticizing the Queen Mother of France, and for heresy. A Faustian figure most of his life, five years before his death, he renounced all learning and ended his days in a simple and pious life, as alluded to in letter 59. (Biographical data: Inglis 96–8.) 86, 196, 206, 211, 242

Ain Soph *or* **En Soph**. *Heb*. ain "not" + soph "limit." The Infinite or Spiritual Light, which appears to us as dark emptiness but from which the universe emanates. 86, 166, 203, 207

Aitareya-Brahmana. *Skt*. One of two liturgical, explanatory texts associated with the Rig Veda. 446

Akasa *or* Akasha. *Skt*. ākāśa "not visible." Space, astral light. 267

Akkadians. A Semitic people of central Mesopotamia in the third millennium BC. 267, 269, 320

Aksakoff *or* **Aksakof** *or* Aksakov, **Alexander Nikolayevich** (1832–1903). A Russian author, philosopher, and investigator of Spiritualism who wrote on Swedenborg, translated Andrew Jackson Davis into German, and in 1874 founded at Leipzig a monthly periodical called *Psychische Studien*. (Biographical data: *CW* 1:444–6; *EOP* 1:16–7.) 33, 44, 45, 47, 52, 70, 73, 102, 126, 141, 154, 170, 171, 194, 195, 213, 214, 235, 250, 259, 263, 270, 285, 311, 330, 331, 340, 361, 465, 468, 469

Albany, New York. Capital of the State of New York. 451

Alden, William Livingston (1837–1908). An editorial writer on the *New York Times* and *Daily Graphic*. He was one of the sixteen "formers" of the Theosophical Society, as Olcott calls those who participated in its formation, as distinct from those who worked for years to assure its stable foundation (*ODL* 1:121–3). (Biographical data: *DAB* 1:150; *ODL* 1:123–4; *WWWA* 1:12.) 106

Alexander II (1818–81). Emperor of Russia, 1855–81, who emancipated the serfs. 42

Alexander the Great (356–323 BC). The king of Macedonia (as Alexander III), who overthrew the Persian Empire and invaded India, spreading Hellenistic culture throughout that part of the world. After his death, his followers continued his cultural expansion elsewhere. He was a legendary figure during his lifetime, and afterwards the subject of many fabulous accounts. Alexander extended his military campaign to India in 327 BC, entering Gandhara (present-day northwestern Pakistan) and moving across the Punjab. Persian history is highly critical of Alexander, and Indian historians do not record his incursion, although several of his soldiers left accounts of their experiences in India. 387

New York State. At her sittings, "spirit hands and faces were shown from the cabinet; and spirit forms, frequently recognized as those of deceased relations, walked about the room and conversed with the sitters" (Podmore 2:96). 233

Angkor. The site of several capitals of the Khmir Empire in Cambodia and of Angkor Wat (temple), famous as the largest religious structure in the world and one of the most elaborate. 285

Anima Mundi. *Lat.* "Soul of the World." The intelligent spirit pervading the universe. *The Theosophical Glossary* identifies it with "the *Alaya* of the Northern Buddhists . . . a radiation of the ever unknown Universal ABSOLUTE." 272, 370, 381

Anna Karenina. A novel by Lev Tolstoy. 3

Anthony, Prof. An otherwise unidentified American with whose philosophical views HPB disagreed. 129, 162

Anthropological Review. The journal of the Anthropological Society of London, vols. 1–8, 1863–70, of which HPB says an English Theosophist had been editor. 435

Antiochus Epiphanes (ca. 215–164 BC). The Greek dynastic king of Syria (175–164 BC) who promoted Hellenic culture and tried to suppress Judaism, thus inciting the War of the Maccabees. His second name means "coming into light, like a god," but he was also called Epimanes, which means "coming into a mad frenzy." Antiochus banned Jewish religious observances and, after an abortive revolution by conservative Jews, captured Jerusalem and raised an altar to Zeus in the Temple, with a statue of himself to which sacrifices were made. Judas Maccabeus organized a military opposition, took the city, and rededicated the desecrated Temple, an act commemorated in the Feast of Hanukkah. 321

Aphrodite. *Gk. myth.* The goddess of sexual love, said to have been born from sea foam (*Gk.* aphros). 169, 171

Apocalypse. *Gk.* "uncovering." The Revelation of John, the last book of the New Testament, a genre of religious literature disclosing secret meanings and especially focusing on end times. 205, 210, 289

apocrypha. *Gk.* "secret, obscure." Religious writings that are not part of the canon of scripture. 205

Apollo. *Gk. myth*. The god of prophesy (among other matters), whose temple at Delphi was tended by the Pythoness, a priestess who delivered oracles while in a state of trance, sometimes said to be caused by breathing vapors from a cleft in the earth under her tripod chair; no such cleft, however, has been found. 214

Apollonius of Tyana (fl. 1st c.). A Greek neo-Pythagorean philosopher who became a semimythical cultural hero in the Roman Empire after interest in him and his travels to the East was promoted by the empress Julia Domna, called "Julia the Philosopher." He was a type of pagan Christ to whom wonder-working powers were attributed and who became the object of veneration. 141, 205, 236, 250, 278

Apuleius, Lucius (ca. 124–after 170). A Platonic philosopher, rhetorician, and author, best known for his narrative fiction the *Metamorphoses*, popularly called *The Golden Ass*. It is an account of the adventures of a young man who has magically been transformed into an ass and is restored to his proper form by devotion to the goddess Isis and initiation into her Mysteries. Apuleius traveled widely in the Mediterranean world and had contact with various initiatory practices, including Egyptian ones, an experience reflected in his work. The book, which includes a telling of the Cupid and Psyche myth, is a combination of mysticism, bawdry, horror, and solemnity. It was influential on later writers from Boccaccio to C. S. Lewis. Apuleius also wrote philosophical treatises on Plato. 352, 357, 359

Ar. The name of a sun god. 266

Arabia. 42, 269

Arabians. 269

Arabic. 319, 442

Ararat. A mountainous region in Armenia, not a single "Mount" as popular tradition has it, where Noah's ark came to rest after the Flood. 267

Archives of the College of Psychic Studies, London. 280

Archives of the Philosophical Research Society, Los Angeles, California. 74

Archives of the Society for Psychical Research, Cambridge, England. 401, 404, 430, 432, 433, 438, 464

Archives of the Theosophical Society, Adyar, India. 7, 12, 37, 65, 77, 78, 90, 97, 106, 108, 126, 137, 140, 146, 151, 161, 171, 184, 185, 191, 194, 261, 328, 337, 342, 355, 392, 412, 423, 443, 451, 461

Archives of the Theosophical Society, Pasadena, California. 484, 493

Archives of the Theosophical Society in America, Wheaton, Illinois. 93, 104, 114, 121, 122, 135, 163, 199, 487

Archon. *Gk.* "ruler." In Gnosticism, one of the governing powers of this world, created with it by the Demiurge; they rule the seven spheres, through which the divine sparks must pass to return to their source. 272

Aristotle (384–322 BC). The Greek philosopher and pupil of Plato who became the most important single influence on Western thought from Classical times to the end of the seventeenth century. His work encompassed botany, chemistry, ethics, history, literary theory, logic, metaphysics, physics, rhetoric, and zoology. HBP characterizes his approach as an inductive one from particulars to universals. 258

Armenia. 5, 267, 269, 320

Armenian. 267

Artaxerxes I, II, *and* **III**. Three Achaemenid kings of Persia who reigned, respectively, 465–425, 404–359, and 359–338 BC. 318

Artemis. A Greek goddess. "Artemis' early worship, especially at Ephesis, identified her as an earth goddess, similar to Astarte" (*New Columbia Encyclopedia* 157), an identification noted by HPB. 287

Art Magic; or, Mundane, Sub-Mundane and Super-Mundane Spiritism (1876). A book attributed by Emma Hardinge Britten to "Chevalier Louis," to whom she acted as translator, but for which her husband, William Britten, is listed by the Library of Congress as "supposed author," although she is widely regarded as its actual author. The book treats some subjects that were of interest to members of the newly formed Theosophical Society. 287, 288

astral light. An invisible region surrounding the planet and corresponding to the linga sharira in the human constitution. It is described as a "picture gallery" (letter 59), that is, what came later to be called the akashic records. It is compared to the nineteenth-century concept of aether or ether and might be also to the twentieth-century concept of a unified field, as it is the source of all energies and the "great agent of Magic" (letter 71). 20, 63, 208, 209, 210, 213, 230, 246, 249, 267, 335

As You Like It. A comedy by William Shakespeare. 229

Athenaeum. An exclusive men's club in Pall Mall, London, founded 1824. 273, 277, 435, 436

Athenaeum. A periodical published in London, 1828–1921. 361

Athens, Greece. 13, 42

Atlantic Monthly. A magazine published in Boston since 1857. 62

Augoeides. *Gk.* augē "a ray of the sun" *and* augazō "to illumine." The auric egg: "the *seventh* principle . . . an almost *immaterial* spirit or the divine Augoeides, *Atma*" (*CW* 3:321); "the brilliant *Augoeides*, the divine SELF" (*CW* 9:257); "the chief 'principle' of all . . . is the 'Luminous Egg' (Hiranyagarbha) or the invisible magnetic sphere in which every man is enveloped. . . . The *seventh* aspect of this individual aura is the faculty of assuming the form of its body and becoming the 'Radiant,' the Luminous Augoeides. It is this, strictly speaking, which at times becomes the form called Māyāvi-Rūpa [illusive form, 'the "double" in esoteric philosophy' (*Theosophical Glossary*)]" (*CW* 12:526). 207, 211, 212

Augustine, Saint (354–430). The Bishop of Hippo, the major church father of antiquity, who transmitted Platonic philosophy to the Christian church. 287

Australia. 260

Austria. 27, 30

Austria-Hungary. The Hapsburg empire from 1867 to 1918. 30

Azotus. A town in northern Judah. 352

Azov, Sea of. An inland sea, a gulf of the Black Sea between the Ukraine and Russia. 5

Aztec. A Mesoamerican culture that flourished in the fifteenth and early sixteenth centuries in central and southern Mexico. Their religion and cosmology included the concepts of cyclicity (with the present earth as the most recent in a series of creations) and multiple simultaneously existing worlds (with the earth between a series of heavens and underworlds). Their pantheon included Quetzalcoatl, the Feathered Serpent, a combination of god and culture hero. 285

Baal. *Semitic* "Lord." A general term for a god; specifically, a western Semitic god of fertility and the weather. 266

Babinet, Jacques (1794–1872). A French physicist who wrote about the phenomenon of a ball lightning that moved inside a house as a cat might and so called a "meteor cat," reported by HPB in *Isis* (1:107). 338

Babylon. The chief city of Babylonia, located about 50 miles south of modern Bagdad. 320

Babylonia. An ancient country in Mesopotamia. 318, 322

Babylonian. 266

Babylonian school. Scholars of the Jewish community of Babylonia who produced the Babylonian Talmud. 298

Bacchic Mysteries. The rites celebrated in honor of the god Bacchus. 283

Bacchus. The Latin name for Dionysos, the Greek god of wine, vegetation, and fertility. 265, 266, 317

Baden Baden. A spa in the Black Forest of Germany, famous as a resort. 28, 42

Bagration-Muhransky, Princess. A family friend whom HPB met in London in 1850. 6

Bal. Presumably a variant of Baal. 266

Balaam. A non-Israelite prophet from Transjordan who is referred to in several books in both testaments of the Bible, as well as in ancient folklore. His name has entered modern folklore and literary allusion in connection with a story recounted in Num. 22.21–35. It tells that Balaam disobeyed a direct command from God not to go to the king of Moab, who was conspiring against the Children of Israel. As Balaam traveled on an ass or donkey to meet the king, an angel with sword in hand blocked his way. Balaam could not see the angel, but the ass could and turned aside. Balaam beat the animal, forcing it to continue. This happened three times, after which the ass, given voice by

God, complained to Balaam for his mistreatment. Then God opened Balaam's eyes so that he too could see the angel, upon which Balaam confessed the error of his ways. From this story, Balaam becomes a symbol of one who cannot see the truth before him, which even an ass can recognize. 294

Baldwin, John Denison (1809–83). A congressman, journalist, and author of *Pre-Historic Nations; or, Inquiries Concerning Some of the Great Peoples and Civilizations of Antiquity, Their Probable Relation to a Still Older Civilization of the Ethiopians or Cushites of Arabia* (New York: Harper, 1869). (Biographical data: WWWA H:37.) 269

Baldwin, Neil. 419, 420, 489, 491

Balkans. 12, 408

Bangladesh. "Land of the Bengalis," a present-day nation in the northeast of the Indian subcontinent, in which the Ganges and Brahmaputra rivers flow together. 6

Banner of Light. A Spiritualist periodical published in Boston, 1857–1907. 32, 64, 65, 66, 67, 70, 75, 76, 85, 94, 99, 103, 104, 110, 115, 117, 118, 119, 121, 139, 143, 144, 171, 172, 195, 198, 200, 222, 224, 229, 236, 237, 238, 257, 258, 272, 273, 277, 290, 295, 296, 410

Bardesanes (154–ca. 222). A Syrian Gnostic poet who converted to Christianity and whose major work is *The Dialog of Destiny, or The Book of the Laws of the Countries*. 298

Bariatinsky, Prince. A nobleman in the court of Emperor Alexander II of Russia. 42

Barkis. A character in the novel *David Copperfield*, by Charles Dickens. 91, 164

Barnabo, Alexander, Cardinal (1801–78). A Papal official concerned with foreign missions. 26, 30

Barnum, Phineas Taylor (1810–91). An American showman famous for circuses and sideshows, to whom is ascribed the proverb "A sucker is born every minute." (Biographical data: *WWWA* H:42.) 193, 194

Baronius, Cesare (1538–1607). A church historian known as the "father of ecclesiastical history," whose major work, the *Annales Ecclesiastici* (1588–1607), traces the history of the church to the year 1198. 130

Barthélemy-Saint-Hilaire, Jules (1805–95). A French politician, journalist, and academic who translated the works of Marcus Aurelius and Aristotle and wrote on Indian religion. 380

bashi-bazook. *Turk.* başı bozuk "irregular soldier" *fr.* baş "head, leader" + bozuk "depraved, corrupt." "Bashi-bazouk . . . a member of an irregular ill-disciplined auxiliary of the Ottoman Empire . . . a turbulent ill-disciplined person" (*Webster's Third*). 282, 284

Bates, Rosa. An Englishwoman, resident in America, who preceded the Founders to England on their way to India and then accompanied them to Bombay. 484

Bathsheba. The wife of Uriah, the Hittite, and the beloved of King David, who sent her husband to be killed in battle in order to marry her. Her son by David was Solomon. 122

Bayard, Pierre Terrail, seigneur de ("lord of Château") (ca. 1473–1524). A French military hero known as *le chevalier sans peur et sans reproche* ("the knight without fear and without reproach"), commemorated in "The Hero" by John Greenleaf Whittier: "O for a knight like Bayard, / Without reproach or fear." His reputation was that of a perfect knight—brave, devout, and generous. 89

Beard, George Miller (1839–83). A physician whose skeptical article on the Eddy phenomena called forth HPB's first published article. (Biographical data: *ANB* 2:407–8; *DAB* 1:92–3; *WWWA* H:47–8.) 33, 37, 38, 39, 40, 48, 76, 142, 162, 172, 295

Beardsley. A portrait photographer of Ithaca, New York. Among his photographs of HPB that she apparently liked (ordering an extra two dozen enlargements) was one with a cigarette in her hand. 198, 199, 259

Beecher, Henry Ward (1813–87). An American Congregationalist minister whose oratorical skills and liberal social views made him the most influential Protestant spokesman of his day. He was an abolitionist, supported a moderate Reconstruction policy after the Civil War, advocated the enfranchisement of women, and supported evolutionary theory and modern biblical criticism. In the 1870s, however, Beecher became the subject of rumors alleging sexual immorality and in 1874 was sued by a former colleague for adultery with the latter's wife, a charge about which the civil jury could not reach agreement, although two ecclesiastical courts found him innocent. (Biographical data: *WWWA* H:49.) 122, 148, 150

Bel. A variant of Baal, applied particularly to the Babylonian god Marduk. 266

Belgrade. The capital of Serbia and later of Yugoslavia. 12

Belgravia. A fashionable residential area of London. 278

Beliy, Elizabeth ("**Liza**") **Petrovna**, *née* von Hahn (1850–1908). HPB's half sister by her father's second marriage to Baroness von Lange. 9, 467, 468

Belus. A sun god. 266

Benajet, Madame. An upper-class Parisian medium. 274

Benares, *now* Varanasi. A holy city on the Ganges in Uttar Pradesh. 341

Benton, J. W. A journalist's error for J. W. Bouton, the publisher of *Isis Unveiled*. 296

Bergen, Jacobs, and Ivins. The law firm that represented HPB in her suit against Clementine Gerebko. 157

Bergmann, Sigmund. The supervisor of a satellite workshop for Edison in lower Manhattan, from whom the Founders hoped to get a phonograph at a reduced price to take to India (Baldwin, *Edison: Inventing the Century* 91). 489

Bering Strait. The narrow body of water between Alaska and Siberia, connecting the North Pacific and Arctic oceans. 286

Berlin, Germany. 486

Berry, Mrs. An Englishwoman who attended séances in London. She is perhaps the artist who produced spirit drawings and received spirit guidance in finding and decorating a house (Podmore 73–5). 18

Besant, Annie. 328

Betanelly, Michael C. A Georgian from the Caucasus who operated an export-import business in Philadelphia. He was interested in Spiritualism and became infatuated with HPB in November 1874. She married him on April 3, 1875; sent him away in late May. In May 1877 he wrote urging her to get a divorce. In 1878 he filed for divorce on the grounds of desertion, and the divorce was granted on May 25. 46, 69, 77, 81, 82, 89, 107, 108, 122, 135, 137, 146, 176, 177, 184, 185, 186, 467

Beyst. Apparently a Hungarian intelligence agency, or perhaps a personal name. The term is transliterated from Russian; its referent is unidentified. 27

Bieloy. *See* Beliy, Elizabeth Petrovna.

Billing, Harry J., Dr. and Mrs. A couple with whom the Founders stayed in England while on their way to India in 1879. Dr. Billing was a member of the 1877 Committee of the Theosophical Society. Mrs. Mary Hollis Billing (as she is also known) was an American medium whose control was "Ski" (or "Skiwaukee") and who was involved in an episode connected with C. C. Massey. (Biographical data: *EOP* 1:604.) 494, 495, 498

Bismarck, Otto Eduard Leopold von, Prince (1815–98). The Prussian unifier and first chancellor of the German Empire, noted for his skill in managing foreign affairs. In domestic politics and social views, he reflected his background as a member of the conservative rural squirarchy. He has been called the "last representative of the ancien régime and cabinet diplomacy." 252

Bjeloybog. *Russ.* "White God." God of the day. 266

Black Sea. A large inland sea south of Russia, north of Turkey, and east of Romania and Bulgaria. 3, 4, 5, 30

Blake, Charles Carter (b. 1840). A lecturer on Comparative Anatomy and Zoology at Westminster Hospital, founding member and Honorary Foreign Secretary of the London Anthropological Society, member of the Anthropological Institute of New York, Anthropological Society of Paris, and Sociedad Antropológica Española, who corresponded with HPB during the first half of 1878. None of her letters to him are known to survive, but all or part of about 10 of his are in the Archives of the Theosophical Society, Adyar. Blake's relationship with HPB fluctuated. When some remarks of hers in *Isis Unveiled* about the Todas (a light-complexioned, tall aboriginal people of southern India) were criticized in the *Spiritualist*, he wrote a letter to the editor of that periodical, dated March 12, 1878 (HPB's scrapbook 7, p. 12), defending her. On September 17, 1878, he sent HPB a postcard (idem) reading: "Captain Burton is now in London and agreed entirely with

HPB re Todas. He will read a paper on Sp[iritualism] in the East on the 2nd of Dec. before the B.N.A.S. [British National Association of Spiritualists]." "Burton" is Sir Richard Francis Burton, author of *The Arabian Nights*, who was elected as a member of the Theosophical Society (*CW* 1:411); his paper for the British National Association of Spiritualists, entitled "Spiritualism in Eastern Lands," was published in the *Spiritualist* 33 (1878): 270-5. Despite his early support on the Todas, Blake was expelled from the Society for publishing derogatory remarks about the Arya Samaj, but was later reinstated. (Cf. *CW* 1:409, 411-2, 424, 436; *ML* 148, 292.) 479

Blavatsky, Nathalia. Apparently a relative of Nikifor Blavatsky's. In her scrapbook (1:124, quoted in *CW* 1:203-4), HPB pasted a newspaper article of March 1876 that cited D. D. Home, to which she added a number of comments, including this: "Mr. D. D. Home . . . has certainly gathered most carefully the dirtiest gossip possible about Nathalie Blavatsky." Jean Overton Fuller (*Blavatsky and Her Teachers* 18, 54-6) has proposed that Nathalia may have been the mother of the child Yury, whom HPB presented as her and Nikifor's ward. Nothing else is known about Nathalia Blavatsky. 9

Blavatsky, Nikifor Vassilyevich (1809-87 or later according to Cranston 133 n.). A member of the Russian landed gentry who served the government in various lower and middle-level civil offices. Shortly after his marriage to HPB in 1849, he became vice governor of the newly formed Province of Yerivan. (Biographical data: *CW* 1:xxxv-xxxvi n. 50.) 4, 5, 7, 9, 24, 29, 41, 146, 267, 301

Blavatsky, Freemasonry, and the Western Mystery Tradition. A monograph by John Algeo. 341

Bloede, G., Dr. A Spiritualist with whom HPB's relationship fluctuated between antagonism, cordiality, and exasperation, as she felt he misunderstood, supported, or misrepresented her and the Theosophical Society. (Cf. *CW* 1:203-4, 260, 393-5.) 252, 253

Bluebeard. In folklore, a husband who marries many wives and kills each before taking another, specifically the murderous husband in a story from Charles Perrault's *Contes de ma mère*

l'oye (*Tales of Mother Goose*, 1697, translated into English by
Andrew Lang in 1888). The character was identified with and
may have been based in part on Gilles de Rais (1404–40), a distinguished French marshal whose career ended with a trial for
Satanism and child murder. 99, 103

Blue Hills. 17, 299, 397, 398, 452

Boaz. The name of the left pillar at the porch of King Solomon's
temple (1 Kings 7.21, 2 Chron. 3.17). 84, 147, 150, 329

Bodleian Codex. A biblical manuscript in the Bodleian Library.
321

Bodleian Library. A library at Oxford University founded by Sir
Thomas Bodley in 1598. 383

Böhme, Jakob (1575–1624). A German mystic and Christian
theosophist who was a major influence on later religious and
philosophical thought. Born in Saxony at a time of great religious and cultural ferment, Böhme had little formal education,
being a shoemaker by trade, but at the age of twenty-five he
had a mystical vision that revealed to him the solution of the
spiritual problems of his age: cosmology, the existence of evil,
and the social and political turmoil around him. He became a
student of Paracelsian alchemy, which he used as a metaphor
for his mystical view of nature and the human soul, and was
suspected of heresy by the governing Protestant authorities.
Four volumes of *The Works of Jacob Behmen* were translated
into English in the seventeenth century by J. Ellistone and
J. Sparrow. 278, 447

Bologna. A city in northern Italy. 13

Bombay *now* Mumbai. A port city and capital of Maharashtra in
western India, where HPB and Olcott first landed in India. 6,
378, 399, 412, 417, 425, 434, 453, 460, 462, 463, 477, 482, 487,
489, 490, 491, 492, 498, 500

Book of Numbers, Chaldean. An ancient Kabbalistic work HPB
frequently refers to (*CW* 15:77), of which she says there are
"perhaps only two or three copies extant, and these in private
hands" (*Theosophical Glossary* 75). 208

Book of the Dead, Egyptian. The name given to a collection
of mortuary texts by Karl Richard Lepsius, a German
Egyptologist, who published the first selection of them in

1842; the collection is also called "The Chapters of Coming-Forth-by-Day." 346, 347

Book of War *or* Book of the Wars of Jehovah. A work quoted in Num. 21.14. 268

Boothby, Mrs. A Boston medium visited by Gen. F. J. Lippitt. 186, 187

Boston, Massachusetts. 32, 38, 39, 60, 90, 94, 100, 113, 117, 137, 138, 152, 159, 171, 184, 185, 189, 191, 193, 214, 242, 255, 445

Bouillon, Godfrey of. *See* Godfrey of Bouillon.

Boutleroff *or* Butlerov, **Alexander Mihaylovich** (1828–86). A Russian chemist who proposed that the characteristics of a molecule result from the arrangement, as well as the number and type, of the atoms composing it, which is the basis of isomers. He was also a psychic researcher, whose lecture on "The Study of Mediumistic Manifestations" was translated by HPB (*CW* 14:497–500). 170

Bouton, J. W. The New York publisher of *Isis Unveiled*. 264, 281, 282, 283, 284, 296, 333, 334, 337, 338, 466

Bowman, Mr. An authority on music, otherwise unidentified. 169

Brahma. *Skt.* Brahmā. The creator of the universe; one of the Trimurti ("three forms" of the Absolute Reality) or trinity, the other two being Vishnu as Preserver and Shiva as Destroyer or Regenerator. 205, 338, 364, 429, 446

Brahman *or* **Brahmin** *or* **Brahmana**. *Skt.* brāhmana. Alternative forms for a member of the highest Indian caste or an adherent of orthodox Hinduism. The form *Brahmin* is usual when applied to "a person of high social standing and cultivated intellect and taste" as in "Boston Brahmin" (*Merriam Webster's Collegiate*) and was "all but universal in popular use" in the nineteenth century (*OED*), but *Brahman* is now the predominant form, reflecting the Sanskrit. 211, 213, 320, 322, 327, 376, 391, 396, 402, 404, 410, 411, 429, 431, 446, 472, 473

Brahmana. Any of the liturgical texts of Hindu scripture that provide guidance for performing the rituals. 446

Brahmanic(al) *or* **Brahminic(al)**. Pertaining to the Brahmans or Brahmanism. 329, 390, 391, 404, 410, 445, 471, 472

Brahmanism *or* **Brahminism**. The religious system of the Brahmans. 344, 351, 379, 445, 469, 470, 471, 474, 499

Brahmanist *or* **Brahminist**. A Brahman or an adherent of Brahmanism. 351, 471, 474, 475

Brahmo Samaj *or* **Brahma Somaj**. *Skt.* "Society of Brahma." A Hindu reform movement inspired by Christian Unitarianism and Islam, founded in 1828 by Ram Mohun Roy as a monotheistic form of Hinduism. Eventually, the group came to reject the authority of the Vedas, the doctrines of avatars and karma, polytheism, and idols. Under Keshab Chunder Sen, the Brahmo Samaj was increasingly Christianized and became active in social reform, education, and opposition to the caste system, oppression of women, and child marriage. Chiefly because of differences of emphasis between native Hindu versus Westernized practices and attitudes, the organization underwent a number of schisms. 431, 496

Brajation, Mme. HPB's grandmother, according to a reporter's account of an interview with HPB, which has many other errors. HPB's maternal grandmother was Princess Helena Pavlovna Dolgorukov; her paternal grandmother was Countess Elizabeth Maksimovna von Pröbsen. This reference is perhaps an error for Princess Bagration-Muhransky (*CW* 1:xxxviii). 41

Brasseur de Bourbourg, Charles-Étienne (1814–74). A French missionary and ethnographer in Mesoamerica who wrote a history of the Aztecs and various other works on Mesoamerican culture. He believed, incorrectly, that he had deciphered the Mayan hieroglyphs. He also translated into French the *Popol Vuh*, the sacred book of the Mayan Quiché Indians, which had been recorded in the Latin alphabet by sixteenth-century Spaniards. 285

Brassó. A Hungarian town (now Brașov in Romania), which HPB visited. 12

Brédif. A French medium whose séances were reported in articles by Nikolay Petrovich Wagner, which HPB translated into English. 171

Britain *or* **Great Britain**. The island including England, Scotland, and Wales. 30, 31, 494

British Columbia, Canada. 285, 286

British India. *See* Mill, James. 392

British Library, Department of Manuscripts, London. 363

British Museum, London. The books and manuscripts formerly housed in the British Museum are now in the new British Library. 242, 243, 477, 498

British National Association of Spiritualists (1873-, after 1882 Central Association of Spiritualists, after 1884 London Spiritualist Alliance, after 1955 College of Psychic Science, after 1970 College of Psychic Studies). A society to promote the interests of Spiritualism. Conferences held in its quarters in 1882 resulted in the formation of the Society for Psychical Research. (Cf. Podmore 2:169, 176-7.) 39, 244, 435, 438

British Theosophical Society. 436

Brittan, S. B. An American, former Universalist minister, follower of Andrew Jackson Davis, and editor of the Spiritualist periodicals *Univercælum*, *Shekinah*, and the *Spiritual Telegraph*. He commented in the *Banner of Light* (October 9, 1875) about H. S. Olcott's views on Spiritualism. (Biographical data: Podmore 1:170-2, and see index.) 198, 200

Britten, Emma Hardinge (1823-99). A London-born medium, exponent of Spiritualism, and author of *Modern American Spiritualism* (1870) and *Art Magic* (1876), who was one of the formers of the Theosophical Society. She and her husband went to Australia and New Zealand in 1878 as Spiritualist missionaries, to found churches and societies. She was noted as an inspirational speaker under spirit guidance (Podmore 1:265-7, 2:133). (Biographical data: *CW* 1:466-7; *EOP* 1:178.) 198, 200, 219, 220, 253, 256, 274, 288, 329

Britten, William. A Spiritualist who married Emma Hardinge Britten in 1870. 172, 173

Broadway, 71, New York. The address of an office shared by Henry S. Olcott and William Quan Judge. 281, 486, 490

Brooklyn, New York. 156, 157, 252, 312

Brown, Elbridge Gerry. The editor of *The Spiritual Scientist*, whom HPB patronized. (Cf. *Canadian Theosophist* 69 [Jan.-Feb. 1989]: 121-9 and 70 [Mar.-Apr. 1989]: 14-7; *CW* 1:45-6; *Golden Book* 16; *ODL* 1:72-4; *Short History* 67-9; *Theosophical History* 4 [Oct. 1992-Jan. 1993]: 115-20.) 38, 39, 60, 61, 94, 117, 118, 119, 122, 125, 128, 134, 135, 140, 152, 169, 171, 179, 180, 181, 182, 185, 189

Brown's lozenges. A brand of cough drops. 146

Bruno *or* **Brun(n)ov, Philipp Ivanovich**, Baron (1796–1875). The Russian ambassador to Great Britain, 1860–74. 29, 30

Brussilov, A. A. de, Gen. The future husband of HPB's niece Nadyezhda Vladimirovna. 416

Buchanan, Joseph Rhodes (1814–99). A professor of physiology at the Eclectic Medical College of New York City who wrote *Manual of Psychometry* in 1885. (Biographical data: *ANB* 3:840–1; *CW* 6:429–30; *DAB* 2:216–7; *EOP* 1:183–4; Podmore 1:155–6; *WWWA* 1:160.) 60, 61, 189, 234, 404

Bucharest. The capital of Romania. 27, 31

Büchner, Ludwig (1824–99). A German doctor of medicine and a philosophical exponent of scientific materialism. His major work, an exposition of atheistic materialism, was *Kraft und Stoff* (*Force and Matter*, 1855), which denied free will and explained consciousness as the product of physical states of the brain, rejecting any distinction between mind and matter. The book caused such outrage that Büchner resigned his appointment as lecturer in medicine at the University of Tübingen. 60, 148, 188, 190, 344

Buck, Jirah Dewey (1838–1916 or 1917). An American homeopathic physician and author, Dean of Pulte Medical College in Cincinnati, President of the American Institute of Homeopathy, and 33° Freemason, who chaired the meeting, held at his Cincinnati home, at which the American Section of the Theosophical Society was organized. (Biographical data: *CW* 3:498–9; *Echoes* 2:453–4; *WWWA* 1:161.) 485

Buckle, Henry Thomas (1821–62). A British historian whose two-volume *History of Civilization in England* (1857–61) was influential in reforming historical writing by emphasizing community rather than individuals, culture rather than politics, and the human relationship to nature rather than morals. 43

buckle and medal phenomenon. The delivery to HPB during a séance at the Eddy farmstead of a medal and "buckle" (pin or clasp) belonging to her father, described by Olcott in *People from the Other World* 355–9. 51, 260

Buda. A Hungarian city on the right bank of the Danube River, the center of government, united with Pest in 1872. 30

Budapest. The capital of Hungary, formed by the union of Buda and Pest in 1872. 30

Buddha. *Skt.* "the awakened one." (1) The title of Siddhartha Gautama, founder of Buddhism. (2) "The Divine or God-like Wisdom" (letter 92). 269, 344, 345, 346, 347, 350, 354, 365, 380, 381, 383, 384, 446

Buddhism. The teachings of the Buddha, summarized in the Four Noble Truths (the existence of frustration, its cause, its ending, and the way to that ending by the Eightfold Path), and the practices implicit in those teachings. 291, 343, 344, 353, 355, 357, 380, 389, 446, 499

Buddhism, Examined in Relation to Its Followers Who Were Living in Siberia. A book by Nil. 343, 355

Buddhist. 268, 279, 286, 290, 291, 312, 329, 343, 345, 346, 351, 353, 368, 370, 372, 380, 389, 410, 433, 446, 474, 475

Buff. The pet dog of Louisa Andrews. 119

Buffalo, New York. 32

Bulwer-Lytton. *See* Lytton (of Knebworth).

Bundy, John C., Colonel (1841–92). The editor of the *Religio-Philosophical Journal* (Chicago). 398

Bunsen, Christian Karl Josias, Freiherr von ("Baron of") (1791–1860). A Prussian diplomat, theologian, and scholar, perhaps the person referred to in letter 71. 267

Burma *now* Myanmar. 7, 380

Burnouf, Eugène (1801–52). A French orientalist best known for his work on Zoroastrianism and the language of the ancient scriptures of that religion. He wrote also on Pali, the language of Theravada Buddhism, and on Sanskrit while professor of that language at the Collège de France. He edited and translated into French the Bhagavata Purana and published a history of Buddhism: *Introduction à l'histoire du bouddhisme indien* (1844), in which he wrote about Nirvana. 380

Burr, F. Ellen. The sister of Frank L. Burr, an editor of the *New York Times*, who wrote a short notice of *Isis Unveiled* in the *Times*, which HPB liked. Olcott then wrote Frank Burr, suggesting that he do a longer review of the book, which he declined to do for lack of knowledge of "elementaries," despite having been convinced of Spiritualism in the early 1850s.

Frank passed Olcott's letter along to his sister, who then wrote Olcott on December 5, 1877, opining that they might be distantly related. In reply, Olcott sent her a copy of his genealogical study, the *Olcott Book*, which led to a further exchange of letters (hers are in the Archives of the Theosophical Society, Adyar), in which she expressed her support of cremation and her dislike of women's adopting their husbands' names. She accepted the diploma Olcott sent her as a "Corresponding Fellow" of the Society and returned the signed pledge. 482, 484, 487, 488, 492

Burr, Frank L. An editor of the *New York Times*. 484

Burr, William Henry. An American reporter, both a court reporter and reporter of the official record of the U.S. Senate (1819–1908). He was a skeptic about Spiritualism but interested in Gnosticism and early Christian history. He wrote several letters to HPB from 11 Grant Place, Washington, DC, dated October 14, 16, 22, 26, November 12, 28, 1877 (in the Archives of the Theosophical Society, Adyar). He borrowed HPB's copy of Jacolliot's *Fils de Dieu* and referred to Higgins's *Anacalypsis* in his letters. (Biographical data: *WWWA* 1:171.) 342, 370, 373

Byron, George Gordon Byron, 6th Baron (1788–1824). An English Romantic poet whose name in the form *Byronic* became a synonym for world-weariness and romantic mystery. Byron's writing and personality captivated Europe; he was widely imitated, especially in Russia, where he was an influence on Mikhail Lermontov, whose novel *A Hero of Our Time* (1840) is about the Byronic hero. 394

C., D. K. An otherwise unidentified correspondent to *Medium and Daybreak* who reported HPB's Cairo Société Spirite and her desire for mediums. 18

Cabala, Cab(b)al(l)ist, Cab(b)alistic(al). *See* Kabbalah, etc.

Caesar, Gaius Julius (100–44 BC). A Roman general and ruler whose name became the word for "emperor" in German (*Kaiser*), Slavic (*tsar*), and other languages. 261, 387

Cagliostro, Alessandro, Count di (1743–95). An Italian mage, alchemist, and hierarch in Egyptian Freemasonry. "Cagliostro" is thought to be a name assumed by Giuseppe Balsamo, an adventurer and charlatan who left a life of poverty in Palermo to travel through the Middle East, studying occultism and alchemy, and who eventually married Lorenza Feliciani, called "Serafina," of Rome. He then traveled through the major cities of Europe as a wonderworker, being especially popular in Paris. In 1789 his wife denounced him to the Inquisition as a heretic, magician, and Freemason. He was arrested in Rome, tried, and sentenced to death, a sentence commuted to life imprisonment in the fortress of San Leo in the Apennine mountains. The identity of Cagliostro and Balsamo has, however, been questioned (*CW* 12:727–30). 141

Cain. A type of the murderous betrayer (Gen. 4.1–15). 44, 282

Cairo, Egypt. 5, 13, 17, 18, 19, 22, 23, 25, 26, 30, 449

Caius Marius: A Tragedy. A play by Richard Penn Smith, premiered in Philadelphia in 1831. 173

Calchas. In Greek mythology, a seer who advised King Agamemnon to sacrifice his daughter Iphigeneia, proposed the wooden horse that allowed the Greeks to capture Troy, and died after the war when he was beaten in a contest of soothsaying; in Shakespeare's *Troilus and Cressida*, a Trojan priest who defected to the Greeks and arranged for his daughter Cressida to be traded to the Greeks in a prisoner exchange, leading to Cressida's betrayal of Troilus; hence a prophet who gives bad advice. 396, 397

Calcutta. A city in eastern India, at one of the mouths of the Ganges River, north of the Bay of Bengal. 7, 410, 428, 472

Calcutta Review. A periodical published by the University of Calcutta, 1844–. 392, 412

California. A state in the far west of the United States. 43, 414, 416, 448

Calmuck. *See* Kalmuck.

Calvin, John (1509–64). A French Protestant reformer whose theology emphasized the sovereignty of God and the depravity of human nature. 354

Cambodia. A country bounded by Thailand on the west, Laos on the north, and Vietnam on the east. 270, 285

Cambridge, Massachusetts. A city settled in 1630 and site of Harvard University, founded in 1636. 59, 95, 187

Cambridge University Library, Cambridge, England. 401, 404, 430, 432, 433, 438, 464

Canaan. A son of Noah's second son, Ham; the eponym of the Land of Canaan; transliterated as "Chanoon" from HPB's Russian, as recorded by V. S. Solovyov. 287, 288

Canaanite. A member of a Semitic people living in and around Palestine about 3000 BC. 266, 269, 286, 287

Canada. 6, 285

Canada, **SS**. The ship on which HPB and Olcott sailed from New York to England. 493

Canadian Theosophist. A journal first published by the Theosophical Society in Canada in 1920. 92, 99, 250, 364, 373, 392, 398, 418, 434, 455, 476, 479, 480

Carbonari. *It. lit.* "charcoal burners." Members of an early eighteenth-century Freemasonic-like secret society in Italy, Spain, and France. The aim of the organization was political freedom. 219

Caribbean. 62

Carlson, Maria. 30, 31

Carrier Dove. A weekly Spiritualist periodical published in San Francisco, 1884–93. 398

Carthage. A Phoenician city on the coast of North Africa, near modern Tunis. Its war with Rome ended in the complete destruction of the city in 146 BC. 173

Cascade. A resort on the southern tip of Oswasco Lake, some twenty miles north of Ithaca, New York. Eugene Corson comments in *Unpublished Letters* (218): "At that time a Mrs. John Andrews, a very excellent woman, the wife of a carpenter, a strong medium for physical manifestations, was holding séances at a little place called Cascade, on Owasco [sic] Lake, where my father and mother had gone for some séances which had proved satisfactory, and they had invited H.P.B. to attend them as their guest. Evidently she had other work on hand and was not especially interested." 90, 114, 115

Caspian Sea. The largest inland sea in the world, with Iran on its

south and Russia and former Soviet Socialist Republics on all
other sides. 3, 410, 492

Cassels, Walter Richard (1826–1907). The lay author of the
anonymously published *Supernatural Religion: An Inquiry into the
Reality of Divine Revelation*, 3 vols. (London: Longmans, Green,
1874–7), a theologically liberal and highly controversial work
that was reprinted many times and elicited many responses.
Speculation on the authorship of the work was rife; HPB's
statement that the author was a Bishop is incorrect.
(Biographical data: *DNB*.) 284

Castor and **Pollux**, *called* the Dioscuri. Sons of the same mother
(Leda), but Pollux was immortal, being the son of Zeus, and
Castor was mortal, being the son of the king of Sparta; when
Castor was killed in battle, Pollux prayed to Zeus that they
might share the same fate, spending alternate days as mortals
in Hades and as immortals on Olympus. Zeus set them in the
heavens as the constellation Gemini. Hence they are symbols
of devoted brothers. 154, 155

Catholic Church. The Roman Catholic Church. 26, 101, 113, 234,
240, 279, 282, 284, 323, 340, 347, 379

Caucasus. A region between the Black Sea and Sea of Azov on the
west and the Caspian Sea on the east, through which the
Caucasus Mountains run southeast-northwest. The mountains
divide the region into two subareas: Ciscaucasia to the north
(Russian territory proper) and Transcaucasia to the south
(Georgia, Azerbaijan, Armenia). The Caucasus is part of the
traditional dividing line between Europe and Asia, the area of
Transcaucasia being generally regarded as Asian rather than
European. 2, 4, 5, 11, 12, 14, 30

"Cave of the Echoes, The." A story by HPB (*CW* 1:338–53). 237

Cayuga Lake. A lake in New York State near the Corsons' house in
Ithaca. 115

Cecil Street. The London location of a flat where HPB lived in
1850 or 1851. 6

Centennial Grounds. Probably Fairmount Park in Philadelphia,
the site of the Centennial Exposition, the first World's Fair in
the United States, opened on May 10, 1876, to celebrate the

one hundredth anniversary of the Declaration of Independence. 177

Central America. *See* America, Central.

Ceylon *now* Sri Lanka. 6, 341, 343, 347, 353, 380, 388

Chaldean. Pertaining to the culture of ancient Mesopotamia, especially the southern part; a member of that culture; the language of that culture. The term early acquired another meaning, however, referring to astrology, soothsaying, occult science, and magic, the sense that HPB most often uses. 204, 267, 268, 269, 286, 298, 302, 319

Chaldean Book of Numbers. *See* Book of Numbers, Chaldean.

Champollion, Jean-François (1790–1832). A French historian, linguist, and Egyptologist who played a key role in the decipherment of Egyptian hieroglyphics by his analysis of the Rosetta Stone. He built upon the earlier work of the Englishman Thomas Young, but it was Champollion who first recognized that most hieroglyphs represent sounds. 132

Champollion-Figeac, Jaques-Joseph (1778–1867). A French librarian and paleographer, the elder brother of Jean-François Champollion. Jacques-Joseph edited several works of his younger brother, the Egyptologist. 132, 286

Cheops. *Gk. form of* Khufu. A twenty-sixth-century BC Egyptian pharaoh, famed as a pyramid builder. 14, 41

Cherson *or* Kherson. A port city on the Black Sea and region in the Ukraine on the Dnieper River. 9

cherub. A winged heavenly being referred to in several books of the Hebrew Bible. 169

Chicago, Illinois. 7

Chicago Times. A daily newspaper, published 1861–81. 97

Child, Henry T. A Philadelphia doctor and Spiritualist who at first attested the genuineness of the Katie King manifestations by Nelson and Jennifer Holmes, even producing a biography of the spirits "John" and "Katie King," supposedly dictated to him by the spirits. But after the confession of their landlady, Eliza White, of impersonating the spirit "Katie King" during faked materializations, Child withdrew his endorsement. Subsequently, HPB charged Child with complicity in the fraud and with attempting to frame the Holmeses with false evidence. He defended himself in an article entitled "After the Storm Comes the Sunshine," which HPB responded to with a mockingly bitter article "Who Fabricates?" 48, 62, 63, 64, 65, 66, 67, 68, 69, 70, 71, 75, 76, 88, 91, 93, 94, 95, 96, 100, 103, 104, 105, 106, 114, 116, 120, 121, 130, 139, 143, 152, 153, 154, 170, 171, 193, 194, 234, 235, 254, 330

Childs, George Washington. An unidentified putative poet, perhaps an error for George William Childs. 177, 183

Childs, George William (1829-94). A philanthropist and the publisher of the Philadelphia *Public Ledger*. (Biographical data: *ANB* 4:812-4; *DAB* 4:70-1; *WWWA* H:104.) 183

China. 470

Chintamon, Hurrychund (*and many other spellings*). A member of the Arya Samaj who was the Founders' first contact on landing in Bombay. When he was discovered to be a political agent of the ruler of Boroda, who had tried to poison the British resident, he was expelled from both the Arya Samaj and the Theosophical Society and fled to England, where he spread suspicion about the Founders and started the "Hermetic Brotherhood of Luxor," which he also brought to America (Ransom 120-1). 399, 400, 402, 417, 418, 426, 431, 433, 435, 439, 442, 451, 453, 456, 459, 460, 461, 463, 492

Chittenden, Vermont. A town near which the Eddy brothers had a farmhouse that was the site of Spiritualist phenomena and where HPB and Olcott met. 32, 33, 35, 36, 37, 46, 48, 50, 79, 80

Chrishna. A spelling of *Krishna* used to emphasize the parallels with Christ. 266

Chrishnavarma. *See* Krishnavarma.

Christ. *Gk.* Christos "anointed." In orthodox Christian theology, an epithet for the unique incarnation of God in human form as Jesus. In HPB's view, "Christ has incarnated, not in Jesus only, but in humanity in its totality" (letter 82). 68, 131, 132, 206, 254, 283, 302, 303, 305, 315, 317, 322, 325, 343, 344, 347, 348, 351, 354, 355, 380, 384, 387, 443, 446, 447, 473, 475, 476

Christian. An adherent of or pertaining to Christianity. 121, 129, 139, 278, 282, 302, 315, 322, 327, 331, 343, 346, 347, 349, 351,

(Biographical data: *ANB* 5:196-7; *DAB* 2:285-6; *WWWA* H:114.)
69, 89, 90, 93, 94, 95, 99, 100, 103, 116, 119, 120, 123, 124,
125, 139, 178, 258

Colenso, John (1814-83). An Anglican Bishop of Natal (now a
province in the Republic of South Africa). While responding to
questions by Zulu converts, he came to realize the historical
inaccuracy of the Bible, a view he expressed in his book, *The
Pentateuch and the Book of Joshua Critically Examined* (1862-79).
That book, his rejection of the doctrine of eternal damnation,
and his tolerance of polygamy among the Zulus led to his trial
for heresy. He was convicted, but the conviction was over-
turned by the Privy Council in England on a question of procedure. A few years later, the South African church was recognized as autonomous, and Colenso was deposed, but continued to serve his Zulu supporters. 344

College of Psychic Studies. The present-day name of an organization founded in 1873 as the British National Association of
Spiritualists. 40

Colombo. The capital of Sri Lanka (Ceylon). 343

Columbian Magazine. A periodical in which Thomas Alva Edison
published his philosophical views. 419

"Comments on 'The "Blessing" of the Brothers.'" An article by
HPB (*CW* 4:354-5). 300

Commodore, **SS**. The ship on which HPB sailed to Constantinople
to escape her husband and family. 5

Compton, Elizabeth J. A medium in Havana, New York, whom
Olcott investigated. 72

Conflict between Science and Religion, The. A book by John William
Draper. 204

Constance, Lake. A lake between Germany, Austria, and
Switzerland, on which Baron de Palm claimed to own
property. 270

Constantine, the Great (ca. 288-337). The first Christian Roman
emperor. Constantine's adherence to Christianity is connected
with a story that exists in several versions. In one, Constantine
had a dream telling him to have his soldiers paint the
Christian monogram ☧ on their shields. In another
Constantine had a vision in which the monogram appeared

in the sky, together with the legend *In hoc signo vinces* "In this sign, you conquer." As a result of his patronage, Christianity became the state religion, although Constantine himself was baptized only on his deathbed. 120, 130, 294, 446

Constantine Monomachus *or* Constantine IX (ca. 1000–55). An emperor of Byzantium. 408

Constantinople *earlier* Byzantium *later* Istanbul. An originally Greek city on the Bosporus Strait between Asia Minor and Europe. 5, 13, 23, 27, 30, 483, 486, 490

Contemporary Review. A monthly periodical published in London and New York, 1866–. 480

Cook, Florence Eliza (1856–1904). An English medium who first materialized the spirit "Katie King" in 1872–4 and was extensively investigated by Sir William Crookes. (Biographical data: *EOP* 1:262–4; Podmore 2:97–9, 152–5.) 61, 62

Cook, Jay. A defendant acquitted by a jury through bribery, according to HPB. 75

Coptic. (1) A modern language descended from ancient Egyptian. (2) Pertaining to the modern descendants of the ancient Egyptians. 5, 132

Corfu, Greece. An island in the Ionian Sea. 483, 486, 490

Cornell University. The university in Ithaca, New York, where Hiram Corson taught. 65, 76, 331, 468

Cornell University, Carl A. Kroch Library, Ithaca, New York. 92, 99

Corson, Caroline Rollins (d. 1901). An American author and translator. She was the French-born wife of Hiram Corson, with whom HPB corresponded in French with some admixture of English. (Biographical data: *WWA*, 1901–2; *WWWA* 1:262.) 109, 113, 114, 115, 116, 120, 128, 151, 161, 164, 197, 199, 200, 234, 237, 251, 259, 467, 468, 469

Corson, Eugene (b. 1855). The son of Hiram and Caroline Corson, who edited HPB's letters to his parents. He was a physician who practiced in Savannah, Georgia. (Biographical data: *WWWA* 4:204.) 199

Corson, Hiram P. (1828–1911). A Spiritualist and English professor at Cornell University with whom HPB corresponded and at whose house in Ithaca, NY, she spent some time writing *Isis*

Unveiled. His published writings treat Latin literature, Anglo-Saxon, Chaucer, Shakespeare, John Milton, Walt Whitman, Robert Browning, Lord Tennyson, and educational and literary theory, but also "Spirit Messages." (Biographical data: *CW* 1:450-3; *DAB* 2:453-4; *WWWA* 1:262.) 65, 66, 69, 71, 76, 85, 89, 90, 91, 92, 97, 99, 104, 108, 111, 114, 115, 116, 121, 122, 124, 128, 139, 140, 143, 151, 154, 161, 163, 164, 171, 174, 175, 182, 195, 197, 198, 199, 200, 202, 222, 229, 231, 232, 233, 251, 252, 253, 256, 259, 331, 332, 336, 337, 464, 468, 469

Cortés, Hernán *or* **Hernando** (1485-1547). The Spanish conquistador who defeated the Aztecs and added Mexico to the Spanish Empire. 286

Cossack. A member of the frontier tribes of southern Russia who served in the cavalry of the Czar's army. 89, 96, 109, 492

Coulomb, Emma Cutting. An Englishwoman whom HPB met in 1871 while she was staying at the Cairo Hotel d'Orient, where Emma was an employee on friendly terms with the owner's son, Alexis Coulomb, whom she eventually married. Emma Coulomb was later to play a significant role in HPB's life. 13

Cox, Edward William (1809-79). An English lawyer, founder of the *Law Times* and of the Psychological Society of Great Britain, a precursor of the Society for Psychical Research, which sought for rational and physical explanations of mediumistic phenomena. (Biographical data: *CW* 1:453-4.) 274

Crawford and Balcarres, Earl of. *See* Lindsay, Alexander William Crawford.

Crickhowell, Wales. The home of "George Holly." 339

Crimea. A peninsula in the Black Sea south of the Ukraine. 5

Crimean War. An 1853-6 war of Russia against Turkey, Britain, and France over hegemony in the Middle East. 29, 31

Crookes, Sir **William** (1832-1919). The discoverer of the element thallium and inventor of the radiometer and the Crookes tube. His study of cathode rays was fundamental in the development of atomic physics. From 1870 until 1874 he investigated the mediumship of Florence Cook (Mrs. E. E. Corner, 1856-1904) and Daniel Dunglas Home (1833-86). Among his many books are *Experimental Investigations on Psychic Force* (1871) and *Researches into the Phenomena of Spiritualism* (1874). (Biographical data: *DSB* 3:474–82; *EOP* 1:280–2; Medhurst, *Crookes and the Spirit World;* Podmore 2:152–9, 237–43, 254–5, 262–3.) 34, 62, 72, 142, 219, 235, 403, 429

"Croquet at Windsor." A translation made by HPB and Alexander Wilder of a Turgenev poem satirizing British support of the Turks (*CW* 1:253–4). 283, 284, 301, 308

Crowell, Eugene (1817–94). A physician and Spiritualist characterized by HPB as "earnest" and "honest." He was the author of *The Identity of Primitive Christianity and Modern Spiritualism* 2 vols. (New York: G. W. Carleton, 1874–5), *Spiritualism and Insanity* (Boston: Colby & Rich, 1877), *The Religion of Spiritualism* (Boston: Colby & Rich, 1878), and *The Spirit World: Its Inhabitants, Nature, and Philosophy* (Boston: Colby & Rich, 1879). 154

crux ansata. *Lat.* "cross with a handle." The Egyptian symbol of life and immortality, incorporated into the seal of the Theosophical Society. 133, 134

Curtis, David A. (1846–1923). A writer, reporter, and agnostic who was the author of an article on the Arya Samaj in *Frank Leslie's Sunday Magazine*. (Biographical data: *WWWA* 1:286.) 487

Cushite. A member of an ancient people inhabiting Cush or Kush, a land in the Nile valley south of Egypt. 269

Cutting, Emma. *See* Coulomb, Emma Cutting.

Cuvier, Georges Léopold Chrétien Frédérick Dagobert, Baron (1769–1832). A French naturalist who became chancellor of the University of Paris. He originated the science of comparative anatomy by classifying animals into phyla based on the structure of their skeletons. He advanced the science of paleontology and identified and named the pterodactyl. His principle of "correlation of parts" proposes that all organs in a body are structurally and functionally interrelated, uniquely characterizing the body by its parts. 147

Cyprus. An island south of Turkey with mixed Greek and Turkish population. 13

Cyrus II *or* "Cyrus the Great" (ca. 585–ca. 529 BC). The king of Persia regarded by the Jews as God's anointed because he respected the cultures and religions of all parts of his vast empire. 318

daemon. *Lat. from Gk.* daimōn, *which also yields* demon, "an evil spirit." In Greek mythology, a supernatural being intermediate between gods and humans, or the guardian spirit or genius of a person. Socrates said he was guided by a certain inner divine principle or *daimênion*, popularly interpreted as his daemon, which warned him against improper action. 293, 307

Daily Graphic*: An Illustrated Evening Newspaper*. A newspaper published in New York, 1873–89. It was the paper that commissioned Olcott to write a series of articles on the Eddy farmhouse phenomena and in which HPB's first published article appeared. 32, 33, 35, 37, 38, 40, 48, 50, 51, 52, 72, 172, 173, 333

daimonion. *See* daemon.

Damodar. *See* Mavalankar, Damodar K.

Dana, David. A brother of the newspaper editor Charles A. Dana, who was at the time editor and part owner of the *New York Sun* (*HPB Speaks* 1:10). 177, 179, 180

Daniel. In the Book of Daniel, a Hebrew prophet deported to Babylon by King Nebuchadnezzar. Following a prophecy by Daniel, the king was turned into a beast that ate grass. 318

Daniels, Cora Linn (b. 1852). She was "a frequent visitor to and correspondent of H.P.B. in 1878" (*HPB Speaks* 1:109). *Who Was Who in America* reports that she was an original member of the Theosophical Society, but that has not been confirmed. The salutation to her as "My dear 'Wide awake'" may be an allusion to the children's periodical *Wide Awake*, published in Boston 1875–93. (Biographical data: *WWWA* 4:227.) 480, 484

Danube. A river rising in the Black Forest of western Germany, flowing eastward across Europe, and entering the Black Sea in Romania. 12, 30, 300, 351

Darius I *or* "Darius the Great" (550–486 BC). A king of Persia noted for his administrative ability, for promoting the rebuilding of the Temple in Jerusalem, and for his invasion of Greece during the Persian Wars. 318

Darwin, Charles Robert (1809–82). The English naturalist whose theory of organic evolution was one of the turning points in European intellectual history. A similar theory was independently developed by Alfred Russel Wallace, who believed that natural selection could not account for all aspects of human evolution. 43, 203, 204, 303

David. The Hebrew king and successor of Saul who became one of the greatest Jewish heroes and the founder of a royal line. Among the various stories associated with him are that of his battle against the Philistines and that of his passion for Bathsheba, which led him to send her husband, Uriah, to be killed in battle, both of which are alluded to by HPB. 87, 122, 282, 284, 317

David Copperfield. A novel by Charles Dickens. 92, 164

Davis, Andrew Jackson (1826–1910). An American Spiritualist known as "the Poughkeepsie Seer." One of the founders of modern Spiritualism, Davis had a clairvoyant experience in 1844, in which he met the Greek physician Galen and the Swedish seer Emanuel Swedenborg, which changed his life. He was a prolific author of works treating cosmology, mystical philosophy, religious interpretation, and social systems. He helped to give Spiritualism a religious orientation and coined the term "Summerland" for the after-death state. (Biographical data: *ANB* 6:164–5; *CW* 1:455–9; *DAB* 3:105; *EOP* 1:301–3; Podmore 1:158–76.) 44, 46, 87, 142, 172

Dawning of the Theosophical Movement, The. A book by Michael Gomes. 62

Dayanand Saraswati *also* **Dayananda** *and* **Sarasvati** (1824–83). Mula Shankara, who adopted the religious name Dayanand Saraswati and founded the Arya Samaj. (Biographical data: Dayanand, *Autobiography*.) 397, 399, 400, 425, 434, 435, 438, 439, 440, 441, 443, 454, 456, 457, 460, 461, 466, 477, 479, 487

Debatable Land between This World and the Next, The. A book by Robert Dale Owen (London: Trübner, 1871). 225

De bello vandalico. A work by Procopius. 287

Dee, John (1527–1608). An English mathematician, astrologer, alchemist, and magician who was advisor to both Queen Mary Tudor and Queen Elizabeth I. 242

DeGraal, Leonard. 421, 422, 423, 489, 491

Demosthenes (384–322 BC). An Athenian statesman widely regarded as the greatest orator of his time. 277

de Palm. *See* Palm, Joseph Henry Louis de, Baron.

Deveney, John Patrick. 421

de Zirkoff. *See* Zirkoff, Boris de.

Dhammapada. *Pali* "Teaching of the Verses" *or* "Dharma Way." A collection of 423 aphoristic verses that is one of the principal Buddhist scriptures. 346

Dhuleep Singh. *See* Singh, Dhuleep, Prince.

diakka. A term used by Andrew Jackson Davis for an ignorant, deceptive spirit that impersonates others at séances; also "shell" or "spook" (*EOP* 331; *Isis Unveiled* 1:218-9; *Theosophical Glossary* 101). 72, 95, 142, 180

Dickens, Charles (1812-70). A popular Victorian English novelist. 35, 88, 92, 164

Dida. The wife of the Great Spirit among the Indians of British Columbia, according to HPB. 286

Dido. In Roman mythology, the daughter of the king of Tyre who founded Carthage and became its queen. She was identified with the tutelary deity of Carthage, the goddess Tanit. In the Aeneid, Virgil recounts her love for Aeneas and her self-immolation when he obeyed Jupiter's command to leave Carthage for Italy, where his descendants were to found Rome. 286

Didona. A name of one of the great goddesses according to HPB. 287

Dinajpur. A town in northeast India (now Bangladesh). 6

Diogenes. The pen name of the unidentified author of a series of articles in the *Spiritual Scientist*, which HPB strongly disliked. The name was taken from the Greek Cynic philosopher (ca. 412-323 BC) who held that virtue consists in simplicity, for the practice of which he lived in a tub, went about in the daylight with a lantern looking for an honest man, and replied to Alexander the Great's question of what the king could do for the philosopher, "Just stand out of my sunlight." 152, 155, 156

Dionysius, *probably* Dionysius the pseudo-Areopagite. An anonymous Christian Neoplatonist, named for Paul's convert at the Athenian Areopagus (Acts 17.34). He was the author of four mystical Greek treatises that transmitted Neoplatonism to later Europe. (Cf. *CW* 14:525.) 206

Dionysos *or* Dionysus. The Greek god of wine, vegetation, and fertility, called Bacchus by the Romans. His mystery rites concerned spiritual ecstasy and life after death. HPB associates him with Osiris, Adonis, sun gods, and Jehovah. 317

Ditson, George Leighton (1812–95). An American diplomat, medical doctor, and member of the Theosophical Society who was one of the signers of the statement "To the Public" published in the *Banner of Light* on April 21, 1877 (*CW* 1:245–6). (Biographical data: *WWWA* H:151.) 197, 199

"Dix, George." The name of one of the spirit controls of Horatio Eddy. 36, 40, 51

Dnepropetrovsk *or* Dnipropetrovsk. The present-day name of HPB's birthplace, Ekaterinoslav. 1

Dnieper River. A river that flows through the Ukraine into the Black Sea. 1

Dobrovolsky, Joseph Florovich Dolivo-. The editor of the periodical *Pravda*. He was related to HPB by marriage through his sister, Yevgeniya Florovna Dolivo-Dobrovolsky, who married one of HPB's cousins, Yevgeniy Feodorovich von Hahn, the Presiding Senator of the Russian Senate. (Cf. *CW* 1:lxxi, lxxiii.) 449, 450

Dogme et rituel de la haute magie. A book by Éliphas Lévi. 250

Dolgorouky, Prince. An unidentified member of the Dolgorukov family who was a mesmerist. 235

Dolgorukov *or* **Dolgorouky** *or* **Dolgorouki** *or* Dolgoruky. The surname of a Russian princely family, perhaps descended from Yury Dolgoruky (1090–1157), a son of Vladimir Monomakh of Kiev (cf. MONOMACH). HPB was related to that family through her maternal grandmother's line. The family included a number of statesmen, military officers, and literary persons.

Dolgorukov, Henrietta Adolfovna de Bandré-du-Plessis. One of HPB's great grandmothers. 2

Dolgorukov, Paul Vassilyevich, Prince. One of HPB's great grandfathers. 2

Dominic, Saint (1170–1221). Founder of the Order of Friars Preachers (Dominicans). 279

Dondukov-Korsakov, Alexander Mihaylovich, Prince (1820–93). A Russian military man and government official who was a friend of HPB's. (Biographical data: *CW* 6:432.) 6, 11

Doubleday, Abner (1819–93). A Union general in the Civil War, firing the first defensive shot at Fort Sumter. He is also credited with the origination of American baseball, although the game has antecedents in both America and England. He served in America as Acting President of the Theosophical Society after the Founders left for India. (Biographical data: *Echoes* 2:454–6; *WWWA* H:154.) 483, 490

Draper, John William (1811–82). A professor at the University of the City of New York (now New York University), specializing in chemistry and physiology. He was also a scholar of intellectual history, his best known work being *History of the Conflict between Religion and Science*, a rationalist work that caused great controversy on its publication in 1874. (Biographical data: *WWWA* H:156.) 72, 204

Druze. A member of a hereditary, esoteric, and heterodox Shiite sect of Islam in Lebanon and Syria. 12, 411, 440

Dubois, Jean Antoine, Abbé (1765–1848). A French missionary who published extensively on Indian religion and culture, such as *Mœurs, institutions et cérémonies des peuples de l'Inde* and *Letters on the State of Christianity in India, in Which the Conversion of the Hindoos is Considered as Impracticable* (1823). 379

Duff M'Duff *or* **McDuff**. *See* McDuff, Duff.

Dufferin and Ava, Frederick Temple Hamilton-Temple-Blackwood, 1st Marquess of (1826–1902). A British diplomat who was governor-general of Canada, 1872–8, and viceroy of India, 1884–8. 285

Dunlap, Samuel Fales (1825–1905). The author of *The Origin of Ancient Names of Countries, Cities, Individuals, and Gods* (1856), *Vestiges of the Spirit-History of Man* (1858), *Sod, the Son of Man* (1861), *Sod, the Mysteries of Adoni* (1861), and *The Ghebers of Hebron: An Introduction to the Gheborim in the Lands of the Sethim, the Moloch Worship, the Jews as Brahmans, the Shepherds of Canaan, the Amorites, Kheta, and Azarielites, the Sun-Temples on the High Places, the Pyramid and Temple of Khufu, the Mithra Mysteries, the Mithra baptism, and Successive Oriental Conceptions from Jordan Fireworship to Ebionism* (1894). 283

Dunlop, D. N. 165

Dupotet de Sennevoy, Jules, Baron (1796–1881). A French disciple of Franz Mesmer and an Honorary Fellow of the Theosophical Society. (Biographical data: *CW* 7:368.) 235

dweller of *or* on **the threshold**. A rare phenomenon in which a kama-manasic shell is so strongly empowered by negative energies that it survives separation from its parent Ego and awaits the latter's reincarnation, when it is drawn by affinity to the latter, whose auric envelop it invades (*CW* 12:636). The term is from Lytton's metaphysical novel *Zanoni*. 202, 275, 276

Dyanand, **Dya Nand**, **Dyn**, etc. *See* Dayanand Saraswati.

Echmiadzin *or* **Etchmiadjene** *now* Ejmiadzin. A city in Armenia twelve miles from Yerevan, the seat of the primate of the Armenian Catholic Church and of a monastery that HPB called "the oldest monastery in Armenia" (*CW* 3:459). 267, 269

Eclectics. An Alexandrian school of theosophical Neoplatonists. 304

Eclectic Theosophist. A bimonthly periodical published by Point Loma Publications, San Diego, California, 1971–95. 363, 484

Eddy, Horatio (1842–1922) and **William** (1832–1932). Brothers whose farm in Chittenden, VT, became the site of séances with the brothers as physical mediums, attracting widespread attention. Olcott wrote a series of newspaper articles on his observations there, later published as *People from the Other World* (1875), and HPB and Olcott met at the Eddy farm. (Biographical data: *CW* 1:461–2; *EOP* 1:385.) 32, 33, 34, 35, 36, 37, 38, 39, 40, 41, 45, 48, 50, 56, 57, 62, 72, 80, 142, 252, 295, 331

Edison, Thomas Alva (1847–1931). "The quintessential American inventor in the era of Yankee ingenuity," as the *Encyclopædia Britannica* calls him. Edison registered more than a thousand patents, his most significant inventions being in the field of electricity: the phonograph, telephone and microphone technology, a telegraphic printer, the electric light bulb, an electric railroad, an electric generator, the alkaline storage battery, and the motion picture. He was a pioneer of research and development laboratories. Less well known is Edison's strong mystical streak. (Biographical data: Baldwin, *Edison: Inventing the*

Century; *WWWA* 1:359.) 418, 419, 420, 421, 422, 423, 424, 428, 450, 488, 489, 490, 491

Edison National Historic Site, West Orange, New Jersey. 421, 422, 423, 489, 491

Edmonds, John Worth, Judge (1799–1874). An early and influential American Spiritualist. Having served in both houses of the New York State legislature, he became a justice on the state supreme court, a position from which he resigned because of controversy over his involvement with Spiritualism. He began as an investigator of the phenomenon but developed mediumistic abilities himself. (Biographical data: *DAB* 3:23–4; *EOP* 1:386–7; Podmore 1:223–5, 230–3; *WWWA* H:165.) 87

Edwin Drood, The Mystery of. A novel being published in serial form by Charles Dickens but left unfinished at his death in 1870. In 1872–73, T. P. James, an uneducated practitioner of automatic writing in Brattleboro, Vermont, produced a second part, longer than the first, completing the novel. The two parts were published together in 1874 (*EOP* 1:331–2, s.v. "Dickens"). 35, 45

Egypt. 5, 12, 13, 14, 16, 18, 19, 25, 27, 30, 41, 43, 141, 271, 285, 286, 319, 449

Egyptian. 219, 269, 307, 317

Egyptian Book of the Dead. *See* Book of the Dead, Egyptian.

Eighth Avenue. *See also* Forty-seventh Street, 302 West, *and* Lamasery. 336, 365, 477

Ekaterinoslav *or* **Ekaterinoslaw**, *later* Dnipropetrovsk. A city in the Ukraine on the bank of the Dnieper River, HPB's birthplace. 1, 296

El. The supreme deity in the Canaanite pantheon, adopted as a name for the Hebrew God. Originally, Yahweh (YHVH) was a subordinate deity to El, to whom El delegated responsibilities for particular matters and nations, but later Yahweh replaced El as the supreme and only God (Bowker 307). 247, 317

elemental. (1) A nature spirit, a semiconscious force of nature. (2) An elementary. In later use the two terms were carefully distinguished, but in earlier times, and in these letters, they were often interchanged. 53, 200, 218, 219, 221, 229, 352, 360, 361

elementary. (1) A cast off astral-mental shell of a dead human being whose spirit has gone to other realms, leaving this shell behind still endowed with some traces of consciousness. (2) An elemental. 59, 169, 188, 198, 204, 206, 207, 208, 210, 211, 212, 221, 225, 226, 229, 233, 235, 236, 240, 243, 244, 246, 247, 248, 249, 255, 275, 276, 354, 360, 361, 365, 372, 387

Elena Blavatskaya. A Russian form of the name Helena Blavatsky. 29, 360, 500

Elephanta. An island in the harbor of Bombay, the site of early cave temples and of a giant sculpture of the Trimurti, the three-headed representation of the gods Brahma, Vishnu, and Shiva. 428

Eleusinian and Bacchic Mysteries. A book by Thomas Taylor. 283, 285

Eleusinian Mysteries. The most famous of the Greek Mysteries, an initiatory rite celebrated at Eleusis, near Athens, in honor of the goddess Demeter. 307

Elias *or* Elijah. An Israelite prophet who was taken to heaven in a chariot of fire, drawn by horses of fire, in a whirlwind (2 Kings 2.1, 11). 204

Elissa. Another name for Dido, queen of Carthage. 287

Elizabeth I (1533–1603). Queen of England. 242

Ellie. A pet name (from "Helen" or Russian "Elena") for HPB, used by "John King." 179, 180, 182, 185

Ellora. A village in western India, where a series of Buddhist, Hindu, and Jain temples were carved out of rock cliffs. 104, 428

Elmo *or* **Erasmus**, Saint (d. 303). An Italian bishop and the patron saint of sailors, for whom is named Saint Elmo's fire, an electrical discharge seen on the masts of ships in stormy weather. 277

Elohim. *Heb. plural of* Eloah "god." God or gods. In the Hebrew scriptures the term is sometimes used in a plural sense with reference to non-Hebrew gods. But its most frequent use is for the God of Israel, interpreted as a "plural of majesty." Theosophical interpreters have pointed to its similarity with the term "Logos," understood as designating, not a divine being, but a divine collective consciousness. (Cf. *CW* 14:200–5.) 207, 322, 327

empyraeum. An obsolete (17th and 18th c.) spelling for *empyrean*, the highest of the heavens, made of fire or light. 155, 169, 171

En Soph. *See* Ain Soph.

England. 6, 21, 31, 34, 41, 61, 80, 214, 227, 235, 241, 277, 282, 315, 338, 341, 356, 399, 431, 434, 435, 438, 439, 441, 442, 449, 457, 461, 482, 491, 493, 494

Ennemoser, Joseph (1787–1854). A physician at the University of Bonn (1820–41), who studied animal magnetism and was the author of *Geschichte der Magie*, translated by William Howitt as *The History of Magic*, 2 vols., 1854. 152, 174

Enoch. A Hebrew patriarch, the father of Methuselah, who "walked with God: and he was not; for God took him" (Gen. 5.21–4). He is therefore coupled with Elias (Elijah) for having been translated to heaven. 204, 205, 213

Ephraim. The younger son of the Patriarch Joseph, and the tribe tracing their ancestry to him. 269

Epictetus (ca. 50–ca. 138). A Stoic philosopher who taught indifference to externals, the existence of good within oneself, and the brotherhood of humanity. 144

Epicurean. A follower of Epicurus (341–270 BC), a philosopher who said that philosophy is the art of making life happy and who subordinated metaphysics to ethics. For him, the highest good was pleasure—not indulgence but serenity. He valued intellectual above physical pleasure and emphasized free will. In popular use, a gourmet or sybarite. 91

Erevan *or* **Erivan**. *See* Yerevan.

Esék. A town in the region of Hungary-Transylvania that HPB visited. 13

Esoteric School. A school HPB founded in 1888. 311

Essays on the Languages, Literature, and Religion of Nepal and Tibet. A book by Brian H. Hodgson. 390

Estonia. 8

Etchmiadjene. *See* Echmiadzin.

ether *or* **aether**. A rarefied element believed to fill outer space and to be the medium for the transmission of light. 83, 196, 203, 205, 206, 207, 210, 213, 246, 272

Ethiopia. 269

Ethiopian. 265, 266, 269, 319

Euclid (fl. 300 BC). A Greek mathematician whose *Elements* of geometry is still typically the model for presenting the subject to students. 258

***Eunomia*, SS**. The ship on which HPB was traveling to Egypt when it exploded and sank. 13, 42, 183

Europe. 5, 7, 24, 71, 162, 233, 240, 252, 259, 270, 286, 321, 361, 402, 429, 433, 437, 440, 447, 457, 479, 494

Eusebius (ca. 263–ca. 339). A bishop of Caesarea and a Church historian. 139, 294

Evans, Mr. Despite C. Jinarajadasa's tentative identification of this man with Mordecai D. Evans, he is probably a different person. 480

Evans, Mrs. The wife of Mordecai D. Evans. 364

Evans, Mordecai D. A member who joined the Theosophical Society on November 8, 1876. 88, 138, 363, 484

Evmonia. *See* Eunomia.

Exchange Street, 18. The Boston address of E. Gerry Brown. 125

Ezekiel. One of the major prophets of the Hebrew scriptures. According to present-day scholars, he was deported to Babylon with other Jews after Nebuchadnezzar captured Jerusalem in 597 BC, and he received prophetic communications from 593 to 571. 318

Ezra. One of the prophets and prophetic books of the Hebrew scriptures. Ezra was an exile in Babylon who returned to Palestine with permission of the Persian king. The Book of Ezra tells of the return of the Jews and the reconstruction of the Temple in the sixth to fifth centuries BC. To preserve purity of religion, Ezra ordered Jews not to marry foreigners. 269, 321, 349

F., Mr. Apparently a reporter for the *Daily Graphic* who interviewed HPB for the newspaper. 38

Fadeef. *See* Fadeyev.

Fadeyev, Andrey Mihailovich de (1789–1867). HPB's maternal grandfather. 2, 3, 4, 14, 41

Fadeyev, Helena Pavlovna Dolgorukova de, Princess (1789–1860). HPB's maternal grandmother. (Biographical data: *CW* 7:304–5 fn.) 2, 9, 41

Fadeyev, Nadyezhda ("**Nadya**" *or* "**Nadejinka/Nadyezhenka**") **Andreyevna de** (1829–1919). HPB's favorite aunt, her mother's sister, but only two years older than HPB. While living in Odessa, in 1870 she received the first known letter from one of the Adepts (KH), informing the family that HPB was well and would return to them in a year and a half (*LMW1* 84–5, *LMW2* 3–5). Many of HPB's letters to her aunt deal at length with their religious differences: Nadyezhda was pious Russian Orthodox, and HPB was anxious not to upset her. (Biographical data: *CW* 1:434–5, fn. 7.) 2, 3, 4, 7, 13, 297, 301, 314, 327, 329, 342, 355, 379, 443, 452, 467

Fadeyev, Rostislav ("**Rostya**" *or* "**Rostia**") **Andreyevich de**, Gen. (1824–84). HPB's maternal uncle. (Biographical data: *CW* 1:255 fn., 3:506–7.) 24, 27, 30, 395

Fales, William S. A law-firm student in Benjamin Tracy's office who served as a translator in Blavatsky's Long Island case and was one of the five persons whose discussions led to the publication of the article on "Rosicrucianism," under the pen name HIRAF, to which HPB replied with her "first *Occult* Shot." Fales was one of the three chief authors of the article and assembled the contributions of the other two, Frederick W. Hinrichs and William M. Ivins. 157

Faraday, Michael (1791–1867). An English scientist specializing in chemistry, electricity, and magnetism. As a young man, he worked with the chemist Sir Humphry Davy at the Royal Institution of Great Britain in London, and in his middle years he worked with Sir Charles Wheatstone on the vibratory aspects of sound shown in Chladni figures (the patterns of powder on a plate, produced by a violin bow). His work on electromagnetism produced the first dynamo and resulted in a theory of electrochemistry. He posited a single universal force of which all known natural forces were manifestations, and he originated field theory—the concept that space is not a mere nothing in which objects are located, but a something that is the medium of electromagnetic forces. In his investigation of Spiritualist phenomena he assumed fraud, whether conscious or unconscious (Podmore 2:9, 145–6). 298, 299

Father Confessor. A priest who hears confessions and is a spiritual guide. 66, 93, 140

Fathers of the Church. *See* Church Fathers.

Fedia *or* **Fedya**. A pet name for "Feodor," specifically for Feodor Nikolayevich de Yahontov, HPB's nephew. 359, 414, 416

Féhervár. A town in Hungary that HPB visited. 12

Fellger, Adolphus. A Philadelphia physician involved in the Katie King controversy (*CW* 1:59). 69

Felt, George Henry. A New York engineer and architect. His lecture on "The Lost Canon of Proportions of the Egyptians, Greeks, and Romans" was the occasion that sparked the formation of the Theosophical Society. He was one of the two first vice presidents of the Society. (Biographical data: *CW* 1:463.) 219, 221, 228, 229, 233, 238, 243

"Few Questions to 'Hiraf,' A." HPB's first occult article (*CW* 1:101–19). 170, 208, 213, 331, 332

Figaro. A French newspaper, first published in 1826. 415

Fiji. 470

Flammarion, N. Camille (1842–1925). A French astronomer who studied especially double and multiple stars and wrote books popularizing astronomy. He was also dedicated, especially toward the end of his life, to psychical research. (Biographical data: *CW* 3:509; *EOP* 1:466-7.) 87, 119, 429

Flammel *or* **Flamel, Nicholas** (ca. 1330–1418). A French notary or public scrivener who is reputed to have discovered a book on alchemy by Abraham, the Jew. Having deciphered this work with the aid of a rabbi, he launched into alchemical experiments with the aid of his wife, Pernelle. They succeeded in producing the Philosophers' Stone, and with the wealth it brought them, they became benefactors for churches and hospitals. (Biographical data: *EOP* 1:465-6.) 133

Flint, Charles R. 157

Florence, Italy. 13

Florsedim. Unidentified. (The ending *-im* appears to be the Hebrew plural.) 268

Fludd *or* Flud, **Robert**, *or* Robertus de Fluctibus (1574–1637). An English mystical philosopher and physician influenced by the teachings of Paracelsus, which he attempted to reconcile with the "New Science" of the seventeenth century. When the Rosicrucian manifestos appeared in the early seventeenth century, Fludd became an enthusiastic supporter and propagandist for them. (Biographical data: *EOP* 1:469; Godwin, *Robert Fludd;* Podmore 1:45–8.) 86, 134, 135, 206

Fort Scott, Kansas. 103

Fort Sumter, South Carolina. The fort at which the first shots of the Civil War were fired under the command of Gen. Abner Doubleday. 483

Forty-seventh Street, 302 West, New York City. The address of the Lamasery at the corner of Eighth Avenue. 280, 289, 312, 336, 362, 365, 390, 392, 421, 422, 453, 464, 478, 485, 487

Four Noble Truths. The fundamental doctrines of Buddhism: that life involves suffering; that suffering has a cause; that suffering has a cure; that the way to the cure of suffering is by following the Noble Eightfold Path. 381

Fourteenth Street and Fourth Avenue, New York City. The site of a house in which HPB lived in 1873 or 1874. 32

Fox sisters. Kate *or* Catharine (1836–92) and Margaret(ta) (1833–93), whose experiences with noises and knockings in their Hydesville, New York, house sparked the Spiritualist movement of the nineteenth century. (Biographical data: *EOP* 1:480–3; Podmore 1:179–88.) 56

France. 7, 21, 29, 31, 34, 113, 227, 236, 341, 348

Frank Leslie's Sunday Magazine. A monthly periodical published under varying titles in New York City, 1877–89. 487

Franklin library. Probably the Library Company of Philadelphia, founded by Benjamin Franklin in 1731 as a subscription or circulating library. 130

Franklin Register and Norfolk County Journal. A newspaper published in Franklin, Massachusetts, 1872–81. 398

free love. The practice of open sexual relations without marriage or other commitment, followed by some early Spiritualists. 46, 214, 227, 232

Freemasonry *or* **Masonic fraternity** *or* **Masonry**. Any of the various organizations with secret rites that assumed their present-day form during and after the eighteenth century. 84, 137, 261, 328, 329, 341, 353, 397, 404, 410, 454, 486

French, Mrs. An unidentified person who received messages through Gen. Lippitt's psychic stand. 186

From the Caves and Jungles of Hindostan. A collection of fictionalized narratives by HPB, under the pen name "Radda-Bai," based on her early experiences and travels in north India, originally published in Russian. 6, 356

Furness, William Henry (1802–96). An author, abolitionist, and Unitarian minister who married HPB and Michael C. Betanelly in 1875. (Biographical data: *WWWA* H:194.) 135

"Further Language from Truthful James." A work by Bret Harte. 229

Galaxy. A magazine, perhaps *Galaxy: A Magazine of Entertaining Reading*, published in New York by William Conant Church, 1866–77 or –78. 62, 139

Gan. The Russian form of the German name Hahn. 2

Ganges. The most important river of India, sacred to Hindus, which flows eastward across northern India (and now Bangladesh) into the Indian Ocean. 276

Gardiner *or* **Gardener** *or* **Gardner**, Dr. The organizer or chairman of lectures by Olcott on elementary spirits and Spiritualism in Boston (*CW* 1:72, 301). 255

Garibaldi, Giuseppe (1807–82). An Italian patriot who led a band of guerrilla "Redshirts" in a fight to unify Italy and free it from foreign rule by the Austrians and the French. HPB's connection with him was through her presence at the Battle of Mentana, in which his forces were defeated by the French. A master of guerrilla warfare, he was inclined to embrace pacifism toward the end of his life, having learned that wars are generally neither justified nor effective. He supported the rights of working people and of women, racial equality, and freethought. 13, 49, 90, 432

Gary, Indiana, *Gazette*. A newspaper in which Thomas Alva Edison published his philosophical views. 419

Gautama. The family name of Siddhartha Gautama, the Buddha. 344, 346, 348, 349, 350, 354, 380, 381, 383, 446

Georgia. A country in the Caucasus, east of the Black Sea, north of Turkey and Armenia, in HPB's time ruled by Russia. 4, 5, 8, 9, 41, 81, 295

Georgian. (1) Pertaining to Caucasian Georgia. (2) A native of Caucasian Georgia. (3) The South Caucasian language of Georgians. 48, 49, 82, 135

Gerebko, Clementine. The woman with whom HPB entered into a partnership to develop land on Long Island for chicken farming and market gardening. When they fell out, HPB sued for recovery of her investment and was successful. 32, 156, 157

Germany. 6, 7, 140, 227, 315, 370

Gibbon, Edward (1737–94). An English historian, known chiefly for his book *The History of the Decline and Fall of the Roman Empire*, which attributes the downfall of Rome largely to the rise of Christianity. Gibbon opposed the American Revolution and favored the French Revolution. 130

Giles, Mr. An otherwise unidentified Bostonian who provided HPB with information about E. Gerry Brown. 117

Girard Street, 1111, Philadelphia. HPB's address in early 1875. 106

gnome. An elemental spirit or force of nature associated with earth. 235, 387

Gnostic. An adherent of or characteristic of Gnosticism. 147, 304, 497

Gnosticism. A system of philosophical thought of late Hellenistic and early Christian times. Gnosticism was not a coherent movement but had a number of variations spread over large areas and long stretches of time, reflecting influences from Jewish mysticism of the sort that later produced Kabbalah, the Hellenistic Mystery schools, Egyptian and Near-Eastern mythologies, Iranian dualism, and Christianity. The common thread of Gnosticism is a belief in salvation by esoteric knowledge, comparable to the Jñāna Yoga of India. Much Gnosticism is also characterized by a dualistic view of spiritual goodness versus material evil. Gnostics developed elaborate myths to express their worldview in symbolic terms. 157, 342

Godfrey of Bouillon (*Fr.* Godefroi de) (ca. 1060–1100). A leader of the First Crusade who, having captured Jerusalem, accepted the crown but refused the title of king and was called instead *Advocatus Sancti Sepulchri* (Defender of the Holy Sepulcher). Tall, handsome, and blond, Godfrey was idolized in legend as the "perfect Christian knight." 89

Gwalior. A city in Madhya Pradesh, formerly a princely state in Central India. Now the city is the winter capital of the state of Madhya Pradesh. 417, 418

Gwikovar. An unidentified young person, apparently of an Indian ruling family, perhaps of the Holkars of Indore. 418

H., Professor. An unidentified pupil of Faraday's. 298

Haas, house of. The house on Polizeyskaya Street, Odessa, where HPB was living with her aunt Katherine Andreyevna de Witte in December 1872. 29

Hades. *Gk. myth*. The underground realm of the god Hades, to which mortals went after death; hence the afterdeath realm where the shells of the dead continue to exist. 57, 86

Hahn, Madame **von**. An unidentified member of HPB's father's family. 314

Hahn, Alexander Petrovich von (1833–4). HPB's younger brother, who died in infancy. 3

Hahn, Alexis Gustavovich Hahn von Rottenstern- (d. ca. 1830). HPB's paternal grandfather. 2

Hahn, Elizabeth Maksimovna von Pröbsen. HPB's paternal grandmother. 2

Hahn, Elizabeth Petrovna von. HPB's half sister. *See* Beliy, Elizabeth Petrovna.

Hahn, Gustav Alexeyevich von (d. ca. 1861). HPB's paternal uncle. 31, 48, 49, 50

Hahn, Helena Andreyevna von, *née* de Fadeyev (1814–42). HPB's mother. 1, 2, 3, 4, 41

Hahn, Leonid Petrovich von (1840–85). HPB's second brother. 3, 4, 370

Hahn, Nikolay Gustavovich von. HPB's cousin by her paternal uncle. 31

Hahn, Peter Alexeyevich von (1798–1873). HPB's father. 1, 2, 3, 6, 32, 40, 41, 52, 156

Hahn-Hahn *and* **Hahn-Hahn von der Rotter-Hahn**. Variants of HPB's family name. 41, 295, 296, 299

Hahn-Hahn, Ida, Countess. According to an error-filled newspaper interview, an author and cousin of HPB's. 41

Hahn von Rottenstern-Hahn, Counts. HPB's paternal ancestors, a German family that settled in Russia. 2

Hamburg, Germany. 42

Hamlet. The title character of Shakespeare's tragic play. 273, 348

Hapsburg Kingdom. The political entity formed by the union of Austria and Hungary from 1867 to 1918. 30

Harbinger of Light. A periodical published in Melbourne, 1870–. 80

Hardy, John. A Boston medium, the husband of Mary M. Hardy. 254

Hardy, Mary M. (*later* Perkins). A Boston medium who produced paraffin casts of the hands of spirits. She and her husband are the subjects of an account by D. D. Home in his book *Lights and Shadows of Spiritualism* (367–70). (Biographical data: *EOP* 1:569.) 254

Hare, David (1775–1842). English educator who worked with the native population of India and was the subject of an 1878 biography by Peary Chand Mitra. 393, 409

Hare, Robert (1781–1858). A distinguished professor of chemistry at the University of Pennsylvania, author of *Experimental Investigation: The Spirit Manifestations* (1855). HPB associated him with Crookes, Flammarion, and Wallace. (Biographical data: Podmore 1:233–6; *WWWA* H:234.) 429

Harley. An unidentified man whom HPB claims to have put "on the truth path." 326

Harper's Weekly. A magazine published in New York, 1857–1976. 402

Harrison, Vernon. 402

Harte, Bret, *orig.* Francis Brett Harte (1836–1902). An American author of the local-color school. Known for his fiction set in California, he was famous for a poem "Plain Language from Truthful James" (1870), also called "The Heathen Chinee." 229

Hartford, Connecticut. 47, 49, 79, 120, 330

Harvard University. 83

Harvey, W. Wigan. 308

Hassan Aga. A merchant from Tiflis, apparently Turkish, who appeared to HPB at Chittenden (Olcott, *People from the Other World* 310–2). 48

Haug, Martin (1827–76). A German expert on Indian and Iranian religious literature and language, such as the *Aitareya Brahmana of the Rig Veda* and the *Book of Arda Viraf*, and the author of *Essays on the Sacred Language, Writings, and Religion of the Parsis*. 446

Hauts phénomènes de la magie, précédés du spiritisme antique, Les. A book by Henri Roger Gougenot des Mousseaux (Paris, 1864). 274

Havana, New York. 72

Hayden, Mr. Apparently a friend of Cora Daniels and an early member of the Theosophical Society from Providence, Rhode Island. 480, 483, 484

Heaven and Hell. A work by Emanuel Swedenborg, *De coelo et ejus mirabilibus, et de inferno, ex auditis & visis*, "Of heaven and its marvels, and of hell, from things heard and seen" (1758). 419

Hebrew. 79, 83, 84, 147, 208, 298, 319, 320, 327, 333

Hegard, Mr. A person concerned with the Henry T. Child controversy. 88

Heidelberg, Germany. 468

Helmont, Jan Baptista van (1577–1644). A Flemish physician, chemist, physicist, and mystic. He discovered carbon dioxide, identified gases as a state of matter in addition to solids and liquids, and coined the term *gas* for them. (Biographical data: *CW* 12:750.) 211, 381

Herald of Odessa. A Russian newspaper in which some of HPB's articles were published. 415, 417

Hermes *or* **Hermes Trismegistus**. *Gk*. Hermēs trismegistos "Hermes thrice greatest." A Greek term for the Egyptian god of wisdom, Thoth, to whom were ascribed various works known collectively as Hermetic books. 204, 205, 214, 286

Hermes, Books of. A class of third-century Gnostic writings attributed to Hermes Trismegistus. 208

Hermetic. Pertaining to Hermeticism or those who espouse it. 195

Hermetic axiom. A statement, in various forms, of the unity of all things and of correspondences between th em. As expressed in the Bowen Notes, it is as follows: "As is the Inner, so is the Outer; as is the Great, so is the Small; as it is above, so it is below; there is but ONE LIFE AND LAW; and he that worketh it is ONE. Nothing is Inner, nothing is Outer; nothing is Great, nothing is Small; nothing is High, nothing is Low, in the Divine Economy." 133, 208

Hermeticism or **Hermetic philosophy**. The doctrines and practices of the books attributed to Hermes Trismegistus. They expressed Gnostic traditions of the first three centuries AD. 196, 246, 248, 278

Herne, Frank (fl. 1870s). An English physical medium with whom Florence Cook first sat. He formed a partnership with Charles Williams to produce impressive phenomena, whose genuineness, however, was suspected. (Biographical data: Podmore 2:78–83, 97–104.) 18, 19

Herodotus (ca. 484–425 BC). A Greek historian whose work is the first attempt at a comprehensive secular narrative of events and who has consequently been called "the Father of History." 265, 266, 269, 287, 318

Herrera y Tordesillas, Antonio de (ca. 1559–1625). The official historiographer of Castille, who wrote a history of the New World (1601). 285

Heth. A son of Canaan, according to Gen. 10.15. 287, 288

Hezelton *or* **Hezleton**. A spirit photographer, like William H. Mumler. 95, 123

Higgins, Godfrey (1773–1833). A British scholar and social reformer who believed in a single ancient universal religion of which all modern forms are developments. He developed that thesis in his major work, *Anacalypsis: An Attempt to Draw Aside the Veil of Saitic Isis; or, An Inquiry into the Origin of Languages, Nations and Religions*, which was a significant influence on HPB, perhaps suggesting the title of *Isis Unveiled*. (Biographical data: Higgins, *Anacalypsis* 1965 reprint 450–64; *CW* 8:458–9; *EOP* 1:598.) 197, 199, 205, 213, 269, 283

Hilarion. A Greek Adept. 13

Hilkiah. A high priest in the seventh century BC who found a Book of the Law in the Temple (2 Kings, 22–3; *CW* 7:374–5). 321

Hindostan. India, especially the northern part where Hindi is spoken. 343, 472

Hindostani *or* **Hindostanee**. The language of Hindostan, Hindi or Urdu. 372, 432

Hindu. A daily newspaper published in Madras, 1878-. 375, 378

Hindu Pantheon. A book by Edward Moor. 269

Hinrichs, Frederick W. A political reformer, chairman of the Brooklyn Committee of the Woodrow Wilson Foundation, and one of the chief authors of the article on "Rosicrucianism," published under the pen name HIRAF. He recorded his recollections of the event in a letter of May 3, 1923, to C. Jinarajadasa, now in the Archives of the Theosophical Society, Adyar. *See* "Few Questions to Hiraf, A."

Hiraf. A pen name used by five acquaintances of HPB's who met to discuss literature, philosophy, and kindred matters. Three of them (William Fales, Frederick Hinrichs, and William Ivins) contributed to a literary spoof on psychism and esotericism, published in the *Spiritual Scientist* under the pen name "Hiraf," an acronym derived from their surnames: Hinrichs, Ivins, Robinson, Adams, Fales, but also suggesting the Masonic figure of Hiram. Two of them, Fales and Ivins, were attorneys who represented HPB in her Long Island court case. Their article introduced in the *Spiritual Scientist* 2 (July 1, 1875): 199, was published in two parts, the first in that issue, page 202, and the second in the following issue (July 8, 1875), pages 212-3. It was entitled "Rosicrucianism," and its acronymous author was given as

HIRAF * * *

The five stars were probably used for their mystical implications but represented the five contributors. HPB responded to the article with what she called her "first *Occult* Shot": "A Few Questions to 'Hiraf'"; she may have arranged publication of the article for that purpose. (Biographical and historical data: *CW* 1:95-100, 101-19; Charles R. Flint, *Memories*, ch. 9.) *See* "Few Questions to Hiraf, A."

Hivite *or* **Hiveen**. A descendant of Canaan. 287, 288

Hoboken, New Jersey. 451

Hodgson, Brian. Author of *Essays on the Languages, Literature, and Religion of Nepál and Tibet* (1874). 389

Hodgson Report. An 1885 report to the Society for Psychical Research on HPB's phenomena, written by Richard Hodgson. (Cf. Harrison, *H. P. Blavatsky and the SPR*; Inglis 359–60.) 401, 402, 418

Holkar. The dynastic rulers of the princely state of Indore. The founder of the line was of peasant origin, Malhar Rao Holkar. 418

Hollis, Mary J. *See* Billing, Harry J., Dr. and Mrs.

"Holly, George." A character in a fictional biography by Gordon Rowe. 339

Holmes, "detective." An otherwise unidentified person who swindled HPB out of $18. 144, 146

Holmes, Nelson *and* **Jennifer** (**"Jennie"**) (fl. 1874). A husband and wife pair of materialization mediums in Philadelphia who claimed to use "John King" and "Katie King" as guides. (Biographical data: *EOP* 1:606.) 47, 58, 61, 62, 63, 64, 65, 68, 69, 70, 71, 73, 74, 75, 81, 82, 85, 88, 90, 93, 94, 95, 96, 104, 110, 125, 138, 144, 153, 155, 186, 193, 235, 254

Home, Daniel Dunglas (1833–86). "The most notable physical medium in the history of spiritualism" (*EOP*). HPB claimed friendship with his wife Alexandrina de Kroll (letter 5) but also disavowed ever having seen her (in a manuscript marginal note to an interview printed in the *Spiritual Scientist*, reprinted as an endnote to letter 10). However, the interview that elicited her disavowal also quotes HPB as saying that in her girlhood she had been an intimate of Home's wife's sister, so the denial of having seen Home's wife may refer only to the time after their marriage. Antagonism developed between Home and both Olcott and Blavatsky, as a result of which she came to regard him with great disdain. Home attacked Olcott and the Theosophical Society in particular in his 1877 work *Lights and Shadows of Spiritualism*. A Mahatma Letter of early 1881 (*ML*, p. 53) refers to Home as "the bitterest and most cruel enemy O. and Mad. B. have, though he has never met either of them." (Biographical data: *CW* 1:469; *DNB* 9:1119–21; *EOP* 1:607–11; Hall *Enigma;* Podmore 2:224–8, and see index.) 19, 42, 43, 233, 252, 254, 258, 260, 274, 308, 360, 361, 362

Honduras. 6

Howitt, William (1792–1879). A British Spiritualist and the translator of *Geschichte der Magie*, by Joseph Ennemoser, as *The History of Magic*, 2 vols. (1854). He, his wife Mary, and their son and daughter were all Spiritualists and developed mediumship, including automatic writing. Howitt was a frequent contributor to the *Spiritual Magazine*. (Biographical data: Podmore 2:163–4, and see index.) 152, 174

HPB Library, Toronto, Canada. 69, 87, 94, 104, 116, 122, 135, 156, 165, 175, 201, 237, 256, 259, 468, 469

HPB Speaks. A collection of HPB's letters, edited by C. Jinarajadasa. 77, 78, 80, 90, 97, 107, 122, 126, 137, 140, 146, 151, 161, 171, 184, 185, 191, 194, 328, 355, 356, 397, 451, 484

Hudson River. A river flowing through New York State and entering the Atlantic Ocean at New York City. 451

Hull. An unidentified referent. 448

Human Nature: A Monthly Journal of Zoistic Science and Intelligence, Embodying Physiology, Phrenology, Psychology, Spiritualism, Psychology, the Laws of Health, and Sociology. A periodical published in London and edited by James Burns, 1867–78, which was the organ of a progressive wing of the British Spiritualist movement. (Cf. Podmore 2:164–6.) 19

Humboldt, Alexander von (Friedrich Wilhelm Heinrich), Freiherr ("Baron") (1769–1859). A German naturalist and explorer who was a pioneer in the development of the modern earth sciences and ecology. 2, 162

Hungary. 12, 27, 30, 486

Huntington township. A community on Long Island and the location of a tract of land that was the subject of legal action by HPB. 156

Hurrychund. *See* Chintamon, Hurrychund.

Huxley, Thomas Henry (1825–95). An English biologist and proponent of Darwinism who coined the word "agnosticism" to designate his attitude toward religion. As a young medical officer in the Royal Navy, Huxley conducted experiments on marine life that led to his election to the Royal Society at the age of 26, although he lacked academic qualifications. Consulted by Darwin before the publication of the latter's revolutionary work, *The Origin of Species* (1859), Huxley became known as "Darwin's bulldog" for his aggressive support of Darwinism. In a famous debate with Bishop Samuel Wilberforce at Oxford in 1860, Huxley turned the bishop's attempt at ridicule against the churchman; that debate has been called science's declaration of independence from theology. In 1876, Huxley visited the United States to speak in Baltimore at the opening of Johns Hopkins University, the first American institution of higher education to specialize in graduate work. When invited to participate in an investigation of Spiritualism by the London Dialectical Society, Huxley declined with this remark: "supposing the phenomena to be genuine, they do not interest me. If anybody would endow me with the faculty of listening to the chatter of old women and curates in the nearest cathedral town, I should decline the privilege, having better things to do" (Podmore 2:147–8). 203, 271, 272, 273, 291, 297

"Huxley and Slade: Who Is More Guilty of 'False Pretences'?" An article by HPB (*CW* 1:226–33). 272

Hyde Park, London. The largest park in London (630 acres), including Kensington Gardens, the Albert Memorial, Marble Arch, and Speakers' Corner, where anyone may orate. 6, 278

Hyksos. A foreign dynasty that ruled Egypt in the eighteenth to sixteenth centuries BC. 350

Hypatia (ca. 370–415). The head of the Neoplatonic school at Alexandria and the first notable woman mathematician, famed for her learning, eloquence, and beauty. Her murder by a mob of monks encouraged by the Archbishop of Alexandria, St. Cyril, marked the beginning of the decline of Alexandria as a center of learning. 396

Iacchus. One of the deities honored in the Mysteries of Eleusis. Little is known about him, but he is sometimes associated with the earth goddess Demeter and sometimes identified with Bacchus. His name was used as a cry during the Eleusinian processions: "Iacche!" 317

Iamblichus or **Jamblichus** (d. ca. 330). A Syrian Neoplatonist and student of Porphyry's whose teachings combined Platonism with Pythagoreanism and Oriental mysticism and magic. His book *On the Egyptian Mysteries* has survived, although his writings on the Greek philosophers other than Pythagoras have not. 214, 236, 249, 278, 352, 357, 359

Ignatieff, Nikolay Pavlovich, Gen. (1832–1908). The Russian Ambassador to Turkey, 1867–77. 28, 30

Illustrated Weekly. A periodical published in New York City, beginning in 1875. 284

"Il Penseroso." A poem by John Milton. 229

Imperial Cross Medium. An epithet for the Spiritualist and medium William Stainton Moses, with allusion to the fact that his spirit control used the signature "Imperator +," hence "Imperial Cross." 273, 278

Inaugural Address. The speech of Henry Steel Olcott delivered on November 17, 1875, at Mott Memorial Hall, New York City, which was the first public meeting of the newly formed Theosophical Society. 218, 220, 222, 223, 228, 229, 231, 238

Incidents in the Life of Madame Blavatsky. A book by A. P. Sinnett. 1, 4, 6, 7, 10, 11, 12, 16, 17, 23, 54, 55, 57, 216, 300, 313, 375, 397

Indépendance belge, L', "Belgian Independence." A periodical published in Brussels, 1843–1940. 43

Index Expurgatorius. A Roman Catholic list of forbidden books. 377, 378

Indian Daily News. A periodical published in Calcutta since 1869. 410

Indian Spectator. A periodical published in Bombay. 442

Indore. The princely state of the Maratha Holkars in central India. 418

Inglis, Brian. 401

Inman, Thomas (1820–76). An English physician who, in addition to various medical works, was the author of *Ancient Faiths Embodied in Ancient Names; or, An Attempt to Trace the Religious Belief, Sacred Rites, and Holy Emblems of Certain Nations, by an Interpretation of the Names Given to Children by Priestly Authority, or Assumed by Prophets, Kings, and Hierarchs* (1868–9), *Ancient Pagan* *and Modern Christian Symbolism Exposed and Explained* (1869), and *Ancient Faiths and Modern: A Dissertation upon Worships, Legends and Divinities in Central and Western Asia, Europe, and Elsewhere, before the Christian Era* (New York: Bouton, 1876). (Biographical data: *CW* 11:579.) 282, 283

International Committee of Spiritualists for the Centennial. An organization mentioned twice by HPB in letters written in 1875, referring to the hundredth-year celebration of the Declaration of Independence in the following year. 154, 170

Introduction of the Science of Universal Theism. A book that Hurrychund Chintamon sent to HPB. 428

Irenaeus, Saint. A second-century Church Father and Bishop of Lyons who wrote *Against Heresies* (*Adversus Haereses*), which supplies much information about early Gnosticism, although colored by polemics. 304, 308

Irish Theosophist. A periodical published by the Irish Theosophist Press, Dublin, 1892–7. 165

Irving Place, 2, New York. The address of the Lotos Club. 261

Irving Place, 16, New York. The house where HPB lived in early November 1874. 37

Irving Place, 23, New York. The house where HPH lived by mid November 1874. 37

Irving Place, 46, New York. The house where HPB lived in August 1875. 219

Irwin, Francis G. *and* **Herbert**. 213

Isidor, Exarch. The bishop of the Orthodox Church in Caucasian Georgia who refused Nikifor Blavatsky an annulment from HPB. 8

Isis. The Egyptian goddess who personifies nature. 164, 216, 274, 278, 331, 332, 362, 367

Isis Unveiled. HPB's first published book, an initial exposition of her views, remarkable for the success it achieved and the influence it exerted. 7, 143, 195, 196, 197, 215, 216, 237, 264, 269, 279, 281, 284, 288, 308, 327, 330, 331, 332, 333, 334, 335, 336, 338, 339, 340, 341, 342, 343, 355, 359, 360, 362, 364, 366, 370, 374, 375, 376, 377, 394, 395, 396, 397, 402, 412, 415, 421, 426, 427, 449, 451, 454, 466, 495, 498

Israel, lost tribes of. Ten tribes forming the northern Kingdom of Israel (as distinct from the two tribes of the southern Kingdom of Judah), who disappeared from history after the Assyrians conquered the northern kingdom in 721 BC. They were probably assimilated by other neighboring peoples, but romantic legends sprang up early and have continued to appear, identifying various peoples with the lost tribes, for example the American Indians according to the Book of Mormon. 268

Italy. 11, 12, 13, 27, 42

Ithaca, New York. The location of Cornell University, where Hiram Corson taught. 65, 92, 99, 119, 151, 164, 182, 195, 200, 202, 229, 331, 332, 336, 465, 468

Ivins, William Mills (1851–1915). A member of the Brooklyn law firm of Bergen and Ivins (later Bergen, Jacobs, and Ivins), in which capacity he represented Blavatsky in her Long Island case. He was one of five friends, three of whom, under the pen name HIRAF, wrote the 1875 article on "Rosicrucianism," to which HPB replied with her "first *Occult* Shot." Later he was active in New York City government (1881–2), was Judge Advocate General of New York State (1885–8), and chaired a committee that wrote a charter (the "Ivins Charter") for New York City (1907–9). (Biographical data: *CW* 1:471; *WWWA* 1:622.) 157, 158

Jachin. The name of the right pillar at the porch of King Solomon's Temple (1 Kings 7.21, 2 Chron. 3.17). 84, 147, 150, 329

Jack. A nickname for HBP that she used with Olcott. 36, 38

Jacob. The Hebrew patriarch who led his family into Egypt at a time of famine. 319

Jacolliot, Louis (1837–90). A prolific French author of novels, travel books, and works on the exotic and esoteric aspects of Indian culture, who worked for a time as a government official in French India. He is frequently cited by HPB in *Isis Unveiled*, *The Secret Doctrine*, and *Collected Writings*. Among his works referenced by HPB are *La Bible dans l'Indie* ("The Bible of India," which argues for the Indic origin of Jewish and Christian beliefs, 1869), *Les Fils de Dieu* ("The Sons of God," 1873), *Christna et le Christ* ("Krishna and Christ," 1874), *L'Initiation et les sciences occultes dans l'Inde et chez tous les peuples de l'antiquité* ("Initiation and Occult Sciences in India and among All the People of Antiquity," 1875), *Genèse de l'Humanité* ("Origin of Humanity," 1876), and *La Femme dans l'Inde* ("Woman in India," 1877). (Biographical data: Caracostea, "Louis-François Jacolliot," *Theosophical History* 9.1.) 287, 288, 347, 353, 376, 378, 402

Jamblichus. *See* Iamblichus.

James, Epistle of. A Christian scripture supposedly written by James, the brother of Jesus. 306

James, T. P. An uneducated American mechanic who claimed to receive messages from Charles Dickens by automatic writing as a continuation of Dickens's unfinished novel, *The Mystery of Edwin Drood*. The work was published in 1874 with Dickens listed as author. (Biographical data: *EOP* 1:331–2 [s.v. "Dickens"].) 35

Japan. 379, 470

Jasher *or* **Yasher** *or* Jashar, **Book of**. An ancient but now lost book of songs quoted in the Hebrew Bible. Two songs are ascribed to the *Book of Jasher:* Joshua's song celebrating his victory over the Amorites, when the sun and the moon stood still (Josh. 10.12–3), and David's lament over the death of Saul and his son Jonathan (2 Sam. 1.17–27). 268, 269

Java. 6

Jeffers, Augusta Sophia. The English governess from Yorkshire who joined the von Hahn family when HPB was about eight. 4

Jehovah. A name for the God of the Hebrew scriptures invented by Christians in the sixteenth century. As Hebrew was written primarily with consonants only, Hebrew scribes (the Masoretes) invented a system of diacritics (lines and dots) to indicate vowel sounds so that the scriptures could be pronounced correctly. However, the name of God, "Yahweh," was considered too holy to be said aloud; and when readers came to its consonant spelling YHVH or JHWH (depending on how one transliterates the Hebrew letters) in the text, they said instead "Adonay" (that is, "Lord"). So the scribes added the diacritics for the vowels of that latter word to the consonants of the name of God as a reminder to readers to pronounce "Adonay." Later Christian translators were unaware of this scribal practice and erroneously supposed the name to be "Yahowah," which they transcribed as "Jehovah." HPB regards the God of the Hebrew scriptures as an amalgamation of various gods of the ancient world, the Logos (or creative principle), archetypal humanity, and the human imagination. 293, 295, 317, 321, 322, 327, 349, 431, 460

Jelihovsky. *See* Zhelihovsky.

Jerome, Saint (ca. 347–420). The Church Father whose translation of the Bible into Latin became the basis for the Vulgate Bible, the official Latin version of the Roman Catholic Church. 385

Jerusalem. 266, 318

Jesuit. A member of the Society of Jesus, a Roman Catholic order founded by St. Ignatius Loyola and established in 1540. It became a force in modernizing the Church, in the Counter-Reformation's combat against Protestantism, and in education, scholarship, and missionary work. The order has long been controversial, being feared and suspected for its members' vow of obedience to the Pope. 196, 289, 376, 478, 479

Jesus. *Gk.* Iēsos, *Heb.* Yehoshua "Joshua." In orthodox Christian theology, the unique incarnation of God, to whom the epithet "Christ" was given. HPB's view was that a mythological persona was constructed around a historical person: "For me Jesus Christ . . . was never a *historical* person. He is a deified personification of the glorified type of the great Hierophants of the Temples, and his story, as told in the New Testament, is an allegory, assuredly containing profound esoteric truths, but still an allegory . . . [based] on the existence of a personage called Jehoshua . . . born at Lüd or Lydda about 120 years before the modern era" (*CW* 9:224–6; *also* 8:189, 380–2 fn.). 206, 279, 282, 287, 302, 305, 316, 320, 323, 348, 349, 354, 377, 430, 467

Jethro. The priest of Midian and father-in-law of Moses (Exod. 3.1). 286

Jews. 147, 265, 269, 287, 317, 318, 319, 349, 460

Jinarajadasa, C. 106, 126, 146, 161, 170, 356, 422, 484

Job. The biblical book treating the problem of suffering. 268

John (the Divine), Saint. The author of the Apocalypse or the Revelation of John. 210

John King. *See* "King, John."

Johnson, Edward H. A colleague of Thomas Alva Edison's who represented Edison when the Theosophists made voice recordings to take to India. 489

Johnston, Vera. *See* Zhelihovsky, Vera Vladimirovna de.

Jones, Sir **William** (1746–94). An English legal authority and philologist who was a judge on the supreme court in Calcutta and founded the Asiatic Society of Bengal. He is best known today as the first proponent of the Indo-European hypothesis, namely, that Sanskrit, Latin, Greek, and many other languages (including English) all developed from a single mother tongue, no longer existing. This hypothesis became the basis for the discipline of comparative linguistics. (Biographical data: *CW* 14:534–5.) 376

Josephus, Flavius (37–ca. 95). The most notable Jewish historian of early times. 265, 318

Joshua, son of Nun. The successor to Moses, director of the Israelites' conquest of Canaan, and most prominent figure in the Book of Joshua. 265, 287

Joy, Algernon. A person whom HPB cites as one who wrote about Henry T. Child. 235

Judaism. 205

Judge, William Quan (1851–96). One of the founding members of the Theosophical Society. Judge was at first Counsel to the Society, became the first General Secretary of the American Section when it was organized in 1886, and edited the *Path* magazine (1886–96). (Biographical data: *CW* 1:472–90; Judge, *Echoes* xix–liii.) 136, 219, 275, 276, 281, 311, 312, 326, 483, 486, 490, 491

Julian calendar. Julius Caesar's reform of the old Roman lunar calendar into a solar one. The Alexandrian astronomer Caesar relied on had miscalculated the length of a solar year by some 11 minutes and 14 seconds. Consequently, by the sixteenth century the Julian calendar was a number of days off the correct solar time, so in 1582 Pope Gregory the Great ordered an omission of ten calendar days that year, October 4 being immediately followed by October 15; he also altered the observation of leap years to keep the calendar more nearly accurate with the solar year. The Gregorian or "new style" calendar only gradually replaced the Julian or "old style" calendar around the world. England adopted it in 1752, and Russia not until 1918. Consequently in dealing with dates recorded in nineteenth-century Russia, it is necessary to convert them to "new style" dates. 1, 9, 52, 183

Jupiter. The Roman god of the heavens, who wielded the thunderbolt, controlled the weather, and was the chief god in the Roman pantheon, identified with Greek Zeus. 287, 316

Justin, Martyr and Saint (ca. 100–ca. 165). A Christian apologist and philosopher who defended Christianity against charges of sedition against the Roman state and whose references to the Gospels are of value to Biblical historians. 316

K Street, 1200, Washington, DC. Gen. Lippitt's address. 193

Kabbalah *or* **Cabala** *or* **Quabalah**. *Heb.* "tradition." Jewish theosophical esotericism and mysticism. 79, 87, 195, 205, 248, 258, 260, 267, 298, 302, 322, 334

Kabbalism. The teaching and practice of Kabbalah. 157

Kabbalist *or* **Cabalist**. An adherent or practitioner of Kabbalah. 195, 203, 212, 231, 257, 350, 353, 447, 497

Kabbalistic(al) *or* **Cabalistic(al)**. Pertaining to the Kabbalah. 59, 79, 188, 206, 207, 211, 244, 267, 268, 387

Kabeiri *or* Cabeiri. A group of deities, probably Phrygian originally, worshiped in Asia Minor, Macedonia, and northern and central Greece. In classical times, they were four: a male pair, Axiocersus and his son Cadmilus, and a female pair, Axiocersa and Axierus. Their cult included rites of purification, fertility, and initiation. 317

Kagan, Anatol. 31, 360

Kali. A Hindu goddess who is the female counterpart of Shiva. She is the terrifying aspect of divine creative energy and represents death, time, and other frightening characteristics of life

that must be faced and overcome before spiritual progress can
be achieved. 445

Kalki. The tenth and final avatar (or incarnation) of the Hindu
god Vishnu, who will come at the end of the present degenerate age (or kali yuga) to purify the world and usher in a new
Golden Age. 475

Kalmuck or **Calmuck**. A Buddhist Mongol people in the area of
Astrakhan, among whom HPB lived as a little girl. 4, 398, 410,
427, 481

kama loka. *Skt.* "desire world." The sphere of existence closest to
that of physical consciousness, in which the remnants of our
personality gradually decay after the death of the physical
body. 57

Kansas. A state in the mid center of the United States. 103

Kapht. According to Alexander Wilder, a name given by Egyptians
to the Phoenicians. 269

Kaphta. According to Alexander Wilder, the place from which
"the Philostians [Philistians?] are said to have migrated." 269

Kapila. The sage-founder of the Sankhya school of Indian philosophy. 381

Kapilavastu. An ancient state in Nepal where the Buddha's father
was king. 348

Kappes, Mr. An artist, who was probably illustrating Olcott's articles for the *Daily Graphic*. 79

Kardec, Allan (1804–69). The Spiritualist pseudonym of Hypolyte
Léon Denizard Rivail, the leading figure in early French
Spiritualism, which is distinguished from Anglophone
Spiritualism by its advocacy of the doctrine of reincarnation.
Kardec's view of reincarnation seems to have been one of a
rebirth of the personality, and it is perhaps that feature which
led HPB to reject his reincarnationist views. His most influen-
tial work was *Le Livre des Esprits* ("The Spirits' Book," 1856).
(Biographical data: *EOP* 1:703; *CW* 5:375–6.) 21, 87, 113, 142,
144, 244, 247, 248

Kardec, Amélie-Gabrielle Boudet. Allan Kardec's wife. 113

Karlsbad *or* Karlovy Vary. A spa in the Bohemian Forest noted for its
thermal springs. Karlsbad is its German name, and Karlovy Vary
its name in the Czech Republic, where it is now located. 467

Karnak. The northern half of the ruins of Thebes on the east bank of the Nile, including the ruins of the Great Temple of Amon, the largest temple complex in Egypt. 132, 134

Kasdim. *Heb.* Chaldeans. According to Gen. 11.31, Abraham departed with his family from "Ur Kasdim" ("Ur of the Chaldees or Chaldeans"). 269

Kashmir. A now disputed area between Pakistan and India. 7, 43

Katherine. An unidentified person whom HPB asks her aunt about. 450

"Katie." The name of several spirit guides, notably "Katie King." (*See also* "King, Katie.") 62

Kaufmann, Konstantin Petrovich (1818–82). A Russian general who was assigned to Turkistan in 1867 to lead the Russian expansion in that area. He became the first governor-general of Russian Turkistan, and his success caused alarm and protest by the British government, which was constantly alert to Russian expansion toward India. 268

Kelley, Edward. An English alchemist and companion of John Dee. 242

Kent, Holy Maid of. An unidentified English medium or mystic. 242

Kerch. A Crimean port city on the Black Sea. 5

Key to Theosophy, The. An introductory book by HPB published in 1889. 311, 419

KH. Kuthumi, the name used for one of HPB's adept teachers. 13, 336

Khedive. Ultimately from a Persian term for "prince," the title of the hereditary rulers of Egypt from 1867 until 1914. They were viceroys of the sultan of Turkey. The first Khedive, still ruling in 1872, was named Isma'il. 25, 27, 30

Kiev. The capital of the Ukraine and in the Middle Ages the capital of Russia. 408

kikimora. *Russ. pl.* kikimori. A hobgoblin in female form. 22, 354

King, Charles William (1818–88). The author of *The Gnostics and Their Remains*, 1864. 283

"King, John." A spirit manifestation who claimed to have been the seventeenth-century buccaneer Sir Henry Morgan. He manifested through a large number of mediums for more than eighty years. HPB's "John King" had the character of a trickster, which supports Olcott's opinion that he "was a humbugging elemental, worked by [HPB] like a marionette" (*ODL* 1:11). Olcott (*ODL* 1:25) also quotes a passage from HPB's scrapbook that supports his opinion, in which she writes of "orders received from T* B* [Tuitit Bey] (an Adept) through P. (an elemental) personating John King." (Cf. *EOP* 1:711–2.) 59, 62, 63, 72, 76, 78, 79, 80, 81, 82, 83, 84, 88, 89, 90, 95, 97, 98, 104, 105, 106, 122, 123, 124, 137, 138, 140, 141, 142, 146, 147, 149, 150, 158, 159, 160, 168, 170, 176, 177, 178, 179, 180, 181, 182, 183, 184, 185, 186, 187, 188, 190, 194, 195, 198, 218, 233, 235, 254, 331, 332, 337

"**King, Katie**." A spirit manifestation claimed to be the daughter of "John King." The manifestations began in Britain in 1872; in America, she notably appeared in the séances of Nelson and Jennifer Holmes in 1874, which have been generally recognized as fraudulent. Manifestations continued to appear for more than a hundred years. (Cf. *EOP* 1:712–3.) 58, 61, 62, 63, 64, 65, 66, 70, 71, 72, 73, 74, 83, 84, 94, 95, 106, 114, 138, 141, 171, 172, 186, 187, 235, 254

Kiriak, Father. A Russian Orthodox priest of whom HPB writes admiringly. 343, 345, 348, 351

Kislingbury, Emily. An Englishwoman who compiled the index for volume 2 of *Isis Unveiled*, served as Secretary of the British National Association of Spiritualists, and eventually as Treasurer of the European Section of the Theosophical Society. 337, 435, 436, 437, 439

Kit Kitich. *Russ.* "Whale, Son of a Whale." A bombastic bully, a stock character on the stage. 271, 272

Kittary, Gen. and Mme. An unidentified couple. 274

Knight, Richard Payne (1750–1824). A Member of Parliament for more than twenty-five years and a gentleman-scholar who published on Priapus, the Greek alphabet, symbolism, and classical sculpture. (Biographical data: *CW* 13:388–9.) 283

Kolozsvár. A town in Hungary that HPB visited. 12

Koran. The sacred book of Islam. 198

Kosovo. A region of Serbia bordering on Albania. 408

Koucheleff Bezborrodke *or* **Besborodka**, Countess. A woman whom HPB knew and whose sister married D. D. Home. 42

Koutcherof, Maxim. A cook in the household of HPB's family. 14, 16

Koutcherof, Piotre. A footman in the household of HPB's family. 14, 15, 16, 17

Kovindasami. *See* Govinda Swami.

Kraft und Stoff, "Force and Matter." A book by Ludwig Büchner. 188, 190

Krishna. *Skt*. "black." An avatar of the god Vishnu, a central figure in the epic Mahabharata and the devotional classic the Bhagavad Gita, who was the object of intense devotional worship. HPB sometimes uses the spelling *Chrishna* to emphasize parallels between Krishna and Christ. 266, 269, 322, 344, 446

Krishnavarma. A visitor from Multan in the Punjab whom HPB describes as being in America in 1878 and with whom she reports that she and Olcott traveled "almost as far as California," otherwise unidentified. 443, 448, 449, 450, 451

Krishnavarma, Shyamaji. *See* Shyamaji Krishnavarma.

Kroble, Countess. *See* Kroll, Alexandrina ("Sacha") de.

Kroll, Alexandrina ("**Sacha**") **de** (d. 1862). The first wife of D. D. Home. 19, 42

kudyani. Native magicians in Caucasian Georgia. 9

Kühlwein. A German former Lutheran minister with whom HPB planned to enter Tibet. He was perhaps a relative of HPB's governess, Antonya C. Kühlwein. 7

Kühlwein, Antonya Christianovna. A governess for HPB and her sister Vera. 4

Kvilecky, Count. A Pole working for the king of Prussia. 28

labarum. The imperial standard of emperors after Constantine the Great (306–37), incorporating into the military standard of the earlier pagan emperors the Greek letters chi and rho (X and P), a monogram for "Christ." (HPB discusses the symbol incidentally in *CW* 9:227 fn. and 14:148–9, 151, 154–5.) 120, 122, 130, 132, 133

"Lablache." A spirit control of Jesse Shepard. 36

Ladakh. A mountainous region in northeastern Kashmir, bordering on Tibet. 7

"Lady of Shalott, The." A poem by Alfred Lord Tennyson. 92

Lahore. The capital of the Punjab. 6, 7

Lamasery. A nickname for HPB and Olcott's residence at 302 West Forty-seventh Street, at the corner of Eighth Avenue, New York. 289, 336, 480

Latin. 82, 135, 171, 186, 259, 288, 308, 333, 403

Laughter and Sorrow. An unidentified book, presumably Russian, that HPB's aunt sent her to read. 379

Lavison, Eduard (d. 1872). The Russian Vice-Consul in Cairo, 1856–72. 25, 30

Lawrence-Archer, J. H., Major. A British officer who brought the Sat Bhai rite from India to England. 341

Lawry, Edwin Wyndham. The author of a letter addressed to Olcott, published in the New York *World*, concerning the duration of a trance state. 200

Leaf, Walter. 35, 46, 52, 73, 74, 127, 144, 174, 194, 195, 196, 214, 215, 251, 260, 264, 271, 289, 312, 341, 362

Lebanon. 12, 23, 333

Lebanon, Mount. 411

Lecs. *See* Leks, Ivan Mikhailovich de.

Lee, Mr. A publisher, otherwise unidentified, who saw Gen. Lippitt's Psychic Stand (a device for recording messages thought to come from the other world). 186

Leh. The chief town of Ladakh. 7

Leipzig, Germany. 428

Leks *or* **Lecs, Ivan Mikhailovich de** (1834–83). Russian Consul General in Cairo, 1868–83. 25, 30

Le Moyne, Francis Julius (1798–1879). A physician and leader in the abolitionist movement who constructed the first crematorium in the United States for his private use, although the first cremation carried out there was that of the Baron de Palm. (Biographical data: *WWWA* H:311.) 261, 280

Lena *or* **Lenochka**. Pet names for "Helena," specifically for Helena Vladimirovna de Zhelihovsky, HPB's niece, the daughter of her sister, Vera. 359, 413, 415, 416

Leskov, Nikolai Semenovich (1831–95). A Russian writer whose novels were concerned with the Russian church and with popular beliefs. He wrote a story dealing with Archbishop Nil. 344

Leslie. An otherwise unidentified person involved in the scandal of "Katie King," Eliza White, and Henry T. Child. 73, 88, 153, 154

Lesseps, Ferdinand-Marie, Vicomte de (1805–94). A French diplomat who built the Suez Canal. 21

Letters from the Masters of the Wisdom. A collection of Mahatma letters, edited by C. Jinarajadasa. 106

Lévi, Éliphas (1810–75). The pseudonym of Alphonse Louis Constant, a French occultist who was a seminal figure in the occult revival of the nineteenth century. (Biographical data: *CW* 1:491–5; *EOP* 1:749.) 212, 235, 247, 250, 258

Leymarie, Mme. The wife of Pierre Gaétan Leymarie. 113

Leymarie, Pierre Gaétan. A French Spiritualist and friend of HPB's, the editor of *La Revue Spirite* ("Spiritualist Review"). 31, 113, 258, 361, 447, 483

Liberty Party. A nineteenth-century American minority political party of which Francis LeMoyne was the vice presidential candidate in 1844. 280

Library of Congress. 484

Life of David Hare. A biography by Peary Chand Mittra. 393

Life of Dayanand Saraswati. A biography by Har Bilas Sarda. 433, 434

Light. An English Spiritualist periodical edited by Stainton Moses, 1881–. 280

Lights and Shadows of Spiritualism. A book by D. D. Home. 256, 361, 362

Limerick, Ireland. 199

Lincoln Spiritual Hall. A Spiritualist meeting place in Philadelphia. 69, 71, 114, 153

Lindsay, Alexander William Crawford, 25th Earl of Crawford and 8th Earl of Balcarres (1812–80). An English nobleman who was famous as a book collector. He also investigated Spiritualism and is referred to in the *Mahatma Letters* and by Podmore (see the indexes). (Biographical data: *DNB*.) 356

Lippincott, Mrs. A Philadelphia woman who hosted a séance by Nelson and Jennifer Holmes. 110

Lippitt, Francis James, Gen. (1812–1902). A lawyer and American Civil War veteran, Spiritualist, and friend of Olcott and HPB. As a young man, he assisted de Toqueville in the preparation of the latter's work *Democracy in the United States* and was attached to the American legation in Paris in 1834–5. (Biographical data: *CW* 1:496–7; Lippitt, *Reminiscences*; *WWWA* 1:734.) (Lippitt's middle initial is sometimes written as "G." by both HPB and Betanelly.) 59, 62, 63, 66, 70, 75, 77, 78, 80, 85, 88, 89, 91, 93, 94, 97, 102, 122, 124, 126, 128, 136, 137, 138, 140, 143, 144, 146, 153, 155, 159, 176, 181, 182, 184, 185, 187, 193, 194, 337

Literaturnoe Obozrenie, "Literary Review." A Russian journal published in Moscow, 1973–. 30, 31

Liverpool, England. 484, 494, 500

Livingstone, David (1813–73). A Scottish missionary and explorer in Africa. Livingstone's efforts to find the source of the Nile, his discovery by H. M. Stanley in 1871, his death in 1873, and the publication of his final journals in 1874 made him a topical figure in the mid 1870s, hence HPB's allusions to him. 50, 127, 278

Liza. A pet name for "Elizabeth," specifically for Elizabeth Petrovna Beliy, HPB's half sister. 9

Logos. *Gk.* "word, thought, reason." The collective order or unifying principle of the universe. 307, 322

London. 5, 6, 17, 19, 29, 40, 83, 100, 114, 125, 127, 138, 141, 143, 145, 154, 160, 178, 187, 191, 193, 216, 234, 250, 271, 272, 274, 277, 278, 326, 339, 353, 355, 357, 361, 364, 388, 389, 401, 409, 410, 428, 434, 435, 436, 437, 439, 450, 454, 459, 477, 478, 483, 484, 486, 490, 491, 498, 500

London *Spiritualist*. *See Spiritualist Newspaper.*

London Spiritualist Alliance. An organization of which Stainton Moses was president (1884–92), the 1884–1955 name of the present-day College of Psychic Studies, founded in 1873 as the British National Association of Spiritualists. 40

Long, Chaille, Col. (1842–1917). A friend of both HPB and one of her uncles, mentioned in her diaries (*CW* 1:422, 424). 449

Longfellow, Henry Wadsworth (1807–82). A popular American poet of the nineteenth century. 119

Long Island, New York. 32, 36, 138, 151, 156, 157, 158

"Lost Canon of Proportion of the Egyptians, Greeks, and Romans, The." A lecture by George Henry Felt. 219

Lotos Club. A prestigious New York club to which Olcott belonged. The club catered to literary interests, its name derived from Tennyson's poem "The Lotos Eaters." (Cf. Prothero, *White Buddhist* 196 n. 1.) 170, 261

Louis XVI (1754–93) *or* XVIII (1755–1824). Kings of France. 262

Lucifer. A monthly periodical of which HPB was the founding editor, published in London, 1887–97. 197, 201, 299, 359, 425

Lucretia *or* **Lucreta.** A byname for Mrs. C. Daniels. 482, 484

Lully, Raymond, *or* Ramón Lull (ca. 1232–ca. 1316). A Catalan philosopher who attempted to convert the Muslims of Tunis to Christianity by debating Muslim scholars. Lully maintained that philosophy, science, and theology were in perfect accord. His major work, *Ars Magna* ("The Great Art") was a defense of Christianity against the teachings of the Muslim philosopher Averroës. Tradition reports that he was stoned to death during his third unsuccessful missionary attempt. 86

"Luminous Circle, The." A story by HPB under the pen name "Hadji Mora" (*CW* 1:177–86). 237

Luther, Martin (1483–1546). The German leader of the Reformation. 354, 466, 487

Luxor. The site of a Temple to Amon-Re at Thebes in Egypt. The term was used as an "adopted name" (letter 59) by HPB for a group of the "Brotherhood, which, having had a branch at Luxor (Egypt), was thus purposely referred to by us under this name [Brotherhood of Luxor]" (*CW* 10:125–6 fn.). However, she also associated the name etymologically with India: "The name Luxor is primarily derived from the ancient Baluchistan city of Lukhsur, which lies between Bela and Kedje, and also gave its name to the Egyptian city" (*Isis* 2:308 fn.). The association of Luxor with Ellora in letter 28 further suggests an Indian connection. 104, 106, 134, 150, 165, 208

Lytton (of Knebworth), Edward George Earle Bulwer-Lytton, 1st Baron (1803–73). An English statesman and author, especially of novels, who entered Parliament at the age of twenty-eight as a Liberal party member but became a Tory through his friendship with Benjamin Disraeli. Lytton's novels, which were a significant source of income for him, were of several types: historical fiction (of which *The Last Days of Pompeii*, 1834, is the best known), Gothic romance (*Pelham*, 1828), novels of English society (*The Caxtons*, 1849), and metaphysical fiction, of which HPB was particularly fond. The last category includes *Zanoni*, 1842; *A Strange Story*, 1862; and *The Coming Race*, 1871. (Biographical data: *EOP* 1:784.) 147, 202

M. *See* Morya.

M. A. Cantab. The pen name of an unidentified correspondent to the *Spiritualist Newspaper*. "M. A. Cantab." signifies that the individual held a Master of Arts degree from Cambridge University. "Cantab." is an abbreviation for Latin *Cantabrigiensis*, "of Cambridge"; compare Stainton Moses's pen name of "M. A. Oxon." 244, 245, 246

Macbeth. A tragic play by William Shakespeare. 222

McCloskey, John, Cardinal (1810–85). Archbishop of New York (1864–85), elevated to Cardinal 1875. (Biographical data: *WWWA* H:343.) 289

McDuff *or* **M'Duff, Duff**. The pen name of the author of a number of religiously satirical articles in the *Religio-Philosophical Journal*. 116, 121

Macroprosopus. *Gk.* macro "great" + prósōpon "face, countenance." A Kabbalistic term for Kether, the first sephirah on the Tree of Life, hence the first manifestation of the Absolute, of which the universe is a reflection. 87

"**Madame Blavatsky Explains**." A letter from HPB to the *Spiritual Scientist* (*CW* 1:186-92). 237

Madame Blavatsky. A book by W. H. Burr. 342, 373

"**Madame Blavatsky: Her Experience—Her Opinion of American Spiritualism and American Society**." A letter from HPB to the *Spiritual Scientist* (*CW* 1:46-9). 173

Madhava Rao, Sir **T.** (1829–91). An Indian statesman who served as Dewan or Prime Minister of Travancore, Indore, and Baroda, and was associated with the Indian National Congress. 375

Madison Avenue, 64. The address of Mott Memorial Hall. 220, 231, 241, 251, 256, 485

Madras. A state and city on the southeast coast of India, *now respectively* Tamil Nadu *and* Chennai. 350, 375, 378, 388

Magi. Originally a tribe of the Medes, later a hereditary liturgical caste of Zoroastrianism. The word "magic" is derived from their name. 318, 320

Magia Adamica. A work by Thomas Vaughan. 196, 209

Magnon, Mme. A French friend of HPB's. 177, 179, 180

Mahabharata. One of the two Indian epics, the other being the Ramayana. The Mahabharata, or "Great Things Pertaining to the Descendents of King Bharata," recounts events before, during, and after a civil war that marked the end of the heroic age of India. The Bhagavad Gita is a part of it. 376, 381, 446

Mahatma Letter. Any letter written by one of the Mahatmas or Adepts, but specifically those in *The Mahatma Letters to A. P. Sinnett*. 356

Maitree-Buddha. Maitreya Buddha, the future Buddha, whose coming will mark the start of a new cycle. 475, 476

Malta. 43

Manglis. A town some thirty miles from Yerevan and the regimental headquarters of the province. 14

Manhattan. One of the boroughs of New York City. 489

Manu. (1) A patron and guardian of one of the human cycles in a manvantara, specifically the progenitor and lawgiver of our cycle. (2) The Law Book that tradition says Manu gave to humanity. 376, 378

Manual of Psychometry. A book by Joseph R. Buchanan. 404

M. A. Oxon. The pen name of Stainton Moses, signifying that he held a Master of Arts degree from Oxford University. "Oxon." is an abbreviation for Latin *Oxoniensis*, "of Oxford." 275, 276, 277

Marble, Mortimer. A member of the Committee of the Theosophical Society in 1877 and a frequent visitor at the Lamasery in 1878. He was one of seven persons that HPB said she had placed "on the true path." 326

"Marie." A spirit guide of Florence Cook. 62

Marius, Gaius (ca. 157–86 BC). A frustrated Roman general and politician who campaigned in Africa, where Carthage had been destroyed by Roman armies in 146 BC. 172, 173

Market Street Railroad. A private transportation company in Philadelphia of which John S. Morton was president. In September 1877, an over-issue of 11,000 shares of stock was discovered, which led to Morton's resignation. 144, 153

Markoff, Yevgueniy Lyovich (1835–1903 or 1904). A Russian writer and first cousin of HPB on her father's side. (Biographical data: *CW* 2:444–6.) 260

Marks, Mr. The lawyer representing Clementine Gerebko, whom HPB sued over property on Long Island. 159, 160

Marquette, L. M. A woman physician who met HPB in Paris in 1873 (*CW* 1:436, *ODL* 1:27–8) and was a member of the Committee of the Theosophical Society in 1877. 265, 268

Martheze, Mr. An unidentified London correspondent of D. D. Home. 361

"Marvellous Spirit Manifestations." HPB's first published article (*CW* 1:30–4). 33, 37

Mary. A maid or washerwoman at the Corson's. 198

Mary. The mother of Jesus. 279, 430

Marya. *Russ.* "Mary." An unidentified Russian girl. 417

Mary Magdalen. One of the inner circle around Jesus. In popular (but unsupported) lore, she is a reformed prostitute and therefore the archetypal penitent. 354

Masha. A pet name for "Marya." 415, 417

Masonry, order of Eastern. *See also* Freemasonry. A group in which HPB was reported as claiming membership. 43

Masorah *or* **Massorah**. *Heb.* "tradition." The system of diacritics (masoretic points) and notes devised by early Medieval Jewish scribes to preserve the correct reading of the Biblical text. Hebrew is traditionally written largely without indication of various linguistic features, including vowels, but only with consonants. The Masorah included a variety of notes to assure a correct text when scribes copied the scriptures. HPB regards the Masorah as exoteric and thus inferior to the esoteric understanding of the Kabbalah. 87, 320, 321, 349

Masorete. One of the scribes who compiled the Masorah. 322, 349

Massey, Charles Carleton (1838–1905). An English barrister who went to Chittenden to investigate Olcott's accounts of the Eddy phenomena. He became a founding member of the Theosophical Society. (Biographical data: *CW* 1:438, 497–9.) 210, 219, 235, 243, 245, 246, 250, 273, 275, 276, 277, 278, 435, 436, 437, 439, 440, 441, 459, 461, 462, 463, 479, 483, 493, 498

Master. A term for an Adept, also called a "Brother." 6, 13, 56, 170, 218, 278, 300, 301, 302, 308, 316, 335, 336, 343, 348, 358, 374, 385, 389, 394, 395, 425

materialism. (1) The belief that physical matter is the only or the ultimate reality. (2) A primary concern with material rather than intellectual or spiritual matters. 101, 112, 113, 201, 217, 243, 396, 403, 441, 447, 486

Matter and Force. Büchner's book *Kraft und Stoff* ("Force and Matter," 1855). 344

Maxim. *See* Koutcherof, Maxim.

maya. The illusions of this world. 382

"**Mayflower**." The name of one of the spirit controls of Horatio Eddy. 36

Meadow Street, 6, Fort. Hurrychund Chintamon's Bombay address. 453, 492

Mecca. The holy city and pilgrimage site for Muslims. 287

Mecklenburg. The Grand Duchy of Germany from which the von Hahns came to Russia. 2

Median(ite). *See* Midian(ite).

Medium and Daybreak, The. A British Spiritualist weekly newspaper published by James Burns, ca. 1869–95. (Cf. Podmore 2:165.) 17, 18, 19

"**Mediums of Boston, The**." A series of articles by "Diogenes" in the *Spiritual Scientist*. 155

Meechum Doss. An Indian yogi who was buried for a month in a state of suspended life. 200

Mejnour. An Adept-like character in Bulwer-Lytton's metaphysical novel *Zanoni*. 208

Memoirs of an Editor. A book by Edward P. Mitchell. 480

Memories of an Active Life. A book by Charles Ranlett Flint. 157

Milton, John (1608–74). An English poet. 229

Milwaukee, Wisconsin. 448

Miracle Club. A precursor of the Theosophical Society, which Olcott attempted unsuccessfully to start in May 1875. 173, 180, 218

Mitchell, Edward P. (1852–1927). The editor-in-chief of the New York *Sun*. His *Memoirs of an Editor* (1924) includes chapter 6 (pp. 158–97), "Meddlings with the Occult," which gives a skeptical account of paranormal matters he investigated: ghosts, hauntings, apparitions, séances, and automatic writing. His poker group included William Quan Judge, and he knew H. S. Olcott through their common journalistic work and mutual friendship with Charles A. Dana (earlier editor of the *Sun* and an original shareholder in the Transcendentalist utopian community, Brook Farm). Mitchell wrote a newspaper account of a bizarre materialization he had witnessed, involving a wedding ceremony between two apparitions, which interested HPB in meeting him (*Memoirs* 188–92). Through an introduction by Olcott, she invited Mitchell to visit her, and subsequently wrote him "several long epistles . . . confiding her thoughts about the troubled ocean of theosophical politics" (*Memoirs* 190). One of those, recorded in *Memoirs*, is letter 129. (Biographical data: *WWWA* 1:849.) 478, 480

Mitchell, Isobel ("Belle") **Buloid** (b. 1835). Olcott's oldest sister and a friend of HPB. 256, 424, 425, 451

Mittra *or* Mitra, **Peary Chand** (1814–83). A Hindu social reformer and author. "One of the earliest members of the Society in India was the Bengali writer Peary Chand Mittra, who was admitted Nov. 9, 1877. Col. Olcott had been in correspondence with him since June 5, 1877" (Gomes, *Canadian Theosophist* 71 [Nov.–Dec. 1990]: 105). 390, 409

Mivart's. A London hotel where HPB stayed, now Claridge's. 6

Modern Priestess of Isis, A. An English translation by Walter Leaf of Solovyov's book about HPB. 35, 46, 52, 73, 74, 127, 144, 174, 194, 195, 196, 214, 215, 251, 260, 264, 271, 289, 312, 341, 362

Moksha. *Skt*. "Liberation; spiritual freedom; release; the final goal of human life" (Grimes 192). 364, 380, 381, 411

Moldavia. A principality in eastern Europe, now divided between Romania and Moldova (formerly part of the USSR). 41

Moleschott, Jacob (1822–93). A physiologist and philosophical proponent of scientific materialism. His major work was *Kreislauf des Lebens* ("The Circuit of Life," 1852). He held that all emotion and thought have a physiological basis, a concept expressed in his motto "no phosphorus, no thought." 148, 150

Moloch. A Middle Eastern god to whom first-born children were sacrificed or dedicated by passing them through fire. 316

Monachesi, Herbert D. A newspaper reporter, one of the formers of the Theosophical Society, and a member of the 1877 Committee of the Theosophical Society, but not active long after. (Biographical data: *CW* 1:500.) 232, 253

Monck, Francis Ward (fl. 1876–8). A British Baptist clergyman (minister of the Baptist Chapel at Earls Barton, Northamptonshire) and medium, popularly given the title "Dr." because of his healing work although he was not a physician. At least once apparently caught in fraud, but otherwise supported by a number of reliable witnesses. (Biographical data: *EOP* 2:870.) 388

Mongolia. 298

Monier-Williams, Sir **Monier** (1819–99). An Indian-born British orientalist, Boden Professor of Sanskrit at Oxford. His major book, *Sanskrit-English Dictionary* (1872), is still the standard work in its field. (Biographical data: *CW* 14:555.) 438, 441, 442, 456, 457, 458, 459, 479

Monomach *or* **Monomakh, Vladimir**. A prince of Kiev to whom the Byzantine emperor Constantine Monomachus gave the imperial Russian crown. 408

Montenegro. The smallest of the Balkan states. 300, 408

Moor, Edward (1771–1848). Author of *The Hindu Pantheon* (1809). 269

More, Henry (1614–87). A philosopher in the school of the Cambridge Platonists who revived Platonism and Neoplatonism in England. More was especially mystical and theosophical. Isaac Newton was his student and was influenced by More's concept of space and time. (Biographical data: *CW* 4:658–61.) 86

More, Robert (Section of Zoroaster). One of the signers of the letter from the Brotherhood of Luxor to Henry Steel Olcott (*LMW2* 12). 167, 170

Morgan, Sir Henry (1635–88). A Welsh sea-raider of the Spanish colonies in the Caribbean, for which activity he was knighted and made deputy governor of Jamaica, where he died wealthy and respected. He was said to have returned as the spirit "John King." 62, 187

Mormon. A member of the Church of Jesus Christ of Latter Day Saints, popularly known as the Mormon Church from its scripture *The Book of Mormon*. In HPB's day, the Mormons were known for their practice of polygamy. 127, 147, 150

Morton, John S. A prominent Philadelphia citizen. HPB says he was the President of the Market Street Railroad and was to be elected "Governor of Philadelphia." 125, 138, 144, 153

Morya *or* **M**. The name used for one of HPB's adept teachers. 6, 64, 218

Moses. The Hebrew lawgiver, prophet, and traditional author of the first five books of the Bible. 271, 286, 317, 319, 321, 350

Moses, William Stainton (1839–92). The most prominent of nineteenth-century English Spiritualists. From being an Anglican clergyman who dismissed Spiritualism, he became himself one of the most remarkable and respected mediums of the time. He edited the Spiritualist periodical *Light* (cf. Podmore 2:177–8) and used the pen name "M. A. Oxon.," which alluded to his Oxford degree. (Biographical data: *CW* 1:500–1; *DNB* 13:1077; *EOP* 2:879–81; *ODL* 1:300–3; Podmore 2:274–88 and see index.) 139, 202, 278, 326, 394

Mott Memorial Hall. The building at 64 Madison Avenue, New York, NY, which was the meeting place for the Theosophical Society after its organization and the venue for Olcott's Inaugural Address on November 17, 1875. 220, 222, 231, 241, 251, 256, 485

Mousseaux. *See* Gougenot des Mousseaux, Henri Roger.

Müller, Dr. A Bishop in India. 348, 355

Müller, Max *or* Friedrich Maximilian (1823–1900). A German-born philologist and Oxford professor. His greatest work was editing the fifty-one volumes of *The Sacred Books of the East*.

(Biographical data: *CW* 5:378–9.) 211, 267, 269, 376, 380, 442, 446, 457

Multan. A city in the Punjab, now Pakistan, nearly 200 miles southwest of Lahore. 443

Mumler, William H. (?–1884). A jewelry engraver who began the practice of spirit photography—the production in photographs of spectral figures believed to be spirits. (Biographical data: *EOP* 2:891; Podmore 2:117.) 95, 123

Mustafa Pasha. The Ottoman military governor of Egypt in the 1870s. 27, 30

"My Books." An article by HPB (*CW* 13:197–8). 330, 333

Mysteries. Secret religious rites in the ancient Greco-Roman period. The Mysteries established a link between the initiate and the god of the Mysteries by things told, things shown, and things done (presumably including myths, sacred objects, and a ritual drama). A common theme of the Mysteries was death and resurrection or life after death. 98, 283, 307, 317, 331, 352, 357, 358

Mystery of Edwin Drood. *See Edwin Drood, The Mystery of.*

" 'Mystical History,' Fragments from HPB's." A biographical account by Vera Zhelihovsky. 11, 12, 17, 21, 23, 31, 54, 57, 216, 313, 375, 397

Nadejinka. A pet name for "Nadyezhda," specifically for HPB's favorite aunt, Nadyezhda Andreyevna de Fadeyev. 380

Nadya. A pet name for "Nadyezhda," specifically for HPB's niece Nadyezhda Vladimirovna de Zhelihovsky or for her favorite aunt, Nadyezhda Andreyevna de Fadeyev. 302, 346, 359

Nadyezhenka. A pet name for "Nadyezhda," specifically for HPB's favorite aunt, Nadyezhda Andreyevna de Fadeyev. 345, 443

Nagkon Wat. Probably Nakhon Si Thammarat, one of the oldest cities of Thailand, which is the site of the Wat Mahathuda temple complex. 285

Nagyvárad. A town in Transylvania that HPB visited. 12

Napoléon Bonaparte (1769–1821). Emperor of the French. 127

Napoli. Naples, Italy. 42

Narayana. A figure in Hindu mythology representing God incarnate in humanity or divinity as the abode and goal of human beings, Vishnu reclining on a serpent as his bed, floating on the milky ocean. 429

Narragansett Bay. A bay of the Atlantic Ocean in the state of Rhode Island. 187

Nassau Street, 84, New York City. The office of the *American Bibliopolist*, which Charles Sotheran edited. 241

Natashka. A pet name for "Anastasia." 450

Nazareth, Israel. 282, 348

Near East. 12

Nebuchadrezzar *or* Nebuchadnezzar II (605–562 BC). The king of Babylonia and builder of the Hanging Gardens of Babylon. He destroyed Jerusalem and carried the Jews into captivity in Babylon. In Dan. 5, the prophet describes the old king's madness, during which he ate grass. 318

Neff, Mary K. 93, 104, 114, 115, 121, 122, 135, 163, 199

Nehemiah (5th c. BC). One of the prophets and prophetic books of the Hebrew scriptures. As governor of Judah under the Persian king, Nehemiah rebuilt the walls of Jerusalem. He also tried to prevent marriages between Jews and foreigners. 269

Neoplatonic. A follower of Neoplatonism, a Neoplatonist. 249

Neoplatonism. A mystical philosophy based on the teachings of Plato. Developed by Ammonius Saccas (2nd–3rd c.), Plotinus (3rd c.), Porphyry (3rd c.), Iamblichus (4th c.), and Proclus (5th c.), it influenced some early Church Fathers and later Western metaphysics and mystical thought. 157

Neoplatonist. A follower of Neoplatonism. 223, 236, 304, 381

Nepal. 6, 353, 357, 383

Nepal Embassy. A group of Nepalese diplomats who visited England in 1850. Much of Nepal's history in the nineteenth century involved efforts to secure the country's independence from, but cooperation with, China, Tibet, and especially British India. 6

nephesh. *Heb.* "breath," hence, like the Greek and Latin equivalents with the same etymological sense (*psyche* and *spiritus*), "vitality" or "soul." Theosophically, the vital animal soul or lower quaternary of human principles. 304, 306

Nerses. The name of several Armenian Patriarchs, here probably Nerses V, who held the post in 1843–57. 267

Neusatz. A town in Austria-Hungary that HPB visited. 12

Nevada. A state in the west of the United States. 448

Nevsky Prospect, 6, St. Petersburg, Russia. Alexander Aksakoff's address. 468

Newark, New Jersey. 280, 483

New Hampshire. A northeast state of the United States. 263

New Haven, Connecticut. 61, 189

New Orleans, Louisiana. 6

Newport, Rhode Island. 187

Newton, Henry Jotham (1823–95). A New York businessman, inventor, manufacturer, and pioneer photographer. He was a Spiritualist who investigated fraud in spirit photography and was president of the first Society of Spiritualists in New York, as well as a forming member of the Theosophical Society and its first treasurer. He and Olcott arranged for the cremation of Baron de Palm, and he was the executor of the Baron's will. (Biographical data: *CW* 1:502–3; *WWWA* H:378.) 214, 237, 270

Newton, H. L. A Boston attorney representing a woman who HPB anticipated would testify falsely against her. 159

Newton, Sir Isaac (1642–1727). The English physicist and mathematician widely regarded as one of the world's greatest scientists. Newtonian physics reigned supreme until the twentieth century and is still the norm for material behavior between the micro and macro levels. 294

New York. (1) A state in the east of the United States. (2) The largest city in the United States. 7, 31, 32, 33, 35, 36, 39, 40, 44, 46, 58, 72, 80, 114, 115, 136, 157, 159, 160, 162, 195, 199, 202, 214, 218, 219, 222, 231, 232, 241, 243, 251, 254, 256, 261, 271, 280, 284, 289, 292, 296, 314, 329, 331, 332, 333, 339, 353, 359, 361, 362, 363, 375, 379, 390, 392, 409, 412, 413, 420, 433, 438, 439, 451, 453, 455, 460, 464, 465, 471, 473, 480, 482, 484, 485, 486, 487, 489, 492, 494

New York Herald. A daily newspaper, published 1840–1920. 301, 339, 340, 431, 467, 488

New York Star. A daily newspaper of this name was published between about 1867 and 1880. The *Daily Star* was published 1868–91. The *Weekly Star* was published 1871–86. 451, 488

New York Sun. A daily newspaper, published 1833–1916, later *New York World Telegram and Sun*. The *Weekly Sun* was published by Charles A. Dana, 1872–94. 32, 183, 236, 237, 339, 467, 469, 473, 476, 477, 478, 482, 484

New York Times. A daily newspaper, published first in 1857. 484

New York Tribune. A daily newspaper, published 1866–1924. 200, 312

New York World. A daily newspaper, published 1860–?1931. A weekly newspaper, published 1860–93. A semiweekly newspaper, published 1860–?1881. 198, 200, 290, 295, 328, 330, 359, 360, 364, 369

Nicene Council. The first general council of the Christian Church, held in 325 at Nicea (modern Iznik, Turkey). Called by the emperor Constantine, the council adopted a creed, condemned the Arian heresy, and defined a canon of scripture. 294

Nicholas I (1796–1855). Emperor of Russia. 23, 42

Niederwalluf on the Rhine. The home of Prince Wittgenstein. 76

Nikolaides, Angelo. A Turkish editor whom HPB reported to be the president of the Constantinople Branch of the Theosophical Society. 483

Nil, *born* Nikolay Fyodorovich Isakovich (1799–1874). Archbishop of Yaroslav and author of a book on Buddhism and shamanistic practices (*Buddhism, Examined in Relation to Its Followers Who Were Living in Siberia*) and other books on religion in Siberia, as well as sermons. 343, 344, 348, 355

Nile, river. 363

Nineteenth Century. A monthly periodical published in London and New York, 1877–1900. 479, 480

Ninth Street, 60 East, New York City. Baron de Palm's address in April 1876. 262

nirvritti *or* **nivritti**. *Skt.* ni- "back" + vrit "to turn." "An infolding or a flowing-back-inwards of that which is outwardly manifested" (Grimes 211). (Cf. letter 100, n. 2.) 381, 383, 389, 390

Noble Eightfold Path. The last of the Four Noble Truths, or basic principles of Buddhism. The Noble Eightfold Path lists the practices that define a Buddhist life: right view, right resolve, right speech, right action, right livelihood, right effort, right mindfulness, and right concentration. 390

North America. *See* America, North.

North American Review. A quarterly (now bimonthly) periodical published in Boston since 1821. 422, 423

North Brook Gardens, Bombay. The address of Mulji Thackersey. 378

Northport, Long Island, New York. The site of the agricultural property for the working of which HPB had entered into a legal arrangement with Clementine Gerebko. 156

Notes on the Scientific and Religious Mysteries of Antiquity; the Gnosis and Secret Schools of the Middle Ages; Modern Rosicrucianism; and the Various Rites and Degrees of Free and Accepted Masonry. A work by John Yarker. 341

nous. *Gk.* "mind, perception." (1) The immortal spirit in a human being, higher manas. (2) The divine mind or third Logos. 291, 305, 307

Nubar Pasha (1825–99). A Christian of Armenian descent who became active in the Egyptian government, eventually serving as Prime Minister. *Pasha* is a title of rank. 25, 30

Nun. The father of Joshua. 287

Nut. An Egyptian deity. As goddess of the sky, Nut is depicted as a woman arching over the earth god Geb. According to HPB, Nut is "the one Spirit of God." (Cf. *Nout* in the *Theosophical Glossary*.) 307

Nychthēmeron. According to HPB, "the space of a day and a night or twenty-four hours." 250

Nysa, Mount. According to HPB, another name for Sinai. 317

Oannes. An amphibious fish-man in Babylonian mythology. He arose from the sea to teach human beings writing and the arts and sciences. 268

od *or* **odyle** *also* odic Force. A universal force that emanates from every object in the universe—including stars, crystals, and the human body—postulated by Karl von Reichenbach. (Cf. *EOP* 2:949; Podmore 1:118–9.) 196, 230

Odessa. 3, 4, 5, 14, 23, 24, 29, 31, 41, 379, 422, 444

O.E. Library Critic. A periodical published in Washingon, D.C. 484

Olcott, Henry Steel (1832–1907). The American agriculturalist, journalist, attorney, and civil rights advocate who was the cofounder and first president of the Theosophical Society. (Biographical data: *ANB* 16:666–7; *CW* 1:503–18; *DAB* 7:10–11; *EOP* 2:952; Murphet, *Yankee Beacon*; Prothero, *White Buddhist*.) 32–40, 43, 45–51, 58, 60–4, 70, 72, 78, 80–2, 84, 102, 104, 106–7, 117–8, 120, 122, 124–6, 128, 135, 139–43, 146, 148, 150, 153, 162, 165, 170, 172–3, 178–9, 189, 193–5, 198–200, 208–9, 213, 218–22, 228–9, 231–3, 235–6, 238, 241, 252–4, 256–8, 261, 270, 273, 275–7, 280–1, 289, 298, 302, 309, 326, 330–9, 341, 354–5, 357, 360–1, 364, 393, 398–400, 407, 420–5, 428, 432, 434, 441, 443, 448–51, 460, 469, 471–2, 474, 477–8, 482–4, 488–91, 493–8

Old, Walter R. 422

Old Diary Leaves. Memoirs by Henry S. Olcott. 33, 35, 37, 38, 46, 58, 135, 150, 218, 219, 222, 270, 330, 331, 332, 333, 334, 335, 336, 338, 339, 361, 407, 420, 425, 491, 500

Olya. A pet name for "Olga." 450

Omniloff. Unidentified, part of a message received on Gen. Lippitt's psychic stand. 187

On Buddhism. *See Buddhism, Examined . . . .*

Onkelos. The translator of the Pentateuch into an Aramaic version close to the literal sense of the original. 298, 322

On Miracles and Modern Spiritualism. A book by A. R. Wallace. 217

Onnofre. A title of Osiris. "One of the titles of Osiris, 'Onnofer' [*Un-nefer*], must be translated 'the goodness of God made manifest'" (*Isis Unveiled* 2:324, quoting K. R. Lepsius, *Königsbuch der alten Ägypter* [Berlin, 1858]). 347

On the Edge of the World. A presumably Russian novel sent to HPB by her aunt. 343

Orange, New Jersey. 253, 256

Orange Street, 565, Newark, New Jersey. The address of Alexander Wilder. 483

Order of St. Ann. A Russian award for service or accomplishment, military or civil. 40, 49

Orestes. *See* Pylades.

Origen (ca. 185–ca. 254). A Christian scholar from Alexandria who was learned in both Greek philosophy and Biblical

Owen, Robert Dale (1801–77). Congressman, social reformer, and Spiritualist, the son of Robert Owen (a British socialist, humanitarian, and founder of the Indiana community of New Harmony). Robert Dale Owen lived for a time in the New Harmony community and was elected to the Indiana legislature and later to Congress, where he sponsored the bill establishing the Smithsonian Institution, afterwards becoming one of its administrators. He advocated birth control, women's rights, abolition of slavery, and support for public education. In 1853 he was appointed Chargé d'Affaires in Naples and while there learned of his father's conversion to Spiritualism. At first he was skeptical, but after meeting the medium D. D. Home in Naples, he investigated Spiritualism and eventually became an active proponent. In 1874 he investigated the mediumship of the Holmeses and the materializations of Katie King. (Biographical data: *ANB* 16:861–3; *CW* 1:518–20; *DAB* 7:118–20; *EOP* 2:969–70; *WWWA* H:390.) 34, 46, 48, 62, 63, 64, 68, 71, 73, 74, 84, 88, 91, 143, 152, 173, 193, 225, 330

Palenque. An ancient city of the Maya in southern Mexico, noted for its temples and sculptures. 285

Palestine. 23, 42, 266, 287, 318, 321

Pall Mall. A street in central London on which many clubs are located. 277, 449

Pall Mall Gazette. A periodical published in London, 1865–1921. 477, 478, 479

Palm, Joseph Henry Louis de, Baron (1809–76). An Austrian nobleman and early member of the Theosophical Society. His funeral was held on May 28, 1876, at the Masonic Temple in New York City; his cremation on December 6, 1876, was the first public one in the United States. (Biographical data: *CW* 14:560.) 261, 263, 270, 271, 277, 279, 280, 285, 353, 482

Palmyra. An ancient city in the Syrian desert, destroyed by the Romans in 272 AD. 23

Panchen Lama. One of the two main Tibetan leaders, the Dalai Lama being the other. The Panchen Lama has his seat at the Tashilhunpo Monastery near Shigatse. Theoretically, the

Panchen Lama is more concerned with spiritual matters and the Dalai Lama with political ones, but in practice the roles have been mixed. 13

Pancoast, Seth (1823–89). A physician, Spiritualist and Kabbalist. He was one of the first two vice presidents of the Theosophical Society and attended HPB during her leg injury. (Biographical data: *CW* 1:520–1.) 165

Panjab. *See* Punjab.

Paracelsus, Philippus Aureolus, *originally* Theophrastus Bombastus von Hohenheim (1493–1541). A Swiss physician and alchemist who pioneered the use of specific chemical remedies for specific diseases, in opposition to the widely accepted theory of unbalanced humors as the cause of ailments. His adopted name, "Para-Celsus," implies "beyond Celsus," the most famous Roman physician. Although in one way an early practitioner of materia medica and an acute observer of medical facts, he combined that material and pragmatic approach with a mystical sensibility and a respect for both traditional folk remedies and the hermetic and alchemical traditions. 196, 211, 235, 333, 387

Paramaguru. *Skt.* "supreme teacher." A term applied by Olcott to the Adept Morya. 336

Paris. 5, 31, 42, 115, 119, 274, 292, 333, 402, 415, 420, 426, 430, 463, 483, 486, 490

Paris, W. A man who visited HPB at the Lamasery and whom she tried unsuccessfully to make "a theosophist of the *inner* ring." 426

Pascal, Blaise (1623–62). A French mathematician and philosopher, to whom Louisa Andrews attributed the saying "Le style c'est l'homme." The exact quotation is "Le style est l'homme même" (The style is the man himself) and is from Georges-Louis Leclerc de Buffon's *Discours sur le style*, delivered on his admission to the French Academy in 1753. 91

Pashkov, Lydia Alexandrovna de, Countess, *née* Glinskaya. A Russian-French writer who traveled through Egypt, Palestine, and Syria. HPB traveled with her briefly in the Near East after leaving Egypt in 1872 (Caldwell, *Esoteric World of Madame Blavatsky* 37, 413). (Biographical data: *CW* 1:521–2.) 23, 30

Pashkovsky, Mr. Perhaps the husband of Countess Pashkov. 25

Path (London). A monthly Theosophical journal published by the Blavatsky Institute, London, 1910–14. 55, 299, 310, 311, 358, 394

Path (NY). A monthly Theosophical journal edited by William Quan Judge, 1886–96. 54, 55, 191, 193, 216, 217, 272, 273, 290, 299, 300, 310, 311, 314, 355, 358, 394, 395, 396, 398, 408, 426, 452

Patriarch. A title of some bishops in the Orthodox Church. 267

Paul, Saint (d. ca. 65). The most important missionary and theologian of apostolic days. HPB says that Paul was an adept of the Greek Mysteries (letter 92) and cites him with respect. 306, 316, 325, 352, 357, 358

Peebles, James Martin (1822–1922). An American Spiritualist, minister, physician, temperance advocate, and abolitionist. He was an editor of the *Banner of Light*, the *Spiritual Universe*, and the *American Spiritualist*. (Biographical data: *EOP* 2:993–4; *WWWA* 1:953.) 403, 410

Peggotty. A character in Charles Dickens's novel *David Copperfield*. 165

peisah. Perhaps a Biblical commentator who writes a literal interpretation or peshat. 349, 355

Pemberton Square, 13, Boston. The address of Gen. Lippitt. 137, 184

Pemberton Square, 27, Boston. The address of a lawyer, H. L. Newton. 159

Pennsylvania, Historical Society of, Dreer Collection, Philadelphia. 364

People from the Other World. Henry S. Olcott's book treating the phenomena at the Eddy Farmstead. 33, 43, 47, 50, 51, 62, 79, 80, 82, 84, 127, 143, 172, 229, 331, 360, 361

périsprit. *Fr.* "psyche, soul." "In the sciences of Spiritualism, an intermediary element between the body and the spirit (astral body)" (*Grand Larousse de la langue française*). 247, 348, 352, 357, 386

Perovsky, Sophie L. (1853–81). A Russian revolutionary who was part of a plot that led to the assassination of Czar Alexander II in 1881. (Cf. HPB's articles "The Assassination of the Czar"

[*CW* 3:121–5], "The State of Russia" [*CW* 3:155–70], and "Trance Mediums and 'Historical' Visions" [*CW* 3:359–65].) 57

Perrault, Charles (1628–1703). A French author best known for his collection of children's stories, *Contes de ma mère l'oye* ("Mother Goose Tales," 1697), including "Bluebeard." 103

Persia. 12, 423

Perth, Australia *or* Scotland. 490

Perty, Maximilian. A professor at the University of Berne who attempted to connect paranormal phenomena with powers latent in the medium's body. (Cf. *CW* 3:236; *EOP* 2:1002; Podmore 2:162.) 249

Pest. A Hungarian city on the left bank of the Danube River, a commercial and industrial area, united with Buda in 1872. 27, 30

Peter, Saint. 352, 357, 358

Peter I, the Great (1672–1725). Emperor of Russia. 127

Petersburg. *See* St. Petersburg.

Pfeiffer, Ida (1797–1858). An Austrian woman who, at the age of 45, decided to travel. Having only modest means, she lived with simple local people and traveled cheaply. Her first trip resulted in a book: *Visit to the Holy Land, Egypt, and Italy* (1844). That work financed her next trip, also recorded in a book: *Journey to Iceland, and Travels in Sweden and Norway* (1846). Her third trip to the Brazilian rain forests, Tahiti, China, India, Persia, Mesopotamia, Russia, Turkey, Greece, and Italy produced *A Lady's Voyage round the World* (1850), which earned her fame as well as income. Her last major trip was to Cape Town, Singapore, Borneo, Java, Sumatra, the Moluccas, the Andes, and the United States, recorded in the equally popular book *A Lady's Second Journey around the World* (1855). Pfeiffer liked India and the headhunters of Borneo, but found little to praise in most of the other places she visited. 50

Philadelphia, Pennsylvania. 46, 47, 58, 60, 62, 64, 65, 66, 69, 70, 73, 78, 80, 81, 83, 85, 88, 92, 94, 99, 100, 107, 108, 124, 125, 126, 128, 135, 138, 146, 151, 153, 155, 158, 159, 161, 163, 164, 165, 173, 174, 176, 183, 186, 187, 188, 193, 199, 235, 254, 465

"Philadelphia 'Fiasco,' or Who Is Who?, The." An article by HPB (*CW* 1:56–72). 65, 72

Philadelphia Press. A daily newspaper, published 1857–80. 339

Philadelphia *Public Ledger*. A daily newspaper, published 1836–1925. 177, 183

Philalethes, Eugenius. *See* Vaughan, Thomas.

Philip. An early Christian missionary of whom the Acts of the Apostles gives an account. 352, 357, 359

Philistine. One of an ancient people living in southwest Palestine. 282, 284

Philological Society of New York. This organization has not been identified. 381

Philostian. No ancient people of this name has been identified. The printed form was probably a typographical error for "Philistian," that is, "Philistine." 269

Phoenician. A Greek term for any of the Canaanites who lived on the Mediterranean seacoast and traded with the Greeks. The great Phoenician cities were Tyre and Sidon in present-day Lebanon. The Phoenicians were famed as navigators, traders, and colonizers over the Mediterranean world; they had cultural connections with Egypt; and their major contribution to European culture was the spread of the alphabet to the Greeks and probably elsewhere. 265, 266, 269, 287, 317, 350

Phrenological Journal and Life Illustrated. A monthly periodical published in New York, 1870–88, devoted to phrenology. Phrenology is the study of the shape of the human skull as a basis for the analysis of character and mental qualities, developed about 1800 by a German physiologist, Franz Joseph Gall. 404, 407, 408

Pico della Mirandola, Giovanni (1463–94). An Italian philosopher, humanist, and Neoplatonist who sought to reconcile Christian and Greek thought, an aim that led him into conflict with the Papacy. 86, 87

Pilate. The Roman governor of Palestine in the time of Jesus. 315

Pillars of Hercules. The promontories on either side of the Strait of Gibraltar. 287

Piotre. *See* Koutcherof, Piotre.

Piraeus, Greece. The port of Athens. 13, 42

Pistis Sophia. A Gnostic treatise of Egyptian origin. HPB wrote notes and commentary on the first part of the *Pistis Sophia* published in her magazine *Lucifer* (*CW* 13:1–81). 250

Plato (ca. 427–347 BC). A Greek philosopher and disciple of Socrates. It has been said that all European philosophy is only footnotes to Plato. 258, 272, 283, 305, 307

Platonism. The teachings of Plato. 284

Platonist. A follower of Plato's teachings. 333

Plotinus (205–70). A Neoplatonic philosopher and disciple of Ammonius Saccas. He traveled to the East to study the philosophies of Persia and India. He was the primary framer of the Neoplatonic philosophy, based on Plato, but elaborated by Plotinus with a cosmology including a theory of emanations, which was the basis of his system. 214, 249

Plutarch (ca. 46–ca. 120). A Greek biographer and essayist best known for his *Parallel Lives*, comparing famous Greeks and Romans in pairs, a work filled with illustrative anecdotes. He also served as a priest of the temple at Delphi. 196, 213, 236, 305, 352, 357, 359

Polizeyskaya Street. The location of the house in Odessa where HPB was living with her aunt Katherine Andreyevna de Witte in December 1872. 29

Pollux. *See* Castor and Pollux.

Polonius. A character in Shakespeare's play *Hamlet*. 273

Poltava. A city in the Ukraine, on the river Vorskla. 4

Pondicherry. A city and territory in the southeast of India, near Madras, founded by the French in 1674. 376

Pontine Marshes. Malarial marshes about 25 miles southeast of Rome. 90

Pope. The bishop of Rome, head of the Roman Catholic Church. 127, 252, 282, 284, 289, 301, 354, 397

Pope Joan. A legendary woman pope, who is supposed to have reigned as John VIII between 855 and 858 (or other dates). There are several versions of the legend, which was taken seriously in the thirteenth to seventeenth centuries but has since been shown to be apocryphal. 257

Porphyry *or* **Porphyrios** (ca. 232–ca. 304). A Neoplatonic philosopher who was a disciple of Plotinus and teacher of Iamblichus. 214, 236, 249, 278, 338, 396

Porter, Mrs. An unidentified medium whom HPB cites as an example of immorality while under control of a "spirit guide." 275

positivist. A philosopher who denies the validity of speculation or metaphysics and maintains that the goal of philosophy is not to explain but to describe experienced reality. The term was coined by the nineteenth-century French philosopher Auguste Comte, from whose thought twentieth-century logical positivism developed. 214, 228

Poti. A port on the Black Sea at the mouth of the Rion River, where HPB began her foreign travels when she ran away from her family and husband. 5, 29, 30

Pratt, Calvin E. The judge in the Suffolk County court that tried HPB's suit against Clementine Gerebko. 157, 160

Pravda. *Russ*. "truth." A Russian daily newspaper published in Odessa, 1877–80, to which HPB submitted articles for publication. One of its editor-publishers was Joseph Florovich Dolivo-Dobrovolsky, the brother of the wife of Yevgeniy Feodorovich von Hahn, a cousin of HPB's. 388, 389, 449

pravritti. *Skt*. "from the verb root vrit = 'to turn' + pra = 'forth' . . . the path of active involvement in the world" (Grimes 248). (Cf. letter 100, n. 2.) 383, 389, 390

Prince of Wales. At the time of these letters, Albert Edward, the eldest son of Queen Victoria, and later King Edward VII. 292, 397, 428

Proarchē *or* Proarchos. *Gk*. The demiurge or subordinate deity who created the material world according to a preexisting plan. (Cf. *CW* 13:43, n. 1.) 276

Procopius (d. ca. 565). A Byzantine official and historian whose *De bello vandalico* treats a war against the African kingdom of the Vandals. 287

Proof Palpable of Immortality. A book by Epes Sargent. 96, 173

Providence, Rhode Island. 483

Pskov *or* **Pskoff**. A city and area in northwest Russia, southwest of St. Petersburg, the location of an estate that Vera Petrovna de Zhelihovsky inherited from her first husband. 8, 9

psyche. The personality or lower quaternary. 306

psychic stand. An invention of Gen. Lippitt's, perhaps a kind of planchette of the Ouija type. It may be the "tipping machine" mentioned in letter 36 and the object of the "patent" mentioned at the end of letter 39. 186

Rig Veda. The oldest of the four Vedas or Wisdom scriptures of Hinduism, consisting of hymns used in liturgical rites. 320, 329, 446

Rite of Adoption. Any of various Freemasonic-like rituals created in France for women. 341

Rituel de la haute magie. A book by Éliphas Lévi. 212

Riverhead, Long Island. The locale of the trial of HPB's case against Clementine Gerebko. 138, 149, 151, 157, 159

Roberts, J. M. A lawyer who, with Olcott and Gen. Lippitt, investigated the Holmes phenomena. 70, 76, 88

Robinson, James. A commercial firm clerk, and one of five men who participated in discussions that led to the publication, under the pen name HIRAF, of the article on "Rosicrucianism," to which HPB replied with her "first *Occult* Shot."

Rochester Knockings *or* Rappings. A phenomenon of knocking sounds in the house of Mr. and Mrs. John Fox and their two daughters, Margaretta and Kate, in Hydesville, near Rochester, New York, in 1848, which began modern Spiritualism. (Cf. *EOP* 2:1099–1100.) 86

Rockies. The Rocky Mountain range, running north to south through the western United States. 7

Romanoffs. The Russian royal family. 414

Romanova. A female member of the Russian royal family. 314

Rome, Italy. Often used metonymically for the Roman Catholic Church. 26, 127, 261, 354, 377, 397

Roosevelt Hospital. The New York hospital where Baron de Palm died. 280

Rosicrucian *or* **Rosecrucian**. (1) A follower of Rosicrucianism. (2) Pertaining to Rosicrucianism or Rosicrucians. 59, 79, 120, 133, 134, 165, 188, 206, 208, 248

Rosicrucianism. The doctrines of various esoteric groups that claim existence from ancient times and membership by various illustrious persons. The origin and aims of the Rosicrucians were first set forth in *Fama fraternitatis* "A Report of the Brotherhood" (1614) and *Confessio rosae cruces* "A Confession of the Rose Cross" (1615), generally thought to have been the works of Johan Valentin Andrea (1586–1654), who used the byname Christian Rosenkreuz. These early works generated great interest in Europe and attracted sympathetic attention from a number of notable persons. There is doubt, however, about the reality of the Rosicrucians described in them. Many modern scholars suspect the works of being fictions with a symbolic (or even satiric) purpose. Yet the interest in Rosicrucianism that sprang from the *Fama fraternitatis* spread in many directions, including Freemasonic, and several organizations of more recent foundation claim connection with the legendary group. Rosicrucian symbolism is widespread in modern esoteric groups as well as in art and literature. (Cf. *EOP* 2:1107–10.) 157

Rutland, Vermont. A town near Chittenden, the site of the Eddy farmhouse. 34

Sabazios. Another name for Bacchus or Dionysos, a mystery god torn into seven pieces (*Isis* 2:487). 317

Sabean *or* **Sabaean**. Pertaining to the people in the land of Saba, in southwestern Arabia, during the first millennium BC. 266

Sacramento, California. 448

Saint-Germain, Comte de (ca. 1710–1784?). An eighteenth-century Adept also identified as Prince Rákóczy, of Transylvania, often associated with Freemasonry. HPB frequently links Saint-Germain and Cagliostro as maligned mages (*CW* 4:339, *SD* 2:156), saying that, after those two, magic died out in Europe because later Adepts, "having learned bitter lessons from the vilifications and persecutions of the past, pursue different tactics nowadays" (*CW* 1:141, *Isis* 2:403). (Biographical data: *CW* 3:523–8; *EOP* 2:1120–1; Fuller, *Comte de Saint-Germain*.) 141

St. John's Wood, London. The location of Annie Besant's house, to which HPB moved in 1890. 328

St. Petersburg. A city in northwest Russia, the cultural center and capital of the country during HPB's lifetime, founded by Czar Peter the Great in 1703 as a "window" to Europe. 3, 5, 8, 19, 25, 36, 57, 102, 178, 184, 195, 274, 422, 453, 468

St. Petersburg University. 494

Saïs. An ancient Egyptian city in the Nile Delta. "The place where the celebrated temple of Isis-Neith was found, wherein was the ever-veiled statue of . . . Isis . . ., with the famous inscription, 'I am all that has been, and is, and shall be, and my peplum no mortal has withdrawn'" (*Theosophical Glossary* 284). 363

Saitic. Pertaining to Saïs. 363

salamander. An elemental spirit or force of nature associated with fire. 211, 387

Sal'ka. A pet name for an unidentified person. 450

Salle Koch. A St. Petersburg "low lager-bier saloon and dance hall." The name appears to be French *salle* "hall" and perhaps a German surname, *Koch*. 36

Salt Lake City, Utah. 127

samaj(a) *or* **somaj(a)**. A society, especially the Arya Samaj. 433, 434, 454, 491

Samaritan. A member of a Jewish community that does not recognize the authority of Jerusalem or the Temple at Jerusalem as the holiest site and that was consequently scorned by the Jews of Judah. 319, 350

Samarkand. A city and region in present-day Uzbekistan. Historically, Samarkand was a stopping point on the Silk Road between China and Europe and a capital of the Mongol Empire under Tamerlane. 267

Sandwich Islands. A former name of the Hawaiian Islands. 127, 470

San Francisco, California. 7

Sanskrit *or* **Sanscrit**. The ancient Indo-European language of India, still used for religious and scholarly purposes. 266, 267, 298, 320, 347, 372, 376, 380, 381, 431, 437, 438, 441, 445, 457, 460

Sansom Street, 3420, Philadelphia. The residence shared by HPB and Michael Betanelly. 78, 108, 128, 135, 137, 138, 144, 146

Saraswati. *See* Dayanand Saraswati.

Saratov, Russia. A port city on the Volga River, where HPB's grandfather was governor of the province. 2, 4, 352

Sarda, Har Bilas. The author of a biography of Dayanand Saraswati. 433, 434

Sargent, Epes (1813–80). A novelist, poet, man of letters, and newspaperman, who developed an interest in Spiritualism. His works on that subject include *Planchette; or, The Despair of Science: Being a Full Account of Modern Spiritualism, Its Phenomena, and the Various Theories Regarding It, with a Survey of French Spiritism* (1869), *The Proof Palpable of Immortality: Being an Account of the Materialization Phenomena of Modern Spiritualism, with Remarks on the Relations of the Facts to Theology, Morals, and Religion* (1875), and *The Scientific Basis of Spiritualism* (1881 [c1880]). (Biographical data: *ANB* 19:279–80; *CW* 3:528–30; *DAB* 8:356–7; *EOP* 2:1127; *WWWA* H:463.) 46, 96, 128, 139, 140, 143, 149, 152, 154, 162, 173, 184, 226

Sasha. A pet name for "Alexander" or "Alexandra," specifically for Alexander Yulyevich de Witte, HPB's nephew. 379, 389, 414, 416, 450

sastra *or* shastra. *Skt.* śāstra, "teaching, doctrine." Religious scripture. 346

Sat Bhai. A Freemasonic order originating in India, for membership in the female branch of which, HPB received a certificate from John Yarker. 341, 350

Saugus, Massachusetts. 32, 353, 445

Saul. The first king of Israel (ca. 1020–ca. 1000 BC). 282, 284, 319

Saville. A London club on Bond Street, of which C. C. Massey was a member. 273, 277

Sayana Mahidhar. A fourteenth-century commentator on the Rig Veda. (Cf. Stutley and Stutley 275.) 457

Schleiermacher, Friedrich Daniel Ernst (1768–1834). A German Protestant theologian who opposed both orthodox theology and the rationalism of his time. 370

School for Scandal. A play by Richard Brinsley Sheridan. 148, 150

Schopenhauer, Arthur (1788–1860). A German philosopher whose views on the pervasiveness of pain and frustration in life and on the renunciation of desire as the only escape from that pain are reminiscent of Buddhism. 381

"Science of Magic, The." An article by HPB (*CW* 1:134–43). 195

Scindia. The family name of the rulers of Gwalior. 417

Scotland Yard. A street in London, formerly the location of the police headquarters; hence, the detective department of the London metropolitan police. 479

scrapbook. Any of the scrapbooks in which HPB pasted copies of her articles and other matters that interested her, often with annotations, as a historical record of the Theosophical Society and her activities. 64, 74, 85, 170, 218, 222, 229, 237, 407, 479

Scribner's Monthly. A periodical published in New York, 1870–81. 76

Secret Doctrine, The. HPB's major work, 1888. 332, 340

Section. A membership division of the early Theosophical Society of either of two types: (1) A unit in a horizontal structure whose members are united by geography, ethnicity, or interest.

Geographical sections of this type (*CW* 9:245) are now called "National Societies" in the Rules of the Theosophical Society; the temporary "Theosophical Society of the Arya Samaj" was called a "vedic Section" (letter from HPB to M. V. Pandia, Mar. 2, 1879). (2) A unit in a vertical structure, through which members might expect to pass: "All who enter our Society pass through different degrees and sections (as in Masonry) from lowest to highest. Promotion depends upon *personal merit* and devotion to the cause" (letter 123); "There are in our societies [Theosophical and Arya Samaj] sections and degrees in which the obligations and attainments differ greatly" (background essay N). The "First Section" of this type was of the general membership and was projected to consist of three degrees with signs, grips, and passwords (letter to Pandia cited above). The "Second Section" consisted of more advanced students (ibid.). A still "Higher Section" consisted of Adepts (letter from HPB to N. de Fadeyev, Feb. 21, 1880). HPB sometimes reversed the numbering and referred to the highest as the "First Section," consisting of the "Brothers." 422, 454, 497

Semitic. A subfamily of languages of which the best known members are Hebrew and Arabic. 266, 285

Sentimental Journey through France and Italy, A. A book by Laurence Sterne. 94, 96

sephirah *or* sefira; *plural* sephiroth *or* sefirot. *Heb.* "number." Any of the Kabbalistic ten emanations of Ain Soph, "the infinite," through which the Divine operates in the world and by which it can be known. 86, 87, 166

seraphim. The highest of the nine orders of angels. 171

Serapis. The name by which an Egyptian Adept was called, taken from that of a popular Ptolemaic Egyptian god combining the attributes of Osiris and Apis (the sacred bull). 170

Serbia. A Balkan country whose capital is Belgrade. 300

Serbo-Turkish War. A war fought by Serbia and Turkey in 1876-7, and joined by Russia in 1877-8. 289

Sermon on the Mount. A major statement of Christ's teaching (Matt. 5-7). 317, 346

Sextilius. A Roman governor of the province of Carthage. 173

Shaker. A member of the religious group called Shakers because of their bodily trembling in religious ecstasy during worship. Spiritualism was practiced by some members of the group. 48

Shakespeare, William (1564–1616). The English playwright. 222, 229, 273

shaman. A religious diviner who has undergone a spiritual initiation that allows him or her to enter into a state of paranormal consciousness and to invoke natural powers for healing and otherwise assisting members of the tribal group. 7, 427

Shepard, Mr. A publisher of the house of Lee and Shepard. 186

Shepard, Jesse Francis Grierson (1848–1927). An American medium and musician whose séances included piano and vocal performances in voice ranges from bass to soprano, sometimes simultaneously, whom HPB regarded as a fraud. He was a prolific and respected author under his last two given names, Francis Grierson. He was also known as "Benjamin Henry Jesse Francis Shepard." (Biographical data: *CW* 1:92–3; *EOP* 2:1172.) 36

Sheridan, Richard Brinsley (1751–1816). An Irish playwright. 150

Shigatse. A city in Tibet where the Adept KH's sister lived, near the monastery of the Panchen Lama. 13

Shimon ben Yohai. *See* Simeon ben Yohai.

shin. *Heb.* The twenty-first letter of the Hebrew alphabet. 166, 208

Shin *or* Shinn, Mr. One of a number of persons—including HPB, Olcott, William Quan Judge, and Alexander Wilder—whose voices were recorded on tinfoil sheets by an early version of Thomas Edison's phonograph on December 15, 1878, before the Founders' departure for India; unfortunately the recordings later deteriorated (*ODL* 1:480). 481

shishimora, *Russ. pl.* shishimori. (1) A crook, rogue. (2) A household spirit, ghost, familiar, elemental. 353

Shwabhavika. *See* Svabhavika.

Shyamaji Krishnavarma *or* **Krishnawarma** (1857–1930). A Sanskrit pandit, lawyer, and politican. As a young man, he was a devoted follower of Dayanand Saraswati and a member of both the Arya Samaj and the Theosophical Society. He studied at Oxford, where he was assistant to the Boden Professor of Sanskrit, Monier-Williams. Later as an associate of Bal

Gangadhar Tilak (who has been called the Father of Modern India), he coined the slogan "Home Rule for India," adopted by Tilak for his Indian Home Rule Society, and was editor of the *Indian Sociologist*. His subsequent political career as a radical nationalist was controversial. (Biographical data: *CW* 1:437 n. 28; Yajnik, *Shyamaji Krishnavarma*.) 438, 441, 449, 451, 455, 456

Siam *and* **Siamese**. *Former terms for* Thailand *and* Thai. 7, 267, 270, 285, 380

Siberia. The Asian part of Russia, from the Ural Mountains to the Pacific Ocean. 4, 7, 286, 427

Siddhartha. The given name of Siddhartha Gautama, the Buddha. 346, 381

Sidgwick, Eleanor Balfour. Henry Sidgwick's wife, who abridged and paraphrased correspondence evidence collected by the Society for Psychical Research for its continuing file on HPB. (Cf. Inglis 360–1.) 401, 404, 430, 432, 433, 438, 464

Sidgwick, Henry (1838–1900). A Cambridge Utilitarian philosopher and one of the founders of the Society for Psychical Research. (Biographical data: *CW* 4:665.) 401

Sidonian. Pertaining to Sidon, a Phoenician city (now Saida, Lebanon). 266

Siémons, Jean-Louis. 77, 92, 103, 107, 150

Sikh. A member of the religion founded in the Punjab in the sixteenth century by Guru Nanak. 417, 418

Simeon ben Yohai, *also* **Simon** *or* **Shimon**, *and* **Jochai** (2nd c.). A Jewish sage, traditionally credited with the authorship of the *Zohar*. 87, 298

Simeon *or* **Simon Stylites**, Saint (ca. 390–459). *Gk.* stylos "pillar." A Syrian hermit who lived for more than thirty-five years on a small platform at the top of a tall pillar. 474

Simon ben Jochai. *See* Simeon ben Yohai.

Simon Magus. A Samaritan Gnostic who was criticized by early Christian writers. 294

Simon Stylites. *See* Simeon Stylites.

Sinai, Mount. The mountain on the Sinai Peninsula on which Moses received the ten commandments from the God of Israel. 317, 321

Sindhia. The family name of the rulers of Gwalior, a princely state formed in the eighteenth century by Ranoji Sindhia, a Mahratta chief. 418

Singapore. A city and island republic on the south of the Malay peninsula. 6

Singh, Dhuleep *or* Dhulip *or* Dalip, Prince (1837–93). The son of Ranjit Singh and, as a child, Maharaja of Lahore (1843–9). After his kingdom was annexed to British India, he lived in England for nearly fifty years. 6

Singh, Mahan *or* Maha. The father of Ranjit Singh. 418

Singh, Ranjit *or* **Runjeet** (1780–1839). "The Lion of the Punjab," the founder and maharaja for nearly forty years of the Sikh kingdom of the Punjab. Expanding the borders of the kingdom, by 1820 he ruled the entire Punjab. His modernized army and government included Sikhs, Hindus, and Muslims, as well as European advisors. After his death, however, the kingdom collapsed because of tribal conflicts. 417, 418

Sing Sing State Prison. A prison in Ossinging, New York, proverbial as a place of incarceration, in 1969 renamed the Ossinging State Correctional Facility. 111, 115

Sinnett, A. P. The editor of *Incidents in the Life of Madame Blavatsky*. 1, 6, 7, 10, 16, 55, 183, 336, 356

sirdar. A chief, an organizer, a Sikh leader. 417, 418

Siva *or* Shiva. *Skt.* "auspicious." One of the principal gods of Hinduism. As part of the Trimurti, he is the Destroyer or Regenerator. 445, 446

Sixteenth Street, 124 East, New York City. A house where HPB lived in 1874–5. 32, 33

Skeleton Key to Mysterious Gates. An early working title for *Isis Unveiled*. 196, 216, 331

sketchbook. A small notebook of HPB's, containing mainly drawings with some annotations (*CW* 1:2–5). 6

Slade, Henry (d. 1905). An American medium known mainly for slate writing, selected by Blavatsky and Olcott to go to Russia for experiments with A. N. Aksakoff. (Biographical data: *CW* 1:525; *EOP* 2:1185–6; Podmore 87–91, 190–3.) 153, 272, 274, 275, 278, 292, 428, 494

Slavonian. A Slavic language. 133, 182, 266

Slavonic. Slavic, a branch of the Indo-European language family including Bulgarian, Czech, Polish, Russian, Serbo-Croatian, Slovene, and Ukrainian. 320

Smith, Richard, Deacon. Unidentified referent. 183

Smith, Richard Penn. The author of the play *Caius Marius*. 173

Société Spirite. *Fr.* "Spiritualist Society." An organization HPB attempted to form in Cairo in 1872 to investigate Spiritualistic phenomena. 17, 18, 19, 20, 21, 22, 23

Society for Psychical Research (SPR). An organization founded in 1882 for the impartial study of paranormal phenomena. (Cf. Haynes, *The Society for Psychical Research, 1882-1982: A History*; Podmore 2:176–7.) 401, 432

Society of Jesus. *See* Jesuit.

Socrates (ca. 470–399 BC). The first of the three foundational philosophers of Greece: Socrates, Plato, and Aristotle. Socrates, who is known primarily through the dialogs Plato wrote, focused on human ethical problems rather than cosmic ones. 211, 258, 293, 307

Sofya. The Russian form of the name "Sophia." 451

Sohar. *See Zohar.*

Solomon. The king of Israel (ca. 962–922 BC) who built the first Temple at Jerusalem and was fabled for his wisdom. 84, 87, 132, 147, 150, 317

Solomon's seal. A pair of interlaced equilateral triangles. The symbol, incorporated into the emblem of the Theosophical Society, is a universal one. 84, 147, 150

Solovyov *or* Solovyoff *or* Solov'ev *or* Soloviov, **Vsevolod Sergueyevich** (1849-1903). A Russian novelist and poet whom HPB met in Paris in 1884. After an initial friendship, following her death, Solovyov published a series of exposé articles entitled "A Modern Priestess of Isis" in 1892 issues of the periodical *Russkiy Vestnik* ("Russian Messenger"). They were compiled and published as a book (*Sovremennaya zhritza Isidi*) in 1893. In 1895 Walter Leaf published an abridged translation of Solovyov's book with some added material "on behalf of the Society for Psychical Research." (Cf. *CW* 6:446 and 7:332-4 fn.) 35, 46, 52, 73, 74, 127, 144, 174, 194, 195, 196, 214, 215, 251, 260, 263, 264, 271, 289, 312, 341, 362

somaj *or* **somaja**. *See* samaj(a).

Sonya. A pet name for "Sofya" (Sophia). 450

Sophocles, Evangelinus Apostolides (ca. 1805–83). A classicist and professor at Harvard University consulted by Gen. Lippitt on ancient letters and symbols. (Biographical data: *WWWA* H:496.) 83, 84, 147

Sotheran, Charles (1847–1902). An English-born journalist and author who came to America in 1874 as a reporter for the *New York World*. He was a forming member of the Theosophical Society and served as its librarian. A prominent Freemason, he was active in Scottish Rite, Memphis Rite, and Swedenborgian Rite bodies. (Biographical data: *WWWA* 1:1157.) 219, 238, 241, 341, 400

South America. *See* America, South.

Southampton, England. A major seaport on the coast of Hampshire. 6

Southampton Row, 15, London. The address of the Spiritualist Institution in the Bloomsbury area of central London. 18

Spencer, Herbert (1820–1903). An English philosopher who established sociology as a discipline and helped to popularize the evolutionary theory of Charles Darwin and Thomas Huxley. 297

Spezzia *or* **Spetsai**. An island off the coast of Greece, near which the powder magazine of the SS *Eunomia*, on which HPB was a passenger, blew up. 42, 183

sphinx. A mythological creature with a lion's body and a human head. The Greek sphinx, associated with riddling, was female and winged. The Egyptian statue at Giza is the portrait statue of a king. 286, 297, 336

spiritism *also* **spiritist** *and* **spritistic**. Spiritualism, also Spiritualist and Spiritualistic, in the narrow sense as "the belief that the spirits of the dead can hold communication with the living, or make their presence known to them in some way, esp. through a 'medium'" (*OED* sense 3). HPB, however, sometimes used both variants, "spiritism" and "Spiritualism," in a broader sense of belief in the existence of a spiritual reality in addition to material reality. 21, 34, 45, 54, 113, 142, 143, 171, 172, 173, 214, 236, 272, 396

Spiritisme dans le monde, Le, "Spiritualism in the World." A book by Louis Jacolliot. 353

Spiritual Association of Philadelphia. An organization of which Henry T. Child was president. 68

Spiritual Hall. *See* Lincoln Spiritual Hall.

Spiritualism. (1) The belief that the spirits of the dead can contact living humans through a person who is especially sensitive to their world (a medium). (2) The belief that spiritual, rather than material, reality is ultimate. 13, 17, 20, 31, 32, 36, 38, 39, 42, 48, 52, 59, 68, 71, 72, 75, 86, 95, 96, 99, 101, 111, 112, 113, 119, 121, 127, 130, 141, 142, 150, 170, 171, 176, 188, 193, 200, 217, 220, 221, 222, 224, 226, 230, 232, 235, 238, 240, 241, 242, 245, 257, 294, 330, 342, 361, 362, 398, 402, 441, 494

Spiritualist Institution. A London site in the Bloomsbury area where Frank Herne and other mediums gave séances. 18

Spiritualist Newspaper: A Record of the Progress of the Science and Ethics of Spiritualism. A weekly periodical published in London, 1869–82, and edited by W. H. Harrison. (Cf. Podmore 2:168.) 100, 103, 117, 143, 154, 235, 241, 243, 244, 245, 250, 300, 435, 493, 498

Spiritual Scientist. A weekly (except monthly during its last volume) periodical published in Boston and edited by E. Gerry Brown, 1874–78. 38, 39, 40, 58, 64, 80, 94, 96, 100, 113, 116, 117, 118, 119, 120, 125, 126, 135, 138, 139, 140, 143, 144, 149, 150, 152, 155, 162, 171, 172, 173, 175, 176, 181, 213, 218, 234, 237, 239, 241, 242, 331

spook. The psychic remains of a dead person after the intelligent spirit of that person has left those remains, also called a "shell." The spook has remnants of the memories and desires of the formerly living person, but no intelligence or spirituality. 11, 13, 16, 17, 20, 22, 56, 57, 151, 192, 274, 385, 387, 388, 389

SPR. *See* Society for Psychical Research.

Springfield, Massachusetts. 61, 93, 110, 114, 189

Springfield Daily Republican. A newspaper published in Springfield, Massachusetts, 1851–1946. 93, 95, 100, 339

St. *Entries beginning with St. are listed under the full spelling* Saint.

Stanhope, Hester Lucy, Lady. A daughter of Charles Stanhope, 3rd Earl, Viscount Stanhope of Mahon, Baron Stanhope of

Elvaston, a radical politician and a scientist. The *Encyclopædia Britannica* calls her "a traveler and an eccentric who became the de facto ruler of a mountain community in western Syria." 2

Stavropol, Russia. The place where HPB's father died and was buried. It is probably the city in a territory of the same name north of the Caucasus Mountains. 40, 50, 260

Sterne, Laurence (1713–68). The English author of *A Sentimental Journey through France and Italy* (1768) and the more popular parodic novel *Tristram Shandy* (1760–67). 94, 96

Storozhenko. A governor of the Province of Tchernigov who was reputed to be a vampire. His story is recounted in *Isis* 1:454-5. 326

"Story of the Mystical, A." A story by HPB under the pen name "Hadji Mora" (*CW* 1:163-73). 237

Strand, the. A street in central London, between the West End and the City, the location of theaters and fashionable shops and hotels. 6

Sturge, A. An Anglican clergyman with whom Blavatsky had "tugs" (*CW* 1:433) or "daily wrangles" (*ODL* 2:3) during their voyage from New York to England but from whom she parted on good terms and with whom she exchanged photographs. 493

Sudan. 41, 43, 50

Suez Canal. 13

Suffolk County, Long Island, New York. The location of the two parcels of land owned by Clementine Gerebko, one of which became the focus of HPB's suit against Gerebko. 156, 157

Summerland. The name given by Spiritualists to the state of the dead. 95, 147, 182, 194, 195

Supernatural Religion. A book by Walter Richard Cassels. 282

Svabhavika *or* **Shwabhavika**. According to HPB, a school of Buddhist philosophy. (Cf. *CW* 2:91 and Reigle, *Doctrine of Svabhāva*.) 353, 370, 383, 389

Swedenborg, Emanuel (1688–1772). A Swedish scientist who underwent a religious crisis in his mid fifties involving dreams and visions. Out of those visions, which continued, came about thirty books in Latin setting forth Swedenborg's percep-tions of the spiritual world. 419, 447

sylph. An elemental or force of nature associated with air. 235, 387

Syria. 12, 23, 42

Syrian. 266, 318, 350

Szeben, Hungary. A town that HPB visited. 12

Taganrog, Russia. A port on the northeast of the Sea of Azov from which HPB began her world travels. 5

Tappan, Cora L. V., *later* Mrs. Richmond (ca. 1840–1923). A Washington, DC, trance medium who was one of the founders of the National Spiritualist Association and its vice president. (Biographical data: *CW* 1:528; Podmore 2:134–9.) 276

Tartar. A Mongolian or Turk, or someone generally of exotic appearance. 7, 286, 498

Tashilhunpo Monastery, Tibet. The seat of the Panchen Lama. 13

Tashkent, Turkistan. The capital of the land now known as Uzbekistan. 268, 269

Tauris. A province in Russia. 9

Taylor, Thomas (1758–1835). An English translator of Plato and author of the *Eleusinian and Bacchic Mysteries* and *The Mystical Hymns of Orpheus*. Blavatsky echoes a shared sentiment, that "others know Greek better, but Taylor knew Plato thousand times better." 283, 285

Taylor, Timothy B. A Methodist minister in Fort Scott, Kansas, who advocated the reconciliation of science and religion and supported Spiritualism. A series of lectures he delivered at the Fort Scott Methodist church in the winter of 1870–1 created a controversy that led to his dismissal from the Methodist ministry in March 1871 on charges of heresy. The lectures were published by the Fort Scott *Monitor* newspaper as a book entitled *Old Theology Turned Upside Down or Right Side Up; by a Methodist Preacher; or Eight Lectures:—Six on the Resurrection of the Dead, One on the Second Coming of Christ, and One on the Last Judgment—Showing from the Standpoint of Common Sense, Reason, Science, Philosophy, and the Bible, the Utter Folly There Is in the Doctrine of the Literal Resurrection of the Body, a Literal Coming of Christ at the End of the World, and a Literal Judgment to Follow*. A second edition of the book, which also contained an additional lecture on "The Magnetic Forces of the Universe," was printed

by the *Banner of Light* Office in Boston the following year
(Malin, "Kansas Philosophers, 1871"). An 1872 appeal to the
Methodist General Conference to reverse the charge of heresy
was unsuccessful. On June 9, 1879, Taylor, who was then living
in Philadelphia, wrote a letter to the editor of the *Banner of
Light*, published in that Spiritualist periodical on July 5, concerning the Spiritualist beliefs of William Lloyd Garrison, the
abolitionist, who had recently died (available on the Web page
<www.spirithistory.com/garriso.html>). Taylor also wrote for
the *Religio-Philosophical Journal*, another Spiritualist periodical.
102, 103

Tbilisi. The present-day name for Tiflis. 4

Teherno-bog. A Slavonian or Russian name for the "Black God—
the Evil, Night-Deity." 266

Temesvár. A town in Hungary that HPB visited. 12

Temple of Solomon. The Temple in Jerusalem, the holiest place
for Judaism. 132, 147, 150, 321, 329

Tennyson, Alfred (1809-92), 1st Baron. English poet laureate. 92

teraphim. *Heb., plural in form, collective in use*. In biblical use, statues
of household gods or deities of local shrines that functioned
as legal title to property, for divinatory uses, etc. HPB in her
correspondence associated them with the empyrean, and the
Theosophical Glossary defines them as "the same as Seraphim, or
the Kabeiri Gods; serpent-images." 155, 169, 171

Thackersey, Mulji *or* **Mooljee** (d. 1880). A member of the
Theosophical Society's General Council whom Olcott had met
on shipboard in 1870 and through whom the Founders came
into touch with the Arya Samaj. 378, 399, 400, 428

Thailand. *See* Siam.

Thaut. *See* Thoth.

Thayer, Mary Baker. A Boston medium, noted for materializing
flowers and other objects from nature, investigated by HPB
and Olcott during the latter part of 1875 (*CW* 1:122). 236, 254,
292

Thebes *or* **Theba**. The capital of the ancient Egyptian empire. 132,
134

Theodidaktos. *Gk*. "god taught." Divinely inspired; a divinely
inspired person. St. Paul used the term in its literal sense in

1 Thess. 4.9: "But concerning love of the brethren ye have no need that one write unto you: for ye yourselves are taught of God [*theodidaktos*] to love one another." It was, however, also used, not in the sense of "instructed by holy scripture," but rather "inspired by God or the gods," as in HPB's comment in *The Key to Theosophy*, sect. 1, fn. 2, "Ammonius Saccas . . . was called *Theodidaktos,* 'god-taught'." 396, 397

Theosophical Forum. A monthly periodical published in New York and edited by Alexander Fullerton, 1889-95. 417

Theosophical Glossary. 134

Theosophical History. A periodical founded and edited by Leslie Price in London, now edited by James Santucci and published in Fullerton, CA, 1985–. 30, 31, 421, 423, 489, 491

Theosophical Nuggets. A periodical published in 1940. 484

Theosophical Quarterly. A periodical published in New York, 1903-38. 308, 328, 390

Theosophical Review. A periodical published in London, 1897–1909, successor to *Lucifer*. 435

Theosophical Society. 3, 32, 37, 65, 77, 78, 90, 97, 106, 108, 121, 122, 126, 134, 135, 137, 140, 146, 151, 161, 163, 171, 184, 185, 191, 194, 195, 198, 199, 200, 201, 209, 213, 214, 217, 218, 219, 220, 221, 222, 223, 227, 229, 231, 238, 239, 241, 242, 243, 244, 250, 251, 255, 256, 259, 261, 270, 289, 311, 328, 329, 337, 341, 342, 353, 355, 361, 363, 364, 375, 387, 390, 392, 396, 397, 399, 400, 401, 404, 412, 413, 417, 418, 420, 422, 423, 429, 431, 435, 438, 441, 453, 459, 460, 464, 465, 477, 479, 485, 490, 491, 493, 494, 498

Theosophical Society of the Arya Samaj of India (*or* **Aryavart**). 397, 400

Theosophic Isis. A monthly periodical published in London, edited by Herbert A. W. Coryn, 1896-7. 339

Theosophist, The. A monthly periodical published in Bombay and Adyar, founded and edited by HPB, 1879-85, thereafter by the President of the Theosophical Society. 7, 61, 106, 171, 300, 328, 355, 356, 412, 422, 423, 491

Theosophy *or* **theosophy**. (1) The teachings and practices associated with the Theosophical Society. (2) A religious philosophy postulating an ancient collective tradition of knowledge and the individual's potential of achieving direct insight into the nature of reality through spiritual discipline (including Gnosticism, Kabbalah, Sufism, and other systems, both Eastern and Western). The two senses are distinguished by many present-day students by the upper-case form for the first (as a proper noun) and the lower-case form for the second (as a common noun). HPB uses the term (without regard to capitalization) in both senses. 87, 201, 217, 339, 340, 395, 396, 402, 435, 478, 493, 497

theurgist. *Gk*. theourgos "miracle worker." One who practices theurgy. 214, 223, 228, 235, 236

theurgy. *Gk*. theourgia "divine work." The practice of a form of "magic" that induces divine action through a human agent. The manifestations of theurgy range from shamanism to the mysticism of the Neoplatonists, in which divine consciousness and powers enter the soul of a human being. In Theosophical terms, it is the linking of the personal consciousness with that of the Augoeides or Divine Self. "To arrive at such an exalted goal the aspirant must be absolutely worthy and unselfish" (*Theosophical Glossary* 329). 233, 286

Thibet. *See* Tibet.

Third Department. A Russian secret police of the mid nineteenth century. 23, 24, 28

Thirty-fourth Street, 433 West. The building in which HPB took a suite of rooms on the first floor and Olcott one on the second floor in November 1875. 263, 332

Thor's hammer. The swastika. 84, 147, 150

Thoth *or* **Thaut** *or* **Thutii** *or* **Tot**. The Egyptian god of wisdom and magic, the messenger and scribe of the gods, identified with Greek Hermes and, as such, called Hermes Trismegistus. "But this word *thoth* does not only mean 'Intelligence'; it also means 'assembly' or *school*. In reality Thoth-Hermes is simply the personification of the voice (or sacred teaching) of the sacerdotal caste of Egypt; the voice of the Great Hierophants" (*CW* 11:534). 205, 213, 286

Thury. A professor at the Academy of Geneva who proposed an "ectenic" force to explain the Spiritualist phenomena of table tilting and developed experiments to test his theory (Podmore 2:187–8). 429

Thutii. *See* Thoth.

Tiberia *or* Tiberias. A town on the Sea of Galilee, built by Herod Antipas and named for the Roman emperor Tiberius. As the center of Jewish learning after the destruction of Jerusalem, the Sanhedrin met there and edited parts of the Mishna and Jerusalem Talmud. 321

Tibet. 6, 7, 13, 267, 270

Tiflis, *now* Tbilisi. A city in Caucasian Georgia, founded about 458 as the capital of the kingdom of Georgia, on the east of the Black Sea just south of the Caucasus Mountains and north of Turkey, Armenia, and Azerbaijan. Conquered over the centuries by Persians, Byzantines, Arabs, and Mongols, the city came under the control of Russia in 1801. 4, 5, 9, 14, 16, 41, 295, 346, 393, 413, 414

Tindall. *See* Tyndall, John.

Tiridates. The name of several rulers of Armenia, notably Tiridates III (late 3rd to early 4th centuries), who adopted Christianity as the state religion and aligned Armenia with Rome rather than Persia. 267, 269

Tischendorf, Lobegott Friedrich Konstantin von (1815–74). A German biblical scholar who discovered fragments of the oldest Greek manuscripts of the Bible in a monastery on Mt. Sinai and, with the support of the Russian government, obtained the rest of the manuscript, called the Codex Sinaiticus, a facsimile of which was published in St. Petersburg in 1862. 321

Tit Titich. *Russ.* "Titus, Son of Titus." *See* Kit Kitich. 272

Tiur, Gen. A Hungarian serving in Italy, otherwise unidentified. 27

Tiverton, Rhode Island. 187

Tolstoy, Lev Nikolayevich, Count (1828–1910). A Russian novelist, philosopher, and mystic. 3

Tot. *See* Thoth.

Tracy, Benjamin Franklin (1830–1915). An American lawyer who served in the Union Army during the Civil War as a brigadier general. His legal career included defending Henry Ward Beecher in the suit against him for adultery, and he was

Secretary of the Navy (1889–93). His law firm supplied a translator for HPB's Long Island case. (Biographical data: *WWWA* 1:1250.) 157

Transylvania. A mountainous area of Romania, formerly of Hungary. 12

Travancore, India. A former princely state, now Kerala. 350, 409, 411

Trimurti. *Skt.* "three forms." The three gods Brahma, Vishnu, and Siva thought of as forms of the same reality, comparable to the Christian Trinity. 322, 446

trinity. The threefoldness of all things, from the divine (the Christian Trinity or Hindu Trimurti) to the human (body, soul, and spirit). 207, 211, 219, 248, 322, 329, 444, 446

Troubetzkoy *or* Trubetskoy, **Yakovlevna**, Princess. Presumably a member of the distinguished Russian noble family that included political activists, religious philosophers, and the linguist Nikolay Sergeyevich. 275

TsGAOR. A Russian archive, the Central State Archive of the October Revolution. 31

Tuitit Bey. An Adept who in 1875 was Olcott's first direct contact with the Brotherhood (*LMW2*, letter 3). 104, 105, 106, 168, 170, 218

Turanian. Any of the Ural-Altaic languages, such as Finnish, Hungarian, Turkish, and Mongolian. 267

Turgenev, Ivan Sergeyevich (1818–83). One of the foremost Russian writers, especially of novels, plays, and short stories. 283, 284, 301

Turkey. 5, 30, 31, 49, 289, 300, 360, 483

"Turkish Barbarities." An article by HPB (*CW* 1:255–60). 360

Turkish War. A war between Russia and Turkey, probably that of 1853–6 (the Crimean War), for service in which HPB's father was awarded a medal. 260

Twain, Mark, *pen name of* Samuel Langhorne Clemens (1835–1910). An American novelist. 273, 482

Tyndall, John (1820–93). A British physicist and successor to Michael Faraday, whose chief research was light, sound, and radiant heat. He was best known as an exponent of science for lay people, serving as "Materialism's chief spokesman . . . . To Tyndall, materialism was a religion. . . . So he urged his fellow-scientists actively to propagate the materialist doctrine, as he was constantly doing himself in popular journals, in order to encourage 'a strong and resolute enthusiasm'" (Inglis 302). His espousal of materialistic explanations made him one of HPB's bêtes noirs. (Cf. Podmore 2:147.) 86, 142, 175, 203, 226, 232, 291, 297, 338, 381, 410

Tyng, Stephen Higginson, Jr. (1839–98). A New York Episcopal priest who organized a conference on the Second Coming (*CW* 3:231 fn.). 473, 475, 476

Tyrian. Pertaining to Tyre, an ancient Phoenician city. 266

Tzereta-Korchay-Tungu Tchichmak-Zuru. A prince of the Kalmucks, according to a comic autobiographical account by HPB. 481

Ukraine. 1, 3, 4, 5

umbra. *Lat.* "a shade or shadow." A spook, the psychic remains of the personality of a dead person. 57

undine. An elemental spirit or force of nature associated with water. 387

Union Square, New York City. The site of a house where HPB lived in 1873 or 1874. 32

United Grand Lodge of England Library, Freemason's Hall, London. 213

Unpublished Letters of Helena Petrovna Blavatsky, Some. 69, 87, 93, 94, 104, 114, 115, 116, 121, 122, 135, 156, 163, 165, 175, 198, 199, 201, 237, 256, 259, 468, 469

Ur of the Chaldees. The place from which Abraham came to Palestine. 213

Ural Mountains. A range of mountains stretching from the Arctic Ocean to the Caspian Sea, taken as the dividing line between Europe and Asia. 4

Uriah. The husband of Bathsheba (2 Sam. 11). 122

Uxmal. An ancient city in the Yucatan peninsula, Mexico, whose ruins include impressive architectural structures. 285

Valia, Valka, Val'ka. Pet names for "Valerian," specifically for Valerian Vladimirovich de Zhelihovsky, HPB's nephew. 359, 415, 416, 450

van der Linden, C. H. An early American member of the Theosophical Society, father of Peter. 453, 455

van der Linden, Peter. An early American member of the Theosophical Society, son of the preceding. 455

Varley, Cromwell Fleetwood (1828–83). An electrical engineer who assisted in the laying of the first Atlantic cable. He considered electrical or magnetic explanations for Spiritualist phenomena, but concluded against such causes. He had contact with D. D. Home, Kate Fox, Florence Cook (Podmore 2:156–7) and other mediums, assisting Sir William Crookes in his investigations of Spiritualism. (Biographical data: *CW* 1:529–30; *EOP* 2:1367–8.) 34

Vaughan, Thomas, *pen name* Eugenius Philalethes, *Gk.* "Well-born Lover of Truth" (1622–66). An English clergyman, author, alchemist, and twin brother of the metaphysical poet Henry Vaughan. Some of his writings were edited by Arthur Edward Waite in *The Magical Writings of Thomas Vaughan (Eugenius Philalethes)* (1888). (Biographical data: *CW* 14:575–6.) 196, 206, 209

Veda. *Skt.* "knowledge," *cognate with English* wit, wis(dom). The oldest religious writings of Hinduism and in any Indo-European language. The Veda consists of four types of writings: Samhita (hymns, the basic texts), Brahmana (guidebooks for performing ceremonies), Aranyaka (treatises for ascetics who live in the forests), and Upanishads (philosophical treatises). The oldest and most important of the texts is the Rig Veda. 205, 376, 381, 399, 437, 445, 446, 457, 458, 461, 463, 471, 485

Veda Bhashya. *Skt.* Veda Bhāṣya "Commentary on the Veda." A commentary on the Vedas by Dayanand Saraswati, setting forth his interpretation of those basic Hindu scriptures. It was written in Sanskrit and Hindi, which the Swami refused to have translated into other languages (including English when Olcott and HPB requested that for publication in the *Theosophist*), as he believed students of the Vedas should learn the Indian languages. He tried unsuccessfully to secure both government subsidy for its publication and its adoption as a text in Indian schools. The work was published in fascicles. 457, 461

Wachtmeister, Constance, Countess (1838–1910). A friend and companion of HPB's at the end of her life. 6

Wagner, Nikolay Petrovich, Prof. (1829–1907). A Russian zoologist and psychic researcher, some of whose articles HPB translated for the *Spiritual Scientist*. (Biographical data: *CW* 6:449.) 162, 170, 171

Waite, A. E. 212

Wales. 339

Wallace, Alfred Russel (1823–1913). A British naturalist who developed the theory of evolution and of the origin of species by natural selection in parallel with Charles Darwin. In 1858, at the age of 35, while thinking about the economic theories of Thomas Malthus, he conceived "the survival of the fittest" as the means by which one species replaces another. He sent a summary statement of his theory to Darwin, who recognized the coincidence with his own thought and used some of Wallace's terms in his book *On the Origin of Species* (1859). Although Darwin is generally credited with the concept of evolution through a struggle for existence because he had developed it in greater detail with more evidence, Wallace independently arrived at the theory and prompted Darwin to publish it. Wallace's chief difference from Darwin was his belief that the higher mental powers of humanity could not have arisen by natural selection, but were the result of an outside spiritual agency. This view was harmonious with Wallace's interest in Spiritualism, which he came to from a materialist background through his investigation of mesmerism, table turning, rapping, telekinesis, spirit photography, automatic writing, materializations, and other phenomena. In 1869, he formed a committee of the London Dialectical Society to investigate such matters. A collection of his papers treating the subject, *On Miracles and Modern Spiritualism*, presented both the theoretical arguments for spiritual phenomena and extensive accounts of the evidence supporting their reality, based on both his personal investigations and those of others. Of his change of mind, he writes in the preface to the first edition (vi–vii): "I was so thorough and confirmed a materialist that I could not . . . find a place in my mind for the conception of spiritual existence, or

for any other agencies in the universe than matter and force.
Facts, however, are stubborn things. . . . By slow degrees a place
was made . . . by the continuous action of fact after fact."
(Biographical data: *DNB* [1912 –21] 546–9; *DSB* 14:133–40;
EOP 2:1385–6.) 34, 86, 203, 217, 362, 403, 429

Ward, Artemus, pseudonym of Charles Farrar Browne (1834–67).
A popular American humorist whose literary character,
Artemus Ward, was the manager of a traveling sideshow and
wrote letters published in newspapers and magazines. Browne
was also famous as a lecturer in the persona of Artemus Ward,
whose wry and comic remarks were delivered with a deadpan
expression. Artemus Ward was one of a number of late nineteenth-century American literary characters (others being Bill
Arp, Josh Billings, and Petroleum V. Nasby) whose style was
characterized by puns, ungrammatical expressions, distorted
misspellings, slang, and incongruously learned vocabulary and
allusions. (Biographical data: *WWWA* H:80.) 95, 96, 177, 183

Wartensee, castles of Old and New. Properties that Baron de Palm
claimed to own. 270

Washington, DC. The capital of the United States. 149, 183, 187,
193, 480, 481, 484

Washington, Pennsylvania. The site of the Le Moyne crematory,
where Baron de Palm was cremated. 261, 280

Washington, George. The first president of the United States.
142

Watkins, John. A London book dealer. 40

Webster. An unidentified man whom HPB claims to have put "on
the truth path." 326

Webster, Dr. A murderer of ca. 1849 who was the "conducting
spirit" in some of Gen. Lippitt's séances. 186, 233

Webster, Prof. An unidentified person. 187

Weisse, John A. A philologist in New York who was a vice president of the Theosophical Society in 1878. 483, 490

Wescott, W. A person whom HPB characterizes as the "leader of
the Choir at the Spirit[ual] Hall" in Philadelphia and who witnessed some dealings of Dr. Child. 69, 93

Westbrook, Mrs. A friend of HPB's in 1876, probably the wife of
Judge Westbrook. 253, 256

Westbrook, R. B., Judge. A vice president of the Theosophical Society in 1877. (Biographical data: *CW* 1:531.) 256

West End, London. A part of central London west of the City, the location of fashionable hotels, restaurants, theaters, department stores, residential areas (Mayfair, Belgravia, Chelsea), clubs, and royal parks. 277

West Indies. An archipelago dividing the Atlantic Ocean from the Gulf of Mexico and the Caribbean Sea. 6

West Orange, New Jersey. The site of Thomas Alva Edison's laboratory and now the Edison National Historic Site. 419, 421, 422, 423, 489, 491

White, Eliza Frances Potter. The landlady of the Holmeses, who was hired by them or by Dr. Child to impersonate the spirit of Katie King. (Biographical data: *People* 438–42.) 63, 64, 67, 70, 88, 90, 94, 95, 103, 154, 155

White Sea. A gulf of the Arctic Ocean in northern European Russia. 423

Whitney, William Dwight (1827–94). A professor of Sanskrit at Yale University and a leading American linguist, lexicographer, and orientalist of his day. (Biographical data: *WWWA* H:578.) 457, 460

"Who Fabricates?" An article by HPB (*CW* 1:75–83). 64, 94, 96, 103, 115, 116, 126, 144, 155, 171

Wiggin, J. H. A Unitarian clergyman who attended HPB's soirees at 46 Irving Place. 219

Wilder, Alexander (1823–1908). An American author, Platonic scholar, physician, and editor, who was involved with the publication and editing of *Isis Unveiled* and contributed to the section titled "Before the Veil." He was a vice president of the Theosophical Society in 1878. (Biographical data: *CW* 1:531-3; *WWWA* 1:1345.) 264, 265, 269, 270, 280, 281, 282, 284, 285, 297, 333, 334, 338, 341, 483, 490, 491

Wilkinson. Secretary to the brother of the Ottoman viceregent of Egypt, otherwise unidentified. 27

Williams, Mr. An artist for the American Publishing Company who did illustrations for Olcott's book *People from the Other World*. 79

Williams, Charles E. (fl. 1870s). A British materializing medium who used the spirit control "John King." He collaborated with Frank Herne and often sat with W. Stainton Moses, who doubted his genuineness. He was often suspected of and sometimes caught in acts of fraud. (Biographical data: *EOP* 2:1404–5; Podmore 2:78–83, 111.) 19, 72

Wilson, Horace Hayman (1786–1860). Editor and continuer of James Mill's *British India*. 392

Wimbridge, Edward (d. 1898). An English architect in New York who accompanied the Founders to India. (Biographical data: *CW* 1:533.) 451

Wisconsin. A state in the northern center of the United States. 270

Witte, Alexander ("**Sasha**") **Yulyevich de** (1846–77). HPB's cousin, the second son of her aunt Katherine, and a Major in the 16th Nizhegorodsky Dragoons (*CW* 1:255 fn., 258 fn.). 389, 416

Witte, Katherine Andreyevna de, *née* de Fadeyev (b. 1819). HPB's aunt and the mother of Count Serguey Witte (*CW* 1:255 fn., 258 fn.). 3, 4, 29, 31, 33, 467

Witte, Serguey Yulyevich de, Count (1849–1915). HPB's cousin, the fourth son of her aunt Katherine, and the Prime Minister of Russia, 1903–6 (*CW* 1:258 fn.). 3

Witte, Yuliy Feodorovich de (d. 1868). HPB's uncle by marriage to her aunt Katherine Andreyevna (*CW* 1:258 fn.). 3, 14, 29

Wittgenstein, Emil-Karl-Ludwig von Sayn-, Prince (1824–78). A Lieutenant General in the Russian Army, a Spiritualist, a close friend of HPB and her family, and a member of the Theosophical Society. (Biographical data: *CW* 1:533–4.) 76, 77, 114, 140, 154, 249, 300, 447

Wood, Mr. A man who thought he saw his dead wife at a séance conducted by Jennifer Holmes. 110

Word: *A Monthly Magazine Devoted to Philosophy, Science, Religion; Eastern Thought, Occultism, Theosophy, and the Brotherhood of Humanity*, edited by Harold W. Percival and published in New York by the Theosophical Publishing Company, 1904–17. 270, 280, 285, 437

Woronseff, Viceroy. According to a newspaper interview, the Russian viceroy in Georgia. 41

Wrangel, Ferdinand Petrovich von, Baron (1794–1870). A Russian explorer and author. 286

Wyld, George (1821–1906). A Scottish homeopathic physician and Unitarian Christian, a founder of the Society for Psychical Research, a president of the London Theosophical Society, and the author of *Theosophy and the Higher Life; or, Spiritual Dynamics* (London, 1880). (Biographical data: *CW* 3:538–9.) 403, 493, 500

Xavier, François *or* Francis, Saint (1506–52). One of the original members of the Jesuit Order and a missionary to India and Japan. 379

Xenophon (ca. 431–ca. 352 BC). A Greek historian. 269

Yago. One of the four Kabeiri gods. 317

Yahontoff, Vera Petrovna de. *See* Zhelihovsky, Vera Petrovna de.

Yahontov, Feodor ("Fedia/Fedya") Nikolayevich de. One of HPB's nephews by her sister Vera Petrovna's first marriage. 416

Yahontov, Nikolay Nikolayevich de. The first husband of HPB's sister Vera Petrovna. 8, 416

Yahontov, Rostislav ("Rostya/Rostia") Nikolayevich de. One of HPB's nephews by her sister Vera Petrovna's first marriage. 416

Yajnik, Indulal Kanaiyalal. 439, 443

Yakut. A character in a story by Nikolai S. Leskov. 345

Yarker, John (b. 1833). An English Freemason who specialized in alternative Masonic Rites. 341, 397, 398

Yaroslavl, Russia. A region on the Volga River. 355

Yasher. *See* Jasher.

Yerevan *or* **Yerivan** *also* **Erevan** *or* **Erivan**. The capital of Armenia. 5, 7, 8, 14, 41, 267, 295

Yevgeniy Ivanovich. An acquaintance of HPB's when she lived in Saratov. 352

Young, Brigham (1801–77). The second president of the Mormon church, who led the Mormons to Utah and established the headquarters of the church at Salt Lake City. Polygamy was practiced as a religious institution by the Utah Mormons;

H. P. BLAVATSKY
COLLECTED WRITINGS

Comprehensive Edition published by

THE THEOSOPHICAL PUBLISHING HOUSE
WHEATON, ILLINOIS, U.S.A.; ADYAR, CHENNAI (MADRAS), INDIA

Large octavos; illustrated with rare portraits;
cloth bound; fully indexed.

Periodicals and Miscellaneous Writings

Vol. I (1874–78) lxxx + 570 pp.

Vol. II (1879–80) xlvi + 590 pp.

Vol. III (1881–82) xxxviii + 583 pp.

Vol. IV (1882–83) xlii + 718 pp.

Vol. V (1883) xxxii + 416 pp.

Vol. VI (1883–85) liv + 481 pp.

Vol. VII (1886–87) xxxiv + 433 pp.

Vol. VIII (1887) xxviii + 507 pp.

Vol. IX (1888) xxx + 488 pp.

Vol. X (1888–89) xxxiv + 461 pp.

Vol. XI (1889) xxxiii + 632 pp.

Vol. XII (1889–90) xxx + 859 pp.

Vol. XIII (1890–91) xxxii + 465 pp.

Vol. XIV (Miscellaneous) xlviii + 733 pp.

Vol XV (Cumulative Index) xiii + 633 pp.

The Letters of H. P. Blavatsky: Vol. 1 (1861–79) xx + 634 pp.

SOFTCOVER EDITIONS
From the Caves and Jungles of Hindostan (1883–86) lv + 719 pp.

Isis Unveiled (1877): Vol. I, [64] + xlvi + (6) + 657 pp.;
Vol. II, iv + (6) + 848 pp.

The Secret Doctrine (1888): Vol. I, [84] + xlviii + 696 pp.;
Vol. II, xx + 817 pp.; Vol. III (Index) 520 pp.

Information concerning further volumes of this series,
which are in preparation, available on request.

OTHER TITLES IN PRINT
The Key to Theosophy
The Voice of the Silence

Available in various editions.

Published by
The Theosophical Society in America
Wheaton, Illinois 60189-0270,
a worldwide, nonprofit membership organization
that promotes fellowship among all peoples of the world,
encourages the study of religion, philosophy, and science,
and supports spiritual growth and healing.

Today humanity is on the verge of becoming, for the first time in its history, a global community. The only question is what kind of community it will be. The Theosophical Publishing House produces titles intended to introduce into humanity a large-mindedness, a freedom from bias, and an understanding of the values of the East and the West and to point the way to human development as a means of service, both for the individual and for the whole of humankind.

For additional titles and online purchasing,
Visit **www.questbooks.net**
For more information about the Theosophical Society,
visit **www.theosophical.org**,
or contact **Olcott@theosmail.net**,
or 630-668-1571.

*The Theosophical Publishing House is aided by
the generous support of the KERN FOUNDATION,
a trust dedicated to Theosophical education.*